SCHOOL OF
ORIENTAL AND AFRICAN STUDIES
UNIVERSITY OF LONDON

London Oriental Series
Volume 30

LONDON ORIENTAL SERIES · VOLUME 30

JOGJAKARTA UNDER SULTAN MANGKUBUMI
1749–1792

A HISTORY OF THE DIVISION
OF JAVA

BY

M. C. RICKLEFS

*Lecturer in the History of South East Asia
at the School of Oriental and
African Studies*

LONDON
OXFORD UNIVERSITY PRESS
NEW YORK   TORONTO   KUALA LUMPUR
1974

Oxford University Press, Ely House, London W. 1

GLASGOW NEW YORK TORONTO MELBOURNE WELLINGTON
CAPE TOWN IBADAN NAIROBI DAR ES SALAAM LUSAKA ADDIS ABABA
DELHI BOMBAY CALCUTTA MADRAS KARACHI LAHORE DACCA
KUALA LUMPUR SINGAPORE HONG KONG TOKYO

ISBN 0 19 713578 1

© *M. C. Ricklefs, 1974*

All rights reserved. No part of this publication may be reproduced, stored in a retrieval system, or transmitted, in any form or by any means, electronic, mechanical, photocopying, recording, or otherwise, without the prior permission of Oxford University Press

*Printed in Great Britain
at the University Press, Oxford
by Vivian Ridler
Printer to the University*

FOR MARGARET
AND MY PARENTS

London Oriental Series

No. 1 PHONETICS IN ANCIENT INDIA
W. SIDNEY ALLEN

No. 2 THE DIACRITICAL POINT AND THE ACCENTS IN SYRIAC
J. B. SEGAL

No. 3 THE MANICHAEAN HYMN CYCLES IN PARTHIAN
MARY BOYCE

No. 4 THE BACKGROUND OF THE REBELLION OF AN LU-SHAN
EDWIN G. PULLEYBLANK

*No. 5 SOCIAL POLICY AND SOCIAL CHANGE IN WESTERN INDIA 1817-1830
KENNETH BALLHATCHET

No. 6 THE HEVAJRA TANTRA
D. L. SNELLGROVE. Two volumes

No. 7 THE GĀNDHĀRĪ DHARMAPADA
Edited with an Introduction and Commentary by JOHN BROUGH

*No. 8 THE HISTORY OF THE CAUCASIAN ALBANIANS BY MOVSĒS DASXURANÇI
Translated by C. J. F. DOWSETT

No. 9 KURDISH DIALECT STUDIES, Vol. I
D. N. MACKENZIE

No. 10 KURDISH DIALECT STUDIES, Vol. II
D. N. MACKENZIE

No. 11 NINETEENTH-CENTURY MALAYA
The Origins of British Political Control
C. D. COWAN

No. 12 THE HEBREW PASSOVER FROM THE EARLIEST TIMES TO A.D. 70
J. B. SEGAL

No. 13 THE MORPHOLOGY OF THE TIGRE NOUN
F. R. PALMER

No. 14 JAINA YOGA
A Survey of the Mediaeval Śrāvakācāras
R. WILLIAMS

* These volumes are out of print.

No. 15 TIDDIM CHIN
A Descriptive Analysis of Two Texts
EUGÉNIE J. A. HENDERSON

*No. 16 NE SHRĪ'S HISTORY OF THE OTTOMANS
The Sources and Development of the Text
V. L. MÉNAGE

No. 17 EASTERN ARABIAN DIALECT STUDIES
T. M. JOHNSTONE

*No. 18 THE NINE WAYS OF BON
Excerpts from gZi-brjid
Edited and translated by DAVID L. SNELLGROVE

No. 19 TIBETAN TEXTS CONCERNING KHOTAN
R. E. EMMERICK

No. 20 SAKA GRAMMATICAL STUDIES
R. E. EMMERICK

No. 21 THE BOOK OF ZAMBASTA
A Khotanese Poem on Buddhism
Edited and translated by R. E. EMMERICK

No. 22 THE 'SŪTRA OF THE CAUSES AND EFFECTS OF ACTIONS' IN SOGDIAN
Edited by D. N. MACKENZIE

No. 23 THE KHOTANESE ŚŪRANGAMASAMĀDHISUTRA
R. E. EMMERICK

No. 24 A DICTIONARY OF THE MON INSCRIPTIONS FROM THE SIXTH TO THE SIXTEENTH CENTURIES
Incorporating materials collected by the late C. O. Blagden
H. L. SHORTO

No. 25 THE FINANCIAL SYSTEM OF EGYPT
A.H. 564–741/A.D. 1169–1341
HASSANEIN M. RABIE

No. 26 THE TREASURY OF GOOD SAYINGS: A TIBETAN HISTORY OF BON
SAMTEN G. KARMAY

No. 27 POPULATION PRESSURE IN RURAL ANATOLIA 1450–1600
M. A. COOK

No. 28 THE MODAL SYSTEM OF ARAB AND PERSIAN MUSIC 1250–1300 (forthcoming)
O. WRIGHT

No. 29 THE *SHEN TZU* FRAGMENTS (forthcoming)
P. M. THOMPSON

* These volumes are out of print.

CONTENTS

ACKNOWLEDGEMENTS		xi
ABBREVIATIONS		xiii
INTRODUCTION		xv
I.	The Historical Background	1
II.	Rebellion and the Division of the Kingdom, 1726–1754	37
III.	The Transition to a Peaceful Division, and the Foundation of Jogjakarta, 1755–1757	67
IV.	Eliminating Options, I: The Failure of Marriage Diplomacy, 1757–1765	96
V.	Eliminating Options, II: The End of Rebellion and the Birth of an Heir in Surakarta, c. 1761–1771	119
VI.	Preparing for a new Age, c. 1768–1775	142
VII.	The New Age in Javanese Literature: Sĕrat Surja Radja, Babad Kraton, and the Literary Renaissance	176
VIII.	The Permanently Divided Kingdom, 1774–1787	227
IX.	Crisis in Surakarta and the Vindication of the Division, 1787–1790	285
X.	The Succession of the Younger Generation, 1791–1792	341
XI.	Jogjakarta and the Dutch	362
XII.	The Consequences of the Permanent Division of Java	414

CONTENTS

APPENDICES

I. Major Officials of the Dutch East India Company in the Later Eighteenth Century — 426

II. Patihs of Surakarta and Jogjakarta in the Eighteenth Century — 428

III. Principal Members of the House of Mataram in the Later Eighteenth Century — 429

IV. Javanese and Western Chronology, A.D. 1749–1792 — 430

GLOSSARY OF JAVANESE WORDS — 432

BIBLIOGRAPHY — 434

INDEX — 447

MAPS

(at end of book)

Central and East Java

The Indonesian Archipelago

ACKNOWLEDGEMENTS

MANY individuals have assisted me in the writing of this book. Four scholars in particular have contributed to my understanding of Javanese history, language, literature, and society in so fundamental a way that without their help this study could not have been completed. Their views sometimes differ markedly from one another, but each in his own way has given me training, advice, criticism, and encouragement which have inspired and sustained me, and which have made possible whatever merit may lie in the following pages. They are Professor C. C. Berg, Dr. H. J. de Graaf, Dr. Th. G. Th. Pigeaud, and Professor P. J. Zoetmulder, S.J. It is an honour to acknowledge my debt to them here.

In Indonesia I was honoured to receive the assistance and co-operation of His Royal Highness S. D. I. S. Kg. Sultan Haměngkubuwana IX, who made available to me the historical resources of his court. His Royal Highness B. P. H. Poeroebojo, Drs. Mudjanattistomo, and Professor Selo Soemardjan gave me their kind advice and assistance. To K. R. T. Widyakusuma and the officials of the Jogjakarta *kraton* I am grateful for their unfailing generosity and patient explanations. The records of the Arsip Nasional Republik Indonesia were made available through the permission of Mr. Mohammad Ali and the constant assistance of Miss Soemartini.

In the Netherlands, Professor M. A. P. Meilink-Roelofsz and the staff of the Algemeen Rijksarchief opened to me the vast resources of their collection, which is the backbone of this study. The incomparable Javanese manuscript holdings of the Leiden University Library also provided several essential sources; I am grateful to Dr. R. Roolvink, former *adiutor interpretis* of the Legatum Warnerianum, and to Mrs. E. M. L. Andriessen-Lück for their help and unfailing kindnesses to me.

In Great Britain, Dr. C. Hooykaas and Professor C. D. Cowan read early drafts of several chapters of this book and gave me valuable assistance. To Dr. Hooykaas I owe special gratitude for initiating me into the Javanese literary idiom in which my sources are written. The British Museum was perhaps the most important single source of Javanese manuscript materials for this research topic. I am thankful to Mr. K. B. Gardner and Dr. G. E. Marrison, and to the staff of the British Museum Department of Oriental Printed Books and Manuscripts, in particular to Mr. J. H. Eisenegger, for their assistance.

Professor O. W. Wolters, Professor Knight Biggerstaff, and Professor George McT. Kahin of Cornell University assisted greatly in making my research possible and have read and given valuable criticisms upon the text of this study. Among the present and former staff of Cornell, I am grateful also to Professor John M. Echols and Dr. Soepomo Poedjosoedarmo for my first introduction to the Javanese language.

My research in England, the Netherlands, and Indonesia from 1967 to 1972 was made possible by generous financial support from the Herbert H. Lehman Foundation, the Foreign Area Fellowship Program, the London–Cornell Project, and the School of Oriental and African Studies. To all of these I am grateful.

The publication of this book has been made possible by a grant from the Publications Committee of the School of Oriental and African Studies.

For the encouragement, advice, criticisms, and support of those named above I shall always be grateful. But since I have not always followed this guidance, I alone am responsible for those errors and weaknesses which remain in this book.

M. C. RICKLEFS

1973

which Dutch East India Company influence in Central Java greatly receded as the Company declined, so the Javanese scene which emerges is relatively untrammelled by foreign intrusions.

One important aspect is not adequately covered in this study, although source materials exist in great abundance. It has not been possible to study and analyse all the statistical records concerning economic affairs. Economics are referred to below where necessary, but the reader should bear in mind that these discussions are usually based not upon analysis of statistics but upon judgements found in non-statistical Dutch and Javanese documents.

11. *Sources*

11. A. *Dutch East India Company documents*

The documents of the East India Company archives are valuable for the historian, but their reliability can be overestimated. Few of the Company's officials knew very well or cared about the Javanese or their language. There was considerable misunderstanding of Javanese affairs, and Dutchmen were often fed deliberately misleading information by their Javanese informants. Furthermore, throughout the archival records runs the constant assumption that Dutchmen were the most important factor in events in Java, a fundamentally inaccurate if understandable cultural presumption. These factors all influence the reliability of Dutch records. The historian must apply to them the same careful standards as he would to any other form of documentation.

The Company's documents were not only influenced by negative factors such as the limitations of Dutch interest, knowledge, and perception. There was also conscious falsification by Company officials. It has been said that propaganda is entirely absent from Company records,[1] but this is too optimistic a judgement. Propaganda can be internal to an organization as well as external, and of the former variety the Company had an abundance. Dutch officials reporting to their superiors sometimes exaggerated the difficulties or dangers of their position to solicit more men, money, and guns, or to convince those above them of their courage. At other times they exaggerated their own control over Javanese situations to demonstrate their competence. Often reports were

[1] Graham Irwin, 'Dutch Historical Sources', in Soedjatmoko, *et al.*, *An Introduction to Indonesian Historiography* (Ithaca, 1965), p. 237.

INTRODUCTION

1. *The Subject*

THE history of the Javanese in the later eighteenth century has not yet received adequate historical attention. The only work of note was published by the missionary and scholar of Javanese C. Poensen in 1901 (see Bibliography). But his work suffered from several shortcomings, most notably the use of a rather biased Javanese source (see II. B. 3 below) and the employment of only published Dutch sources. His was a pioneering effort, but it has remained the standard reference only because of the absence of any successors. All general histories of Indonesia and the few general articles on the period have taken their information from Poensen, with the occasional introduction of materials from other published sources. By a fresh investigation of published and unpublished materials the present study hopes to take Poensen's work a step further.

The period is interesting and important for several reasons. It offers the opportunity to observe the establishment of a new court and kingdom, Jogjakarta, and the reign of a significant ruler, Sultan Mangkubumi. Like Poensen's study, this work concentrates upon Jogjakarta. It still remains for full-scale studies of Surakarta and the Mangkunĕgaran and of the Dutch-controlled coastal territories in the same period to be written. The period immediately precedes one of considerable conflict between Javanese and Europeans and therefore provides an important background to those later episodes.

Perhaps one of the most important aspects of the period lies in its general historical significance. The later eighteenth century is the earliest period in Javanese history which has voluminous and contemporaneous documentation in both Dutch and Javanese. For the first time the historian can build up with some confidence a picture of how Javanese state life actually functioned at a particular time. Care has been taken here to ensure that important sources are as far as possible confined to those written before the end of the eighteenth century, in order to avoid the considerable problem of later interpolations. And this was a period during

ABBREVIATIONS

LOr	Leiden University Oriental manuscript.
MN	Pangeran Adipati Mangkunĕgara I (Mas Said).
NBS	Netherlands Bible Society (Nederlands Bijbe Genootschap) manuscript, on loan to the Leiden University Library.
PB III	Susuhunan Pakubuwana III of Surakarta.
PB IV	Susuhunan Pakubuwana IV of Surakarta.
Sĕmarang	As sender or recipient of a letter cited in footnotes: Governor and Director of Java's Northeast Coast and Council, Sĕmarang.
TBG	*Tijdschrift van het Bataviaasch Genootschap van Kunsten en Wetenschappen.*
VBG	*Verhandelingen van het Bataviaasch Genootschap van Kunsten en Wetenschappen.*
VKI	*Verhandelingen van het Koninklijk Instituut voor Taal-, Land- en Volkenkunde.*
VOC	Verenigde Oostindische Compagnie, the Dutch East India Company.

ABBREVIATIONS

AN	Arsip Nasional, Djakarta.
Batavia	As sender or recipient of a letter cited in footnotes: Governor-General of the Dutch East India Company and Council of the Indies, Batavia.
BEFEO	Bulletin de l'École Française d'Extrême Orient.
BK	Babad Kraton. BM Add. MS. 12320.
BG	Jasadipura I, Babad Gijanti. 21 vols. Batavia, 1937–9.
BKI	Bijdragen tot de Taal-, Land- en Volkenkunde.
BM	British Museum, London.
B. Mang.	Babad Mangkubumi. LOr 2191.
BTDj	W. L. Olthof (ed. and trans.). Babad Tanah Djawi, in Proza, Javaansche Geschiedenis. 2 vols. 's-Gravenhage, 1941.
BTDj(BP)	Balai Pustaka. Babad Tanah Djawi. 31 vols. Batavia, 1939–41.
de Graaf, GI	H. J. de Graaf. Geschiedenis van Indonesië. 's-Gravenhage, 1949.
dJ	J. K. J. de Jonge and M. L. van Deventer (eds.). De Opkomst van het Nederlandsch Gezag in Oost-Indië. Verzameling van onuitgegeven Stukken uit het Oud-Koloniaal Archief. 16 vols. 's-Gravenhage, 1862–1909.
GG	Governor-General of the Dutch East India Company.
H.XVII	The 'Heeren XVII', Directors of the Dutch East India Company, Amsterdam.
HB I	Sultan Haměngkubuwana I of Jogjakarta (formerly Pangeran Arja Mangkubumi).
JSEAH	Journal of Southeast Asian History.
JSEAS	Journal of Southeast Asian Studies.
KA ... (OB ...)	Used in citing documents from the Algemeen Rijksarchief, The Hague. 'KA' gives the number of the volume in the Koloniaal Archief series. 'OB' gives the year of the same volume in the series of Overgekomen Brieven en Papieren.
KITLV	Koninklijk Instituut voor Taal-, Land- en Volkenkunde, Leiden.

falsified for the more mundane reason that ignorance, incompetence, inefficiency, or dishonesty required covering-up. This conscious falsification is somewhat more difficult to control than the negative limitations described above, but the records often exist in sufficient volume and Company officials often made enough contradictory statements in their individual self-interests for suspicious areas to be ascertained.

But the Company records also have strengths which make them the historian's most valuable tool. Except when Company officials were directly involved in Javanese intrigues they rarely had a vested interest in Javanese politics. Their reports are therefore often more impartial than contemporary Javanese sources. Their information sometimes came from several Javanese individuals with widely varying views of a particular person or event, thus making possible a balanced picture. The comments of these Javanese participants are often reflected in Dutch records, sometimes quoted in translation in them, and occasionally available in Javanese originals. Thus, Dutch documents are sometimes a means to approach indigenous Javanese sources as well. And the Dutch records provide the luxury of constant and accurate dating, which Javanese sources often lack and without which the historian can hardly function for he cannot place events in their proper relationships to one another.

II. A. I. *Algemeen Rijskarchief, The Hague*

The vast archival collection of the 'Koloniaal Archief' was the main body of Dutch documentation for this study. It was necessary to concentrate upon those volumes which were most important for internal Javanese history from among the several thousand housed in The Hague. They are the subseries 'Batavias Inkomend Briefboek' in the series of 'Overgekomen Brieven en Papieren'. These contain copies of all letters from the Governor and Council of Java's Northeast Coast at Sĕmarang to Batavia, often enclosing original reports and correspondence from Dutch Residencies at the courts and translations of items in Javanese. This series thus contains most of the information about Javanese affairs available to the Dutch. Eighty-eight volumes were employed, being one to four volumes for each year from 1755 to 1792. The series of 'Gemeen & Secret Afgaand Briefboek van Batavia' was consulted but found to be of little value for this study.

II. A. 2. *Arsip Nasional Republik Indonesia, Djakarta*

The Indonesian National Archive houses a miscellaneous collection from this period, much of it salvaged from the fire of the Sĕmarang Stadhuis in 1850 which destroyed the bulk of the Sĕmarang archive.[2] This collection has the advantage of containing several Javanese originals of treaties, reports, and correspondence. The volumes consulted are listed in the Bibliography.

II. A. 3. *Published Documents*

Several published documents are listed in the Bibliography. The most important group of such records is the invaluable de Jonge and van Deventer series of archival sources in sixteen volumes.[3] These volumes suffer from the disadvantages of all Company documentation described above in II. A. in somewhat exaggerated degree in that the records selected by de Jonge and van Deventer tend to originate in levels of the Company higher than the court Residencies or the Sĕmarang Government, and are thus less detailed and more removed from Javanese affairs.

II. B. *Javanese sources*

Javanese records offer several problems for the historian. They often argue special points of view to reflect favourably upon their author, patron, or main hero. There is a considerable problem of interpolation, with new versions of events finding their way into texts each time they were rewritten. Hence contemporaneousness is an important test of historical relevance. The language of Javanese sources, which were almost exclusively written in verse, is sometimes exceedingly vague. In this study the Javanese texts are given in footnotes whenever they are not over long, so that they may be compared with the English summaries or translations. The volume of Javanese records is a considerable problem. The four most important sources for this study, *Babad Gijanti*, *Babad Mangkubumi*, *Sĕrat Surja Radja*, and *Sĕrat Sakondar*, together contain over 3,500 pages of Javanese verse. The two *Babad Tanah Djawi* versions of *Babad Kraton* and the major Surakarta *Babad* contain some 4,000. Whereas it may be possible to glance over pages of Dutch records in search of relevant pas-

[2] J. A. van der Chijs, *Inventaris van 's Lands Archief te Batavia (1602–1816)* (Batavia, 1882), p. 155 n. 1.

[3] J. K. J. de Jonge and M. L. van Deventer (eds.), *De Opkomst van het Nederlandsch Gezag*. Full reference in Bibliography.

INTRODUCTION

sages, it is virtually impossible to skim documents written in a script in which words are not divided from one another.

But the advantages of Javanese source materials far outweigh the disadvantages. It is possible to gain from them an internal view of Javanese affairs which may not be free of bias but which cannot be accused of ignorance or indifference. The history of the Javanese courts simply cannot be written without careful attention to these records.

There are basically two types of narrative Javanese sources, the 'historical' and the 'mythical', for want of better terminology.[4] Whether Javanese poets would have accepted the validity of this distinction is a question best left to be considered elsewhere. There are also many important sources of a non-narrative nature, such as legal texts, letters, and land lists. But it is the narrative sources which predominate for most historical periods. The 'mythical' texts are those which do not describe real historical events, such as the earlier portions of the *Babad Tanah Djawi* versions, *Sĕrat Sakondar*, and *Sĕrat Surja Radja*. These texts are invaluable for reconstructing myths, cultural values, and idealized perceptions of actual situations. To be of historical value, however, one must be sure that they derive from the time and place to which their contents are supposed to appertain. The 'historical' texts are those which purport to describe actual events. They often lack sufficient dating to be used independently of Dutch records, but their description of events, their political history, is often more accurate than a survey of the secondary literature on Javanese historiography might suggest. The debate on the question of the historical accuracy of Javanese sources has concerned primarily the *Babad Tanah Djawi*. Very little of this debate has considered those texts which are solely 'historical' in nature and which derive from the period they describe or shortly thereafter, such as *Babad Gijanti* and *Babad Mangkubumi*. When compared with Dutch records, these sources seem on the whole not to require extraordinary analytical tools to be of use to the careful historian.

II. B. 1. *Babad Gijanti*

The 'historical' text of most importance for the period 1746–57 (Chapters II–III) is the *Babad Gijanti* by Raden Ngabei Jasadipura

[4] Cf. G. W. J. Drewes, 'Over werkelijke en vermeende Geschiedschrijving in de Nieuwjavaansche Litteratuur', *Djåwå*, vol. 19 (1939), pp. 244–57.

I. The dates of his life are somewhat uncertain and *Babad Gijanti* is not dated, but it seems reasonable to accept that Jasadipura I was a contemporary of the events he described here and that the text was written before c. 1803, at the latest. Jasadipura I was a court poet of Surakarta, one of the greatest in the history of Modern Javanese literature, and *Babad Gijanti* is a major literary work as well as an important historical source. Although much of its twenty-one volumes cannot be checked with Dutch records, which are less well informed, it seems to be accurate as literal history within the limits set out in II. B. Jasadipura I's main hero was Sultan Mangkubumi, Mas Said (Mangkunĕgara I) being also a heroic figure. Susuhunans Pakubuwana II and III are depicted less sympathetically. The edition published by Balai Pustaka has been used here (see Bibliography).

II. B. 2. *Babad Mangkubumi*

The most significant Javanese source for Mangkubumi's reign after 1755 (Chapters III–X) is *Babad Mangkubumi*, which was apparently written by his son the Crown Prince, later Sultan Hamĕngkubuwana II, in two segments. The first and major part was completed in 1773, the remainder being added after the Sultan's death in 1792.[5] Thus it is a description of the period by a contemporary at the centre of court affairs. Not surprisingly, it is favourable to Mangkubumi and to the Crown Prince, often violently critical of Mangkunĕgara, indifferent to Pakubuwana III, and opposed to Pakubuwana IV. It is tolerably well-written verse and much of it is accurate history, although it will be seen in the body of this study that sometimes history has been reshaped. The manuscript of this text (LOr 2191) was presented to Leiden University Library in 1874 by Mr. W. H. de Jong, Contrôleur in the Binnenlandsch Bestuur, having been acquired by him in Banjumas.[6] It appears to be a Jogjakarta *kraton* copy, finely written with illuminated initial pages. It is written on Dutch paper of late-eighteenth- or early-nineteenth-century manufacture, and consists of 549 pages.

[5] See below, pp. 167–9 n. 87.
[6] M. J. de Goeje, 'Aanwinsten der Verzameling van Oostersche Handschriften te Leiden', *De Nederlandsch Spectator*, 21 November 1874, pp. 379–80.

INTRODUCTION   xxi

11. B. 3. *Poensen's Babad*

Poensen's article of 1901 (see Bibliography) was based upon a prose manuscript (now LOr 5765) of Pakualaman origin.[7] It appears to have been written after Pakualam I's installation in 1813, to judge from its contents. It is not very accurate on the reign of Mangkubumi, but since Poensen's article is available in published form and has been the standard reference for over seven decades, it has been used for comparison here. It is favourable to Mangkubumi, and antagonistic to the Jogjakarta Crown Prince, Mangkunĕgara, Pakubuwana II, Pakubuwana III, and Pakubuwana IV.

11. B. 4. *Babad Pakĕpung*

The crisis of 1790 in Surakarta (Chapter IX) is the subject of *Babad Pakĕpung* (Sana Budaja MS. 123), a short text of 61 pages. It is undated and its authorship uncertain. It was perhaps written in Surakarta early in the nineteenth century by Raden Ngabei Jasadipura II (alias Raden Padjangwasista, alias Raden Ranggawarsita I, alias Raden Tumĕnggung Sastranagara).[8] The Sana

[7] See also M. C. Ricklefs, 'On the Authorship of Leiden Cod. Or. 2191, Babad Mangkubumi', *BKI*, vol. 127, no. 2 (1971), pp. 264–5.

[8] There is some dispute over the genealogy of the Jasadipuras and Ranggawarsitas. This equation of Jasadipura II and Ranggawarsita I is the version most accepted now by Javanese scholars. See Tjabang Bagian Bahasa, Djawatan Kebudajaan pada Kementerian P.P. & K., Jogjakarta, *Riwajat Kjahi Jasadipura I: Pudjangga Djawa di Surakarta* [Jogjakarta, 1952], p. 1.

The text of *Babad Pakĕpung* makes 'Jasadipura' seem to be a leading figure in the court intrigues (incorrectly, it seems; see p. 338 n. 117). This must be Jasadipura I, who would have been an adult member of court circles. It also says that 'Jasadipura' was ignored by PB IV because of his youth (p. 1), and this young 'Jasadipura' must be Jasadipura II. Later (pp. 14–15) the text mentions 'Mas Ronggawarsita' (Ranggawarsita I/Jasadipura II), the scribe of the Crown Prince, as a distinct person from Jasadipura (I), the head of the scribes:

B. *Pakĕpung* (Sana Budaja MS. 123), pp. 14–15, Canto IV (Ḍanḍanggula):

5. dene ingkang kĕni anunulis
   mung kakalih lijane tan kĕna
   amung tjarik Kadipaten
   Mas Ronggawarsiteku
   lawan tjarik kilen satunggil
   mung pun Djajasasmita
   dene lurahipun
   Ki Ngabei Waladana
   titinḍihe Jasadipura Ngabei
   tinambuh kalih pisan.

This suggests that the text was written by someone of the Jasadipura-Ranggawarsita line, whose role is emphasized, and that it was perhaps Ranggawarsita I/Jasadipura II. There is, however, no entirely adequate evidence for this.

Budaja MS. is, however, of much more recent date, being written on lined notebook paper. It is not a highly accurate text, although it preserves several interesting details. Nevertheless it is a useful source for comparison with Dutch and Jogjakarta texts. It is violently opposed to the Susuhunan's *santri* advisors.

II. B. 5. *Chronogram lists*

Chronogram (*sĕngkala*) lists provide concise and often illuminating descriptions of major events as well as the dates of their occurrence. The following were consulted:

BM Add. MS. 12323 (B), a Surakarta list, beginning with the year 1 and ending in 1815. Since it was part of John Crawfurd's collection it can have been copied no later than his departure from Java in 1816. It is a reliable source for the Surakarta period to 1815.

BM Add. MS. 12325 (C), a Jogjakarta text of little accuracy extending from early mythical history to 1813. It is also from Crawfurd's collection and hence no later than 1816 in date.

Babad Sangkalaning Momana, a Jogjakarta list originally composed in 1865 by Pangeran Arja Surjanagara, a distinguished littérateur of the House of Pakualam, and subsequently added to by others down to 1912. The text (a MS. in the Museum Pusat, Djakarta, consulted in a copy provided by Dr. H. J. de Graaf) is thus not contemporaneous to the period of this study. It was consulted because it is sometimes considered one of the major examples of this genre, but it was found not to be very reliable as a source for this period.

Sĕrat Djumĕnĕngan Sampejan-Dalĕm Ingkang Sinuhun Kangdjĕng Sultan Hamĕngkubuwana I, a Jogjakarta *kraton* list (MS. A. 22) extending from the birth of Sultan Mangkubumi to 1910. It was consulted merely because it is housed in the court of Mangkubumi's successors, but it proved to be inaccurate.

II. B. 6. *Laws and Treaties*

Several published legal and treaty texts have been employed (see Bibliography). For this study particular use was made of BM Add. MS. 12303, 'A Journal kept by the late Sultan of Java'. This volume was kept, apparently for reference, by Sultan Hamĕngkubuwana II of Jogjakarta, the Crown Prince during most of the period of this study, and was captured by the British forces who deposed him in 1812. This manuscript thus preserves unedited laws and treaties just as they were known to the Jogjakarta court, and obviates the possibility that Dutch texts might differ from those known to the Javanese.

11. B. 7. *Versions of the Babad Tanah Djawi*

This text, beginning with Adam and extending into 'historical' times (seventeenth century or after), is available in several manuscript and published versions, of which three are most commonly cited in this study:[9]

Babad Kraton (BM Add. MS. 12320) was written in the court of Jogjakarta in 1777–8 by Raden Tuměnggung Djajengrat, a son-in-law of Sultan Mangkubumi. It has been employed here primarily as a statement of *kraton* tradition in Jogjakarta during Mangkubumi's reign. It is a massive text, containing 170 cantos in over 1,400 large pages (717 folios), and was carried away from the Sultan's court by the British in 1812. It is free from problems of doubtful origin, later interpolation, or editing for external consumption.

The major Surakarta *Babad Tanah Djawi* has been used for comparison. It was begun in the reign of Susuhunan Pakubuwana IV (1788–1820) but the present version dates from 1836, when it was copied for the Dutch Government 'Java Institute' in Surakarta. The published Balai Pustaka edition of thirty-one volumes (see Bibliography) has been employed up to 1745–6. The portion of the manuscript from that time to the end of the text in 1768 was never published, and reference is therefore made also to the original eighteen-volume manuscript (LOr 1786).

The Meinsma *Babad Tanah Djawi* is a heavily edited prose condensation of the major Surakarta *Babad*. It is not an acceptable primary source for historical research, but it is the text most commonly consulted by those who know Javanese because it is published in transliteration and it is the only one consulted by those who do not because it is also available in Dutch translation. References are always to the edition and translation by W. L. Olthof (see Bibliography).

[9] For a more full discussion of these texts and their interrelationship, see M. C. Ricklefs, 'A Consideration of Three Versions of the Babad Tanah Djawi, With Excerpts on the Fall of Madjapahit', *Bulletin of the School of Oriental and African Studies*, vol. 35, pt. 2 (1972), pp. 285–315.

xxiv JOGJAKARTA UNDER SULTAN MANGKUBUMI

11. B. 8. *Sĕrat Surja Radja*

The mythical text summarized in Chapter VII is the Jogjakarta *pusaka* text *Kangdjĕng Kjai Surja Radja*, written by the Crown Prince of Jogjakarta (Sultan Hamĕngkubuwana II) in March 1774. The date and authorship of the original *Surja Radja* text of 1774 seem beyond doubt, and it therefore represents a reliable source for *kraton* myth at an important time in Jogjakarta's history. Other versions have also been employed for comparison.[10]

11. B. 9. *Sĕrat Sakondar*

The version of the Baron Sakendar story summarized in Chapter XI is that in BM Add. MS. 12289, *Sĕrat Sakondar*. As part of Crawfurd's collection it can have been written no later than 1816, and was perhaps composed between 1808 and 1812. It seems to be of Jogjakarta *kraton* origin.[11] Thus, it was composed shortly after the period described here, but it is the oldest version known to this writer and the closest to the Jogjakarta *kraton* myth of Sultan Mangkubumi's day.

Several other texts of the Baron Sakender story of later date were used for comparison.[12]

11. B. 10. *Other Javanese Sources*

Other Javanese texts have played more minor roles in the present study and some have merely been mentioned in passing. All of these will be found in the Bibliography.

111. *Orthography and Transliteration*

All spellings of Javanese names and words follow eighteenth-century usage as far as possible. Quotations from Javanese sources are spelled as in the original, even where this involves forms which are no longer considered standard. Plurals of Javanese words have been formed by adding the English 's' or 'es'. The only significant departure from these orthographic standards is the name of the city of Jogjakarta. The form used here corresponds to current usage, but there is a large number of variant spellings. *Ngajogjakarta (Adiningrat)* would be the correct formal style in eighteenth-century usage. The current style has been adopted here for the sake of simplicity.

[10] See p. 193 n. 54, and pp. 194–5 n. 59.
[11] See Chap. XI, especially p. 337.   [12] See pp. 377–8 n. 38.

INTRODUCTION

The system of transliteration for Modern Javanese follows that in Dr. Pigeaud's Javanese–Dutch dictionary (see Bibliography), with the following exceptions: *oe* here becomes *u*, *é* and *è* become *e*, *e* (*pĕpĕt*) becomes *ĕ*. This system satisfies the need for accuracy while at the same time being close to current Javanese practice and requiring no special characters. At the time of this writing, rules for the new official orthography for Javanese are not yet available.

Consonants are pronounced rather as they are in English, the major exceptions being the alveolar *ḍ* and *ṭ*. *Dj* is pronounced like English 'j' in 'job'; *tj* like 'ch' in 'chair'; *j* like English 'y'; *ng* like 'ng' in 'sing'.

Vowels are pronounced as follows: *a* is like the 'a' in 'father' in closed syllables, but like the 'au' in 'caught' in open final syllables; *e* is like either the 'e' in 'set' or the 'a' in 'fate'; *ĕ* is like 'e' in 'fallen'; *i* like 'i' in 'machine'; *o* is rather like 'o' in 'old'; *u* like 'u' in 'rule'.

Words in other languages (Old Javanese, Sanskrit, Arabic) follow currently acceptable systems of transliteration. Malay passages occurring in Javanese texts and in Javanese script are transliterated according to the system for Javanese.

IV. Dates

Four systems of dating are used in this study. The solar Śāka era used since Old Javanese times and its successor lunar era (from 1633) are for the sake of convenience classified together as the Javanese era (A.J.). It was this system of chronology in which the Javanese thought. The Islamic *Anno Hijrae* (A.H.) was also employed by the Javanese courts, but much less frequently than A.J.

Whenever a date is given without any indication of the era (A.J. or A.H.), it is a date in the Christian calendar (A.D.). A table of conversions from A.J. to A.D. for the period of Mangkubumi's reign will be found in Appendix IV.

I
THE HISTORICAL BACKGROUND

THE 'Hindu-Javanese' period of Indonesian history bequeathed to the world a series of famous temples, often magnificent in design and exquisite in detail. Their outlines are well known to many Indonesians and foreigners, scholars and tourists alike. These structures have been seen as the quintessential expression of a Javanese Classical Age, and a great body of scholarship has been erected over their ruins. The Old Javanese and Sanskrit literature of this period has also attracted scholarly attention. With the fall of the kingdom of Madjapahit in the late fifteenth or early sixteenth century, the Hindu period of Javanese history came to an end. But it was not barbarians who now took centre stage. Nor was it the beginning of a Javanese 'Dark Age'.

The Islamic successor kingdoms were heirs to the sophisticated culture of Madjapahit, which they adapted to their own genius. The new age produced no Barabuḍur, but built instead the mosques of Děmak and Kudus, the royal grave-sites at Imagiri, and the pleasure-garden *cum* fortress of *Taman Sari*. Sanskrit and Old Javanese literature gradually disappeared; the books of the succeeding centuries were in Modern Javanese, but are no less worthy of scholarly attention than their 'classical' precursors. Indeed, in some ways, the distinction between the Old and Modern periods of Javanese history is more an historiographical and linguistic convention than an historical reality.

The decline and fall of Madjapahit is shrouded in mystery. There are few reliable documents from the latter years of the kingdom shedding light on the final collapse. Any reconstruction of these years depends largely upon Chinese notices, which speak of warfare early in the fifteenth century,[1] and upon the story of discord, death, and confusion which seems to be suggested in the Middle Javanese *Pararaton*,[2] from Bali. According to Modern

[1] W. P. Groeneveldt, 'Notes on the Malay Archipelago and Malacca, Compiled from Chinese Sources', *VBG*, vol. 39, pt. 1 (1877), pp. 36–7.
[2] See J. L. A. Brandes (ed.), 'Pararaton (Ken Arok) of het Boek der Koningen

Javanese tradition, the kingdom fell in the Javanese year (Śāka/ A.J.) 1400, equivalent to A.D. 1478,[3] and this date is traditionally taken as the beginning of the Islamic period in Java. If Madjapahit did fall in 1478, however, it is undeniable that a 'Hindu' power-centre continued to exist for some time thereafter. There are Hindu-Javanese inscriptions from A.J. 1408 (A.D. 1486)[4] and Portuguese sources mention a 'heathen' ruler in the second decade of the sixteenth century.[5] Historical precision about the last years of Madjapahit is thus impossible at the present time. It is clear, however, that its fall was coincident with a development only slightly less obscure, the rise of Javanese Islam as a political force.

The beginnings of Islam in Java are vague, but the religion certainly claimed adherents on the island before the end of the Madjapahit period. In 1416, Ma Huan, the secretary of the great Ming admiral Cheng Ho, wrote that there were three types of people in Java: Muslims from the West, Chinese (some of whom had embraced Islam), and the native Javanese, whom he rather flamboyantly described as savages believing in devils.[6] Archaeological evidence gives a rather fuller picture of this situation. The oldest Islamic gravestone found on the coast of Java dates from

---

van Tumapel en van Majapahit' (2nd. ed.; ed. N. J. Krom), *VBG*, vol. 62 (1920); see especially chaps. xi–xviii.
For the standard description of these events, see N. J. Krom, *Hindoe-Javaansche Geschiedenis* ('s-Gravenhage, 1931), chap. xiii.

[3] Brandes, 'Pararaton', p. 40. The date is also found in several Modern Javanese *babads* and *sĕngkala*-lists; see below, p. 177 n. 8.
See also G. P. Rouffaer, 'Het Tijdperk van Godsdienstovergang (1400–1600) in den Maleischen Archipel: Wanneer is Madjapahit Gevallen?', *BKI*, vol. 50 (1899), pp. 111–99.
On all these matters, see the forthcoming monograph by Dr. H. J. de Graaf, with notes by Dr. Th. G. Th. Pigeaud, to be entitled, 'De eerste Moslimse Vorstendommen op Java: Studiën over de staatkundige Geschiedenis van de 15de en 16de Eeuw'.

[4] OJO 91, 92, 93, 94/5, in N. J. Krom (ed.), 'Oud-Javaansche Oorkonden. Nagelaten Transscripties door wijlen Dr. J. L. A. Brandes', *VBG*, vol. 60 (1913), pp. 212–26.

[5] On these Portuguese sources, see Krom, *HJG*, pp. 452–61. Krom did not have available the important records of Tomé Pires, which also distinguish the heathen ruler of the interior from the 'Moors' of Java's coast; see Armando Cortesão (ed. and trans.), *The Suma Oriental of Tomé Pires and the Book of Francisco Rodrigues* (2 vols.; London, 1944), vol. i, pp. 174 ff.

[6] Ma Huan, *Ying-yai Sheng-lan*, in W. W. Rockhill, 'Notes on the Relations and Trade of China with the Eastern Archipelago and the Coast of the Indian Ocean during the Fourteenth Century,' *T'oung Pao*, vol. 16 (1915), p. 242. Also in Groeneveldt, 'Notes', pp. 49–50.

1419.[7] The deceased, one Malik Ibrahim, had been born in Persia and had probably journeyed to Java as a trader. But Islam was not limited to the coast. The Tralaja gravestones, found in the region of the Madjapahit *kraton*, suggest the presence of Javanese Muslims at the centre of the Hindu-Javanese kingdom as early as A.J. 1298 (A.D. 1376), during the reign of the great Hajam Wuruk.[8] A gravestone dated A.J. 1370 (A.D. 1448) marks the burial at Trawulan of a Muslim dignitary traditionally said to have been a queen of Madjapahit. She is referred to in Javanese tradition as *Putri Tjĕmpa*, the Princess from Champa, one of the wives of Madjapahit's last ruler, Brawidjaja.[9]

The means by which Islam spread in Java cannot easily be ascertained from available evidence.[10] It is, therefore, a question likely to attract much speculation. It is clear that the religion spread gradually over several centuries. The role of the Islamic

[7] J. P. Moquette, 'De Datum op den Grafsteen van Malik Ibrāhīm te Grissee', *TBG*, vol. 54 (1912), pp. 208–14.
I am ignoring here the late-eleventh- or early-twelfth-century tomb at Leran, since the date when this gravestone was imported to Java may be much later than the date of its inscription; see J. P. Moquette, 'De oudste Mohammedaansche Inscriptie op Java, n.m. de Grafsteen te Leran', *Handelingen van het eerste Congres voor de Taal-, Land- en Volkenkunde van Java* (Weltevreden, 1921), pp. 391–9; and Paul Ravaisse, 'L'Inscription coufique de Léran à Java', *TBG*, vol. 65 (1925), pp. 668–703.

[8] L.-Ch. Damais, 'Études javanaises: I, Les Tombes musulmanes datées de Trålåjå', *BEFEO*, vol. 48 (1957), pp. 353–415.

[9] See Bataviaasch Genootschap van Kunsten en Wetenschappen, *Rapporten van de Commissie in Nederlandsch-Indië voor Oudheidkundig Onderzoek op Java en Madoera, 1907* ('s-Gravenhage, 1909), pp. 42–51. Krom, *HJG*, p. 452, expresses scepticism about the dentification of the deceased as the Putri Tjĕmpa.
See also *BTDj*, trans., pp. 18–19; and *BK*, f. 52ᵛ. In the latter text she is called 'Pramesjari ing Darawati'. *BK*, f. 66ʳ, explains that 'Ni Mas Ratu Dyariwati' was the wife of Brawidjaja, formerly called 'Putri Tjĕmpa': . . . Ni Mas Ratu / Dyariwati ingkang nama / Putri Tjĕmpa punika purwane dingin / kang garwa Brawidjaja.
She is also called Darawati in the *Sĕrat Kaṇḍa*; Brandes, 'Pararaton', pp. 223, 226.
On the question of Islam in Champa, see G. Coedès, *The Indianized States of Southeast Asia* (ed. Walter F. Vella; trans. Susan Brown Cowing; Honolulu, 1968), pp. 238–9.

[10] For a summary of the writing on this topic, see G. W. J. Drewes, 'New Light on the Coming of Islam to Indonesia?', *BKI*, vol. 124, no. 4 (1968), pp. 433–59. See also D. G. E. Hall, *A History of South-East Asia* (3rd ed.; New York, 1968), pp. 213–18, and the literature which Professor Hall cites there.
Epigraphic materials are discussed in Louis-Charles Damais, 'L'Épigraphie musulmane dans le Sud-Est Asiatique', *BEFEO*, vol. 54 (1968), pp. 567–604.

trader, who married locally in Java and converted his wife to his faith, ultimately leading to the establishment of nuclear Islamic settlements, must have been significant in some areas of the island. One suspects this form of proselytization would have been most common in coastal areas less incorporated into the sophisticated Hindu-Javanese culture of Madjapahit.

In the cultural heartland of Central and East Java it seems less likely that the peripatetic Muslim trader would have commanded sufficient prestige to convert any but the lower levels of society. In such areas, the agent of conversion among the élite may perhaps have been the mystical teachers of the Sufi brotherhoods (*ṭarīqah*), who may also have been connected in some way with the Islamic trading guilds.[11] There is, however, no specific evidence to confirm this suggestion. The lack of austerity in the Sufi understanding of Islam may have made the new creed more readily acceptable to the Javanese élite, who were accustomed to a religion based upon a complex pre-Hindu animism infused at higher social levels with the Indic philosophies of Hinduism and Buddhism.

Javanese tradition calls the early Muslim leaders in Java *walis* (saints). They are normally said to have been nine in number (the *wali sanga*), but their names are not always the same.[12] It is un-

[11] See A. H. Johns, 'Sufism as a Category in Indonesian Literature and History', *JSEAH*, vol. 2, no. 2 (July 1961), pp. 10–23; and 'Muslim Mystics and Historical Writing', in D. G. E. Hall (ed.), *Historians of South East Asia* (London, 1961), pp. 37–49. But see also Drewes, 'New Light', p. 453.

[12] *BK*, f. 75r, lists them as Sunans Ngampel-Děnta, Kudus, Murja, Benang (i.e. Bonang), Giri, Kalidjaga, Lěmbahbang (i.e. Lěmah Abang), Gunungdjati, and Walilanang.

In *BTDj*, trans., pp. 20–46, are found Ampel-Děnta, Kudus, Bonang, Giri, Kalidjaga, Siti Djěnar (i.e. Lěmah Abang), Gunungdjati, and Walilanang.

In his classic series of articles 'De Heiligen van Java', D. A. Rinkes dealt with four of the nine: Seh Siti Djěnar, Sunan Gěsěng, Ki Paṇḍan Arang of Těmbajat, and Pangeran Panggung; *TBG*, vol. 52 (1910), pp. 556–89; vol. 53 (1911), pp. 17–56, 269–300, 435–581; vol. 54 (1912), pp. 135–207; vol. 55 (1913), pp. 1–201.

T. J. Bezemer (ed.), *Beknopte Encyclopaedië van Nederlandsch Indië* ('s-Gravenhage, 1921), lists the following under 'Heiligen': Malik Ibrahim (Maulana Maghribi), Sunan Ngampel (Raden Rahmat), Sunan Bonang (Makdum Ibrahim), Sunan Giri (Raden Paku), Sunan Gunungdjati, Sunan Kudus, Sunan Muria, Sunan Dradjat, and Sunan Kalidjaga.

In *Sěrat Kaṇḍa* (Brandes, 'Pararaton', p. 227) are listed Sunans Giri, Tjěrbon (i.e. Gunungdjati), Gěsang, Mědjagung, Undung (i.e. Kudus), Bonang, Dradjat, Kalidjaga, and Seh Lěmahbang.

See also Dr. Pigeaud's shorter summary of the *Sěrat Kaṇḍaning Ringgit Purwa* (LOr 6379), where there are mentioned Sunans Ngampel-Děnta, Undung (Kudus), Dradjat, Iskak (Giri), Bonang, Tjěrbon, Kalidjaga, Seh Siti

certain when the historical personages behind these legends lived. Although they are described as contemporaries, their deeds cover the late fifteenth and sixteenth centuries, and in the case of several of these spiritual lords they extend into the seventeenth century. Many of the *walis* seem to have been of non-Javanese origin and were often connected with particular port-towns of the Javanese *pasisir*.[13]

It would probably be wrong to see these *walis* as street-corner preachers. Rather, they were perhaps more likely mystics who gave their teachings to small groups of selected students, attracted to them for their learning and magical prowess. But again, this can only be supposition. The Meinsma *Babad Tanah Djawi* comments, 'At that time, many Javanese wished to be taught the religion of the Prophet and to learn supernatural powers and invincibility.'[14] Wondrous tales are told of the *walis*' ability to walk on water, to change rice to sand or, rather more profitably, earth to gold.[15] Their grave-sites are considered to be repositories of great spiritual power and are still sites of pilgrimage.[16]

The best-known version of Javanese historical tradition, that contained in the nineteenth-century Surakarta Major *Babad Tanah Djawi* and the Meinsma prose *Babad Tanah Djawi*, ascribes to the *walis* a significant role under the leadership of Raden Patah of Bintara in the defeat of Madjapahit. The older recension of this tradition contained in the eighteenth-century Jogjakarta *Babad Kraton* presents a somewhat different picture, and gives only passing reference to military action. In general, it minimizes the conflict between the new and the old religions and omits entirely

---

Djěnar, and Pangeran Panggung; Th. G. Th. Pigeaud, *Literature of Java* (3 vols.; The Hague and Leiden, 1967–70), vol. ii, pp. 362–3.

[13] See H. J. de Graaf, *Geschiedenis van Indonesië* ('s Gravenhage, 1949), p. 81.

[14] *BTDj*, text, p. 46: Ing waktu punika tětijang Djawi katah kang sami rěměn nggěguru lampah ing agami Rasul tuwin nggěguru kadigdajan sarta katěguhan.

[15] See de Graaf, *GI*, p. 81.

[16] As late as 1775, it was necessary for the Dutch East India Company to require a special undertaking from the officials in charge of the holy grave-site of Sunan Giri at Grěsik that they would not allow Sunan Giri's holy *kris* to fall into unauthorized hands, which might employ it to foment rebellion; Contracts of Ardjanagara and Astranagara, Regents of Grěsik, 30 June 1775, in KA 3362 (OB 1777).

to mention the *walis* in connection with the fall of Madjapahit.[17] It is thus uncertain what role the *walis* may have played in the obscure historical processes which led to the end of Madjapahit. Nevertheless, it is probably correct to assume that they had significant temporal as well as spiritual authority, and that if there was a major military assault on Madjapahit they would presumably have been involved in some way. The legendary tales surrounding these divines probably also give a roughly accurate picture of Javanese religion in the early years of the Islamic period: mystical, unorthodox by modern standards, and probably not so very different from Hindu-Javanese practices. Pre-Islamic beliefs survived the 'conversion', and still survive today.[18]

That is not to say that more orthodox Islam was not known in Java in the sixteenth century. A Javanese *primbon* (notebook, handbook) of sixteenth-century origin was brought back to the Netherlands by the first Dutch expedition to the Indies (1595–7).[19] The most recent editor of this important manuscript, Professor G. W. J. Drewes,[20] agrees with the previous view of Professor Kraemer that the text shows no significant 'adaptation to Javanese surroundings'. It is an orthodox mystical document which might be found in any Islamic land.[21] The text formerly known as the *Sĕrat Bonang*, because of an incorrect attribution to Sunan Bonang of Tuban,[22] is also believed to be a sixteenth-century document.[23] Professor Drewes has also recently re-edited this text, pointing out the erroneous nature of the ascription to Sunan Bonang, and suggesting

[17] A discussion of these three sources, with texts and translations on the fall of Madjapahit, will be found in Ricklefs, 'Consideration'.
[18] See Clifford Geertz, *The Religion of Java* (Glencoe, 1964); and H. A. van Hien, *De Javaansche Geestenwereld* (3 vols.; Batavia, [1933–5]).
[19] On this first expedition, see G. P. Rouffaer and J. W. Ijzerman (eds.), *De eerste Schipvaart der Nederlanders naar Oost-Indië onder Cornelis de Houtman, 1595–1597* (3 vols.; 's-Gravenhage, 1915, 1925, 1929); and J. C. Mollema, *De eerste Schipvaart der Hollanders naar Oost-Indië, 1595–1597* ('s-Gravenhage, 1935).
[20] The text (LOr 266) has been thrice published: by J. G. H. Gunning (Leiden, 1881), by H. Kraemer (Leiden, 1921), and most recently by G. W. J. Drewes, *Een Javaansche Primbon uit de Zestiende Eeuw* (Leiden, 1954).
[21] Drewes, *Primbon*, pp. 3–4.
[22] See B. J. O. Schrieke (ed.), *Het Boek van Bonang* (Leiden, 1916). Sunan Bonang was one of the nine *walis*; see above, n. 12.
For a descriptive catalogue of other mystical texts said to be connected with Sunan Bonang, see G. W. J. Drewes, 'Javanese Poems dealing with or attributed to the Saint of Bonaṅ', *BKI*, vol. 124, no. 2 (1968), pp. 209–40.
[23] See Schrieke, *Bonang*, pp. xii–xvi; and Drewes, *Primbon*, p. 7.

BACKGROUND 7

that the book is more properly called 'The Admonitions of Seh Bari'. Like the *primbon*, this work too is orthodox Islamic mysticism, but by listing various heresies then current on Java it suggests that there were others who were less doctrinally correct.[24]

The most famous Javanese heretic of these early years was Seh Siti Djĕnar, one of the nine *walis*. Whether or not the legend of Siti Djĕnar is historically accurate, it can perhaps give a feeling for the historical context of early Javanese Islam. He was supposedly condemned to death by a synod of the *walis* for teaching the secret mystical truth (*ngelmu gaib*) that Allah and His Creation, including man, were One. When Siti Djĕnar was first summoned to the synod, he told the emissaries, 'Know, you two, that Siti Djĕnar does not exist, now it is Allah who appears; report this.'[25] Before Sunan Giri, he declared, 'There is no Friday, there is no mosque, only Allah indeed exists. There is nothing other which now has existence.'[26]

This account not only suggests that mystical strains of Islam were current on Java, but suggests also the continuing strength of pre-Islamic conceptions of Reality. The identity of the Self with the God-head is a common theme of the ancient Upanishadic philosophy, and is basic to Hindu thought. In the *Chandogya-Upanishad*, Svetaketu is told by his teacher,

In the beginning there was existence, One only, without a second. He, the One, thought to himself: Let me be many, let me grow forth. Thus out of himself he projected the universe; and having projected out of himself the universe, he entered into every being. All that is has its self in him alone. Of all things he is the subtle essence. He is the truth. He is the self. And that, Svetaketu, THAT ART THOU.[27]

Indo-Iranian influences on Islamic philosophy led to the perseverance of this mystical theme within the faith of the Prophet, as well. But what was orthodox in Hinduism might be heresy in

[24] See G. W. J. Drewes (ed. and trans.), *The Admonitions of Seh Bari* (The Hague, 1969).
[25] Rinkes, 'Heiligen II', *TBG*, vol. 53 (1911), p. 20: Wruhanira sira kalih / Seh Siti Djĕnar sĕpi / saiki Allah kang wudjud / wus sira umatura.
[26] Ibid., p. 22: tan ana ran Djumuwah / miwah tan ana kang masdjid / ia amung Allah kang ana sanjata / noranana lianira / ingkang maudjud saiki.
Rinkes's text is from a late-nineteenth-century manuscript from Sĕmarang; see ibid., p. 18 n. 1.
[27] Swami Prabhavananda and Frederick Manchester (eds. and trans.), *The Upanishads, Breath of the Eternal* (New York, 1963), pp. 68–9. Emphasis in original.

Islam. Like Siti Djĕnar after him, the tenth-century Persian mystic al-Ḥallāj was martyred for declaring his identification with the God-head. He wrote,

> I am He whom I love, and He whom I love is I.
> We are two souls dwelling in one body.
> When thou seest me, thou seest him:
> And when thou seest Him, thou seest us both.[28]

This denial of any distinction between God and man, in its most extreme form the denial of any difference between God and the *kafir* (infidel), is a common and widely-accepted heresy in Modern Javanese mystical texts.[29] Indeed, it is a moot point whether Siti Djĕnar was condemned to death for the heretical nature of his doctrine, or simply because he had made that doctrine public, to the uninitiated.

Thus it seems clear that Hindu-Javanese mystical concepts were able to survive the 'conversion' to Islam, thereby suggesting the cultural continuities which linked Old and Modern Java. Professor Zoetmulder has observed that Modern Javanese mystical writings often explain their teachings with terminology borrowed from Sivaite mysticism.[30] That this is so is a comment not only upon the durability of Hindu-Javanese culture, but upon the ecumenicity of religious mysticism as well. In general, it would seem to be incorrect to see the adoption of Islam by the Javanese as a definitive turning-point in Javanese cultural history.

With the new faith came a new kingdom, its capital at Dĕmak on the north coast of Java. The history of Dĕmak is, however, shrouded in legends and semi-historical tales of dubious veracity, and it is impossible at this time to describe its history with any confidence.[31] Even the dates for the kingdom are uncertain, although it is probable that Dĕmak was the main political force on Java during much of the first half of the sixteenth century.

The collapse of Madjapahit probably left a legacy of confusion, local aspirations, and divided loyalties. Judging from later, better-

[28] Quoted in Philip K. Hitti, *History of the Arabs* (London, 1968), pp. 435–6.
[29] See P. J. Zoetmulder, *Pantheisme en Monisme in de Javaansche Soeloek-Litteratuur* (Nijmegen, 1935), especially chap. ix, 'Radical Monisme', and chap. xii, 'De Leer der Walis'. See also the texts quoted in Drewes, 'Javanese Poems'.
[30] P. J. Zoetmulder, 'Die Hochreligionen Indonesiens', in P. Zoetmulder and Waldemar Stöhr, *Die Religionen Indonesiens* (Stuttgart, 1965), pp. 304–5.
[31] Dr. H. J. de Graaf's new monograph, 'De eerste Moslimse Vorstendommen', will deal with Dĕmak history.

BACKGROUND

documented periods, Java was probably riddled with small dynasties, and Děmak was probably no more than the main power in a fragmented political situation.[32] *Babad Kraton* describes the situation in these terms:

> XIII: 16. . . .
> Adipati Bintara
> was named ruler of all of Madjapahit,
> becoming the first Islamic Ruler
> over all of the Land of Java,
> 17. reigning in Děmak
> . . .
>
> 18. . . .
> It is told, after a period
> 19. of ruling as King of Děmak,
> his government was exceedingly honoured
> by the Rulers of the Land of Java, all.
> All the Rulers submitted
> to the Lord of Děmak;
> all the troops submitted as well.
>
> 20. We will not speak of how long
> was the reign of Sultan Děmak;
> the *walis* all assented,
> approving.[33]

[32] Portuguese sources also suggest this was the case. See Cortesão, vol. i, pp. 182–98.

[33] *BK*, ff. 74ᵛ–75ʳ. Canto XIII (Pangkur):

> 16. . . .
> Adipati Bintara
> pan djuměněng Ratu ngrad ing Madjalangu
> dadi purwa Ratu Islam
> sadaja ing Tanah Djawi
>
> 17. djuměněng aneng ing Děmak
> . . .
>
> 18. . . .
> katjatur sampun alami
>
> 19. djumněng Sang Ratu Děmak
> langkung keḍěp parentahira Nrěpati
> marang ingkang para Ratu
> Tanah Djawa sadaja
> para Nata pan sami sujud sadarum
> datěng Sang Prabu ing Děmak
> wadya-bala sujud sami

This passage suggests the fragmentation of early-sixteenth-century political reality on Java, although the reference to the 'Rulers of the Land of Java' could be taken as mere poetic convention. The new Lord of Děmak, Raden Patah, must have required a consensus of other power-centres in order to rule. And these other power-centres, particularly the coastal port-states, are represented in the *Babad Kraton* passage not only by the 'Rulers', but more importantly by the *walis*, who assented to Děmak's position. It is of interest here that Seh Siti Djěnar is associated by tradition with the Pěngging area of Central Java, which is said to have been an opponent of Děmak. Thus, his martyrdom before a synod of the remaining *walis*, who were supporters of the Děmak hegemony, should perhaps be seen as having a political as well as a sectarian significance.[34] Dr. de Graaf believes that the third ruler of Děmak, Sultan[35] Trěnggana (?*c*. 1505–?1546), presided over the kingdom's Golden Age, but that the realm again fell apart after his death.[36]

Such political fragmentation is a consistent theme of Javanese history, and times of true political unity would appear to have been the exception rather than the rule. This is so, it seems, at least to some extent because of the geography of Java. The island can be readily divided into a series of more-or-less isolated plains and valleys, separated from one another by volcanic mountain ranges. This perhaps produced strong senses of local identity and centrifugal forces which could easily threaten the hegemony of any kingdom claiming sovereignty over the island. The successful ruler ensured his control of the island by military pressure when necessary and, at other times, by ruling in a manner which did not threaten the autonomy of provincial dignitaries and thereby force

    20. tan kawarna laminira
           sadjěněnge Sultan Děmak aněnggih
           kang para wali adjurung
           angastreni sěmana
           . . . .

[34] Rinkes, 'Heiligen II', *TBG*, vol. 53 (1911), pp. 45–7.
[35] I am following Modern Javanese convention in using the title 'Sultan' for the rulers of Děmak. It is open to question whether any of them actually held this title; see H. J. de Graaf, 'Titels en Namen van Javaanse Vorsten en Groten uit de 16e en 17e Eeuw', *BKI*, vol. 109 (1953), pp. 66–7.
[36] De Graaf, *GI*, pp. 92–4. The date 1505 has been communicated to me by Dr. de Graaf. He formerly assigned the beginning of this reign to 1521. He now believes there may have been an interruption of the reign, ending in 1521.

BACKGROUND 11

them into rebellion. These themes will be considered more fully at the end of this chapter.

The manner in which the kingdom of Padjang now came to exercise hegemony over Java is not discernible from documents presently available. It is significant, however, that with Padjang the *kraton* had returned from the more Islamic *pasisir* to the old cultural heartland of Central Java. Here the likelihood of Islamic traditions influencing the affairs of the court was probably even less than had been the case during the short period of coastal predominance. The investiture of the first Sultan of Padjang is traditionally assigned to the year A.J. 1503 (A.D. 1581). This date, however, seems too late for the accession of the first ruler, and was probably contrived by later Javanese writers to fit an idealized chronological pattern of dynastic change.[37] Dr. de Graaf suggests that the first ruler of Padjang, one Djaka Tingkir, must have functioned as ruler for some time before receiving the title of Sultan, if indeed he ever received it.[38] *Babad Kraton*, adding to the documentary confusion, describes a period when 'Sultans' reigned at both Děmak and Padjang, during the reign of Sultan Prawata of Děmak (?1546–?1561).[39] Thus, it is again difficult to unravel the web of legends surrounding historical events. It does seem probable, however, that Padjang was never more than *primus inter pares* in a politically disintegrated situation, and that even this qualified authority was short-lived.[40]

By about 1578, a regional power-centre had been established in the Mataram area, near present-day Jogjakarta.[41] Here Javanese history had come full circle. The homeland of the eighth- and

[37] See below, p. 179 n. 18.
[38] See H. J. de Graaf, 'De Regering van Panembahan Sénapati Ingalaga', *VKI*, vol. 13 (1954), pp. 24–5; and 'Titels en Namen', pp. 69–73.
[39] *BK*, ff. 83ʳ–83ᵛ. De Graaf, *GI*, p. 481, gives A.D. 1546 as the year of Sultan Trěnggana's death. *BK* has no *sěngkala* for this event, but gives A.J. 1483 (A.D. 1561) for the death of Sultan Prawata, on f. 90ʳ.
[40] Cf. de Graaf, 'Sénapati', pp. 67–9.
[41] The date A.D. 1578 is calculated by Dr. de Graaf ('Sénapati,' p. 54) on the basis of the statement that the *kraton* which fell in A.J. 1600 (A.D. 1677) had existed for one century. Thus, he takes the original foundation of Mataram to have been in A.J. 1500 (A.D. 1578). There are a number of objections which might be raised to this procedure, the foremost being that the figure of one hundred years (see below, pp. 180–1, n. 20) is found in chronicles written in the eighteenth and nineteenth centuries, and may have been added later to make history more orderly. Nevertheless, it is probably true that by about A.D. 1578, Mataram had begun to be at least a significant regional power.

ninth-century kingdom of Mataram was again to be the focal point of royal authority in Java. For the next four centuries, the House of Mataram would rule as Javanese monarchs, first in Mataram itself (Kuṭa Gĕḍe, Kĕrta, Plered), then in Padjang (Kartasura, Surakarta) and finally, in regal bifurcation, in both (Surakarta, Jogjakarta). It is only with the history of Mataram that it gradually becomes possible for the historian to speak with greater confidence.

The beginnings of Mataram are hardly less obscure than the events of the preceding century. Dr. de Graaf has published a monograph on Panĕmbahan Senapati Ingalaga (?1574–1601), traditionally considered the first ruler of Mataram, which is based upon both indigenous and external documentation for the nebulous events of those years.[42] Professor Berg has argued, however, that Senapati in fact never existed, and was solely a creation of later years, designed to give Sultan Agung (1613–45) a fictitious royal genealogy.[43] It is true, as Professor Berg points out, that the feats ascribed to Senapati bear a resemblance to those of Sultan Agung. It is also notable that some Javanese sources date the death of Senapati's father, and therefore Senapati's accession to authority over Mataram, in A.J. 1535 (A.D. 1613),[44] which was in fact the date of Sultan Agung's succession. This suggests that at least some elements of the traditional story of Senapati's reign may be antedated versions of Agung's feats. But Dr. de Graaf has replied to Professor Berg's arguments with evidence which demonstrates that Mataram was a major power at least some two decades before Agung became ruler.[45] It therefore seems most unlikely that Senapati was entirely a product of later dynastic myth-making.

[42] The events of Sénapati's reign summarized here are based upon Dr. de Graaf's 'Sénapati'.

[43] C. C. Berg, 'Twee nieuwe Publicaties betreffende de Geschiedenis en de Geschiedschrijving van Mataram', *Indonesië*, vol. 8 (1955), pp. 97–128, especially pp. 110–12.

[44] *BTDj* (*BP*), vol. iv, pp. 76–7; *BK*, f. 110r; BM Add. MS. 12323 (B), f. 34r; *BTDj*, trans. p. 72, text p. 70.

A.J. 1535 was given not for the death, but for the ascension of Kjai Gĕde Mataram, Senapati's father, in J. W. Winter, 'Beknopte Beschrijving van het Hof Soerakarta in 1824', *BKI*, vol. 54 (1902), p. 27; but see also Rouffaer's n. 4 on p. 99 of the same article.

[45] Dr. de Graaf has answered Prof. Berg's objections in 'De Historische Betrouwbaarheid der Javaanse Overlevering', *BKI*, vol. 112 (1956), pp. 55–73. Willem Lodewijks' map of Java, showing Mataram as a major power before the end of the sixteenth century, is a particularly important piece of evidence.

BACKGROUND

The *babad* stories are anything but sober historical accounts. They claim that a falling star spoke to Senapati, foretelling the greatness of Mataram and of Senapati's descendants. Acting upon this prophecy, he proceeded to establish liaison with the powerful Goddess of the Southern Ocean, in whose underwater palace he spent three days and nights learning how to call up the armies of the spirits, as well as pursuing more intimate studies.[46] There are various romantic versions of the events leading up to the subsequent conflict with the ruler of Padjang, which is said to have ended in a Mataram victory in the shadow of Tjaṇḍi Prambanan.[47] This event probably took place late in the 1580s.[48]

Senapati's reign is described as a series of campaigns, largely against the eastern *pasisir*. His most powerful rival seems to have been Surabaja, which was not to be subdued until the third decade of the seventeenth century. In general, the port-cities of the *pasisir* were probably still powerful and largely independent when Senapati died in 1601.[49] There is no evidence that Senapati had exercised any very permanent control outside of Central Java, and he should not be seen as sovereign over the island. That was to be the role of his grandson Sultan Agung. But this first prince of Mataram did, it seems, establish Mataram as a powerful regional force, and thereby lay the foundations for later imperial greatness, a sufficiently significant part to have played in the Javanese historical drama.

New actors were meanwhile stumbling on to the stage. In 1596 there arrived at Bantĕn in West Java four small ships, their crews weakened by scurvy and beset by dissension and incompetent leadership. The first Dutchmen had reached Indonesia.[50] It was to be many years before the Dutch played any role in the internal history of Java, but this first expedition is nevertheless of great significance for the historian of Java. Thereafter, increasingly regular and progressively more reliable Dutch documentation is available as a check upon indigenous records. This begins to be

---

[46] See *BTDj*, trans. pp. 78–82, text pp. 75–9. See also A. B. Cohen Stuart (ed. and trans.), *Geschiedenis van Baron Sakéndhèr, een Javaansch Verhaal* (Batavia, 1850), text p. 98, trans. pp. 94–5 and 155–7 n. 89; *BTDj (BP)*, vol. v, pp. 20–35; and p.398 below.
[47] See de Graaf, 'Sénapati', pp. 80–5.   [48] Ibid., pp. 89–90.
[49] Ibid., p. 129.
[50] See Rouffaer and Ijzerman, *Eerste Schipvaart*; and Mollema, *Eerste Schipvaart*. See also de Graaf, *GI*, pp. 138–41.

a significant source of information in the reign of Senapati's son and successor Panĕmbahan Seda ing Krapjak (1601–13). Krapjak's reign, like that of his father, was largely taken up with military efforts against rebellions and the competing powers of the *pasisir*.[51] The reports of the Dutch fleet which touched at Djĕpara in 1602 confirm the existence of a state of war between Mataram and Dĕmak, an ally of Surabaja.[52] As late as the 1620s Dutch accounts picture Surabaja as a great and powerful city, with dependencies along the eastern *pasisir*, perhaps as far inland as Kĕḍiri, and even on the southern coast of Borneo. Her merchantmen were seen from Malacca to the Moluccas.[53] The Dutch factory at Grĕsik (1602–15) observed a series of Mataram expeditions against Surabaja,[54] but when Krapjak died the great city was not yet subdued.

The reign of Panĕmbahan Krapjak is significant not only for martial exploits. Javanese tradition also assigns Krapjak the role of a great builder, overseeing the construction of various buildings and the walls of the *kraton* at Kuṭa Gĕḍe.[55] He was perhaps a patron of literature as well. A nineteenth-century *sĕngkala*-list says that in the last year of his reign, Krapjak ordered the writing of a history of Dĕmak.[56] Thus, with Krapjak, the House of Mataram was perhaps taking on the trappings and style of a house of kings. The *kraton* was enlarged and embellished, and chronicles compiled. The family was, it seems, beginning to rise above the level of Panĕmbahan Senapati, the rebel soldier and imperial aspirant. Advisers, nobility, and the inherited bureaucracy of older power centres which had come under Mataram control, such as Dĕmak and Padjang, must have exerted a civilizing influence upon the parvenu dynasty. As it became more civilized in the traditions of a Javanese royal house, the dynasty's claim to legitimacy grew more credible, for it was essential in order to be a successful monarch to behave in what was recognized as a kingly

[51] See H. J. de Graaf, 'De Regering van Sultan Agung, Vorst van Mataram, 1613–45, en die van zijn Voorganger Panembahan Séda-ing-Krapjak, 1601–13', *VKI*, vol. 23 (1958), chap. i. [52] Ibid., pp. 6–8.
[53] Ibid., pp. 13–18. [54] Ibid., pp. 18–21. [55] Ibid., pp. 22–3.
[56] *Babad Sangkalaning Momana* (Museum Pusat, Djakarta), p. 245: A.J. 1534, Ingkang Sinuhun ngĕrsakakĕn amurjani Babad ing Dĕmak, ingkang ngladosi tjarik Pandjang Mas. I am grateful to Dr. de Graaf for supplying me with a copy of this important text. An error in de Graaf, 'Sultan Agung', p. 23, gives this date as A.J. 1535 (A.D. 1613). The correct date is A.J. 1534 (A.D. 1612), as Dr. de Graaf's first reference on that page states.

fashion. A more full discussion of this aspect of royal authority will be found at the end of this chapter.

Even the location of the new court may have been important. Surrounded by eighth- and ninth-century temples, in which the eighteenth-century rulers of Mataram are known to have taken pride, the new monarchs may have felt inclined to emulate the former splendour of the ancient kings. It is possible that these ancient temples housed small groups of hermits, always respected by the Javanese. Perhaps such figures, too, helped the new rulers of Central Java to understand what it meant to be lords over the land dominated by the powers of Mount Mĕrapi and the Goddess of the Southern Ocean.

Panĕmbahan Krapjak was succeeded by his son, remembered in tradition as Sultan Agung (1613-45), one of the truly great figures of Javanese history.[57] It was Sultan Agung who consolidated the Mataram empire on Java, and no other Javanese dynasty was ever to replace it. He brought recalcitrant Javanese princes to heel in a series of campaigns, culminating in the fearful siege and surrender of Surabaja in 1625.[58]

But Agung found his pre-eminence on Java was also threatened by a new, non-Javanese, factor, the Dutch East India Company. Relations between Mataram and the Company had been volatile from the start[59] and, when the Company's headquarters was established at Batavia in 1619, it was natural that the Javanese monarch should consider the possibility of subduing this new political force. The two sieges of Batavia in 1628 and 1629 were, however, colossal failures for the Javanese,[60] and Mataram did not again attack the Dutch in their headquarters. Dr. de Graaf comments that this was 'a turning point in the history of the city [Batavia], of Java, indeed of all of Indonesia'.[61] It will be seen that the Dutch Company in later years would come to threaten the very existence of a Javanese state.

Sultan Agung's defeat before the walls of Batavia precipitated renewed troubles within his kingdom,[62] probably the result of a general questioning of his authority as monarch because of his

[57] The title Sultan was adopted only late in the monarch's reign. I am employing it here simply as a form of shorthand to avoid confusion, and in accordance with Javanese convention.
[58] See de Graaf, 'Sultan Agung', pp. 28-52, 77-99.
[59] See ibid., pp. 53-76, 144-5. [60] Ibid., pp. 145-63.
[61] Ibid., p. 151. [62] See ibid., pp. 193-200.

demonstrated inability to subordinate the Dutch. As in other times of crisis, the familiar centrifugal forces again appeared. Discontent was successfully put down by a series of executions, but the fragmentary records concerning this opposition suggest some of it was of more than temporary significance. The Central Javanese malcontents were apparently led by wandering religious mystics centred on the Těmbajat area, the grave-site of Ki Paṇḍan Arang (Sunan Bajat), the *wali* of Central Java.

Such religious antagonism to the rulers of Java was not uncommon in the Mataram period, and was a result partly of the uneven process of conversion to Islam. The disavowal of the ruler's divinity by Islam may suggest itself as a factor here, perhaps making it easier for non-royal persons to claim sacral authority than would theoretically have been possible in the Hindu-Javanese era. Such a judgement, however, depends upon an understanding of the king's position in pre-Islamic Java which cannot at the present time be demonstrated convincingly. There is no evidence that the Hindu-Javanese ruler's divinity made the countryside any less prone to rebellion than in later centuries. This need not have been so even in theory, much less in practice. The Hindu-Javanese ruler was a god, but by performing appropriate rituals a rebel could equally partake of divinity.[63] In the Islamic period the king was in theory no longer divine, but neither could a rebel become a god. It can be argued in more general terms that in a time of religious transition the process of redefining the bases for moral judgements increases the likelihood of discordant ethical interpretations coming into conflict, thus making it more likely that rebellion will employ religious justifications. Thus, in Islamic Modern Java, perhaps dissident élites were more likely to inscribe religious mottos upon the banner of rebellion, rather than employing more clearly dynastic or local appeals. It may also be supposed that in Old as well as Modern Java, local religious notables in the countryside were natural leaders of popular discontent in turbulent times. The nature of this problem was probably very little affected by the change of religion, and it must have faced Hindu as well as Islamic Javanese rulers.

---

[63] Indian literature on kingship generally took the view that only good kings achieved the status of a divine being (*deva*), thus making rebellion not difficult to justify in religious terms; see J. Gonda, *Ancient Indian Kingship from the Religious Point of View* (Leiden, 1966), pp. 33–5.

BACKGROUND

Sultan Agung may have been aware of such problems, and perhaps attempted to assert a greater sacral authority. In 1624 he adopted the title *susuhunan*, which was particularly associated with the *walis*, and in 1641 he solicited the title of Sultan from Mecca.[64] He also took other steps to increase his spiritual strength. A Javanese text tells how Agung was instructed in the secret mystical sciences (*ngelmu gaib*) by the spirit of Sunan Bajat, and in 1633 he visited Tĕmbajat, the recent trouble-spot, and erected a gateway at the holy grave-site.[65]

In the same year, indeed perhaps while he was at Tĕmbajat, Sultan Agung demonstrated his Islamic piety and authority by taking a step which literally changed Javanese history for the rest of time. He officially abandoned the solar calendrical system and regularized the use of the Islamic lunar year of 354/5 days. The reasons for this change in chronometry are uncertain. Dr. de Graaf suggests it is to be seen as an expression of Agung's religious conviction.[66] It seems reasonable to conjecture that this was also an attempt by the Sultan to avail himself of the spiritual power of Islam, at a time when his position probably seemed threatened. Conceptions of time are important in Java, and Agung's introduction of the new calendar would have been a powerful step, bringing the calendar into line with the new Islamic age. It is perhaps a comment on the early history of Islam in Central Java that the princes of Mataram had not bothered to do so before.

Sultan Agung was too perspicacious to believe that calendars and titles alone could end the problem of religiously-based insurrection. About 1636 he sent the son of the last independent ruler of Surabaja, related to the family of the *wali* Sunan Ngampel-Dĕnta, at the head of a Mataram force which defeated and captured Sunan Giri. Giri, whom the Protestant Dutch had described as the Javanese 'Pope', was a focal point for opposition to Mataram and a refuge for defeated opponents.[67] Although Sultan Agung was to have no further cause to fear the power of Giri, his descendants would not be so fortunate. During the Trunadjaja wars later

---

[64] De Graaf, 'Sultan Agung', pp. 127–9, 264–8.
[65] Ibid., pp. 200–4. The *Babad Nitik* story to which Dr. de Graaf refers is to be found in Rinkes, 'Heiligen IV', *TBG*, vol. 53 (1911), pp. 490–6; see also p. 437, and photos II and III on the gateways at Tĕmbajat, and Appendix III, giving the Javanese text of the *Babad Nitik*.
[66] De Graaf, 'Sultan Agung', p. 204.
[67] Ibid., pp. 205–20. See also n. 16 above.

in the seventeenth century Giri was again to play the role of spiritual rival to the power of Mataram.

When Sultan Agung died, the *Babad Tanah Djawi* says, the weeping in the *kraton* was like rolling thunder, and outside the rumblings of Mt. Měrapi merged with the roar of a rainstorm.[68] He is remembered in Javanese historical tradition as the great conquerer, the pious Muslim, the opponent of the Dutch. He did, indeed, achieve the unification of the Mataram empire, and his reign was one of the greatest, if not the greatest, in Modern Javanese history. But subsequent events were to show how much in a state such as Mataram depended upon the person of the ruler, and how fragile was the unity achieved by Agung in the hands of lesser men. Furthermore, Sultan Agung had struck a blow at the sources of Javanese prosperity. The devastation and depopulation of the coastal trading ports and the destruction of rice-lands and irrigation systems which resulted from his wars must have caused more damage to Javanese trade and agriculture than the Dutch could ever have achieved. It is uncertain whether this resulted from a conscious policy to destroy the independent wealth of the troublesome *pasisir*, or was an unintended consequence of the warfare and of Agung's wish to cut off the rice supply being shipped to his rivals in Batavia.[69] In any case, it meant the beginning of an isolation of Central Java from the outer islands, a process of turning inward, which the Dutch may have hastened by their activities in the Moluccas, and from which only the Dutch could profit.

It is a truism that dynasties rarely produce rulers of a consistently high stature, and Agung's son conformed to this rule. His reign was a catastrophe. Susuhunan Amangkurat I (1646–77) began his reign with a series of slaughters of old opponents, including his brother Pangeran Alit, who was supported against the Susuhunan by a group of divines. The Susuhunan prepared a further massacre for the latter, and it is claimed that five to six thousand men, women, and children were cut down within one-half hour.[70] The Dutch ambassador Rijklof van Goens remarked upon 'the strange manner of their government . . ., which is

[68] *BTDj*, trans. p. 146.
[69] See B. J. O. Schrieke, *Indonesian Sociological Studies, Selected Writings of B. Schrieke* (2 vols.; The Hague, 1955–7), vol. i, pp. 59–60, 74–6.
[70] For the details of all these events, see H. J. de Graaf, 'De Regering van Sunan Mangku-Rat I Tegal-Wangi, Vorst van Mataram, 1646–1677' (2 vols.), *VKI*, vols. 33, 39 (1961, 1962), vol. i, pp. 23–34.

inconceivable to us, by which the old are murdered in order to make place for the young'.[71] What van Goens did not appreciate was that this behaviour was equally unacceptable by Javanese standards, and was symptomatic of the impending disintegration of the kingdom.

Behind this carnage lay more significant events, of which murder was only the most obvious and unpleasant symptom. The unity of the kingdom was again breaking down, and divisions appeared within the royal house and throughout the countryside. It seems that the Susuhunan's attempts to exert authority by assassination and to centralize the administration of the kingdom by decree threatened and alienated ever more Javanese notables, thus destroying the consensus without which a king could not govern. Eventually the ruler could not use his armies against delinquent sectors of the kingdom because he dared neither leave the court himself nor entrust the command of his troops to anyone else.[72]

Amangkurat I attempted to institute complete royal control of the *pasisir* trade and, when this seemed unsatisfactory, he commanded the requisition or destruction of all Javanese shipping.[73] It is probable that the Susuhunan was jealous and suspicious of the independent wealth which might go to the coastal trading centres, and was willing to destroy the *pasisir* if he could not control it.

Amangkurat I's tyranny exacerbated the natural centrifugal forces inherent within Mataram, which were a result of both geographic and religious irregularity. According to the Meinsma *Babad Tanah Djawi*,

> In those days everything which His Highness desired was in conflict with the *adat* (custom); he often employed violence against others, and continually held executions in public. The *bupatis, mantris,* and *sĕntanas* stole one another's appanages; the order in the kingdom was destroyed all the more.[74]

The Crown Prince soon became the focus of a plot against his father, and in the 1670s a great rebellion broke out in his favour,

[71] H. J. de Graaf (ed.), *De Vijf Gezantschapsreizen van Rijklof van Goens naar het Hof van Mataram, 1648–1654* ('s-Gravenhage, 1956), p. 67.
[72] GG to H.XVII, 16 Dec. 1659, in dJ vi, p. 81.
[73] See de Graaf, 'Mangku-Rat I', vol. i, chaps. viii–xii, xiv.
[74] *BTDj*, text p. 154: Kala sĕmantĕn Sang Nata sabarang karsanipun ewah kalijan adatipun, asring mĕsesa tijang, tansah nggĕlarakĕn sijasat. Para bupati mantri tuwin para sĕntana sami lampah alap-alapan ing kalĕnggahanipun, sakĕlangkung rĕsah tataning nĕgari. Cf. *BTDj* (*BP*), vol. xi, p. 28.

led by the Madurese prince Trunadjaja, who drew much of his initial support from the *pasisir* and raised the flag of Islam. The *kraton* fell to the rebels in 1677, and Amangkurat I died while fleeing from the defeated capital. The Crown Prince had meanwhile fallen out with Trunadjaja, and now succeeded his father as Susuhunan Amangkurat II (1677–1703).[75]

Trunadjaja would almost certainly have been victorious, and gone on to found a new dynasty on Java, had not Amangkurat I, shortly before his death in 1677, turned to the Dutch East India Company for assistance.[76] For the first time, Dutch forces intervened in Central Java and succeeded in restoring Amangkurat II to power over his father's kingdom. The new ruler was obligated to repay the costs of the Dutch war effort, but the court had lost its treasury to the rebels and, when Trunadjaja's stronghold at Kĕḍiri was taken in late 1678, the Mataram treasure was looted by the victors. Thus, with no funds to use in repayment, Amangkurat II ceded to the Company the ports of the *pasisir* and all their incomes until his debt was redeemed.[77] Now, with the acquisition of territorial power on the fringes of the Javanese kingdom, for the first time the Dutch were becoming involved in the turbulent political life of the Javanese. The initial identification of Amangkurat II with his Dutch mentor Admiral Speelman was so complete that rumours spread suggesting that the new Susuhunan was the Admiral's son and not Javanese at all.[78] The *Babad Tanah Djawi* preserves a remarkable description of the new monarch's appearance, which was said to resemble that of a Dutch Governor-General on a trip to Java.[79]

The Susuhunan established a new *kraton* at Kartasura in 1680,[80] the remains of which are still to be seen to the west of Surakarta. The new court was occupied by five rulers over a period of sixty years, throughout which Java was afflicted with almost con-

---

[75] For details, see de Graaf, 'Mangku-Rat I', vol. ii.
[76] See the Contract of 28 Feb. 1677, in dJ vii, pp. 79–83.
[77] Contract of 19 Oct. 1677, in dJ vii, pp. 163–6. See also Bataviaasch Genootshap van Kunsten en Wetenschappen, *Dagh-Register, Gehouden int Casteel Batavia vant Passerender daer ter Plaetse als over geheel Nederlandts India* ('s-Hage, 1887–1931), *1677*, pp. 366–7; *1678*, pp. 746–9.
[78] Such rumours are mentioned in both Dutch and Javanese sources. See *BTDj* trans. pp. 203–4, 206–8; *Dagh-Register 1680*, p. 687.
[79] *BTDj*, trans. pp. 208–9; text p. 202: Sang Prabu Mangkurat, jen dipunsawang, kados Gurnadur-Djendral ngĕdjawi.
[80] See *BTDj*, trans. p. 205; *Dagh-Register 1680*, p. 687.

tinual disorder. Historians of Java have traditionally divided the Kartasura years into a number of periods: the rebellion of Surapati (1686–1703), the First Javanese War of Succession (1703–8), the Second Javanese War of Succession (1718–23), and the Chinese War (1740–5).[81]

All the wars and rebellions of the Kartasura period originated in similar circumstances and, from the point of view of Mataram history, the age should be seen as a unit dominated by common themes. First, court intrigues within the royal family produced a state of near-permanent anarchy. Second, armed rebellion apparently fed upon the *pasisir* and East Javanese aversion to the authority of Central Java, which was probably entwined with a third factor, the tensions between the more- and less-self-consciously Islamic segments of Javanese society. All of these motifs were associated with a newer, fourth element, the involvement of the Dutch. Some princely rivals thought in terms of a traditional struggle over the succession, in which Dutch forces could be useful, and failed completely to grasp the essentially disruptive nature of the Dutch presence. The position of the Dutch Company was meanwhile expanded and consolidated through a series of contracts and concessions with which the Javanese rulers repaid their obligations. The Company hoped by further involvement to be able to impose a solution which would guarantee peace and stability.

A closer examination of the dynamics of Javanese history in the sixteenth and seventeenth centuries is necessary to see the significance of the collapse of the state in the Kartasura period, which is the immediate background to the foundation of Jogjakarta.

The years of rebellion demonstrated the fragility of the geographical unity forged by Sultan Agung. The country fell to pieces during the Trunadjaja rebellion, and nothing that the kings of Mataram or the Dutch could do was able to put it back together again.

More importantly, the rebellion of Trunadjaja and the subsequent troubled years also serve to illustrate the limitations imposed upon the exercise of royal authority by Javanese political conditions. The geographic fragmentation and local traditions,

[81] e.g. de Graaf, *GI*, pp. 233–62. Dr. de Graaf departs somewhat from the conventional terminology for these years.

including varying degrees of adherence to Islamic ideals, meant there might easily be a reluctance to acknowledge royal authority, which could then only be ensured by resorting to military action. But the assembling and maintenance of an army at the same time required the acquiescence of local notables who provided men or at least allowed the king's army to pass without hindrance. Armies of occupation far from the court were a physical impossibility.

Therefore, the king needed a consensus to rule. He must be recognized and accepted by members of the royal family, local aristocrats throughout the countryside, and religious leaders, who together comprised the Javanese 'élite'. It was essential for the king to be seen by them as the legitimate sovereign whose rule it was in their interest to accept. Without such general acceptance, the king could hardly maintain himself. The potential sources of rebellion were so many that even in the best of times the kingdom might fall apart. Even a ruler of the stature of Sultan Agung repeatedly had to deal with disloyalty or rebellion. Such rebellions could only be put down successfully if a large enough number of local aristocrats, princes, and other notables were sufficiently opposed to the rebellion to send their men to march in the royal armies. The number of those who sided with the rebel, who hindered the royal forces in their passage, or who simply stood aloof from the struggle would have to be small. As long as the acceptance of the ruler's authority was nearly unanimous, local dignitaries were unlikely to support the occasional rebel for fear of subsequent royal wrath backed up by large numbers of troops. But if even a small number of dignitaries, princes at court, or religious leaders should agree to oppose the king's authority, a still larger number might withdraw from the contest to await its outcome. From these the king could expect only nominal gestures of obeisance, but few or no troops or taxes, and little or no assistance, until he had sufficiently demonstrated his potential for survival. Under these circumstances, the king's ability to bring his opponents to heel was further decreased, with the probable result that still more notables might join either the rebel camp or the group observing the course of events before committing itself. Thus, even a relatively small amount of opposition, if not immediately dealt with, might ultimately lead to the total collapse of royal power. The king's main preoccupation was therefore to prevent the emergence of such disaffected groups of notables.

Royal authority in Mataram rested upon a balance of legitimacy and local autonomy. This can be understood only if a distinction is preserved between the 'magical and religious implementation of kingship' and the 'technical implementation of kingship', as Mr. Moertono has recently done in his study of Modern Javanese politics.[82] On the one hand, the pomp and glory, the religious and supernatural props of legitimation, were elaborated and emphasized, in order to raise the monarch's visible status and prestige to a level which suited his imperial pretensions. His court was known to house the holy regalia (*pusaka*), large collections of spiritually powerful weapons, books, conveyances, and musical instruments, and all the glitter and finery suitable to a king. The rulers of Mataram also claimed the special protection of the Goddess of the Southern Ocean, who had promised her support to Senapati's descendants. All of this made the king's authority over Java seem a cultural axiom. One could not lightly mobilize a large army of troop levies against such an imposing figure.

But while the king's cultural prestige was emphasized, his administrative power was limited. The ideal king refrained from interfering in the day-to-day administration of the countryside, which was in the hands of largely autonomous officials and dignitaries. More than this, the king was also limited by custom in taking decisions even within his own court. He must consult with the members of his family and with his advisers, and it seems he was expected to take no administrative decision without their agreement. In the following chapter will be found a rather pointed lesson on this subject given to Susuhunan Pakubuwana II. The Javanese sources often describe courtly gatherings in which the king solicits the advice of his courtiers on some issue. While

---

[82] See Soemarsaid Moertono, *State and Statecraft in Old Java: A Study of the Later Mataram Period, 16th to 19th Century* (Ithaca, 1968). See also my review of Mr. Moertono's monograph in *JSEAS*, vol. i, no. 1 (March 1970), pp. 116–17.

The Javanese political system described in this chapter may be compared with the very similar institutional principles of the Malay Sultanates; see J. M. Gullick, *Indigenous Political Systems of Western Malaya* (London, 1965), pp. 44–54. But see also the rather different situation in the state of Kĕdah, which was conscious of external threats and partly for that reason maintained a much firmer central authority; Sharom Ahmat, 'The Political Structure of the State of Kedah, 1879–1905', *JSEAS*, vol. 1, no. 2 (Sept. 1970), pp. 115–28.

See also the Balinese ideas of kingship discussed in Peter John Worsley, *Babad Buleleng: A Balinese Dynastic Genealogy* ('s-Gravenhage, 1972), especially pp. 26–7, 41–9, 68, 70–1.

maintaining all due reverence for the ruler and for the avoidance of overt conflict within the court, a free exchange of ideas is often described, and courtiers and princes sometimes successfully argue a view in opposition to that of the king, who then changes his mind. These sessions end with a royal pronouncement of the consensus (*mupakat*) of the meeting, to which the courtiers normally reply 'Sandika' ('Whatever you wish!'). Sometimes, however, individuals may respond 'Datan lěnggana' ('I will not oppose you'), which seems to suggest that opposition was a recognized possibility.[83] By allowing for consultation and argument, this decision-making process recognized and accounted for the countervailing powers and centrifugal forces within Javanese political life. This lessened the likelihood of the king taking steps which would alienate his supporters and precipitate the collapse of the state.

The truly powerful monarch, a rare figure in Javanese history, was one who successfully employed the opportunities of kingship to manipulate and balance the interests of lesser notables, thereby directing the political system to his own ends. But not even the most powerful king could be a despot and long remain upon the throne. The more-or-less autonomous dignitaries and locally influential leaders were attracted by the legitimate glory of the king, in whose reflected light they might bask. But their day-to-day autonomy was not threatened. So long as this was the situation, they had much to gain and little to lose by accepting the ruler's sovereignty, except of course for those who aspired to be kings themselves. The monarchy provided an atmosphere of legitimacy, unity, and stability, and provided the means of channelling the collective interest in maintaining peaceful political and economic life. The numerous local aristocrats, princes, and religious leaders thus contributed to the consensus which supported the king's authority. They were further connected to the royal house by an intricate series of marriage alliances, which gave a wide range of individuals a further interest in the preservation of royal authority

---

[83] Examples of such sessions may be found in several texts, e.g. *B. Mang.*, pp. 230, 338, 455–6, 476, 502, 530–1, 544–6.
  On the similar relationship of the ruler to his advisers in India, see Gonda, *Ancient Indian Kingship*, pp. 1–2, 134–6; and A. L. Basham, *The Wonder that was India: A Survey of the Culture of the Indian Sub-Continent before the Coming of the Muslims* (New York, 1959), pp. 87–8.
  Islamic political thinking did not expressly recognize similar restraints upon royal authority.

for the sake of themselves and of their descendants who would be members of the royal house as well. On audience days at the court, these princes and officials gathered to pay homage to the ruler, their glittering many-coloured costumes looking 'like scattered flowers', as the Javanese texts sometimes say. Their very presence was a form of legitimation, and contributed further to the ruler's visible glory, which was already responsible in large part for their presence.

But this was a system which was easily upset. When things went well they went very well, feeding upon their own success. But when things went badly they went very badly indeed. The quickest way to upset the balance was for the king to lose the essential consensus. This might happen in two ways: either by being too much a king, or by being not enough a king. If his visible glory were below standard, if his treasury were inadequate, or if he were unable to deal with persistent rebellions, it would seem most unlikely that this man could be the protégé of the Goddess of the Southern Ocean. If he showed insufficient concern for the maintenance of religion or the welfare of his subjects, he was also not worthy of the position he held. In these circumstances, his authority was likely to decline and the kingdom to collapse. Conversely, if the king attempted too much, perhaps trying actually to govern and administer daily affairs throughout his kingdom, he would rapidly alienate those upon whose support he depended and, again, the fragile state structure was likely to fall.

It seems clear that Amangkurat I's mistake was to be too much a king. His attempts to centralize the administration of the whole island alienated those upon whom his existence as monarch depended, from coastal trading interests to spiritual notables and, finally, the Crown Prince and his party. As a result, the gentle balance was tipped, and the kingdom collapsed.

Such was the somewhat precarious system of Modern Javanese politics up to the late seventeenth century. Thereafter, these factors continued to be of importance, and continued to define both the successful and the unsuccessful king. The successful monarch must balance the opposing interests within his kingdom without threatening their essential autonomy. And he must appear to be a kingly person, embodying the Javanese personal virtues of moderation, restraint, beauty, and so on, while also meeting the standards of imperial glory. Such a man was not to appear for several decades, and in his absence the divisions within the

Javanese élite which erupted in the reign of Amangkurat I were to become ever greater and more violent. It was not until the emergence in the 1740s of Pangeran Mangkubumi (later Sultan Hamĕngkubuwana I) that someone appeared who seemed to a very large number of the Javanese élite to meet the standards of kingship, and who also had the opportunity to become king.

After 1677, however, a new and disruptive factor appeared in Javanese politics with the large-scale military intervention of the Dutch East India Company in Central Javanese affairs. The impact upon the Javanese of this intervention is, however, easily misconstrued, for it is possible to be misled by a conceptual framework based upon late-nineteenth- and twentieth-century political life, thereby asking entirely the wrong questions of the historical evidence. Dutch involvement in seventeenth- and eighteenth-century Java must be seen within its appropriate historical context, which was very different from that of later periods. One must particularly appreciate the peripheral nature of Dutch involvement. Until the early nineteenth century the Dutch rarely attempted to impose their standards upon Javanese society, and they were not significant political factors except in their important role as a military force whose support was valuable to some Javanese intrigants. Largely because of this peripheral nature of the Dutch involvement, the Javanese élite reaction was by no means unanimous.

Some Javanese certainly opposed the Dutch East India Company, while others were willing to ally themselves with it. It is important to understand, however, that this did not mean these Javanese were either 'anti-Dutch' or 'pro-Dutch' in the sense in which those terms apply to more recent nationalist episodes. In general, opposition to or alliance with the Dutch was not, it seems, necessarily a choice made upon a particular individual's view of the Dutch nation, race, or culture. It would be no more correct to conclude without some specific evidence that a particular Javanese insurgent opposed the Dutch simply because they were Dutch, than it would be to make the entirely nonsensical assertion that Pakubuwana I (1703–19) opposed Amangkurat III (1703–8) because the latter was Javanese. There was not yet in the eighteenth century the sense of cultural conflict which was to emerge in response to more aggressive European policies in the nineteenth century.

There was certainly some Islamic aversion to the Dutch as infidels (*kafir*), but one feels that this was of distinctly secondary significance throughout the eighteenth century among the Central Javanese élite who were the arbiters of courtly politics. It is difficult to reconstruct precisely what such courtly notables intended on those occasions when they did use the term *kafir*. It seems not unreasonable, however, to suggest that for them this was a term which typified the differences between Dutch and Javanese, which included not only religion but race, colour, dress, manners, and so on. A *kafir* was what a Dutchman was. But it seems inappropriate to assume this reflected any real religious intolerance, except in those few cases in which there is some evidence to suggest this was the case. It may be pointed out here that to ascribe to the Javanese élite an orthodox Islamic hatred of the infidel would fail to explain two other facts of Javanese history: that even among the opponents of the Dutch *kafirs* there was no noticeable tendency to take an equally negative view of the *kafir* Javanese of the Těnggěr mountains or of the infidel Balinese, and that on the other hand that area of Java which adjusted most readily to Dutch *kafir* authority was precisely the more deeply-Islamized *pasisir*.

The reader should be aware of the general way in which the courtly élite viewed the Dutch, so that it will be possible to understand how they judged the Dutchmen who appear in the following pages. There are no Javanese texts from the eighteenth century or earlier specifically evaluating the Dutch, but they appear frequently both in Javanese *babad*-literature and in such pseudo-historical texts as *Sěrat Baron Sakenḍer* and *Sěrat Surja Radja*.[84] From such sources it may be possible to deduce the early Javanese view of the Europeans.

Generally speaking, the Javanese courtly élite seem to have looked upon the Dutchmen as 'clowns'. But as with other aspects of Javanese culture, it would be easy to place the wrong interpretation upon this term. In Western society, the clown is only sometimes more than a butt of fun, occasionally perhaps rising to the status of a tragic figure or of a revealing mirror of reality. But in Javanese culture the most famous clowns are not only the

---

[84] See Cohen Stuart, *Baron Sakéndhèr*. *Sěrat Surja Radja* is discussed and summarized in Chapter VII below. The Baron Sakenḍer story is summarized in Chapter XI.

purveyors of atrocious puns, of a coarse or gentle humour, and sometimes of the most abominable behaviour, but are also wise and even divine figures. With their comic aspects they combine powerful spiritual qualities which may seem inconsistent to the Westerner, but which are for the Javanese merely two diverse but inseparable aspects of the entire phenomenon.

To understand this perception, one must turn to the shadow theatre (*wajang*) for models, as the Javanese élite themselves must instinctively have done. In the *wajang*, the *panakawans* (literally 'retainers') are both clown-servants and divine protectors and advisers to the main characters of the plays. The most important and popular of these clowns is Sĕmar, an obese waddling character who is constantly breaking wind and engaging in off-colour songs and stories. Yet he is said by the puppeteer (*ḍalang*) to be in fact the god Sang Hjang Ismaja, the most powerful of gods, who could rule the world if he wished. His advice to the heroic Pandawas contains the highest wisdom.[85] The other main *panakawan* figures, Petruk, Gareng, Bagong, Togog, and Saraita, are also noted for their bizarre physical appearance and behaviour, combined with immortality and flashes of a sort of folk-wisdom.[86]

The early Dutchmen must immediately have reminded the Javanese of these clown-figures, and indeed a Westerner visiting Java today may find children happily calling him by one of the clowns' names. To the Javanese, these Dutchmen were bizarre in appearance: white-skinned, hairy, large, and singularly ill-dressed for a tropical climate. Their behaviour, too, was atrocious, simply because it did not conform to Javanese practice. When greeting someone, they stood up to show respect rather than dropping to the ground so as to be lower than the other. They doffed their hats in greeting, rather than covering their heads; they shook hands, sat on chairs, spoke Malay, and perspired freely.

[85] See the *ḍalang's* descriptions of Sĕmar translated in James R. Brandon (ed.), *On Thrones of Gold: Three Javanese Shadow Plays* (Cambridge, Mass., 1970), pp. 120, 311; and in Boedihardja, 'Grepen uit de Wajang', *Djåwå*, vol. 2 (1923), pp. 22–3. The latter is translated into English in Claire Holt, *Art in Indonesia: Continuities and Change* (Ithaca, 1967), p. 144.

See also J. Kats, *Het Javaansche Toneel*, vol. i: *Wajang Poerwa* (Weltevreden, 1923), pp. 40–1, 115–16; Benedict R. O'G. Anderson, *Mythology and the Tolerance of the Javanese* (Ithaca, 1965), pp. 22–3; Hardjowirogo, *Sedjarah Wajang Purwa* (Djakarta, 1952), p. 97; Holt, pp. 144–5.

[86] See Kats, *Wajang Poerwa*, pp. 40–1, 104, 115–16; Anderson, *Mythology*, pp. 42–4; Hardjowirogo, pp. 98–100, 131–2; Holt, pp. 144–5.

Much of this behaviour has now become part of the comic behaviour of the *wajang* clowns. The Dutch also drank prodigious amounts of beer and strong liquor, a social usage which so struck the Javanese that the *babads* often record its occurrence. Although Javanese princes normally had no religious objection to the consumption of alcohol, and would themselves take drink on formal occasions, the Dutch consumption of alcohol was so great in quantity and informal in manner that it apparently contributed to the Javanese perception of the Dutch as clowns.[87]

The eighteenth-century Jogjakarta *Babad Kraton* obliquely compares the Dutch with one of the bizarre god-figures of the *wajang*. In this case, however, the comparison is not to one of the *panakawans* but to the god Narada. He is the elder brother, adviser, and emissary of Baṭara Guru (the god Siwa), but he is depicted in the *wajang* as an obese and physically unrefined character. His appearance is not unlike that of Sĕmar, with whom he also shares a humorous manner. Yet he is a god, and a source of great wisdom.[88] In *Babad Kraton* Narada often speaks in the Malay language, just as the Dutch did. And at one point in the early mythical stories about Watu-Gunung, the latter's bereaved

[87] On Dutch alcoholic consumption, see C. R. Boxer, *The Dutch Seaborne Empire, 1600–1800* (London, 1965), p. 208, where Professor Boxer quotes Governor-General J. P. Coen in 1620: ' "Our nation must drink or die" . . . and he was not referring to water.' See also ibid., pp. 208–9, 219, 233.

Babad references to Dutch drinking are not uncommon, although because of the courtly bias of the *babads* many of these references are to stately occasions when the Dutch proposed a series of formal toasts. For examples, see *B. Mang.*, pp. 267, 277, 335, 409–11, 472, 475; Poensen, 'Mangkubumi', p. 317 n. 2. See also *B. Mang.*, p. 310, where Sultan HB I dines with his military commanders, and shares a drink of Jenever (*djĕnewrĕ*) with them!

See also the interesting description of the conflict arising from the differences between Dutch and Javanese protocol in 1677, in *BTDj*, text pp. 178–9; trans. pp. 184–5.

Malay authors were also struck by many of the Dutch habits which the Javanese found characteristic, including drinking; see A. L. V. L. van der Linden, *De Europeaan in de Maleische Literatuur* (Meppel, 1937), pp. 10–11. See also C. Skinner (ed. and trans.), 'Sja'ir Perang Mengkasar (The Rhymed Chronicle of the Macassar War) by Entji' Amin', *VKI*, vol. 40 (1963), pp. 78–9, 186–7, where drunkenness is among the pejorative characteristics ascribed to the Dutch.

See also the Balinese sculpture depicting the curious appearance of a Dutchman of the East India Company, seated as if on a chair, with hat on and one leg hitched over the other knee, in de Graaf, *GI*, facing p. 232; and the humorous North Balinese temple relief picturing an obese mustachioed Dutchman seated in a chair with his legs crossed, drinking beer, in Miguel Covarrubias, *Island of Bali* (London, 1937), between pp. 202 and 203.

[88] See Anderson, *Mythology*, p. 31; Hardjowirogo, p. 13.

wife (Dewi Sinta) is addressed in Malay by Narada, who is invisible. She snaps back, in a delightful anachronism, 'Who's speaking, invisible, just like a Dutchman?'[89]

Thus this unusual appearance and behaviour apparently led the Javanese élite to perceive of the Dutch in terms drawn from *wajang* clown-figures, of whom the Dutch apparently reminded them. But the divine aspect of these *wajang* figures is as important as the comic. It is not surprising, then, to find that the Dutchmen whose behaviour the Javanese often found comical were also respected, even feared, characters. This was so even in the latter half of the eighteenth century when, as will be seen below, at least some Javanese came to be aware that Dutch military power was declining as a result of the Company's economic setbacks. Thus the Javanese view of the Dutch did not depend entirely upon their assessment of Dutch military power.

The impression gained from the Javanese texts, which is consistent also with the descriptions of Javanese behaviour preserved in Dutch records, that the Javanese both laughed at and respected the officials of the Dutch Company, is thus seen to be entirely consistent within the perspectives of Javanese culture. The apparent contradictions of this attitude derive only from an anachronistic assessment of pre-nineteenth-century Java as if it were a modern nationalistic culture, in which the colonial enemy was both better known and more obtrusive than in pre-nationalist times. In the pages that follow, the Dutch will appear in many guises: as the butt of Javanese humour, as the feared foe, as the respected advisers. Each Dutchman was an individual, and his relations with each Javanese prince or official were as unique as any other human relationship. But individual relationships are influenced by general presuppositions. Javanese–Dutch relations can only be understood within the cultural context in which the Dutch took up their roles as characters on the Javanese stage.

But if the Dutch could be understood within a traditional Javanese framework, their presence in Java was none the less disruptive. In times of dissolution in the past, new Javanese monarchs had emerged by exercising superior martial abilities and by commanding the loyalty of larger armies than their opponents. Now it was possible for a pretender who was unable to win such

---

[89] *BK*, f. 8ʳ. Canto I (Ḍanḍanggula), verse 85: sapa sintěn angandika tan kaeksi / dening kaja Wělonda.

a contest to solicit the support of Dutch Company forces and to emerge as the man who controlled the *kraton*, but who was perhaps without the consensus necessary to exercise sovereignty over the kingdom. When such men sat upon the throne of Mataram, their very presence there was an added impetus to rebellion and to the dissolution of the kingdom. Each step taken by the Dutch to maintain such monarchs, who seemed to them legitimate by standards of hereditary succession, tended to increase the centrifugal tendencies in Java, a process which the Company was unable to understand. This had little to do with Javanese aversion to the Dutch, although there were certainly sectors of Javanese society, especially in the more self-consciously Islamic areas, which did object to the infidel intrusion. Among the Central Javanese courtly élite, however, this factor was very rarely of importance. The process here was rather more subtle.

The Company had sufficient influence to prevent the normal denouement of a dynastic crisis in Java, that is, the emergence from the ranks of rebellion of a single ruler who had the necessary consensus to govern the kingdom. By giving their support to the ruler who seemed 'legitimate' because of his heredity, the Dutch could successfully prevent the emergence of a new monarch, but they could neither entirely suppress rebellion nor impose a consensus in favour of their candidate. Thus, they could prevent the traditional resolution of such crises, but they had neither the power nor indeed the perception or inclination to introduce any alternative political solution. This meant that the political system could collapse as easily as had ever been the case, but that it could not be put together again. In other words, the Company could not create *ex nihilo* the consensus which their candidate required to hold his kingdom together and the absence of which continually spawned rebellion, but they were perfectly capable of preventing the final overthrow of the monarch. It should be noted here that, although the Company's military power was widely used, the Dutch need not be particularly powerful in order to disrupt Javanese politics in this way. They need only be present. In times of war, a relatively small European force with indigenous Indonesian levies could if necessary defend a single position against much larger Javanese armies. And in the intermittent times of peace, the very presence of the Dutch held the promise of the possible arrival of large numbers of Company troops. Even in the last decade of its existence the Company was capable of mustering a respectable expeditionary force for a limited period of time. Therefore, even late in the eighteenth century when the Company's precarious financial position was appreciated by many Javanese, it seems the presence of Dutchmen even in very small numbers may have convinced much of the courtly élite that a 'final solution' of the political crisis was impossible. And at all times, regardless of the potential or actual number of Company troops, the Dutch were still regarded as 'clowns', whom Javanese looked upon both with mirth and with genuine fear and respect. Their support of a ruler was therefore a factor of considerable significance, quite apart from the question of Dutch military strength.

The Dutch were 'spoilers'. They could disrupt a system which they did not understand, but they could neither control nor replace it. This threatened that the political crisis into which the Dutch moved might become chronic and incapable of solution.

There would seem to have been two possible theoretical solutions to this crisis. First, the single ruler whom the Dutch considered legitimate and pliable enough not to threaten their commercial interests, and whom therefore they were willing to support, might happen also to be a man who commanded a sufficient Javanese following to reign over Mataram in his own right. This would have been the happiest of outcomes, but it did not occur. There may indeed be a contradiction hidden here. It has been noted that one of the essential ways for a Javanese monarch to command a consensus of the élite throughout the kingdom was to give the appearance of being a king. This royal appearance was itself enhanced by the display in battle and on audience days of the consensus of notables supporting the king. Once the initial Dutch intervention had taken place, however, all subsequent monarchs were observed to require Dutch military support to maintain themselves upon the throne. That they were seen to require Company assistance in battle may perhaps have demonstrated that they lacked a Javanese consensus. If the political system recognized the essentiality of a consensus in support of the monarch, as seems to have been the case, then the lack of a consensus must by definition have meant the loss of legitimacy. If this was so, the ruler possessed less of the legitimate glory the reflection of which other notables desired to be. It is tempting, therefore, to see a causal relationship between the presence of

Dutch military assistance and the loss of Javanese support for the kings. Yet, although such an interpretation is attractive, it does not seem entirely appropriate. Such an attitude would have been inconsistent with the regard in which the Dutch were held by both their allies and their enemies. It is true that whatever the Dutch were, they were obviously not Javanese. They could not, therefore, replace the consensus of Javanese notables which was essential to the maintenance of the monarchy, if that consensus had already been lost. Yet it would seem inappropriate to see the loss of a Javanese consensus as a direct result of Dutch support. The reasons would be more appropriately sought among factors within Javanese society not directly related to the issue of the Dutch role. It is nevertheless true that throughout the Kartasura years the Company's support was given to the incumbent monarchs, who usually lacked sufficient Javanese support to function successfully as kings. It was not until the middle of the eighteenth century that princes emerged, especially Mangkubumi and Mas Said, who had fought against but could not be defeated by the Dutch. When one of these, Mangkubumi, was finally recognized by the Company as Sultan, he became the first monarch who had both Dutch recognition, albeit grudgingly, and a firm Javanese consensus. It was only then that a resolution of the political crisis became possible. But Mangkubumi was not the only monarch whom the Dutch were to recognize, and the ultimate solution was still not to be the emergence of a single ruler.

The second theoretical solution was in fact the one which was eventually to emerge. This was that the state of political dissolution should itself be regarded as the permanent and rightful state of Javanese politics. In past centuries the kingdom had not infrequently been split into two or more principalities ruled by two or more 'kings', until one of the contestants had sufficient backing to depose the others. This had apparently been the situation during much of the sixteenth and early seventeenth centuries, during the Trunadjaja war, and during the Wars of Succession and the Chinese War of the Kartasura period. It would again be so in the years after 1749. This state of affairs had always been temporary, and one ruler had always eventually emerged as the dominant figure. During such periods of division, the state system reflected political realities as successfully as it did during periods of unification. If the largely autonomous local notables, princes, and religious leaders were not sufficiently behind one of the royal contenders to enable him to crush the opposition, then it was perfectly natural that there should be several 'kings' living in a state of warfare or uneasy tension until one of them had sufficient support to launch the final campaign.

Perhaps these periods of division were tense, and all desired them to end, partly because they posed a serious crisis of legitimation. The king who attracted support must still meet the two standards of Javanese kingship. In its 'technical implementation', he must not threaten the autonomy of his supporters. While the kingdom was divided this hardly posed a problem. The follower who felt threatened merely shifted his allegiance to another 'king' who promised more lenient overlordship. Therefore, either a king did not threaten his followers' essential autonomy or he risked losing even the partial support he commanded. If this occurred, he simply ceased to be a 'king', and was eliminated from the contest by the remaining contenders, either by being allowed to submit and become a vassal himself or by being helped to a more eternal kingdom.

But in the legitimative aspect of kingship the crisis was immense. If there were, say, three 'kings' in opposition to one another, could they all be protégés of the Goddess of the Southern Ocean, could each set of *pusakas* be the true set, could all three be the 'shadow of God upon the earth'? Clearly only one could be the true king and eventually it would be he who emerged victorious. But so long as there were other contenders, no single 'king' could command the unequalled lustre of kingship which was so important an element in making it worth the while of lesser notables to recognize him. Javanese notables would support the one among the contenders who not only posed the least threat to their autonomy, but whom they also believed to be the legitimate ruler. If sufficiently large numbers believed one of these kings to be the true monarch, he would soon have the power necessary to destroy his rivals. As the likelihood of his success became more apparent, supporters of the other contenders would recognize in him the signs of legitimacy, and swell still more the number of his followers. When, with ever-growing army, the successful contender had removed the opposition, his victory would be hailed as irrefutable evidence of the wisdom of having chosen his side as the legitimate one. The Javanese dignitaries would have been indifferent to the circular nature of this reasoning. As was noted above, when things went well, they went very well indeed, and fed upon their own success.

As the years of the eighteenth century passed it became ever more unlikely that a single ruler would emerge in this traditional fashion. This was true in large measure because of the Dutch presence. It will be seen in the following chapter how, by the 1740s, this led to almost total disintegration of the kingdom. If the situation was not to be resolved, then it must be stabilized unless endemic warfare was ultimately to exhaust the island, as well as to bankrupt the Dutch East India Company. The Dutch came to the conclusion by the middle years of the eighteenth century that it was impossible to keep Java united as a single state under the rule of their candidates for the throne. The Javanese several years later came to the same conclusion. The following pages attempt to analyse how the Javanese courtly élite eventually came to believe that there might never again be a single ruler of Mataram. Having come to this conclusion, however, this courtly élite were confronted by a crisis of legitimation of a kind never before faced in Javanese history. If there were permanently to be more than one king, traditional views of the state must somehow be revised to legitimate what in previous centuries had always been a temporary circumstance, a development which had always been seen as an anomaly against the ideal of a unified monarchy.

The development of a new view of the rightful structure of the Javanese state took several decades, and will be considered in detail in the following chapters. Contrary to the schools of thought which have seen the Dutch as being in control of Javanese affairs since the establishment of Batavia in 1619, this crisis of the late seventeenth and eighteenth centuries was the first time that the Dutch presence had any significant impact upon the affairs of the Javanese state. And this was not a colonial crisis, nor was the reaction a nationalist one. Indeed, the effect of the Dutch presence was so subtle, if devastating, that the Javanese appear never to have identified the Dutch East India Company as the essential disruptive element preventing the resolution of a traditional dynastic crisis. The Javanese élite apparently never saw the Dutch presence as being particularly dangerous or oppressive, except in so far as the Company might place its military power at the disposal of one's enemies. The Company was not seen as dangerous simply because it was foreign. The result of this was that the Javanese continued to consider relations among themselves as the primary issue. Indeed, after the mid-eighteenth century, the signs of the Company's weakness were sufficiently apparent and the withdrawal of large Dutch forces from Central Java so obvious that the Javanese can be excused not having recognized the Dutch as their central problem. This meant that the Javanese never contemplated a third potential solution to their crisis: temporary unity among themselves to drive the Dutch from Java, after which they might work out their internal problems to their logical and traditional conclusion.

Thus the history of this dynastic crisis, and of its resolution, is essentially autonomous Javanese history.[90] The presence of the Dutch may be seen as the essential disruptive force, but they neither controlled nor understood the Javanese political currents with which they dealt. What mattered was simply the fact of the Dutch presence preventing the resolution of the crisis, not decisions taken at Sĕmarang, Batavia, or in the Netherlands which only occasionally had any relevance to the course of events in Central Java. While the Dutch could prevent the usual outcome of a Javanese dynastic crisis, they could not impose any other solution. Initiative still lay with the Javanese, in whose hands alone lay the possibility of analysing and resolving the new problems of the kingdom.

[90] Cf. J. C. van Leur, 'Eenige Aanteekeningen betreffende de Mogelijkheid der 18e Eeuw als Categorie in de Indische Geschiedschrijving', *TBG*, vol. 80 (1940), pp. 544–67.

II

REBELLION AND THE DIVISION OF THE KINGDOM
1726–1754

It was a somewhat lamentable kingdom to which Susuhunan Pakubuana II (1726–49) succeeded, and in his reign culminated the problems which had plagued Java for so long. The court was split by intrigue, the countryside sundered by rebellion. It was this ruler's inglorious task to preside over two great rebellions, the fall of the Kartasura *kraton*, the final cession of the *pasisir* to the Dutch, and, upon his deathbed, the cession to the Dutch of sovereignty over the entire kingdom of Mataram.[1]

But the weakness of the Javanese state was paralleled by the growing debility of the Dutch East India Company. By the time Pakubuwana II succeeded, the Company was already in serious financial difficulties, and the continuing cycle of warfare and intervention in Java increased Dutch financial burdens while preventing the peaceful conditions necessary for trade.[2] By the middle of the eighteenth century the Company's army was in a weak condition,[3] and the Dutch records abound in woeful comments on the state of the Company in general. It continued to decline until its dissolution at the end of the eighteenth century. By 1761, the departing Governor of Java's Northeast Coast was moved to lament, 'Oh! had the Company remained a merchant.'[4]

Court cabals surrounded Pakubuwana II from the beginning and constantly threatened the relative peace of the early years of his reign. This prompted the Dutch to assist in the banishment of troublesome dignitaries from the court, including most notably

[1] For further details of the reign, see de Graaf, *GI*, pp. 249–64.
[2] On the decline of the VOC, see ibid., pp. 165–8; Boxer, *Dutch Seaborne Empire*, pp. 268–94; Hall, *History*, pp. 330 ff.; dJ x, pp. i ff.
[3] See P. J. F. Louw, *De derde Javaansche Successie-Oorlog (1746–1755)* ('s-Hage, 1889), pp. 9–15.
[4] Hartingh, Memorie, 26 Oct. 1761, in dJ x, p. 371. See also Batavia to H.XVII, 17 Oct. 1761, in dJ x, pp. 328–30.

the Susuhunan's brother Pangeran Arja Mangkunĕgara who was taken to Batavia in 1728 and eventually exiled overseas, the *patih* Danurĕdja who was banished from Java in 1733, and his successor Natakusuma who was exiled to Ceylon a decade later. But such banishments could not ameliorate the underlying political disintegration of the Javanese state, and the situation remained highly volatile, requiring only an appropriate catalyst to spring again into flame. This was provided in 1740. In that year, mutual suspicion between the Chinese and Dutch residents of Batavia bred ominous rumours throughout that city, and finally in October 1740, minor conflicts developed into a full-scale massacre of the Chinese there.

Roving bands of Chinese escaped the holocaust in Tanah Abang and moved eastwards on Java, attacking and harrassing Dutch posts along the coast, finally besieging the main Dutch position at Sĕmarang. At this point, a court faction in Kartasura convinced the Susuhunan to aid the Chinese and even carried out a successful assault on the Company's garrison at the court. But the fortunes of war soon turned against the Chinese forces, and simultaneously a pro-Dutch faction gained the ear of the vacillating Susuhunan, who now desired Batavia's forgiveness, which was granted. But the insurrection continued to spread, accumulating supporters from the Javanese as well as the Chinese population, and eventually it engulfed the court itself. The Kartasura *kraton* fell to rebels in June 1742. The fleeing Susuhunan begged the Dutch to assist in his restoration, in return for which he would allow the Company to chose the *patih* and to control the *pasisir*. Since these two were considered to be the cause of much of the court's instability and the origin of much rebellion, the proposal must, as Dr. de Graaf has commented, have 'sounded like music to Batavia's ears'.[5]

The rebellion was broken in 1743 with the submission to the Dutch of the rebel Susuhunan, a thirteen-year-old grandson of the deposed Susuhunan Amangkurat III (1703–8) named Mas Garĕndi (Sunan Kuning).[6] The Dutch exiled him to Ceylon.

[5] De Graaf, *GI*, p. 259.
[6] Amangkurat III was deposed and banished to Ceylon by the Dutch in 1708. The VOC supported instead the claims of Susuhunan Pakubuwana I (1703–19), the grandfather of Pakubuwana II. Amangkurat III died in Ceylon in 1737, and his family then returned to Java. On these events, see ibid., pp. 238–41.

REBELLION AND DIVISION, 1726-1754

Two years later, the restored Susuhunan Pakubuwana II built a new *kraton* at Surakarta,[7] and Java must have seemed at peace. But this renewed stability was illusory, and the disorder in Java was by now almost complete. Ten years later, the Governor of Java's Northeast Coast, Nicolaas Hartingh, observed that the Javanese nation

is in itself fickle, and by the multitude of princes very inclined to rebellion; for it cannot in truth be said that since the Company's first move Java has even for ten years been peaceful and quiet, or cleared of rebels.[8]

Several princes of the House of Mataram had joined the Chinese insurrection, and when it came to an end in 1743, a number of these princes did not submit. Two in particular remained in the hills: Mas Said, son of the exiled Pangeran Mangkunĕgara and nephew of the Susuhunan, and Pangeran Singasari, the Susuhunan's half-brother.[9] Both were to play important roles in the following years of chaos.

Dutch intervention in Javanese affairs had from the start only exacerbated the underlying problems of disunity among the élite. Their efforts on behalf of Pakubuwana II now had the same familiar effect, and precipitated the last great period of destruction in Java before the nineteenth century. In 1743 the Susuhunan repaid the Dutch for their assistance by signing over all of Madura and Balĕmbangan, Surabaja, Rĕmbang, Djĕpara and other ports on the coast, and by agreeing that the Dutch might take possession of a strip along the coast 600 roods deep, whenever it pleased the Company to do so. For the time being, this area was left under the Susuhunan's control.[10]

Court intrigues meanwhile continued to proliferate and minor rebellion persisted in the countryside. It is difficult to be sure of the course of events within the *kraton* walls, but it seems that Pakubuwana II promised that whoever drove the rebels from

[7] See Soepomo Poedjosoedarmo and M. C. Ricklefs, 'The Establishment of Surakarta, a Translation from the *Babad Gianti*', *Indonesia*, no. 4 (Oct. 1967), pp. 88–108.
[8] Sĕmarang to Batavia, 1 Nov. 1756, in dJ x, p. 313.
[9] On the family of PB II, see *BG*, vol. i, pp. 42–3. See also n. 18 below.
[10] PB II–VOC Treaty, 11 Nov. 1743, in dJ ix, pp. 434–47; also in [G. W. van Imhoff], 'Reis van den Gouverneur-Generaal van Imhoff, over Java, in het Jaar 1746', *BKI*, vol. 1 (1853), pp. 292–306.

Sokawati[11] would be repaid with control of 3,000 *tjatjahs* (households) in that area. The ruler's half-brother Pangeran Arja Mangkubumi, later the first Sultan of Jogjakarta, accepted the challenge and, in 1746, proceeded to defeat the forces of Mas Said, thereby taking military control of Sokawati. When Mangkubumi came to claim the lands as Pakubuwana II had promised, however, the *patih* Pringgalaja opposed the grant. Personal animosity between Pringgalaja and Mangkubumi now once again threatened the peace.[12]

Into the midst of this volatile situation came Governor-General G. W. van Imhoff (1743–50), whose journal[13] records two main accomplishments during his trip to Central Java. First, van Imhoff exercised the option to take control of the 600-rood-deep territory along the *pasisir*, as stipulated in the treaty of 1743. Second, he agreed with Pringgalaja's argument that to give Mangkubumi control of Sokawati would be to give the latter too much power, and van Imhoff convinced the Susuhunan to withdraw his promise. At the same time, he advised Mangkubumi before a court gathering to check his ambitions. As a result, Mangkubumi went into rebellion (19 May 1746).[14]

Javanese sources suggest that other issues were involved in Mangkubumi's rebellion as well as his claims to Sokawati and the blow to his prestige of a public reprimand. The cumulative effect of seven decades of chaos and the resultant influential position of the Dutch in Javanese court affairs were threatening basic organizational traditions of the Javanese state.

[11] Sokawati is no longer used as the name of the district. It is to the northeast of Surakarta, and is now known as Sragen.
[12] See Louw, *Successie-Oorlog*, pp. 7–8; C. Poensen,'Mangkubumi. Ngajogyakarta's eerste Sultan. (Naar Aanleiding van een Javaansch Handschrift)', *BKI*, vol. 52 (1901), pp. 231–8.
An interesting variation of this story, the veracity of which is difficult to judge, is in Thomas Stamford Raffles, *The History of Java* (2 vols.; London, 1830), vol. ii, pp. 247–8.
[13] See van Imhoff, 'Reis'.
[14] See ibid., pp. 397–403; Poensen, 'Mangkubumi', pp. 231–8; dJ x, pp. xl-xli; Hartingh, Memorie, 26 Oct. 1761, in dJ x, pp. 365–6; Batavia to H.XVII, 31 Dec. 1746, in dJ x, pp. 62–4; van Imhoff, Kort Begrip, 9 June 1746, in dJ x, p. 94; Louw, *Successie-Oorlog*, pp. 6–8.
Sěrat Babad Pakunĕgaran (BM Add. MS. 12283), f. 105^r, correctly dates Mangkubumi's departure Thursday, 27 Rabingulakir, Dal, rupa swara obah ing djagad (A.J. 1671), which is 19 May 1746.
Babad Sangkalaning Momana, p. 267, wrongly dates Mangkubumi's departure in A.J. 1672.

Babad Gijanti[15] describes the meeting between van Imhoff and the Susuhunan, who is depicted as a weak and vacillating character. According to this text, when van Imhoff raised the subject of the leasing of the *pasisir* the ruler was surprised, not having suspected that the Company would in fact claim those lands. He asked that the Governor-General be patient while he first consulted the advisers (*pra najaka*) of the kingdom on the matter. Van Imhoff replied that the advisers were not to be trusted. Had not the Susuhunan joined the (Chinese) rebellion against the Dutch only a few years before because of the bad advice of his courtiers?[16] His Highness was the ruler, and no one could defy his wishes. Under this pressure, the unhappy Susuhunan submitted to the request.

After this meeting, Pakubuwana II summoned his two first ministers (*patih*), Pringgalaja and Sindurĕdja, and his brother Mangkubumi, informing them that he had leased the *pasisir* to the Company:

> IV: 19. His Highness said softly,
> 'Know, Mangkubumi,
> that Grandfather [Governor-] General has arrived,
> asking for the leasing of the *pasisir*.
> I, younger brother, have already agreed
> to the Company's request,
> because I was intimidated by the discussion.'
> The Honoured Pangeran [Mangkubumi] spoke softly,
> 'My Lord, but this is not fitting.'
>
> 20. 'Are you not aware
> that the role of a ruler
> carries the obligation to reign only?
> Executive power in the kingdom
> is with the *patih*,
> *najakas* and *tumĕnggungs*,
> along with the *sĕntanas*;
> it is these who have the duty
> to use power extending in the length and breadth.

[15] *BG*, vol. i, pp. 32–50.
[16] Cf. van Imhoff, 'Reis', pp. 398–9. Van Imhoff says that PB II raised objections to his proposals, but van Imhoff pointed out to the Susuhunan 'that under his rule Java has almost never remained at peace for a dozen years, largely because the ruler cannot possibly control and keep everything in order from the interior, and has to leave his ministers alone, who misuse his authority to their own advantage, and thus continually generate the discontented and the rebels...'.

21. 'Indeed, there is yet no *adat*
for the ruler himself to negotiate.'
His Highness said softly,
'Yes, that is true, younger brother.
But when I met [with the Governor-General]
I asked [him] to be patient, without success.'[17]

[17] *BG*, vol. i, pp. 34–5, Canto IV (Sinom):

19. Sang Nata alon ngandika
    wruhanira Mangkubumi
    jen praptane kaki Djendral
    minta anggaḍuh pasisir
    sun jaji wus marĕngi
    Kumpĕni pamitanipun
    wit kapĕngkok witjara
    Djĕng Pangeran matur aris
    ḍuh Pukulun dene ta botĕn kadosa

20. punapa tan kaengĕtan
    lamun djĕnĕnging Narpati
    mung darma mĕngku kewala
    bangbang lumalum ing nagri
    jĕkti wontĕn papatih
    najaka para tumĕnggung
    tuwin para sĕntana
    punika kang darbe wadjib
    amasesa angalangna angudjurna

21. inggih dereng wontĕn adat
    Ratu papadon pribadi
    Sang Nata alon ngandika
    ija bĕnĕr sira jaji
    nanging sun duk papanggih
    minta sareh datan antuk
    . . . .

Cf. *Sĕrat Babad Pakunĕgaran*, ff. 103ᵛ–104ʳ, Canto XXXIV (Ḍanḍanggula).
PB II speaks to Mangkubumi:

38. Marma jaji sira sun timbali
    wruhira Djendral ingkang prapta
    wong pasisir sakabehe
    maksa kudu djinaluk
    sun sĕmbaja pikir tan nganti
    abutuh sun pinĕksa
    apĕs djĕnĕng ingsun
    dadya sun turut kewala
    wong pasisir digaḍuh marang Kumpni
    besuk mulih maring wang

39. matur runtik Pangran Mangkubumi
    botĕn pĕnĕd ing karsa Paduka
    santana datan tinaros
    . . . .

Mangkubumi also complained that the amount of money which Pringgalaja and Sindurĕdja proposed to ask from the Dutch in exchange for these lands was insufficient. The taxes from the *montjanĕgara* (outer regions) were in arrears, and the wealth of the central districts of Padjang, Mataram, Bagĕlen, and Kĕḍu was inadequate to support the *kraton*. Nevertheless the lowest figure, the 20,000 reals per annum proposed by Sindurĕdja, was accepted by the Susuhunan.

According to *Babad Gijanti*, Mangkubumi was greatly upset by these events, which he felt to be a misfortune for all of Java. He pondered what would be the outcome for the *kraton* if it were separated from the *pasisir*; there would undoubtedly be troubles. Returning to his residence, the prince consulted his own advisers, who bemoaned the fact that of the nine Pangerans still at court, only Mangkubumi was consulted by the Susuhunan. This was, they said, a sign of the troubles facing the kingdom.[18] This complaint was a clear comment upon the Susuhunan's isolation from those who should traditionally have been his advisers, and upon the general breakdown of the decision-making process within the court, under Dutch pressure. If the Pangerans were not consulted, their interests could not be represented and taken into account. In such a situation, it was natural that the princes should reconsider the wisdom of continuing to support the Susuhunan.

Pringgalaja had meanwhile gained the ear of the Governor-General, who consequently intervened in the dispute over Mangkubumi's claim to Sokawati.[19] *Babad Gijanti* claims that the Dutch commandant von Hohendorff advised Pakubuwana II to reduce Mangkubumi's lands temporarily to 1,000 *tjatjahs* to appease the Governor-General. Pakubuwana II supposedly accepted this

[18] The nine were Pangerans Danupaja, Adinagara, Adiwidjaja, Mangkubumi, Rongga, Mataram, Sĕlarong, Panular, and Bei. Pangerans Buminata and Singasari were in rebellion, along with Mas Said and others; see *BG*, vol. i, pp. 42–3. This list is essentially confirmed in a VOC list of the ruler's brothers dated Nov. 1743, in AN Solo 42; Dr. de Graaf has very generously provided me with a transcript of this document. In this list there is found one Pangeran Dipasanta, who is said to have been 'excused from service' because of his infirmity (*gebreckelijkheijt*), and was perhaps no longer alive in 1746. There was also a Pangaran Prangmadana in 1743, then 18 years old, who may have become the Pangeran Bei of *BG*. The 1743 list also includes one Pangeran Ngabei Loringpasar, who was reported by van Imhoff ('Reis', p. 415) to have died by 1746, and whose son had joined the rebels.

[19] *BG*, vol. i, pp. 41–50. The story of the appanage being reduced to 1,000 *tjatjahs* is also to be found in *Sĕrat Babad Pakunĕgaran*, ff. 104^v–105^r.

solution, but the modern historian should perhaps regard this tale with some scepticism.

With the reduction of the promised 3,000 *tjatjahs* Mangkubumi's position at the court became untenable. According to *Babad Gijanti* he asked the Susuhunan's permission to leave Surakarta, and received his brother's valedictory blessing. Again, one may doubt that the departure took quite this form, but it is not inconceivable in the Javanese context.

With the departure of Mangkubumi began the conflagration which Dutch historians have called the Third Javanese War of Succession (1746–55). Clearly the immediate cause of the rebellion was Pringgalaja's success in reducing Mangkubumi's power and influence by preventing him from controlling the large appanage in Sokawati. But it seems Mangkubumi also objected to the expanding Dutch control of Javanese territory and to the separation of the *pasisir* from Central Java. Fifteen years later, after Mangkubumi had become Sultan of Jogjakarta, the Dutch Governor at Sĕmarang wrote that the Company's possession of the coasts

is a gnawing worm in [the Javanese rulers'] bosoms . . . It is even said that [Pakubuwana II], who died so wretchedly from heartbreak as well as from vermin, always had the impression that the cession was only for one year or three, to underwrite the war . . . which I leave as it is, although the present ruler [Pakubuwana III] has often heartily held forth about it to me as well as to others. And with what aversion and emotion the Sultan agreed thereto at my first encounter [in 1754] is to be found in my notes about that; indeed he gave it clearly to be known that his brother had no qualification whatsoever for such a surrender, at the very least could not abridge the rights of his successors.[20]

The Dutch occupation of the *pasisir* meant that after 1746 Javanese *kraton* history becomes almost exclusively the history of the interior provinces of Central Java. The horizons of the Central Javanese courtly élite were shrinking.

The Sĕmarang Governor's comment also hints at a third impetus to rebellion, which emerges clearly from the *Babad Gijanti* account. The Susuhunan was not in fact the absolute monarch the Dutch believed, or wished, him to be. He had no authority

[20] Hartingh, Memorie, 26 Oct. 1761, in dJ x, pp. 361–2. Cf. *Sĕrat Babad Pakunĕgaran*, f. 103^r, where the Governor-General is quoted as saying that the *pasisir* would later be returned to the Susuhunan (see also the stanzas from this text reproduced in n. 17 above).

REBELLION AND DIVISION, 1726-1754

to take a major decision such as the surrender of the *pasisir* without previous consultation with the dignitaries of the kingdom. Mangkubumi is quoted in *Babad Gijanti* as saying that there was no *adat* for such behaviour; such a monarch had no place in Javanese custom. But Dutch pressure seems to have forced upon the wretched Pakubuwana II a role similar to that which Amangkurat I had attempted to play, the absolute monarch who might decide the fate of his far-flung subjects according to his personal whim. This unacceptable authoritarianism had contributed to the collapse of the kingdom in 1677 and now, seventy years later, it also contributed to the rebellion of Mangkubumi. It is notable that the Dutch memorandum cited above suggests that by 1761 the Dutch were coming to be aware of this obscure but fundamental aspect of the Javanese state. The Governor pointed out that in the matter of contractual obligations between the Company and the rulers,

the burden lies entirely on the shoulders of the *patihs*, for everything about negotiation, according to their doctrine, tends towards the decline of a ruler.[21]

Van Imhoff in 1746 did not suspect the extent to which a Javanese monarch's authority was circumscribed by customary limitations. These were a formal expression of the need to maintain an élite consensus in order to hold the kingdom together. Being unaware of this, van Imhoff quite unintentionally forced the Susuhunan to violate Javanese royal custom in such a way as to make rebellion the likely outcome. Once again the delicate balance upon which the state depended was disturbed, and the countryside burst into flame.

Thus, *Babad Gijanti* suggests that personal ambition was not the sole motivation for Mangkubumi's rebellion. Ethical issues concerning the nature of royal authority were also at stake. If the Susuhunan were to take decisions without prior consultations in the traditional fashion, the interests of dignitaries such as Mangkubumi were directly threatened. The author of *Babad Gijanti*, Raden Ngabei Jasadipura I, was an admirer of Mangkubumi although himself a Surakarta court poet.[22] It is not surprising, then,

---

[21] Hartingh, Memorie, 26 Oct. 1761, in dJ x, p. 367.

[22] It is not true, as Poensen suggests ('Mangkubumi', p. 235), that *BG* is written 'from a Surakarta standpoint', and therefore should differ in interpretation from his Jogjakarta (Pakualaman) text. Jasadipura's admiration of

that *Babad Gijanti* provides this apologia for the insurrection. Yet it is significant that another chronicle written on the initiative of Prince Mangkunĕgara I (Mas Said), who was later Mangkubumi's arch-enemy, gives essentially the same version of these events.[23]

After leaving Surakarta, Mangkubumi joined forces with the rebel Mas Said and gave his daughter Ratu Bĕndara in marriage to him to seal the alliance. The two princely rebels now proceeded to ravage Central Java. By the end of 1746, Mangkubumi's following was said to have reached about 3,000 men, and late in 1747 his army, then said to total 13,000 including 2,500 cavalry, butchered a handful of Dutch troops at Grobogan.[24]

In May 1748, Pringgalaja promised Pakubuwana II that he would march against the rebels, and the Susuhunan could look forward to victory within the month. When the assembled troops of Surakarta marched out to destroy the enemy, however, Mangkubumi and Mas Said outflanked them and swept down upon the city, burning a number of houses and threatening the *kraton* itself before withdrawing to the hills of Sokawati. Shortly thereafter, Mangkubumi drove deep into the Company's coastal areas, driving the Dutch forces before him and killing the Dutch Resident of Djuwana. Mas Said and Mangkubumi, at the head of armies numbered in thousands, were successfully checked by Dutch troops in the coastal regions, but it was impossible for the Company's limited forces to defeat such vast armies decisively.[25]

Mangkubumi is quite clear. See also Soebardi, 'Raden Ngabehi Jasadipura I, Court Poet of Surakarta: His Life and Works', *Indonesia*, no. 8 (Oct. 1969), p. 100.

[23] *Sĕrat Babad Pakunĕgaran*, ff. 102^v–105^r. This text is dated A.J. 1705 (A.D. 1779); it therefore dates from a period when MN and HB I had already been bitter enemies for several decades. See n. 17 above.

A very brief translation (perhaps inaccurate) of a Javanese text published in 1839 emphasizes the withholding of Sokawati as the main reason for Mangkubumi's rebellion. The text seems, however, to be extremely superficial and of little historical value; see 'Vertaling van een Javaansch Handschrift, behelzende eene Geschiedkundige Schets der Splitsing van het Rijk van Soerakarta en der Stichting van het Rijk van Djockjokarta', *Tijdschrift voor Neêrland's Indie*, vol. 12, pt. 2 (1839), pp. 204–11.

[24] Louw, *Successie-Oorlog*, pp. 16 ff.; Poensen, 'Mangkubumi', pp. 238 ff.; [H. de Munnik], 'Kort Verhaal van de Javasche Oorlogen, welke met onderscheidene Prinsen gevoerd zijn, sedert den jare 1741, tot den algemeenen Vrede, gesloten in den jare 1757', *VBG*, vol. 12 (1830), pp. 75–254. On the attribution of the 'Kort Verhaal' to Hartingh's secretary Hermanus de Munnik, see dJ x, p. 373 n. 1.

[25] Louw, *Successie-Oorlog*, pp. 20–3.

Pakubuwana II had by now ruled for more than two decades over his turbulent kingdom. As the months of 1749 passed, it became clear that his days were numbered. In a traditional kingdom such as Java, few questions are more crucial than that of succession. Accordingly both the Dutch and the rebel princes took steps to prepare for the great event which would come when the wretched Susuhunan, not yet forty years old, drew his last breath.

Mangkubumi apparently hoped he could forestall the succession of the Susuhunan's sixteen-year-old son, Mangkubumi's nephew, by declaring himself ruler of Java. In preparation he took up residence some forty-five miles to the southwest of Surakarta at a place named Jogja, near the old *kratons* of Kuta Gĕḍe and Plered.[26] The choice of location was significant. When van Imhoff stopped at Jogja during his tour of 1746 he learned that the area was considered by some to be 'the centre of Mataram'.[27] Mangkubumi had now returned to the area which gave the dynasty its name, and where its glory had been founded.[28] He also made contact with the Dutch Governor of the Northeast Coast, the former Surakarta commandant von Hohendorff, but he failed to win any concessions on the question of the succession in Surakarta.[29] P. J. F. Louw, the historian of this war, judged that peace would have been possible in 1749 if the Dutch had given in to Mangkubumi on the succession, but neither Batavia nor von Hohendorff realized 'that it was fire with which they were playing'.[30]

The Company, with a rigidity typical of its view of Javanese affairs, was determined that the Susuhunan's son should succeed. It is hardly surprising that the Dutch did not wish Mangkubumi or his son to become Susuhunan, for they had little reason to expect this would produce a co-operative court. But it was equally unreasonable to expect that peace would return to Java without a settlement with the rebellious princes. While war continued, the Company could not pursue its mercantile interests, and its military resources were inadequate to restore the essential peace by force.

[26] Ibid., p. 24. For a summary of evidence on the history of Jogja before it was occupied by Mangkubumi, see Poensen, 'Mangkubumi', p. 267.
[27] Van Imhoff, 'Reis', p. 407. See also ibid., p. 408, where van Imhoff says some considered 'Passar gedee' to be 'het middelste van de Mattarm'.
[28] Surakarta was located not in Mataram, but in Padjang.
[29] Louw, *Successie-Oorlog*, pp. 26–7.   [30] Ibid., p. 27.

Some sort of settlement with the rebels would ultimately be required, but the Company was not yet prepared to consider this. Drifting uneasily between the Scylla of exhaustion or defeat and the Charybdis of concession, the Dutch waited for Pakubuwana II to die.

Throughout October and November 1749, the Susuhunan's illness grew worse. The Company strengthened its Surakarta garrison, hoping to be able to hold the court until the succession could be accomplished. News that the Crown Prince was also ill did nothing to soothe frayed nerves.[31] Early in December, Governor von Hohendorff left Sĕmarang with a company of dragoons and some Balinese troops for Surakarta, in order to regulate the succession.[32] When he saw the Susuhunan on 8 December, he found the ruler's physical condition so horribly deteriorated that Pakubuwana II was virtually unrecognizable and unable to bestir himself. Von Hohendorff was much moved by the pitiable scene, and asked Pakubuwana II if he had any medication or wished to have any, and indeed from what illness he was suffering. After a time, the dying man replied only that he was pleased to be able to see von Hohendorff before he died, but he had no interest in medicine since he knew well that he must die. The following day he was persuaded to submit to an examination by two Dutch doctors who had accompanied the Governor. They discovered that the Susuhunan was already stiff and without feeling below the abdomen. He rejected all attempts to convince him there was hope of recovery.

It was impossible for von Hohendorff to consult with the Susuhunan on matters of state concerning the succession and the rebels. With his end so near, Pakubuwana II had no wish to concern himself with worldly cares. He apparently desired a trusted friend to relieve him of the burdens of state, and this he found in von Hohendorff, who had served for many turbulent years at the *kraton*. Eight years before, in 1741, then-Captain von Hohendorff had undertaken the hazardous task of commanding the tiny Dutch garrison at Kartasura, whose predecessors had been so recently attacked upon the Susuhunan's authority. He

---

[31] Louw, *Successie-Oorlog*, pp. 27–31.
[32] The following description of events is taken from von Hohendorff's Dagregister, 31 Dec. 1749. Dr. de Graaf has very generously provided me with a transcript of this document from the Djakarta AN.

had subsequently fought in defence of Pakubuwana II's rights against the rebel Susuhunan in the Chinese War, and had advised the Susuhunan on the subsequent establishment of the new Surakarta *kraton*. As commandant at Surakarta, von Hohendorff had been involved in the negotiations with the Governor-General in 1743 and 1746. In 1748 he had left to become the first Governor of the Northeast Coast at Sĕmarang (1748–54).[33] Now, back in Surakarta to witness the Susuhunan's death, von Hohendorff was presented with a remarkable proposition.

Pakubuwana II proposed that, since von Hohendorff was at the court, it would be better if the latter simply took control of the kingdom himself. Mataram was being offered to the Dutch. Von Hohendorff tried to dissuade the Susuhunan, probably because the proposal was so unexpected and apparently revolutionary in nature that von Hohendorff could think of no other reaction. The Susuhunan persisted, however, and as his fever grew worse, von Hohendorff withdrew without answering the proposal, advising the Susuhunan to consider further.

On the tenth of December von Hohendorff was again received by Pakubuwana II, who persisted in his intention to surrender the burdens of his kingdom to the Dutch Governor. Having now had time for reflection, von Hohendorff agreed that the proposal was most advantageous. He insisted, however, that an oral agreement was insufficient basis for such a step. Furthermore, the cession must be absolute. Pakubuwana II agreed, adding that even if he were to be granted a few more years of life, he only wished to live them in peace, without worldly cares. Von Hohendorff hastened to his lodging to draw up a contract to regularize the cession, but was shortly called back to the ruler, whom he found in tears. Pakubuwana II asked if von Hohendorff had compassion for him and, having been assured that this was so, asked that von Hohendorff then have compassion for his children as well. The few possessions he would leave behind which did not belong to the state should be divided among them, and the contract which was being drawn up should not omit to say that the Susuhunan commended all his children to the protection of the Company.

The next day, 11 December 1749, the Susuhunan signed and sealed the act of cession, by which the entire kingdom of Mataram

[33] See dJ ix, pp. 412, 426, 433 n. 1; dJ x, p. xlvi; Soepomo and Ricklefs, 'Establishment of Surakarta'.

was turned over to the Dutch.[34] It seems remarkable that Pakubuwana II should have done this. Indeed, it has been suggested that the Susuhunan only intended the cession to be temporary, in accordance with the Javanese practice whereby a dying man entrusts his goods to a friend to ensure their safe transmission to his heirs. It was, according to this argument, only a Dutch misconception of Javanese practice which led this treaty to be considered a formal cession of sovereignty. While this is an eminently logical explanation in itself, and may perhaps be correct, it is nevertheless not supported by historical materials available at present. An analysis of both Dutch and Javanese texts of the agreement, in the light of von Hohendorff's report and of comments in *Babad Gijanti*, suggests that the Susuhunan in fact wished the Dutch Governor to undertake two tasks. One of these was to transmit to the ruler's children the goods which were their inheritance, and to take those children under his care. This was clearly a case of a dying man entrusting his possessions to a friend to ensure their transmission to his heirs. In the conspiratorial atmosphere of the Surakarta *kraton*, the Susuhunan believed von Hohendorff to be the man to undertake this task for him. But there was a distinction between this matter and the question of the kingdom itself, which the treaty appears to have ceded to the Company without reservation.[35] There is, however,

---

[34] The Dutch text is in dJ x, pp. 159–60. Both the Dutch and the Javanese texts are published in Soekanto, *Sekitar Jogjakarta, 1755–1825* (*Perdjandjian Gianti—Perang Dipanagara*) (Djakarta, [1952]), pp. 178–81. The Javanese text is also in Soeripto, *Ontwikkelingsgang der Vorstenlandsche Wetboeken* (Leiden, 1929), pp. 188–9; Soeripto's text is not the original and shows minor differences from Soekanto's.

[35] See Soekanto, *Sekitar Jogjakarta*, p. 15 n. Dr. Soekanto asks whether the VOC was the *legal possessor* of Mataram ('Apakah Kompeni *jang punja dengan sah* negara Mataram?') and concludes that this was not so. He argues that it was not PB II's intention to grant sovereignty to the Dutch, but rather he was simply acting in accordance with the Javanese *adat* in entrusting (*menitipkan*) his kingdom to the Company to ensure its transmission to his son. Von Hohendorff's diary, however, indicates that the Susuhunan made a distinction between his kingdom and his personal possessions; it was the transmission of the latter to his heirs he asked von Hohendorff to ensure. This distinction also appears in the texts of the contract (see n. 34 above). The Dutch text says:

Ik Soesoehoenan Pakoeboewono ... bekenne en verklare met desen openlijk ... het Mattaramsche rijk ... met ap- en-dependentie alle gezag, magt en authoriteijt, welke it tot dato hebbe gehad, over te geven aan de Doorlugtige O. Ind. Comp. ... doende overzulks bij dezen daarvan vollen afstand en verklaere van nu af aen, daar op geen de minste pretensie meer te

inadequate documentation of the Susuhunan's precise intentions in this latter question largely because of completely differing sets of interests. The legal issues which concerned the Dutch in the eighteenth century and historians in the twentieth were

> hebben of te houden; maar 't Rijk . . . bij deezen uijt eijgen vrije en onbedwongen wil gecedeert en overgegeven te hebben aan voorz. doorlugtige Comp. . . . bevelende mijne na te laten kinderen voornamentlijk den Kroonprins pangeran Adipattij Anom, in de protexie en bescherming van de voorm. Doorlugtige Oost Indische Comp.
>
> The Javanese text reads:
>
> Kawula Kangdjěng Susuhunan Pakubuwana . . . angakěni sarta amratelakakěn kalajan iklasing manah . . . karaton Matawis . . . sarta sawěwěngkonipun sědaja, kang ing mangke sampun kawula asta, punika sadaja sami kaaturakěn ḍumatěng Kumpni kang agěng . . . inggih sawab padamělan punika, mila kalampahan kautjulakěn sadaja, kawula botěn pisan jen aděrbeja karsa agadaha malih, nanging ta wau karaton . . . ing mangke sukanipun manah kawula, botěn awit jen kaparipěksaha, kaaturakěn ḍumatěng Kumpni. . . . Inggih sakalangkung gen kawula anitipakěn putra-putra kawula kang kantunkantun punapa dening Pangeran Adipati Anom kawula lindungakěn ḍumatěng aub ing Kumpni . . .
>
> Both texts thus seem to make a distinction between the kingdom and the ruler's children: the kingdom (het Mattaramse Rijk, Karaton Matawis) was 'handed over' (over te geven, kaaturakěn; *note, not*: katitipakěn) to the Company while the Susuhunan's children were 'entrusted to the care of the Company' (bevelende . . . in de protexie en bescherming van, anitipakěn . . . lindungakěn ḍumatěng aub).
>
> Nor does a comparison of the two texts support the suggestion made privately to the present author that the Javanese and Dutch versions diverge on the question of the cession. It also cannot be argued that the treaty was signed under duress, since von Hohendorff's diary indicates that the suggestion came from the Susuhunan and that the text of the agreement was read to him three times and discussed before he signed it. It should be pointed out that the ruler was apparently mentally alert until shortly before his death.
>
> *Babad Gijanti* also indicates that it was PB II who first suggested that von Hohendorff should take over responsibility for the Susuhunan's children; see vol. vi, p. 31: . . . / Sri Narendra gja engět wardaja / ririh ḍawuh andikane / Gupěnur ija sukur / dene sira těka pribadi / prakara sutanira / ki Dipati iku / ja mongsa boḍowa sira / sadurunge sauwise pasrah mami / ija marang ing sira. In *BG*, vol. vi, p. 32, von Hohendorff addresses a court gathering, announcing that the *kraton* has been turned over to him by PB II: . . . / paḍa mijarsakěna / jen mangke Sang Prabu / seleh karaton maring wang / . . .
>
> It seems impossible to argue that, at least in formal legal terms, the treaty does not cede full sovereignty to the VOC, in both Dutch and Javanese versions, without putting intolerable strains upon both the semanticist's and the lawyer's art. Dr. Soekanto's argument that such a cession could not have been intended because such an act was 'not rational' is, perhaps, not entirely to the point. Pakubuwana II was not in a physical or mental state to be much concerned about temporal standards of rationality. In any case, such a cession was no less rational than the cession of the *pasisir* in 1743 and 1746, the legality of which Dr. Soekanto

probably quite irrelevant to Pakubuwana II and his contemporaries, who undoubtedly saw the issues in rather more immediate terms. The long-term implications of the arrangement may have had little significance to the Javanese in 1749, living in a troubled world in which nothing seemed lasting. If Pakubuwana II considered the issue in terms of sovereignty, which seems unlikely, he would probably have come to the conclusion that no piece of paper adorned with red lacquer seals could make the Dutch *de facto* sovereigns over Mataram. Only men and gunpowder could accomplish that, and of these commodities the Dutch supply was to be inadequate until the nineteenth century. And in any case, the Javanese idea of sovereignty did not imply the sort of direct control which is implied in Western political thinking. Thus to some extent the debate over sovereignty deals in a subject which was unlikely to have had the significance for eighteenth-century Javanese which it may hold for others.

Armed with the Susuhunan's authority to regulate the succession, von Hohendorff decided it best to install the new ruler immediately, while Pakubuwana II still lingered on. Accordingly von Hohendorff invited the Crown Prince to a meeting on the evening of 13 December, an encounter which von Hohendorff, with all his experience of Javanese court intrigue, must nevertheless have found disconcerting. He asked the young prince whether he brought any news from the *kraton*, whether he had seen or spoken with his father. The Crown Prince said he had not. Why, von Hohendorff asked, did he hold himself distant from his father at such a time? The imperial heir replied that such a visit was likely to cause him more discomfort than pleasure, since Pakubuwana II had recently not only forbidden him to enter the *kraton* but had attempted personally to assault him with a *kris*, being suspicious of an affair between the Crown Prince and one of the royal concubines. The Governor, much surprised at this, asked if his father had not spoken with the prince since his illness began

---

does not deny although it was equally irrational and equally in conflict with Javanese *adat*.

A more important source of misunderstanding between PB II and the VOC was the difference in their conceptions of 'sovereignty'. In the period covered by this present study, the latter half of the eighteenth century, the effect of this treaty and of the differing perceptions of the implications of VOC sovereignty was negligible. In the nineteenth century, however, this would change drastically, and would lead to considerable conflict.

concerning affairs of state, and whether the Susuhunan had not expressed his interest in seeing his son succeed him. No, was the reply. Von Hohendorff asked the Prince whether he did not aspire to succeed his father and to govern Mataram under the stipulations which the Company would lay down. The Crown Prince said he did. Since the conversation at last seemed to be going in the right direction, the Prince was given copies of the treaties of 1743 and 1746, and the cession his father had signed two days previously. Having read them, he declared that he had no objection to becoming Susuhunan under the conditions contained therein. The next day he signed an agreement which stipulated in precise legal language what the *Babad Gijanti* expressed more succinctly: the Governor-General and the Batavia Council of the Indies installed the new Susuhunan.[36] The Crown Prince acknowledged that he became ruler not through right of inheritance, but because the Dutch East India Company chose him for the position.[37]

On the fifteenth of December, the Crown Prince was declared by von Hohendorff to be the new ruler of Surakarta, Susuhunan Pakubuwana III (1749–88), the vassal of the Dutch East India Company. Von Hohendorff recorded the Javanese population's surprise at the young ruler's subordination to the Dutch on the day of his accession. On the Governor's right, the position of honour, stood not Pakubuwana but the Dutch commander Toutlemonde. The ruler stood in a lower position, on von Hohendorff's left. Upon the Governor's suggestion, the new Susuhunan and his ministers of court then paid final respects to the dying Pakubuwana II,[38] who finally found his peace on 20 December.[39]

Thus ended one of the most catastrophic reigns of Javanese history. But history is not always a linear progression. The year 1749 was in many ways the nadir of the decline of Mataram and

[36] *BG*, vol. vi, p. 32: lamun wong gĕdé-gĕdé Bĕtawi / tuwan Djendral ngadĕgakĕn Radja.

[37] Von Hohendorff, Dagregister, 31 Dec. 1749 (see n. 32 above). The text of the agreement signed by the Crown Prince is in dJ x, pp. 160–2.

[38] Von Hohendorff, Dagregister, 31 Dec. 1749 (see n. 32 above). *BG*, vol. vi, pp. 31, 32, dates the accession Monday, 4 Sura, Alip (A.J.) 1675. Monday, 15 Dec. 1749, was 5 Sura in the new 'Thursday Calendar'. *BG* was, therefore, still using the 'Friday Calendar' for this event. On this calendrical problem, see n. 42 below.

[39] Von Hohendorff, Surakarta, to Batavia, 21 Dec. 1749, in dJ x, p. 156; and Dagregister, 31 Dec. 1749 (see n. 32 above). See also *BG*, vol. vi, p. 37; Batavia to H.XVII, 31 Dec. 1749, in dJ x, p. 153 (where PB II's death is said to have occurred on 16 December, which is wrong).

the high-water mark of Dutch influence in eighteenth-century Java. Thereafter, the declining power of the Company, both financial and consequently military, made it more and more difficult for the Dutch to sustain an extended intervention in Java. While they remained an important factor in the calculations of Javanese politics, their presence was to become less obtrusive, particularly after 1755. At the same time, forty-five miles to the southwest of Surakarta, a new kingdom was in the process of creation which was to provide much of the impetus for a renaissance of traditional Java.

Von Hohendorff had been moved to the precipitous installation of Pakubuwana III largely because of ominous rumours that Mangkubumi had been declared Susuhunan in Jogja. Dutch sources report that this was done on 11 December 1749, the very day that Pakubuwana II surrendered the kingdom.[40] There is, however, some confusion about this date. The Dutch had heard rumours of such a declaration as early as July 1749, although this information was apparently inaccurate.[41] Javanese texts agree that the accession occurred in the month of Sura A.J. 1675 (11 December 1749–9 January 1750), which is confirmed by a later Dutch reference as well. A comparison of the various documents suggests that this event probably took place on 1 Sura A.J. 1675, but that because Jogja had not followed Surakarta in adjusting the calendar by one day, this was in fact 12 December 1749, the day after the cession of the kingdom.[42]

[40] Von Hohendorff, Dagregister, 31 Dec. 1749 (see n. 32 above). See also dJ x, pp. xlvi–xlvii. [41] See Louw, *Successie-Oorlog*, pp. 24–6.
[42] *BG*, vol. vi, pp. 27, 28, says Mangkubumi became Susuhunan on Friday, 1 Sura, Alip [A.J. 1675]. But 1 Sura, A.J. 1675, actually fell upon Thursday (11 Dec. A.D. 1749). This was, however, the beginning of the so-called 'Thursday Calendar' in the complicated Javanese chronometry. If Jogja continued to use the old 'Friday Calendar' when Surakarta adopted the 'Thursday Calendar', 1 Sura would indeed have fallen on a Friday. In that case, the date would be 12 December A.D. 1749.
It is likely that Jogja continued to use the 'Friday Calendar'. Mangkubumi's letter to von Hohendorff (in his Dagregister, 31 Dec. 1749) is dated Monday, 4 Muharram, which date would only be possible in the 'Friday Calendar'. In the 'Thursday Calendar' 4 Muharram would have been Sunday. See also n. 38 above, which shows that *BG* was also still using the 'Friday Calendar' for this period.
The declaration of von Hohendorff's emissary to Mangkubumi, Muhamad Djuwana, cited in his Dagregister, 31 Dec. 1749, also suggests that the date was 12 December.
Sĕrat Djumĕnĕngan S.D.I.S. Kg. Sultan Hamĕngkubuwana I (Jogja kraton

REBELLION AND DIVISION, 1726-1754

Mangkubumi is said to have been urged to claim the throne of Mataram by the growing number of princes and officials who had left Surakarta to join him at Jogja, and he emphasized to the Dutch that his claim to the throne rested upon his selection by these dignitaries of Mataram.[43] Mangkubumi thus claimed an élite consensus which by traditional standards should have enabled him to replace the Surakarta Susuhunan as the true monarch of Mataram. Indeed there were said to have been fewer officials and dignitaries present at the accession of Pakubuwana III than were present when Mangkubumi took the traditional royal titles,[44] *Susuhunan Pakubuwana Senapati Ingalaga Ngabdurahman Sajidin Panatagama*, to which *Babad Gijanti* adds, 'who was the true ruler, established in and administering the land of the island Java'.[45] It was not unusual for Javanese rebels to claim royal titles.

MS. A. 22), p. 1, dates Mangkubumi's accession Friday-Lěgi, 3 Sura, Alip A.J. 1675, and itself wrongly converts that date to 13 December A.D. 1749. Friday-Lěgi was 2 Sura in the 'Thursday Calendar' (12 December) or 1 Sura in the 'Friday Calendar' (also 12 December). This manuscript, written early in the twentieth century A.D., has a number of inaccurate dates, and its reliability is often open to question. But the use of 'Friday-Lěgi' again points to 12 December as the correct date.

Babad Sangkalaning Momana, p. 267, gives only the year Alip, A.J. 1675, for this event.

See also de Munnik, Report, 1 Aug. 1763, in KA 2986 (OB 1764). According to de Munnik, in 1763 HB I celebrated the anniversary of his accession in July. Since this anniversary would certainly have followed the Javanese and not the Western calendar, and since Sura, A.J. 1689, began on 12 July A.D. 1763, this may be taken as evidence that the accession in fact took place in Sura, i.e. in December A.D. 1749, and not in July A.D. 1749, which would have been Radjab or Saban, A.J. 1674, and is in conflict with all the Javanese materials.

Poensen, 'Mangkubumi', pp. 243-5, attempted to reconcile the conflicting information on the date of the accession, but the result was not very satisfactory.

See also below, p. 80 n. 31.

[43] *BG*, vol. vi, pp. 13-20, 22-3, 25-9. In his 4 Sura letter to von Hohendorff (Dagregister, 31 Dec. 1749; see n. 32 above), Mangkubumi emphasized that he had been chosen as ruler by the dignitaries of the kingdom.

[44] See Louw, *Successie-Oorlog*, p. 33; dJ x, p. xlvii; Raffles (1830), vol. ii, p. 250.

[45] The titles are given in *BG*, vol. vi, p. 28, which adds: ingkang tuhu Narendra / mandireng aměngku / talatah ing nuswa Djawa.

Mangkubumi's letter to von Hohendorff, cited in his Dagregister, 31 Dec. 1749 (see n. 32 above), dated 4 Muharram, uses the titles *Susuhunan Pakubuwana ing Mataram Abdul Rahman Sajidin Panatagama*.

In Poensen's Pakualaman *babad* ('Mangkubumi', p. 238), the title is given as *Kangdjěng Sunan ing Mataram*.

Thereafter, Mangkubumi is usually referred to in Javanese sources as *Sunan Kabanaran*, after the name of his residence.

But by taking the name Susuhunan Pakubuwana, with the particular titles associated with the House of Mataram, Mangkubumi was announcing in particular that he claimed the throne of the kingdom as the successor to the previous Pakubuwanas, and that he had sufficient support to be considered the ruler, rather than his young nephew at Surakarta, who owed his throne not to the support of the Javanese but to the Honourable Gentlemen of Batavia. From the Javanese point of view, Mangkubumi's reign thus began in 1749. The fact that the Dutch were not forced to recognize him for six more years is inadequate historical justification for the customary dating of his rule from 1755. The latter year was one of almost unparalleled significance for Mangkubumi, but it was not the beginning of his reign.

By mid-December 1749, the Javanese kingdom had once again been divided between rival kings. The process leading to this division was essentially the same as it had been on previous occasions. For one reason or another, a sufficient number of the Javanese élite chose to support a rebellious prince rather than the incumbent ruler. What the Javanese could not have known in 1749 was that neither of these two kings was to emerge victorious, that neither would be finally defeated. This was the last time Java was to be divided in this way, for it was never again to be reunited, at least until modern times. But for several more years the Javanese élite continued to believe that the divided circumstance was the same as it had always been, and that the solution would be the one with which they were familiar, the eventual emergence of a single monarch. In the ensuing contest for support between Pakubuwana III and Mangkubumi, legitimation was a key issue, and it soon became abundantly clear that in this Mangkubumi had great advantages over his young nephew.

The last shreds of support for the Surakarta Susuhunan were quickly eliminated when, after his succession, the Company arrested the six princes remaining at the *kraton* who had not been sagacious enough to join the rebels. They were sent to Sĕmarang to be banished, thereby eliminating even the token appearance of élite consensus which the Susuhunan had hitherto been able to display. It was apparently the Company's assumption that since it was princes who went into rebellion, if there were no princes there could be no more rebels. The Susuhunan also agreed to turn over to the Company his five younger brothers when the eldest had reached the age of ten. Of his five remaining uncles, brothers of the dead Susuhunan Pakubuwana II, all were now in rebellion.[46] The warfare resumed with a renewed fury in 1750. The Company's assumption that the regular succession of Pakubuwana III would somehow damp the fires of rebellion was shown to be pitifully misconceived. The Dutch were soon facing armies estimated to be 60,000 strong, which was probably a somewhat exaggerated figure, while the Company's forces were being reduced by the guerilla-tactics and by epidemics.[47] In July 1750, forces under Mas Said, now Mangkubumi's chief general and *patih*, and Pangeran Singasari, again attacked Surakarta and were driven off only after the Company's forces had suffered serious losses.[48] The warfare continued to demonstrate the constantly growing power of the rebels. By 1752, Mangkubumi was able once more to drive into the Company lands in the *pasisir*.[49] In keeping with the age-old pattern of rebellion, insurrections were erupting from Madura to Bantĕn.[50] The Dutch seemed on the verge of inundation.[51]

The Company decided in 1752 to alter the formal arrangements for controlling the Susuhunan, restoring to him some authority over lower officials. He was also to be allowed to sit on the throne by himself, with the Dutch Resident at a lower level rather than sitting beside him as he had done since the ruler's installation at the hands of the Governor. It was hoped that these measures would increase popular respect for the ruler and discourage the spread of rebellion.[52] But the rebellion could not be stopped. Batavia could not give to the Susuhunan the authority which was denied him by the rebellious élite.

Yet the rebel princes were now beginning to realize that so long as the Dutch defended Pakubuwana III, he could not be eliminated from the political context. The warfare which had

[46] Von Hohendorff, Dagregister, 31 Dec. 1749 (see n. 32 above); Louw, *Successie-Oorlog*, p. 33; Batavia to H.XVII, 31 Dec. 1749, in dJ x, p. 153; von Hohendorff, Surakarta, to Batavia, 21 Dec. 1749, in dJ x, p. 157.
[47] Louw, *Successie-Oorlog*, p. 37.
[48] Ibid., p. 38. On Mas Said as *patih*, see Poensen, 'Mangkubumi', pp. 238–39; and *BG*, vol. vi, p. 29.   [49] Louw, *Successie-Oorlog*, p. 52.
[50] Ibid., pp. 49 ff. See also Batavia to H.XVII, 8 April 1751, in dJ x, pp. 183–4.
[51] See Louw, *Successie-Oorlog*, pp. 53–4.
[52] Ibid., pp. 63–4. Raffles (1830), vol. ii, p. 251, describes the practice of the Resident sitting upon the throne beside the Susuhunan as 'an indelicate assumption which had previously given the greatest disgust to the Javans'.

been almost continuous since the Chinese War and which had devastated much of the Javanese countryside was unlikely to succeed in deposing the Susuhunan. The participants in this fighting now began occasionally to consider whether other courses of action might not be more productive. Desultory contacts with the rebels led to the beginning of negotiations between von Hohendorff and Mas Said in October 1752. A split had developed between Mas Said and his father-in-law Mangkubumi, presumably because of conflicting personalities and ambitions. The negotiations were not immediately successful, but the Dutch and the rebels had clearly begun to tire of trying to defeat one another completely. Mangkubumi's personal hatred of von Hohendorff probably accounts for the lack of contact between those two.[53]

Pakubuwana III was meanwhile becoming a very lonely man. In 1752, his few remaining officials complained that they were so impoverished they could not even fulfil their responsibilities in caring for the ruler's horses and his elephant. Officials continually disappeared from the court only to reappear among the rebels, a process which reached its consummation when the Crown Prince himself joined Mas Said in 1753. Von Hohendorff told Batavia that he hardly knew 'how the government of the present unfortunate and pitiable ruler is to be maintained any longer'.[54] Batavia responded to this with the suggestion that Mas Said be offered the position of Crown Prince. The latter replied that he wished to be made Susuhunan.[55] The warfare continued.

Von Hohendorff was by now aware that his long-standing personal involvement in Javanese affairs, and in particular the hatred Mangkubumi felt for him, made successful negotiations impossible. He therefore asked to be relieved of his responsibilities as Governor of the Northeast Coast and in April 1754 was replaced by Nicolaas Hartingh. Hartingh reputedly not only knew Javanese, but had a reputation for understanding Javanese affairs as well.[56] The Dutch also adopted a new and more realistic

[53] Louw, *Successie-Oorlog*, pp. 67–8, 70–1 ff.   [54] Ibid., pp. 56, 73.
[55] Ibid., pp. 77–81.
[56] Ibid., pp. 82–5. See Mangkubumi's denunciation of von Hohendorff on the occasion of his meeting with Hartingh at Pĕdagangan, in *BG*, vol. xvi, p. 64.
On the doubtful knowledge of indigenous languages on the part of VOC officials who were believed by their colleagues to be proficient in them, see J. Gonda, 'Eenige Grepen uit de Geschiedenis der Beoefening van de Maleische Taal- en Letterkunde', *Verslag Provinciaal Utrechtsch Genootshap van Kunsten en Wetenschappen* (1935), pp. 94–7.

REBELLION AND DIVISION, 1726-1754   59

diplomatic approach: Mangkubumi was to be conciliated even if it meant recognizing him as next successor to the throne of Mataram or granting him control over a part of Java.[57]

Negotiations soon began between Hartingh and Mangkubumi, and military action abated. An important intermediary in these contacts was one Seh Ibrahim, also referred to as Tuwan Sajid Běsar or Sarip Běsar. Javanese texts describe him as a Turkish merchant sent by the Company to calm Mangkubumi's heart, or as an Arab emissary of the Sultan of *Rum* (i.e. Turkey) with authority to adjudicate the Javanese disputes.[58] The Dutch speak of 'the so-called or titled Turkish High Priest Said Ibrahim or Sarif Bazar', or 'the Turkish priest (Bapa Sarif Besar)', and mention his 'spiritual authority'.[59] Who this man was, whence he came, and how he became an important figure in the negotiations of 1754 is impossible to say at the present time. He must remain one of the more mysterious and romantic characters of the shadowy history of this period.

In April 1754, Mangkubumi told Hartingh, via Seh Ibrahim, that his ancestors had ruled all of Java but that he would be satisfied if the Company merely granted him the title of Sultan Mataram and provided him with a reasonable income. Pakubuwana III might remain in Surakarta and he, Mangkubumi, would allow the Company to retain the *pasisir* and would assist the Dutch against Mas Said.[60] Clearly Mangkubumi had come to recognize the temporary impossibility of defeating both Mas Said and the Dutch-supported Susuhunan. He was prepared to move instead to the traditional *modus vivendi* in such situations of accepting a peaceful division of the kingdom until such time as his support should be sufficiently overwhelming to launch a final unifying campaign. It will be seen below that Mangkubumi was familiar with the historical precedents for such a temporary division. This was not such a major change of policy as it might seem to the outside observer. Mangkubumi was not giving in to the Dutch,

[57] Louw, *Successie-Oorlog*, pp. 85-6.
[58] *BG*, vol. xiv, pp. 61 ff.; Poensen, 'Mangkubumi', pp. 263-4; A. C. Vreede, *Catalogus van de Javaansche en Madoereesche Handschriften der Leidse Universiteits-Bibliotheek* (Leiden, 1892), p. 87.
Sultan Ngrum is a familiar figure in a number of Javanese mythical stories.
[59] Hartingh, Kort Verslag, 1 Nov. 1756, in dJ x, p. 307; Louw, *Successie-Oorlog*, p. 74 (see also pp. 83, 85, 86, 89, 93).
[60] Ibid., p. 89.

for he had not been fighting them. It was true that they had been on the side of his enemy the Susuhunan, but the Company was not itself his main opponent in the real struggle, which was to forge an élite consensus. Indeed, for some two years even the Susuhunan had not been Mangkubumi's primary enemy. In this contest for élite support Mas Said had become a very much more dangerous competitor. Now Mangkubumi was willing to accept a partition of Java between himself, the Susuhunan, and the Dutch, one of the benefits of which would be that the power of the Company would now come to his assistance in the war against Mas Said.

The diplomatic manœuvring which commonly accompanies such affairs continued for some months, but Mangkubumi's communication of April 1754 was to be the basis for the settlement. He soon clarified his position by demanding one-half of the kingdom. Batavia considered this to be an acceptable solution so long as the lands were in the east (Madiun, Pranaraga, etc.) and so long as there was no absolute right of succession by Mangkubumi's heirs to his authority.[61]

The war which had devastated Java for nearly nine years was now nearing an end. In September, Hartingh met personally with Mangkubumi at Pĕdagangan in Grobogan. The Dutch Governor found his erstwhile adversary clad in a white jacket and a 'common painted Javanese garment' (presumably a *kain* of *baṭik*), wearing two *krises*, with a 'priestly cap' wound about with a fine linen handkerchief sewn with small gold lace upon his head. Mangkubumi's retinue was clad in similar fashion. This white attire, in some ways reminiscent of that later worn by Mangkubumi's great-grandson the rebel Dipanĕgara, may perhaps suggest a significant Islamic element in the rebel court. It is more likely, however, that this was a courtly form of battle-dress.[62]

[61] Louw, *Successie-Oorlog*, pp. 90–6. Mas Said continued to demand all of Java; ibid., p. 91.
[62] Hartingh, Dagregister, 18 Sept. 1754 and ff., in dJ x, p. 287. The Pĕdagangan meeting is also described in *BG*, vol. xvi, pp. 49, 62–5, where Mangkubumi is clearly pictured as a king. In *BG* it is Mangkubumi who receives Hartingh, in the VOC record the reverse.

Another interpretation of the white attire is possible, but seems less likely to be correct. It might be suggested that Mangkubumi saw himself as a suppliant in search of justice. It was customary in Java for a subject who believed himself to be the victim of injustice at the hands of his superiors to clothe himself in white and sit in the sun on the *alun-alun* before the *kraton*, until the ruler took notice of his presence and summoned him to present his case directly to the monarch.

Hartingh discussed first the matter of titles, Mangkubumi eventually agreeing that it would be inappropriate to have two Susuhunans Pakubuwana, and instead the title of Sultan Mataram was accepted by both sides. Mangkubumi and his advisors pointed out that three Sultans ruled in Tjirĕbon and two had ruled over Java in the days of Padjang and Mataram in the sixteenth century. They said that the Javanese language knew no other title with the same significance, thus implying, it seems, that the title was somehow particularly appropriate to a divided kingdom. It is difficult to see any justification for such an interpretation of the title, if indeed this is what Mangkubumi meant. By the eighteenth century the Javanese courtly *babads* did anachronistically describe the rulers of Dĕmak and Padjang as 'Sultans' and during the supposed hegemony of those kingdoms in the sixteenth century Java had often been fragmented. But the first Javanese ruler known actually to have called himself Sultan was Sultan Agung. And he had taken that title not in the early years of his reign when Java was still divided between Mataram and the *pasisir* alliance led by Surabaja, but in 1641 when his kingdom was effectively united. Nevertheless, Mangkubumi seems to have left

This practice, known as *pepe*, required the wearing of white, probably because the suppliant was essaying a most dangerous course in presenting his case against his superiors directly to the king, who might decide against him and command severe punishment. The suppliant was thus in the realm of danger and even death, and it was appropriate that he should be clad in the purity of white. Perhaps, then, Mangkubumi saw himself in a similar situation, seeking justice from the Dutchman who stood above PB III, doing *pepe* before the powerful Governor of Sĕmarang. And Hartingh's report does, indeed, suggest that Mangkubumi displayed considerable anxiety at meeting him. Yet such an interpretation nevertheless seems most unlikely. It is not supported by Javanese sources, and in general the role of suppliant would seem to have been entirely inconsistent with Mangkubumi's confidence in his royal standing.

The most likely explanation is that the rebel courtiers were dressed for war. Hartingh, who could not of course have been expected to appreciate the subtleties of Javanese dress, nevertheless commented that this clothing 'could not exactly be seen as a sign of peace, seeing that this attire had been assumed by him some time ago'. *BG*, vol. xvi, p. 63, says merely that 'His Highness then had donned his garments, attiring himself in battledress': Sang Nata wus abusana / ngrasuk kapradjuritan. This 'battle-dress' (*pradjuritan*) is described by Gericke and Roorda as 'a kind of uniform with *bĕbĕd* [*kain* about the lower body and legs] and *tjĕlana* [trousers] and *klambi sikĕpan* [a jacket worn when armed], *udĕng* [headkerchief], one *kris* in the belt and one hanging on a belt'. The similarity between this and Hartingh's description is obvious, and makes it very likely that this was a form of battle-dress, as *BG* says. See J. F. C. Gericke and T. Roorda, *Javaansch-Nederlandsch Handwoordenboek* (rev. ed.; ed. A. C. Vreede and J. G. H. Gunning; 2 vols.; Leiden, 1901), vol. ii, p. 241.

Hartingh with the impression that he believed 'Sultan' to be a fitting title for a ruler in a divided kingdom.[63]

Again Mangkubumi asked for one-half of Pakubuwana's realm,[64] but he rejected the Dutch proposal that he should control the eastern areas: no ruler had ever had his capital there, he said. This latter statement was simply untrue. Clearly what Mangkubumi meant was that no king of the House of Mataram had ever had his court anywhere but Central Java. Before clarifying what areas he did wish to rule in his new Sultanate, however, Mangkubumi insisted that he and the Governor should swear an oath of loyalty and friendship between himself and the Company. When this had been done, Mangkubumi seemed to be more at ease, but he nevertheless continued to temporize over the question of what regions he claimed. Hartingh overheard him speaking in Javanese to his *patih* about the *pasisir*, and warned that any request to control that area would be in vain. The matter was postponed until the following day.[65]

The Javanese *pasisir* officials who accompanied Hartingh were subsequently interrogated about the size of their areas by Mangkubumi's *patih*. Hartingh saw this as confirmation of an intent to demand the *pasisir*, and again sent warning that such a request had no hope of success. Yet when Mangkubumi discussed the matter with Hartingh he submitted a list of areas which included sections of the coast. Hartingh explained in strong terms that Batavia would never agree to that, and Mangkubumi eventually dropped the request. He would be satisfied with one-half of Central Java with the title of either Susuhunan or Sultan. Mangkubumi again mentioned the example of the late sixteenth century, when Java was divided between Padjang and Mataram, as the precedent for this division. With regard to the *pasisir* he finally asked only that he receive one-half of the 20,000 reals paid annually by the Dutch for its lease, which Hartingh indicated would naturally follow from the division of the kingdom.[66]

---

[63] Hartingh, Dagregister, 18 Sept. 1754 and ff., in dJ x, pp. 289–90, 291, 293. It does not appear to be historically correct that there were at any time two 'Sultans' in Padjang and Mataram. Mangkubumi, however, apparently believed this to have been the case. *BK*, ff. 83^r–83^v, describes a period when Sultans supposedly reigned in both Děmak and Padjang. On the general problems of Javanese royal titles, see de Graaf, 'Titels en Namen'.
[64] Hartingh, Dagregister, 18 Sept. 1754 and ff., in dJ x, p. 290.
[65] Ibid., pp. 290–1.   [66] Ibid., pp. 291–4.

Mangkubumi also raised the issue of who would succeed Pakubuwana III in Surakarta, hoping for a guarantee that the Susuhunan's position would fall to his own descendents upon vacancy. If the Dutch agreed to this, Java might in time be reunified without further warfare. Hartingh said he would submit this request to Batavia, along with the proposals concerning the procedure for dividing the lands and royal regalia.[67]

Mangkubumi, his sons, and his high officials promised they would help the Dutch to defeat Mas Said. A Dutch guard consisting of Captain C. Donkel and twenty dragoons was left behind to seal the new friendship and as a guarantee that the Company would in her turn aid Mangkubumi against the common enemy.[68] The animosity between Mangkubumi and Mas Said was by now at least two years old, and Mas Said had recently inflicted serious defeats upon his father-in-law.[69] The importance of this development cannot be overemphasized. Had it not been for this, it seems unlikely that Mangkubumi would have been willing to treat with the Dutch for a settlement, since his support among the Javanese élite would then have been nearly unanimous. But many of that élite, when forced to chose between the two rebels, had chosen the popular and flamboyant Mas Said. Mangkubumi continued throughout most of his life to see Mas Said as his main enemy, rather than the Susuhunan, which was an accurate assessment of the Javanese political situation.

Batavia subsequently examined the reports of the Pědagangan negotiations, and judged Mangkubumi's demands to be excessive. He was to be offered one-half of Java, with the title Susuhunan, and his descendants were to be granted the right of succession in the area, but it must be in the eastern areas of the island sufficiently distant from Surakarta. The question of the right of succession in Surakarta was to be postponed. The proposal to divide the money for the *pasisir* was approved.[70] But Mangkubumi still refused to accept the repeated proposition that he become a Susuhunan of East Java. He insisted upon the area of Mataram itself where, as he pointed out to Hartingh in September, he had already ruled for five years as Susuhunan.[71]

Finally Batavia submitted. Mangkubumi, in conjunction with

[67] Ibid., pp. 294–5.
[69] See Louw, *Successie-Oorlog*, pp. 70 ff.
[71] Ibid., pp. 100–3.
[68] Ibid., pp. 295–6.
[70] Ibid., pp. 100–2.

Dutch forces, had begun to fight Mas Said with considerable success, but the Company feared he might again unite with his son-in-law if his demands were not met. This thoroughly unrealistic apprehension suggests how little Batavia understood of the dynamics of the Javanese political scene. It was agreed that he would hold Mataram and one-half of Central Java. Batavia had already begun to refer to Mangkubumi as 'Sultan Hamĕngkubuwana'.[72]

Susuhunan Pakubuwana III had had no voice in these negotiations, and was in no position to object to the dismemberment of his kingdom. He was without support except for the Dutch, whose decision he had no choice but to follow.[73] When Hartingh informed him of the proposals for a settlement with Mangkubumi, who was to receive the title Sultan, Pakubuwana III simply agreed.[74] The scene was set for the formal partition of Java into two kingdoms.

The subsequent bipartition of Java in 1755 has been seen as the culmination of a perfidious Dutch imperialist design beginning with the acquisition of sovereignty in 1749: *divide et impera*. Raffles wrote of the 1749 episode:

The reduced state of the Susuhunan's authority before his death and the distracted condition of affairs, afforded an opportunity too favourable to be overlooked by the Dutch, of at once attaining the grand object of all their political interference, the sovereignty of the country. A weak prince on his death-bed was, under existing circumstances, easily brought to any terms, in the hope of continuing even the nominal succession in his family.[75]

Such judgements ascribe too great a role to Dutch policy, the primary object of which was in any case not sovereignty but profit. It is clear from the developments between 1746 and 1755 that the Dutch were not in a position to determine the course of history. Rather, the events of those years are explicable only in terms of the political forces at work among the Javanese. The cession of formal sovereignty in 1749 was suggested by the Susu-

[72] Louw, *Successie-Oorlog*, pp. 104–5. The course of the negotiations of 1754 is also described in Batavia to H.XVII, 31 Dec. 1754, in dJ x, pp. 227–34.

[73] See the comments on PB III's circumstances in April 1754, in Hartingh, Kort Verslag, 1 Nov. 1756, in dJ x, p. 307.

[74] Louw, *Successie-Oorlog*, pp. 103–4; PB III to Batavia, 16 [Sura A.J.] 1680 (2 Nov. 1754), in dJ x, p. 298.

[75] Raffles (1830), vol. ii, pp. 248–9.

REBELLION AND DIVISION, 1726-1754

hunan, not the Dutch. And the division of Java in 1755 was to be carried out on Mangkubumi's terms, not Hartingh's. And all of this was because of the collapse of royal authority among the Javanese and the shift of the political consensus from the ruler to the rebels. Indeed, the treaty of 1755 merely recognized and formalized a division of the kingdom which had already existed since Mangkubumi's accession in 1749, and with which the Dutch had originally little to do. As Louw has observed, for the East India Company the treaty of 1755 was less a matter of policy than of necessity.[76] From Mangkubumi's point of view it may even be wrong to see the treaty of 1755 as primarily a Javanese–Dutch settlement. Mangkubumi's main enemies were never the Dutch, but always his Javanese opponents, first Pakubuwana II and III and, by 1755, Mas Said. The Dutch were a powerful military force who were exceedingly dangerous to have as enemies and who could be troublesome as allies. But the object of the warfare had been to gain control of Java, not to expel the Dutch. And this struggle was far from finished. Only the nature of the competition was to change in the 1750s, moving from full-scale warfare to a less destructive *modus vivendi*. That is not to say the Dutch did not benefit from the arrangements, nor that they had no influence whatsoever. But the Company was too weak in the face of overwhelming Javanese political forces to play a determinative role.

Historical hindsight has also ascribed another significance to the division of Java which it did not have in 1755. The system of two main courts has survived into the twentieth century, thus giving the impression of a permanent arrangement. But in 1755, it was not intended to be permanent. Even the Dutch were unsure what the future might hold, thus accounting for their confusion on the question of succession. At first they were uncertain whether Mangkubumi's descendants were to have the right to succeed him, and later they were undecided about who should succeed Pakubuwana III in Surakarta.[77] The latter, a young man in ill health, was not to produce a male heir until late in the 1760s. Thus the possibility of a peaceful reunification remained open.

Mangkubumi's position seems clear, both from the documents on the negotiations of 1754 and from subsequent events. He knew

[76] See Louw, *Successie-Oorlog*, p. 32 n. 3, and pp. 105-6, 122-3.
[77] By 1757, the VOC had begun to speak of the division as permanent; see Batavia to H.XVII, 31 Dec. 1757, in dJ x, p. 314.

well that Javanese history contained precedents for the division of the kingdom; he must have been further aware that division was never permanent. His references to the contemporaneous existence of rulers in Padjang and Mataram late in the sixteenth century had a double significance. That duality had been temporary, ending in the ascendancy of Mataram. Moreover, the Dutch had now agreed that he would hold Mataram, while Surakarta was located in the area still called Padjang. The possibility of repeating the course of events which had ended in Mataram hegemony two centuries before could hardly have escaped Mangkubumi's notice. In Surakarta as well, much later events would clearly reveal a great reluctance to accept the partition as permanent.

The overriding problem of Javanese politics in the latter half of the eighteenth century was to be that of division. Java must either be reunited or, if that should prove impossible, new steps must be taken to regularize the situation. The way in which the Javanese state reacted to this problem is the main concern of the following chapters.

At the end of January 1755 Governor Hartingh left Sĕmarang for Central Java to arrange the peaceful partition of the kingdom. With that trip began the history of Jogjakarta and of Java divided, for the transition from warfare to peaceful conditions was ultimately to make it possible for the state of division to become permanent. Important Javanese figures had already begun to believe that for the time being that part of the conflict which concerned Mangkubumi and the Susuhunan would not be fought to its logical conclusion. In this lay the first step towards a belief that the conflict might never be resolved.

III

THE TRANSITION TO A PEACEFUL DIVISION AND THE FOUNDATION OF JOGJAKARTA
1755–1757

NICOLAAS HARTINGH left Sĕmarang on 29 January 1755, and by the time he returned from Central Java on 21 February the kingdom of Mataram had been formally divided into two.[1] In this process, a later Javanese *babad* says, Hartingh 'acted as *ḍalang*',[2] the puppeteer in the Javanese *wajang*-theatre. This *babad* reflects the later views of Prince Pakualam I (1813–29), who was not unskilled in using European influence to his own advantage. It may, therefore, anachronistically exaggerate the role of Hartingh. For the *ḍalang* in Java is more than a puppeteer. He gives life to his characters, speaks for them, causes them to act. He is the manipulator, and in Javanese mystical literature is sometimes explicitly likened to God, the Creator who is yet One with his Creation. It is remarkable that a Javanese text, even a much later one, should have placed a European in such a position. Yet it must be said that the role of the Dutch was indeed not unlike that of a *ḍalang* in the transition from warfare to peace in 1755. They had neither created the original characters nor set the plot in motion, but now they were certainly playing the role of manipulator, bringing the warfare to a peaceful conclusion which it might not have reached had there been no Dutchmen in Java. They had made the division of Java necessary by preventing the overthrow of Pakubuwana II and III, and had made it possible by causing the Susuhunan to surrender formally one-half of his

[1] The following description of the Gijanti and Djatisari meetings is taken from Hartingh, Dagregister, 26 Feb. 1755, in KA 2757 (OB 1756), unless another source is indicated. Extensive selections from Hartingh's Dagregister are to be found in Louw, *Successie-Oorlog*, pp. 107–21.

[2] Poensen, 'Mangkubumi', p. 264 n. 1: ingkang minangka ḍalang. Poensens' translation, 'de beraadslagingen leidde', does not make clear the importance of the word *ḍalang*.

kingdom to the rebels. In these final negotiations on the division, Hartingh did act as the manipulator, as a kind of *ḍalang*. It is therefore of interest that at least one Javanese source, albeit a later one, should have so explicitly recognized this role.

Hartingh paused first in Surakarta, where Pakubuwana III reaffirmed his willingness to cede half the kingdom to Mankubumi. He objected to the obvious corollary that the 20,000 reals paid annually for the lease of the *pasisir* must also be divided, but he gave in to Hartingh's insistence. With Java so thoroughly devastated by the wars, this money was virtually the only source of income either ruler was to have for some time.[3] Since the kingdom was now also to be split into two, each ruler's income from the land would also be halved. Thus these annual funds from the Dutch took on a still greater importance. Whether or not the Javanese rulers approved in principle of the Dutch possession of the *pasisir*, the only alternative would be to forfeit the income which the Dutch paid for its lease, which was unthinkable. The Dutch coastal position was therefore probably strengthened as a by-product of the wars and the consequent division of Central Java, which made Dutch money all the more essential to the functioning of each court. Pakubuwana III's reluctance to share these funds was as understandable as the necessity that they be shared.

Hartingh proceeded to the village of Gijanti, below Mt. Lawu to the southeast of Surakarta, where Mangkubumi had established temporary court. On the ninth of February, Hartingh and Mangkubumi met privately in the latter's residence, with only the translator Kartabasa (Ki Běstam) and Mangkubumi's *patih* Natakusuma present. Hartingh submitted the draft treaty to Mangkubumi, who approved it except for the fifth section. This would have prevented the ruler from requiring his *bupatis* and *wědanas* ('regenten') to appear at the *kraton* if they were unwilling to do so. Instead they might send a member of their family or another dignitary. Only with the approval of the Company could they be forced to appear on pain of dismissal. This proposal struck at a basic institution of the kingdom, for an official's personal appearance at court was virtually the only way to confirm his obedience. Indeed, failure to appear normally indicated rebellious intent. At the very least the absence of one or more important

---

[3] See Hartingh, Kort Verslag, 1 Nov. 1756, in dJ x, p. 310.

courtiers called into question the strength of the consensus supporting a ruler. Mangkubumi asked how it would be possible to govern and to maintain order under such a restriction. Recognizing the justice of this objection, Hartingh agreed to change the article. In the final treaty, Mangkubumi merely promised not to take revenge on any of these officials for actions during the war.

In this meeting Mangkubumi also raised the question of the succession in Surakarta. What would happen should Pakubuwana III die without a male heir? Hartingh replied that it was not yet the time to determine that since the Susuhunan was still young and appeared capable of producing many children. Mangkubumi smiled and replied that, indeed, time would tell. Once again the possibility of a peaceful reunification of the kingdom seemed to be left open.

By the 1743 treaty between Pakubuwana II and the Company, the Javanese monarch appointed his *patih* with the approval of the Dutch.[4] Mangkubumi's choice for this post was therefore also a matter for negotiation. Pangeran Natakusuma had been functioning as Mangkubumi's *patih* up to the time of the Gijanti meeting and was clearly a trusted adviser. But he was in frail health and Mangkubumi did not wish to retain him in that post. Furthermore, Mangkubumi reportedly told Natakusuma that he could not be *patih* because twice before the kingdom had been brought to ruin by *patihs* named Natakusuma.[5] Instead Mangkubumi wanted to appoint his brother-in-law, the *bupati* of Banjumas, Raden Tuměnggung Judaněgara.[6] Initially Judaněgara was unwilling to relinquish his position in Banjumas, possibly because of the dangers of being *patih* at the centre

[4] Text in dJ ix, pp. 434-47. The similar regulation concerning the 'hoofdregenten' (*najakas*) was never enforced; see G. P. Rouffaer, 'Vorstenlanden', *Adatrechtbundels*, vol. 34, p. 262.

[5] According to the account of this meeting in Hartingh's Dagregister, HB I was referring to events during the reigns of Amangkurat I (1646-77) and Pakubuwana II (1726-49). I am unaware of a *patih* Natakusuma in the former reign, although there was a Pangeran Natakusuma involved in the intrigues at the beginning of the reign of Amangkurat II (1677-1703). The *patih* Natakusuma of PB II was exiled to Ceylon by the Dutch for his role in the 'Chinese War' of the 1740s and was returned to Java in 1758 upon the request of HB I.

The present Natakusuma had also been HB I's *patih* at the Pědagangan meeting; see Hartingh, Dagregister, 18 Sept. 1754 and ff., in dJ x, p. 289.

[6] The subsequent discussions between Hartingh and HB I on the selection of Judaněgara are also described in *B. Mang.*, pp. 9 ff., ending with the introduction of Judaněgara as the *patih* Danurědja on p. 34.

of court intrigue. It had been a not-uncommon practice of Javanese rulers, particularly of Susuhunan Amangkurat I, to raise to a higher office those who were marked for assassination, thereby cutting them off from many of their former supporters. It is entirely possible therefore that Judanĕgara, who has assisted the Dutch in the wars,[7] actually feared for his life. In any case, his reluctance is probably a reflection of the general disillusionment and distrust among the Javanese dignitaries after the years of chaos. But Mangkubumi was not to be diverted and his sister, Judanĕgara's wife, helped to convince her husband to accept the post.

Hartingh at first did not wish Judanĕgara to give up the administration of Banjumas, but he too submitted to Mangkubumi's will. He did not doubt that Judanĕgara would protect the Company's interests at the court, since his troops had aided the Dutch in the recent hostilities. Judanĕgara was subsequently proclaimed *patih*, with the name Danurĕdja (I), and he was to serve Mangkubumi with distinction until the latter's death. He was perhaps one of the most able *patihs* of Mataram history. It was agreed that his son would succeed him as *bupati* of Banjumas, which was under the control of Surakarta.

Mangkubumi asked Hartingh to introduce Judanĕgara publicly as the new *patih*. The Dutchman refused, saying that Mangkubumi should introduce him for it was Mangkubumi upon whom Judanĕgara would depend in the future. Mangkubumi insisted that Hartingh had the right to make the announcement, since he was the 'third ruler of Java', but Hartingh did not agree. Mangkubumi's attitude at first seems out of character for him, and the reasons for it are indeed somewhat unclear. His apparent willingness to accept the Dutch as the 'third ruler', governing Batavia and the *pasisir*, was probably connected with a recognition of the importance of the 10,000 reals the Company was to pay him annually for the lease of the coast. And if since his rebellion of 1746 Mangkubumi had not been defeated, neither had he succeeded in decisively defeating the Company. Since the initial negotiations of 1754 he had appeared ready to abandon his objections to the Dutch position on the coast, if only as a *modus vivendi*. It will also be seen in Chapter XI that one of the features of the Batavia–Jogjakarta relationship as it came to be seen from the Javanese

[7] See Louw, *Successie-Oorlog*, p. 41.

TRANSITION TO PEACE, 1755-1757 71

side was the central position of the *patih* as one of the two men (with the Resident) who owed loyalty to both sides. Thus from this point of view also, Hartingh's introduction of the *patih* may have seemed particularly appropriate. But Hartingh would not agree.

The physical division of the kingdom was also carried out at Gijanti, with a formality and precision which previous periods of division had presumably never entailed. The phenomenon of an agreed peaceful partition was probably unique at this time in Javanese history. It is to be presumed that in the past divided kingdoms had become so not by treaty, but by the temporary exhaustion of their constituent armies. Pakubuwana III was represented in this by the Resident Abrahams, Ngabei Tirtanĕgara, and Mangkubumi's arch-enemy Pringgalaja. According to *Babad Mangkubumi*, Mangkubumi was represented by Judanĕgara in these negotiations, at which the Dutch Captain and Resident C. Donkel was also present. Mangkubumi directed that the division must be exact, without so much as a finger's-breadth of difference.[8] The final division did in fact differ slightly, but Mangkubumi was satisfied with his slight advantage.

In the *montjanĕgara* (outer regions) Mangkubumi received control of 33,950 *tjatjahs* (households), while Pakubuwana III retained 32,350. Each ruler had 53,100 *tjatjahs* in the central area. The Susuhunan's territory in the *montjanĕgara* was generally to the west (Banjumas) while Mangkubumi's was in the east, but in the latter area the boundaries of the two kingdoms were intricately entwined. In the central areas (Kĕḍu, Mataram, Bagĕlen, Padjang, Sokawati, etc.) there was a hopeless cadastral confusion, with villages belonging to the two kingdoms dangerously intermixed.[9] If the population estimates were at all accurate, in 1755 the two rulers controlled some 172,500 *tjatjahs*. Hageman estimated there were six persons to each household, thereby arriving

[8] *B. Mang.*, pp. 5-8. The division of the kingdom is the main concern of the opening sections of *B. Mang.*

[9] The details of the division are to be found in Bijlage no. lvii, dJ x, pp. 373-5. The demographic information upon which the division was based could hardly have been of very great accuracy.

A map of the division showing the situation *c.* 1760 is to be found at the end of A. K. Pringgadigda, *Geschiedenis der Ondernemingen van het Mangkoenagorosche Rijk* ('s-Gravenhage, 1950) or in his *Dhoemadhos saha Ngrembakanipoen Pradja Mangkoenagaran* (Surakarta, 1939). See also Rouffaer, 'Vorstenlanden', pp. 236, 316.

at a figure of 1,035,000 for the population of Java excluding the Dutch-controlled coasts.[10] If one takes the lowest reasonable figure of four individuals per household, which may be more realistic,[11] the total population controlled by the two rulers was only 690,000. In either case, there were obviously considerable areas neither populated nor under cultivation, which perhaps made the cartographic confusion less politically dangerous than it might have been in a more densely-populated island. But on the other hand, the untilled countryside might easily harbour marauders, and the maze of involuted boundary-divisions proved to be a source of great instability.

The negotiations having been successfully concluded, there remained the formal acts of installing Mangkubumi as Sultan and signing the peace settlement. This was done on 13 February. While the *Qur'ān* was held over his head, Mangkubumi swore the oath, saying God and the Prophet Muḥammad should curse him and his descendants if ever they broke the agreement. Having agreed to a temporary division of Java at least in part in order to have Dutch assistance against Mas Said, Mangkubumi was concerned that the Dutch should also fulfil their part of the bargain. He solicited from Hartingh an admission that he could consider himself released from his oath if the Company failed to uphold its part of the agreement. Upon Mangkubumi's insistence, Hartingh then formally swore on behalf of the Company to maintain the contract. It was then signed and sealed. Both Hartingh's diary and *Babad Mangkubumi* say that some of Mangkubumi's officials had no seals to affix and must simply sign instead.[12] The rebel leaders had not yet had the leisure to acquire the accoutrements of a courtly life.

[10] J. Hageman, 'Geschied- en Aardrijkskundig Overzigt van Java, op het Einde der Achttiende Eeuw', *TBG*, vol. 9 (1860), pp. 267, 310, 315. Hageman calculates a total for all of Java and Madura in 1755 of 1,509,000. These figures do not include Batavia and the West Java Sundanese area.

[11] This was the estimate used by van Imhoff in 1746; 'Reis', p. 409. Sometimes a *tjatjah* was also estimated to equal five persons; see P. J. Veth, *Java, Geographisch, Ethnologisch, Historisch* (3 vols.; Haarlem, 1875–82), vol. ii, p. 492 n. 2; and dJ xi, p. lxxviii n. 2.

[12] See *B. Mang.*, p. 11. For a photographic reproduction of the last page of the Gijanti contract, see Soekanto, *Sekitar Jogjakarta*, p. 9. There seven signatures are to be seen but only five seals. Those with seals are 'Sultan Pakubuwana' (i.e. HB I), the Crown Prince, Pangeran Ngabei Leringpasar, Pangeran Natakusuma, and Pangeran Arja Pakuningrat. Those without are Raden Adipati Danurĕdja and Raden Tumĕnggung [Rongga] Prawiradirdja.

TRANSITION TO PEACE, 1755-1757

By the Gijanti Contract,[13] Mangkubumi was named Sultan over one-half of Central Java, which he recognized to be a fief from the Company. His sons were granted right of succession. His *patih* and high officials were required upon appointment to go personally to Sĕmarang to take an oath of allegiance to the Company. All such appointments were to be made with the approval of the Dutch. These requirements were, however, in fact only observed with regard to the *patih*.[14] Mangkubumi further promised to take no revenge on any officials for their actions in the recent war. He denied any pretensions to Madura or the *pasisir* and agreed to receive one-half of the 20,000 reals the Dutch paid annually for the coast. He would also deliver up specified agricultural products at prices fixed by the contract, but it is unclear whether these deliveries were in fact made. The economic aspect of this treaty could be studied in the voluminous Dutch records on such matters, but it has not been possible to undertake such a study here. There are, however, occasional comments in Dutch sources suggesting that at least in some years there were considerable problems in getting agricultural products from the Central Javanese kingdoms. Mangkubumi also promised to uphold the treaties between the Company and previous Javanese monarchs. If he failed to abide by the terms of the contract, his lands would revert to the Dutch to dispose of as they saw fit. Most importantly for Mangkubumi, there was to be an alliance between the Sultan and the Dutch, and between the Sultan and the Susuhunan.

Hartingh then took Mangkubumi's hand and placed the new Sultan Hamĕngkubuwana I upon his throne. *Babad Mangkubumi* somewhat effusively says, 'All of Java submitted.' Seated upon his throne (*Ḍampar Kĕntjana*) Mangkubumi is said to have looked like the god Wisnu. Strangely, the date for this accession in *Babad Mangkubumi* is wrong.[15] From his throne, the Sultan

---

[13] 13 Feb. 1755, text to be found in dJ x, pp. 298-303.
[14] Rouffaer, 'Vorstenlanden', p. 262.
[15] *B. Mang.*, p. 29, Canto V (Asmaradana), verse 1: . . . rat Djawa samja sumujud / lir pendah Wisnu Bĕṭara. In V: 8, *B. Mang.* quotes the VOC declaration: Ing mĕngko Djĕng Sultan ugi / tĕtĕp djumĕnĕng Narendra / mĕngku rat Djawa sĕparo / . . .

For the date, *B. Mang.*, p. 32, gives Monday, 29 Djumadilakir, Ehe, purnasṭa rasaning katong, which can only be A.J. 1681; that year was, however, Wawu not Ehe.

The correct Javanese equivalent for Thursday, 13 February A.D. 1755, would be Kĕmis-Kliwon, 1 Djumadilawal, Be, A.J. 1680, in the 'Thursday Calendar'.

announced the appointment of Judanĕgara as *patih*, with the name and title Raden Adipati Danurĕdja. He also made other court appointments, making officials of his advisers and generals. Hartingh had suggested some days before that the Sultan should meet with the Susuhunan to seal the reconciliation, and Mangkubumi had agreed.[16] On the fifteenth of February, Hartingh, the Sultan, and their entourages proceeded to Djatisari, midway between Gijanti and Surakarta. There the two rulers, uncle and nephew, met as equals. Mangkubumi arrived first and took his place at a table at which Hartingh presided. Pakubuwana III arrived shortly thereafter, to the sound of Mangkubumi's *gamĕlan*.

Both monarchs found the encounter such a difficult and emotional experience that neither could speak. Hartingh broke the silence by welcoming, in Javanese, his 'beloved brothers', telling them that the hour everyone had so long wished for had arrived. Peace was restored and the beautiful land of Java was to be delivered from the ravages of war. He took their hands, raised them from the table, and Mangkubumi and Pakubuwana III finally greeted one another. Both monarchs promised they would work together against Mas Said and, to set a seal upon the occasion, a glass of beer was drunk.[17]

On this occasion Pakubuwana III presented the Sultan with a *kris*. From his vantage point at the head of the table Hartingh heard Mangkubumi ask whether the *kris* was a *pusaka* (holy regalia). Pakubuwana III replied that it was not, but that it had been carried by Pakubuwana II. Javanese sources, however, identify this weapon as Kjai Kopek, handed down from the *wali* Sunan Kalidjaga and later one of the three *pusaka agĕng* (great

If the Sultan was still using the 'Friday Calendar' (see above, pp. 54-5 n. 42) the date would have been 29 Rabingulakir.

BG, vol. xvii, p. 47, gives Rabingulakir without a date, Be, mur sarira ngojag bumi [A.J. 1680]. See also the discussion of this *sĕngkala* in Balé Poestaka, *Babad Gijanti, Pratélan Namaning Tijang lan Panggénan* (Batavia, 1939), p. 95 n. 2.

Sĕrat Djumĕnĕngan S.D.I.S. Kg. Sultan Hamĕngkubuwana I (Jogja kraton MS. A. 22), p. 1, is thoroughly confused. It gives Kĕmis-Pon, 29 Djumadilawal, Be, A.J. 1680, or 14 March A.D. 1755, both of which dates are wrong.

Babad Sangkalaning Momana, p. 268, gives only the year, Be, A.J. 1680.

[16] Hartingh's proposal of this meeting is also to be found in *B. Mang.*, pp. 34-5.

[17] The description of the meeting in *B. Mang.*, pp. 41-4, is similar to that in Hartingh's Dagregister, but it is interesting to note that in the Javanese text Hartingh addresses HB I and PB III not as 'brothers' but as 'father' and 'son' respectively (kang rama lan kang putra).

regalia) of Jogjakarta. The Javanese texts say its identity was made known at Djatisari and perhaps Hartingh simply misunderstood the Susuhunan's statement. In the nineteenth century it was said that Mangkubumi had at first doubted the authenticity of the *kris*, but that it was later confirmed when the former *patih* of Pakubuwana II returned from Ceylon and identified it.[18]

It was particularly significant that this *kris* should have been ascribed to Sunan Kalidjaga. According to the courtly *babads* it was Kalidjaga who had convinced the Sultan of Padjang in the sixteenth century to give Mataram to Ki Pamanahan, after he had promised the land but had then failed for a time to fulfil his promise. Mataram later went on to win hegemony over Java from Padjang. It was these events to which Mangkubumi specifically referred as the precedent for the division of 1755. Indeed, these *babad* stories have some striking similarities to the events of the mid-eighteenth century, when Pakubuwana II (of Surakarta, in Padjang) had promised to give certain lands to Mangkubumi, had then failed to do so, but had been persuaded in the end to surrender Mataram. According to the Javanese texts, the two broken promises were separated by precisely two centuries, and the Javanese certainly believed that events tended to repeat themselves in cycles of centuries. There are, of course, important differences between the two episodes as well. But in both cases the final cession of Mataram had been achieved by the intervention of an outsider from the *pasisir*. In the sixteenth century it had been Kalidjaga, whose grave-site is at Kadilangu near Děmak. In the eighteenth century it was the Dutchman from Sěmarang. It was therefore fitting that it was Sunan Kalidjaga's *kris* which changed hands, for it was symbolic of the division itself and of the means by which it had been arranged.[19] Whether the traditions

---

[18] B. Mang., pp. 41–2; BG, vol xvii, p. 78; BG, vol. xviii, p. 13; Babad Sangkalaning Momana, p. 268; J. Groneman, De Garěběg's te Ngajogyâkartâ ('s-Gravenhage, 1895), pp. 55, 59.

[19] See BTDj, trans. pp. 55–65, text pp. 53–63; BTDj (BP), vol. iv, pp. 31–56; BK, ff. 93^r–102^v.

The death of Arja Panangsang, for which Mataram was to be given to Ki Pamanahan as reward for his part in the attack, is dated A.J. 1471 (A.D. 1549). The defeat of Mas Said, for which Sokawati was to be given to HB I and which immediately preceded HB I's rebellion, occurred in A.J. 1671 (A.D. 1746) (see above, p. 40 n. 14).

Among the most obvious differences between these two episodes are the absence of an eighteenth-century parallel to Ki Pandjawi, who received control

concerning the sixteenth century had an influence upon the formalities of division in 1755, or whether the latter influenced the way in which the sixteenth century was described in the *babads*, all the extant copies of which were composed after 1755, is impossible to say.

Javanese oral tradition supplements the 1755 episode by saying that a general division of the *pusakas* took place at Djatisari. This is not confirmed by the eighteenth-century sources used in this study, but an accumulation of *pusakas* would have been necessary before the Sultan could firmly establish his court. No Javanese monarch could establish authority without gathering about him all such legitimate props of kingship, which were among the few forms of authority within the monarch's personal control in times of peace.

Finally it was time for the two monarchs of Java to take leave of one another, which presented as great a protocol problem as had their moment of meeting. Neither wished to be the first to leave, thus implying he was inferior to the other and was receiving the other's permission to depart, the normal means of withdrawing from the royal presence. In this situation, for which there were no Javanese precedents, there could be no Javanese models of behaviour, an acutely embarrassing *contretemps*. But the Javanese had for some time observed the curious social behaviour of the Dutch and this seems to have offered a solution. Recognizing the

---

over Pati (unless the VOC could be seen in this role), and the absence in the sixteenth century of a character analogous to Pringgalaja.

It should be noted that the *babads* also say that Sultan Agung's acceptance of the existence of Batavia (i.e. a division of the island between the VOC and the Javanese) took place in A.J. 1571 (A.D. 1649). This date is certainly fictitious, being 20 years after the last siege of Batavia and 4 years after Agung's death. It seems to be dated so as to fit the idea of the island undergoing some sort of process of division in the years A.J. 1471, 1571, 1671. See *BTDj*, trans. p. 143, text p. 139, for the event of A.J. 1571. *BTDj* (*BP*,) vol. x, p. 16, has the *sěngkala wong apěrang anatas ing buta tala*, which is unclear but presumably is supposed to be A.J. 1571. BM Add. MS. 12323 (B), ff. 35^v, 40^r, has the events of A.J. 1571 and 1671, but not that of A.J. 1471. *Babad Sangkalaning Momana* has none of these dates.

On the general influence of century-cycles on Javanese perceptions, see Chap. VII below.

The other two *pusaka agěng* of Jogjakarta, Kjai Plered and Kjai Běṭok, were also involved in the events surrounding the episode of A.J. 1471 (A.D. 1549). The former was the weapon which killed Arja Panangsang and the latter was the weapon of Panangsang's earlier victim Sunan Prawata. See the Javanese sources cited at the beginning of this note, and Groneman, *Garěběg's*, pp. 55–60.

TRANSITION TO PEACE, 1755-1757 77

essential foreignness of the idea of two equal kings meeting one another in a peaceful fashion in the middle of Java, the participants took refuge in foreign models of behaviour. Hartingh reported that the rulers drank a glass (of beer, presumably) and then

> clasped their hands and said farewell by repeatedly putting their heads on one another's shoulders, thus as it were giving the kiss of unity and brotherly love, which met with the admiration of everyone, for such is something uncommon between such potentates and has never been seen in Java; indeed, the dignitaries on either side stood up staring in amazement and prophesied to them that something good would come of this event.[20]

Then Hartingh accompanied the Susuhunan back to Surakarta, while the Sultan returned to his temporary residence at Gijanti. Never again in the period of this study did two Javanese rulers expose themselves to the difficulties of a personal encounter.

The formalities of division had been completed, but the strains upon the traditional conceptions of the state were obviously very great. There was not even an accepted *adat* for two equal rulers to greet one another. In the nineteenth century, forms of protocol were apparently devised to deal with this delicate situation. This involved the apparent acceptance of the Susuhunan of Surakarta's position as being somewhat higher than that of the Sultan of Jogjakarta. Surakarta came to be thought of generally as the senior court (*ingkang sĕpuh*) and Jogjakarta as the junior (*ingkang anem*).[21] But this was not so in 1755. In the discussions recorded in the *babads* there is a repeated emphasis on the necessity of maintaining exact equality in the division of the kingdom and at the Djatisari meeting.[22] It is repeatedly mentioned that Mangkubumi was in fact the elder of the two rulers (*ingkang sĕpuh*) while his nephew Pakubuwana III was the younger (*ingkang*

---

[20] This is also quoted in Louw, *Successie-Oorlog*, p. 121. *BG*, vol. xviii, p. 16, describes the leave-taking without detail, as does *B. Mang.*, p. 44.

[21] See L. W. C. van den Berg, *De Inlandsche Rangen en Titels op Java en Madoera* ('s-Gravenhage, 1902), p. 98; Rouffaer, 'Vorstenlanden', p. 262; Poensen, 'Mangkubumi', p. 240 (it should be remembered that Poensen's *babad* was probably written in the nineteenth century). See also W. B. d'Almeida, *Life in Java, With Sketches of the Javanese* (2 vols.; London, 1864), vol. ii, pp. 98–9, on the annual meeting between Susuhunan and Sultan, and Veth's somewhat sceptical rehearsal of the story in *Java*, vol. iii, pp. 616–17 and p. 617 n. 1.

[22] See *B. Mang.*, pp. 5–43.

anem).²³ Again the precedent of the sixteenth-century partition of Padjang may have been in Mangkubumi's mind, for the chronicles say that the ancestor of the House of Mataram, Ki Pamanahan, was older (*sĕpuh*) than Ki Pandjawi, and for that reason he chose the less populated area, the forest of Mataram, destined to be the victorious principality.²⁴

There was even a confusion of titles. The 'correct' form for the Sultan was *Kangdjĕng Sultan Hamĕngkubuwana Senapati Ingalaga Ngabdurahman Sajidin Panatagama Kalipatulah*. Pakubuwana III continued to employ the official seal used since the time of Pakubuwana I (1703–19) with the titles *Kangdjĕng Susuhunan Pakubuwana Senapati Ingalaga Ngabdurahman Sajidin Panatagama*.²⁵ But there are examples of the Sultan using the name Pakubuwana and of the Susuhunan using both the name Hamĕngkubuwana and the title *Kalipatulah*, which has subsequently come to be used only in Jogjakarta.²⁶ The problem was partly one of language usage, for in eighteenth-century Javanese the distinction between the syllables *pa* and *ma* was sometimes ignored, the vowels *a* and *ĕ* were regularly interchanged, and the nasal *ng* was often omitted in

---

²³ e.g. *B. Mang.*, pp. 5, 35; and numerous places in *BG*, vol. xvii, pp. 70–9; vol. xviii, pp. 1–16.

²⁴ See *BTDj*, text p. 59, trans. pp. 61–2; *BK*, ff. 100ʳ ff.

²⁵ These titles are taken from the texts and the red lacquer seals on original documents in the Djakarta Arsip Nasional.

See PB III to Palm, 24 Sawal A.J. 1713 (9 Aug. 1787), in Solo 26, 'Soerakarta Brieven 1754–91'; HB I to Greeve, 10 Mulud A.J. 1717 (Nov. 1790), in Java's Noord-Oost Kust 162, 'Bijlagen 1790'; HB I–PB III Contract Ratification, 2 Nov. 1773, in Djokja 42.

See also PB I–VOC Contract, [A.D. 1708?], in Solo 52; and PB II–VOC Contract, 13 Nov. 1743, in Solo 53. The seal of the Pakubuwanas contained only the words *Kangdjĕng Susuhunan Pakubuwana Senapati Ingalaga 1726*. The fuller form of PB III's title is cited in the texts of the documents. It is notable that 1726 is the date of the accession of PB II, but it is in the Western rather than the Javanese calendar.

B. Mang., p. 30, Canto V (Asmaradana), verse 9, gives the Sultan's titles as 'Sultan Mangkubuwana Dji / Senapati Ingalaga / Ngabdurahman Sajidine / Panatagama Kalipah / tolah Nagri Mĕntaram / . . .' The minor differences in form here are largely due to the requirements of the poetic meter.

²⁶ See Soeripto, *Vorstenlandsche Wetboeken*, pp. 42, 239; Vreede, *Catalogus*, pp. 87 n. 1, 110 n. 1, 123 n. 1; *Babad Sangkalaning Momana*, p. 268; NBS 75 (6), in Pigeaud, *Literature*, vol. ii, p. 728. HB I's signature on the Gijanti treaty is 'Sultan Pakubuwana'; see photo in Soekanto, *Sekitar Jogjakarta*, p. 9.

This confusion also appears on several translations of letters in the Algemeen Rijksarchief, although some of these cases may be Dutch copyists' or translators' errors. e.g., Sultan 'Paccoeboeana' to Batavia, 5 Rĕdjĕb (27 March 1757), in KA 2802 (OB 1758).

writing. The introductory syllable *ha* could also be dropped. Thus, until the Javanese began to formalize the distinctions in royal titles, there was little difference among *haměngku, hamangku, mangku, paku*, and so on.[27]

The fact that these distinctions were not regularized until long after 1755 suggests that the Javanese state system was not yet equipped to cope with a situation of bifurcated sovereignty. Furthermore, it indicates what is demonstrated more clearly by the subsequent course of events, that the division was not yet accepted as permanent.

The new Sultan now possessed a kingdom, officials, and regalia. He lacked only two things to establish himself as a monarch: a capital city and money. The latter he acquired by convincing Hartingh, with some difficulty, to advance him one-half of the 10,000 reals due annually for the lease of the *pasisir*.[28]

There was some misunderstanding concerning the selection of a site for Mangkubumi's court. On the eleventh of February he had asked Hartingh whether he might go to Mataram to select a permanent location, to which Hartingh simply replied, 'Yes, why not?' Three days later, after the Sultan's accession, Danurědja reported Mangkubumi's intention to move to Mataram, but Hartingh objected. He did not wish Gijanti to be abandoned since it was the key to the joint campaign against Mas Said. Mangkubumi might make a brief trip to Mataram to select a location, but should move there permanently only after Mas Said was defeated. Mangkubumi then informed the Governor that this was in fact his intention. He was sending one of his officials to select a site, which he would later visit for a few days to approve.[29]

Mangkubumi's emissary Djajawinata was sent to Mataram shortly after the Djatisari meeting. He established a temporary court (*kraton pasanggrahan*) at Gamping (on the western side of present-day Jogjakarta) for use until the permanent *kraton* site was ready at Jogja, where Mangkubumi had earlier taken residence

---

[27] J. L. A. Brandes also commented on this confusion; see 'Bladvulling: Eenige foutieve Eigennamen in de door Meinsma uitgegeven Prozabewerking van den Babad Tanah Djawi', *TBG*, vol. 35 (1893), p. 128. See also Poensen, 'Mangkubumi', pp. 246–7, 246 n. 2; and n. 70 below.

[28] Hartingh, Dagregister, 26 Feb. 1755, in KA 2757 (OB 1756). Also in Louw, *Successie-Oorlog*, pp. 119–20.

[29] Hartingh, Dagregister, 26 Feb. 1755, in KA 2757 (OB 1756); partially quoted in Louw, *Successie-Oorlog*, pp. 115, 119.

in 1749.³⁰ Hartingh's objections do not appear to have prevented the Sultan from moving from Gijanti to Gamping. It is unclear when he moved from there to the *kraton*. *Babad Mangkubumi* gives a date equivalent to 6 November 1755.³¹ Dutch records suggest that the move actually took place in February 1756, but that the court was not officially named *Ngajogjakarta Adiningrat* until April.³² In the *kraton* itself the foundation date is expressed in a depiction of two serpents entwined, representing the chronogram 'two snakes feel as one' (*dwi naga rasa tunggal*). This is the Javanese year 1682, which began only in late September 1756. Perhaps these various dates refer to different stages in the construction and occupation of the new court. Apparently the official occupation of the court (6 November 1755) was several months before the actual move.

The name Ngajogjakarta was apparently derived from or at the very least had obvious similarity to the Sanskrit name *Ayodhyā* (in Modern Javanese, *Ngajodya*), the capital city in the epic *Rāmāyaṇa*.³³ Although Islam was apparently of some importance

---

³⁰ See Hartingh, Dagregister, 26 Feb. 1755, in KA 2757 (OB 1756); Poensen, 'Mangkubumi', p. 266; *B. Mang.*, pp. 50 ff.

For a summary of the earlier history of the Jogjakarta area, see Poensen, 'Mangkubumi', p. 267; see also *BG*, vol. xix, p. 24. Jogjakarta was built upon a site formerly known as the forest of Bringan (*alas Bringan*). This was presumably the location of the game preserve of Panĕmbahan Seda ing Krapjak (*krapjak Bĕringan*) which Dr. de Graaf was unable to locate ('Sultan Agung', p. 23).

³¹ *B. Mang.*, pp. 96–7, says that HB I took possession of his *kraton* (*ngĕdaton*) and renamed it Ngajogjakarta Adiningrat on Kĕmis-Lĕgi, Sapar (without a date), Wawu, tjondrasṭa nĕm Ratu, which is A.J. 1681 (A.D. 1755). The only time when Kĕmis and Lĕgi coincided in Sapar A.J. 1681 was on 1 Sapar in the 'Thursday Calendar', which was 6 November A.D. 1755. Since there would have been no Kĕmis-Lĕgi in the month of Sapar following the 'Friday Calendar', it seems that HB I had by this time adjusted the calendar by one day to introduce the 'Thursday Calendar' (see above, pp. 54–5 n. 42).

³² The letters from Jogjakarta Resident C. Donkel to Hartingh are all datelined 'Cratong Passangrahan' until 9 Feb. 1756. After 12 Feb. 1756 they are date-lined 'Djokjo', and after 14 April 1756 'Djokjocarta'; see AN Djokjo 32, 'Djokjakarta Brieven naar Samarang, 1746–61'.

See also Sĕmarang to Batavia, 26 Feb. 1756, announcing the Sultan's move to his 'vaste residentie plaats Djokjo', and 8 April 1756, announcing the court had been renamed 'Djokjocarta Diningrat', in KA 2779 (OB 1757).

³³ See Hageman, 'Overzigt', p. 153; cf. Veth, *Java*, vol. ii, p. 493.

The *Rāmāyaṇa* was known in Old Javanese, in which version the city was called *Ngajoḍyā*; see H. Kern (ed.), *Rāmāyaṇa, Oudjavaansch Heldendicht* ('s-Gravenhage, 1900), p. 2. Modern Javanese versions of this text were subsequently produced, the most famous being the *Sĕrat Rama* ascribed to Jasadipura I. This has been published several times, most recently by Bale Poestaka

TRANSITION TO PEACE, 1755-1757

to Sultan Haměngkubuwana I, the continuing influence of pre-Islamic tradition is evident. The *Rāmāyaṇa* perhaps had a particular attraction because of its Wisnuite nature. The Sultan was sometimes described in *Babad Mangkubumi* as 'looking like Wisnu'.[34] Wisnu's role as saviour of the world in troubled times seems to have been well known in Java. Furthermore, Wisnu was especially connected with the warrior class, particularly in his eighth incarnation as Krěsna, a character well known in Java from the *wajang*-theatre as well as from literature. In Modern Javanese *babads*, Wisnu was also made the first ruler of Java.[35] Professor Berg has suggested that Jogjakarta functioned as the 'Wisnuite' *kraton* in a centuries-old cycle of courts, alternating

---

in 1925, ed. J. Kats. In this text the city is called *Ngajodya* (e.g. Canto I, verse 14).

This latter version of the *Sěrat Rama* is dated A.J. 1750 (A.D. 1822) (Canto I, verse 1: sirneng tata paṇḍita siwi) and is thus considerably later than the founding of Jogjakarta. The earliest dated MSS. of *Sěrat Rama* known to me are the *Rama Badra Djawi* (LOr 2105), *Sěrat Rama* (NBS 4), and *Sěrat Rama* (NBS 149), all dated A.J. 1746 (A.D. 1818). An *Asṭa Brata* fragment of the Rama story (NBS 87–XXIV) is dated A.J. 1711 (A.D. 1784). Although none of these MSS. is as old as Jogjakarta, there were surely older Modern Javanese texts of the story as well as extant copies of the Old Javanese text from which the name of the capital city would have been known.

The late date of the Rama texts, excepting the *Asṭa Brata* fragment, incidentally raises the question of the propriety of ascribing these versions to Jasadipura I (see Pigeaud, *Literature*, vol. ii, p. 713; E. M. Uhlenbeck, *A Critical Survey of Studies on the Languages of Java and Madura* ['s-Gravenhage, 1964], p. 138). Although the details of the lives of Jasadipura I and II, and of the Ranggawarsitas as well, are obscure, it seems that the elder Jasadipura died *c*. 1803. On Jasadipura's life, see Soebardi, 'Jasadipura I', pp. 81–4.

The name *Ajogja* was apparently used for the Jogjakarta area even before it was occupied by HB I; see Poensen, 'Mangkubumi,' p. 267; *BG*, vol. xix, p. 24.

[34] e.g. *B. Mang.*, pp. 29, 145. On pp. 179 and 338 he is called *Sang Murti*, one of the names used in Java for Wisnu.

[35] See Brandes, 'Pararaton', p. 66; Basham, *Wonder*, pp. 302–7; Schrieke, *Sociological Studies*, vol. ii, pp. 83–6; *BTDj*, text p. 7, trans. p. 7; *BTDj(BP)*, vol. i, p. 8; *BK*, f. 2ʳ. See also G. W. J. Drewes, *Drie Javaansche Goeroe's: Hun Leven, Onderricht en Messiasprediking* (Leiden, 1925), pp. 153–4; Anderson, *Mythology*, p. 14.

See also C. F. Winter, Sr., *Javaansche Zamenspraken*, vol. ii (Amsterdam, 1858), p. 258, where the *Sěrat Djajabaja* is explained. Here Mataram is called the 'age of (supernatural) power' (djaman kala sakti) and it is then explained that *kala sakti* is a name for Wisnu and that Mataram is called this because in that time everyone was practising warfare, like Wisnu: Nagari ing Matawis dipunwastani djaman kala sakti, kala sakti punika djudjulukipun Sang Hjang Wisnu,, kala samantěn Ratu ing Matawis saabdinipun sadaja sami rěměn ulah kapradjuritan, kados Baṭara Wisnu,,

between Buddhist and Wisnuite rulers, in which the Wisnuite age was a time when the kingdom was divided. Further research and analysis are required before it will be possible to assess the applicability to the Modern Javanese situation of Professor Berg's reconstruction of Old Javanese dynastic theory. But if his understanding of pre-Islamic theory is correct, it is not unlikely that it should also prove to be applicable in the eighteenth century.[36]

There is nothing very remarkable in an Islamic Javanese ruler occupying a 'Wisnuite' court. The idea that Islamic and Hindu traditions were mutually exclusive resulted from pressures for orthodoxy, particularly in the heartlands of these faiths. It would be inappropriate to apply *a priori* such theoretical philosophical standards to the Javanese circumstance. The materials which survive from the eighteenth-century Javanese courts clearly suggest that the thought that Islam and Hinduism were mutually exclusive was unlikely to have occurred with much urgency to the Javanese court élite. It is interesting here that Mangkubumi's son, who became Crown Prince in 1758 and eventually succeeded as the second Sultan of Jogjakarta, was likened in *Babad Mangkubumi* not to Wisnu but to the *Qur'ānic* hero Joseph.[37] The *Sĕrat Jusup*, rather freely adapted from the story of Joseph in Egypt in Sura XII of the *Qur'ān*, was one of the most popular of Javanese romances and seems to have had a special status. It was often written on palm-leaves, like Old Javanese texts, when virtually everything else was being written on paper and bound in the modern fashion.[38] Thus, together the Sultan and the Crown Prince were seen to evoke two heroic figures, Wisnu and Joseph, who were to some extent representative of the two great cultural traditions, Hinduism and Islam, so successfully synthesized in Modern Javanese courtly culture.

[36] Professor Berg has discussed this problem with me on several occasions. The roots of the theory are to be found in C. C. Berg, 'Het Rijk van de Vijfvoudige Buddha', *Verhandelingen der Koninklijke Nederlandse Akademie van Wetenschappen, Afd. Letterkunde*, vol. 69, no. 1 (1962), especially pp. 133–4, 196–7. Professor Berg has further developed this theory in 'Māyā's Hemelvaart in het Javaanse Buddhisme', *Verhandelingen der Koninklijke Nederlandse Akademie van Wetenschappen, Afd. Letterkunde*, vol. 74, nos. 1 and 2 (1969), pp. 52–3, 128, 138–9.
[37] e.g., *B. Mang.*, pp. 267, 273, 276, 387.
[38] On the *Sĕrat Jusup*, see Pigeaud, *Literature*, vol. i, pp. 217–19. For a summary of a Jusup text from eighteenth-century Surakarta, see Vreede, *Catalogus*, pp. 26–31.

When he became Sultan in 1755 and proceeded to his new capital city, Mangkubumi was probably already in his forties,[39] an age his wretched brother Pakubuwana II had never reached. As a young man he had witnessed the intrigues and warfare during the reigns of his father Susuhunan Amangkurat IV (1719–26) and of his brother until he had chosen the role of insurgent prince himself. For nearly nine years he had led his armies across Java and he had emerged a leader of great vigour and ability. He had forged in battle the consensus which had already made him a ruler in 1749. Now he was to rule for nearly four more decades, outliving his nephew Pakubuwana III. Dutch opinions of the character of Haměngkubuwana I varied according to the extent of his co-operation at any particular time, but he was undoubtedly a remarkable man. His most notable physical trait was the habit of answering importunate Dutch requests or queries with an enigmatic smile.[40]

Although until now Sultan Mangkubumi has received little attention in the scholarly literature on Java, he was certainly one of the most able rulers of Modern Javanese history. Indeed, although further research is required before it will be possible to judge the qualities of the various Javanese monarchs, a preliminary estimation suggests that only Sultan Agung and Sultan Mangkubumi, alone among all the rulers of the House of Mataram to the end of Dutch rule in Indonesia, truly merit the appellation 'great'. Both understood the possibilities and the limitations of Javanese kingship and both successfully manipulated the king's position to their own greater glory, leaving at their deaths kingdoms more stable and powerful than they had found at their accession. Both were successful generals and this battle-field experience was very likely important in forming their abilities to read men and to use them wisely, so essential to achieving greatness as a king of Java.

This is not to say, however, that it is always easy to have a very clear view of Mangkubumi as a personality. The king's traditional role was not that of a policy-maker or a problem-solver, but rather that of one who prevented the emergence of problems

[39] Various sources on the date of HB I's birth provide conflicting information. He was apparently born sometime between A.D. 1709 and 1717. See Rouffaer, 'Vorstenlanden', p. 260; Poensen, 'Mangkubumi', p. 230; and Sĕrat Djuměněngan S.D.I.S. Kg. Sultan Haměngkubuwana I, p. 1.

[40] See Hartingh, Memorie, 26 Oct. 1761, in dJ x, p. 365. For a selection of Dutch judgements on HB I, see Poensen, 'Mangkubumi', pp. 280–3.

by the manipulation of the traditional techniques of kingship. Thus even a great ruler was, in times of peace, a somewhat distant figure who embodied the unity of the realm but for whom it was dangerous to impose too much upon the Central Javanese élite—princes, regional dignitaries, and religious notables—who supported him. Thus, in the following pages, as Mangkubumi moves from war to peace, he may begin to recede somewhat as a human figure, except on those occasions when circumstances require his personal action.

The new Sultan was a great builder in the honoured tradition of a Javanese king. Indeed, the construction of large and spectacular buildings was an essential element in demonstrating his right to be recognized as monarch. The small *desa* which Jogja must have been was rapidly transformed into a capital city, the focal point of which was the new *kraton*. Hartingh wrote that Mangkubumi was a great lover of new buildings as part of his concern 'to install himself as ruler'. He caused fountains, rock-works, and water-works to be constructed and then pulled down and reconstructed if unsatisfactory.[41]

To the south and west of the *kraton* was built *Taman Sari*,[42] a Xanadu worthy of Coleridge's verse. Its system of artificial lakes with underwater tunnels and false islands is a remarkable sight even in its present condition of collapse. Originally the 'water castle', as the Dutch called it, was accessible by water from the *kraton* itself and was connected by a broad canal with a second large basin and false island to the south of the court (*Pulo Gĕḍong*). In 1788 Mangkubumi treated the Governor of Sĕmarang to a tour of this fabulous complex aboard a gilded boat.[43] There were sunken

[41] Hartingh, Memorie, 26 Oct. 1761, in dJ x, p. 365. See also *BG*, vol. xix, pp. 24 ff.

[42] I am most grateful to Drs. Mudjanattistomo of Jogjakarta, a scholar and lover of *Taman Sari*, for conducting me on a tour of its ruins. A description of the site is also to be found in Veth, *Java*, vol. iii, pp. 631–3, where the construction of *Taman Sari* is wrongly ascribed to HB II. When Veth described the site it was already in very bad condition. See also H. D. H. Bosboom, 'Het verdwenen Waterkasteel te Djokdjokarta (uit oude Papieren)', *TBG*, vol. 45 (1902), pp. 518–29; J. Groneman, 'Het Waterkasteel te Jogjåkartå', *TBG*, vol. 30 (1885), pp. 412–34; Denys Lombard, 'Jardins à Java', *Arts Asiatiques*, vol. 20 (1969), pp. 145–54.

The *Taman Sari* complex is to be seen (marked L, M, N,) on map III of P. J. F. Louw and E. S. de Klerck, *De Java-Oorlog, 1825–1830* (6 vols.; 's-Hage, 1894–1909).

[43] Greeve, Dagregister, 20 Aug. 1788, in KA 3708 (OB 1789).

bathing-pools for the Sultan's wives and adjacent chambers from which the monarch might observe them. His sleeping-chamber contained a carved bedstead appearing to float upon the water, with a similar bed for his favourite wife beside it. Soaring archways stood above the entrances, with tree-lined bathing-pools below.

Taman Sari was not only a pleasure garden. Its design strongly suggests that it was also intended as a last position of defence should the kraton ever be attacked. On a more exotic level, there is clear evidence that the complex also had a religious and mystical significance. One of the most remarkable buildings was the Sumur Gumuling, accessible only by an underground passage. It is a large construction consisting of circular galleries on two floors, with a central courtyard surmounted by four converging staircases, joining in the middle and leading in a single set of steps to the second floor. Below the central point of the staircase have been found old kris blades, leading to the conjecture that the building may perhaps have had a religious significance. Some sources, including a Dutch account of 1791, clearly suggest that Sumur Gumuling was intended as a kind of mosque, although the precise use of the various parts of the building remains somewhat unclear. A recent writer has suggested further that the myth of the Goddess of the Southern Ocean may have played a part in Taman Sari,[44] a suggestion which is consistent with the extensive use of water in the complex. A more precise indication of this is contained in the Jogjakarta texts Babad Kraton and Sĕrat Surja Radja, which quite clearly suggest that Taman Sari was the name of a place sacred to the Goddess.[45] If this is true, its construction was not only a means whereby Mangkubumi could display his royal style and standing. It was also a way of maintaining the link with the Goddess of the Southern Ocean which was believed to have been established by Senapati and Sultan Agung. Taman Sari should be seen, therefore, as an important step in establishing the Sultan's legitimacy as a monarch of the House of Mataram.

[44] See Bosboom, 'Waterkasteel', pp. 519–25, 528; and Lombard, 'Jardins', pp. 146–7, 154, 170–2.

[45] Sĕrat Surja Radja (Jogja Kraton MS. F. 7; dated A.J. 1841), pp. 71–4 (Canto XI); here the kingdom of the Goddess of the Southern Ocean is visited by disease and misfortune and she retires in a worried state to a mosque in 'Taman Sari'. The Surja Radja story is discussed below, in Chap. VII. In BK, f. 282^r, is described Sultan Agung's visit to the Goddess late in his life, which takes place in 'Taman Sari'. In the same story in BTDj(BP), vol. x, p. 34, is mentioned 'Taman Asri'.

Babad Mangkubumi dates the beginning of the construction of this fabulous water palace in A.J. 1683 (A.D. 1757–8). The position of the event in the text indicates that this date may, however, be incorrect. Another source gives the rather more likely date A.J. 1684 (A.D. 1758–9).[46] The construction of the whole of *Taman Sari* must have occupied many years. It was apparently abandoned sometime after the death of Hamĕngkubuwana I in 1792, for unknown reasons. There may have been mystical factors which led subsequent rulers not to use the area. But perhaps more mundane considerations influenced the decision. The system of pools must have provided a vast breeding ground for mosquitoes, making it an unhealthy location. And the architectural technique was primitive, particularly in the arches, so that the buildings may simply have fallen into disrepair and been abandoned.

In the months after the Gijanti settlement the Sultan appointed the officials who were to govern his kingdom. The *patih* Danurĕdja, at the centre of the administrative system, has already been discussed. A somewhat more obscure official was the *patih djĕro* (inner *patih*) who was charged with administrative responsibilities within the *kraton* walls. Because of the nature of this post its occupant was little known to the Dutch. Sometime in the mid-1760s the Sultan appointed one Kjai Urawan to this position, with the title and name Tumĕnggung Sindurĕdja. When Sindurĕdja died sometime in the late 1770s he was succeeded by his son with the title and name Raden Rija Sindurĕdja.[47] Another influential and trusted adviser was Raden Tumĕnggung Ronggaprawiradirdja, who after abandoning the life of rebellion was named *bupati-wĕdana* (chief administrator) of the *montjanĕgara* (outer lands). He was Mangkubumi's brother-in-law and thus

---

[46] *B. Mang.*, p. 144. The *sĕngkala* is sinome sarira manis Nĕrpati. The event is preceded by the death of the first Crown Prince, which occurred on 6 Sept. 1758, which was in fact at the beginning of A.J. 1684; see Donkel to Sĕmarang, 7 Sept. 1758, in AN Djokjo 32, 'Djokjokarta Brieven naar Samarang, 1756–61'.
A.J. 1684 is given in Groneman, 'Waterkasteel', p. 414. *Babad Sangkalaning Momana*, p. 270, dates the beginning of construction in Ehe, A.J. 1685, also in connection with the death of the first Crown Prince. This date is wrong, however, since that death occurred in A.J. 1684.

[47] See *B. Mang.*, pp. 230–3, 445; Louw and de Klerck, *Java-Oorlog*, vol. i, p. 88, citing *Babad Dipanĕgara*.
Sindurĕdja is mentioned occasionally in Dutch archival material; see HB I–PB III Contract, 28 Nov. 1768, in KA 3169 (OB 1770); Lapro to Sĕmarang, 22 March 1772, in KA 3256 (OB 1773). See also Rouffaer, 'Vorstenlanden', p. 279, on the post of *patih djĕro*.

also the brother-in-law of Danurĕdja. His family were to serve as heads of the *montjanĕgara* and military commanders for the Sultanate for several generations. His great-grandson Sĕntot later became *senapati* (commander-in-chief) to the rebel Dipanĕgara and ended his days in the service of the Dutch.[48] According to the later *Babad Dipanĕgara* the first Sultan was also served by one Pĕkih Ibrahim as *pĕngulu* (head religious functionary). The *babad* says, 'These three: the ruler, the *patih*, and the *pĕngulu* had only one will, and for this reason Jogjakarta experienced the greatest prosperity.'[49]

Slowly the Sultan's authority over his court and people, many of whom had so recently renounced the undisciplined life of rebellion, was established. A number of rebels submitted to him and were accepted as his subjects.[50] The forms of kingship were augmented by acquiring *pusakas* and by elaborating the Sultan's visible status. In the latter he was assisted by Dutch provision of trumpeters, elephants, Persian horses, and a coach.[51] The Dutch commented on Mangkubumi's concern in all these things to follow 'the example of the previous rulers of the Mataram empire'.[52]

In Surakarta conditions improved. Pakubuwana III had been virtually friendless in 1754 but after the end of the war with Mangkubumi courtiers began to return to him. As they did so, the Susuhunan began for the first time to become a true Javanese ruler supported by an élite consensus. Many of the dignitaries who had

[48] Sĕmarang to Batavia, 13 Dec. 1755, in KA 2757 (OB 1756); *BG*, vol. xvii, p. 68; *B. Mang.*, pp. 45–6. See also Louw and de Klerck, *Java-Oorlog*, vol. i, p. 88, citing *Babad Dipanĕgara*; Soekanto, *Hubungan Diponegoro-Sentot* (Djakarta, [1959]); de Graaf, *GI*, pp. 395–7.
In *B. Mang.*, p. 366, HB I recommends Ronggaprawiradirdja to the future HB II, *c.* 1765.
[49] Quoted in Louw and de Klerck, *Java-Oorlog*, vol. i, p. 88.
[50] Sĕmarang to Batavia, 25 Jan. 1755 and 13 Dec. 1755, in KA 2757 (OB 1756); id., 1 Nov. 1756, in dJ x, p. 310; Hartingh, Dagregister, 26 Feb. 1755, in KA 2757 (OB 1756); Hartingh, Memorie, 26 Oct. 1761, in dJ x, p. 367.
[51] Hartingh, Dagregister, 26 Feb. 1755, in KA 2757 (OB 1756); Sĕmarang to Batavia, ultimo Feb. 1755 16 May 1755, and 9 Sept. 1755, in KA 2757 (OB 1756); HB I to Batavia, 5 Dulkangidah A.J. 1684 (1 July 1759), in KA 2861 (OB 1760); Sĕmarang to Batavia, 20 June 1760, in KA 2889 (OB 1761); id., 19 Aug. 1760, in KA 2888 (OB 1761); id., 9 June 1761 and 23 July 1761, in KA 2919 (OB 1762); Poensen, 'Mangkubumi', p. 303; *BG*, vol. xxi, pp. 59 ff.; *Babad Sangkalaning Momana*, p. 269.
[52] Sĕmarang to Batavia, ultimo Feb. 1755, in KA 2757 (OB 1756). See also Hartingh, Dagregister, 26 Feb. 1755, in KA 2757 (OB 1756); van der Burgh, Memorie, 19 Sept. 1780, in dJ xi, p. 402.

left the court in the years of rebellion had apparently done so only because it seemed political suicide to remain on the losing side in Surakarta. Now, when it was clear that Surakarta would not be destroyed at least for the time being, these dignitaries came back. As a result Pakubuwana III became more than a Dutch-defended nonentity. Mangkubumi could not have been pleased at these signs of vitality in the Susuhunan's court, but he had agreed to a peaceful partition with Surakarta and he did nothing now to break the agreement. With this sudden emergence of Pakubuwana III as a serious factor in Javanese royal politics, which was probably unexpected by the Sultan, the possibility began to grow that the partition of the kingdom might evolve as a long-range compromise solution to the problem of élite disunity. The Susuhunan's deteriorated residence was rebuilt and the court rapidly took on a renewed pomp. He, too, received the elephants, trumpeters, etc., which the Dutch provided.[53] In 1761 Hartingh commented that the Susuhunan was 'a good-natured man, but somewhat dull and dishevelled', and much under the influence of his wife, a half-sister of the prince of Madura.[54]

Relations between Pakubuwana III and Haměngkubuwana I were made easier by the death of Pringgalaja in October 1755. The Sultan's hatred of the man is amply documented in both Dutch and Javanese sources, and Pringgalaja's passing was mourned by neither ruler. *Babad Gijanti* candidly says that he was poisoned. His replacement as the Susuhunan's *patih* was Raden Adipati Mangkupradja, formerly head of Kědu and the oldest of the Surakarta *wědanas*.[55]

[53] Hartingh, Dagregister, 26 Feb. 1755, in KA 2757 (OB 1756); Sěmarang to Batavia, ultimo Feb. 1755, in KA 2757 (OB 1756); id., 8 April 1756, in KA 2779 (OB 1757); id., 1 Nov. 1756, in dJ x, p. 307; PB III to Batavia, 2 Běsar Ehe A.J. 1684 (27 July 1759), in KA 2861 (OB 1760); Hartingh, Memorie, 26 Oct. 1761, in dJ x, p. 361.

[54] Hartingh, Memorie, 26 Oct. 1761, in dJ x, p. 361. See also Hartingh, Dagregister, 26 Feb. 1755, in KA 2757 (OB 1756).

[55] PB III to Batavia, 20 Oct. 1755, in KA 2757 (OB 1756); Sěmarang to Batavia, 10 Oct. 1755, 1 Nov. 1755, and 13 Dec. 1755, in KA 2757 (OB 1756); Batavia to Sěmarang, 31 Dec. 1755, in KA 912 (Afgaand Briefboek 1755).
HB I's dislike of Pringgalaja is evident throughout the earlier pages of *B. Mang.* His death and replacement by Mangkupradja are to be found in *B. Mang.*, pp. 95-6.
BG describes the death by poisoning in vol. xix, p. 23. See also Vreede, *Catalogus*, p. 88; and *BG*, vol. xix, p. 36.
BG, vol. xix, p. 23, dates the event Monday, 27 Běsar, Be [A.J. 1680], which

TRANSITION TO PEACE, 1755–1757

In April and May 1756 Mangkupradja and Danurĕdja went to Sĕmarang and then exchanged visits to the respective courts, in the course of which differences already arising from the chaotic land division were settled. The settlement which was ultimately reached was called the 'Book of Klĕpu' (*Sĕrat Buk Kalĕpu*)[56] after the *desa* in which the main meeting took place.[57] It was to be the basis for all later discussions of land questions until 1773–4, when a new land regulation was agreed. It did nothing, however, to alleviate the baroque complexities of the boundaries and disputes over land questions were to continue for two more decades.

The increasing stability of Central Java was only relative. The pacification of Mangkubumi, who had been the major rebel leader, immediately ameliorated the island's strife-torn condition. But lesser rebellions continued and the difficulties of agricultural recovery were compounded by these rebellions as well as by the failure of the rains in 1755.[58] The rebels were particularly strong in the east of Java and the Company was obliged to threaten its

---

was 4 October A.D. 1755. That date was, however, a Saturday. Pakubuwana III's letter to Batavia of 20 Oct. (see above) gives the date 29 Bĕsar, Be or 8 October A.D. 1755. Although 29 Bĕsar was a Monday, it was 6 Oct., not 8 Oct. See Hartingh's description of Mangkupradja in his Memorie, 26 Oct. 1761, in dJ x, p. 364.

[56] Sĕmarang to Batavia, 8 April 1756, in KA 2779 (OB 1757); Donkel to Sĕmarang, 14 April 1756 and 21 May 1756, in AN Djokjo 32, 'Djokjokarta Brieven naar Samarang, 1756–61'; Hartingh, Memorie, 26 Oct. 1761, in dJ x, pp. 366–7.
On the basis of Jogjakarta documents, Rouffaer, 'Vorstenlanden', p. 241, dates the *Sĕrat Buk Kalĕpu* 11 Sura, Alip, A.J. 1683 (26 Sept. A.D. 1757). I suspect this is a ratification date. The VOC documents make it clear that land questions were discussed in April–May 1756, although negotiations may have continued for some time thereafter. *Babad Sangkalaning Momana*, p. 269, dates the meeting in A.J. 1682.

[57] It is not entirely clear which of the many *desas* named Klĕpu this was, although it was most probably the Klĕpu in sub-district Polanhardjo, district Dĕlanggu, Klatĕn regency. This is apparently the village mentioned in several places in *BG*, e.g. vol. iv, p. 60; vol. vi, pp. 8, 55, 58, 79; vol. viii, pp. 56, 57; vol. xx, p. 11. Fourteen *desas* named Klĕpu are listed in W. F. Schoel (ed.), *Alphabetisch Register van de Administratieve- (Bestuurs-) en Adatrechtelijke Indeeling van Nederlandsch-Indie*, vol. i: *Java en Madoera* (Batavia, 1931). See also Sĕmarang to Batavia, 18 July 1768, in dJ xi, p. 83.

[58] Sĕmarang to Batavia, 8 April 1756, in KA 2779 (OB 1757). See also id., 25 Jan. 1755 and 9 Aug. 1755, in KA 2757 (OB 1756); id., 16 Sept. 1755, 16 Nov. 1755, and 13 Dec. 1755, in KA 2756 (OB 1756); id., 1 Nov. 1756, in dJ x, p. 312.

Javanese coastal officials with severe punishment if they showed no greater exertions against the insurgents.[59] Many of the rebels were religious mystics (*tapas*) whose charisma some Javanese found irresistible. Nevertheless, in the course of 1755 the troops of the Dutch and the two Javanese rulers made considerable progress and a number of rebels lost their heads.[60]

Mangkubumi's rebel half-brother Pangeran Singasari escaped when Kĕḍiri fell to the Company and its allies,[61] but Pangeran Buminata, also called Bintara, submitted to Dutch forces in June 1755. He feared to return to either the Sultan or the Susuhunan, against both of whom he had rebelled at various times. He was instead banished by the Company. He died in Ceylon in 1783, and Pakubuwana III then refused even to allow the return of his descendants to Java. With him were captured a *kris* and a pike, both *pusakas*, which the Dutch divided between the two rulers.[62]

The most powerful unsubdued rebel was Mas Said, Mangkubumi's son-in-law and his *patih* in the early years of his rebellion. He was also variously known as Raden Mas Arja Surjakusuma, Pangeran Prangwadana, Susuhunan Adiprakosa, and Pangeran Adipati Mangkunĕgara. He emerges from the records as a man of great energy. A *babad* written later in his life suggests further that, unlike many other Javanese of this period, Mas Said had a particular dislike of the Dutch *qua* Dutch.[63] He showed throughout his life that he was less willing to tolerate their presence even as allies than was, for instance, Mangkubumi. Hartingh said that Mas Said was small in stature but 'fire and vivacity radiate from

[59] Sĕmarang to Batavia, 26 Feb. 1756, in KA 2779 (OB 1757).
[60] Id., ultimo April 1755, 16 May 1755, and 9 Aug. 1755, in KA 2757 (OB 1756); id., 1 Nov. 1756, in dJ x, pp. 311–12; id., 8 April 1756, in KA 2779 (OB 1757).
[61] Hartingh, Djĕpara, to Batavia, 17 June 1755, in KA 2757 (OB 1756).
[62] Hartingh, Surabaja, to Batavia, ultimo June 1755, in KA 2757 (OB 1756); Sĕmarang to Batavia, 10 Oct. 1755, in KA 2757 (OB 1756); id., 26 Feb. 1756 and 8 April 1756, in KA 2779 (OB 1757); id., 22 Feb. 1783, in KA 3543 (OB 1784); id., 8 March 1783, in KA 3545 (OB 1784).
Buminata was first sent to Banda. How and when he was moved to Ceylon is unknown to me. The story of Buminata to his banishment to Banda is also to be found in *BG*, vol. i, pp. 6, 59; vol. v, pp. 16, 40; vol. vi, p. 33; vol. xiv, p. 25; vol. xix, p. 12.
Poensen, 'Mangkubumi', pp. 249–50, was confused by the two titles used by this prince.
[63] *Sĕrat Babad Pakunĕgaran* (BM Add. MS. 12283), dated A.J. 1705 (A.D. 1779). There are several references, for instance, to the 'arrogance' of the Dutch (e.g. f. 101ʳ: pijangkuh Kumpni).

his eyes'.⁶⁴ His forces dwindled after the Gijanti settlement as some of his supporters were attracted away from him to a less perilous existence at one of the two peaceful *kratons*. The Dutch hoped for a quick kill. But the Company learned a bitter lesson when the rebel overwhelmed a Dutch force in October 1755, and killed Captain van de Poll, hero of the Madura campaign ten years before.⁶⁵

Mangkubumi spared no efforts to assist in the defeat of his erstwhile ally, personally leading his troops into the field. Hartingh observed that the Sultan

is the most interested in the extermination of this marauder, out of expectations of sole sovereignty over Java, which he hopes for and has his eye on, as he made clearly known at the first conference at Pĕdagangan.⁶⁶

For Mangkubumi the original impetus to come to peace with the Company and the Susuhunan was largely so that their forces might be united against Mas Said. Until the sudden emergence of Pakubuwana III as a credible ruler after the Gijanti treaty, Mas Said had seemed the only serious competitor in the struggle for 'sole sovereignty over Java', which Hartingh correctly identified as Mangkubumi's goal. Now he hoped for the final annihilation of his enemy. But Mangkubumi, too, received a rude shock in February 1756, when Mas Said nearly succeeded in burning the new *kraton* at Jogjakarta.⁶⁷

Nevertheless Mas Said's forces were insufficient to gain his goal of the conquest of Java. He therefore entered into negotiations with the Dutch in 1756. He refused to submit to either of the Javanese rulers as the Dutch urged him to do and pressed instead for control of one-third of the kingdom. The Dutch, however, were unwilling to see another equal partition of Java, a plan against which the Sultan in particular objected. At one point the Company

⁶⁴ Hartingh, Memorie 26 Oct. 1761, in dJ x, p. 363. It is difficult to accept Poensen's uniformly negative assessment of MN's character, which resulted from an uncritical acceptance of the viewpoint of his Pakualaman *babad*; see 'Mangkubumi', pp. 232, 264–5.

⁶⁵ Sĕmarang to Batavia, 17 Oct. 1755, in KA 2757 (OB 1756). See also dJ x, pp. xxxvii, lxxvii. The death of van de Poll is also described in *B. Mang.*, p. 101.

⁶⁶ Sĕmarang to Batavia, 8 April 1756, in KA 2779 (OB 1757). See also id., 1 Nov. 1756, in dJ x, p. 309.

⁶⁷ Id., 26 Feb. 1756, in KA 2779 (OB 1757). See also Poensen, 'Mangkubumi', p. 268.

wished to withdraw from the affair altogether. Hartingh told the two *patihs* that the costs of the war were considerable, and since Java was beginning to flourish again could not the Susuhunan and the Sultan defeat Mas Said themselves? The *patihs* replied that they were able to resist the rebel but were not capable of defeating him without Dutch assistance.[68]

By February 1757 Mas Said, Pakubuwana III, and the Company had moved toward mutually acceptable bargaining positions. Only the Sultan remained unwilling to compromise. The Company and the Susuhunan wanted peace; Mangkubumi still wanted victory. Mas Said sent a brother to Surakarta to assess the situation and it was soon evident that his peaceful submission to the Susuhunan was possible.[69] Pakubuwana III agreed to meet Mas Said outside the city of Surakarta, which the latter was unwilling to enter because of the proximity of the Susuhunan's troops and of the Sultan's forces under Ronggaprawiradirdja. At this meeting Mas Said submitted to the Susuhunan.

A conference was held with Governor Hartingh at Salatiga in mid-March 1757, where Mas Said swore allegiance to the Susuhunan, the Company, and the Sultan, who was represented by Danurĕdja and the Resident Donkel. He received the title *Kangdjĕng Pangeran Adipati Hamĕngkunĕgara Senapati Ingajuda*, with control over 4,000 *tjatjahs* of the Susuhunan's territory. He established his princely residence within the city of Surakarta. The Sultan provided no lands for Mangkunĕgara's maintenance,[70]

---

[68] Sĕmarang to Batavia, 1 Nov. 1755, 16 Nov. 1755, and 13 Dec. 1755, in KA 2757 (OB 1756); D. W. Freijer, Batavia, to MN, 31 Dec. 1755, in KA 912 (Afgaand Briefboek 1755); Sĕmarang to Batavia, 26 Feb. 1756, 8 April 1756, and 10 May 1756, in KA 2779 (OB 1757). There are numerous other letters in KA 2756 (OB 1756) and KA 2779 (OB 1757) concerning these events. See also *B. Mang.*, pp. 97–8.

[69] Sĕmarang to Batavia, 16 Feb. 1757 and 10 March 1757, in KA 2802 (OB 1758). See also Batavia to Sĕmarang, 26 Feb. 1757, in KA 914 (Afgaand Briefboek 1757).

[70] Sĕmarang to Batavia, 29 March 1757, in KA 2802 (OB 1758); Batavia to H. XVII, 31 Dec. 1757, in dJ x, pp. 314–17. See also dJ x, pp. lxxviii–lxxix; and *B. Mang.*, pp. 132–8.

The full form of MN's title is to be found on his seal on a 'Geschrift' of 1790 in AN Java's Noord-Oost Kust 162, 'Bijlagen 1790'. Only after the death of MN did his descendants acquire the regular use of the additional title *Arja*; see Rouffaer, 'Vorstenlanden', p. 267. Nevertheless, *Arja* appears among MN's titles in van der Burgh, Memorie, 19 Sept. 1780, in dJ xi, p. 406.

The same confusions mentioned above concerning the Susuhunan's and the Sultan's titles also applied to Mangkunĕgara. He was consistently called Paku-

and reportedly had only scorn for the settlement.[71] The animosity between these two men was to be a continuing theme of the subsequent decades. As with the earlier division of the kingdom in 1755, so also the permanence of Mangkunĕgara's appanage was uncertain. It was not until 1792 that his descendants were guaranteed the right of succession, thus making the Mangkunĕgaran into an autonomous principality.

Mangkunĕgara's new status in the Javanese political structure was an irregular one. He had hoped for total conquest of the kingdom and when this proved unattainable had then desired equality of status with the Susuhunan and the Sultan. His powerful position among the Javanese élite would seem to have justified such a status. He presumably accepted a lesser position only because the entire idea of a peacefully and formally divided kingdom was itself highly irregular and was seen merely as a temporary expedient until such time as reunification would be possible. But he shared with Mangkubumi, Pakubuwana III, and the remaining Javanese élite the bitter lessons of many years of unproductive warfare. He, too, had arrived at the conviction that although reunification of Java was the only acceptable outcome of the strife, warfare would not attain it at least for the time being. He was willing to turn to a form of competition which stopped short of the full-scale use of arms. In so doing, he joined a political structure which over the years would take on permanency as the élite more and more gained a vested interest in its maintenance. Eventually, Mangkunĕgara would join the Sultan and the Susuhunan in realizing that no means but warfare could reunite Java and that, since the élite had firmly renounced warfare after the years of inconclusive destruction, Java would therefore not be reunited.

For the Sultan the submission of Mangkunĕgara was a major defeat. His main competitor had been not killed, but bribed into

---

nĕgara in these early years, and a chronicle written in his court in 1779 has the title *Sĕrat Babad Pakunĕgaran* (BM Add. MS. 12283) as does another written eighteen years later, *Babad Pakunĕgara* (Raffles Jav. MS. 16, Royal Asiatic Society, London). See also P. A. 'Paccoenagara' to Batavia, [March 1757], in KA 2802 (OB 1758); HB I to van Ijsseldijk, 9 Sura Djimawal A.J. 1717 (19 Sept. 1790), and HB I to 'Adipattij Pakoenagoro', 14 Sura Djimawal A.J. 1717 (24 Sept. 1790), in AN Java's Noord-Oost Kust 162, 'Bijlagen 1790'. See also the reference to 'Paku Nagara' in Raffles (1830), vol. ii, p. 247; and Brandes, 'Bladvulling', p. 128.

[71] See *B. Mang.*, pp. 132–6. Cf. Poensen, 'Mangkubumi', pp. 271–2.

submission by his 'allies' of Surakarta and Batavia. The major incentive to the treaty of Gijanti, the destruction of Mas Said, had come to nothing.[72] Mangkubumi was now trapped in a situation which had become quite different from what he had expected. Instead of remaining as the sole contender for the throne of Mataram who had a substantial consensus among the Javanese, he not only still had opponents, but had even lost relative support. Several dignitaries had remained with Mangkunĕgara and would now join him to live in Surakarta. And the Susuhunan, although never as powerful as the Sultan, must now be taken more seriously in political calculations than ever before. Further steps had been taken on the path towards a more permanent division of Java.

With Mangkunĕgara's submission the major rebellions in Java ended for the first time in nearly two decades. There were still malcontents and marauders roaming the countryside but the notables of Javanese history had been forced to renounce major military action as a means of contention. Not even the combined forces of Surakarta, Jogjakarta, and the Company could defeat even the weakened army of Mangkunĕgara; nor could any one of the Javanese princes succeed in defeating all opponents. It was stalemate. Inverting the Clausewitzian formula, now politics was to become warfare by other means. Neither the Susuhunan, the Sultan, nor Mangkunĕgara yet accepted that Java was permanently divided, but all understood that reunification by conquest was unlikely to succeed. This was so not only because of Dutch military intervention, but also because none of the three had been able to unite all of the Javanese political élite and popular sentiment behind him.

The Company was exhausted and greatly relieved to be able to demuster its indigenous troop levies.[73] With the end of the warfare which had devastated Java almost continually for eighty years, the necessity for large-scale Dutch military action was gone and it was to be more than thirty years before the Company again launched a major expedition into the Central Javanese heartland. Although the Dutch were still an important element in the

---

[72] HB I later told Hartingh that he was averse to not keeping his word and said that the Dutch often broke theirs. Hartingh denied that this was so, which HB I merely answered with a grin; Hartingh, Memorie, 26 Oct. 1761, in dJ x, p. 365.

[73] Batavia to H.XVII, 31 Dec. 1757, in dJ x, pp. 316–17; Batavia to Sĕmarang, 28 March 1757, in KA 914 (Afgaand Briefboek 1757).

Javanese situation their influence now became more peripheral. The Company was able to turn its attention to its increasing debt and, ultimately, to its approaching bankruptcy.

The Javanese could now consider the question which decades of chaos had not answered: how was the kingdom to be governed, and by whom?

IV

ELIMINATING OPTIONS, I: THE FAILURE OF MARRIAGE DIPLOMACY
1757–1765

IN the late 1750s and early 1760s, the three main Javanese princes continued to hope that Java would be reunited. But they were firm in their conviction that warfare had been tried as a means to this and had failed. They were undoubtedly encouraged in this view by their supporters and courtiers throughout the countryside who enjoyed the benefits of peace. For the first time in decades it was possible to construct a relatively stable administration and to reap the fruits of Java's abundant resources. No one was anxious to be plunged again into the chaos of full-scale civil war. But if warfare on such a grand scale had been renounced, there remained other courses of action, other options. For nearly nine years after the peace of Salatiga, Hamĕngkubuwana I, Pakubuwana III, and Mangkunĕgara I played a complex game of political intrigue often interrupted by violence betraying the true intensity of the conflict. The complexities of this period and the heavy emphasis on harem politics led the missionary scholar C. Poensen to conclude that the interest of Mangkubumi's story ended in 1757. He complained that the chronicle he was reading thereafter contained nothing more than 'all sorts of particulars of the court- and family-life of the Sultan'.[1] But it was precisely in such events that the true significance of this period lay.

Having abandoned all-out rebellion, the most traditional means of becoming sovereign and of reunifying the kingdom, the leading contenders turned to another traditional technique, political marriage. Marriage was inextricably connected with succession, the most important issue of all. If one could successfully marry

---

[1] Poensen, 'Mangkubumi', p. 284.

one's child to the offspring of a ruler, there was a chance that one's grandchild at least might eventually succeed to the throne. In mid-eighteenth-century Java, two further factors were of particular significance. Pakubuwana III produced several eminently marriageable daughters, but it was to be many years before a son survived. There was thus a possibility of reunifying the kingdom in the next generation if the Houses of Jogjakarta and Surakarta could be united in marriage. Although all previous rulers of Mataram had had direct connection in the male line to preceding sovereigns, Javanese custom did allow for succession through the female line. If an official died without a son, his domain might go to his daughter with a guardian or husband in charge; if she had a son, he would inherit.[2] Thus if the Crown Prince of Jogjakarta could be married to a daughter of Pakubuwana III, he might find himself ruling both Surakarta and Jogjakarta after the death of his father-in-law and father. Or, if he produced a son from such a union, that son might become heir to both *kratons*. It would still remain for any such ruler of a reunited Java to demonstrate that he could maintain a consensus of the élite. But none of the main contenders in eighteenth-century Java doubted that he could do so if given the opportunity. And there is clear evidence, discussed below, that Mangkubumi at least was willing to take drastic action to ensure that his successor would also be a man who could do so. A second factor, one which produced the greatest *cause célèbre* of the period and very nearly plunged Java into renewed warfare, was that Mangkunĕgara had been married since the years of rebellion to Mangkubumi's eldest daughter. He had, therefore, a potential means of legitimizing either succession in or conquest of Jogjakarta. If he should gain a claim through marriage to the Surakarta throne as well, he would be doubly dangerous.

In these years more mundane problems also concerned the rulers, who were constantly fending off financial embarrassment. The devastated countryside took time to recover, and meanwhile the Susuhunan and the Sultan asked the Company for rights to birds' nests- and tobacco-sales to bolster their incomes.[3] There was a recurring and serious shortage of copper coins throughout

[2] See C. F. Winter, Sr., *Javaansche Zamenspraken*, vol. i (ed. T. Roorda; 5th ed.; Leiden, 1911), p. 23.
[3] See Sĕmarang to Batavia, 1 April 1757 and 8 Nov.1757, in KA 2802 (OB 1758); HB I to Batavia, 3 Sapar A.J. 1682 (Nov. 1757), in KA 2802 (OB 1758); Batavia to H.XVII, 31 Dec. 1757, in dJ x, p. 317.

the latter years of the eighteenth century.[4] Such financial difficulties continued to make the Dutch payments for the lease of the *pasisir* essential to both *kratons*. While there is no suggestion that either monarch was particularly happy that the coast was beyond his control, their financial requirements continued to contribute to the permanence of the Dutch position there. Indeed, the *pasisir* had always been such a difficult area for the Mataram kings to administer that the 10,000 reals from the Dutch was probably more regular and very likely more profitable than the incomes they might have received had they ruled the coasts themselves. But the great political issue of the day was still the attempt to solve the problem of the division of Central Java short of a full-scale resort to arms.

It was necessary that consideration be given to the Dutch position, and Hamĕngkubuwana I very early began to regulate his relations with the Company to his advantage. The overriding principle for the Sultan would appear to have been the maintenance of a friendly alliance with the Governor-General in Batavia, but the absolute rejection of any implied limitation upon his sovereignty within his kingdom. This conflicted with the Dutch view that they were sovereign and the Javanese rulers their vassals by virtue of the treaty of 1749. The Sultan had agreed to Dutch sovereignty in the Gijanti treaty, and treaties were taken very seriously by the Javanese. But it must be emphasized that the Javanese view of sovereignty would not thereby have admitted Dutch pretensions to control over internal Jogjakarta affairs. In like manner, the Sultan's sovereignty over his kingdom did not apparently imply a right to meddle in the internal administration of each *bupati's* domain. This therefore was less a conflict over the question of sovereignty itself than over what the recognition of sovereignty entailed. While the Company was so weak, however, it had neither the means nor the desire to attempt any real control in Central Java. The Company wanted above all peace and stability, at the cheapest possible price. As a result, for a dynamic ruler like Mangkubumi the opportunities for complete

[4] See Sĕmarang to Batavia, 30 Oct. 1762, in KA 2957 (OB 1763); id., 16 Jan. 1763 and 9 April 1763, in KA 2986 (OB 1764); HB I to Batavia, 30 Rĕdjĕb (15 Feb. 1763), in KA 2985 (OB 1764); Sĕmarang to Batavia, 20 Dec. 1783, in KA 3545 (OB 1784); Batavia to H.XVII, 31 Dec. 1784, in dJ xii, p. 64; id., 29 Dec. 1787, in dJ xii, pp. 125–6; dJ xi, pp. lxxix ff.

The shortage of currency was of course a serious problem for the Company as well as for the Javanese monarchs.

independence were very much greater than they had been since the beginning of the eighteenth century. It is essential to grasp this fact in order to see Javanese history in the latter half of the eighteenth century in its appropriate context. Throughout his reign the Sultan's manipulation of the relationship with the Dutch was rather more able than that of his Surakarta counterparts. Mangkubumi revealed an accurate understanding of the realities and limitations of Dutch power and sometimes took delight in the unmistakable signs of the Company's military weakness. He was, therefore, never quite trusted by Batavia in this period. Pakubuwana III, on the other hand, was generally submissive and co-operative. Mangkunĕgara, the most fiery of the three, rarely lost an opportunity to express his disdain for the Company whenever there was nothing to be gained from being suppliant. The Dutch were consequently ready to blame him for whatever troubles occurred.

The Sultan clearly appreciated and enjoyed the Company's straitened circumstances. For instance, it was the custom for the Dutch garrison to fire cannon salutes whenever the Sultan, his mother, or his wives appeared, when letters were received, and so on. When the Company complained that this was costing considerable powder, the Sultan replied with a smile, saying surely the Dutch were not short of powder.[5] After the Gijanti settlement Mangkubumi had successfully put off sending an embassy to pay his respects in Batavia. When Danurĕdja finally led such a mission in late 1758, Hartingh wrote to Batavia asking that the emissaries be sent back as quickly as possible, for he did not like Danurĕdja to be absent from the court.[6]

But more immediately important than the Dutch to Mangkubumi was the situation within his own court. If Pakubuwana III's problem was a lack of sons, the Sultan's problem was a superfluity. He had over thirty children before his death, including at least sixteen sons.[7] Rivalry among these sons subsequently

---

[5] Hartingh, Memorie, 26 Oct. 1761, in dJ x, pp. 369–70.

[6] HB I to Batavia, 3 Sapar A.J. 1682 (Nov. 1757), in KA 2802 (OB 1758); Sĕmarang to Batavia, 20 Oct. 1758, in KA 2830 (OB 1759); Batavia to H.XVII, 30 Dec. 1758, in dJ x, p. 320; *B. Mang.*, pp. 140–1.

[7] See Louw and de Klerck, *Java-Oorlog*, vol. vi, pp. 458, 465; Dwidjosoegondo, *Serat Dharah inggih 'Seseboetan Radèn'* (Malang, 1941), pp. 97–8; *Putra-Dalĕm Sinuwun Sapisan* (Jogja Kraton MS. A. 24); Poensen, 'Mangkubumi', pp. 298–9, 312–13. The sons of HB I are listed below, p. 352 n. 31.

produced many of the crises of the early nineteenth century, and a number of them were involved in the intrigues which led to the Java War (1825–30).

The first Crown Prince, Raden Mas Ĕnṭo, had been named during the years of rebellion,[8] but his behaviour left much to be desired. The Sultan's parental affection was considerably strained in late 1755 when he was obliged to march to Kĕḍu in order to require his son's submission. The young prince had engaged in an outing in the course of which he had murdered seven Chinese.[9] His misbehaviour did not end then, and in April 1758 Hartingh again commented on troubles caused by the prince.[10] A later *babad* says the Crown Prince's sins included ignorance of Javanese literature, pride and conceit, filial impiety, and relations with Chinese women. He visited the ruins of Barabuḍur to see 'the thousand images' although there was a prophecy that this would bring immediate misfortune to a prince, for there was an image of a *satrija* (knight) in a cage.[11] Although the last is a most interesting misconception of the Buddha-images in their *stupas*, the entire passage seems considerably exaggerated. The source is a chronicle reflecting the viewpoint of Prince Pakualam I (1813–29), who was libellously critical of all of Mangkubumi's children excepting, not surprisingly, himself. Nevertheless there can be no doubt that the Crown Prince's behaviour was unacceptable. Mangkubumi could have no confidence in such a son as a potential heir to a reunited throne of Mataram, or even to his half of the kingdom.

The Sultan's patience was at an end. In late August 1758, he invited his son to dine with him and there apparently poisoned him. The prince's life dragged on for eight days, on each of which the Sultan and the Resident, Major Donkel, visited him. Finally he died after having received his father's forgiveness and blessing, and was buried at the royal grave-sites at Imagiri. Hartingh later appositely observed that the episode demonstrated that 'His Highness is not to be played with'.[12]

[8] See *BG*, vol. v, p. 46.
[9] Sĕmarang to Batavia, 9 Sept. 1755, in KA 2757 (OB 1756); Hartingh, Kort Verslag, 1 Nov. 1756, in dJ x, p. 310; see also Poensen, 'Mangkubumi', p. 287.
[10] Sĕmarang to Batavia, 11 April 1758, in KA 2831 (OB 1759). See also id., 18 Sept. 1758, in KA 2831 (OB 1759).   [11] Poensen, 'Mangkubumi', p. 287.
[12] Donkel to Sĕmarang, 7 Sept. 1758, in AN Djokjo 32, 'Djokjokarta Brieven naar Samarang, 1756–61'; Hartingh, Memorie, 26 Oct. 1761, in dJ x, p. 365. The death of the Crown Prince is reported, without details, in *B. Mang.*, p. 143.

ELIMINATING OPTIONS I, 1757-1765   101

Mangkubumi did not choose his next eldest son, Pangeran Arja Ngabei, to succeed as Crown Prince. The reasons for this are not entirely clear, but Dutch and Javanese sources suggest variously that Ngabei had been involved in a scandal with one of the Sultan's concubines, that his mother's status was too low, and that he was intellectually below standard.[13]

Instead the Sultan named his youngest son at that time, Raden Mas Sundara or Raden Mas Timur, as heir. He was then eight to ten years old, and was ultimately to succeed as Sultan Haměngkubuwana II (1792-1810, 1811-12, 1826-8).[14] The traditional title for a Crown Prince of Mataram was given to him, *Kangdjěng Pangeran Adipati Anom Haměngkuněgara Sudibja Radja Putra Nalendra Mataram*,[15] a title sufficiently similar to that of Pangeran Adipati Mangkuněgara to cause occasional confusion in some sources. The subsequent problems of his turbulent reign as the second Sultan of Jogjakarta have given him a 'bad press' in

[13] Louw and de Klerck, *Java-Oorlog*, vol. i, p. 31 n. 3; Poensen, 'Mangkubumi', p. 286; Donkel to Sěmarang, 28 Sept. 1758, in AN Djokjo 32, 'Djokjokarta Brieven naar Samarang, 1756-61'; Sěmarang to Batavia, 20 Oct. 1758, in KA 2830 (OB 1759); Ossenberch, Memorie, 13 May 1765, in dJ xi, p. 36.

[14] HB I to Batavia, 29 Sura Ehe (1 Oct 1758), in KA 2830 (OB 1759); Sěmarang to Batavia, 20 Oct. 1758, in KA 2830 (OB 1759); Batavia to H.XVII, 30 Dec. 1758, in dJ x, p. 320.

This is also the order of succession which the Dutch agreed to at the time of the Gijanti treaty, 13 Feb. 1755; text in dJ x, pp. 299-300.

HB I's mission to Batavia of 1758 brought news of these events and carried back Batavia's approval of the new Crown Prince; HB I to Batavia, 29 Sura Ehe (1 Oct. 1758), in KA 2830 (OB 1759); Batavia to HB I, 11 Dec. 1758, in KA 915 (Afgaand Briefboek 1758); HB I to Batavia, 20 March 1759, in KA 2861 (OB 1760).

In *B. Mang.*, p. 144, the young prince is called Raden Mas Timur; this section is quoted below, p. 169 n. 88. On the age of the young prince there is considerable agreement; he was apparently born *c.* 1749-50; see Poensen's summary of published information in 'Mangkubumi', p. 289; Sěmarang to Batavia, 20 Oct. 1758, in KA 2830 (OB 1759); *B. Mang.*, p. 144 (cited below, p. 169 n. 88); Rouffaer, 'Vorstenlanden', p. 260.

The standard discussion of the reign of HB II is C. Poensen, 'Aměngku Buwånå II (Sěpuh). Ngajogyåkartå's tweede Sultan. (Naar Aanleiding van een Javaansch Handschrift)', *BKI*, vol. 58 (1905), pp. 73-346. His reign is much in need of further research.

[15] The title is taken from the Crown Prince's seal on a letter to van Ijsseldijk of 1790, in AN Djokjo 34, 'Djokjokarta Brieven naar Samarang, 1770-1780'.

See also the form of the title given in *B. Mang.*, p. 187: Kangdjěng Pangeran Dipati Anom Haměngkuněgara ingkang Sudibja Ngrěnggani Maharadja Putradji Ngajogjakarta; and in *Kg. Kj. Surja Radja* (2 vol. MS. in Prabajěksa, Jogjakarta), vol., i, p. 2: Kangdjěng Gusti Pangeran Adipati Anom Haměngkuněgara kang Sudibja Atmarinadja Sudarma Mahanalendra.

published European and Javanese sources, but the first Dutch judgements were not unfavourable. In 1765 the Sĕmarang Governor, who respected the Sultan, observed that the Crown Prince 'already demonstrates in his conduct the truth of the saying that the fruit does not fall far from the tree'.[16] He might have added that fruit falling far from the tree in Jogjakarta was likely to be poisoned rather than allowed to flourish. The most telling testimonial to the Crown Prince's capabilities was the fact of his retention in his position by a father who had apparently not scrupled at the elimination of the previous incumbent.

Early in 1759 the new Crown Prince was circumcised, and immediately Mangkubumi set in motion the new politics of the reunification of Java through marriage. He desired that his son should marry a daughter of the Susuhunan. To ascertain the possibility of such a union he sent to Surakarta Raden Aju Djuru, wife of the former *patih* of Pakubuwana II who had recently returned from exile in Ceylon.[17]

During the years of rebellion the Company had on several occasions banished recalcitrant Javanese dignitaries to places outside Java. Raden Adipati Natakusuma had been banned because as *patih* to Pakubuwana II he had led the pro-Chinese court faction. In 1749 he had been joined in Ceylon by Mangkubumi's brothers Adinĕgara, Ngabei, and Danupaja.[18] Apparently even before the Gijanti settlement Mangkubumi had requested Natakusuma's return to Java, along with the surviving members of the families of the princes. After considerable misgivings and procrastination in Batavia, Natakusuma and several members of the royal house were returned to Jogjakarta in May 1758, thereby adding further to the visible status of the Jogjakarta *kraton*.[19]

[16] Ossenberch, Memorie, 13 May 1765, in dJ xi, p. 36.
[17] Donkel to Sĕmarang, 17 Feb. 1759, and 3 March 1759, in AN Djokjo 32, 'Djokjokarta Brieven naar Samarang, 1756–61'. See also *BG*, vol. xxi, p. 83.
[18] There is some confusion in the VOC records concerning how many other Pangerans were in exile in Ceylon. The Dutch also used Banda and the Cape of Good Hope as places of banishment (as well as several other less important locations) and exiles from throughout Indonesia were to be found in such places. On the banishment of these princes in 1749, see p. 56 above. See also *BG*, vol. vi, pp. 33, 37.
[19] It seems the request was first made at the Pĕdagangan meeting. On the return of these dignitaries, see Sĕmarang to Batavia, 16 May 1755, in KA 2757 (OB 1756); Batavia to Sĕmarang, 1 July 1755, in KA 912 (Afgaand Briefboek 1755); Sĕmarang to Batavia, 8 April 1756, in KA 2779 (OB 1757); Batavia to Sĕmarang, 30 April 1756, in KA 913 (Afgaand Briefboek 1756); Sĕmarang to

ELIMINATING OPTIONS I, 1757-1765   103

Upon his return Natakusuma was renamed Pangeran Djuru by the Sultan,[20] and he became a respected senior adviser on courtly affairs. He is credited with having confirmed the identity of the *pusaka-kris* given by Pakubuwana III to Haměngkubuwana I at Djatisari,[21] and with having diverted the Sultan from marrying a descendant of Sunan Kalidjaga because it conflicted with the *adat*.[22] Djuru himself had a very large collection of weapons which were kept at Batavia and restored to him on his return,[23] and which may have included *pusakas*. His importance to the young court of Jogjakarta was further enhanced by his experiences outside Java. The Pakualaman *babad* says he was particularly valuable for his knowledge of how to get along with Europeans.[24]

Djuru's adventures in Ceylon were of great interest to the Javanese. One wonders whether the Dutch, who were constantly worried about the anti-European potential of Islam, were wise to select Ceylon as a place of exile, for the island was on the main pilgrimage route from Indonesia to Mecca. *Babad Gijanti* contains a description of the Pangeran's experiences in Ceylon, which his wife told to Pakubuwana III on the occasion of her visit to Surakarta. There, she said, the exiles became students of mystical teachers named Sajid Musa Ngidrus and Ibrahim Asmara, whose magical powers achieved wondrous things. At the great recitations of the *Qur'ān* each Friday, Javanese fruits and delicacies were magically transported to Ceylon. Ship-captains from Surat, the Bengal coast, and Sělangor were among the pilgrims who visited these teachers.[25] Such tales, whether true or not, undoubtedly

---

Batavia, 2 July 1756, in KA 2779 (OB 1757); Batavia to HB I, 26 April 1758, in KA 915 (Afgaand Briefboek 1758); Sěmarang to Batavia, 11 April 1758, in KA 2831 (OB 1759); Batavia to Sěmarang, 26 April 1758, in KA 915 (Afgaand Briefboek 1758); Sěmarang to Batavia, 10 May 1758 and 24 May 1758, in KA 2830 (OB 1759); *B. Mang.*, pp. 141–3; *BG*, vol. xxi, pp. 49 ff.; Poensen, 'Mangkubumi', pp. 265–6.

[20] *B. Mang.*, p. 143; *BG*, vol. xxi, p. 71; Poensen, 'Mangkubumi', pp. 265–6.
[21] Groneman, *Garěběg's*, p. 59.
[22] Donkel to Sěmarang, 15 July 1759, in AN Djokjo 32, 'Djokjokarta Brieven naar Samarang, 1756–61'. The prospective bride was a daughter of Pangeran Widjil ('Pangerang Woettjel') of Kadilangu.
[23] Batavia to Sěmarang, 26 April 1758 and 16 June 1758, in KA 915 (Afgaand Briefboek 1758). Djuru complained that a number of items were missing, including 90 pikes set with gold, a *gamělan*, and some flintlocks.
[24] Poensen, 'Mangkubumi', pp. 284–5.
[25] *BG*, vol. xxi, pp. 84–7.

enhanced the prestige of the returned exiles, particularly in religious affairs. According to *Babad Gijanti*, Pangeran Djuru was made head of the religious officials in Jogjakarta.[26]

Despite Djuru's prestige, his wife's attempted arrangement of a marriage between the Susuhunan's and the Sultan's children was unsuccessful. Early in 1760 Pakubuwana III requested that Pangeran Djuru himself might visit Surakarta and the Sultan approved, asking him again to raise with the Susuhunan the question of the marriage. But the old Pangeran, too, returned to Jogjakarta without having succeeded. Pakubuwana III insisted that his daughter was too young for marriage,[27] which may have been true in a sense, since the Susuhunan himself would only have been about twenty-seven years old in 1760. But the Crown Prince of Jogjakarta was also a child and a royal child-marriage would not seem to have been unusual.

Mangkubumi also met opposition in his attempt to form a marriage link with the Panĕmbahan of Madura, whose sister was married to the Susuhunan. The Madurese prince seemed amenable to forming far-flung marriage alliances, and was himself proposing to wed a princess of Bima. But Batavia opposed the Sultan's plan, and the subsequent documentary silence indicates that the Company was successful in encouraging the Panĕmbahan not to accommodate Mangkubumi.[28]

In non-marital affairs things were going rather better. Despite the continuation of small-scale rebellions in the countryside, both rulers' courts were flourishing in the years 1759–62, and relations between the two were peaceful. Both maintained a friendly attitude toward the Dutch and there was a mutual flow of gifts between Batavia and Central Java.[29] Consistent with the growing internal stability within his kingdom, the Sultan was able

[26] *BG*, vol. xxi, p. 71.
[27] Donkel to Sĕmarang, 8 Jan. 1760 and 30 Jan. 1760, in AN Djokjo 32, 'Djokjokarta Brieven naar Samarang, 1756–61'. Djuru's trip to Surakarta is the last event described in *BG*; see vol. xxi, pp. 107–22.
[28] Sĕmarang to Batavia, 16 Feb. 1757, in KA 2802 (OB 1758); Batavia to Sĕmarang, 26 Feb. 1757 and 4 March 1757, in KA 914 (Afgaand Briefboek 1757); Sĕmarang to Batavia, 10 March 1757 and 1 April 1757, in KA 2802 (OB 1758).
[29] See Sĕmarang to Batavia, 22 Nov. 1759, in KA 2861 (OB 1760); id., 19 Sept. 1762, in KA 2957 (OB 1763); id., 8 Dec. 1762, in KA 2986 (OB 1764). There are several letters demonstrating the good relations between the VOC and the rulers to be found in KA 2919 (OB 1762), KA 2920 (OB 1762), KA 2956 (OB 1763), and KA 2957 (OB 1763).

to carry out in 1760 a major reorganization of his administration, appointing new officials and redrawing boundaries. The hand of Danurĕdja is probably to be seen in this, for the able *patih* continued to maintain his position of influence with the Sultan.[30] The reorganization was a technical administrative act, and is of interest here primarily as an indication of the Sultan's growing authority in the countryside and, perhaps, of the first signs of a new problem in Javanese politics: an increasing number of princes and dignitaries to be supported by a decreased amount of land. This will be discussed in more detail below.

In 1762 Mangkubumi received a mission from the Sultan of Bantĕn, but there was no apparent pan-Islamic significance in this. The Bantĕn ruler simply wished Mangkubumi to provide him with wooden pantiles, a saddle, a *ḍalang*, and a boat. But since the coastal timber-producing areas were under Company control, Jogjakarta was as inadequately endowed with suitable timber as Bantĕn, a fact with which Mangkubumi believed the Sultan of Bantĕn to be well acquainted. He therefore had to act as intermediary in asking Batavia to provide the vessel, which the Company agreed to do.[31] But the fact that the mission from Bantĕn had come to Jogjakarta clearly indicated that Mangkubumi's status as a Javanese monarch was not doubted by another Indonesian ruler.

Yet all was not as calm as appearances sometimes suggested in these years. Tensions persisted, particularly between Hamĕngkubuwana I and Mangkunĕgara. And the Sultan was also beginning to chafe under the political limitations which were imposed upon him by the Company's position. After the end of the wars, the Company's role was still very much the same as it had been before. The Dutch could not control the Javanese or force them to do that which they were unwilling to do. They could, however, prevent the rulers from undertaking other actions they might have attempted had they not feared the chaos of renewed

[30] Donkel to Sĕmarang, 30 Jan. 1760 and 19 Feb. 1760, in AN Djokjo 32, 'Djokjokarta Brieven naar Samarang, 1756–61'. There are several other letters from Donkel in 1760 in this volume on these administrative rearrangements.

[31] Van der Sluijs to Sĕmarang, 25 June 1762 and 5 July 1762, in AN Djokjo 33, 'Djokjokarta Brieven naar Samarang, 1761–64'. The Sultan of Bantĕn requested a boat described in the Dutch as a 'prauw pantjaling'. A *prau* is simply a boat or ship, while *pĕntjalang* is a Malay word defined by H. C. Klinkert, *Nieuw Maleisch-Nederlandsch Woordenboek, met Arabisch Karakter* [Leiden, 1893], as a large native trading-ship.

warfare and the potential hazards of renewed Dutch intervention. The Company caused the Javanese princes' horizons to shrink.

In May 1762, the new Governor of Java's Northeast Coast, W. H. van Ossenberch, made the customary tour to Central Java. At Jogjakarta he was presented with the Sultan's demand that Mangkunĕgara be exiled from Java. The Company rejected the proposition, which apparently resulted from the Sultan's suspicion that his son-in-law was intriguing to get the Susuhunan's throne for his own son on the death of Pakubuwana III. The Dutch rejection understandably put the Sultan into a 'peevish humour'.[32] His allies in Batavia had not only failed to carry the campaign against Mangkunĕgara to a successful conclusion, but now even refused to arrest and banish him when he was available for arrest in Surakarta. The reasons for the Sultan's indignation would have been understandable to all but the Dutch. They wrongly believed that the struggle for supremacy had ended in 1757, whereas it had merely changed in tactics. But if the Dutch were now willing to defend Mangkunĕgara, the Sultan could hardly march on Surakarta and attempt to capture him, a course which was in any case unlikely to have been successful given the very real support Mangkunĕgara had among the Javanese élite.

The Sultan also asked van Ossenberch that two of his favorites, Sumadiwirja and Ranamĕnggala, be given positions in Pĕkalongan and Pĕmalang. The Dutch reacted strongly against this proposition as well, since these areas were within the Company's coastal domain. The difficulties were compounded when Batavia at first confused the Pĕmalang matter with quite a different proposal concerning Malang, in the mountains south of Surabaja, over which the Sultan desired to have complete control. This misunderstanding was caused by the fact that the Javanese in the eighteenth century did, indeed, refer to Malang sometimes as 'Pamalang',[33] and Batavia's fury over the 'error' of the innocent Resident at Jogjakarta was quite unjust. In any case, the Dutch were unsure whether Malang might not also be within their jurisdiction, since Batavia wrongly believed it lay to the east of the meridian of Pasuruan, the boundary of Dutch territory established in the treaty of 1743.[34] The problem was somewhat academic,

---

[32] Batavia to H.XVII, 31 Dec. 1762, in dJ x, pp. 386–7.
[33] e.g. *B. Mang.*, pp. 360, 361, 368, 399, 417, 421.
[34] See PB II–VOC treaty, 11 Nov. 1743, in dJ ix, p. 438.

since neither the Company nor the Javanese rulers were in control of Malang, then in the hands of the rebel Pangeran Singasari and the descendants of Surapati. The Governor of Sĕmarang had no interest in the area and was quite happy to let Mangkubumi or the Susuhunan attempt to take it. But the Company felt it must reject Mangkubumi's attempt to place his courtiers in official positions in the coastal area.

The whole issue was so prejudiced by these misunderstandings that it seems to have grown out of proportion. Until late 1764 the Sultan continued to reiterate the request, even repeatedly sending the two young men to Sĕmarang in the company of Danurĕdja or the Resident to argue the case. Sumadiwirja was the son of the former Adipati of Pĕkalongan who, Mangkubumi said, had been the first person to advise him to make peace with the Company. In Hartingh's time the post had not been returned to the former incumbent and now the Sultan merely asked that the son be given the position 'or at least be kept in mind'. He asked for Ranamĕnggala a position controlling 1,000 *tjatjahs*, a sizeable domain. The Company's refusal to consider these requests made the Sultan ever more angry, a reaction not ameliorated by the equally forthright rejection by the Dutch of his repeated insistence that Mangkunĕgara be exiled. The Dutch began to fear the Sultan might contemplate taking measures against them, possibly in conjunction with the Susuhunan or Mangkunĕgara, a prospect so unlikely that it seems remarkable the Dutch considered it. Van Ossenberch was so concerned that he asked Batavia to approve the Sultan's requests regarding the young courtiers even after Batavia had firmly rejected them. But Batavia was unmoveable.[35]

Why the Sultan made the proposals at all is not certain. He may have hoped to gain some influence over affairs in the *pasisir* by placing his favourites there, as the Dutch feared. But it seems

[35] On these disputes, see Sĕmarang to Batavia, 30 Oct. 1762, 11 Nov. 1762, and 20 Nov. 1762, in KA 2957 (OB 1763); van der Sluijs to Sĕmarang, 12 Nov. 1762, in AN Djokjo 33, 'Djokjokarta Brieven naar Samarang, 1761–64'; Sĕmarang to Batavia, 8 Dec. 1762, in KA 2986 (OB 1764); Batavia to H.XVII, 31 Dec. 1762, in dJ x, pp. 386–8; Sĕmarang to Batavia, 23 June 1764, 4 Aug. 1764, 10 Nov. 1764, and 14 Nov. 1764, in KA 3016 (OB 1765); Ossenberch, Memorie, 13 May 1765, in KA 3048 (OB 1766). The section concerning Sumadiwirja and Ranamĕnggala is edited out of the version of van Ossenberch's Memorie in dJ xi, pp. 22–40, but may be found in another published text, ed. R. W. Tadama, in *Berigten van het Historisch Genootschap te Utrecht*, vol. 5, pt. 2 (1857), pp. 200–1.

more likely that he simply had insufficient lands to parcel out in appanages to his courtiers, and hoped to find places for them in the Dutch-controlled areas. Further evidence on the later land settlements of the 1770s, discussed in Chapter VI, also indicates that the shortage of good land was a problem in the truncated Central Javanese kingdoms. It was essential for stability that princes and courtiers receive adequate land in order to give them a vested interest in the political order. With the *pasisir* gone to the Dutch and Central Java split in two, there was a serious danger that some dignitaries either would receive domains inadequate to support an appropriate life-style, or would receive no grants at all except by paring away appanages already given to others. This posed the threat that groups would emerge of those disaffected notables who were always the greatest source of rebellion. The problem was further exacerbated by the fact of peace itself, for this meant that far fewer dignitaries were being killed or exiled. Furthermore, there was a general growth of population already under way. A full economic analysis of the very voluminous Dutch and Javanese records on such matters as land grants and agricultural production would be necessary to assess the dimensions of this problem. Pending such an investigation, it seems reasonable to assume that this hunger for land very likely lay behind the Sultan's request for Sumadiwirja and Ranaměnggala and that this was a general problem throughout this period.

There were also problems in 1762 within the Surakarta *kraton*, where the Susuhunan was unable to control the web of intrigue surrounding him.[36] The good-natured ruler was dominated by his wife, the sister of the Paněmbahan of Madura, and dared order nothing which she opposed. He was also somewhat inclined to drunkenness and other unseemly intemperances, although a few years earlier the Dutch observed that neither of the rulers used opium.[37] The ruler's wife was a clever woman who employed her powers over the Susuhunan to take freedoms he allowed no one else. She was soon to be accused of the most infamous behaviour. The languid old *patih* Mangkupradja had demonstrated an affection for the Company, but betrayed a notable inability to execute the Susuhunan's commands. Indeed, one of the constant

[36] The following description of affairs in the Surakarta kraton is from Sěmarang to Batavia, 23 July 1762, in KA 2957 (OB 1763).
[37] Hartingh, Kort Verslag, 1 Nov. 1756, in dJ x, p. 313.

ELIMINATING OPTIONS I, 1757-1765　　109

themes of the reign of Pakubuwana III was the incompetence of his *patihs*. An inability to choose capable men for such a central position reflected unfavourably upon the Susuhunan's general command of the arts of kingship.

Such troubled waters were ideal for indulging Mangkunĕgara's conspiratorial talents. He attempted to bring the Susuhunan into disrepute with the court in hopes of gaining the throne for himself on the death of its incumbent. At the same time he was ingratiating himself with the Susuhunan, whom the Dutch attempted to dissuade from an 'all-too-great familiarity with that prince'. The Dutch felt that many Javanese dignitaries would choose Mangkunĕgara's side in a dispute, not least because of their continuing loyalty and affection for his father Pangeran Arja Mangkunĕgara, the brother of Pakubuwana II and Mangkubumi, who had been banished to Batavia in 1728 and later moved to Ceylon and eventually to the Cape of Good Hope.[38]

In August 1762, Pakubuwana III took steps to regain some of his authority. Unable to endure any longer his wife's tyranny, he divorced her. The Susuhunan accused her of repeated adultery, and was finally moved to action when she insisted that he put to death one of his other women. It seems he very nearly killed his domineering wife on the spot.[39] Twenty years later evidence came to light suggesting that the Susuhunan had also made contact, perhaps via Mangkunĕgara, with a mystically-inclined rebel in East Java in hopes of procuring a discreet means to bring about his wife's death.[40] She was not killed, however, but simply sent away from the court, and in fact she came to outlive her former husband by about six weeks.[41]

After ridding himself of his wife's influence the Susuhunan

[38] Hartingh, Memorie, 26 Oct. 1761, in dJ x, p. 363. See also de Graaf, *GI*, pp. 249-50.
[39] Beuman to Sĕmarang, 8 Aug. 1762, in KA 2957 (OB 1763); PB III to Sĕmarang, 17 Sura A.J. 1688 (Aug. 1762), in KA 2957 (OB 1763).
[40] See Sĕmarang to Batavia, 19 Aug. 1762, in KA 2957 (OB 1763); trans. Jav. letter, Tumĕnggung Wirawidigda to Panĕmbahan Dewa Ratu, seen at Surabaja 8 May 1782, in KA 3519 (OB 1783); and Sĕmarang to Batavia, 23 June 1782, in KA 3519 (OB 1783). There is some doubt about the authenticity of this letter found in 1782 and said to date from 1762.
[41] There was considerable confusion about what should be done with the woman. Eventually she went to Kudus, the Bupati of which she married. She died in Kudus in November 1788, some six weeks after the death of PB III. See Sĕmarang to Batavia, 10 Aug. 1762, in KA 2957 (OB 1763); id., 20 Dec. 1767, in KA 3107 (OB 1768); id., 10 Nov. 1788, in KA 3708 (OB 1789).

seemed to take a greater control over the affairs of his kingdom.[42] To replace his Madurese wife he married a daughter of Pangeran Djuru, the former *patih* who had returned from Ceylon to Jogjakarta. Apparently the girl had been promised in marriage to the Jogjakarta Crown Prince, but the Sultan was willing that she be married instead to the Susuhunan.[43] He may have agreed because the marriage seemed to offer a potential means of exerting some influence over the Susuhunan through the daughter of Djuru.

The animosity between Mangkunĕgara and the Sultan continued to worsen during these affairs in Surakarta, which the Sultan believed Mangkunĕgara to be using to increase his influence there. Hamĕngkubuwana's suspicions were strengthened by the sudden announcement in September 1762 of marriage between Mangkunĕgara's son and the eldest daughter of the Susuhunan, after the Sultan had failed to arrange such a marriage for his own son.[44] Mangkunĕgara's family now stood dangerously close to control over the succession in Surakarta. Mangkubumi insisted to the Company that they must beware Mangkunĕgara's machinations, but the Dutch were now beginning to see this enmity as a most useful means of preventing the reunification of Java against themselves. They consistently rejected out of hand the Sultan's insistence that Mangkunĕgara be exiled.[45]

The twin themes of personal hatred between the Sultan and Mangkunĕgara and the involuted marriage-politics met in one person, the Sultan's eldest daughter and Mangkunĕgara's wife, Ratu Bĕndara. Mangkubumi had invited his daughter and Mangkunĕgara to visit Jogjakarta shortly after the peace of Salatiga in 1757. But Mangkunĕgara was understandably reluctant to undertake such a trip and he and his wife remained in Surakarta.[46] There were rumours in 1758 that such a visit would take place,[47] but in fact the Sultan did not see his daughter until she alone visited

[42] Ossenberch, Memorie, 13 May 1765, in dJ xi, p. 32.
[43] Sĕmarang to Batavia, 19 Sept. 1762, in KA 2957 (OB 1763).
[44] The marriage was not solemnized until December. Sĕmarang to Batavia, 19 Sept. 1762, in KA 2957 (OB 1763); id., 8 Dec. 1762, in KA 2986 (OB 1764). See also Ossenberch, Memorie, 13 May 1765, in dJ xi, p. 34.
[45] Hartingh, Memorie, 26 Oct. 1761, in dJ x, p. 363; Sĕmarang to Batavia, 23 July 1762 and 11 Nov. 1762, in KA 2957 (OB 1763).
[46] Sĕmarang to Batavia, 1 June 1757, in KA 2802 (OB 1758).
[47] Id., 1 Sept. 1758, in KA 2831 (OB 1759); Donkel to Sĕmarang, 2 Sept. 1758 and 9 Sept. 1758, in AN Djokjo 32, 'Djokjokarta Brieven naar Samarang, 1756–61'.

him for the first time in June 1761, after he had promised in advance to give her control of 600 *tjatjahs* as she desired.⁴⁸

In 1763, Ratu Běndara became the focus of a crisis which very nearly resulted in full-scale warfare between Mangkuněgara and the Sultan. The incident illustrates the extent to which personal animosities, political ambitions, considerations of prestige, and affairs of the heart could be inextricably and explosively entwined in an apparently simple course of events. It struck chords so deep within Javanese life that the Dutch could hardly understand the crisis, much less influence its outcome. Javanese and Dutch sources agree⁴⁹ that the conflict began with a visit by the Jogjakarta Crown Prince to Surakarta, where he hoped to see his prospective bride, one of the Susuhunan's daughters. There he was humiliated and insulted by Mangkuněgara. When the Crown Prince returned to Jogjakarta, he was followed by his elder half-sister Ratu Běndara who, upon her arrival, announced that she had no intention of returning to her husband. He was accused of mistreating and humiliating her, and of being incapable of fulfilling his conjugal duties.

Mangkuněgara claimed his wife was being held in Jogjakarta against her will, and soon both Surakarta and Jogjakarta troops were being stationed in the countryside. The Sěmarang Head-Administrator Hermanus de Munnik went to Jogjakarta in July 1763, where he found the Sultan protesting his innocence. Ratu Běndara insisted that her presence there was her own decision freely arrived at, but so long as she was in her father's city there was no way of knowing whether the statement was true. The Sultan insisted that divorce was the only solution. De Munnik got little more from the Sultan than a guided tour of *Taman Sari*. He attempted but found it impossible to bribe the *pěngulu* to give a legal decision in Mangkuněgara's favour and feared that Mangkubumi might ultimately send his daughter back to Mangkuněgara

⁴⁸ Van der Sluijs to Sěmarang, 9 May 1761 and 16 June 1761, in AN Djokjo 32, 'Djokjokarta Brieven naar Samarang, 1756–61'.

⁴⁹ The description of the Ratu Běndara affair given here, up to van Ossenberch's trip, is drawn from the following sources: *B. Mang.*, pp. 200–30, 234–9, 268–344; Poensen, 'Mangkubumi', p. 273–8; Munnik, Sěmarang, to Batavia, 23 June 1763, in KA 2986 (OB 1764) (see also dJ x, p. 394 n. 2); van der Sluijs to Sěmarang, 25 June 1763, in AN Djokjo 33, 'Djokjokarta Brieven naar Samarang, 1761–64'; Sěmarang to Batavia, 15 July 1763, in KA 2986 (OB 1764); PB III to Batavia, 1 Aug. 1763, in KA 2986 (OB 1764); HB I to Batavia, 1 Aug. 1763, in KA 2986 (OB 1764); Munnik, Report, 1 Aug. 1763, in KA 2986 (OB 1764).

dead. In Surakarta the Susuhunan meanwhile encouraged Mangkunĕgara to turn the dispute over to Sĕmarang's good offices.

The Sultan was furious with the Dutch for pressing him to relinquish his daughter and angrily shouted at the Resident van der Sluijs, 'If the Company wants to name Mangkunĕgara Sultan and take the half of the kingdom of Java from me, good luck!' His voice was so loud that the guards at the *kraton*'s inner gates came rushing in, and Danurĕdja was greatly upset.[50] Mangkubumi and the Javanese élite knew that the dispute was, among other things, over the question of the influence through political marriage which Mangkunĕgara might some day wield in Jogjakarta. It had implications for the very existence of the Sultanate in Mangkubumi's line. Mangkunĕgara had been for many years, and was still, the Sultan's major competitor in the struggle for supremacy over Java. Several opportunities to rid himself of this competitor had already slipped through the Sultan's fingers because of the incompetence, from his point of view, of his Dutch allies. Mangkunĕgara had not been killed by the Dutch after 1755. Nor would they arrest and exile him after 1757. They had not even prevented the marriage the previous year between Mangkunĕgara's son and Pakubuwana III's eldest daughter. Now the Dutch seemed to be saying that Mangkunĕgara's marriage to the Sultan's eldest daughter should also be preserved. Mangkubumi's loss of patience with the Company was understandable, although the Company nevertheless failed to understand it. Not surprisingly, their attempted mediation had no effect upon Mangkubumi, except to increase his impatience. On the same day that he brought the *kraton* guards running in, the Sultan rudely refused the customary offer of a drink from the Resident, saying that he wanted nothing to do with Dutch drink. Danurĕdja petitioned the Resident to be relieved of his impossible position as *patih*, caught between the angry Sultan and the Dutch.[51]

The Company believed that if open hostilities began, they would most likely result in a victory for Mangkunĕgara, who was thought to be popular among many of the Jogjakarta dignitaries.[52] This is a difficult matter to judge, but it does indeed seem that Mangkubumi's control of his officials was relatively firm, which

[50] Van der Sluijs to Sĕmarang, 25 June 1763, in AN Djokjo 33, 'Djokjokarta Brieven naar Samarang, 1761-64'. [51] Ibid.
[52] Sĕmarang to Batavia, 1 Aug. 1763 and 2 Aug. 1763, in KA 2986 (OB 1764).

might have been a virtue in moderation were it not for the fact that in a divided kingdom officials could always abandon a too-demanding ruler for one less strict.

In September and October 1763, Governor van Ossenberch went to Central Java to arbitrate the dispute before it destroyed the peace. By then hostilities had begun on a minor scale and neither Mangkubumi nor Mangkunĕgara would compromise.[53] Apparently the Susuhunan, who alone of the three Javanese princes had no prospect whatsoever of benefiting from a new war, I pressed Mangkunĕgara to be more amenable. According to *Babad Mangkubumi*, Pakubuwana III advised Mangkunĕgara to accept the proposals for divorce, for if he gave rein to his anger he would find himself facing three enemies: Mataram, the Company, and God. Mangkunĕgara supposedly replied,

LII: 9. ...
'It is so, my young Lord,
10. 'To battle the Law of God,
that is what I fear.
Therefore will I submit
to the wish of My Lord.'[54]
...

[53] Sĕmarang to Batavia, 13 Sept. 1763, in KA 2986 (OB 1764); id., 13 Oct. 1763, in KA 3016 (OB 1765); Ossenberch, Secret Rapport, 12 Nov. 1763, in AN Djokjo unnumbered volume containing Jogjakarta Contracts; Sĕmarang to Batavia, 12 Nov. 1763, in KA 3016 (OB 1765).
[54] *B. Mang.*, p. 341, Canto LII (Kinanṭi): (PB III addressing MN:)
8. ...
inggih tamtonipun kangmas
mangaler-ngidul tan polih
jen kangmas dados kroḍanja
satĕmaha mĕngsah katri
9. karijin mĕngsah Mĕntarum
kaping dwi mĕngsah Kumpni
ping tiga mĕngsah ing Suksma
Pangeran Mangkunĕgari
matur ing raji Sang Narpa
inggih punika Ri Adji
10. mĕngsah kukum ing Jwang Agung
punika kang kula djrihi
mila kawula sumongga
ing karsa Paduka Adji
....

B. Mang., pp. 224–5, describes an earlier occasion when PB III warned

It seems likely that Mangkunĕgara feared the combined forces of the Sultan and the Dutch more than the Law of God. He had long before come to the conclusion shared by other leading Javanese figures that warfare in which the Dutch allied themselves with one's enemy was unlikely to have a successful outcome. Mangkunĕgara may have disliked the Dutch but he could not readily contemplate renewed warfare against both them and the Sultan. Indeed, had he attempted such a hazardous course, many of his supporters would probably have refused to follow him. The Sultan's furious intransigence had now compelled the Company to abandon any idea of forcing Ratu Bĕndara to return to her husband, and Mangkunĕgara could not therefore hope that the Company would dare to take his side if he initiated full-scale hostilities. Consequently, he now grew more co-operative. For the first time Mangkunĕgara may have begun to appreciate more fully the implications of his subsidiary position, more than just a prince but less than a king. With a limited amount of land and manpower under his administration, and with the majority of the Javanese élite enjoying the benefits of the restoration of peace, he could rarely succeed in a game of military bluff.

It became clear that Mangkunĕgara would reluctantly accept a divorce if it were agreed that Ratu Bĕndara would not remarry so long as her former husband still lived. Van Ossenberch doubted that the Sultan would accept this stipulation and was pleasantly surprised when he appeared to do so. The divorce was duly arranged and in December 1763 Mangkunĕgara lost his connection by marriage to the House of Jogjakarta.[55]

The denouement of this affair only occurred two years later, but already the Sultan had won. His daughter remained in Jogjakarta for the rest of her life. It seems unlikely that she was forced to do so, although Mangkunĕgara insisted until his death that this was the case. If the Sultan had held her against her will, it would have been unwise for him to entrust to her the preparation of all his food, as he did in 1778 when he was concerned for a time lest

---

MN he would face three enemies, but they were then said to be HB I, the VOC, and PB III himself, not God. MN seems to have found this a less fearsome alliance.

[55] Sĕmarang to Batavia, 15 Nov. 1763 and 2 Dec. 1763, in KA 3016 (OB 1765).

the Crown Prince's ambition outstrip his filial piety.⁵⁶ Such an arrangement indicated mutual trust.

It was subsequently discovered that the divorce of Ratu Běndara and Mangkuněgara had been on the Sultan's terms, for he had not in fact promised that she would not remarry. When van Ossenberch's successor had occasion to reread Mangkubumi's letter on that subject, he found that the Governor had been misled. The Sultan had merely said, 'With regard to the remarriage of Ratu Běndara, you needn't worry, for as yet she has no wish to marry.'⁵⁷

The hostilities which had begun during the Ratu Běndara affair ceased in December, and captured *desas* were returned to their rightful sovereigns during the first months of 1764.⁵⁸ Central Java was generally peaceful throughout 1764 and 1765.⁵⁹ Although Mangkuněgara was unhappy about the loss of his wife, for whom his affection appears to have been genuine, he remained at peace.⁶⁰

The divorce had been a serious blow to Mangkuněgara's prestige and political ambitions. But it also seriously damaged the Sultan's ambitions, for it dealt a crippling blow to his marriage diplomacy. In October 1762, Pakubuwana III had again agreed that one of his daughters might marry the Jogjakarta Crown Prince when she came of age,⁶¹ but the agreement came to nothing during the Ratu Běndara affair. The Susuhunan did not feel he could oblige the Sultan while the latter remained so obstinate towards Mangkuněgara.⁶² After the divorce settlement in December 1763, Hamengkubuwana I again tried to conclude the marriage, but the

---

⁵⁶ Van Rhijn to Sěmarang, 22 Aug. 1778, in KA 3420 (OB 1779).

⁵⁷ HB I to Sěmarang, 12 Oct. 1763, attached to report of December 1765, in KA 3049 (OB 1766). For the Surakarta understanding of the agreement, as given in LOr 1786, see Vreede, *Catalogus*, p. 98 n. 1.

⁵⁸ Sěmarang to Batavia, 16 Dec. 1763, in KA 3016 (OB 1765); Batavia to H.XVII, 31 Dec. 1763, in dJ x, pp. 394-5; Sěmarang to Batavia, 3 Jan. 1764, 30 Jan. 1764 and 7 April 1764, in KA 3016 (OB 1765); Batavia to H.XVII, 31 Dec. 1764, in dJ xi, p. 18.

⁵⁹ Sěmarang to Batavia, 23 June 1764, in KA 3016 (OB 1765); id., 25 Jan. 1765, in KA 3049 (OB 1766).

⁶⁰ Sěmarang to Batavia, 16 Dec. 1763 and 30 Jan. 1764, in KA 3016 (OB 1765); MN to Ossenberch (2 letters), [May] 1765, in KA 3048 (OB 1766); Ossenberch, Memorie, 13 May 1765, in dJ xi, pp. 32-3; MN to Batavia, 5 Puasa A.J. 1687 [*sic*; error for A.J. 1691] (16 Feb. 1766), in KA 3078 (OB 1767).

⁶¹ Sěmarang to Batavia, 30 Oct. 1762, in KA 2957 (OB 1763).

⁶² Munnik, Report, 1 Aug. 1763, in KA 2986 (OB 1764); Sěmarang to Batavia, 2 Aug. 1763, in KA 2986 (OB 1764).

Susuhunan continued to postpone it.[63] The Dutch correctly believed that the Sultan intended the proposed union to be a means by which his son could succeed in Surakarta should the Susuhunan die without male progeny. The Company was therefore of two minds whether to intercede on the Sultan's behalf, as he asked. Governor van Ossenberch approved of the marriage, but he could not move the Susuhunan to carry it out.[64]

The Crown Prince of Jogjakarta paid a second visit to Surakarta in April 1765, but the desired marriage was no closer after his trip. The Dutch reported that he was politely received and that the bitterness between the courts had decreased.[65] Javanese sources, however, describe great tension during this trip. Because of his continuing anger at the loss of his wife, Mangkunĕgara supposedly threatened the Crown Prince, forcing the Susuhunan to intervene and insist that such matters must be settled by Sĕmarang. Pakubuwana III begged that Jogjakarta and Surakarta remain at peace. On the occasion of a *wajang-topeng* (masked dance) performance, at which the Susuhunan danced the role of Pandji, the young Crown Prince was too embarrassed to dance, professing that he had not yet learned. The Susuhunan said he, too, was no expert and the Crown Prince then accepted the invitation to join him. But the performance provoked Mangkunĕgara's anger when the Susuhunan and the Crown Prince became too tired to continue. The situation became so tense, says the *babad*, that the Crown Prince's entourage prepared against possible hostilities on their return trip to Jogjakarta, for it seemed that the Susuhunan would be unable to curb Mangkunĕgara. They arrived home safely, however, having been met by an escort from Jogjakarta.[66]

The difference between the Dutch and the Javanese sources is difficult to reconcile. The *babad* story has several striking similarities with the description of the prince's first trip to Surakarta in 1763, which also involved a dance performance.[67] It is possible

[63] Sĕmarang to Batavia, 2 Dec. 1763 and 23 June 1764, in KA 3016 (OB 1765).
[64] HB I to Sĕmarang, 8 Dulkangidah A.J. 1690 (May 1765), in KA 3048 (OB 1766); Ossenberch, Memorie, 13 May 1765, in dJ xi, pp. 32, 34.
[65] Sĕmarang to Batavia, 20 May 1765, in KA 3049 (OB 1766).
[66] *B. Mang.*, pp. 255–98. This trip is also described in Poensen, 'Mangkubumi', pp. 299–300. Poensen confused this second trip of the Crown Prince with the first, when Ratu Bĕndara returned to Jogjakarta.
[67] *B. Mang.*, pp. 200–13.

that the author of *Babad Mangkubumi*, who was apparently the Crown Prince himself, combined elements of the two events to make more dramatic history. If the tensions had been as great in 1765 as the *babad* suggests, it is strange that the Company documents do not reflect this. Nevertheless it is certain that Mangkunĕgara's anger was at least a potential threat to the peace at this time. Van Ossenberch wrote in May 1765 that he had lost more than one night's sleep on that account.[68] Perhaps the Dutch Residents were unaware of the potential for hostilities, or if they did realize the possibility it may have been omitted somewhere in the bureaucratic channel from the courts via Sĕmarang to Batavia. There is nothing unlikely about both incidents, of 1763 and 1765, having taken place at a performance of the dance, in which art the adult Mangkunĕgara would have been more accomplished than the youthful Crown Prince. He would therefore have been in a position to be insulting about the young prince's more amateur efforts.

Van Ossenberch's successor as Governor at Sĕmarang, Johannes Vos (1765–71), did not share his predecessor's inclination to favour a marriage between Surakarta and Jogjakarta. On his customary visit to the courts in October 1765, he encouraged the Susuhunan not to allow the marriage unless Ratu Bĕndara were returned to Mangkunĕgara.[69] But the Sultan would not return Ratu Bĕndara. Indeed, it may have been beyond his powers to do so if her determination was as genuine as the documents suggest. Finally the entire proposal was abandoned. Hamĕngkubuwana I told Vos that his son would marry a girl from Jogjakarta.[70]

In December 1765, the Jogjakarta Crown Prince married a daughter of Pangeran Pakuningrat of Jogjakarta. But if Mangkunĕgara or the Dutch were inclined to view this as a sign of defeat for the Sultan and of victory for themselves, they learned that the Sultan had not entirely lost his mastery of the situation. At the same time, Ratu Bĕndara married one Pangeran Dipanĕgara.[71] The Sultan innocently rejected the indignant Dutch

[68] Ossenberch, Memorie, 13 May 1765, in dJ xi, pp. 32–3.
[69] Sĕmarang to Batavia, 15 July 1765 and 15 Nov. 1765, in KA 3049 (OB 1766); Batavia to H.XVII, 31 Dec. 1765, in dJ xi, pp. 46–7.
[70] Sĕmarang to Batavia, 15 Nov. 1765, in KA 3049 (OB 1766).
[71] The wedding festivities for the Sultan's two children are described in B. Mang., pp. 367, 373–5, 378–97.
Dipanĕgara was the son of the dead Pangeran Ngabei Saloringpasar; HB I

objections that he had promised she would not remarry by pointing out, quite correctly, that he had promised no such thing.[72] The Susuhunan was displeased, and Mangkunĕgara furious.[73]

With the marriage of the Crown Prince to a Jogjakarta wife, the Sultan had in effect abandoned the attempted reunification of Java through marriage. For the second time since the Treaty of Gijanti, Mangkubumi's plans had ended in a major defeat. Mangkunĕgara had not been killed, and now the houses of Jogjakarta and Surakarta had not been joined in marriage. He had, however, achieved a partial success. By the remarriage of Ratu Bĕndara to a Pangeran of the Sultanate, he had at least ensured that Mangkunĕgara could not use marriage to claim the Sultan's throne.

Thus, after several years of tension and intrigue, another step had been taken towards a more permanently divided kingdom, another option eliminated. Marriage diplomacy had failed to solve the problem of division. But the succession in Surakarta remained one of the central issues of Javanese politics for several more years, for the Susuhunan had not yet produced a male heir. His eldest daughter was now married to Mangkunĕgara's son, and that prince's line thus seemed most strategically placed to control the succession. This situation also meant more than ever that Mangkunĕgara and his family must be eliminated if the Sultan hoped somehow to reunite the kingdom. But other matters concerned the Javanese in the 1760s as well, and in the following chapter it will be seen that changes occurring both inside and outside the courts were to contribute to an increasing sense of stability as the decade passed.

---

to Batavia, 22 Djumadilakir Alip A.J. 1691 (5 Dec. 1765), in KA 3049 (OB 1766); Poensen, 'Mangkubumi', p. 266. He died in July 1787; Siberg, Memorie, 18 Sept. 1787, in dJ xii, p. 86.

The date of the wedding was 19 Djumadilakir Alip A.J. 1691 or 2 Dec. A.D. 1765; see B. Mang., p. 385; HB I to Batavia, 22 Djumadilakir Alip A.J. 1691 (5 Dec. 1765), in KA 3049 (OB 1766); Sĕmarang to Batavia, 9 Dec. 1765, in KA 3049 (OB 1766).

[72] There are several letters relating to this matter in KA 3049 (OB 1766). See especially HB I to Sĕmarang, Nov. 1765; and HB I to Batavia, 22 Djumadilakir Alip A.J. 1691 (5 Dec. 1765). See also Batavia to H.XVII, 31 Dec. 1765, in dJ xi, p. 47.

[73] Sĕmarang to Batavia, 9 Dec. 1765, in KA 3049 (OB 1766); Batavia to H.XVII, 31 Dec. 1765, in dJ xi, p. 47.

V

ELIMINATING OPTIONS, II: THE END OF REBELLION AND THE BIRTH OF AN HEIR IN SURAKARTA
c. 1761–1771

IN the years immediately after the Ratu Běndara crisis, there was a somewhat unaccustomed quiet about court life in Central Java. Gifts continued to flow from the Dutch to the Javanese monarchs, and Dutch records note the flourishing state of Surakarta in particular.[1] Relations with the Company had not been much affected by the matrimonial diplomatics of the rulers. In late 1764 the Sěmarang Governor commented on his generally friendly relations with Surakarta and Jogjakarta, despite the Sultan's 'well-known hot-tempered constitution'.[2]

Mangkubumi was, however, growing less concerned to cultivate the Dutch as allies. They had failed to rid him of Mangkuněgara, which was the main result he had hoped from the alliance. He had no intention of breaking with Batavia, which provided him with money, guns, and a flow of courtly paraphernalia, and which was for the Javanese a prestigious ally to have. Nor apparently did he have any particular objections to the Dutch race. But if the Company was to be of little military use to him, the Sultan was not much interested in being useful to them. The Dutch now

---

[1] PB III to Batavia, 4 Rědjěb Be A.J. 1688 (20 Jan. 1763), in KA 2985 (OB 1764); Ossenberch, Memorie, 13 May 1765, in dJ xi, p. 34; PB III to Batavia, 5 Puasa Alip A.J. 1687 [*sic*; error for A.J. 1691] (16 Feb. 1766), in KA 3078 (OB 1767).

[2] Sěmarang to Batavia, 10 Nov. 1764, in KA 3016 (OB 1765). On further aspects of relations between the VOC and the Javanese princes, see Sěmarang to Batavia, 11 March 1764, in KA 3016 (OB 1765), reporting HB I's dislike of the Second Resident at Jogjakarta, Luzac (HB I is referred to as 'tiresome'). See also the letters from HB I, PB III, and MN to Sěmarang, May 1765, in KA 3048 (OB 1766), on the occasion of van Ossenberch's replacement by Vos; and *B. Mang.*, pp. 361–3, on the same event, where the date A.J. 1717 is wrong, as is the attribution of the Batavia letter to GG Jacob Mossel (actually GG, 1750–61; P. A. van der Parra was GG in 1765).

began to learn that the extensive limitations theoretically imposed upon the Sultan by the Gijanti treaty could not prevent significant and irritating signs of independence. Military strength was ultimately the key to politics in Java, and it was precisely in that area that the Company found itself balked by the Sultan.

The Dutch garrisons at the courts required permanent fortresses, but the story of their construction was long and frustrating. In early 1765 the Sultan finally agreed to the oft-repeated Dutch request to provide materials for a brick fortress at Jogjakarta.[3] At that time the Dutch 'fortress' hardly merited the name, there being only one wooden building and none of stone or brick. Van Ossenberch believed that in case of a crisis the garrison would have been safer in an open field.[4] Later in 1765 Johannes Vos, the new Governor at Sĕmarang, optimistically prophesied that the brick fortress would be completed before the end of 1766,[5] but at the end of his tenure in 1771 he reported that there had been little progress.[6]

In 1772 J. R. van der Burgh, Vos's successor, again said that both rulers were happy to construct fortresses for the Company at their own expense,[7] and in 1774 Amsterdam was told that both projects were being 'diligently pushed forward'.[8] In 1775 a Dutch engineer's report said the exterior of the Surakarta fortress was complete, the interior buildings were making excellent progress, and the Susuhunan had graciously provided the Dutch with cannon. But the Jogjakarta fortress was moving so slowly that at the same rate it could hardly be done in five years. The Sultan continually employed his subjects in building projects for his own pleasure, leaving the Dutch fortress without a sufficient labour force. Nor were there enough cannon in Jogjakarta.[9]

The same curious pattern of optimistic prophecies followed by pessimistic reports continued for nearly two more decades. At the

[3] Sĕmarang to Batavia, 6 March 1765, in KA 3049 (OB 1766). On the progress of the Jogjakarta fortress, see also Poensen, 'Mangkubumi', pp. 293–5.
[4] Ossenberch, Memorie, 13 May 1765, in KA 3048 (OB 1766). Partially printed in dJ xi, pp. 36–7; full text (ed. R. W. Tadama) in *Berigten* (1857), p. 198.
[5] Sĕmarang to Batavia, 20 May 1765 and 15 Nov. 1765, in KA 3049 (OB 1766).   [6] Vos, Memorie, 24 July 1771, in dJ xi, p. 173.
[7] Sĕmarang to Batavia, 28 Aug. 1772, in KA 3256 (OB 1773).
[8] Batavia to H.XVII, 31 Dec. 1774, in dJ xi, p. 273. Poensen, 'Mangkubumi', p. 295, commented that this was merely 'het oude gezang'.
[9] Sĕmarang to Batavia, 5 Dec. 1775, in KA 3336 (OB 1776).

ELIMINATING OPTIONS II, c. 1761–1771

end of 1776 both fortresses were supposedly receiving their finishing touches,[10] but nevertheless in 1778 the Jogjakarta Resident was ordered to exhort the Sultan to finish the fortress there as quickly as possible.[11] The continual building projects of the Sultan and, by 1778, of the Crown Prince as well, were said to be responsible for the lack of progress. The problem was compounded by suspected profiteering on the part of the Jogjakarta officials who provided the Dutch with building material.[12]

By 1779 the Surakarta fortress was finally declared to be ready for occupation in the following year, but the Jogjakarta project, after fourteen years of construction, 'has made little progress'.[13] In 1780, when the Dutch were fearing an English attack, the Jogjakarta Resident assured his superiors that the fortress there was then being 'worked upon with greater diligence than before'.[14] Yet when van der Burgh turned over the Sĕmarang Governorship to J. Siberg in the same year, he told him that the Sultan's and the Crown Prince's pleasure-constructions were the reason that the fortress was still not completed.[15]

Siberg, like new officials before him, was confident of greater success. In 1781 he loaned the Sultan 10,000 reals for four years, although Mangkubumi was already in debt to the Company for that amount. In return the Sultan said he had ordered his *patih* Danurĕdja to speed up work on the fortress, to please the Governor-General and Council of the Indies.[16] When he made the customary visit to the courts, Siberg sent to Batavia a most optimistic assessment of the state of the fortress,[17] and in 1785 told Batavia that the Jogjakarta project was not only nearly finished, but of an exceptionally high standard.[18] But in 1787 he informed his successor, Jan Greeve, that the construction of the Jogjakarta fortress was less than a success. He hoped it would be finished in another two years.[19]

---

[10] Sĕmarang Politicque Resolutien, 14 Dec. 1776, in KA 3389 (OB 1778).
[11] Sĕmarang to Batavia, 18 April 1778, in KA 3418 (OB 1779).
[12] Id., 24 Dec. 1778, in KA 3418 (OB 1779).
[13] Id., 20 Dec. 1779, in KA 3447 (OB 1780).
[14] Id., 30 April 1780, in KA 3476 (OB 1781).
[15] Van der Burgh, Memorie, 19 Sept. 1780, in dJ xi, p. 417.
[16] Sĕmarang to Batavia, 15 March 1781, in KA 3494 (OB 1782); HB I to Sĕmarang, 1 Mulud Alip A.J. 1707 (Feb. 1781), in KA 3494 (OB 1782); Sĕmarang to Batavia, 15 March 1781, in KA 3492 (OB 1782).
[17] Sĕmarang to Batavia, 5 Sept. 1781, in dJ xii, p. 5.
[18] Id., 1 March 1785, in KA 3597 (OB 1786).
[19] Siberg, Memorie, 18 Sept. 1787, in dJ xii, p. 91.

Greeve reported at the end of 1787 that the slow procurement of timber was partly to blame for the fact that carpentry work at Jogjakarta was sometimes at a standstill.[20] In the following year he reported nothing could be done on a proposal to construct three fortresses guarding the road to Jogjakarta until the fortress at the court was completed.[21] Greeve visited Jogjakarta in 1788 and found the fortress 'in a very clean and well-regulated situation', although a few changes were required. Perhaps pushing his luck, he then spoke to the Sultan about building the three forts on the way to Jogjakarta, but the Sultan proved to be unwilling to undertake this on his own expense. Greeve was uncertain whether to ascribe this 'to his fickle nature or to his thriftiness, which exceeds all imagination'.[22]

The last report on the fortress from the reign of the first Sultan was sent by the Jogjakarta Resident in 1790. In that year the people of the *montjanĕgara* had spent ninety days working on the fortress, which was then said to be very near completion.[23]

This tale of procrastination is a comment not only upon the Sultan's increasing independence and the limitations of the Dutch position. It also suggests something of the workings of the Company's bureaucratic machinery. It is not clear when the Dutch garrison moved into its fortress, or at what point the buildings became of any real military value. It is clear, however, that Hamĕngkubuwana I prevented the Company from establishing a defensible military position in Jogjakarta for much, if not all, of his reign. This was not because the Sultan was unable to provide the resources for constructing the fortress. Although he did face serious economic problems, his construction of the *kraton*, *Taman Sari*, and similar buildings, and in 1785 of massive fortifications around the *kraton*, suggests that means were availabe for the construction of the Dutch fortress as well. This, however, the Sultan was unwilling to see built, for reasons which were presumably connected with his estimation of the relative advantages and disadvantages of a strong Dutch garrison in his city. Fortunately for the Company, there was no need for major military action in Central Java until nearly the end of the Sultan's life, and then its object would be Surakarta, as will be seen in Chapter IX.

[20] Sĕmarang to Batavia, 31 Dec. 1787, in KA 3705 (OB 1789).
[21] Id., 9 May 1788, in KA 3708 (OB 1789).
[22] Id., 29 Aug. 1788, in KA 3708 (OB 1789).
[23] Id., 12 April 1790, in KA 3802 (OB 1791).

ELIMINATING OPTIONS II, c. 1761–1771   123

Rebellions did continue in Java in the late 1750s and the 1760s, but after the submission of Mangkunĕgara they had been of a minor nature. Some of the apparent rebels in Central Java were undoubtedly partisans of the rulers. Thus, when hostilities which had arisen during the Ratu Bĕndara crisis abated late in 1763, the Dutch were aware that many of the so-called *kramans* (rebels) were troops of the Sultanate, whom Mangkubumi then recalled.[24] But there were genuine rebels as well, many of whom were religious leaders of great influence who could easily assemble a following. The significance of the religious element in rebellion was such that the Sĕmarang Governor Johannes Vos seems to have believed the Javanese words *tapa* (ascetic, man of religion) and *kraman* (rebel) to have been synonymous.[25] Several rebels were also connected either to the House of Mataram or to some other distinguished Javanese family.[26] And most of the major insurgents in this period were at one time or another connected with Malang, where Surapati's descendants and Pangeran Singasari controlled a virtually independent domain.

One of the most important rebels of the 1760s was Raden Mas Guntur, also known as Raden Wiratmĕdja. He was descended from a long line of distinguished trouble-makers, beginning with his great-great-grandfather Susuhunan Amangkurat II (1677–1703). His great-grandfather was Susuhunan Amangkurat III (Sunan Mas, 1703–8), who was defeated in the First Javanese War of Succession and exiled by the Dutch in favour of Susuhunan Pakubuwana I (1703–19). Two sons of Sunan Mas, Pangeran Tĕpasana and Pangeran Wiramĕnggala, were brought back to Java at the request of Pakubuwana II, who reportedly desired *pusakas* which they possessed. Both rebelled again, and both were put to death in 1742, the former at Kartasura and the latter at Sĕmarang. Pangeran Tĕpasana had two notable sons. One was Raden Mas Garĕndi (Sunan Kuning), who as a child became the rebel Susuhunan supported by the Chinese insurgents; he was

---

[24] Sĕmarang to Batavia, 16 Dec. 1763, in KA 3016 (OB 1765); Batavia to H.XVII, 31 Dec. 1763, in dJ x, pp. 394–5.
[25] Vos, Memorie, 24 July 1771, in dJ xi, p. 162, refers to 'een voor lange al overledene Javaanse tapa of craman'. See also Batavia to H.XVII, 31 Dec. 1773, in dJ xi, p. 246 and n. 1.
[26] See the comments on the 'lean princes and court dignitaries' and the problems of peace in Java, in Batavia to H.XVII, 31 Dec. 1762, in dJ x, p. 385.

exiled to Ceylon in 1743. The other was Raden Mas Wiratmědja, the father of the rebel Raden Mas Guntur. Guntur had married a daughter of Mangkunĕgara about the time of the latter's submission in 1757, and had then become a subject of Pakubuwana III. He also took his father's name, Wiratmědja.[27]

In August 1761, Guntur and his wife left Surakarta and made their way eastwards, plundering in the Blora and Djipang area. Jogjakarta and Surakarta troops were soon in pursuit of the rebel band, both showing an unusual alacrity in pursuit. Dignitaries who appeared favourable to Guntur were severely punished; one such unfortunate official's head was taken to the Surakarta *alun-alun* (square before the *kraton*) for public display. By the end of 1761 Guntur had successfully taken refuge in the mountainous Malang area, but in early 1762 he came down into Tjĕngkalsewu in north-central Java, and then went southwards to Madiun. His forces, however, were continually being weakened by the attacks of the Javanese rulers' troops. In July 1762 he asked the Dutch to make him *wĕdana* over the lands to the east of Mount Lawu, i.e. the Madiun area, but the Governor of Sĕmarang simply sent Guntur's emissaries to the Susuhunan, who decapitated them, threw their bodies in the river, and impaled the heads on bamboo poles on the *alun-alun*. Suspicions grew that Mangkunĕgara was secretly assisting his son-in-law's rebellion, but before any action could be taken in this regard Guntur was captured and killed by Surakarta forces in September 1762. His wife was returned to her father, Mangkunĕgara.[28]

The unusual vigour with which Guntur had been pursued suggests both Hamĕngkubuwana I and Pakubuwana III believed his rebellion to be of more than usual significance. *Babad Mangkubumi* says he wished to do battle with the two rulers, hoping

---

[27] Van Suchtelen, Lijst der thans in wezen zijnde kinderen, broeders, en susters ... van de Soesoehoenan P. B. II., Nov. 1743, in AN Solo 42 (transcript provided to me by Dr. H. J. de Graaf); Lapro to Sĕmarang, 9 May 1772, in AN Djokjo 34 'Djokjokarta Brieven naar Samarang, 1770–1780'. See also *BG*, vol. xiv, p. 59; vol. xxi, pp. 41, 43. Guntur's submission was reported in PB III to Batavia, 6 Rĕdjĕb A.J. 1682 (28 March 1757), in KA 2802 (OB 1758).

[28] On Guntur, see Sĕmarang to Batavia, 16 Aug. 1761, 15 Sept. 1761, 31 Oct. 1761, 13 Nov. 1761, and 22 Dec. 1761, in KA 2920 (OB 1762); id., 23 April 1762, 23 July 1762, 19 Aug. 1762, and 19 Sept. 1762, in KA 2957 (OB 1763); Batavia to H.XVII, 31 Dec. 1762, in dJ x, pp. 385–6; *B. Mang.*, pp. 150–79.

to share in the control of Java.²⁹ Undoubtedly his descent from Amangkurat II made him a particularly dangerous figure, as did his marriage to a daughter of Mangkunĕgara, whose role in the affair remains unclear. *Babad Mangkubumi* also suggests Guntur possessed *pusakas* handed down from Amangkurat II,³⁰ which would have made his rebellion all the more threatening and his capture all the more desirable.

The possible significance of Guntur's rebellion is also suggested by a document which the Dutch discovered in 1772, when a second 'Raden Wiratmĕdja' appeared in the Dĕmak area and was killed there.³¹ Since the original of that name was apparently killed ten years before, the new rebel was presumably a descendant or partisan of Guntur who took his name and reputation, as was not uncommonly done. It is, of course, also possible that the 'Guntur' killed by the Susuhunan's troops earlier had been falsely identified. The document suggests that Guntur wished to expel the Dutch and to reunify Java in a Kartasura restoration. Its dating is uncertain, although it seems to have been written either between 1730 and 1738 or, rather more likely, in the year of Guntur's rebellion, 1761.³² It took the form of a letter from Guntur's

²⁹ *B. Mang.*, pp. 150–1, Canto XXI (Midjil):

    28. jwantĕn trah ing Mangkuratan nĕnggih
        Mas Guntur raning wong
        engĕt nagri Djawi tumut darbe
        . . .

    29. . . .
        ajun tanḍing djurit
        mĕngsah kalih Ratu

    30. arsa madĕg aneng montjanagri
        . . . .

³⁰ *B. Mang.*, p. 366. There were said to have been two *krises*, one named Kjai Bontit. There are several problems here. The event is wrongly placed in the chronicle between the succession of Vos as Governor of Sĕmarang (ibid., p. 362) and the marriage of the Crown Prince (ibid., pp. 367 ff.), both of which events took place in 1765. Furthermore, the victory over Guntur is ascribed to Jogjakarta troops (see also ibid., pp. 368–71) although the VOC documents cited in n. 28 above say the victory belonged to Surakarta forces. The Dutch, however, also mention a *kris* belonging to this man, which was said to have been taken to Surakarta; Sĕmarang to Batavia, 24 Dec. 1762, in KA 2986 (OB 1764).

³¹ Sĕmarang to Batavia, 9 May 1772, in KA 3256 (OB 1773). See also id., 24 Dec. 1762, in KA 2986 (OB 1764), denying rumours that Wiratmĕdja (Guntur) was still alive.

³² The text is dated Saturday, 25 Sura, Dal, without the year. It was said by the Dutch to be in Kartasura court handwriting ('in teekening van het Carta

grandfather Pangeran Těpasana to other members of his family, and said in part,

Above all you must... remind our son Mas Garěndi [Sunan Kuning] and grandson Mas Guntur and also my nephew Mas Said [Mangkunĕgara I] in holy secrecy that they are descendants of the Court of Mataram and for that reason should conduct themselves as the most magnanimous of all in Java, even though they should suffer the greatest poverty as a result.

Herewith I bless my son Gunawan [i.e. Guntur?] and wish from my heart that he may carry the title of Pangeran Adipati and that he may come out of the northern mountains with victorious weapons and that he may hold that title over the lands of Děmak and Grobogan, that all of Java shall be obedient to him, and that as ruler he will reside in the court of Kartasura. The blessings of the forefathers of Adilangu, Serang[an?], Děmak, Sěsela, Giri, Tuban, Gěgěsang, Ampel, Bonang, Murja, Kalidjaga, Kudus, Kalinjamat, Madjapahit, and Tjěmpa be and remain over him for the rest of his days. And if today or tomorrow he should become Susuhunan ['Keijser'], I pray to God that his rule shall be fortunate and that he may remain steadfast in his faith.

Remember what I told the General, that the Company shall possess Java no longer than to the ninth generation from me, and then Kartasura shall be restored to its previous prosperity.[33]

This invocation of practically every important *pasisir* name connected with the history of Javanese Islam suggests the importance of religion to the author of this document. The significance of Kartasura, symbolizing the glory of the unified Javanese kingdom,

---

Soerase hof'), and itself claims to be by Pangeran Těpasana, who died in 1742. The last Dal-year before A.D. 1742 was A.J. 1663 (A.D. 1738) and the text would therefore appear to have been written in that year or before. Mangkunĕgara seems to have been born about 1724 (see Poensen, 'Mangkubumi', p. 228) and since he is mentioned in the letter, it must have been written thereafter. Thus the date would appear to have been either Dal, A.J. 1655 (A.D. 1730) or Dal, A.J. 1663 (A.D. 1738). But it is noteworthy that 25 Sura, Dal, A.J. 1687 (26 Aug. A.D. 1761) would have been a few days after Guntur left the Surakarta court, and the document may have been originally fabricated or simply recopied and therefore redated at that time. At no time since the introduction of the lunar calendar by Sultan Agung, however, had 25 Sura in a Dal-year in fact fallen upon a Saturday.

[33] Javanese Geschrift, 25 Sura, Dal, as appendix to Sěmarang to Batavia, 9 May 1772, in KA 3256 (OB 1773). The letter is available only in Dutch translation. *B. Mang.*, p. 153, says that Guntur changed his name to 'Pangeran Anom' after leaving Surakarta. Although the Javanese letter mentions the title 'Pangeran Adipati' and not 'Pangeran Anom', both the references may refer to the title of a Mataram Crown Prince, 'Pangeran Adipati Anom'.

ELIMINATING OPTIONS II, c. 1761–1771

is also clear. For the writer, the restoration of that glory meant a return to Kartasura and the expulsion of the Dutch. This was not unlike the appeal of Trunadjaja to Amangkurat II some eighty years before to avoid the Dutch Christians and take the court to Madjapahit so all of Java might know that he was king.[34] The writer of the above letter saw the centre of Java as Kartasura rather than Madjapahit, but he, too, hoped for a restoration of Java's greatness which would recreate the glorious past and rid the island of the infidel. The anti-Dutch and pro-Kartasura appeals of the Těpasana letter suggested the uniting of two themes which were as dangerous for the Javanese rulers as for the Dutch. It was desired not only to expel the infidel, but to reunite the kingdom as well. This was something neither the Susuhunan nor the Sultan could allow anyone but himself to do. In the case of a descendant of the Amangkurats, such ideas were far too dangerous to be tolerated. Guntur had to be eliminated.

Shortly after Guntur's death in 1762 another rebel appeared who was even more clearly in the tradition of the religious insurgent, as was suggested by his name, Abdul Kadir.[35] Whether or not he had anything to do with the Qādirite order, he was apparently a man with considerable religious charisma. The materials on Abdul Kadir are somewhat confusing. His career began in Kědu early in 1763, but there is conflicting information on whether he was a subject of the Susuhunan or of the Sultan. In any case, he attacked areas belonging to Pakubuwana III and then took refuge in the Mt. Ungaran area south of Sěmarang. In April 1763, he defeated Javanese and European troops sent against him by the Company, and thus greatly increased his following. The Kaliwungu and Kěndal areas west of Sěmarang

[34] H. J. de Graaf, 'De Opkomst van Raden Troenadjaja', *Djåwå*, vol. 20 (1940), p. 86, or id., 'Gevangenneming en Dood van Raden Truna-Djaja, 26 Dec. 1679–2 Jan 1680', *TBG*, vol. 85 (1952), pp. 290–1.
[35] The Persian mystic 'Abd-al-Qādir al-Jīlānī (1077–1166) was one of the most revered of Muslim saints. He is connected in the history of Sufi mysticism with the first *ṭarīqah* (brotherhood). He was an extremely popular figure in Indonesia, particularly in the more strongly Islamic areas of West Java (Bantěn) and in Atjeh. The miracles connected with his life were described in several texts in Malay, Sundanese, and Javanese; see G. W. J. Drewes and Poerbatjaraka, *De Mirakelen van Abdoelkadir Djaelani* (Bandung, 1938), and Hitti, *History of the Arabs*, pp. 436–7. Although Abdul Kadir Djaelani, as he was known in Indonesia, was more popular in Bantěn than in Central Java, some MSS. concerning him are of Central Javanese origin, e.g. LOr 7489 and NBS 77; see Pigeaud, *Literature*, vol. ii, pp. 442, 729.

were largely under his control. The Susuhunan showed a particular anxiety to destroy the rebels, and put their home village in Kĕḍu to the sword. But it was Company forces who finally defeated them in late April. Abdul Kadir escaped, however, and was said to have taken refuge in Kĕḍu under the Sultan's protection.[36]

During 1764 suspicions grew that either the Sultan or the Jogjakarta Crown Prince was protecting the rebels.[37] Abdul Kadir himself may have died during this time, or retired peacefully to a hermitage, for interest then shifted to his two sons. The Dutch records call them 'Bagechus' and 'Semaun' or 'Koeda' and 'Smaun'.[38] They were apparently the same as the 'Bagus Kuda' and 'Sĕmangun' described in *Babad Mangkubumi* as 'sons of a true sage'. But they were 'possessed by evil spirits, both wishing to become ruler'.[39] This was, it seems, the point at which royal patrons deserted their protégés. Anything was forgiveable except *lèse majesté*. The two sons of Abdul Kadir were said by the Dutch to be accompanied by one Sĕtjawalantĕn ('Sitjowilanten'), former *patih* of the first Crown Prince of Jogjakarta, who had been poisoned in 1758.[40] Sĕtjawalantĕn does not figure in *Babad Mangkubumi*, but there is one Sĕtjajuda there,[41] as well as in the Pakualaman *babad*, where he is said to have been married to a descendant of the Amangkurats.[42]

Jogjakarta troops displayed a suspicious reluctance to do battle with these rebels, who were finally defeated by the Susuhunan's troops in January 1765. Sĕtjawalantĕn was killed and both Bagus Kuda and Sĕmangun were turned over to the Dutch, who interrogated them. Their confessions clearly implicated both the Sultan

[36] Sĕmarang to Batavia, 9 April 1763, 21 April 1763, 25 April 1763, and 28 May 1763, in KA 2986 (OB 1764).
[37] See Batavia to H.XVII, 31 Dec. 1765, in dJ xi, p. 45, and ibid., n. 1.
[38] Sĕmarang to Batavia, 25 April 1763, in KA 2986 (OB 1764); id., 25 Jan. 1765, in KA 3049 (OB 1766).
[39] *B. Mang.*, p. 345, Canto LII (Kinanṭi):

37. Atmadjeng panḍita tuhu
Kjai Gĕng Tinab kang siwi
Bagus Kuda kang anama
arinja Sĕmangun nami
kasurupan ing drubiksa
prasamjarĕp dadya Adji.

I am at a loss to explain the name Kjai Agĕng Tinab, which is unknown to me from any other source on Abdul Kadir.
[40] Sĕmarang to Batavia, 25 Jan. 1765, in KA 3049 (OB 1766).
[41] *B. Mang.*, p. 345.   [42] Poensen, 'Mangkubumi', pp. 297–8.

ELIMINATING OPTIONS II, c. 1761-1771   129

and the Crown Prince of Jogjakarta, but van Ossenberch continued to doubt these accusations. The Sultan and his court were already apparently developing a capacity to convince the Dutch that their version of events was the correct one. Van Ossenberch sent the two rebels for punishment to the Sultan, upon whose order they were executed.[43]

The confusions surrounding such rebels are not easily dispelled. Nevertheless it seems that Abdul Kadir and his sons were of considerable significance, although the documentation is only fragmentary. They had connections with the world of Islam and very likely to the House of Mataram as well, either as its protégés or through descent or marriage. No indisputable evidence ever appeared regarding the Jogjakarta *kraton*'s relationship to these rebels, and Governor van Ossenberch persistently denied that there was any involvement. Nevertheless it is very likely that the Sultan or his son had extended them protection. Like Sultan Agung before him, perhaps Sultan Mangkubumi was attempting to control and to turn to his advantage religious forces which might otherwise endanger his throne and subjects. The *Babad Mangkubumi* story of the rebels' aspirations to become ruler may provide either the reason they were abandoned by the Sultan or, equally likely, an *ex post facto* justification of the somewhat embarrassing necessity to execute them. The *babad* version of their deaths has them defeated by Company troops, and their heads taken to Sĕmarang.[44] Thus *Babad Mangkubumi* absolved the Sultan and the Crown Prince of responsibility for their defeat or execution.

After the defeat of Mas Guntur and Abdul Kadir,[45] attention shifted to the cauldron of rebellion at Malang. Malang had never been controlled by either the Dutch or the Javanese rulers, and

[43] Sĕmarang to Batavia, 25 Jan. 1765, 6 March 1765, and 20 May 1765, in KA 3049 (OB 1766). See also *B. Mang.*, pp. 345-6.

[44] *B. Mang.*, p. 346.

[45] There were several more minor rebels as well. On one or more rebels called Panĕmbahan, see Sĕmarang to Batavia, 23 July 1762, in KA 2957 (OB 1763); id., 25 April 1763, in KA 2986 (OB 1764); id., 20 Sept. 1764, in KA 3016 (OB 1765).

On Pangeran Natanĕgara, see Sĕmarang to Batavia, 30 Oct. 1762, in KA 2957 (OB 1763).

On Ngabei Djajalĕlana, see Sĕmarang to Batavia, 30 Oct. 1762, in KA 2957 (OB 1763); Vos, Memorie, 24 July 1771, in dJ xi, p. 162.

On Wiradirĕdja, see Sĕmarang to Batavia, 24 Dec. 1762, in KA 2986 (OB 1764).

since early in the eighteenth century the descendants of the Balinese rebel Surapati had lived there as a virtually independent power. Family connections and geographical proximity to Bali made for continuing contacts with the Hindu culture of that island and with its quarrelling princely families, thus probably increasing the explosive potential of Balĕmbangan, lying between Malang and Bali, as well as impeding the progress of Islam in the area. An investigation of the internal history of Balĕmbangan and Malang in the late eighteenth century would be most instructive, but is impossible here.[46] Malang is considered here for its importance in the history of the divided Central Javanese kingdom.

The Malang rebels were of consequence to the Company and to the Javanese rulers not simply because any independent rebel kingdom was dangerous to stability. In addition, Malang was the headquarters of Pangeran Singasari, alias Pangeran Arja Prabudjaka or Prabudjaja, a son of Susuhunan Amangkurat IV (1719–26) and therefore half-brother to Mangkubumi and half-uncle to Pakubuwana III. In 1743, when about sixteen years old, Singasari had rebelled from the court of his half-brother Pakubuwana II at Kartasura.[47] During Mangkubumi's rebellion he had at times fought on the side of the future Sultan and Mangkunĕgara,[48] but after the Gijanti settlement he had submitted neither to the Sultan nor to the Susuhunan.

So long as Singasari remained in Malang, there existed another potential contender for the throne of Mataram whose genealogy and past history were as impeccable as any of the Javanese élite. He had never joined the divided state structure which had emerged in the 1750s as an interim solution to Java's problems. There always remained the possibility, therefore, that Singasari might still attempt what Mangkubumi and Mangkunĕgara had abandoned trying to do. He might drive down from the mountains of Malang, gather a large following from among the élite,

[46] For a summary of the materials on these matters, see de Graaf, *GI*, pp. 233–7, 240–1, 272–5.

[47] See Verijssel, Rapport, 14 Dec. 1743, in AN Solo 42; and van Suchtelen, Lijst der thans in wezen zijnde kinderen, broeders, en susters ... van de Soesoehoenan P.B. II., Nov. 1743, in AN Solo 42. Dr. H. J. de Graaf has provided me with copies of both these documents.

[48] See Louw, *Successie-Oorlog*, pp. 38, 60. See also *BG*, vol. i, p. 6; vol. vi, p. 6; vol. viii, p. 47.

and sweep away the system of division and the three princes who had joined it, along with their Dutch protectors. Such a course of events was extremely improbable, for Singasari was even less likely in the 1760s to achieve a unification of the élite and to defeat all who would oppose him than Mangkubumi and Mangkunĕgara had been in the 1740s and 1750s. But this cannot have prevented the Sultan, the Susuhunan, and Mangkunĕgara from being concerned about even such a remote possibility. Although for several years Singasari had not tested the strength of his following on the field of battle, he was still recognized as an influential figure whose potential to disrupt the Central Javanese *modus vivendi* was not to be underestimated. For the Sultan, as for the other two main princes of Central Java, it was desirable that Singasari should submit to him and thereby contribute to the stability of his authority. Failing this, Singasari would best be eliminated.

Between 1757 and 1762 Sultan Mangkubumi had repeatedly invited Singasari to submit to him, and had promised him a fitting income and status at Jogjakarta. Singasari had replied with a friendly correspondence, for instance informing the Sultan of the impending circumcision of his eldest son in 1760 and receiving a cash gift in reply. But he showed no inclination to abandon the mountains of Malang.[49] Nor could Pakubuwana III persuade him to settle at Surakarta.[50]

In the 1760s relations between the Sultan and Singasari began to change, a process which the Dutch understood only imperfectly. Javanese sources, with their limited concern for chronology, are also somewhat difficult to understand. Nevertheless the broad pattern of events seems clear. According to *Babad Mangkubumi*, about 1762 the Sultan apparently began to lose patience with Singasari's failure to come to Jogjakarta to settle. More ominously, this *babad* indicates that under the influence of Wiranĕgara, one of Surapati's descendants, Singasari began to have imperial

[49] Donkel to Sĕmarang, 13 May 1757 and 5 March 1758, in AN Djokjo 32, 'Djokjokarta Brieven naar Samarang, 1756–61'; Sĕmarang to Batavia, 11 April 1758, in KA 2831 (OB 1759); Donkel to Sĕmarang, 18 Dec. 1760, in AN Djokjo 32, 'Djokjokarta Brieven naar Samarang, 1756–61'; Hartingh, Memorie, 26 Oct. 1761, in dJ x, p. 333; Sĕmarang to Batavia, 19 Sept. 1762, in KA 2957 (OB 1763).

[50] Sĕmarang to Batavia, 11 Nov. 1762 (wrongly dated 11 Oct. in archive copy), in KA 2957 (OB 1763). See also Batavia to H.XVII, 31 Dec. 1766, in dJ xi, pp. 55–6.

aspirations. He took the royal-sounding title *Pangeran Prabudjaja Adi Senapati Ingalaga*, and gave to his son the title of a Crown Prince of Mataram, *Kangdjĕng Pangeran Adipati Anom Hamĕngkunĕgara*. Mangkubumi probably feared that Singasari now intended to make his bid for the throne of Mataram and he ordered Ronggaprawiradirdja to march against Singasari.[51]

These events are reflected, although not confirmed, in Dutch documents. In May 1762 the Sultan asked van Ossenberch to be allowed to take control of Malang. At that time the proposal became confused with other requests concerning Pĕmalang.[52] Once these confusions were cleared up, van Ossenberch had no objections to such an attempted conquest, although Batavia wrongly believed Malang was to the east of the meridian of Pasuruan, and therefore Company territory.[53]

There was some military action in 1762. It does not, however, seem to have been the bloody assault by Dutch, Jogjakarta, and Surakarta troops described in *Babad Mangkubumi*, where the fighting is compared to Surapati's assault on Captain Tack seventy-six years before.[54] Rather, Singasari and the Surapati descendants marched into the Kĕḍiri area, after the Susuhunan's official there had marched away ostensibly to help defend Blitar from Singasari. Singasari was then surrounded in Kĕḍiri by troops of both Javanese rulers, but succeeded in escaping to the mountains.[55] Until early in 1765, it seems the rebels were relatively quiet in their virtually inaccessible mountain refuges.

At the beginning of 1764 it was rumoured that Singasari would submit to the Sultan. Van Ossenberch doubted this, for he believed that Singasari's 'apprehensions of an unpleasant reception

[51] *B. Mang.*, pp. 239–48. In ibid., p. 357, Wiranĕgara's appearance is compared to the collosal *wajang*-figure Kumbakarna (see Anderson, *Mythology*, pp. 17–18). See also n. 57 below.

The major Surakarta *Babad* (LOr 1786) indicates that Singasari occupied Madjapahit as his capital, and that the Dutch were willing to recognize him as a ruler with the title *Panĕmbahan Erutjakra*, a title associated with the Javanese messianic figure of the Just Ruler (*Ratu Adil*); see Vreede, *Catalogus*, pp. 95, 98.

[52] See pp. 106–7 above.

[53] Sĕmarang to Batavia, 11 Nov. 1762 (wrongly dated 11 Oct. in archive copy) in KA 2957 (OB 1763); Batavia to H.XII, 31 Dec. 1762, in dJ x, p. 388.

[54] *B. Mang.*, pp. 250–5. The reference to Captain Tack is in ibid., p. 253. See also H. J. de Graaf, *De Moord op Kapitein François Tack, 8 Febr. 1686* (Amsterdam, 1935).

[55] Sĕmarang to Batavia, 24 Dec. 1762, 16 Jan. 1763, and 1 Aug. 1763, in KA 2986 (OB 1764); id., 30 Jan. 1764, in KA 3016 (OB 1765).

are not unfounded'.⁵⁶ This judgement may, however, have been wrong. *Babad Mangkubumi* indicates that Singasari was again offered the protection of Jogjakarta. He was invited to submit to the Sultan or, if this was not his wish, he might take refuge in the Jogjakarta *montjanĕgara* if he should be defeated by the Dutch. Then a false battle was arranged and 'fought' between Ronggaprawiradirdja's troops and the Malang forces, which the former appeared to lose.⁵⁷

By mid-1765, evidence was mounting that at least some Jogjakarta officials were in contact with the Malang rebels, although van Ossenberch and his successor Vos would not be convinced of the Sultan's responsibility.⁵⁸ Hamĕngkubuwana I produced various somewhat flimsy excuses for not sending out troops, or for calling them back after minor clashes with the enemy. In 1765 he wanted Ronggaprawiradirdja to be present at Jogjakarta for the *Garĕbĕg Mulud* festivities and therefore recalled him to court.⁵⁹ More than once the Sultan used the somewhat remarkable explanation that he could not send out troops since they were needed *inter alia* for the construction of the Company's fortress. Perhaps more truthfully, he said the troops were eating the land bare but had no visible effect on the rebels. It was also found impossible to achieve any real co-operation between the Surakarta and Jogjakarta troops.⁶⁰ Thus it seems that, at the very least, the Sultan had no enthusiasm at this time for the pursuit of Singasari. At the most, he may have had an understanding with him, although *Babad Mangkubumi* is unreliable on other aspects of the Singasari story and may not be a trustworthy source on this matter.

⁵⁶ Sĕmarang to Batavia, 30 Jan. 1764, in KA 3016 (OB 1765).

⁵⁷ *B. Mang.*, pp. 347–59. There follows a story of a victory by the Malang forces over Surakarta troops at Kĕḍiri, and finally the death of Wiranĕgara from illness is reported; ibid., pp. 359–61. The problems of using *B. Mang.* and similar *babads* are illustrated by the fact that the Dutch reported Wiranĕgara had died in 1757; Sĕmarang to Batavia, 19 Sept. 1762, in KA 2951 (OB 1763); and id., 17 Jan. 1771, in KA 3229 (OB 1772). It is impossible to say in such matters whether the Dutch or the Javanese sources are likely to be the more accurate.

⁵⁸ Ossenberch, Memorie, 13 May 1765, in dJ xi, p. 36; Sĕmarang to Batavia, 20 Dec. 1767, in KA 3107 (OB 1768).

⁵⁹ Sĕmarang to Batavia, 15 July 1765, in KA 3049 (OB 1766). On the *garĕbĕg* celebrations, see Groneman, *Garĕbĕg's*; and Soedjono Tirtokoesoema, *De Garebegs in het Sultanaat Jogjakarta* (Jogjakarta, 1931).

⁶⁰ Sĕmarang to Batavia, 6 March 1765, 15 July 1765, and 15 Nov. 1765, in KA 3049 (OB 1766); Batavia to H.XVII, 31 Dec. 1765, in dJ xi, p. 46; Sĕmarang to Batavia, 16 June 1766, in KA 3078 (OB 1767); Batavia to H.XVII, 31 Dec. 1766, in dJ xi, p. 56.

Singasari was a revered individual among the Javanese, who were apparently reluctant to fight descendants of the royal house.⁶¹ As with Mas Guntur and Abdul Kadir, he was also an important religious figure, it seems. *Babad Mangkubumi* calls his battles against the Dutch a Holy War (*prang sabil*),⁶² which was not a common term in the eighteenth-century court texts. Among the rebels in the Malang area were several Muslim 'priests', as the Dutch incongruously called them, including at least one Malay and a 'Moor', by which was presumably intended a non-Indonesian Muslim.⁶³ There is even a somewhat remote possibility that Singasari had been heard of in Mecca, and was believed there to be Susuhunan of Java. Three Arabic letters, ostensibly from a Palembang Muslim in Mecca, were turned over to the Dutch in 1772. They exhorted the three Javanese princes to Holy War against the infidels, and were addressed to the Sultan of Mataram, Pangeran Pakunĕgara (i.e. Mangkunĕgara),⁶⁴ and Susuhunan Prabudjaka in 'Solocarta' (i.e. Surakarta).⁶⁵ It seems possible that this last confused title indicated some knowledge of Prabudjaka (Singasari) on the part of an Indonesian in Mecca. It should be noted that *Babad Mangkubumi* also calls Singasari 'Sunan' of Malang.⁶⁶

But Singasari's fate was to be the same as that of other rebels in the 1760s. Whereas twenty or even ten years before such people were cultivated allies of Mangkubumi and Mangkunĕgara, in the 1760s they had lost their usefulness. The major *dramatis personae* had become part of a new and relatively peaceful system, the rules of which were still being evolved. In this new situation, people like Singasari were an embarrassment and a danger. Rebels could expect only very limited indulgence from one of the Central Javanese princes before being abandoned to their fate or even

---

⁶¹ See Sĕmarang to Batavia, 11 April 1758, in KA 2831 (OB 1759); id., 15 Nov. 1765, in KA 3049 (OB 1766).   ⁶² *B. Mang.*, p. 399.

⁶³ It is not always clear what relationship particular rebels may have had with Singasari. See Sĕmarang to Batavia, 20 Dec. 1767, in KA 3107 (OB 1768); id., 20 Oct. 1768, list of captured rebels, in KA 3140 (OB 1769); id., 18 Nov. 1769, in KA 3169 (OB 1770). See also Batavia to H.XVII, 21 Oct. 1768, in dJ xi, p. 87 n. 2; id., 31 Dec. 1773, in dJ xi, p. 246, and ibid., n. 1, on the problem of possible non-Islamic factors.

⁶⁴ See above, pp. 92–3 n. 70.

⁶⁵ The letters are available only in Dutch translation, dated 22 May 1772, in Sĕmarang to Batavia, 3 June 1772, in KA 3256 (OB 1773). See also below, pp. 150–4. The author appears to have been somewhat confused about the political situation on Java.   ⁶⁶ *B. Mang.*, p. 398.

ELIMINATING OPTIONS II, c. 1761–1771

turned upon by their former benefactor. Moreover, although the Dutch Company was militarily weaker than before, it could now concentrate its forces on a single foe at a time.

In 1767 and 1768 the Dutch launched a series of expeditions against the Balěmbangan area, at a time when the Balinese were temporarily distracted by internal disputes on their own island.[67] Ultimately Javanese and Dutch troops succeeded in assaulting the forces of Pangeran Singasari. On 16 July 1768, the Company's forces captured Singasari himself in the rugged mountains along the south coast of Java. With him were taken various members of his family, including a daughter who subsequently attempted to kill the Dutch commandant Meijer with a *kris*.[68] Singasari was taken to Surabaja, where he indicated a desire to submit to the Susuhunan. The latter wished nothing to do with his troublesome uncle, however, and asked the Company to exile him from Java. From the Sultan came an even stronger denunciation of Singasari as a 'rotten member' which must be amputated.[69] He was therefore sent on to Batavia for banishment, where he died in chains before he could be sent abroad.[70]

The *Babad Mangkubumi* version of Singasari's capture illustrates a greater concern for the Sultan's honour than for historical accuracy. Like the description of the deaths of Abdul Kadir's sons, this story absolves the Sultan of responsibility for ceasing to patronize Singasari and for demanding his banishment. The chronicle claims that the Dutch offered to make Singasari ruler over one-third of Java. He was sufficiently attracted by this offer to agree to negotiations at Surabaja. Upon his arrival there, the perfidious Europeans got him drunk and put him to bed. Singasari subsequently awoke to the sobering realization that he was a prisoner: the doors had been locked from the outside. He was then put on board ship and sent to Batavia.[71]

This version of events in effect made Singasari responsible for

---

[67] There is a considerable correspondence on these expeditions, particularly in KA 3106 and 3107 (OB 1768) and in KA 3139 and 3140 (OB 1769). See also de Graaf, *GI*, p. 273; Sěmarang to Batavia, 18 July 1768, in dJ xi, pp. 77–83; R. F. van Niepoort, Memorie, 9 July 1784, in dJ xii, pp. 53–5.

[68] Meijer, Mudal, to Coop â Groen, Surabaja, 20 July 1768, in KA 3140 (OB 1769) (partially quoted in dJ xi, p. 81 n. 1). See also Batavia to H.XVII, 21 Oct. 1768, in dJ xi, p. 88 n.

[69] Sěmarang to Batavia, 27 July 1768 and 5 Aug. 1768, in KA 3140 (OB 1769).

[70] Batavia to H.XVII, 21 Oct. 1768, in dJ xi, p. 88 n.; id., 31 Dec. 1770, in dJ xi, p. 133.

[71] *B. Mang.*, pp. 404–12.

his own fate. In wishing to become third ruler of Java he was guilty of offending the authority of the Sultan. As was suggested with regard to Abdul Kadir's sons, *lèse majesté* was perhaps the one unforgiveable crime. When Mangkubumi was told of Singasari's capture, he is supposed to have said to Danurĕdja,

> LXIV: 7. . . .
> 'As for younger brother Singasari,
> because he insisted on rebelling,
> Danurĕdja, against me,
> let us have no more [of him]!'[72]

Java must not be divided again nor, of course, must it be united by anyone but the Sultan of Jogjakarta. Anyone guilty of such schemes was undeserving of protection; such a person was a 'rotten member' requiring amputation, as the Sultan had said of Singasari. Thus the Sultan was not answerable for Singasari's fate.

This *Babad Mangkubumi* story is not supported by available Company documentation. That is not to say that the Dutch were above the arrest of an enemy during negotiations. Sunan Mas had been captured in this way in 1708 and Pangeran Dipanĕgara would be taken in the same fashion in 1830.[73] But it seems this did not happen to Pangeran Singasari, who surrendered after a military assault. The *babad* version is apparently sheer invention.

After Singasari's capture the Sultan and the Susuhunan lost interest in Malang. Governor Vos discovered, somewhat to his dismay, that it lay to the south-west of Pasuruan and therefore did not belong to the Company according to the 1743 boundaries. Nevertheless both rulers made it known that they had no objection to Dutch control of the area.[74] It is possible, although unlikely, that the Javanese monarchs were as ignorant of Malang's precise position as Batavia had been.

---

[72] *B. Mang.*, p. 417, Canto LXIV (Ḍanḍanggula):

> 7. . . .
> dene jaji ing Singasari
> ḍasar kudu balila
> Danurdja maring Sun
> lah uwis adja dinawa
> . . . .

[73] See de Graaf, *GI*, pp. 241, 397–8.

[74] Sĕmarang to Batavia, 23 Dec. 1769, in KA 3169 (OB 1770). The 1743 treaty had given the Dutch all of the Balĕmbangan area lying east of a line drawn due south from Pasuruan. Malang is in fact to the west of that line. For the text of the treaty, see PB II-VOC Treaty, 11 Nov. 1743, in dJ ix, p. 438.

ELIMINATING OPTIONS II, c. 1761–1771

For over two years the remnants of Surapati's descendants succeeded in escaping capture. During that time the Sultan co-operated with the Company in pursuing them, although rumours persisted that subjects of Jogjakarta were protecting the rebels. Finally, in January 1771, Jogjakarta troops captured the last of the Malang insurgents. The Sultan delivered them to the Company at Sĕmarang.[75] *Babad Mangkubumi* claims the Sultan had repeated his offer of protection to the rebels. When they had taken refuge with Ronggaprawiradirdja, however, they were uncertain about being conducted to Jogjakarta. They finally agreed to go there, but shortly after their arrival the Sultan delivered them over to the Company. There is no explanation of this behaviour.[76]

The capture of Singasari and of the last of Surapati's descendants marked the end of an era in Javanese history. Surapati's family had been a law unto themselves for nearly ninety years. Singasari had submitted to no one for a quarter-century. Within a few years the last pockets of resistance would be wiped out in Balĕmbangan.[77] The rebellions which had hardly ceased for a century, and which had been probably in part a continuation of pre-Islamic traditions of independence in East Java, would now come to an end. There were still to be rebels and trouble-makers in Java, some of whom would be of considerable significance. But the day of the great rebels of the House of Mataram was over until the nineteenth century. With the end of the great princely rebels, another option to accepting the division of Mataram as a long-range solution to the problem of élite disunity had been eliminated. Barring the sudden and unexpected appearance of a truly messianic figure, there was simply no one left to offer a focus of loyalty alternative to the Susuhunan, the Sultan, and Mangkunĕgara. None of these three had succeeded in unifying

[75] Sĕmarang to Batavia, 30 Aug. 1768, and 20 Oct. 1768 list of captured rebels, in KA 3140 (OB 1769); id., 21 April 1769, in KA 3169 (OB 1770); Sĕmarang to HB I, 20 Dec. 1769, in KA 3169 (OB 1770); Sĕmarang to Batavia, 4 Oct. 1770 and 15 Dec. 1770 list of captured rebels, in KA 3199 (OB 1771); id., 15 Dec. 1770, in dJ xi, p. 123; Batavia to H.XVII, 31 Dec. 1770, in dJ xi, p. 129; Sĕmarang to Batavia, 17 Jan. 1771, in KA 3229 (OB 1772); HB I to Sĕmarang, received 17 Jan. 1771, in KA 3229 (OB 1772).

It is entirely likely that relatives of the Surapati line survived, but the main line of descent seems to have ended. Two rebels said to have been of this family were turned over to the Dutch by PB III in August 1772; Sĕmarang to Batavia, 28 Aug. 1772, in KA 3256 (OB 1773).

[76] *B. Mang.*, pp. 413–18, 420–36.   [77] See de Graaf, *GI*, pp. 274–5.

Java in the past, and none was likely to do so in the future. A major milestone had been passed. It is significant that the major Surakarta *Babad Tanah Djawi* ends its eighteen-volume history of Java with the capture of Singasari and a simultaneous eruption of Mt. Kĕlut.[78] For the author of this text, Singasari's end was a fitting close to a monumental history which had begun with Adam. The eruption of Kĕlut underlined the importance of the event: supernatural phenomena had accompanied it. The segment of the major *babad* known as *Babad Prajud* ('Chronicle of Usurpation'), describing the troubled years since Mangkunĕgara's submission in 1757, also ends with Singasari's fall.[79]

The fall of the Malang rebels was, for the Javanese, the end of an era in a more literal sense as well. As in other cultures, so in Java the perception of time is largely correlative to the numerical system used to define it. There is a tendency to see units of time, especially centuries, as distinct segments of history. The capture of Singasari in A.D. 1768 may suggest little beyond the bare events. But for the Javanese this occurred early in A.J. 1694. The seventeenth century of the Javanese Era was drawing to a close. There existed theories of history, the subject of Chapter VII, which disposed the courtly élite to assume that the turn of the century would be an important time of change. Other events at about this time, also discussed below, suggest this was indeed a significant time for the Javanese courts.

Between 1766 and 1770 relations between Surakarta and Jogjakarta, and between both courts and the Company, had been generally friendly. The animosities of the Ratu Bĕndara affair seem to have been largely forgotten, and there was a rather unusual shared interest in the suppression of rebellion.[80]

[78] LOr 1786, vol. xviii, pp. 402–5. See also Vreede, *Catalogus*, pp. 70–99; and Pigeaud, *Literature*, vol. ii, p. 25. The text was begun in the reign of PB IV of Surakarta (1788–1820) and finished in 1836 in the reign of PB VII (1830–58). The original Leiden MS. was romanized by J. Soegiarto and from that romanization Balai Pustaka published its 31-volume *Babad Tanah Djawi* (1939–41), again in Javanese script. The published Balai Pustaka version, however, ends with the establishment of Surakarta in 1745–6, omitting the remainder of the MS. text. See Ricklefs, 'Consideration', p. 289.

[79] LOr 6755, *Babad Prajud*. See Pigeaud, *Literature*, vol. ii, p. 412. Apparently the 'usurpation' of the title refers to the continuous usurpation of lands belonging to others during this period.

[80] See Sĕmarang to Batavia, 12 March 1766, in KA 3078 (OB 1767); Batavia to H.XVII, 31 Dec. 1766, in dJ xi, p. 55; id., 31 Dec. 1767, in dJ xi, p. 74; Sĕmarang to Batavia, 18 July 1768, in dJ xi, p. 82; Batavia to H.XVII, 31 Dec.

ELIMINATING OPTIONS II, c. 1761-1771

As the Sultan grew older, however, he began to show concern for the succession. Subsequent developments suggest that this, too, was perhaps influenced by the perception of the approaching end of an age. He at times believed he would not live long, or at least so he told the Dutch.[81] This proved to be a gross underestimation of his vitality. Nevertheless his concern for the succession was real, and it seems likely that the failure of his attempts at political marriage had only increased his anxiety for the future. It was even rumoured that he intended to step down in favour of the Crown Prince when the latter reached maturity, spending the rest of his years in religious seclusion in *Taman Sari*.[82] This would have been a possible means of ensuring a regular succession. The Dutch believed that if the Sultan should die, the Jogjakarta Crown Prince and Mangkunĕgara would contend for the Jogjakarta throne, and the death of the Susuhunan would produce similar conflict between Mangkunĕgara and the Sultan for the Susuhunan's position.[83] In either case the outcome was likely to be violent. But Batavia wished to make no formal regulations for succession, believing that uncertainty would make the Javanese princes and their offspring more malleable.[84] This thinking was perhaps in error: uncertainty was more likely to increase instability than to make the situation more controllable.

The Sultan's 'beloved son',[85] the Crown Prince, betrayed few of the troublesome tendencies which would later make his reign as Sultan the object of much European vituperation. During Johannes Vos's years at Sĕmarang (1765-71) the Prince 'governed himself very well'.[86] In 1771 the Sultan commended his son to the Dutch and requested a wife for him from the Company's *pasisir*

1768, in dJ xi, p. 92; Sĕmarang to Batavia, 4 Oct. 1770, in KA 3199 (OB 1771); Batavia to H.XVII, 31 Dec. 1770, in dJ xi, p. 130.

[81] Van der Sluijs to Sĕmarang, 9 May 1761, in AN Djokjo 32, 'Djokjokarta Brieven naar Samarang, 1756-61'.

[82] Ossenberch, Memorie, 13 May 1765, in dJ xi, p. 36.

[83] Ibid., pp. 37-8.

[84] Batavia to H.XVII, 31 Dec. 1765, in dJ xi, pp. 47-8.

In 1792 the Governor of Sĕmarang, van Overstraten, took the more realistic view that it was better to make clear whom the VOC viewed as Crown Prince in order to remove any reason for hope from other ambitious princes; see Sĕmarang to Batavia, 25 April 1792, in dJ xii, p. 257.

[85] Ossenberch, Memorie, 13 May 1765, in dJ xi, p. 35.

[86] Vos, Memorie, 24 July 1771, in dJ xi, p. 172.

lands 'so he can then call himself a son of the Company'.[87] The Governor approved this request, but the first girl proposed by Sĕmarang, from a distinguished Javanese coastal family, was not felt by the Sultan to be suitable and he politely refused her.[88] This affair would seem to have been a curious extension of Javanese marriage diplomacy to a commercial power usually unmoved by such matters. Apparently the Sultan hoped to cultivate the Company's favour toward his son, for he never underestimated the value of having Batavia as an ally so long as such an alliance was profitable to himself. He may have wished to have some influence among the *pasisir* Javanese as well. But Vos's successor, J. R. van der Burgh (1771–80), was to have ample reason to be dissatisfied with the Crown Prince and the proposed marriage was never arranged.

The designs upon the Surakarta succession nurtured by Mangkunĕgara and Hamĕngkubuwana I had to undergo drastic revision in 1768. In the evening of 31 August 1768, a son was born to Susuhunan Pakubuwana III by a major wife.[89] The child survived the perils of early infancy and by about 1771 it had become clear that there was to be an heir to the Surakarta throne.[90]

The birth of the Surakarta Crown Prince entirely changed the political context of Central Java. Both Mangkunĕgara and Mangkubumi must have received the news with considerable dismay. Barring the untimely demise of the young heir, neither the Sultan nor Mangkunĕgara would see his descendants upon the Susuhunan's throne. Such an outcome had already been rendered improbable for the Sultan by the failure of his marriage politics before 1765; now it had been rendered impossible. Nor would Mangkunĕgara's family become more than the secondary princes of Surakarta, even which relatively humble status was not yet

---

[87] HB I to Sĕmarang, received 17 Jan. 1771, in KA 3229 (OB 1772).
[88] Sĕmarang to HB I, 17 Jan. 1771, in KA 3229 (OB 1772); Vos, Memorie, 24 July 1771, in dJ xi, p. 172.
The young lady was a daughter of the Regent of Paṭi, Raden Arja Mĕgatsari.
[89] PB III to Batavia, 26 Djumadilawal Dje A.J. 1694 (9 Oct. 1768), in KA 3139 (OB 1769).
The date of the birth was 18 Rabingulakir. It is not entirely clear who was the mother of the child, the future PB IV. An early Surakarta *sĕngkala* list, BM Add. MS. 12323 (B), identifies her only as the Ratu Kĕntjana (f. 43ʳ), who had been raised to that title in A.J. 1688 (A.D. 1762). She had previously been known as Raden Aju Kilen (f. 42ʳ).
[90] See Vos, Memorie, 24 July 1771, in dJ xi, p. 169.

assured to his descendants. Even Mangkunĕgara's success in 1762 in marrying his son to Pakubuwana III's eldest daughter had now come to nothing. His apparent control over the Surakarta succession had become meaningless, for now the Susuhunan had produced a male heir who could succeed directly, regardless of to whom his other children were married. Another milestone on the route to a permanent division of Java had now been passed; another alternative path had been blocked.

By the end of the 1760s the Central Javanese courtly élite had learned several rather disheartening lessons, the last of which had been the birth of the Surakarta Crown Prince. They had concluded in the 1750s that warfare would not reunify Java. Subsequently they had also learned that marriage diplomacy was of no avail. Meanwhile the system of division itself had allowed the devastated island again to prosper, and the inertial weight of the system must have increased with each peaceful harvest. Major rebels who were outside the system and who might challenge it had disappeared in the course of the 1760s. Thus, political possibilities were now reduced to two major courses. One would be forcefully and violently to attempt again to impose the hegemony of one of the three principals upon the others. But the Javanese élite must all have known that this was at the very best a hazardous course which was unlikely to end in success. No one had even the degree of nearly-unanimous support which in the 1750s had proved insufficient to win Mangkubumi hegemony over Java. And the Dutch could still throw their support to the losing side and prevent the final victory of any one contender, as they had always done. But there remained a second option: to accept that the formal division of Mataram was a viable long-term solution to the very old and traditional problem of disunity among the élite. Mangkunĕgara at first seemed to incline again toward the former and more violent approach, which was appropriate to both his status and his temperament. But the Sultan and the Susuhunan tended now toward the latter course of stability.

VI
PREPARING FOR A NEW AGE
c. 1768–1775

As the end of the seventeenth century of the Javanese Era approached,[1] the Central Javanese political situation moved towards greater stability. The end of the major rebellions, particularly symbolized by Pangeran Singasari's capture, was a major step forward. This event, along with the birth of the future Pakubuwana IV, both within about six weeks in 1768, symbolized the beginning of this progress towards a more regular and peaceful political life.

The general direction of events described in the preceding chapters had moved more and more towards the acceptance of the division of Mataram as a long-term rather than as a temporary solution. But this was unprecedented in the Javanese experience, for division had always been a temporary and anomalous, if a constantly recurring, circumstance. If division was now to become permanent, the Javanese state must somehow adapt its traditional standards to this untraditional situation. In the realm of administration, the formal structure of division must be assembled. And in the field of legitimation, division must be explained and made to seem right to the courtiers of each ruler; it must be shown not to offend cosmic standards of harmony lest each ruler lose much of the legitimative lustre which attracted followers to him. In Chapter VII will be discussed detailed theories of history which led the Javanese to suspect that now, as the century drew to a close, change could be expected. That chapter will suggest how those theories were valuable in legitimizing the division of Java, to which the Javanese élite had been forced to turn as a permanent form of settlement. In the present chapter the formal structure of ad-

[1] The reader may wish to refer to Appendix IV, giving date conversions for the Javanese calendar. For more detailed expositions, see the article 'Tijdrekening' in *Encyclopaedia van Nederlandsch-Indië* (9 vols.; 's-Gravenhage, 1917–1940) or Balai Poestaka, *Djidwal memindahkan tahoen Djawa dan 'Arab ketahoen Maséhi* (Batavia, 1932).

ministration will be considered. Here, important steps were taken to reduce the level of instability in Javanese political life. These steps were apparently taken at least in part because of the expectation of changes to come at the end of the century, which made each of the three main princes wish to defend himself against the possibility that these changes would unseat him. At the end of this period, as the new century began, Java would have substantially completed her own stabilization, a process in which the Dutch played only an indirect role. The result was to give the divided kingdom a peaceful and efficient system of administration which would for the first time provide a basis for a permanent partition.

The greatest general impediment to political stability was the lack of any formalized relationship between the two courts. Conflicts continually arose for which there were no means of settlement except warfare or appeal to the arbitration of an outside power, the Dutch East India Company. There were no customary means for two *kratons* to deal with one another on a permanent and equal basis. This problem, if never entirely resolved, was considerably ameliorated in the years after 1768, thereby further contributing to political tranquillity. By the end of this transitional period extending well into the 1770s, the administrative foundations had been laid for a permanently divided Javanese kingdom.

The first steps in this direction were taken with regard to the incessant land disputes. The complex land boundaries established at Gijanti in 1755 and at Klĕpu thereafter had often caused turmoil. The system was prone to local disputes which easily ended in violence; it was a relatively simple matter for a Javanese notable to plunder or usurp villages belonging to his enemies. The last time this had happened on a significant scale was during the Ratu Bĕndara affair of 1763. Then, the hostilities between Mangkunĕgara and the Sultan had very nearly ended in full-scale warfare.[2]

Most of the *desas* taken during the Ratu Bĕndara affair were returned to their rightful sovereigns in the course of 1764. Mangkunĕgara was accused of retaining certain villages belonging to Jogjakarta, but the crisis soon passed. It is interesting that Mangkunĕgara responded to a reprimand from Pakubuwana III by writing to the *bupati* of Sĕmarang, Sura Adimĕnggala, to protest his

[2] On Klĕpu, see p. 89 above; on the Ratu Bĕndara crisis, see pp. 110–15 above.

innocence.³ This was consistent with a tendency apparent in Javanese court life since the previous century to appeal to the outsider Europeans or their representatives to settle internal quarrels. This was necessitated by the fact that the Javanese state still offered no other means to settle conflicts between powerful princes short of warfare or the threat of warfare.

In 1767 and 1768, Mangkunĕgara again helped himself to villages belonging to Jogjakarta. Hamĕngkubuwana I, growing wise, timid, or diplomatic with age, turned to the Dutch and asked them to organize a conference to settle the dispute. Governor Vos did not wish to concern himself with this incident, but he was subsequently approached by both rulers about a general conference on land problems. The increase of population since the end of the wars had, in any case, made a revision of the Book of Klĕpu necessary. This project Sĕmarang approved and subsequently the *patihs* and Dutch Residents at the two courts met in Central Java late in 1768.⁴

The resultant land contract was not signed in Central Java. The *patihs* and Residents proceeded to Sĕmarang for that ceremony. On 28 November 1768, in the *dalĕm* (residence) of Sura Adimĕnggala, the new contract was duly signed and sealed. Previous agreements on the subject were turned over to the Secretary of the municipal administration (*Secretaris van Politie*), who destroyed them. Thus was supposedly achieved a new regulation for the population not included in the Book of Klĕpu. But after the signing a new claim was immediately submitted by Pakubuwana III's side, which Danurĕdja rejected for the Sultan's. Both parties agreed to turn the question over to Governor Vos, who decided in favour of the Sultan. This was then made a part of the contract.⁵

---

³ Sĕmarang to Batavia, 7 April 1764, in KA 3016 (OB 1765). As *bupati* of Sĕmarang, Sura Adimĕnggala was the chief Javanese official in the Company's coastal lands.

⁴ Sĕmarang to Batavia, 18 July 1768, in dJ xi, pp. 82–3; id., 21 April 1769, in KA 3169 (OB 1770). The meeting was planned to be held at Kadisono ('Cadessana') which was not, as Vos said, half-way between the two courts. It is in the Sleman district north-west of Jogjakarta.

⁵ HB I–PB III Contract, Sĕmarang, 28 Nov. 1768, in KA 3169 (OB 1770). See also BM Add. MS. 12323 (B), f. 43ʳ, on the meeting between the *patihs*, followed by the trip to Sĕmarang: Dipati Mangkupradja, Dipati Danurdja panggijan ing Kalĕpu [*sic*], pabĕn bumi tanpa dados, ladjĕng mring Sĕmawis, Ngahad 12 Rabingulakir, tjatur wĕdana ngojag bumi [A.J. 1694] Dje.

PREPARING FOR A NEW AGE, c. 1768-1775   145

The land problem was still not settled to everyone's satisfaction. Although Vos sent an encouraging report to Batavia on the subject,[6] further negotiation was already required towards the end of 1769. That meeting had to be postponed for the fasting-month (Puasa), and for the replacement of the incompetent Surakarta *patih*.[7] The old Mangkupradja had served Pakubuwana III since the death of Pringgalaja in 1755, and was known to be a friend of the Company. He had never been notable for his competence, however, and his inability seems to have kept pace with his advancing age.[8] In late 1769, Pakubuwana III claimed to have discovered that Mangkupradja was delaying the land settlement and falsifying his reports. He resolved to have a new *patih*, and Batavia subsequently approved the selection of one Sasradiningrat, who in April 1770 became the third *patih* to serve Pakubuwana III.[9]

The new land negotiations were hampered by an apparent lack of information about the situation in outlying districts and by unnecessary quibbling and 'hair-splitting', as Vos called it.[10] Nonetheless, another contract was finally signed and sealed under Vos's supervision at Sĕmarang on 28 November 1770. In January, the two rulers ratified it.[11] Yet even after more than two years of negotiation and two contracts the land problems were still not

[6] Sĕmarang to Batavia, 21 April 1769, in KA 3169 (OB 1770).
[7] Sĕmarang to HB I, 11 Nov. 1769, in KA 3169 (OB 1770); HB I to Sĕmarang, received 24 Nov. 1769, in KA 3169 (OB 1770); Sĕmarang to PB III, 15 Dec. 1769, in KA 3169 (OB 1770). Puasa A.J. 1695 began in late December 1769 and ended in late January 1770.
[8] See Sĕmarang to Batavia, 23 July 1762, in KA 2957 (OB 1763); Ossenberch, Memorie, 13 May 1765, in dJ xi, pp. 34-5.
[9] Sĕmarang to HB I, 11 Nov. 1769, in KA 3169 (OB 1770); HB I to Sĕmarang, received 24 Nov. 1769, in KA 3169 (OB 1770); PB III to Sĕmarang, 13 Dec. 1769, in KA 3169 (OB 1770); Sĕmarang to PB III, 15 Dec. 1769, in KA 3169 (OB 1770); PB III to Sĕmarang, received 22 Dec. 1769, in KA 3169 (OB 1770); Sĕmarang to Batavia, 23 Dec. 1769, in KA 3169 (OB 1770); id., 21 April 1770, in KA 3198 (OB 1771).
B. Mang., pp. 368-71, claims that Mangkupradja fell from PB III's favour because of his lack of military success against the Malang rebels and Mas Guntur. Like much of the rest of this part of the chronicle, this story is sheer invention, and chronologically rather confused.
[10] Sĕmarang to HB I, 11 Nov. 1769, in KA 3169 (OB 1770); Sĕmarang to Batavia, 23 Dec. 1769, in KA 3169 (OB 1770).
[11] Sĕmarang to Batavia, 4 Oct. 1770, in KA 3199 (OB 1771); HB I-PB III Contract, Sĕmarang, 28 Nov. 1770, in KA 3199 (OB 1771) (see also dJ xi, p. 123 n. 1); Sĕmarang to Batavia, 15 Dec. 1770, in dJ xi, p. 123; Batavia to H.XVII, 31 Dec. 1770, in dJ xi, p. 131; Sĕmarang to Batavia, 17 Jan. 1771, in KA 3229 (OB 1772); Vos, Memorie, 24 July 1771, in dJ xi, pp. 167-9.

completely resolved. Clearly an entirely new land regulation would ultimately be required. For the time being, however, the situation had been improved.

Mangkunĕgara was not in the congenial mood which the Sultan and the Susuhunan seemed to share. Early in 1772, after several years of relatively peaceful behaviour, he considered taking the initiative again in a manner which caused panic among the Company's officials. The extent and purpose of the prince's plotting were never clarified. The initial reports to the Dutch were almost certainly exaggerated, and the Company overreacted. But it seems certain that, at the very least, Mangkunĕgara was conspiring to increase his independence of the Susuhunan.

In mid-January 1772, Mangkunĕgara wrote to the new Governor at Sĕmarang, van der Burgh, replying to the latter's New Year wishes. He said he was well enough, but would be a good deal better if he could regain Ratu Bĕndara. And furthermore would van der Burgh please intervene with the Susuhunan to give Mangkunĕgara certain lands, and with the Sultan to pay off a debt which was said to be outstanding.[12] If the Governor was taken aback at Mangkunĕgara's aggressive response, he would shortly have still greater cause for concern.

Rumours soon spread that Mangkunĕgara was in contact with rebels in Balĕmbangan, and that he was harbouring what were said to be remnants of the Surapati family. He was said to be conspiring *inter alia* with the old *patih* Mangkupradja and with Judanĕgara of Banjumas, the son of Danurĕdja of Jogjakarta. There was considerable scepticism about some of these reports, but the Surakarta Resident van Straalendorff began to take them seriously. His fears focused upon the annual celebration of the *Garĕbĕg Bĕsar* in March 1772. Apparently the Susuhunan feared Mangkunĕgara had some evil design on van Straalendorff's life, and advised him not to appear in public at the *Garĕbĕg* festivities. The Susuhunan would not appear either.[13]

[12] MN to Sĕmarang, 15 Jan. 1772, in KA 3256 (OB 1773).
[13] Gondelagh, Pasuruan, to Sĕmarang, 12 Dec. 1771, in KA 3256 (OB 1773); van Straalendorff to Sĕmarang, 27 Jan. 1772, in KA 3256 (OB 1773); Sĕmarang to Batavia, 7 March 1772, in KA 3256 (OB 1773); van Straalendorff to Sĕmarang, 13 March 1772 and 14 March 1772, in KA 3256 (OB 1773); Lapro to Sĕmarang, 16 March 1772, in KA 3256 (OB 1773).

Garĕbĕg Bĕsar is celebrated on 10 Bĕsar, which in A.J. 1697 should have fallen upon Sunday, 15 March 1772. The Dutch records, however, indicate that the celebration was on 14 March.

Van Straalendorff determined to feign illness to avoid the *Garěběg*. He sent his adjutant first to Pakubuwana III and then to Mangkunĕgara to announce his sudden indisposition. At Mangkunĕgara's *dalĕm* the adjutant announced himself and was asked his purpose in coming. He replied it was necessary to speak to Mangkunĕgara in person, whereupon he was required to enter. Once inside the residence, his reception was less than cordial. He had first to pass between two rows of pikes, at the end of which he discovered the corpulent Mangkunĕgara dancing in front of his people. While the unfortunate adjutant looked on, the prince ordered his troops simultaneously to load their carbines, blunderbusses, and pistols. Only then might the adjutant announce that the Resident would not appear at the *Garěběg* because of illness, and that the Susuhunan would also not be present. Mangkunĕgara sagely observed that this was a rather sudden illness, adding that he would not attend the *Garěběg* himself if the Susuhunan were not going to be present.[14] Withdrawing from the *dalĕm*, the adjutant must have felt that the rumours about Mangkunĕgara were not entirely unfounded.

The following day van Straalendorff somewhat unwisely went to see Mangkunĕgara himself. He did so in order to deliver a letter from van der Burgh to the prince, advising him that Sěmarang's intercession on his behalf was possible only if he remained true to the Company. Mangkunĕgara expressed surprise that the Resident's illness allowed him to go out, but the resolute adjutant pointed out that the Company's orders must be followed whether one was ill or not. This moral example did not much impress the prince, who told van Straalendorff to go home since he was ill. Mangkunĕgara would send his reply later.[15]

Mangkunĕgara informed van Straalendorff the next day of his continuing attachment for the Company.[16] But rumours continued to proliferate, and Governor van der Burgh at Sěmarang soon began to believe them, his credence encouraged by the behaviour of Mangkunĕgara before *Garěběg Běsar*.

It was rumoured, investigated, denied, and then rejected that the Sultan was involved in the plot with Mangkunĕgara, whatever

[14] Van Straalendorff to Sěmarang, 14 March 1772, in KA 3256 (OB 1773). For Mangkunĕgara's physique, see Vos, Memorie, 24 July 1771, in dJ xi, p. 169.
[15] Van Straalendorff to Sěmarang, 16 March 1772, in KA 3256 (OB 1773); Sěmarang to Batavia, 18 March 1772, in KA 3256 (OB 1773).
[16] Van Straalendorff to Sěmarang, 16 March 1772, in KA 3256 (OB 1773).

it might be.[17] A nephew of the Sultan, Pangeran Arja Kusumajuda of Jogjakarta, was implicated, defended by the Sultan, arrested by him, then again set free. But in 1775 he died suddenly and mysteriously.[18] It seems he had indeed been in contact with Mangkunĕgara, but the details were never discovered by the Dutch.

In this tense situation, the Company was deeply concerned for its own military position, the garrison at Sĕmarang then being so weak that the corps of dragoons had not a single officer. Preparing for the worst, Batavia ordered late in March that Mangkunĕgara should be arrested if it seemed necessary to do so, although there was still no proof of any of the accusations.[19]

The prince wrote to van der Burgh in April expressing innocent concern about the common gossip going around. He denied there was any truth in these tales and said, 'I rely entirely on the Company, for it is my father and mother in life and in death.' This picture of innocence was somewhat marred by Mangkunĕgara's request that he be free to choose when or whether to appear before the Susuhunan in audience, which he disliked being compelled to do.[20] This was in conflict with his agreement in 1757 to appear on regular audience days,[21] and the Company could not agree to his new request. It seems the purpose of the entire exercise may have been to achieve this greater independence of the Susuhunan.[22] If so, the attempt failed, although changed circumstances eighteen years later would crown a similar attempt with success.

By April the fears of the Company and the Susuhunan were subsiding, and Mangkunĕgara was not arrested. The earlier re-

[17] Sĕmarang to Batavia, 18 March 1772, in KA 3256 (OB 1773); Lapro to Sĕmarang, 22 March 1772, in KA 3256 (OB 1773).
[18] Lapro to Sĕmarang, 19 March 1772, in KA 3256 (OB 1773); Sĕmarang to van Straalendorff, 21 March 1772, in KA 3256 (OB 1773); Lapro to Sĕmarang, 22 March 1772, in KA 3256 (OB 1773); Danurĕdja, Relaas, received Sĕmarang 29 March 1772, in KA 3256 (OB 1773); Sĕmarang to Batavia, 1 April 1772, in KA 3256 (OB 1773); Lapro to Sĕmarang, 8 April 1772 and 11 April 1772, in KA 3256 (OB 1773); HB I to Sĕmarang, received 13 April 1772, in KA 3256 (OB 1773); Sĕmarang to Batavia, 20 April 1772, in KA 3256 (OB 1773); id., 31 Dec. 1775, in KA 3362 (OB 1777).
[19] Sĕmarang to Batavia, 18 March 1772, in KA 3256 (OB 1773); id., 5 July 1777, in KA 3391 (OB 1778).
[20] MN to Sĕmarang, 12 April 1772, in KA 3256 (OB 1773).
[21] See Batavia to H.XVII, 31 Dec. 1757, in dJ x, p. 316.
[22] See Sĕmarang to Batavia, 20 April 1772, in KA 3256 (OB 1773).

PREPARING FOR A NEW AGE, c. 1768-1775   149

ports and rumours were seen to have been exaggerated.[23] But in May the Susuhunan accused two members of his family and the demoted *patih* of a plot which may or may not have involved Mangkunĕgara. Indeed, this new plot may have existed nowhere but in the Susuhunan's imagination, encouraged by his brother Pangeran Purbaja. In any case, the supposed plotters, not including Mangkunĕgara, were arrested and exiled from Java. Pakubuwana's brother Danupaja and his nephew Martasana joined the perpetual colony of Javanese aristocrats on Ceylon, where Martasana's father had also been sent in 1749. Mangkupradja was sent to the island Edam in the bay of Batavia, where he died.[24]

The true nature of Mangkunĕgara's plots, if indeed they had existed at all, was never discovered. It is clear, however, that he and the Susuhunan were at odds in 1772, and that Mangkunĕgara was unhappy with the restrictions imposed upon him by his subsidiary position at Surakarta. He was apparently apprehensive for his future at the court, an anxiety perhaps encouraged by the approaching end of the century. This problem will be considered below.

In July and August 1772, van der Burgh made the customary new Governor's tour of the courts. There he was able to reconcile Mangkunĕgara and the Susuhunan, thus taking another step towards a new *adat* which would make possible the administration of a divided kingdom. Pakubuwana III complained that Mangkunĕgara had not appeared at his audience for seven years, that the prince's armed entourage was too numerous, and that in various ways he failed to pay appropriate respect to the Susuhunan. Mangkunĕgara claimed in defence that the Susuhunan and his court officials subjected him to continuous minor insults unworthy of his status, ancestry, and age. He protested the misfortunes his family had suffered, particularly the loss of Ratu

[23] Lapro to Sĕmarang, 26 March 1772, in KA 3256 (OB 1773); Sĕmarang to Batavia, 1 April 1772, 20 April 1772, and 9 May 1772, in KA 3256 (OB 1773).
[24] PB III to Sĕmarang, 20 Sapar A.J. 1698 (received 23 May 1772), in KA 3256 (OB 1773); Sĕmarang to PB III, 24 May 1772, in KA 3256 (OB 1773); van Straalendorff to Sĕmarang, 26 May 1772, in KA 3256 (OB 1773); Sĕmarang to Batavia, 3 June 1772, in KA 3256 (OB 1773); PB III to Sĕmarang, 19 Rabingulawal A.J. 1698 (received 23 June 1772), in KA 3256 (OB 1773); Sĕmarang to Batavia, 5 July 1772, in KA 3256 (OB 1773); van der Burgh, Memorie, 19 Sept. 1780, in dJ. xi, p. 407.
Martasana's father Adinĕgara was among the princes exiled when PB III became Susuhunan in 1749.

Běndara, claiming that after her loss he had been given permission to appear at court or not, according to his wish. He begged the Company's protection and grace for himself and in particular for his children. This concern for his children suggests that Mangkuněgara, like the Sultan, was beginning to consider the problems of succession and inheritance.

Van der Burgh succeeded in reconciling this conflict, in which matters of dignity were the central question. Pakubuwana III granted Mangkuněgara the lands he wished, thus raising his status, and Mangkuněgara abandoned his financial claim against the Sultan. He swore to appear at the Susuhunan's audiences and not to employ an entourage greater than his status allowed. These and related matters were made into an agreement dated 17 July 1772.[25] At the same time, Mangkuněgara returned to Jogjakarta a daughter of Ronggaprawiradirdja who had fled and taken refuge with him.[26] Thus the peace, which had seemed to be threatened, was buttressed by a new regulation of the relationship between Mangkuněgara and the Susuhunan. This had been achieved by the Company performing the mediatory role. Like Hartingh at Gijanti, van der Burgh was playing the *ḍalang*.

Although Mangkuněgara behaved properly after this new agreement, the Dutch were concerned for the future. Van der Burgh believed that sooner or later the prince would again cause trouble, either if one of the rulers should die, or if Mangkuněgara should succumb to the influence of religious trouble-makers.[27] Such religious figures were not apparently involved in the troubles of 1772,[28] but in May 1772 fresh evidence of attempted spiritual influence upon Mangkuněgara was discovered.

A *hadji* (pilgrim) returned from Mecca to Surakarta in 1772, where he suddenly died. Among his possessions were found three letters in Arabic, ostensibly from a Palembang Indonesian in

---

[25] Sěmarang to Batavia, 28 Aug. 1772, in KA 3256 (OB 1773). See also dJ xi, p. xxxvii; and Batavia to H.XVII, 31 Dec. 1772, in dJ xi, p. 325.

[26] Sěmarang to Batavia, 28 Aug. 1772 and 24 Sept. 1772, in KA 3256 (OB 1773).

[27] Sěmarang to Batavia, 20 April 1772, in KA 3256 (OB 1773).

[28] At one point 2 *ḍukuns* (shaman) appeared in the reports concerning the plots, but their presence in a particular area was not connected to Mangkuněgara's suspected machinations. They were said to be the butt of local jokes for the inefficacy of their magic. See Danurědja, Relaas, received Sěmarang 29 March 1772, in KA 3256 (OB 1773); Anggatruna, Relaas, received Sěmarang 29 March 1772, in KA 3256 (OB 1773).

Mecca addressed to the Sultan, the Susuhunan,[29] and Mangkunĕgara. The Surakarta *patih* turned over these letters, with a banner inscribed in Arabic, to the Dutch Resident, claiming that no one else knew of their existence.[30] The Company had reason to hope this was the case. The letters to the Susuhunan and the Sultan encouraged them to defend the Islamic faith against the infidels, for which Paradise would surely be their reward.[31] The Dutch felt this to be of no unusual significance. The letter to Mangkunĕgara, however, aroused their concern.

The letter-writer invoked God's blessing and forgiveness upon Mangkunĕgara, assuring him that,

> Even more shall God forgive the sins of the most pious persons who are like Pangeran Mangkunĕgara, whom He has created to gain such great honour in the world, as well as because Your Highness is a royal descendant of the House of Mataram, to which God and His Prophet Muḥammad give grace overflowing. Thus Your Highness' justice is known everywhere. Moreover may it please Your Highness to consider the words of the *Qur'ān*, that a few people can indeed overcome a great force.[32]
>
> Furthermore, may it please Your Highness to consider that in the *Qur'ān* stand written the following words, saying thus,
>
> That if someone dies in Holy War[33] you must not say that he is dead, for God has said that the soul of such a man enters a great dove which

---

[29] The possibility that this letter may have been intended for Pangeran Singasari was discussed above, p. 134.

[30] Sĕmarang to Batavia, 3 June 1772, in KA 3256 (OB 1773). The Arabic inscription makes little sense in the romanized Dutch version: 'Erahman Erachim Mohamat Rassoel Loesah [Loelah?] Abdulla.'

[31] 'Palembangar Samat', Mecca, to 'Sulthan in de Mattaram, zoon van den Soesoehoenang Dipatte'; and 'Palembangar Abdul Samat', Mecca, to 'Soesoehoenang Praboedjoko te Solocarta, zoon van den Soesoehoenang Praboedjoko, Sulthan van het Javase Rijk'; Dutch translations dated 22 May 1772, in Sĕmarang to Batavia, 3 June 1772, in KA 3256 (OB 1773).

[32] Cf. *Qur'ān*, Sura VIII, The Spoils, 65 ff. (Arberry's translation, vol. i, pp. 204–5):

> O Prophet, urge on the believers to fight. If there be twenty of you, patient men, they will overcome two hundred; if there be a hundred of you, they will overcome a thousand unbelievers, for they are a people who understand not.
>
> Now God has lightened it for you, knowing that there is weakness in you. If there be a hundred of you, patient men, they will overcome two hundred; if there be of you a thousand, they will overcome two thousand by the leave of God; God is with the patient.

[33] The Dutch text has 'oorlog van besigie', which I take to be an error for 'oorlog van religie', i.e. 'war of religion' or Holy War.

takes it directly to Heaven. . . .³⁴ And thus must such more and more be in Your Highness' heart, for it [the soul of one fallen in Holy War] is like a flower whose fragrance is smelled from sunrise to sunset. Yea, even all of Mecca and Medina, with the Malay Lands, wonder at the pleasing fragrance of it. And all men pray to God that Your Highness may triumph over all your enemies. May Your Highness ponder the saying of Muḥammad, who said, kill all those who do not follow the Islamic faith, unless they should come over to Your Highness [ten sij denselven tot uwE geloofd koomen].³⁵

Therefore, the writer of this, Seh Muḥammad, has a great desire, if it should please the Omnipotent, to see the appearance of Your Highness' feet; the reason I wish to see Your Highness is that the news of your goodness shines forth like a diamond. . . . Have courage that you shall always be fortunate if you exert yourself in the fear of God; fear not misfortune and flee all evil; if someone does such, he shall see heaven without clouds and earth without uncleanliness . . .

The author then conveyed a *djimat* (amulet) from 'Siti Fatimah, daughter of Abdullah', which would ensure victory on the battlefield, thereby protecting the Islamic faith. This was presumably a reference to the banner found with the letters. This *djimat* was sent, the letter said, because in Mecca it was known that Mangkunĕgara was feared in battle; he should use it with God's blessing for the destruction of his enemies and all those who were not Muslims. Mangkunĕgara was also sent the blessings of

the old God-fearing of Mecca and Medina, namely Ibrahim, Imām Shāfi'ī, Imām Ḥanafī, Imām Malikī, and Imām Ḥanbalī, and also from all the others of these places who unanimously wish that the blessings of the Prophet and of His four great apostles Abū Bakr, 'Umar, 'Uthmān, and 'Alī may remain always upon Your Highness' person.³⁶

---

³⁴ Cf. *Qur'ān*, Sura III, The House of Imran, 163-4 (Arberry's translation, vol. i, p. 94):
  Count not those who were slain in God's way as dead, but rather living with their Lord, by Him provided, ...
Qur'ān, Sura XLVII, Muḥammad, 5 ff. (Arberry's translation, vol. ii, p. 220):
  And those who are slain in the way of God, He will not send their works astray.
  He will guide them, and dispose their minds aright, and He will admit them to Paradise, that He has made known to them.

³⁵ Cf. *Qur'ān*, Sura II, The Cow, 185 ff. (Arberry's translation, vol. i, p. 53):
  . . . then, if they fight you, slay them—such is the recompense of unbelievers—but if they give over, surely God is All-forgiving, All-compassionate.

³⁶ 'Abdul Ragman', Mecca, to 'Pangerang Pacoe Nagarra, koning van het

PREPARING FOR A NEW AGE, c. 1768-1775

Even after the hazards of triplicate translation and quintuplicate copying,[37] this letter remains of interest. Its clear encouragement of Mangkunĕgara's proud and bellicose nature, and its emphasis upon the religious basis for action, might have threatened the stability of Central Java. Of the three main Javanese aristocrats, Mangkunĕgara was the least well-placed, the most volatile, and the most feared by both the Dutch and other Javanese. He was more likely to resort to violence than either the Sultan or the docile Susuhunan, having the least to lose and the most to gain from any new upheaval. That the most incendiary of the Arabic letters should have been addressed to him suggests his reputation was known and appreciated among those who were sufficiently pious to undertake the pilgrimage to Mecca. The spectre of a rebellious Mangkunĕgara leading a Holy War was ominous, but when religious xenophobia finally found a patron in Java in the late 1780s, it was not to be he. It is further apparent that, whoever the author of the letter may have been, he was not a Wahhābī, at whose door historians have tended to deposit some anti-European Islamic movements in the Indonesian world later in the eighteenth and early in the nineteenth centuries.[38] A Wahhābī would have tolerated neither the use of *djimats* nor the references to any schools of law other than the Ḥanbalī. In any case, the possibility of Wahhābī ideas being communicated from Mecca to Java so early in the career of Muḥammad ibn-'Abd-al-Wahhāb (1703-92) and over thirty years before the Wahhābī capture of

---

Javase Rijk', Dutch translation dated 22 May 1772, in Sĕmarang to Batavia, 3 June 1772, in KA 3256 (OB 1773).

[37] There were apparently (and not surprisingly) no Dutchmen who knew Arabic. The original letters were therefore translated by the Javanese translator Kartabasa into Javanese. Then the Dutch translator C. P. Boltze rendered them into Dutch. A copy would then have been sent to Batavia, where another copy would have been made and sent to Holland. The result is the preservation of only the final copy, in somewhat difficult Dutch. From this has emerged my English version, making the third translation and the fifth copy from the Arabic original. The Dutch destroyed the original documents (see n. 40).

This Kartabasa, incidentally, was not the same Kartabasa (Ki Bĕstam) who served Hartingh at Gijanti. The latter had died in 1762; Sĕmarang to Batavia, 20 Nov. 1762, in KA 2957 (OB 1763).

[38] The 1788-90 crisis in Surakarta was attributed by M. L. van Deventer to the Wahhābīs (dJ xii, pp. xi-xxii), a suggestion which I feel is probably incorrect (see Chap. IX below). On the question of the Sumatran 'Padris' and Wahhābīya, see Anthony Reid, 'Nineteenth Century Pan-Islam in Indonesia and Malaysia', *Journal of Asian Studies*, vol. 26, no. 2 (Feb. 1967), pp. 272-3.

Mecca (1803) seems very slight.[39] Perhaps the writer was acquainted instead with the Naqshbandī order. But it seems most likely that, in the best of mystical traditions, his knowledge transcended the distinctions between different orders and schools or, alternatively, that his understanding was insufficient to grasp the distinctions. It is notable that the writer did not criticize the Javanese monarchs for their conduct as Muslims, which was to become a theme of later Islamic agitation. There was nothing very 'revivalist' about this letter.

The Dutch were no doubt relieved that these epistles had been intercepted before reaching their destinations. The documents were subsequently destroyed upon Batavia's orders,[40] to prevent their becoming known. It is not impossible, however, that the sense of the messages, if not the letters themselves, may have been communicated. The letters to the Sultan and the Susuhunan introduced two 'priests', Hadji Běsari and Muḥammad Idris. It was the former who died, leading to the discovery of the letters and the banners. But the Dutch documents mention neither the fate of the second man nor that of the *djam-djam* water (holy water) from Mecca which was mentioned in the letter to the Sultan. Perhaps this Muḥammad Idris was still alive and able to deliver the seditious communications orally or in copy. If so, it did not immediately affect the course of events in Java. The 1770s saw the beginning of major steps towards political stability on the part of the Javanese monarchs. The incendiary messages from Mecca did not impede this progress.

The letters were nevertheless a significant historical landmark. They were the first evidence to come to light of an attempt from the world of international Islam to foment Holy War in Java in the second half of the eighteenth century. The letters' authority was purely Islamic, their author a *hadji*, not a *pangeran*. There was no reference to any of the indigenous traditions of Javanese Islam, nor to the glorious epochs of Javanese dynastic history. Never again during the period up to the deaths of Haměngkubuwana I, Pakubuwana III, and Mangkuněgara I did the Dutch uncover such unequivocal evidence of this nature. It was not, however, an isolated example of anti-Europeanism. In succeeding

---

[39] For a brief statement on the Wahhābī movement, see Hitti, *History of the Arabs*, pp. 740–1.

[40] Sěmarang to Batavia, 28 Aug. 1772, in KA 3256 (OB 1773).

decades, anti-Dutch religious movements were to appear in Java as well as elsewhere in the archipelago. It is not impossible that other *hadjis* in the eighteenth century brought back inflammatory views like those in the three Arabic letters, perhaps reinforcing potential indigenous antagonisms towards the Dutch. When these antagonisms reached crisis proportions in the years 1787-90, however, it was to be a much more Javanized religion than that of the letters of 1772. And then its targets would be not only the Dutch, but also the Javanese rulers who tolerated the Company's presence.

At the Central Javanese courts, a more regularized state system was meanwhile evolving. Both the Sultan and the Susuhunan wished to end the petty conflicts and occasionally major clashes which had typified the divided kingdom since 1755. This could only be done by accepting the division itself, unless one of the rulers dared to attempt a reunification by force of arms. The approaching end of the seventeenth century of the Javanese Era perhaps encouraged steps to solve the problems of division; a new age was shortly to dawn. The influence of traditional conceptions of chronological and dynastic change is most clear in the field of literature.[41] But in literature, law, and land, in princes and public buildings, evidence suggests that the transition to the new century, from about A.J. 1690 to A.J. 1703 (A.D. 1764-77), was a major event.

One of the factors in the evolution of the new system may have been Sultan Mangkubumi's apparent unwillingness to allow the Dutch to continue as mediators in Javanese affairs. Although he, like the Susuhunan and Mangkunĕgara, had sometimes been willing to use the Dutch to settle disputes, there was nevertheless an element of independence whenever Dutch intercession was not to his advantage. When Ratu Bĕndara remarried in 1765, the Sultan denied the right of the Dutch to intervene. He told Vos that the latter had apparently misunderstood the Sultan's previous statement to van Ossenberch that he 'needn't worry' about Ratu Bĕndara wishing to remarry. The Sultan said these words had meant only that he would behave according to God's Law, according to which a divorced woman was allowed to remarry; the disagreement related only to the Javanese, he said, and if the Susuhunan didn't understand the content of the faith he, Mangkubumi,

[41] See Chap. VII below.

could convince him.⁴² Subsequently the Sultan informed Batavia that the entire affair was conducted in accordance with Islam, which Pakubuwana III knew as well as himself.⁴³ In other words, he was rather pointedly informing the Company that theirs was not the authority to interpret Islamic law, which was a matter for the Javanese alone.

In 1773 Mangkubumi made the point even more directly. Two criminals had been apprehended at Surakarta and sent by the Susuhunan to van der Burgh at Sĕmarang. Since both claimed to be the Sultan's subjects, van der Burgh had sent them on to Jogjakarta for judgement.⁴⁴ The Sultan informed the Dutch Resident that he would prefer such matters to be settled between himself and the Susuhunan, without the intervention or cognizance of the Company. Van der Burgh ordered the Resident to ignore the Sultan's comment and to maintain the system of Dutch mediation 'in order not to give the rulers the idea of independence'.⁴⁵ He clearly saw the far-reaching significance of the Sultan's proposal.

Despite van der Burgh's desire to maintain the Company's mediatory role, agreements were being made between the rulers which tended in fact to remove the Dutch from the day-to-day workings of the Javanese state system. They still remained important as the final arbiters of disputes which could be settled in no other way, as the Javanese were to recognize in an agreement of 1790. But for the many less difficult but potentially no less dangerous disputes, there was now evolving a system which did not require constant European involvement. These agreements were often reached with the knowledge, approval, and mediation of the Company, but they were generally of a self-regulatory nature which did not then require further Dutch intervention. The unceasing cadastral controversies were among the first to be the subject of such major transactions.

⁴² HB I to Sĕmarang, Nov. 1765, in KA 3049 (OB 1766). The Ratu Bĕndara affair is described on pp. 110–15 above.

⁴³ HB I to Batavia, 22 Djumadilakir, Alip A.J. 1691 (5 Dec. 1765), in KA 3049 (OB 1766).

⁴⁴ HB I to Sĕmarang, 2 Bĕsar A.J. 1698 (received 27 Feb. 1773), in KA 3281 (OB 1774); Sĕmarang to Batavia, 5 April 1773, in KA 3281 (OB 1774). One of the two criminals was said merely to be a rebel (*kraman*); he was declared innocent by the Sultan and set free. The other had crept armed into PB III's residence, and was banished by HB I to an inhospitable area of Patjitan, near the south coast.

⁴⁵ Sĕmarang to Batavia, 5 April 1773, in KA 3281 (OB 1774).

PREPARING FOR A NEW AGE, c. 1768-1775

The land conferences of 1768-70 had not achieved a permanent settlement of the boundary problems, although they had considerably ameliorated them. Small differences persisted and grew.[46] By early 1772, the Dutch were again attempting to mediate territorial disputes, but with little success. The Sultan intransigently insisted on having a particular area only, it seemed, because Mangkunĕgara controlled it. At the same time, both the Susuhunan's and the Sultan's representatives displayed an entirely unhelpful cunning, in which art van der Burgh somewhat unusually thought the Susuhunan's people to be the more accomplished. Some years later van der Burgh singled out the Sultan's ministers for their 'unbelievable hair-splitting' in these matters. The latter judgement was more normal for the Dutch, who usually believed Surakarta to be the more malleable and reasonable court of the two. Soon Surakarta, Jogjakarta, and Sĕmarang commissioners were jointly attempting to record the lands of Kĕḍu and Bagĕlen, in order to determine what belonged to each ruler and what each actually possessed.[47]

Both Pakubuwana III and Hamĕngkubuwana I now asked van der Burgh to assist in drawing up entirely new land registers.[48] This was clearly the only possible solution to the acrimonious boundary disputes. The shifting of villages back and forth across boundaries, some by agreement and others by conquest, and the growth of population in Central Java since 1756, had rendered the Book of Klĕpu and the subsequent agreements based upon it unreliable guides to the real situation. The Dutch spoke of the Book of Klĕpu as 'grown very obscure through erasure and striking-out'.[49]

In late February 1773, just over a week before *Garĕbĕg Bĕsar*, A.J. 1698, Hamĕngkubuwana I and Pakubuwana III wrote separately to van der Burgh at Sĕmarang. They told him that they had commanded the registering of all lands under their control. These registers would then be sent to Sĕmarang where the two sides could settle any differences.[50] At the same time, various disputed

---

[46] See Sĕmarang to Batavia, 25 April 1771, in KA 3229 (OB 1772); Batavia to H. XVII, 31 Dec. 1771, in dJ xi, p. 221.

[47] Sĕmarang to Batavia, 7 March 1772, in KA 3256 (OB 1773); van der Burgh, Memorie, 19 Sept. 1780, in dJ xi, p. 397. Van der Burgh was particularly critical of what seemed to be the dishonesty of Danurĕdja.

[48] Sĕmarang to Batavia, 28 Aug. 1772, in KA 3256 (OB 1773).

[49] Batavia to H.XVII, 31 Dec. 1772, in dJ xi, p. 235.

[50] HB I to Sĕmarang, 2 Bĕsar A.J. 1698 (received 27 Feb. 1773), in KA 3281 (OB 1774); PB III to Sĕmarang, 2 Besar A.J. 1698 (received 26 Feb. 1773),

areas were already being returned to their rightful overlords.[51] Such land registers had probably been a regular feature of the administrative system since long before the eighteenth century. There had been a major census of the kingdom in the reign of Sultan Agung, if *Babad Sangkalaning Momana* is to be trusted,[52] and census-taking was also known in other Indonesian kingdoms, including Palembang and Bantĕn.[53] Presumably some sort of census must have been compiled before the division of the Javanese kingdom at Gijanti. Thus the technique of compiling the lists would have presented no unaccustomed problems, and it was not in this that Dutch assistance was required. The settling of conflicting claims, however, would have been virtually impossible had either side been unwilling to co-operate, in which case the Dutch would again have had to mediate. But there was now, it seems, a greater willingness in both Javanese courts to settle finally the land disputes.

There were certainly disputes and conflicts over the rightful disposition of lands,[54] but nevertheless the new registers were completed by late 1773. They were signed and sealed at Sĕmarang on 2 November 1773 by the *patihs* and Residents on behalf of the rulers.[55] On 26 April 1774 the Susuhunan and the Sultan ratified the agreements, in which they again acknowledged their lands to be a fief of the Company. The Book of Klĕpu had now become obsolete, and was replaced by this 'New Book' (*Sĕrat Ébuk*

---

in KA 3281 (OB 1774). The date 2 Bĕsar A.J. 1698 was equivalent to 24 Feb. A.D. 1773.

[51] Sĕmarang to Batavia, 5 April 1773, in KA 3281 (OB 1774).

[52] *Babad Sangkalaning Momana*, p. 249: Angka 1560, taun Be [A.D. 1638] . . . pametangipun siti Tanah Djawi . . .

Lists of land areas and populations are found on ibid., pp. 249–54. See also de Graaf, 'Sultan Agung', p. 222 n. 2.

There are several lists of land areas under various court dignitaries found in Dutch Company records, which could only have come from similar lists in Javanese. Such Javanese lists are also to be found in BM Add. MSS. 12341, 12342, and 14397.

[53] See LOr 2052, 2055, and 7709, Bantĕn Sultanate census, A.J. 1696 and after; and CB 146 (5–8), Palembang census materials, probably eighteenth century; in Pigeaud, *Literature*, vol. ii, pp. 64–5, 461, 784–5.

[54] See van der Burgh, Memorie, 19 Sept. 1780, in dJ xi, p. 397.

[55] Original copies of the 2 November agreement are to be found in AN Djokjo 42, 'Register der landen van den Sultan (met het tractaat van 2 November 1773)' and AN Solo 43, 'Register der landen van den Soesoehoenang . . .'

PREPARING FOR A NEW AGE, c. 1768-1775   159

Anjar).⁵⁶ Although the new century (A.J. 1700, beginning on 14 March A.D. 1774) began in the interval between the signing and the ratification, neither of these documents betrays an interest in that event. The Dutch and the Javanese texts of both agreements are dated in the Christian era, rather than with the equivalent Javanese dates (16 Ruwah A.J. 1699 and 14 Sapar A.J. 1700).

The new land lists showed a moderate total population increase on Java since 1755.⁵⁷ Whereas the number of *tjatjahs* (households) under the Javanese rulers recorded at Gijanti had been 172,500, in 1773–4 the total was 202,090, an increase of about 17 per cent in two decades. Converted to a population figure, the total of 202,090 households would have included 808,360 individuals at a rate of four per *tjatjah*, or 1,212,540 if the somewhat less likely estimate of six per household were used.⁵⁸ This increase in population was almost entirely accounted for in the core regions (*nĕgara agung*) surrounding the courts (Mataram, Gunung Kidul, Padjang, Matĕsih, Laroh, Sokawati, Kĕḍu, Bagĕlen, Patjitan, Kaduwang, Banjumas, etc.), where the *tjatjahs* grew from 106,200 in 1755 to 138,940 in 1773–4, an increase of over 30 per cent. In the *montjanĕgara* the figures actually showed a total decrease of almost 5 per cent. This picture was somewhat distorted by the inclusion of several areas in the calculation for the *nĕgara agung* in 1773–4 which had been counted as *montjanĕgara* in 1755, notably Kaduwang, Banjumas, Pamĕrden, and Patjitan. If these had been calculated with the *montjanĕgara* in 1773–4, the population loss there would be reduced considerably while the growth of the *nĕgara agung* would be a somewhat smaller percentage figure.

The population estimates which result from this data are, of course, as unreliable as the figures upon which they are based. And the comparison of two sets of somewhat unreliable figures, from 1755 and 1773–4, is hardly a scientifically satisfying process. What is more important are the general trends which appear from this data.

It is clear, first of all, that the population of Java had increased since the restoration of peace in the 1750s. It continued to do so after 1774, and by about 1795 the increase over 1755 was of the

⁵⁶ The Dutch text of this contract is to be found in dJ xi, pp. 259–61. An incomplete copy of the Javanese text is in BM Add. MS. 12303, 'A Journal kept by the late Sultan of Java [HB II]', ff. 82ʳ–83ʳ.

⁵⁷ The 1773–4 lists are summarized in dJ xi, pp. liv–lvi n. 1. The 1755 list is in dJ x, pp. 373–5.

⁵⁸ See dJ xi, p. lxxviii n. 2.

order of 45 per cent. The growth in the Dutch *pasisir* areas, however, was apparently almost five times as rapid as in the Javanese kingdoms.[59]

Secondly, the concentration of resources around the capital cities is apparent. The *nĕgara agung* accounted for virtually all of the population increase. The greater security of these central regions in the years between 1755 and 1773–4 was undoubtedly a factor. The *montjanĕgara* had harboured rebellious groups during most of those years, and the proximity of the ruler's troops in the *nĕgara agung* may have attracted population, as well as making possible more settled agriculture. But the confusing boundary divisions of the central area often caused hostilities there as well. It seems probable that many Javanese were attracted closer to the *kratons* for reasons having less to do with military than with psychological security.

Finally, the inclusion of areas in the *nĕgara agung* which were formerly considered *montjanĕgara* was a significant development. It seems that the *nĕgara agung* was primarily parcelled out to princes and dignitaries in appanage, while the *montjanĕgara* was under the jurisdiction of *bupatis*, nominally controlled by the ruler via his *patih*.[60] The inclusion of Kaduwang within the *nĕgara agung* was therefore a logical redesignation, since it had become the appanage of Mangkunĕgara. The encroachment of the *nĕgara agung* upon this and other areas of the *montjanĕgara* suggests that more and more dignitaries needed supporting, since the incidence of exile and death in battle had declined considerably, and the additional lands for this purpose had to be carved out of the *montjanĕgara*, thereby becoming part of the *nĕgara agung*. The Sultan's attempt to place two of his favourites on the coast in 1762–4 may have resulted from this same kind of pressure for land.[61] This pressure, as well as the general increase of population, must have been an impetus to the expansion of the area under cultivation. Dutch records comment upon the Sultan's particular assiduity in restoring ruined lands, and his industry in the quiet appropriation of unclaimed areas.[62]

[59] See Hageman, 'Geschied- en Aardrijkskundig Overzigt', p. 267.
[60] See Rouffaer, 'Vorstenlanden', pp. 236, 242–3; Moertono, *State and Statecraft*, pp. 102–3; Selosoemardjan, *Social Changes in Jogjakarta* (Ithaca, 1962), pp. 23–7. [61] See above, pp. 106–7.
[62] See Sĕmarang to Batavia, 7 March 1772, in KA 3256 (OB 1773); Siberg, Memorie, 18 Sept. 1787, in dJ xii, p. 82.

PREPARING FOR A NEW AGE, c. 1768-1775

The most remarkable aspect of the new land settlement was that it apparently worked. In the years after 1774, minor hostilities did erupt occasionally, and when this occurred villages were taken. But the incessant boundary disputes which had typified Central Java before 1773-4 in fact seem to have come to an end.[63] At the end of his incumbency in 1780, Governor van der Burgh looked back with pride on this settlement, which he somewhat unjustly depicted as a personal achievement. Since the agreement, he said,

each has peacefully possessed his own, and . . . a few small differences over the boundaries which have developed between their respective subjects have been settled directly by the *patihs* and Residents at the courts.[64]

In 1783 the two rulers peacefully exchanged 357 *tjatjahs*, without the animosity and bloodshed which such a matter might have occasioned ten years before.[65]

The land settlement of A.D. 1773-4 (A.J. 1699-1700) was thus a major landmark on the road to a permanently divided kingdom. Not only had the land holdings of the two courts been newly listed, but procedures had been agreed for settling future disputes. This new land settlement was, however, only one aspect of the major process of regulating the division of the kingdom.

In this same period, a series of legal agreements between the courts established a new juridical structure appropriate to a divided kingdom. While Rouffaer's and Soeripto's belief that the legal codes of the eighteenth century were based on previous codifications[66] is undoubtedly true, the new codes were nevertheless

[63] See Sěmarang to Batavia, 31 Dec. 1774, in KA 3337 (OB 1776).
[64] Van der Burgh, Memorie, 19 Sept. 1780, in dJ xi, p. 397.
[65] Sěmarang to Batavia, 20 Dec. 1783, in KA 3545 (OB 1784).
[66] Rouffaer, 'Vorstenlanden', pp. 335 ff.; Soeripto, *Vorstenlandsche Wetboeken*, pp. 118-19, 129, 151, 169, and elsewhere.

Dr. Soeripto's thesis (1929) is the standard work on the eighteenth-century law codes, and the reader desiring detailed information on the subject should seek there. It is clear, however, that a very great deal more research is required before Javanese law will be completely understood, as Soeripto himself seemed to feel (see pp. 1-2). Some of Soeripto's conclusions are highly speculative, based more on certain intellectual biases of the author than on knowledge.

For instance, he argues on the one hand that the Javanese codes are 'Indonesian' in character, rather than Indian or Muslim (see p. 176). But at the same time, he dates his hypothetical 'Unḍang-unḍang Mataram' in 1677 because the *kraton* first signed a treaty with the VOC in that year (p. 15), the implication being that law codes were inspired by the Dutch. This perhaps reflects the intellectual dilemma of a Javanese sympathetic to Indonesian nationalism who

an important departure. One of their main functions was to regulate juridical affairs between the two moieties of a divided kingdom, a situation which had never before required judicial regulation. Although some legal procedures had possibly been agreed upon by the two courts fairly soon after the division of 1755,[67] the extant versions of these bilateral arrangements date not from the time of the division, but from the period beginning in A.J. 1697 (A.D. 1771). By A.J. 1699 (A.D. 1773) a major codification had been completed and agreed upon. It seems that the resulting law codes should be seen, along with the new land settlement, as part of the process of accepting the kingdom's division on a more permanent basis.

The *Anggĕr-Agĕng* (Great Law Code) was the first to be codified. Soeripto typefies it as a 'general quasi-international

---

was writing a thesis in Dutch in Leiden University. The thesis is dedicated to 'the fighters for and the friends of the Indonesians', the latter term being still rather emotive in 1929. This dilemma is made more clear on p. 180, where he says of the codes, 'In wezen zouden ze dan in hoofdzaak Indonesisch zijn gebleven, eclectisch verrijkt met gedachten uit het Nederlandsch recht. Hun karakter zou dus wel Indonesisch zijn geweest, maar met eenige Nederlandsche trekken, om later door den tijd (dus historisch) en door de evolutie in het wezen van den Indonesiër zelf te groeien tot een hoogere eenheid. Het heeft echter niet zoo mogen zijn.' His argument that 'Javanization' of the law codes also began in 1677 (see p. 178) would seem to have no documentary justification whatsoever. It may be true, but there is no way to show this was so. The paucity of documentation is the major stumbling-block here.

It is also not surprising that a native of Surakarta should take the view that Jogjakarta legal texts were simply copies of Surakarta texts (see pp. 4, 150). This underestimates the joint Surakarta–Jogjakarta nature of some of the codes. On this question, see also Rouffaer, 'Vorstenlanden', p. 341 n. 1.

My intention here is not to attempt a new statement on the eighteenth-century laws, but merely to show them to have been a part of a larger process regularizing the division of the kingdom. In so doing, I have used Soeripto's Surakarta texts and a volume of Jogjakarta codes, BM Add. MS. 12303, 'A Journal kept by the late Sultan of Java', which was apparently kept for reference by HB II and captured by the British forces who deposed him in 1812.

For an annotated bibliography of publications on Javanese law, see Uhlenbeck, *Critical Survey*, pp. 142–4. For further MSS. on the subject, see Pigeaud, *Literature*, vol. iii, Index, under the names of the codes.

[67] The texts of the *Anggĕr-Agĕng* seem to refer to a legal agreement made at Gijanti. See Soeripto, *Vorstenlandsche Wetboeken*, pp. 70, 82, 232, 262; 'Journal', BM Add. MS. 12303, ff. 39ʳ, 63ᵛ.

There are also Jogjakarta laws dated before A.D. 1771–3. See NBS 75 (6), *Undang-undang*, dated A.J. 1691 (A.D. 1765), in Pigeaud, *Literature*, vol. ii, p. 728; another copy of this MS. is in CB 126, in Pigeaud, *Literature*, vol. ii, p. 780.

Internal legal regulations of some sort must always have existed.

PREPARING FOR A NEW AGE, c. 1768-1775

lawbook',[68] that is, a general regulation of relations between subjects of the two courts. This code was agreed between Danurĕdja and Sasradiningrat on 6 Sura A.J. 1697 (21 April A.D. 1771), and subsequently renewed in A.J. 1708, 1712, 1715, and 1719 (A.D. 1782, 1786, 1789, 1792). The immediately available versions of this code differ somewhat, all being copies not of the original text but of the later versions.[69] Nevertheless it can be said that the general purpose of the code was to establish detailed legal procedures for settling crimes or disputes which crossed the boundaries between Surakarta and Jogjakarta. It established punishments for standard categories of crime, and determined legal jurisdiction in various circumstances.

At the beginning of A.J. 1699 (11 Sura, i.e. 4 April A.D. 1773), the *Anggĕr-Arubiru* (Law on Disturbing the Peace) was codified.[70] Its purpose was above all to end the disputes between Jogjakarta and Surakarta subjects over land claims. It was thus an aspect of the general land settlement achieved in A.J. 1699-1700. It was renewed in A.J. 1708 and 1712 (A.D. 1782, 1786), on the same days as the renewal of the *Anggĕr-Agĕng* in those years. The *Anggĕr-Arubiru* prescribed punishments for those who appropriated lands illegally, the severity of the punishment to vary with the delinquent's rank. It also laid down punishments for interfering with rice fields, waterworks, or roadways. Each *patih* was empowered to confiscate clothing which was forbidden to the subjects of his king (*awisaning Ratu*) should a subject of the other *kraton* wear such attire while visiting in the *patih's* capital city, the boundaries of each city being carefully defined.

[68] Soeripto, *Vorstenlandsche Wetboeken*, p. 8.
[69] Surakarta copies are to be found in ibid., pp. 70-80, 82-105, 232-8, 262-86. See also ibid., pp. 80-1 and 104 n. 1, on the date.
Jogjakarta copies are in 'Journal', BM Add. MS. 12303, ff. 39^r-45^v, 63^v-78^v.
The texts are dated Saturday, 6 Sura A.J. 1697. That date (21 April A.D. 1771) was, however, a Sunday.
See also Rouffaer, 'Vorstenlanden', pp. 339-40. Rouffaer's view that this law code and the others which followed it resulted from VOC initiatives does not seem acceptable; see ibid., p. 339, and Rouffaer's note to Winter, 'Beknopte Beschrijving', p. 122.
[70] For texts, see Soeripto, *Vorstenlandsche Wetboeken*, pp. 140-5, 145-8, 250-4; 'Journal', BM Add. MS. 12303, ff. 78^v-81^r; T. Roorda (ed.), *Javaansche Wetten* (Amsterdam, 1844), pp. 225-31.
The date Sunday, 11 Ruwah (28 Oct. A.D. 1773) appears on several copies, but this is probably a mistake for 11 Sura, which was a Sunday whereas 11 Ruwah was a Thursday.
See also Rouffaer's comments on this code in 'Vorstenlanden', pp. 343-4.

The stipulation in the *Anggĕr-Arubiru* regarding forbidden attire (*awisaning Ratu*, perhaps more commonly known as *larangan-Dalĕm*) is of particular interest. It is uncertain when this became part of the *Anggĕr-Arubiru*, although it can have been added no later than the first decade of the nineteenth century. Most likely it was part of the original text.[71] It suggests that the *awisaning Ratu* in the two courts were different, so that a subject of one ruler might inadvertently wear a forbidden item in the other king's territory. This is the first evidence of a disparity in customs between Surakarta and Jogjakarta which has subsequently become an essential part of Javanese life. In speech, dress, manners, literature, and the arts, Surakarta and Jogjakarta differ. It is probably safe to assume that this resulted partly from a conscious effort to establish two independent identities, although such matters cannot easily be documented. It had very likely begun before the 1770s, with roots perhaps extending back to differing local usages long before the Gijanti treaty of 1755. Yet it is interesting that a Surakarta *sĕngkala* (chronogram) list suggests that a new style of *kris* hilt was decreed to be *awisaning Ratu* just in A.J. 1697 (A.D. 1771).[72] It cannot be said, however, whether any other

[71] Soeripto's translation (*Vorstenlandsche Wetboeken*, p. 148) of Roorda's text (*Javaansche Wetten*, pp. 230–1) is inaccurate. The Surakarta *patih* named in Roorda is Danuningrat, not Djajaningrat. And there are only two dates at the end of the text, A.J. 1699 and 1708. The A.J. 1712 date is found on other copies but not on Roorda's. Thus it would seem that the section on *awisaning Ratu* must have been added at least by the time of the second copy of A.J. 1708 (A.D. 1781). The *patih* at that time, however, was still Sasradiningrat, who had earned PB III's fury and was in the process of being replaced by Sindurĕdja. Danuningrat was *patih* in the years A.D. 1804–10, even after the date of the third version of the *Anggĕr-Arubiru* of A.J. 1712 (A.D. 1786).

The *awisaning Ratu* section is also in 'Journal', BM Add. MS. 12303, f. 80ʳ⁻ᵛ, where the Surakarta *patih* mentioned is Djajaningrat and the dates are A.J. 1699, 1708, and 1712. Djajaningrat was indeed *patih* at the time of the renewal in A.J. 1712 (A.D. 1786). The names of the Jogjakarta *patihs* are of no assistance, since they have all been named Danurĕdja.

It can be asserted unequivocally that the clause was inserted some time before A.D. 1812, when the British captured B.M. Add. MS. 12303.

It seems to me, however, that documentary problems notwithstanding, there is no reason not to assume that the *awisaning Ratu* section was included in the original text of A.J. 1699 (A.D. 1773).

See also Rouffaer's note 61 in Winter, 'Beknopte Beschrijving', pp. 161–4.

[72] BM Add. MS. 12323 (B), f. 43ᵛ: Duk salin wangun Ukiran Tunggak-Sĕmi, Isen, 25 Mulud, Wawu 1697.

Winter, 'Beknopte Beschrijving', pp. 77–8, lists the Surakarta *awisaning Ratu*, including 'Oekiran Toengak Semie—(greep van een kris, van die naam en fatsoen)'.

PREPARING FOR A NEW AGE, c. 1768-1775   165

items of forbidden apparel were also decreed at this time. Whatever its origins and development, the existence of two different styles in the Sultan's and Susuhunan's courts was an important, if obscure, aspect of the growing permanence of the division.

These law codes from the years A.J. 1697-9 (A.D. 1771-3) thus formalized relationships between the two halves of the formerly united kingdom.[73] By so doing, they made the regular administration of a divided kingdom possible, perhaps for the first time in Modern Javanese history. The dating of these land and legal settlements at the end of the seventeenth century of the Javanese Era may have been entirely fortuitous. There were several non-calendrical reasons for the rulers to wish a more regularized system, among them advancing age, greater experience, and perhaps growing resignation. But it was not only in legal matters that the transition to the new century seems to have been important.

Construction at the new court of Jogjakarta was a continuous affair, but around the turn of the century in the Javanese Era an unusual number of important buildings were erected. At the end of A.D. 1775 (late A.J. 1701), van der Burgh said that the Sultan

occupies and exhausts his subjects ceaselessly with building all sorts of

[73] Other codes may have been written in this period as well. See Soeripto, *Vorstenlandsche Wetboeken*, pp. 156-8; Rouffaer, 'Vorstenlanden', pp. 341-2.
  I am not considering the *Nawala-Pradata* here. While it is true that the Surakarta *Nawala-Pradata* was decreed on 30 Sura A.J. 1697 (15 May A.D. 1771), I do not have a Jogjakarta text from the same period. It seems, in any case, that the *Nawala-Pradata* should be considered as separate from the joint Surakarta–Jogjakarta codifications of A.J. 1697-9. The Surakarta text does, it is true, concern problems involving subjects of the Sultan or Mangkunĕgara, but this is not the case with the later Jogjakarta version in BM Add. MS. 12303. Both versions are primarily concerned with internal legal administration. The Jogjakarta manuscript differs considerably, as was pointed out by S. Keyzer in 'De Javaansche Handschriften to London', *BKI*, vol. 2 (1854), p. 335. Rouffaer did not see the BM text, but believed Keyzer ('Vorstenlanden', pp. 340-1); Soeripto did not see the BM text, and did not believe Keyzer (*Vorstenlandsche Wetboeken*, pp. 42-5). The Jogjakarta MS., however, was from the reign of HB II, being dated A.J. 1723 (A.D. 1796), and is therefore not of concern in the present study.
  For texts of the *Nawala-Pradata* (Surakarta), see Soeripto, *Vorstenlandsche Wetboeken*, pp. 21-9, 30-9, 239-43, 255-61. The Jogjakarta *Nawala-Pradata*, containing 19 articles, is in 'Journal', BM Add. MS. 12303, ff. 56^r-60^v. Other Jogjakarta *Nawala-Pradata* texts are known but there does not seem to be a version dated c. A.J. 1697-9. The text which Soeripto discusses (*Vorstenlandsche Wetboeken*, p. 42) with its thoroughly confused dating may perhaps be from that period, but it seems highly unlikely that this text of 21 articles should have preceded the BM text of 19 articles or Soeripto's A.D. 1795 text of 17 articles, as Soeripto himself observes.

... constructions for his pleasure, and demolishing and reconstructing them if they should not satisfy intentions or expectations.[74]

Javanese sources generally agree that the Sultan's new *Prabajěksa* (royal residence) was constructed in A.J. 1695 (A.D. 1769),[75] in which year may also have been built the *Siti Inggil Ler*,[76] the raised terrace on the north of the *kraton* where the Sultan appeared in state. In A.J. 1696 (A.D. 1770) was built the *Gědong Pulo Arga* (presumably a construction in *Taman Sari*).[77] The great mosque (*Masdjid Agěng*) on the west side of the northern *alun-alun* was erected in A.J. 1699 (A.D. 1773)[78] and the *Sěrambi*, the front portal to the mosque where a religious court held session, was built in A.J. 1701 (A.D. 1775).[79]

An early-nineteenth-century Surakarta *sěngkala*-list records the construction of several buildings in that city as well. It dates the mosque (*Masdjid Agěng*) and its pillars (*saka guru*) in A.J. 1690 (A.D. 1764), the *Siti Inggil* in A.J. 1691 (A.D. 1765), the *kraton* walls (*pagěr bumi*) in A.J. 1692 (A.D. 1766), the new *Prabajěksa* in A.J. 1693 (A.D. 1767), a new *pěndapa* (hall) in A.J. 1697 (A.D. 1771), and the new Dutch fort (*lodji*) in A.J. 1699 (A.D. 1773).[80] It is difficult to say how many of the dates for buildings in either Jogjakarta or Surakarta are correct, but the Dutch records confirm that there was considerable construction activity, at least in Jogjakarta.

Both rulers also showed considerable concern for the problem of succession at this time, as did the Company. When van der Burgh visited the courts in A.D. 1772 (A.J. 1698), Mangkubumi

---

[74] Sěmarang to Batavia, 15 Dec. 1775, in KA 3336 (OB 1776).
[75] B. *Mang.*, pp. 418–19; *Sěrat Djuměněngan S.D.I.S. Kg. Sultan HB I*, p. 3; *Babad Sangkalaning Momana*, p. 271, dates this Dal A.J. 1694, but A.J. 1694 was Dje, A.J. 1695 was Dal. BM Add. MS. 12325 (C), f. 48ʳ, dates the *Prabajěksa* A.J. 1695, and adds that the *Sri Měnganti Kilen* [sic] was also built then; I regard this MS. as being rather unreliable.
[76] According to *Sěrat Djuměněngan S.D.I.S. Kg. Sultan HB I*, p. 3. It is not mentioned in other texts. This MS. contains some erroneous information on other matters and should probably not be trusted.
[77] B. *Mang.*, p. 420. It is not mentioned in other sources.
[78] B. *Mang.*, p. 420; *Babad Sangkalaning Momana*, p. 271; *Sěrat Djuměněngan S.D.I.S. Kg. Sultan HB I*, p. 3; BM Add. MS. 12325 (C), f. 48ʳ.
[79] B. *Mang.*, p. 420, where the *sěngkala* is difficult (see n. 87 below); *Babad Sangkalaning Momana*, p. 271; *Sěrat Djuměněngan S.D.I.S. Kg. Sultan HB I*, p. 4; BM Add. MS. 12325 (C), f. 48ʳ.
[80] BM Add. MS. 12323 (B), ff. 42ᵛ–44ʳ. See also Raffles (1830), vol. ii, p. 264.

lost no opportunity to impress upon him his wish that the Crown Prince's right to succession in Jogjakarta should be confirmed by the Company,[81] the young prince then being in his early twenties.[82] Batavia did, in fact, make regulations for the succession late in 1772, in order that the Sĕmarang Governor and the Residents at the courts need not refer to their superiors should one of the rulers die suddenly. But these orders were to be kept secret in sealed envelopes, to be opened only if they should be needed.[83] The Sultan had to content himself with the usual assurance that Batavia's approval would probably fall upon the Crown Prince, provided his conduct was satisfactory.[84]

There is some reason to suspect that the Sultan even contemplated abdication at about this time. Some years previously Dutch sources had reported a rumour that Mangkubumi would step down when the Crown Prince had achieved his majority.[85] The prince was to be twenty-four years old in A.J. 1700 (A.D. 1774) and the Sultan may have considered abdicating in his son's favour at that point, for the age of twenty-four was just three *windus* (eight-year cycles) and may have been a significant age for a prince, perhaps corresponding to the Western idea of majority.[86] Literary evidence also suggests that the Sultan may have planned to step down. *Babad Mangkubumi* was said to have been written by the Crown Prince in A.H. 1187 (A.J. 1699, A.D. 1773), and the events described after that date seem to have been added in a rather brief manner to a first and more substantial part of the chronicle which had been finished in that year.[87] This suggests

[81] Sĕmarang to Batavia, 28 Aug. 1772, in KA 3256 (OB 1773).
[82] The Crown Prince had been born about A.D. 1749-50. See above, p. 101, n. 14.
[83] Batavia to H.XVII, 31 Dec. 1772, in dJ xi, p. 236. All records of these orders were apparently destroyed; see dJ xi, pp. xxxviii and 236 n. 2.
[84] Sĕmarang to Batavia, 28 Aug. 1772, in KA 3256 (OB 1773).
[85] Ossenberch, Memorie, 13 May 1765, in dJ xi, p. 36.
[86] Cf. *Het Triwindoe-Gedenkboek Mangkoe Nagoro VII* (2 vols.; Soerakarta, 1939-40). This volume was produced in celebration of three *windus* of rule by MN VII, rather than in observation of an age of three *windus*.
[87] *B. Mang.*, p. 1, Canto I (Midjil):

    1. Midjil Ri Sang Wiranom murwani
       wau kang tjarijos
       Srĕrat Babad Mĕntaram wijose
       Pranarendra ngrat Djawa winuni
       kĕng minulja sami
       kalipah Jang Agung

that in A.J. 1699 the reign of Mangkubumi was expected to end in the near future and that it was therefore appropriate that a chronicle of the reign should be composed. At the beginning of

 2. ing ri Akad purwanja tinulis
   dera Sang Wiranom
   djam sĕdasa endjang ing wantjine
   ping salikur tanggalnja narĕngi
   Madilawal sasi
   Alip taunipun

 3. mongsa kanĕm kang windu Tjetra di
   wukunja gumantos
   mapan Wukir sĕngkalane mangke
   paṇḍita sṭa amudja sĕmedi [A.H. 1187]
   . . . .

The 'Sang Wiranom' referred to here as the author of the text appears to be the Jogjakarta Crown Prince. See also ibid., p. 454, where he is called 'Djĕng Sang Prawiranom'. For a more detailed discussion of the date and authorship of this text, see Ricklefs, 'Authorship'.

The section giving the construction projects around the turn of the century (ibid., pp. 419–20) ends with the difficult sĕngkala for the Sĕrambi, 'sudjalma ingkang muluk apan samja amudja sĕmedi'. The date for the Sĕrambi must be A.J. 1701, which is known from other sources (see n. 79 above), but I fail to see how it can be derived from this sĕngkala. But it will be observed that this sĕngkala is similar to that given for the writing of the babad itself, 'paṇḍita sṭa amudja sĕmedi'. I suspect that the original text of B. Mang., written in A.H. 1187/A.J. 1699/A.D. 1773, may have ended at around this point. This section of B. Mang. is unusually condensed, as is another later section (ibid., pp. 436–7) on the replacement of Vos by van der Burgh (A.D. 1771) and Lapro by van Rhijn (A.D. 1773). Thereafter the text seems to skip five or six stanzas in one stanza (LXVI: 20; see n. 102 below). This leaves me with the suspicion that at around this point there was a break in the writing of the book, which was then taken up later. Certain matters of style give a similar feeling of discontinuity, but it is impossible to be certain.

The belief that the MS. consisted originally of a babad written in A.H. 1187/A.J. 1699/A.D. 1773, with another section added later in order to complete the story of the reign of HB I up to his death (A.D. 1792), is supported by the fact that the bulk of the MS. concerns the period before A.J. 1699/A.D. 1773, comprising what seems to have been the original MS. The later sections are very much more brief. The entire MS. consists of 549 pp. (there is some minor misnumbering of pages) and 84 cantos, covering the period A.J. 1681–1719/A.D. 1755–92. The first (original) section seems probably to have ended somewhere between pp. 418–20 (Canto LXIV) and pp. 436–7 (Canto LXVI). There is no point at which a definite break can be established (a transitional section was presumably added with the new passages). It may be reasonable to assume, however, that Canto LXIII (pp. 412–17) may be the last complete canto of the original MS., telling of the sending of Pangeran Singasari in chains to Batavia and of the return of the Jogjakarta troops from the montjanĕgara (A.J. 1694–5/A.D. 1768–9). If this is accepted at least as being sufficiently correct to demonstrate the point that the emphasis of this MS. falls disproportionately upon the period before A.J. 1699/A.D. 1773, then it will be seen that these first cantos cover only

PREPARING FOR A NEW AGE, c. 1768-1775

A.J. 1700, the Crown Prince was credited with the authorship of the great prophetic pseudo-history *Sĕrat Surja Radja*, the text specifically mentioning that his age was twenty-four and that he was 'designated to succeed the Ruler'. This reference to the succession may have meant that this was to take place in the near future.[88] It was also at about this time that the Crown Prince

---

13 out of the 37 years covered in the whole text (c. ⅓), yet they comprise 417 of the total 549 pages (c. ¾) and 63 of the 84 cantos (c. ¾). The remaining ⅔ of HB I's reign is covered in ¼ of the pages, comprising ¼ of the cantos. The fact that ¾ of the text covers only ⅓ of the reign strongly suggests that the remaining part was added much later, in less detail, only to complete the story. The suggestion follows that the original MS. was conceived as a complete history of the reign of HB I, which was expected to end at about the time of writing.

[88] *Kangdjĕng Kjai Surja Radja* (2 vol. MS. in Prabajĕksa, kraton Jogjakarta), vol. i, p. 7, Canto I (Asmaradana):

> 5. . . .
> Sri Nalendra ing Matarum
> pan kaṭah atmadjanira
>
> 6. nging Putra ingkang satunggil
> kang dadya tĕlĕng ing drija
> ginaḍang sumilih Katong
> ajusja padlikur warsa
> . . . .

Cf. *B. Mang.*, pp. 143-4, on the naming of the Crown Prince in 1758, Canto XX (Ḍanḍanggula):

> 45. . . .
> saksurude Pangran Dipatya
> sanadyan kaṭah amangke
> atmadjengira Prabu
> mung kang dadya tĕlĕng ingkang sih
> Djĕng Den Mas Timur nama
> langkung sih Sang Prabu
> apan baḍe gĕntanana
> mring kang raka djumĕnĕng Pangran Dipati
> Anom Mĕngkunĕgara
>
> 46. Kangdjĕng Raden Mas Timur ing mangkin
> ingkang jusja dawĕg wolung warsa
> . . . .

These two sections from *Kg. Kj. Surja Radja* and *B. Mang.* (which are also discussed in Ricklefs, 'Authorship', pp. 268-70) are parallel passages, both about the Crown Prince of Jogjakarta and both in books apparently written by him. It should be noted that although the *B. Mang.* passage is about the succession of the Crown Prince in 1758 (i.e. at the time which was then being described) the Javanese phrase 'baḍe gĕntanana (i.e. gĕntenana)' would usually be translated in the future tense: 'will replace.' Yet it is obviously about events at that time, not in the future. The same is true of the *Surja Radja* phrase 'ginaḍang sumilih

began to take a more active part in the affairs of the court. Dutch sources comment for the first time late in A.D. 1778 (A.J. 1704) that the Crown Prince had now joined his father as an initiator of grand building projects.[89]

All of this tends to suggest that the conjunction of the new century and the Crown Prince's possible 'majority' was significant for Jogjakarta politics. Perhaps the Sultan was asking the Dutch to confirm, not that his son would succeed after his own death, but that he might succeed in or about A.J. 1700 (A.D. 1774). The possible theoretical reasons for such a wish will be considered in Chapter VII. If this was the case, it would account for Hamĕngkubuwana's concern for the succession at this time, a concern also shared by Pakubuwana III and Mangkunĕgara I. While speculation is among the lesser historians' virtues, it seems possible that a plan to abdicate in favour of the Jogjakarta Crown Prince had to be abandoned because the Dutch would not give a firm assurance to recognize the succession. They would not do so because they understood the Sultan's comments to refer to the eventual possibility of his own death, whereas he may actually have wished reassurance with regard to an abdication in the very near future. In the absence of a firm Dutch statement, abdication must have seemed a perilous course which would only give the enemies of Jogjakarta, particularly Mangkunĕgara, an opportunity to attempt a *coup* of one sort or another. More than once the Dutch had proved themselves unpredictable allies when it came to dealing with Mangkunĕgara. It may have seemed wiser, therefore, for the Sultan to remain firmly in control in Jogjakarta. Whatever the case, contemporary evidence does suggest that there may have been, for a time at least, an expectation within the Jogjakarta *kraton* that the Sultan's reign was about to end.

Pakubuwana III also wished Batavia's confirmation of his son as heir. The Susuhunan's general health was not good and van der Burgh worried more about the untimely demise of the forty-year-old Susuhunan than of the Sultan, then in his late fifties or early sixties. Moreover, the Surakarta Crown Prince was still

---

Katong', which therefore should perhaps be taken to mean 'designated to replace the King (very soon, or now)' rather than 'designated to replace the King (at some distance in the future)'.

The *Surja Radja* text is discussed in greater detail in Chap. VII.

[89] Sĕmarang to Batavia, 24 Dec. 1778, in KA 3418 (OB 1779).

PREPARING FOR A NEW AGE, c. 1768–1775

a child, unlike the heir in Jogjakarta, thus making the situation in Surakarta altogether less stable. Apparently the Susuhunan was considering officially installing his son as Crown Prince in late A.J. 1700 (December A.D. 1774) but did not then act.[90]

Early in A.J. 1701 (A.D. 1775), Pakubuwana III wrote to the Governor-General and Council of the Indies at Batavia, announcing his intention, with their permission, to declare his son Crown Prince within the year.[91] Since the Susuhunan was clearly not to be diverted from his plan, the Dutch felt it best to approve.[92] Van der Burgh privately told Batavia that the title *Pangeran Adipati Anom* (Crown Prince) did not necessarily guarantee the bearer would succeed as ruler,[93] a view which the Susuhunan was very unlikely to have shared. Within two months, the Crown Prince of Surakarta had been announced.[94] Mangkunĕgara expressed to the Resident his surprise that the Susuhunan had waited so long to declare his son *Pangeran Adipati Anom*.[95] Since the Susuhunan seems in fact to have acted with considerable haste, Mangkunĕgara may have meant he was surprised that the Susuhunan had waited until A.J. 1701, rather than carrying this out in A.J. 1700.

Mangkunĕgara also chose this period to attempt to confirm the position of his children. In A.J. 1700 (A.D. 1774) he wrote to Sĕmarang, saying that he was growing old and his life might end at any time. He wished, therefore, to commend to the protection

[90] Id., 28 Aug. 1772, in KA 3256 (OB 1773); id., 31 Dec. 1774, in KA 3337 (OB 1776). The Dutch reported that PB III was awaiting the outcome of an illness from which MN was suffering before installing his own son as Crown Prince. I fail to see any very obvious logic here.

[91] PB III to Batavia, received at Sĕmarang 11 April 1775, in KA 3337 (OB 1776). The letter refers to 'this year or 1701' ('dit jaar of 1701'). The 'or' must be a Dutch translator's attempt to get around the problem of two calendrical systems, rather than a particle marking the existence of two alternative years in which the Crown Prince could be installed. The year A.J. 1701 began on 4 March A.D. 1775, and thus when the letter was written it was already A.J. 1701 (11 April A.D. 1775 was 9 Sapar A.J. 1701).

[92] Sĕmarang to Batavia, 17 April 1775, in KA 3337 (OB 1776); Batavia to H.XVII, 30 Dec. 1775, in dJ xi, p. 284.

[93] Sĕmarang to Batavia, 17 April 1775, in KA 3337 (OB 1776).

[94] This was done in June A.D. 1775, which was roughly equivalent to the month of Rabingulakir A.J. 1701; Sĕmarang to Batavia, 31 Dec. 1775, in KA 3362 (OB 1777).
BM Add. MS. 12323 (B), f. 44ʳ, gives 8 Rabingulakir A.J. 1701 for the installation of the Crown Prince.

[95] Sĕmarang to Batavia, 17 April 1775, in KA 3337 (OB 1776).

of the Company his son Pangeran Arja Prabu Amidjaja, as well as all his other children and grandchildren. He said he trusted in the Company and was sure of its affection for him, but he nevertheless wished a letter from the Governor-General confirming this.⁹⁶ He sent a list of his children, including sixteen sons and fifteen daughters. At the head of the list was his eldest son:

Raden Mas Suramulja, now renamed Pangeran Arja Prabu Amidjaja, twenty-four years old. Of him I ask the Company that he may assume my place.⁹⁷

Since Javanese is a language which does not always clearly indicate tense, it is uncertain whether Mangkunĕgara wished his son to succeed immediately or upon his own death. The Company certainly assumed it was the latter. But it is notable that Mangkunĕgara's son, like the Sultan's, was twenty-four in A.J. 1700. Perhaps Mangkunĕgara wished to step down at the turn of the century in favour of his son, as the Sultan may have wished to do.

The Susuhunan was unwilling to agree to Mangkunĕgara's wish that his son should inherit his large appanage, all of which was carved out of the Susuhunan's lands. Nor had Batavia intended Mangkunĕgara's position to be a permanent principality to be handed down to his descendants. Mangkunĕgara had also requested an appanage for his second son from the Susuhunan, and another for his third son in the Company's *pasisir* lands. None of these requests was granted. Instead the Governor-General wrote to Mangkunĕgara assuring him in general terms of the Company's affection for himself and his children, so long as their conduct was correct. Two of his daughters were married off to sons of distinguished Javanese families from the Dutch-controlled *pasisir*. But there was no firm guarantee of Mangkunĕgara's position or of his son's right of inheritance.⁹⁸

Mangkunĕgara nevertheless reacted as if the Company had committed itself to the maintenance of himself and his family.

⁹⁶ MN to Sĕmarang, received 23 Oct. 1774, in KA 3337 (OB 1776). This letter would have been written in the month Ruwah A.J. 1700, although the Dutch copy does not include the date. MN was not, in fact, in good health at this time.
⁹⁷ List of children of MN, received at Sĕmarang 28 Dec. 1774, in KA 3337 (OB 1776). Dutch translation only.
⁹⁸ Sĕmarang to Batavia, 31 Dec. 1774 and 17 April 1775, in KA 3337 (OB 1776); Batavia to H.XVII, 30 Dec. 1775, in dJ xi, p. 283; Sĕmarang to Batavia, 31 Dec. 1775, in KA 3362 (OB 1777).

PREPARING FOR A NEW AGE, c. 1768–1775

Early in A.J. 1701 (April A.D. 1775), at the same time as Pakubuwana III informed the Dutch that he was going to raise his son to Crown Prince, Mangkunĕgara wrote to Sĕmarang thanking the Company for finding husbands for his two daughters. He also expressed his gratitude for what he took to be confirmation of his title *Pangeran Adipati*.[99] To the Governor-General he wrote,

> Now that I see myself confirmed in that rank [of *Pangeran Adipati*] by the Company and protected therein by the same, I find that my condition is rather better than before, and for that reason I trust that, should I come to die, my children shall succeed me.[100]

In fact the permanent status of the Mangkunĕgaran principality was not confirmed until A.D. 1792. Nevertheless Mangkunĕgara chose to behave as if it had been confirmed in A.D. 1775, at the beginning of the new Javanese century. But if he had ever considered stepping down in favour of his son, he had clearly abandoned the plan.

As the new Javanese century began, the Javanese courts enjoyed a deep and unaccustomed peacefulness,[101] fostered by a series of events over several years. The most notable landmarks had been the end of the Malang rebels (A.J. 1694–6, A.D. 1768–70), the birth of an heir to the Susuhunan (A.J. 1694, A.D. 1768), the new land settlement (A.J. 1694–1700, A.D. 1768–74), and the general regulation of relationships between the Javanese principals, notably between Mangkunĕgara and the Susuhunan (A.J. 1698, A.D. 1772) and between Surakarta and Jogjakarta (A.J. 1697–9, A.D. 1771–3). *Babad Mangkubumi* speaks of the peace and prosperity of Jogjakarta at the turn of the century:

> LXVI: 19. . . .
> Described now the land of Ngajogja:
>
> 20. Ever more prosperous was the land;
> all that was planted, grew;
> all that was bought was cheap.

---

[99] MN to Sĕmarang, received 11 April 1775, in KA 3337 (OB 1776).

[100] MN to Batavia, 11 April 1775, in KA 3337 (OB 1776). The date 11 April 1775 is equivalent to 9 Sapar A.J. 1701.

[101] See Batavia to H.XVII, 31 Dec. 1773, in dJ xi, p. 246; id., 31 Dec. 1774, in dJ xi, pp. 272–3; id., 30 Dec. 1775, in dJ xi, pp. 283–4; Sĕmarang to Batavia, 31 Dec. 1775, in KA 3362 (OB 1777); Batavia to H.XVII, 31 Dec. 1776, in dJ xi, p. 286.

Resident van Rhijn was ever more proficient
In serving every wish of His Highness.[102]

The Central Javanese political situation was becoming more stable. It seems that the idea of a permanent division was coming to be accepted by the Javanese courts; the existence side by side of two Javanese rulers was ceasing to be a volatile situation. This may have had little or nothing to do with the turn of the century in the Javanese Era. All three principals were growing older, and perhaps wiser or more tired, and this may have been sufficient impetus to end the uncertain state of affairs, particularly since it was now apparent that there was an heir to the Surakarta throne. Furthermore, any options to the partition of the kingdom had been progressively eliminated since the 1750s. Thus events seemed to move unerringly towards the acceptance of a permanent division of Mataram. Yet the coincidence of so many stabilizing developments at the end of the Javanese seventeenth century is striking and suggests something rather different from the unplanned, inertial growth of the idea of a permanent partition. Now decisions on the subject had been taken and were being acted upon in the Javanese *kratons*. The administrative measures described in this chapter were the result of positive political decisions which made the division workable on a permanent basis. The following chapter will consider some of the traditional ideas which encouraged such steps.

Javanese politics were not, however, entirely a matter for the Javanese. The Dutch Company was certainly not in control of Javanese affairs, but it was in a position of influence. This influence may, for instance, have been sufficient to prevent the

---

[102] *B. Mang.*, p. 437, Canto LXVI (Asmaradana):

19. . . .
    warnanĕn nagri Ngajogja
20. langkung ardjaning nĕgari
    sabarang tinanĕm mĕdal
    murah kang tinumbas kabeh
    Oprup Pang Reng langkung wignja
    ngladosi sakarsendra
    . . .

This description is not dated, but it is preceeded by the installation of J. M. van Rhijn as Resident (A.D. 1773–86) and by the visit of van der Burgh to the courts (July–Aug. 1772). It is followed by the tale of Pangeran Rongga of Djadjar (A.D. 1778). Thus, logic would suggest it is meant to describe the period between A.D. 1772/3 and 1778, i.e. A.J. 1698 to 1704.

Sultan resigning his throne to his son in A.J. 1700, a plan which Mangkunĕgara had possibly shared with regard to his son. But in non-political matters the Company had virtually no influence, and in such affairs also the importance of the change of the century is suggested. It is hinted at by the unusual construction activity at the *kratons* in A.J. 1690–1701 (A.D. 1764–75). Such buildings were important legitimizing measures, contributing to the ruler's visible status and to the sense of stability within his court. In these same years the Dutch reported that the Sultan was concerned to solicit from them a pair of pistols as *pusakas*, as well as a carriage, a Persian horse, and female slaves.[103] Van der Burgh observed at the beginning of A.J. 1699 (April A.D. 1773) that

The Sultan is mindful of everything which fosters his glory and ambition, and is also very attentive that in all things there is an equality between himself and the Susuhunan.[104]

Such evidence suggests that the Jogjakarta *kraton* was in these years giving particular attention to the forms of legitimation and stability.

It is in the field of literature, the subject of the following chapter, that the significance of the new century is most clearly seen. Here it was not a question of possible vague perceptions that a new age was dawning, such as might be found even in industrialized countries in the present time. Rather a very specific received tradition of political change at the turn of each century was maintained. It no longer fitted real events, but tradition can create a kind of reality of its own. In the eighteenth century, Jogjakarta literature in particular seems to have striven to recreate a traditional reality unchanged since Madjapahit. In so doing, the Jogjakarta *kraton* could become a continuation of that tradition, which was ultimately the only form of legitimation possible in Java. This would be the final step in turning the partition of Java from a temporary *modus vivendi* into a legitimate and durable long-range solution to the inability of the Javanese élite to unite.

[103] Sĕmarang to Batavia, 5 June 1774, in KA 3310 (OB 1775); id., 17 April 1775, in KA 3337 (OB 1776); id., 31 Dec. 1775, in KA 3362 (OB 1777).

[104] Sĕmarang to Batavia, 5 April 1773, in KA 3281 (OB 1774). Van der Burgh was arguing for the addition to the VOC establishment at Jogjakarta of a Second Resident, so it would be the same as that at Surakarta, where the Second Resident accompanied MN on formal occasions. The Sultan was displeased that there was no Second Resident at his court to accompany the Crown Prince on such occasions.

VII

THE NEW AGE IN JAVANESE LITERATURE: SĔRAT SURJA RADJA, BABAD KRATON, AND THE LITERARY RENAISSANCE

THE turn of a century was an important time of change in Javanese tradition, an idea which might be generally accepted in societies elsewhere in the world. But in Java there was a rather specific application of such concepts. Traditional Javanese historiography tended to schematize political change, forcing it into a rigid pattern based on the turn of a century. It seems possible that this schematization then had a reciprocal effect upon political behaviour, which tended to fit the pattern. Events had been rewritten to become tradition, and the tradition then moulded events to fit itself. Paucity of early documentation makes it impossible to reconstruct the course of these developments, although certain suggestions may be made. On the other hand, a plethora of relatively recent materials, from the eighteenth century and after, prevents a complete analysis of the problem of schematization in Javanese historiography at this time. It can be shown, however, that a historiographical schema based upon the turn of the century existed in Java in the late eighteenth and early nineteenth centuries, and almost surely before. It can further be suggested that this schema helps to explain otherwise puzzling developments in eighteenth-century Jogjakarta.

The pattern of interest here was a simple one, although it may have been part of a larger and more complex system.[1] At the end of each century ('oo), Javanese chronicles record that a dynasty or court ended, and after an interval of three years a new dynasty or court began ('03). Among modern scholars, both Dr. de Graaf[2]

---

[1] See also pp. 5–6, n. 19 above, on the pattern A.J. 1471–1571–1671, and n. 36 below.

[2] De Graaf, 'Historische Betrouwbaarheid', p. 58.

and Professor Berg[3] have observed the existence of such patterns, as did others before them, including Brandes and Veth.[4]

Some Javanese texts extend the pattern far back into Javanese history, with certain variations. One important nineteenth-century *sĕngkala*-list, for instance, dates the establishment of the kingdom of Padjadjaran in A.J. 1200 (A.D. 1278) and its fall in A.J. 1300 (A.D. 1378).[5] The foundation of Madjapahit, the construction of Barabuḍur or of the *Masdjid Watu* (Stone Mosque) at Salatiga were sometimes also dated A.J. 1300 (A.D. 1378).[6] These were, however, somewhat eccentric extensions of a pattern which was most consistently applied beginning only with the fall of Madjapahit.

Madjapahit was said to have fallen in A.J. 1400 (A.D. 1478). This is perhaps the most widely-known date in Javanese history, since it is taken to be the beginning of the Islamic period. It poses problems upon which there has been much debate.[7] Whether or not all of the implications which have been drawn from the putative events of A.J. 1400 (A.D. 1478) are correct, the fact remains that it is a standard date in Modern Javanese texts.[8] It may indeed be very

[3] C. C. Berg, 'De Weg van Oud- naar Nieuw- Mataram', *Indonesië*, vol. 10, no. 5 (1957), pp. 420–1; id., 'Kraton-Bouw in de Wildernis', ibid., vol. 10, no. 6 (1957), pp. 517, 528; id., 'Vijfvoudige Buddha', p. 232 n. 31.

[4] J. Brandes, 'Iets over een ouderen Dipanagara in Verband met een Prototype van de Voorspellingen van Jayabaya', *TBG*, vol. 32 (1889), p. 419 n. 1; Veth, *Java*, vol. iii, p. 615.

[5] *Babad Sangkalaning Momana*, pp. 228, 229.

[6] BM Add. MS. 12323 (B), f. 33ᵛ, dates Barabuḍur (Rĕtja Buḍur), the Masdjid Watu Salahtiga, and the fall of Padjadjaran in A.J. 1300, and the foundation of Madjapahit in A.J. 1301.

BM Add. MS. 12325 (C), f. 44ᵛ, dates the Salatiga mosque in A.J. 1300, but dates Barabuḍur in A.J. 1218, the fall of Padjadjaran in A.J. 1360, and the foundation of Madjapahit in A.J. 1361, which is clearly nonsensical.

Brandes, 'Dipanagara', p. 419, mentions A.J. 1300 as a date sometimes given for the foundation of Madjapahit.

On the curious problem of an old ruin at Salatiga, now unknown, see H. J. de Graaf, 'De verdwenen Tjandi te Salatiga', *BKI*, vol. 114 (1958), pp. 117–20, especially p. 119 on Buddingh's report that the *tjanḍi* was built by Prabu Birawa in A.J. 1300.   [7] See Chap. I above, and Ricklefs, 'Consideration'.

[8] *BK*, f. 74ᵛ, has a mistaken *sĕngkala*, the import of which is discussed below (see n. 32); *BTDj* does not have this date, nor has *BTDj(BP)*.

BM Add. MS. 12323 (B), f. 33ᵛ: sirna ilang karjeng bumi, Be 1400.
BM Add. MS. 12325 (C), f. 44ᵛ: sirna ilang kĕrtining bumi, 1400.
Babad Sangkalaning Momana, p. 234: Be 1400.
Raffles (1830), vol. ii, p. 257: 1400.
Winter, 'Beknopte Beschrijving', p. 36, says that the Javanese became Muslims in 'Djee 1403', which shows that he knew of the theory but either confused it somewhat or had been told a slightly eccentric version.
See also Brandes, 'Pararaton', pp. 229–30, citing a *Sĕrat Kanḍa* text.

old, for it is mentioned for the death of the Madjapahit ruler in his *kraton* in the Middle Javanese *Pararaton*,[9] the manuscripts of which have dates as old as A.J. 1522 and 1535 (A.D. 1600, 1613).[10] Professor Berg has even suggested in the course of his reconstruction of Old Javanese dynastic theory that the end of the Madjapahit dynasty in A.J. 1400 was implicitly calculated in the *Nāgarakĕrtāgama* and other Old Javanese materials written before the event.[11] Without considering the complex philological problems involved here, it may be said that while this at first seems highly improbable, such a prophecy may have been current two centuries later, at which time it may have been a factor in the fall of the *kraton* in A.J. 1600 (A.D. 1677). Thus, there is at least a possibility that the fall of the Madjapahit dynasty in A.J. 1400 was expected some years before.

The last date in the *Pararaton*, immediately following the death of the last ruler, is A.J. 1403 (A.D. 1481) for the *guntur pawatugunung*.[12] This was apparently a volcanic eruption, which Professor Berg has interpreted as an event welcoming the arrival of a new dynasty or new ruler.[13] This view would seem to be correct. Such natural phenomena have long been, and are still, believed in Java to announce a rightful succession.[14] Furthermore, A.J. 1403 is

[9] Brandes, 'Pararaton', p. 40: Bhre prabhu sang mokta ring kaḍaton i çaka çunya-nora-yuganing-wong, 1400.

[10] See ibid., inleiding, p. 3, and pp. 40–1. There are other MSS. as well, but the A.J. 1400–3 dates are in the oldest.

[11] See Berg, 'Vijfvoudige Buddha', pp. 72–95; id., 'Māyā's Hemelvaart', pp. 191, 214–15, 696. Professor Berg has been kind enough to discuss this and related questions with me on several occasions.

[12] Brandes, 'Pararaton', p. 40: Tumuli guntur pawatu-gunung i çaka kayambara-sagareku, 1403.

[13] Berg, 'Vijfvoudige Buddha', pp. 77 ff., 237 n. 36; id., 'De Weg van Oud-naar Nieuw-Mataram,' pp. 421–2.

[14] Cf. *Nāg.* I: 4, on the accession of Hajam Wuruk; translation in Th. G. Th. Pigeaud, *Java in the 14th Century: A Study in Cultural History* (5 vols.; the Hague, 1960–3), vol. iii, p. 4:

2. ... the tokens of his being superhuman, wonderful, were:

3. an earthquake, the earth rumbled, rain of ashes, thunder, flashes of lightning turning about in the sky,

4. the mountain Kampud collapsed, annihilated were the bad people, the rascals, dead without a gasp.

Cf. also Selosoemardjan, *Social Changes*, p. 23, describing the arrival of the new Sultan (HB IX) in Jogjakarta in 1939. He had been met by his dying father, HB VIII (1921–39) in Batavia, but the old Sultan lost consciousness on the train

given in several Modern Javanese sources as the year in which the first ruler of the new kingdom at Dĕmak was invested.[15] It seems, therefore, that the '00–'03 cycle is perhaps as old as A.J. 1522–35 (A.D. 1600–13), when the early *Pararaton* manuscripts were written in Bali.

The death of the third and last ruler of Dĕmak is said in one Javanese text to have occurred in A.J. 1500 (A.D. 1578). This date is not, however, commonly found in other Javanese sources.[16] It seems not to be historically reliable, but rather contrived to fit the pattern. Dr. de Graaf believes the third Dĕmak king to have died about A.D. 1546.[17]

The investiture of the first ruler of Padjang was dated in A.J. 1503 (A.D. 1581), another year which does not seem historically correct. It is a common date in Modern Javanese texts.[18]

---

to Jogjakarta and died a few days later: 'When the unconscious Sultan, escorted by his son, was carried from the train at Jogjakarta's railway station, a clap of thunder exploded in the clear sky, during dry weather and while the sun was shining brightly. This unusual phenomenon of mother nature made a deep impression upon Jogjakarta's people, and it created the belief that the young Crown Prince must be endowed with exceptional qualities.'

[15] *BK* does not have a *sĕngkala* for this event, nor does *BTDj* have this date.
BM Add. MS. 12323 (B), f. 33ᵛ: ngadĕg ing kita Dĕmak, gĕni mati siniram ing djalmi, Alip 1403.
BM Add. MS. 12325 (C), f. 44ᵛ, gives two dates, one for the accession of Sultan Dĕmak (suta mati gawening wong, 1401) and another for the accession of Sultan Bintara (Ehe, bahning matingranu iku, 1403) who is the same person; this MS. is at times rather wildly confused.
Babad Sangkalaning Momana, p. 234: Wawu, 1401, kraton ing Dĕmak, djumĕnĕngipun Raden Patwa, djudjuluk Sultan Bintara . . . Alip, 1403, tĕtĕp djumĕnĕngipun Sultan Bintara, kaiden Sunan Giri.
Raffles (1830), vol. ii, pp. 254, 257: 1403.

[16] *Babad Sangkalaning Momana*, p. 240: Ehe 1500, seda Sultan Bintara, kang kaping tiga, djumĕnĕngipun Adipati Andajaningrat ing Padjang, kraton ing Padjang.

[17] De Graaf, *GI*, p. 94.

[18] *BK* seems not to have a *sĕngkala* for this, unless A.J. 1503 is intended in the otherwise nonsensical statement that the mantri (3) was captured (5); see f. 107ᵛ, Canto XXI (Sinom), 61: djumnĕnga Sultan Padjang / punika babade uni /rĕke mantri winisaja / punika babade dingin.
BTDj, text p. 68, trans. p. 70: A.J. 1503.
BTDj(BP), vol. iv, p. 71: rĕsi titiga wisajeng djanma [A.J. 1537!].
BM Add. MS. 12323 (B), f. 34ʳ: adĕging kita Padjang, Dal 1503.
Babad Sangkalaning Momana, p. 241: Dal 1503, djumĕnĕngipun Adipati ing Padjang, kaiden Sunan Giri.
Raffles (1830), vol. ii, pp. 254, 258: 1503.

JOGJAKARTA UNDER SULTAN MANGKUBUMI

In the seventeenth century, Dutch documents are available to check the Javanese dynastic theory, with remarkable results. The great rebellion of Trunadjaja culminated in his conquest of the Plered *kraton* in A.D. 1677, equivalent to A.J. 1600. The theory of dynastic change was fact. The full date given in Javanese texts does not accord exactly with Dutch documents on this event,[19] but it is sufficient that a *kraton* had indeed fallen in A.J. 1600 (A.D. 1677). The *babads* suggest also that Susuhunan Amangkurat I knew in advance that this would happen because the century was about to end. He is quoted as saying that he knew it to be God's will that Mataram should end after one hundred years.[20]

[19] *BK*, f. 355ʳ: malĕm Akad, 18 Sapar, sirna ilang rasane ingkang bumi [1600].
BTDj, text p. 168, trans. p. 174: malĕm Akad, 18 Sapar, Be 1600.
BTDj(BP), vol. xii, p. 32: malĕm Akad, 18 Sapar, Be, sirna ilang rasane ingkang bumi [1600].
BM Add. MS. 12323 (B), f. 36ʳ: malĕm Ngahad, 18 Sapar, sirna ilang rasaning Ratu, Be 1600.
BM Add. MS. 12325 (C), f. 46ʳ.: Dal [*sic*], sirna ilang obah ing djagad, 1600; this MS. says that it was Sultan Agung who fled the *kraton*!
Babad Sangkalaning Momana, p. 260: Ngahat-Wage, 8 [*sic*] Sapar, Be 1600.
Raffles (1830), vol. ii, pp. 260–1: 1600.
On the problems of reconciling the Dutch sources, which date the flight from the court 28 June 1677, with the Javanese date 18 Sapar (22 April), see de Graaf, 'Mangku-Rat I', vol. ii, pp. 188–91.

[20] *BK*, f. 354ᵛ, Canto LXXXVI (Durma):

27. . . . / Sri Narendra Matawis
28. sampun wikan lamun djangdjining Pangeran / tan kĕna owah gingsir / jen kita Mataram / pan sirna djĕnĕngira / Sri Narendra ing Matawis / wus anarima / jen titah ing Jang Widi
29. Sri Narendra karsane atilar pura / kengsĕr saking Matawis / tan kĕna tinambak / rĕngkane ing Mataram / pan sampun ḍatĕng ing djangdji / wus satus warsa / djĕnĕnge ing Matawis.

BTDj, text p. 168: Nanging Sang Nata mbotĕn karsa mĕdali pĕrang, sabab sampun sumĕrĕp ing pĕpĕsṭen ing Allah, jen nĕgari Matawis sirna pan-djĕnĕnganing Ratu, sarta sampun djangkĕp satus taun karaton ing Matawis; Sang Prabu punika djumĕnĕng Ratu wĕkasan (see trans. p. 174).
BTDj(BP), vol. xii, pp. 31–2 (Durma): Sri Narendra Matawis // wus uninga lamun djangdjining Pangeran / tan kĕna den gingsiri / jen kita Mataram / pan sirna djĕnĕngira / Sri Narendra ing Matawis / pan anarima / marang titah ing Widi // Sri Narendra akarsa atilar pura / kengsĕr [text has kengkĕr] saking Matawis / tan kĕna ingampah / Nagri Mataram rĕngka / pan sampun tĕka ing djangdji / ing satus warsa / djĕnĕnge ing Matawis.

Before Mangkurat's flight from the court, the rebel conspirators were said to have met and come to the conclusion that, as the year had changed (to A.J.

The Susuhunan's statement may, of course, be apocryphal, since none of the chronicles is available in versions older than the eighteenth century. In any case, the statement offers several problems. If the Susuhunan was referring to the '00–'03 cycle, he should have mentioned a period of ninety-seven years. In fact, the chronicles do not assign either the date A.J. 1500 (A.D. 1578) or A.J. 1503 (A.D. 1581) to the foundation of Mataram. Dr. de Graaf could arrive at a date for that foundation only by assuming the statement of Amangkurat I to be literally true, and subtracting one hundred years from A.J. 1600 to give A.J. 1500.[21] The problem can be resolved by suggesting that Amangkurat meant Mataram had finished its century of dominance in a general sense, not that a period of exactly one hundred years had ended. Unfortunately, the Javanese texts would bear such an interpretation only with difficulty. It would be fruitless to speculate further until more is known of the Javanese materials concerning these events. What is important here is simply that the eighteenth- and nineteenth-century chronicles correctly dated the fall of Plered in A.J. 1600, and that the event may have been expected to happen in advance of the date.

1600), Mataram was old and the time had come for its fall. See *BK*, f. 351ᵛ, Canto LXXXV (Pangkur):

22. . . . tan winarna laminipun / sampun agěnti warsa / Paněmbahan Madurětna wus arěmbug / kalajan Radja Makasar / arsa nginggahi Matawis

23. miwah Paněmbahan Rama / angrěmbagi sětu kalawan pasṭi / ing Mataram wus sěpuh / mangsane jen rěngkaha . . .

Cf. *BTDj(BP)*, vol. xii, p. 25 (Pangkur): tan kawarna laminipun / ja ta agěnti warsa / Paněmbahan Madurětna wus arěmbug / . . . / lan Radja Galengsong sira / minggah ḍatěng ing Matawis // miwah Paněmbahan Rama / angrěmbugi satu kalawan pasṭi / ing Mataram pan wus sěpuh / ungsume jen rěngkaha.

Cf. *BTDj*, text p. 167 (see trans. p. 172): Mbotěn antawis lami nuntěn gěntos taun. Trunadjaja, Radja Galengsong, Paněmbahan Kadjoran sami pirěmbagan nggenipun baḍe mbĕḍah něgari Matawis.

See also Professor Berg's comments on the phrase *gěntos taun* in 'Kraton-Bouw', pp. 516–17. While Professor Berg is right in stressing the importance of the year A.J. 1600, it seems to me unnecessary to argue that *taun* here means 'century' rather than 'year'. Shortly before this statement in the chronicles the year A.J. 1599 is mentioned (see *BTDj*, text p. 164, trans. p. 170), and it seems that *gěntos taun* simply means 'the year changed', i.e. to A.J. 1600, which year did indeed have a special significance.

[21] De Graaf, 'Sénapati', p. 54.

The new *kraton* of Kartasura was founded in the month Ruwah A.J. 1603,²² again in keeping with the dynastic theory. In this case the date accords well with that given in Dutch records, September A.D. 1680.²³

The congruity of dynastic theory and political reality in A.J. 1600–3 (A.D. 1677–80) is noteworthy. It would lead one to suspect these events were the model for the theory, were it not for the fortuitous preservation of the *Pararaton* on Bali, suggesting the '00–'03 cycle to be older than A.J. 1600. If in the seventeenth century the theory preceded the fact, the possibility must be considered that the latter was influenced by expectations derived from the former.²⁴

The applicability of this cycle in A.J. 1700–3 (A.D. 1774–7) seems at first doubtful. No *kraton* fell in A.J. 1700; none was founded in

²² *BK*, f. 395ʳ: Wednesday-Pon, 7 Ruwah, Alip, tri sirna rĕtuning djagat [1603].

BTDj, text p. 199, trans. p. 205: Wednesday-Pon, 27 Ruwah, Alip 1603.

BTDj(BP), vol. xiii, p. 33: Ruwah (without date), Alip, mantri sirna obah ing rat [1603].

BM Add. MS. 12323 (B), f. 36ʳ: Ruwah (without date), lir ngambara ngrasa wani, Alip 1603.

BM Add. MS. 12325 (C), f. 46ʳ: Alip, mantri sirna rasa wani, 1610 [*sic*! The chronogram actually means 1603].

Babad Sangkalaning Momana, p. 261: Alip 1603.

Raffles (1830), vol. ii, pp. 254, 261: 1603.

²³ See *Dagh-Register 1680*, p. 687; Batavia to H.XVII, 29 Nov. 1680, in dJ vii, p. 52. Dr. de Graaf has informed me that a letter by Jacob Couper, dated 15 October 1680 (in KA 1249), gives different dates for the trip to Wanakĕrta (Kartasura), and that the dates given in both *Dagh-Register* and dJ are unlikely, given travelling conditions in Java at that time. It is not possible at this time to reconcile these conflicting materials. In any case, most of the possible dates for the foundation of Kartasura, both Dutch and Javanese, fall within a period of a few days, particularly between 21–3 Sept. 1680. The Javanese dates are confusing, however, for neither 7 nor 27 Ruwah was Wednesday-Pon.

²⁴ This is the view taken by Professor Berg in 'Kraton-Bouw', pp. 516–17, 528. See also his 'Vijfvoudige Buddha', p. 313, on Gadjah Mada as a 'planner of future history', determining future dynastic events by promulgating the 'Greater Madjapahit' dynastic theory. But see also ibid., p. 255 n. 45, where Professor Berg takes the apparent existence of a schematized history as a reason to question the historical value of the information contained in the source. He is undoubtedly wise to be sceptical, but the same logic would lead to rejection of the historical veracity of the A.J. 1600–3 (A.D. 1677–80) events, were they not documented by the Dutch. If one takes the view that dynastic theory can affect political events, one cannot then reject information about those political events simply because they can be shown to fit the theory. Professor Berg considered this problem very briefly in the context of his comments on the latter part of the *Pararaton*; see his essay 'The Javanese Picture of the Past', in Soedjatmoko *et al.*, *Introduction*, p. 109.

A.J. 1703. It will be suggested below, however, that this cycle may be of assistance in understanding developments in Jogjakarta at this time.

It would also seem unlikely that the theory could be preserved in A.J. 1800–3 (A.D. 1871–4), in the truly colonial era of Javanese history, without being fully understood by the early Dutch orientalists. Yet this may have been the case.[25] In a book published in A.D. 1878 (i.e. A.J. 1808) a Dutch observer wrote,

> Every hundred years . . . the *kraton* is demolished and rebuilt anew in another place. In Solo [Surakarta] this ought to have taken place a short time ago, but the [Dutch] government had no inclination thereto, because of the great costs which it entailed for us and for the Susuhunan, and got out of it. It was made clear to the Susuhunan that, in order to remain near the *kraton*, the fort and the residency would also have to be moved at the Susuhunan's expense, and that was too much for His Highness.[26]

Although this writer does not say when the Susuhunan had desired to move his court, it seems likely that it was in the period A.J. 1800–3.

Outside the *kratons* the late nineteenth century was a time when many looked forward to the end of an era in a more general way. In Jogjakarta such attitudes were no doubt encouraged by an unusually destructive earthquake in June A.D. 1867 (A.J. 1796), which caused several hundred deaths and severely damaged the city, including the *kraton* itself.[27] The more Islamic malcontents on Java sometimes expected the *Ratu Adil* (Just Ruler) to appear at the end of the thirteenth century in the Islamic Era (A.H. 1300 was A.D. 1882).[28] Others expected his appearance in A.J. 1800 (A.D. 1871).[29] One strongly anti-Islamic text, the *Sĕrat Dĕrmagaṇḍul*,

---

[25] I have often been told in the Jogjakarta *kraton* that many important aspects of *kraton* life were always kept secret from the Dutch in the days before independence. Such matters may still be kept from the outsider.

[26] E. van Rijckevorsel, *Brieven uit Insulinde* ('s-Gravenhage, 1878), p. 80. Veth, *Java*, vol. iii, pp. 615–16, cited van Rijckevorsel's comments, but did not suggest that this was a matter involving calculations in the Javanese calendar of a specific traditional pattern.

[27] Veth, *Java*, vol. iii, pp. 617, 619.

[28] *Pralambange Tanah Djawa*, LOr 6536, predicted the coming of the *Ratu Adil* in A.H. 1297–9 (A.D. 1879–81); see Pigeaud, *Literature*, vol. ii, p. 391. See also Drewes, *Drie Javaansche Goeroe's*, pp. 166–7, on a text referring to A.H. 1200 (A.D. 1785) as a turning-point.

[29] Drewes, *Drie Javaansche Goeroe's*, p. 131, comments that the Djajabaja prophecies were a particular problem in Java from the A.D. 1870s. Brandes,

predicted the end of the Islamic period of dominance on Java four centuries after the fall of Madjapahit. The text's opposition to Islam, however, apparently led to the calculation of the date in the old solar calendar (thus, A.D. 1878, four solar centuries after A.D. 1478), rather than in the newer Javanese system of solar followed by lunar years (thus, A.J. 1800/A.D. 1871, four Javanese solar/lunar centuries after A.J. 1400/A.D. 1478).[30] The nineteenth century is still largely *terra incognita* to the historian of Java, however, and it is not yet possible to say whether the old dynastic theory was still preserved in its specific form.[31]

The eighteenth-century *kratons*, however, obviously knew of this tradition, for it is preserved in their documents. Such documents also make it possible to suggest the way in which the Jogjakarta *kraton* perhaps employed the old belief that a kingdom ended in '00 and another began in '03 to legitimize its existence. It was Jogjakarta, the new court, the second court, which had the most anomalous legitimative position. Surakarta's antecedents led easily via Kartasura back to Sultan Agung, thence to Madjapahit and on to the mythical forbears of the kings of Java. But where was the smooth line of succession which led to Jogjakarta? It had been founded after Surakarta but was yet not its successor. It

---

'Dipanagara', pp. 373, 384–5, 387, gives a nineteenth-century *pralambang* predicting the coming of a just ruler in A.J. 1800 (A.D. 1871), who would then reign for 100 years; see also Drewes, *Drie Javaansche Goeroe's*, pp. 136–7.

The 100-year cycle of *kratons* and the prophecies of a just ruler in A.J. 1700, 1800, or 1901 (*sic*) were important in the Djajabaja prophecies; see J. A. B. Wiselius, 'Djåjå Båjå, zijn Leven en Profetieën', *BKI*, 3rd series, vol. 7 (1872), pp. 172–217, especially p. 212.

[30] G. W. J. Drewes, 'The Struggle between Javanism and Islam as Illustrated by the Sĕrat Dĕrmagaṇḍul', *BKI*, vol. 122, no. 3 (1966), pp. 325–7, 362. Professor Drewes does not comment on the unusual use of the solar calendar, but his implicit deduction that the date intended was A.D. 1878 rather than A.J. 1800/A.D. 1871 seems to be correct. It may be, however, that some earlier prophecy concerning A.J. 1800 was rewritten to suit the opening of the Prabalingga *Hoofdenschool* in A.D. 1879.

[31] Professor Sartono Kartodirdjo has contributed a valuable monograph on a West Javanese insurrectionary movement in the 19th century, 'The Peasants' Revolt of Banten in 1888, its Conditions, Course, and Sequel, A Case Study of Social Movements in Indonesia', *VKI*, vol. 50 (1966). This includes a note on such movements in Central and East Java (ibid., pp. 269–73). Professor Sartono is, however, concerned with social groups which were not closely connected with Central Javanese *kraton* tradition and, while various millenary traditions were involved in these troubles, it is not entirely surprising that the '00–'03 cycle does not appear in his materials. See also Professor Sartono's *Tjatatan tentang Segi-segi Messianistis dalam Sadjarah Indonesia* (Jogjakarta, 1959).

was thus Jogjakarta which stood most in need of legitimation. It may not be entirely accidental, therefore, that the literary materials concerning the years A.J. 1700-3 (A.D. 1774-7) are almost entirely from Jogjakarta. On the other hand, it cannot be overemphasized that the fortuitous preservation, recognition, and availability of historical materials is the major factor in research into such obscure matters as the interplay between Javanese myth and politics two hundred years ago. Perhaps similar materials existed in Surakarta, but have not survived, lie unnoticed, or are kept from modern scholarly attention in the interest of a living tradition.

The Jogjakarta *kraton* saw the past as a series of cycles, as is suggested by the preservation of the *kraton*-cycle in Jogjakarta chronicles. Indeed, the traditional Javanese view of history was generally cyclical. Similar literary motifs reappear in the chronicles in varying contexts associated with different characters. Dates are sometimes confused as well. The Jogjakarta *Babad Kraton*, for instance, gives a mistaken chronogram for the fall of Madjapahit (A.J. 1400/A.D. 1478) which is in fact the date for the fall of Plered (A.J. 1600/A.D. 1677).[32] Perhaps the two events were sufficiently similar for the author that he was either confused or simply unconcerned about the century in which they occurred.

As the cycle came round again, and A.J. 1700 (A.D. 1774) approached, there were perhaps many in the Javanese courts who wondered what the new century would bring. Would a *kraton* fall, and if so, which would it be? What new court would be founded in A.J. 1703 (A.D. 1777)? Political events leading up to that time, described in the preceding chapter, show clearly an increasing concern in both Jogjakarta and Surakarta to create the means of stability. It seems possible that this was so precisely because each court was apprehensive of the turn of the century as a time when its existence might be challenged, as had been that of every court in existence at the turn of a century since Madjapahit, according to their dynastic theory. But neither ruler was willing to renew the inconclusive fratricide of the A.D. 1740s and 1750s. Even Mangkunĕgara was apparently becoming less volatile. Thus, if neither

[32] *BK*, f. 74ᵛ, Canto XIII (Pangkur): 14. sirna ilang rasaning rat / sĕngkalane duk bĕdah ing Madjapahit.

Sirna-ilang-rasaning-rat gives the date for the fall of Plered, A.J. 1600. This can be confirmed by comparison with the chronograms given for that event in other texts; see Ricklefs, 'Consideration', p. 314 n. 22.

ruler was willing to attack the other, the measures which they took, each to guarantee his own stability, willy-nilly guaranteed that of their counterpart as well. They were becoming committed to the partition of the kingdom.

An early-nineteenth-century *sĕngkala*-list from Surakarta describes a series of natural phenomena in the late A.J. 1690s of the kind which heralded the end of a century and the fall of a *kraton*.[33] It lists ash-rains in A.J. 1695 (A.D. 1769), an eruption of Mt. Mĕrapi in A.J. 1696 (A.D. 1770), the collapse (?*djugrug*) of Mt. Prau in A.J. 1697 (A.D. 1771). In A.J. 1698 (A.D. 1772) a triple sun supposedly appeared, and there was a great light in the skies with lightning-bolts in the centre. In the same year the (Sala) river branched eastwards.[34] It is impossible to say whether any of these things actually occurred. Certainly this Surakarta source contrasts markedly with the Jogjakarta *Babad Mangkubumi*, which describes the peace and prosperity of that city around the turn of the century.[35] The latter depiction is more in accordance with the impression gained from Dutch documents. But the Surakarta list does suggest that the Susuhunan's court was as apprehensive of the changes which might come with the new century as Jogjakarta seems to have been, even though further literary evidence on the matter is entirely from the latter court.

When A.J. 1700 began (14 March A.D. 1774) the end of the era was at hand.[36] It has already been noted that it was in the previous

---

[33] Cf. *BTDj* on the natural phenomena late in the reign of Amangkurat I, as A.J. 1600 approached, which were 'a sign that the kingdom would fall'; *BTDj*, text p. 154, trans. p. 159. See also de Graaf, 'Mangku-Rat I', vol. ii, p. 34, on an eruption of Mĕrapi in A.D. 1672 (A.J. 1595); cf. *BTDj*, text p. 150, trans. pp. 155–6. See also Sartono Kartodirdjo, 'Peasants' Revolt', pp. 166–8; and Wiselius, 'Djåjå Båjå', p. 186.

[34] BM Add. MS. 12323 (B), ff. 43ᵛ–44ʳ:

Kala djawah-awu, Kĕmis ping 23 Sijam, Be 1696.
Ardi Mĕrapi murub, djawah-awu kĕrikil, Djumungah 7, Dulkangidah, Be 1696.
. . .
Djugrug Gunung Prau, Rĕbo 16 Sawal, Wawu 1697.
. . .
Surja kĕmbar djadjar tiga, tedja kĕmbung, tĕngah mawi obar-abir, Kĕmis 5 Sapar, Djimakir 1698.
. . .
Bĕnawi kasiḍat mangetan, Rabingulakir, Djimakir 1698.

[35] *B. Mang.*, p. 437. Text cited above, p. 174, n. 102.

[36] At least two MSS. of the prophecies of Djajabaja describe the period A.J. 1670–1700 (A.D. 1745–74) as a 'time of confusion' ended by the coming of a just

year, A.J. 1699, that the Jogjakarta Crown Prince had been credited with composing the chronicle of his father's reign.[37] Perhaps he had written the history of the reign because it was about to end, as had the reigns of previous rulers at the turn of the centuries. But for the first time in three hundred years, no one would attempt to overthrow a *kraton* by force. Armed rebellion had been renounced at Gijanti and Salatiga, and since the capture of Pangeran Singasari there was no one likely to play the role of Raden Patah, Djaka Tingkir (Sultan Padjang), and Trunadjaja. Yet the question remained of what the future would bring, until A.J. 1703 when the new era would have begun. It was suggested in the previous chapter that the Sultan considered abdication in favour of his son. He might have wished to do so in order for there to be a new ruler, thereby doing minimum injustice to the old pattern. But he did not do so, possibly because the political position of the Dutch, with its implicit military sanction, dissuaded him from a step which the Dutch seemed unwilling to recognize, just as the presence of the Company had also made a dynastic war unlikely.

Thus the Javanese courts faced a dilemma. The laws of history, the patterns of the past, would not be fulfilled except by the improbable step of one of the kingdoms voluntarily dissolving itself for a new united kingdom to be founded in A.J. 1703 (A.D. 1777). It seems that this dilemma was resolved, at least in Jogjakarta, through the medium of literature. If the historical pattern was not fulfilled by political reality, it could be ritually observed in literature. The maintenance thereby of the old pattern was probably desirable not only because the pattern was believed to represent living laws of history, but also because it must have carried with it the implication that the court which existed after A.J. 1703 (A.D. 1777) would be the rightful kingdom for the new age. Thus the old pattern which threatened the existence of a court in A.J.

---

ruler in the form of Si Tandjung Putih. It will be noted that this period, A.J. 1670–1700, begins just before the rebellion of Mangkubumi (A.J 1671/A.D. 1746), and ends with the new century. Another MS. describes a similar period for A.J. 1770–1800. See Wiselius, 'Djåjå Båjå', p. 212 (it will be noted that Wiselius's conversions from the Javanese to the Western calendar are incorrect).

The period A.J. 1670–1700 is perhaps also related to the idea of the island undergoing a process of division in A.J. 1471, 1571, and 1671, at the beginning of the 'time of confusion' (see pp. 5–6, n. 19 above).

[37] *B. Mang.*, p. 1. Text cited above, pp. 167–8, n. 87. See also Ricklefs, 'Authorship'.

1700 could confirm that court's legitimacy in A.J. 1703. This use of literary activity to compensate for or to correct the problems which faced the Javanese courts was symptomatic of the Javanese response to the limitations placed upon the spectrum of political possibilities by the Dutch presence, however remote that presence on a daily basis.

Of the various *sĕngkala*-lists consulted in this study, only one has an entry for A.J. 1700. *Babad Sangkalaning Momana* notes under that date:

> Kangdjĕng Gusti [the Crown Prince of Jogjakarta] began the composition of *Sĕrat Surja Radja*; at that time his age was twenty-four years.[38]

This book, *Sĕrat Surja Radja*, is still kept in the Jogjakarta *kraton*. Since A.D. 1948 it has been preserved as a *pusaka* in the Sultan's private residence (*Prabajĕksa*), with the appellation *Kangdjĕng Kjai Surja Radja*. It is the oldest book in the Jogjakarta *kraton* and the only book to be counted amongst the *pusakas*.[39] The two-volume text is heavily illuminated with gold-leaf and is among the most beautiful of Javanese manuscripts.[40]

The *Sĕrat Surja Radja* is a complex mythical tale of battles and adventures royal. It shares many motifs with a wide range of Javanese *belles-lettres* and historical literature. Several of its characters are well known from the *wajang*-theatre as well. But the text is more than *belles-lettres*. On one level, at least, *Sĕrat Surja Radja* is apparently a grand pseudo-historical or prophetical allegory, concerning the actual situation of Jogjakarta in the eighteenth century. Not surprisingly, the great problems concerning the mythologized Jogjakarta of *Sĕrat Surja Radja* were a divided kingdom and a thoroughly mythologized Dutch East

---

[38] *Babad Sangkalaning Momana*, p. 271: Angka 1700, taun Ehe, Kangdjĕng Gusti awit jasa Sĕrat Surja Radja, ingriku juswa 24 warsa.

[39] This information was provided to me by B. P. H. Poeroebojo, for whose continuous assistance during my time in Jogjakarta I am most grateful.
The book *Sĕrat Surja Radja* was moved from the *kraton* library to the *Prabajĕksa* in 1948 because its supernatural force was suspected to be the cause of much illness and several deaths among the court officials in that year. The move to the *Prabajĕksa* was in order to control the book's power.

[40] I was able to examine this book only through the gracious permission of S.D.I.S. Kg. Sultan Hamĕngkubuwana IX, who spared no effort to facilitate my research in his *kraton*. I wish to record here my gratitude for all his kindnesses to me.

India Company. During the preceding century the Company had considerably distorted the course of Javanese history, preventing a Javanese military solution of the problems of the state. Now, it seems, the Crown Prince's book prophesied the final solution of the division and of the Dutch problem: unity and victory for the Javanese, made possible by the superior culture of Javanese Islam. Then might the Dutch be accommodated and everyone live happily ever after in the new century.

Sĕrat Surja Radja is only one of several Javanese books which are known or seem to be allegorical. Professor Berg has proposed that the Old Javanese Arjunawiwāha is 'the history of Erlangga's life-story, transposed into epic form',[41] a suggestion which has been accepted and occasionally extended by others.[42] In his forthcoming book on Old Javanese literature, Professor Zoetmulder suggests that the ultimate victory of Erlangga had perhaps not been achieved when Mpu Kanwa composed the Arjunawiwāha. Professor Zoetmulder, who has elsewhere commented on the spiritual power of words in Old Javanese culture,[43] here suggests that,

through the magic power of his literary activity, in which Arjuna and Erlangga were identified, [Mpu Kanwa] hoped to contribute to the attainment of this final victory.[44]

The Sĕrat Surja Radja of A.J. 1700 was perhaps designed to do something similar.

Many centuries after the Arjunawiwāha, the episodes of the Java War (A.D. 1825–30) were also to inspire allegory. Babad Dipanagaran Surja Ngalam is a mythologized history of Prince Dipanĕgara, in which Sultan Hamĕngkubuwana III (A.D. 1810–11, 1812–14) is called 'Prabu Indrapuri' and the other main characters also received mythical pseudonyms.[45] Various characters of the

[41] C. C. Berg, 'De Arjunawiwāha, Er-Langga's Levensloop en Bruiloftslied?', BKI, vol. 97, no. 1 (1941), pp. 19–94; quotation from p. 39.
[42] See J. E. van Lohuizen-de Leeuw, 'The Beginnings of Old-Javanese Historical Literature', BKI, vol. 112 (1956), pp. 383–94.
[43] In Zoetmulder and Stöhr, Religionen, pp. 262–3. See also ibid., p. 273, on Old Javanese literary works as 'Sprach-Caṇḍi'.
[44] I am grateful to Professor Zoetmulder for allowing me to cite his manuscript here.
[45] LOr 6488. The 'code' of the allegory is explained in a note written in Malay. See Pigeaud, Literature, vol. ii, p. 383.

Dipanĕgara episode were also sometimes identified with specific figures of the *wajang* theatre. Dr. Pigeaud was told that a Jogjakarta prince of the late nineteenth century ordered a set of *wajang-kulit* puppets in classical dress and style, but with the faces of principals of Jogjakarta history, particularly Prince Pakualam I (A.D. 1813–29) and his contemporaries.[46] During the Indonesian Revolution (A.D. 1945–9), *wajang-pantjasila* sometimes depicted events in a similar mythologized way. In at least one case, the Dutch Queen Wilhelmina was depicted as the demonic Baṭari Durga.[47] Clearly the Javanese were accustomed to portray real events in mythical terms, as is sometimes done even now by the *wajang* puppeteer (*ḍalang*). Perhaps many of the Javanese manuscripts presently believed only to be mythical tales would prove to be allegory if the 'code' of characterization could be understood.

That the *Sĕrat Surja Radja* of A.J. 1700 was about Jogjakarta seems reasonably clear. The names and titles of many of the lower officials, the regalia and *kraton* buildings in the book derive from the real situation of the eighteenth century, not from the mythical age it purports to describe. The mythical ruler of the story is described in terms similar to those used for Sultan Hamĕngkubuwana I. The young prince of *Sĕrat Surja Radja* and the Jogjakarta Crown Prince are also given similar titles, and the mythical prince is said to look like Joseph, a comparison the Crown Prince also applied to himself in *Babad Mangkubumi*.[48]

The ruler of Java in *Sĕrat Surja Radja* is called Surja Djaja Amisesa, a mythical name used elsewhere as a pseudonym for the Sultans Hamĕngkubuwana of Jogjakarta. This is seen in another Jogjakarta *kraton* manuscript, *Sĕrat Suluk Surja Djaja*

---

[46] See Dr. Pigeaud's comments on the decorations on DevAth DvT V 1, *Buku Kĕḍung Kĕbo*, in his *Literature*, vol. ii, p. 869.

The nineteenth-century *wajang* set has been described by Dr. Pigeaud in a letter to the author, 16 December 1969. Dr. Pigeaud had not seen the puppets himself.

[47] Seno Sastroamidjojo, *Renungan tentang Pertundjukan Wajang Kulit* (Djakarta, [1964]), p. 47.

[48] For the descriptions of the Sultan and of the mythical ruler, see n. 62 below.

On the titles for the young prince, see n. 70 below. For the references to the young prince as Jusup, see *Kg. Kj. Surja Radja*, vol. i, pp. 10, 14; vol. ii, p. 4. For *B. Mang.* references to the Crown Prince as Jusup, see above, p. 82, n. 37. Other phrases such as Sang Pĕkik, Sang Prawiranom, and Sang Anom for the young prince and the Crown Prince are also shared by *Kg. Kj. Surja Radja* and *B. Mang.*; on these, see also Ricklefs, 'Authorship'.

*Amisesa.*⁴⁹ When a *kraton* official read this book in A.D. 1950 he appended this note:

Sĕrat Suluk Surja Djaja Amisesa. Telling the adventures of Kangdjĕng Sultan Surja Djaja Amisesa Dipaningrat Njakrakusuma Kalipatulah the Fifth, who adorned the *kraton* of Madjapahit Adiningrat, wearing the decoration Tjakraning Surja, the Lion of the Netherlands, and the Legion of Honour.

Beginning with the tale of Rĕtna Manik Rasa, child of Sang Maha Rĕsi [Honoured Great Hermit] of Mt. Lĕngkara . . .

Ending with the tale of King Gonda Sukma Misesa, Senapati Ngalaga Kabir Mukminin, who was about to replace his father-in-law, becoming Ruler adorning the *kraton* of Ngendra-Buwana, paying obeisance to Kangdjĕng Sultan Surja Djaja Amisesa Dipaningrat Njakrakusuma Kalipatulah the Fifth, who adorned the *kraton* of Madjapahit Adiningrat.

That which was called the Edict of Kangdjĕng Sultan of Madjapahit Adiningrat, which was read when the King of Ngendra-Buwana was made Ruler, was dated with the *tjondra-sĕngkala*: Four Hermits were the Teachers of the King (1774) [A.D. 1845].

If the Royal Passing-Away is dated of S.D.I.S. Kg. Sultan Hamĕngkubuwana the Fifth of Jogjakarta, it was the year Dal, 1783 [A.D. 1854–5], thus the year 1774 was calculated nine years before that Royal Passing-Away.⁵⁰

⁴⁹ Jogja kraton MS. F. 1. The body of the MS. is presently in poor condition and virtually illegible.

⁵⁰ Ibid., note on first page: Sĕrat Suluk Surja Djaja Amisesa. Njariosakĕn, lampahanipun Kangdjĕng Sultan Surja Djaja Amisesa, Dipaningrat Njakrakusuma, Kalipatulah ingkang djumĕnĕng kaping V, saha ngrĕnggani Karaton Maespati Adiningrat, ngagĕm bintang Tjakraning Surja, Lejo Nedĕrlan, sarta Lesijun pan Ir.

Wiwitan, njariosakĕn Rĕtna Manik Rasa putranipun Sang Maha Rĕsi ing Wukir Lĕngkara. . . .

Wĕkasan, njariosakĕn Prabu Gonda Sukma Misesa, Senapati Ngalaga, Kabir Mukminin, ingkang nĕmbe sumilih ing marasĕpuh, djumĕnĕng Nata angrĕnggani Karaton Ngendra-Buwana, sowan bĕkti Kangdjĕng Sultan Surja Djaja Amisesa, Dipaningrat Njakrakusuma, Kalipatolah ingkang djumĕnĕng kaping V, saha ngrĕnggani Karaton Maespati Adiningrat.

Ingkang kasĕbut sĕrat palĕkat saking Kangdjĕng Sultan ing Maespati Adiningrat, ingkang kawaos, nalika Prabu ing Ngendra-Buwana, kadjumĕnĕngakĕn Nata, mawi dipunpengĕti tjondra-sangkala: tjatur rĕsi panḍita Dji (1774).

Manawi apengĕti Surud-Dalĕm, Sampejan-Dalem Ingkang Sinuhun, Kangdjĕng Sultan Hamĕngkubuwana, ingkang djumĕnĕng kaping V, ing Ngajogjakarta, amarĕngi taun Dal, 1783, dados taun: 1774, kapetang kirang 9 taun saking Surud-Dalĕm wau.

Wĕdana Kawindrawidjaja
27–III–1950.

While the details of the story are unclear, it is obvious that this *kraton* official understood the name Surja Djaja Amisesa V to be a mythical pseudonym for Sultan Haměngkubuwana V (A.D. 1822–6, 1828–55) and the events of the mythical story to be related to the history of Jogjakarta.

It seems possible that the subsidiary Javanese kingdoms which appear in *Sĕrat Surja Radja* represented Surakarta and the Mangkunĕgaran. It would be unwise to insist this was so, however, for there are so many characters and place-names in the text that it is difficult to follow the narrative thread or to be sure of locations and relationships.

But the kingdom of *Tanah Sabrang* (The Land Overseas) quite clearly represented the Dutch, although only Javanese names were used for them. In *Sĕrat Surja Radja* the people of Tanah Sabrang are said to be infidels (*kopar*, i.e. *kafir*),[51] and their troops perhaps include those on ship as well as on foot.[52] Other more conclusive descriptions of Tanah Sabrang as the Dutch may exist on pages of the original text which it was not possible to read.[53] The description is, however, quite unequivocal in later versions of the *Surja Radja* story.

Selections from the *Surja Radja* were employed by the Sultan's *ḍalang* as a text for performances of the arrow-dance (*bĕksa djĕmparing*) and lance-dance (*bĕksa djĕbĕng*) during the British occupation of Java (A.D. 1811–16). By that time the Javanese were acquainted not only with the Dutch, but with the English government and the French Napoleonic administrations of Daendels and Janssens (A.D. 1808–11) as well. It is therefore understandable

---

[51] *Kg. Kj. Surja Radja*, vol. i, 34 pages from the end; vol. ii, p. 14. On the necessity of this somewhat bizarre form of page reference, see n. 59 below.

[52] There are several such references, e.g. ibid., vol. ii, p. 15, Canto IV (Asmaradana):

27. . . . ngling Sang Nata pira kehnja
28. gamanja kang nglanggar mami
    umatur Rahaden Ngarga
    kapalan kalih kĕṭine
    kang djawi ingkang nganḍarat
    . . . .

It is possible, however, that the *kapalan* here are not naval forces but cavalry, since *kapal* in Javanese can mean either 'ship' or 'horse'.

[53] On the unusual research conditions surrounding the reading of this MS., see n. 59 below.

NEW AGE IN JAVANESE LITERATURE

that the ruler of Tanah Sabrang in these short versions of *Surja Radja* has 'French and English troops'.[54]

In a complete version of *Surja Radja* written in the Jogjakarta kraton in A.J. 1841–3 (A.D. 1911–12) the descriptions of Tanah Sabrang leave little doubt of its identity. Here, too, the people of Tanah Sabrang are infidels.[55] Moreover, like the Dutch East India Company, Tanah Sabrang has troops from Tĕrnate, Makasar, and the Buginese,[56] as well as naval forces.[57] Its leaders doff their hats (*tĕpijo*, from Portuguese *chapeo*), speak Malay, and are described as 'Officers' (*Upĕsir*); Sĕmarang is also mentioned.[58]

---

[54] *Sĕrat Konḍa*, also called *Sĕrat Gĕnḍing Bĕksan*, consisting of selections from *Sĕrat Surja Radja*, BM Add. MS. 12325 (B), f. 12ʳ: Pradjurit Prĕsman lan Anggris. Also mentioned on several other pages.

See my 'Inventory of the Javanese Manuscript Collection in the British Museum', *BKI*, vol. 125, no. 2 (1969), p. 252, where I mistakenly cite the first text ('B1') as *Sĕrat Purwa Radja*. The MS. has *Sĕrat Surja Radja*, as does 'B2'.

See also a similar Javanese tale, the *Sĕrat Achir ing Djaman*, ending in a battle between the Javanese and the kings of Holland, England, France, and Bengal, and finally in the conversion of the *kafir* rulers; summarized in S. van Praag, *Onrust op Java. De Jeugd van Dipanĕgara. Een Historisch-Literaire Studie* (Amsterdam, 1947), pp. 228–34.

[55] *Sĕrat Surja Radja* (Jogja kraton MS. F. 7), p. 857, Canto C (Pangkur):

25. . . .
    pan wus tjampuh kang juda
    Eslam Kapir samja sudiranipun
    langkung inguni ramenja
    nanging Wong Sabrang kalinḍih.

See also ibid., pp. 956, 966, and elsewhere.

[56] Ibid., p. 851, Canto C (Pangkur):

5. . . .
    Sri Narendra Pudja Dewa [ruler of Tanah Sabrang]
    dukanja jajah sinipi

6. Sang Nata Tĕrnate lawan
    ing Makasar Bugis katrinireki
    kinen bantu ing apupuh
    . . . .

Balinese troops are also mentioned later, e.g. pp. 864, 867, 869.

[57] Ibid., p. 875, Canto CIV (Durma):

5. Sawadyanja prakapalan sami tiwas
    . . . .

Cf. n. 52 above.

[58] Ibid., pp. 871–2, Canto CIII (Gurisa) (in Javanese script):

1. Sarĕng matur mring Sang Radja
    sarwi bukak tĕpijonja
    mentak ampun ḍengan tuwan

194   JOGJAKARTA UNDER SULTAN MANGKUBUMI

Short of calling Tanah Sabrang 'Holland', the author of this version could hardly have identified it more clearly.

The original text of *Sĕrat Surja Radja* would thus appear to be a mythologized consideration of the problems faced by Jogjakarta at the start of the new century. It is therefore a mine of information on the *kraton's* perception of its problems, and on the potential solutions to them. Not all mines are easily worked, however, and this one is among the most difficult, not only because of the nature of its treasure but because of research conditions as well.[59]

    saja abilang sĕkarang
    radja-radja suda linggar
    sauḍara lari lantas
    tĕrlalu rang Djawa banjak
    sĕkarang ḍĕkĕt dimukak.

Sang Radja Drusman (Tanah Sabrang) also replies to this report in Malay:

2. . . .
    pĕrsetan banjak bitjara
    ḍija kira takut lawan
    brapa banjak urang Djawa
    saja tidak takut lawan

3. kaluk ḍija takut lijat
    Samarang Djawa sĕmua
    saja sĕnḍiri jang lawan
    kaluk ḍapĕt tangkĕp sadja
    saja tampĕr tamtu basah
    tempo kita Tanah Sabrang
    suḍa tiḍak bole lawan
    sama tunḍuk ḍengĕn kita

4. sĕkarang ini anglanggar
    suḍah aḍa Tanah Djawa
    tiḍak brani ḍengĕn lawan
    kita malu djuk pulang
    para Upĕsir sĕdaja
    djrih mulat kruḍaning Radja
    . . . .

[59] Because the MS. is a *pusaka* it cannot be made readily available for research purposes. On each appearance it must be brought in ceremonial procession from the *Prabajĕksa* to the *Bangsal Manis*, on a suitable day and accompanied by appropriate offerings (*sadjen*) borne by *kraton* officials. The organizational and financial complications of such ceremonial meant that I could read this MS. only on a few occasions, and then seated somewhat uncomfortably on the marble floor of the *Bangsal Manis*, surrounded by *kraton* officialdom.

To maximize my limited opportunities, I adopted the somewhat artificial rule that I would take extensive notes and transcriptions from the first and last thirty pages (approximately) of each of the two volumes. I read as a result some

NEW AGE IN JAVANESE LITERATURE 195

The text of this book, in its A.J. 1700 form, begins with a *manggala* (proem) in praise of the Crown Prince, the Sultan, and the book *Surja Radja*. This proem illustrates the place of the book in *kraton* affairs, and the way in which its contents were understood

---

120 pages of the MS., which must total about 1,000 pages (unnumbered). These pages, selected from the beginning, middle, and end of the text, I hoped would enable me to describe the development of the story. The limitations of this approach are obvious. Yet my experience with the library copy of *Surja Radja* (kraton MS. F. 7, dated A.J. 1841–3/A.D. 1911–12), which I read in its entirety (1,029 pages), led me to suspect that much of the original MS. would, like the later MS., consist of elaborate poetic descriptions of the beauties of nature, the colourful life of the court, and the sanguinary horrors of battle. I hoped, therefore, that the method I adopted would spare me unnecessary poetic digressions, while allowing me to understand the essentials of the text.

The result of this approach was generally satisfactory, excepting that I would like to have read more of the first volume in order to be certain whether it contains the lengthy lessons on Islamic mysticism found in kraton MS. F. 7 (Cantos II–X, and ff.) and the victory over the other Javanese kingdoms (Cantos XIII–LXXXVI).

It should be noted, incidentally, that the *pusaka* MS. of A.J. 1700 was not the original text of the story, although it is the oldest copy extant. Eighteen pages from the end of the second volume the scribe began a new canto, but then mistakenly copied four and one-half stanzas of the preceding canto a second time, then stopped, and began his new canto again. This could only have happened if he were copying literally from another book and lost his place while turning the page (to p. 17 from end of vol. ii). There are also several places where lines have been left out and later inserted in the margin as correction. The introductory *manggala* (cited below) says this was copied from an original by the Crown Prince, presumably to produce a more beautiful work of art; this would explain the obvious evidence that this is a second copy. I am confident, however, that the *pusaka* MS. is in fact the version of A.J. 1700, produced in more artistic form from a text in the Crown Prince's autograph, or from a copy written by a court poet according to the Crown Prince's general directions. The paper is of the heavy Dutch variety, watermarked 'J. H. & Z', in use in the late eighteenth century on Java. Furthermore, the text has only the date A.J. 1700, whereas kraton MS. F. 7 has the date it was written (A.J. 1841–3) and the dates of previous versions, A.J. 1700, 1785. The *pusaka* MS. also names the author only as Crown Prince, whereas kraton MS. F. 7 calls him Crown Prince but also refers to him as Sultan HB II. The fact that he is not referred to as Sultan in the *pusaka* suggests it was written before his accession, while he was still Crown Prince.

Another copy of *Surja Radja* is BG 164, Museum Pusat, Djakarta. It is dated Dal, widigbya kang djahning mahendra ngrat (A.J. 1743/A.D. 1815), and in appearance is more like the original MS. than kraton MS. F. 7. It, too, describes the author as Sultan HB II, indicating its origin after his accession. Unfortunately, I only became aware of the existence of this MS. a few days before leaving Indonesia and could only examine it very briefly.

It should be noted that LOr 8604, *Sĕrat Surja Radja*, bears no relation to the Jogjakarta *Surja Radja* texts described here. It is a history beginning with Adam and the prophets, and continuing into post-Madjapahit history and nineteenth-century Jogjakarta history.

by the court literati, who knew that this was very much more than just a good mythological story:

Be it known, this is the *pusaka* of Kangdjĕng Gusti Pangeran Adipati Anom Hamĕngkunĕgara [the Crown Prince], the Illustrious, Royal Son of his father the Great King. That is, Kangdjĕng Sultan Hamĕngkubuwana Senapati Ingalaga Ngabdurahman Sajidin Panatagama Kalipatolah, of the island Java, who adorns the City Ngajogjakarta Adiningrat. And praised exceedingly in this book, indeed, is the perfect heart of Kangdjĕng Sultan; may he receive the blessing of Allah the Most High in this world and in the world to come, and the blessing of the intercession of Kangdjĕng Nabi (Prophet) Muḥammad—God bless Him and grant Him peace.

Be perfect the praise of his heart when, indeed, Kangdjĕng Gusti [the Crown Prince], great of intent, creates the secrets of knowledge (*ngelmu*) and the ordering of the kingdom, contained in *Sĕrat Surja Radja*.

And let there be no misunderstanding, for this book has many meanings, which are contained in this *Surja Radja*, yea which are rendered into verse, causing the withered heart to flower, and which are made a mirror, a reminder of knowledge (*ngelmu*) and of the ordering of the kingdom.

Now, while that Honoured Royal Son creates a pleasure-garden in this *Surja Radja* excellent, we are precise, not as if negligent of our vow, true in soul and body [?], as if standing firm in the sea.

Indeed, he is destined to remain enveloped with the Attributes of the Majesty of God, the Beauty of God, the Perfection of God, the Omnipotence of God, and the Attributes Omnipotent, Willing, Knowing, Living, Hearing, Seeing, Speaking, Being One.

Be perfect the perseverance in wisdom (*ngelmu*), indeed, of those who are ordered to copy this book from the original creation of Kangdjĕng Gusti, that is, the scribes named Sĕstraprawira and Wirjawidjaja. Now, the writing which is enclosed in illumination is done by himself [the Crown Prince] and the embellishment of the illumination and the stanza-headings are done by himself.

Now, those who are ordered to gild and to paint [the illuminations] are the wives, the women, and the serving-girls of the Crown Prince's Residence, and he who was ordered to bind [the book] is named Nur Wahid.

It was written on Monday-Pon [*sic*; error for Monday-Lĕgi], the eighth day of the month Muharram [the first month] of the year: 1–7–0–0 [21 March A.D. 1774].[60]

[60] *Kg. Kj. Surja Radja*, vol. i, p. 2:
Pratanḍa pusaka Kangdjĕng Gusti Pangeran Adipati Anom, Hamĕngkunĕgara kang Sudibya Atmarinadja sudarma Mahanalendra. Anĕnggih Kangdjĕng

The first canto of the book (pp. 6 ff.) begins with the date of the writing, given correctly as Soma-Manis (Monday-Lĕgi), with the chronogram *purna linang ing paṇḍita*, A.J. (1)700. There follows praise of the Sultan of Jogjakarta and of the Crown Prince, most beloved of his many children, then twenty-four years old.[61] Then begins the story of the book. The reader should remember that what seems merely to be a romantic tale was, for the court of Jogjakarta, a book containing 'the secrets of knowledge and the ordering of the kingdom':

In Java is a king ruling an Islamic nation, the King of Purwa Gupita (or Purwa Tjipta), Maharadja Surja Amisesa by name, who is 'as if he had descended from Paradise' and 'embodies the sun and the moon'.[62]

Sultan Hamĕngkubuwana Senapati Ingalaga Ngadurahman [sic] Sajidin Panatagama Halifatolah ing Nusa Djawa kang angrĕnggani Nagri Ngajudjakarta Adiningrat. Lawan ta pinudyeng sastra antyan tuhu manah kang sampurna Kangdjĕng Sultan, mugi antuka sih kanugrahaning Allahu Tongala ing donja rawuh ing aherat, sarta kang barkat safangat, Kangdjĕng Nabi Muhamad, salalahu ngaleji wasalam. Malipurna pamudyanireng ati manawi anĕnggih Kangdjĕng Gusti maha sadya mangirtya sandining ngelmi mjang pranataning pradja tumrap in Surat Surja Radja. Lan sampun wetĕn [sic] kaliru ing tampane sawab surat puniku akeh rasane dene kang wus tumrap ing Surja Radja puniku. Mapan, kinarja sasĕkar mĕkar wigaring manah lawan kinarja paesan, pangengĕt-engĕt, ing ngelmu mjang pranataning pradja. Dira Sang Narpa Putra kapja maudyana ing Surja Radja antyan, kita puniki titis tan mantreng wikara pratignja tuhu djiwa majongga lir tan, djrak [i.e., lir ta andjrak?] ing sagara. Puniku tuhu pasṭi tĕtĕp, kalimputan ing sifat Djalalolah,, Djamalolah,, Kamalolah,, Kaharolah,, lan sifat, Kodrat,, Iradat,, Ngelmu,, Hajat,, Samak,, Basar,, Kalam,, Wahdanijat.

Malipurna panohiding ngelmu anĕnggih kang kinen anurun surat sangking wit pangirtyanireng Kangdjĕng Gusti. Nĕnggih prijaji tjarik awasta Sĕstraprawira lan Wirjawidjaja dening sastra kang munggeng ing wadana kaasta prijongga tuwin rĕngganing wadana lawan pada pan kaasta prijongga. Dening kang kinen maraos jungging para garwa para prijaji para manggung ing Kadospaten, dening kang kinen njamak awasta Nur Wahid. Kala sinurat ing dina Sĕnen-Pon tanggal ping walu sasi Muharam ing Taun Ehe angkaning warsa 1-7-0-0.

[61] Text cited above, p. 169, n. 88.
[62] *Kg. Kj. Surja Radja*, vol. i, p. 8, Canto I (Asmaradana):

13. ...
    lir piturun saking sjarga.
    . . . .

15. Tuhu Prabu andjasmani
    ing surja kalawan tjondra
    . . . .

[*Footnote 62 continued overleaf*

The King has two sons, the older named Dasakusuma, who is married to Princess Kumalawati, daughter of Udajana, the ruler of a part (*saperang*) of the *pasisir* and *montjanĕgara*. The younger son is Djajakusuma, married to Dyah Pudjasmara, daughter of a *paṇḍita* (teacher, wise man) from Mt. Rasamulja, whose name is Sang Danasukma. The King decides to divide his kingdom between his sons, the older (Dasakusuma) to become ruler in Danaradja, controlling the area to the east of the river (*bĕngawan*) with the name Surja Amidjaja. The younger son (Djajakusuma) will succeed in Purwa Gupita (or Purwa Kaṇḍa) with the title Surja Wisesa. (Vol. i, Canto I: 11–32)

After seven months the King dies and his two sons succeed over the divided kingdom (*nĕgara kalih*). The older ruler, Surja Amidjaja, begets two children. The younger, Surja Wisesa, begets four, his oldest son Pudjakusuma (Sang Pĕkik) having the appearance of Joseph come down from Paradise. Then Surja Wisesa dies after fifteen years of rule, and his elder brother Surja Amidjaja then retakes that part of the kingdom (Purwa Gupita) and moves his capital there, thus depriving of his heritage the young Pudjakusuma, who then lives under his uncle's rule. Eventually he becomes displeased with his fate, and turns to religious practices, meditating upon the Omnipotent God (*Allah kang Murba-Wisesa*). A voice comes to him assuring him his wishes will be fulfilled, but the time has not yet come. (Vol. i, Canto I: 32–52)

Purwa Koṇḍa (Purwa Gupita) is now beset by misfortunes, which arouse the concern of Surja Amidjaja. He calls together his court and asks the wise men about the cause of the misfortunes. After a lengthy discussion, the ruler's anger turns against Pudjakusuma, who is killed upon the ruler's order, along with his companions Supala and Supali. (Vol. i, Canto I: 52–IV: 27)

Pudjakusuma's sister Pudjarĕsmi and her siblings hear the terrible news, but are defeated when they attempt to attack the ruler in revenge. The angry Surja Amidjaja now sends his forces against the *paṇḍita* at Rasamulja (home of Pudjakusuma's grandfather) whom he believes to be in league with the party of the dead prince. (Vol. i, Canto IV: 27–V: 11)

Note, the same phrases are used to describe HB I on ibid., p. 7, Canto I (Asmaradana):

    4. Tuhu jen Prabu linuwih
       andjasma ing surja tja[n]dra
       . . . .

    5. . . .
       tuhu jen pĕkik warnane
       lir piturun saking sjarga.
       . . . .

The *paṇḍita* of Rasamulja, also called *panĕmbahan ing Giri*, is the son of the former *paṇḍita* (and therefore uncle to the dead Pudjakusuma), renowned for his asceticism. His name is Danasukma (II). The history of these *paṇḍitas* began with a saint (*walijolah*) from Arabia named Djatiwisesa, who came to Java and practised asceticism on Rasamulja. After strenuous asceticism, a voice spoke to him saying it was God's will that neither his son nor his grandson were destined to rule Java. But his great-grandson (*bujut*, i.e. Pudjakusuma)[63] would be entitled to rule Java, and Tanah Sabrang would pay him tribute (*ambulu-pĕti*). All his great-grandson's descendants were destined to become *Pakuningbumi* (cf. Pakubuwana, Mangkubumi, etc.). Upon his death, Djatiwisesa was succeeded by his son Danasukma (I), who was born not of woman, but of God's will.[64] After nine years succeeded Danasukma (II), whose sister married the ruler of Purwa Gupita (Djajakusuma). (The text is here rehearsing the events already described leading to Pudjakusuma's misfortune.) (Vol. i, Canto V: 11–39)

The emissaries from the ruler of Purwa Gupita (Surja Amidjaja) now arrive at Rasamulja. A furious battle follows, which Purwa Gupita loses, as it also loses a second assault, defeated by the magical power of the *paṇḍita*. (Vol. i, Canto V: 39–48)

The bodies of the dead Pudjakusuma and his companions are meanwhile being carried by the river down to the ocean, accompanied by horrific natural phenomena. The bodies float glistening on the sea. Sang Panĕmbahan Giri (Danasukma II) arrives in the midst of the ocean, for he knows what has been preordained by God. He takes up the bodies: it matters not that they have been killed, for the radiant brightness of life (*tjahja*) is still to be seen. Much moved by the sight of the slain bodies, Danasukma (II) speaks of God's will, and orders the bodies to rise, once, twice, without success. On his third summons, Pudjakusuma revives, and bows in obeisance at the feet of his saviour. Tearfully he relates his misfortunes. The *paṇḍita* then advises him to return to Purwa Gupita and approach the ruler (Surja Amidjaja) to calm his anger. Pudjakusuma does not wish to obey, fearing for his safety, but the *paṇḍita* begins to lecture him on the duties of a servant of

---

[63] The line of descent is Djatiwisesa—Danasukma I (Pudjakusuma's grandfather)—Danasukma II (Pudjakusuma's uncle) and Pudjasmara (Pudjakusuma's mother)—Pudjakusuma.

[64] *Kg. Kj. Surja Radja*, vol. i, p. 23, Canto V (Pangkur):

26. . . .
   sira ana tanpa bijang
   midjil karseng Jwang pribadi

27. nora kalawan lantaran
   . . . .

the king. (Vol. i, Canto VI: 1–VII: 2. The end of this portion of the manuscript.)

It is impossible to say what events occur in this manuscript between Pudjakusuma's salvation and when the story is taken up again at the end of the first volume.[65] It may be possible to infer from the later manuscript of A.J. 1841–3 (A.D. 1911–12),[66] however, that Pudjakusuma now sets off on a long series of adventures, in the course of which he receives teachings in Islamic mysticism and kingship (Cantos II–X). These emphasize the unity of opposites and of servant and master (*kawula-gusti*); the heretical view is taken that there is no difference between God and the infidel (*kapir*) (Canto X: 28–9). The prophecy is repeated that Pudjakusuma will rule Java and Tanah Sabrang, controlling everything to the east of Persia (Canto X: 7). Then the Goddess of the Southern Ocean appears, here called Rĕtna Dewati. She is the queen of the spirits, thousands of years old, but can be either young or old depending on whether the moon is new or old (Cantos XI–XII).[67] There follows a series of battles with other Javanese potentates, in which the Goddess joins. The course of these wars is confusing, but they seem to end in a victory for Pudjakusuma (Cantos XIII–LXXXVI). Then begins the tale of Tanah Sabrang, which occupies the remainder of the book (Cantos LXXXVII–CXXIV). The first volume of the original *Surja Radja* of A.J. 1700 seems to end during the contest for supremacy on Java, apparently after the Javanese have suffered losses at the hands of Tanah Sabrang:[68]

There have been battles with the infidel, and many have died. Sang Putra (Pudjakusuma) receives news that more forces, of unknown origin, are marching against him. News comes to him that the king Sang Asmara (of Tanah Sabrang?) has marched into the *pasisir* lands belonging to Purwa Gupita, and has destroyed all the cities belonging to the Dipati of Gonda Pura (?). It is then decided to establish a *kraton* in Purwa Radja, and the forest is cleared (*babad*) for that purpose. Raden

---

[65] See n. 59 above on the reasons for the break in the narrative at this point, and again after vol. ii, Canto VI: 9.

[66] Jogja kraton MS. F. 7.

[67] I am grateful to S.D.I.S. Kg. Sultan Hamĕngkubuwana IX for confirming that Rĕtna Dewati is a name for Kg. Ratu Kidul when she is young, i.e. before the middle of each month.

[68] The large number of new personal and place names which appear at the end of this volume makes for much confusion.

Putra (Pudjakusuma) occupies the *kraton* and the city flourishes. There is talk of revenge against the people of Sabrang. (Vol. i, Canto X from end–Canto VIII from end: 7)

At Mt. Wilaja to the south of Purwa Radja is a hermitage, the home of one Sidiwĕtjana. After his death, his two children, including the beautiful Dyah Enḍangrĕtnasasi, go to Purwa Radja to pay obeisance. A love affair develops, and she is eventually wedded to the ruler (Pudjakusuma). (Vol. i, Canto VIII from end: 7–Canto VI from end)

The brother of Enḍangrĕtnasasi, named (Wasi) Djajamurtjita, now leads the troops against the enemy area at Gadjah Oja in the *pasisir*, which he conquers and plunders, much to the joy of Sang Pĕkik (also, Ri Sang Dipaningpupuh, Sang Prawirengpupuh, etc., i.e. Pudjakusuma). The court then joins in a hunt on the *alun-alun*, where the wild animals are driven by Djajamurtjita (called Raden Wukir). (Vol. i, Canto V from end–Canto II from end)

Later, at a court gathering a letter is received from *Sinuhun Giri*, announcing that Sang Pĕkik (Pudjakusuma) is to become ruler like his late father (Djajakusuma). Dyan Anom (also Sang Prawiranom, i.e. Pudjakusuma) obeys, and is made ruler. He dines with the Muslim divines (*paralim, para kaum*). (Vol. i, last Canto)

The second volume begins with the celebrations of the new ruler's accession on Monday-Pon, 4 Muharram, Alip (without the year being mentioned). Like Solomon in appearance, he is declared to be *Pakuning Alam-donja*. He looks like Joseph come down from Paradise. Then is read the letter from *Radja Panḍita Giri*, giving the prince royal titles. The prince, named Djajasumadi (? i.e. Pudjakusuma),[69] is to be called

[69] I am unable satisfactorily to explain the name Djajasumadi. It seems this must either be an alias for Pudjakusuma, or at least a descendant of Pudjakusuma. Otherwise the accession as *Pakuning Alam-donja* would be inconsistent with the previous prophecies in the *Kg. Kj. Surja Radja*.

On the first page of ibid., vol. i, before the text begins, a list of names is written in a rough hand which has the appearance of a genealogy. Pudjakusuma does not appear in it, but Djajasumadi is the seventh name: Prabu Purwa Konḍa ingkang,, 1 [i.e. Prabu Maharadja Surja Amisesa],, Putra Raden Djajakusuma,, 2 [i.e. Prabu Surja Wisesa, Pudjakusuma's father],, Putra Raden Senakusuma,, 3,, Putra Raden Tedjakusuma,, 4,, Putra Kusumawidjaja,, 5,, Putra Raden Djajamisadi [sic],, 6,, Putra Raden Dja[ja]sumadi,, 7,, Putra Raden Djaja Asmara,, 8,, Putra Raden Danusĕmara,, 9,,

Near the end of the later text of the story, kraton MS. F. 7, p. 1025, Canto CXXIV, verses 12–14, Djajasamadi [sic], who looks like Joseph, is the son of Surja Wisesa (Ruler of Purwa Ginunggung, i.e. Purwa Gupita) by Kusumaningaju (sister of Prabu Sindurarĕdja), and is destined to succeed as ruler; in verse 18, he becomes ruler.

It would be unwise to attempt to fill the gaps in my understanding of this text with clever guesses. Mysteries such as the name Djajasumadi are better left as they are, in the interest of understanding the general historical significance of the writing of *Kg. Kj. Surja Radja*.

Radja Surja Djaja Amisesa Muhamad Djenal Ngasik Ngarifin.[70] All pay obeisance to the new king, and the people are happy. (Vol. ii, Cantos I-II)

Turning from the new ruler of Purwa Radja, the text tells of king Pontjasona (of Tanah Sabrang), who has ruled for a long time in Purwa Ginupit (i.e., Purwa Gupita, now apparently controlled by Tanah Sabrang), famous in Java and Sabrang.[71] He is fortifying his *kraton*. A voice has come to him, saying that if he wishes himself and his descendants to remain rulers in Java, he must destroy the *djimat* (amulet) of Java, the grave-site (*pasarejan*) at Giri-Rasamulja. If not, his kingdom will fall. His attempt to destroy the site is, however, foiled by the magical disappearance of it.[72] Pontjasona now hears of the successes of his enemy Djajasumadi (i.e. Pudjakusuma, now Surja Djaja Amisesa), who has attacked Pontjasona's lands, among which are the *montjanĕgara* and *pasisir* (*pontjanagri pasisir*). He tells his *patih* Beganonda that he does not believe this Djajasumadi (Pudjakusuma, Surja Djaja Amisesa) to be the true prince of Java (*putreng Tanah Djawa*). Beganonda agrees, saying that person has died long ago and it is inconceivable that he should live again. Pontjasona announces that he will defeat the ruler of Java, for the Javanese are no match for the

---

[70] This title is a mystery to me. It is not among the royal titles of the House of Mataram. It is significant, however, that in the beginning of the text the Jogjakarta Crown Prince gives himself the same title (*Kg. Kj. Surja Radja*, vol. i, p. 8, Canto I, Asmaradana):

> 7. Djumĕnĕng Pangran Dipati
> Anom Hamĕngkunĕgara
> Muhamad Djenal Ngasike
> . . . .

[71] *Kg. Kj. Surja Radja*, vol. ii, p. 9, Canto III (Durma):

> 1. Enĕngĕna Sang Prabu ing Purwa Radja
> gĕnti ingkang kawarni
> Prabu Pontjasona
> kang wus ngaḍaton lama
> aneng ing Purwa Ginupit
> wus kasub ing rat
> Sabrang lirna ing Djawi.

Thus, Purwa Gupita and Purwa Radja are two distinct *kratons*.

[72] Ibid., vol. ii, p. 10, Canto III (Durma):

> 7. Mila Ri Sang Pontjasona karsanira
> nugjani ing sjareki
> nging sarĕng linakjan
> kang pasarejan arsa
> rinusak tan dya tan keksi
> pan dadya wana
> . . . .

people of Tanah Sabrang, with which his advisers agree.[73] Then comes the news that Djajasumadi (Pudjakusuma) has received the titles of a Javanese king (Surja Djaja Amisesa), and that he is indeed the prince whom Pontjasona believed to be dead. Pontjasona orders his troops to war. (Vol. ii, Canto III–IV: 13)

The ruler of Purwa Radja (Pudjakusuma) meanwhile takes advice from Djajamurtjita on how he should go to war in the path of God (*sabilolah*) against the infidels. A battle plan is decided, and on Friday-Wage the troops are to depart. But first there are festivities in the court, with the troops dancing and the *gamĕlan* and *wajang* performed. (Vol. ii, Canto IV: 13–VI: 9. The end of this portion of the manuscript.)

In the last pages of Volume II, the war between Java and Tanah Sabrang is under way. Their forces are equally matched and the bloody tide of battle flows back and forth. The Goddess of the Southern Ocean[74] is on the side of the Javanese, but the spirit forces and magical power (*sĕkti*) of Tanah Sabrang are equal. (Vol. ii, Canto X from end–Canto II from end)

Suffering losses and unable to achieve a victory, the Javanese are ordered by the Goddess (Prabu Kĕnja) to recite the *Qur'ān* and pray to God for victory. The field residence (*pasanggrahan*) of the leader of Tanah Sabrang (called Sang Sri Pontjarĕsmi) is then struck by earthquake and storm, striking fear in the hearts of Pontjarĕsmi and his troops. The Javanese take the offensive and soon the city Purwa Rukma (under Tanah Sabrang) is besieged by the (Javanese) spirit-troops, who have meanwhile been victorious in the south against the demon armies

---

[73] Ibid., vol. ii, pp. 11–12, Canto III (Durma):

27. Sri Sudibya latah sarwi angandika
 sireku jaji kalih
 kagunggung musuhnja
 mĕngko [text has mĕkong] jen sidajaha
 Ratu ing Djawa sadasih
 mongsa kongsija
 kalah mring djĕnĕng mami

28. dadi nora paḍa lan wong Tanah Sabrang
 Sri Sindura ngabĕkti
 Radjeng Tanah Djawa
 kalamun katimbanga
 lan Nata saniskareki
 nadyan watĕna
 sasra lir Nateng Djawi

29. datan padya-padya jen anjamenana
 lawan kakang Nĕrpati
 . . . .

[74] Here called Prabu Rara Rat Djawi, Sang Rĕtna, Prabu Kĕnja, Sang Dewi, Sang Prabu Wanodya, Sang Rĕtna Dewi, Sang Rĕtna Tanah Djawi, Sang Prabu Dewi, Prabu Rara Surja Dewati, etc.

of Purwa Rukma. The Javanese king, however, orders that the city be not destroyed, but merely frightened.[75] (Vol. ii, Canto II from end: 26–last Canto: 3)

Now the ruler of Purwa Rukma falls seriously ill. His court and his city are greatly disturbed by his illness, their courage gone. No amount of medicine can cure the ruler, nor can the friendly king of spirits (*Nalendra djin*) help him. The court prays in vain to their god (*Dewa*) to drive the enemy from the city and to cure their king. On the eve of Friday-Lĕgi, the ruler sends away his wives and prays in solitude to his god (*Dewagung, Dewa kang Luwih Masesa*) that he might be cured and the city made to prosper, the enemy driven from its walls. Suddenly a disembodied voice speaks to him, saying:

10. . . .
    So, O King, you ask the *Dewa*

11. to be cured of your illness
    and for all such wishes.
    It has not been granted because
    of this: your sphere,
    all of it,
    and the praying to the *Dewa*,
    it is the wish of God
    should be laid waste. Change your faith
    to Islam, call upon
    Allah, the Most High.

12. This god does not exist,
    rather Allah the Most High be praised
    in the form
    which is one,
    Who created the worlds,

---

[75] *Kg. Kj. Surja Radja*, vol. ii, 10 pages from end to 9 pages from end, Last Canto (Ḍanḍanggula):

2. . . .
    lan Nagri Purwa Rukmine
    sĕmana wus kinĕpung
    kasrambahan tĕpang kang baris
    dĕnawa ingkang mĕnang
    prang baris neng kidul
    mila karsanja Sang Nata
    ingkang nagri datan ginĕmpur tumuli
    ginirisan kewala

3. aja kongsi rĕsak kang nĕgari
    . . . .

transient and eternal;
all of it, completely
is governed by Allah.
And pay homage to the Prophet
Muḥammad, the Emissary

13. of Allah the Most High.
    If you observe not
    the Islamic faith,
    your *kraton* is destined
    to be destroyed by the enemy,
    you will disappear with
    your wives, children, and servants.
    If you follow Islam
    your enemies will surely withdraw themselves
    and you shall be healed.

14. The Islamic faith
    is above, below are the believers in gods.[76]

[76] Ibid., 8 pages from end, Last Canto (Ḍanḍanggula):

10. . . .
    lah kaki Adji sira nanĕḍa Dewa
11. amuljaha ing laranireki
    mjang salirnja ing satjiptanira
    tan katrima sawab dene
    mĕngko djagatireku
    saniskaranira puniki
    mjang pamudyaning Dewa
    karsaning Jang Agung
    rinutjat salin sarengat [text has sarengjat]
    gama Islam anĕbuta sira kaki
    ing Allahu Tongala
12. noranana Pangeran puniki
    nanging Allah Tongala sinĕmbah
    ing dalĕm wudjude mangke
    ka[ng] saka(ng) tunggal iku
    kang dadekĕn alam puniki
    kabir lan sahir ika
    sangkĕp sadajeku
    kawisesa direng Allah
    karo dening angestokĕna ing Nabi
    Mukamad kuutusan [*sic*]
13. ning Allahu Tongala puniki
    jen sira kaki nora ngestokna
    maring agama Islame
    pasṭi kratonireku
    gĕmpur dening mungsuhireki

When the ruler hears this his heart is full of wonder. But he hesitates because he knows nothing of the practices of Islam. He asks God (*Widi*) for help, and the voice returns: Allah the Most High has granted the *Qur'ān* and the books (*kitab*), containing all the ways of Islam. These volumes then appear before the ruler, and his illness is immediately cured. He rises, opens the *Qur'ān* and *kitab* to read them, and his heart is enlightened like the sun. Perfecting his understanding of the faith, he now remains the ruler, a Saintly King (*Ratu Waliolah*). His wives, children, courtiers, and all within Purwa Rukma embrace Islam. (Vol. ii, last Canto: 3–21)

When the besieging forces learn of this conversion they are furious. They attack the *kraton* of Purwa Rukma, but are driven back by a volcanic eruption. They then attempt another assault, again thrown back by the volcano. Then all the troops withdraw. The ruler of Purwa Rukma (here Purwa Kĕntjana) and his subjects rejoice that they have been saved by Allah. (Vol. ii, last Canto: 21–34)

The ruler of Purwa Rukma now goes to Prabu Pontjarĕsmi (king of Tanah Sabrang) and pleases him with his report on the course of the war. Pontjarĕsmi is, however, amazed at the tale of the miraculous cure and the salvation of the city of Purwa Rukma through conversion to Islam. Pontjarĕsmi himself has been ill, and constantly praying to the *Dewa* to be cured. Now he, too, converts to Islam along with his court, and the already-converted ruler of Purwa Rukma becomes their *guru* (teacher). Pontjarĕsmi is healed. (Vol. ii, last Canto: 34–43)

The enemy (Javanese) forces wish again to attack Pontjarĕsmi, but the Javanese ruler (called the Holy Supreme Ruler, Ri Sang Tunggul Nalendra) orders the troops withdrawn. The Javanese king sends an emissary to the Goddess of the Southern Ocean (Prabu Rara Surja Dewati) informing her by letter of all the happenings, and of his commands. She withdraws all her forces, but does so cautiously lest the enemy attempt to follow. (Vol. ii, last Canto: 43–50)

Now the two former enemy kings meet. The ruler of Tanah Djawa goes to the ruler of Purwa Rukma (i.e. Pontjarĕsmi, the supreme king of Tanah Sabrang), unaccompanied by his troops, escorted only by two companions. Now their religions are one; they deliberate together on

---

      sira sirna kalawan
      garwa putra wadu
      jen sira wus klakon [text has klaklon] Islam
      mungsuhira amasṭi mundur pribadi
      sira anuli mulja

14. agama Islam iku ta kaki
      luwih luhur anḍap wong dĕdewan
      . . . .

NEW AGE IN JAVANESE LITERATURE

mystical knowledge (*ngelmu*). The ruler of Purwa Rukma (Tanah Sabrang) gives to the Javanese king, his younger brother (*ari*), products from his island Ngambar Sari, which lies near the island Java. These include iron, gold, silver, lead, cloves, silk, and jewels. Then the two rulers exchange documents (*srat*) bearing their seals (*tjap*). Now the ruler of Purwa Rukma wishes to return home, as does his younger brother the king of Java. They depart, returning separately to Purwa Rukma (under Tanah Sabrang's domain) and Purwa Gupita (again the Javanese capital), taking with them all their gifts. The kings are pleased. (Vol. ii, last Canto: 50-9. End of *Kg. Kj. Surja Radja*)[77]

[77] I find these last stanzas unclear in part. The text is as follows: *Kg. Kj. Surja Radja*, vol. ii, last 3 pages, Last Canto (Ḍanḍanggula):

50. ...
    risampunira mangkana
    tjinarita Sang Prabu ing Tanah Djawi
    lawan ing Purwa Rukma

51. papanggijan pijambak Sang Adji
    pan agěntos lajarinajaran
    ḍumatěng pasanggrahane
    nging tan běkta wadya gung
    amungakěn kang parpat kalih
    wadya tan auninga
    dene mangke sampun
    tunggil ing sarengatira
    mila těpang ing karsa kadwinja malih
    samja sakuṭunira

52. tur samja musawaratan ngelmi
    pan adawa lamun tjinarita
    denja panggijan Sang Katong
    wontěn malih winuwus
    pulo ḍěkět ing Tanah Djawi
    nging kareh Purwa Rukma
    wijarireng pulo
    antawis bumi salěksa
    těngranira ingkang pulo Ngambar Sari
    Bopatinja sadjuga

53. ingkang pulo pamědalireki
    keh warnanja wěsi mas salaka
    mjang timah pala tjěngkehe
    salir gijanggi iku
    tuwin tjinḍe sěsamineki
    lan mawi mědal rětna
    ing mangke puniku
    kapatěḍakěn arinta
    Nateng Djawi saklangkung panrimaneki
    mila kang raka Nata

54. mangkatěn karsanja sawab dening
    liněpaskěnireng batosira

Thus ends the holy and confusing book *Sĕrat Surja Radja*. It would be folly to attempt to interpret every detail of the story, even if it could be fully understood. Certain aspects of this book

    dira wit Gami Sutjine
    purwanira apupuh
    lan kang raji dan tĕpang kapti
    lan malih sarĕng juda
    lan mĕngsahireku
    inggih samja tinondjok srat
    djuga-djuga nanging witnja katut dening
    kang raka Purwa Rukma

55. dadya raji angrentjangi djurit
    mila kapisungsungan ing pulja
    lawan kang putra estrine
    ingkang dadya garweku
    Radja Putra ing Tanah Djawi
    ing mangke pan binĕktan
    nan Bopati tjatur
    lawan mantri kawandasa
    sapradjurit salĕksa kaṭahireki
    kang estri tan kaetang

56. nanging Sang Prabu ing Purwa Rukmi
    darbe pamĕḍĕt ḍatĕng arinta
    mĕnggah kaprabon ing Katong
    kang raji Bandjar nĕngguh
    kadjawinja dadana nagri
    punika pinalampah
    ing raji Sang Prabu
    prituwin garwa lan putra
    ingkang kantun neng nĕgari Bandjar Rukmi
    puniku pinalampah

57. katĕḍakna raji Bandjar Rukmi
    pan adawa lamun tjinarita
    Sang Nata kalih kalije
    wus saeka ing kalbu
    ing pamĕnḍĕt wus panggih adja [adji?]
    pan nampeni-nampenan
    saha prataṇdeku
    surat-surat mawi ĕtjap
    risampunja mangkana Sri Purwa Rukmi
    arsa kondur mring pradja

58. ingkang raji Prabu Tanah Djawi
    pan kasarah manawi akarsa
    lumiring ing raka Katong
    utawi ladjĕng kondur
    ingkang raka nurut sakapti
    ning Sri Katong Djawa
    arsa ladjĕng kondur
    ḍumatĕng ing Tanah Djawa

do, however, seem clear and are sufficient to understand its place in Jogjakarta history. Sĕrat Surja Radja appears clearly to have been a prophetic device to solve the problems of Jogjakarta, but there are several possible ways in which the power of the book may have been intended to function. Perhaps the book was a pseudo-history, to change the past, replacing the real history of division and foreign intervention with a pseudo-history of reunification of the kingdom and the domestication of the Dutch through their conversion to Islam. Thereby a state myth that Jogjakarta was the *kraton* of a unified Java, with friendly relations with the foreign but Islamic Dutch Company, that friendship sealed by a contract, could be made true. It had not happened in the real world but through the act of writing *Surja Radja* it had happened 'magically', which was perhaps sufficient for the purposes of state theory. This does not, however, seem to be a very adequate interpretation.

Perhaps, rather than a pseudo-history the book was meant to change the contemporary situation in A.J. 1700. The kingdom had been divided and the infidel foreigners had fought a long series of wars, all of which was true and was admitted to be true. But at the moment of writing, through the book's power that situation was resolved. Problems which had not been soluble in the world of politics were dismissed in literature and could therefore be ignored. But this, too, seems an inadequate explanation.

In this writer's opinion, it is most likely that the *Sĕrat Surja Radja* was prophecy. It looked to the future. The kingdom was divided and the foreign infidels had taken the lands of the Javanese kings, but *Surja Radja*'s mythologized future history told

---

       risampunja mangkana Sang Nata kalih
       bubar sing pasanggrahan

59. samja kondur ḍumatĕng nĕgari
     Purwa Rukma lan Purwa Gupita
     sawadya gumrah sjarane
     tan karwarna ingĕnu
     gantjangakĕn tjaritaneki
     wus prapta ing nĕgara
     sagung kang pasungsung
     mjang pamĕnḍĕt sadajanja
     mapan sampun kintuki-kintunkĕn sami
     suka galih ing Nata.

The kingdom of Bandjar Rukma referred to in these last stanzas must be Tanah Sabrang. In Jogja kraton MS. F. 7, the kingdom of Tanah Sabrang is called Bandjar Binangun or Bandjar Rukma.

what was to happen. It is notable that the Jogjakarta Crown Prince, the book's author, seems clearly to have identified himself with the mythical prince Pudjakusuma.[78] It was he, Pudjakusuma and therefore by literary implication the Crown Prince, who was heir to a divided kingdom, who died and was raised again. It was he who was instructed in religion and kingship and who went on to reunify the kingdom.[79] He led the crusade against the infidel foreigners and, after the intervention of God, met in friendship with the converted foreign king, signed a document, affixed his seal, and lived happily ever after. A prophetic and spiritually powerful *scenario* had been established in which the Crown Prince of Jogjakarta was to be the saviour.

It seems possible that this role the Crown Prince was to play was associated with the plan which the Sultan may have cherished to abdicate in favour of his son in A.J. 1700. If that plan had existed, however, it was abandoned, perhaps because the Dutch appeared unwilling to recognize the young prince as the next Sultan.[80] It is of interest in this regard that, although no Surakarta materials like *Surja Radja* have been identified, Mangkunĕgara's son who also became twenty-four in A.J. 1700 had the name Prabu Amidjaja, a mythical name similar to the Surja Amidjaja of *Sĕrat Surja Radja*.[81] Perhaps, then, similar ideas were cherished by Mangkunĕgara, whose need of legitimation was perhaps even greater than the Sultan's.

If *Sĕrat Surja Radja* was originally prophecy, this may explain the continued rewriting of the text in the Jogjakarta *kraton* into the twentieth century. If it were intended to change the past, one application of retrospective magic should have sufficed. Perceptions of problems change, however, and the court ultimately came to appreciate European religious intransigence. When the text was rewritten in A.J. 1841–3 (A.D. 1911–12) the ending was changed. In this later version, the foreign king is no longer con-

[78] See nn. 48, 70 above.

[79] If I am correct in assuming that the pages I did not read in vol. i of *Kg. Kj. Surja Radja* contain materials similar to those in Jogja kraton MS. F. 7, Cantos II–LXXXVI. See n. 59 above.

[80] See above, pp. 167–70. At least two MSS. of the *Pralambang Djajabaja* prophesied the accession of a just ruler in A.J. 1700; see Wiselius, 'Djåjå Båjå', p. 212.

[81] See above, p. 172. Cf. the names given in *babads* to the early semi-mythical rulers of Java, e.g. Djaja Midjaja, Lĕmbu Amidjaja; see *BTDj*, text pp. 11–12, trans. pp. 11–12.

verted but instead annihilated after a long series of rather incredibly bloody battles.[82]

It seems, then, that *Sĕrat Surja Radja* was a powerful prophetic document to deal with the crisis of A.J. 1700.[83] Had it been merely a plan for action it would not have required the complex mythological story nor would it have been likely to have the special status implied by its artistic refinement, its authorship by the Crown Prince, and its ultimate recognition as one of the *pusakas* of the Sultanate. It is impossible to reconstruct with complete confidence exactly how the book's power was intended to function and it is unclear whether, when, or how the Crown Prince actually expected the events he prophesied to move from the realm of literature to that of fact. But the conclusion seems unavoidable that *Sĕrat Surja Radja* was one of the measures taken to surmount the threat to the kingdom which came with the turn of the century.

The year A.J. 1700 was, however, only the beginning of the traditional period of change. A new *kraton* should emerge in A.J. 1703 as the *kratons* of Dĕmak, Padjang, and Kartasura were believed to have appeared in previous centuries. Again, in the world of real events the pattern was not maintained. No new *kraton*

[82] *Sĕrat Surja Radja*, Jogja kraton MS. F. 7, pp. 972 ff. I am unable to say which ending is to be found in *Surja Radja*, MS. BG 164, Museum Pusat, Djakarta (see n. 59 above).

[83] If my understanding of this book is correct, it may have an oblique significance for Old Javanese studies as well. Anyone familiar with the latter field will be aware of the scholarly debate over the historical value of the *Nāgarakĕrtāgama*. Put in eighteenth-century terms, the problem is whether the 'historical' sections of the *Nāgarakĕrtāgama* represent a chronicle (albeit a very short one) like the Modern Javanese *babads* or a mythological book not unlike *Sĕrat Surja Radja*. In the eighteenth century we have the luxury of a vast amount of Dutch and Javanese material, enabling us to say that, for instance, *Babad Mangkubumi* is 'real' if sometimes inaccurate history while *Sĕrat Surja Radja* is mythologized history, even though the institutions of the kingdom and many of the names of lesser officials are clearly drawn from the real situation of the eighteenth century. Were *Sĕrat Surja Radja* the only extant document from eighteenth-century Java, we would be hard put to know whether there had ever been a prince Pudjakusuma who reunified the kingdom, or a foreign infidel invader who converted to Islam. Given the paucity of fourteenth-century documentation, the question whether the *Nāgarakĕrtāgama* is more like a *babad* or *Surja Radja* is virtually insoluble. But one could learn a great deal about life in the eighteenth-century *kratons* from *Sĕrat Surja Radja's* descriptions of audiences, hunts, ceremonies, etc. Similarly, even if the political events of the *Nāgarakĕrtāgama* are contrived, its author would surely have drawn his descriptive materials from the court life which was familiar to him. The *Nāgarakĕrtāgama* would therefore have great historical value even if one were convinced that it is not itself a work of history.

was founded in that year (A.D. 1777). But there was a major act of creation.

In the month Ruwah, A.J. 1703, precisely in keeping with the old pattern, a *babad* was written in Jogjakarta. So far as is known to the present author, it is the oldest dated and complete version of the major *Babad* tradition, beginning with Adam and the early semi-mythological history of Java and extending into Mataram times.[84] Certainly chronicles of this type were written before A.J. 1703. Such texts must have been among the books always kept by Javanese rulers and dignitaries.[85] One such chronicle was bought by the Company translator J. Gordijn from his old Javanese teacher in Surakarta in A.D. 1750. This *babad* extended from Adam to Kjai Gĕḍe Sĕsela, ancestor of the House of Mataram, and the portion of the text to the beginning of Madjapahit times was published in Dutch translation in A.D. 1779–81.[86] But it appears that no complete Javanese text of this type verifiably older than the Jogjakarta *babad* of A.J. 1703 (A.D. 1777) is presently known.

The Jogjakarta *babad* manuscript is untitled, but a reference in its last canto suggests that *Babad Kraton* (Chronicle of the *Kratons*) would be an appropriate title. Its author was Raden Tumĕnggung Djajengrat, a descendant of the House of Mataram and son-in-law to the Sultan. He began the book on Sunday-Pon, 25 Ruwah A.J. 1703[87] (28 September A.D. 1777) and eventually

---

[84] See Ricklefs, 'Consideration'.

[85] See the Dutch references of A.D. 1677 and 1707 to the Susuhunan's 'old books and papers', cited in de Graaf, 'Mangku-Rat I', vol. ii, p. 153, and 'Historische Betrouwbaarheid', p. 57.

[86] Josua van Iperen, 'Begin van eene Javaansche Historie, genaamd, Sadjara Radja Djawa,' *VBG*, vol. 1 (1779), pp. 134–72; vol. 2 (1780), pp. 262–88; vol. 3 (1781), pp. 117–33.

[87] The author's name is given in *BK*, f. 715ᵛ, Canto CLXX (Midjil):

   3. ingkang ajasa surat puniki
      Babad ing Karaton
      widji Mataram kamantu Ngradjeng
      Djajengrat silihira wawangi
      trahireng Bupati
      nama Dyan Tumĕnggung.

The beginning of the text is in ibid., f. 1ᵛ, Canto I (Ḍanḍanggula):

   1. Anglir silĕm tĕmbang Madugĕnḍis
      lajang babad duk wiwit sinurat
      ing Dite-Épon dinane
      Prangbakat wukunipun

finished it eight months later. The massive fourteen-hundred-page manuscript was discovered in the *kraton* and carried away by the British forces who deposed Sultan Hamĕngkubuwana II in A.D. 1812.[88]

The text of *Babad Kraton* is interesting and important in the context of *babad*-studies in general, but it need not be reviewed here. Two elements of the text are, however, significant to this study. First, the date of its writing (Ruwah A.J. 1703) suggests that the author had in mind the theory of the '00–'03 cycle, which is enshrined in its pages. At the end of the period of change, when the new *kraton* should theoretically have been founded and a new age should have begun, *Babad Kraton* was written to record the past, the old age.

The second relevant aspect of *Babad Kraton* is the selection of its stopping-point. Javanese chronicles tend generally to end with the events immediately prior to the date of the text's composition. When this is not so, as in the case of *babads* about Dĕmak, Padjang, Sultan Agung, etc., which were composed in the eighteenth and nineteenth centuries, the poet's selection of subject is significant in so far as it reveals something of his perceptions of historical development, of the units into which Javanese history falls. The

---

    sasi Saban tanggalnja
    nĕnggih sĕlawe taun Ĕdal
    pan sĕngkalanipun
    damar muluk wiku djagat [AJ 1703]
    . . . .

The reader may be curious to know why this was not written on the same day (7 or 27 Ruwah) as the founding of Kartasura in A.J. 1603. The complex Javanese chronological system is to blame here, for the Javanese deal not only in centuries of 100 lunar years, but also in *windu*-cycles of 8 lunar years, lunar months, solar months (*mangsa*), *wuku*-cycles of 30 weeks of seven days each, seven-day weeks, and five-day weeks, the latter two together giving a repeating 35-day cycle. Furthermore, from time to time the entire calendar is shifted by one day, as for instance in 1749 when the 'Friday Calendar' was replaced by the 'Thursday Calendar' (see p. 54 n. 42). The propitiousness or otherwise of a particular day is determined by the conjunction of these various systems, and since the cycles are of different lengths and in only a few cases divisible one by the other, the relationship among them is constantly changing. Therefore, a particular conjunction of elements may have made a date in A.J. 1603 propitious for founding the *kraton*, but a different combination on the same date in A.J. 1703 would not necessarily have been favourable for beginning a *babad*.

[88] According to a note in John Crawfurd's hand at the front of the MS. See Ricklefs, 'Inventory of the Javanese Manuscript Collection in the British Museum', p. 251, under *Add. 12320*.

author of *Babad Kraton* ended his chronicle not with the events immediately prior to A.J. 1703, nor with the capture of Pangeran Singasari (A.J. 1694/A.D. 1768), which the later author of the major Surakarta *babad* was to see as the natural division.[89] Rather, the text of *Babad Kraton* proceeds from Adam to the fall of Kartasura in A.J. 1667 (A.D. 1742). But this was not originally the case.

Babad Kraton has not one, but two endings, and they are most important. The first was intended to be superseded by the second but it was inadvertently left in the body of the manuscript as evidence of an important change of mind. In mid-February A.D. 1778, Djajengrat brought his *babad* to a close at a point just after the foundation of Kartasura in A.J. 1603 (A.D. 1680). At this point, Java was still divided between Padjang, where Amangkurat II ruled Kartasura, and Mataram, where his brother Susuhunan Ngalaga (Pangeran Pugĕr, later Susuhunan Pakubuwana I) occupied the old court and had not yet submitted. The text closed with a special admonition to the reader to consider the year of its completion, A.J. 1704 (Tuesday-Kliwon, 19 Muharram A.J. 1704/17 February A.D. 1778).[90] Thus, the original text ended with

[89] *Babad Tanah Djawi*, LOr 1786. See above, p. 138.
[90] The pages of the *BK* MS. run as follows:
F. *398*ʳ: Canto XCVIII (which begins on f. 393ᵛ and includes the foundation of Kartasura on f. 395ʳ), beginning in the middle of stanza 41 and ending in stanza 44, followed by the date of completion and the admonition to the audience (Ḍanḍanggula):

  44. . . .
      kunĕng wadya Kartasura
      kawarnaha para punggawa Matawis
      ngundurakĕn arahan

  45. titi tamatira duk tinulis
      aneng tadjug wĕntu lahor ika
      Anggara-Kasih dinane
      anĕnggih wukunipun
      Maḍasija mongsaningreki
      kapitu pan ingetang
      sasine winuwus
      Muhkaram tanggal sangalas
      taun Ĕbe angkaning warsa winilis
      dadya sĕngkalanira

  46. warna sirna panḍita ning djalmi [A.J. 1704]
      inggih punika sĕngkalanira
      kang matja mjarsa sagunge
      dipunsami ametung
      sirah-tĕnggak tusaningreki
      densami ngekadasa

the foundation of Kartasura in the midst of a division of Java in A.J. 1603. This suggests that the author was perhaps seeking a precedent for the fact of division in A.J. 1703 (A.D. 1777), which he found in the previous century. Closing his chronicle in A.J. 1704, he left his audience with a picture of Java divided at the previous turning of the recurring cycle of centuries.

A precedent for division had been found, but it was apparently recognized immediately that it was the wrong one. Java had indeed been divided when Kartasura was founded, but it had not long remained so. Susuhunan Ngalaga had been driven from Mataram before the end of A.J. 1603 and had submitted to his brother shortly thereafter. Thus, Java had been reunited in the previous cycle, even if *Babad Kraton* did not describe its reunification. Moreover, it had been reunited by Padjang (Kartasura). Whereas Mangkubumi could use the division of the sixteenth century as a precedent for the partition at Gijanti, since that had ended in reunification by Mataram,[91] he was not likely to accept as a precedent the division of the seventeenth century which had ended in victory for Padjang (Kartasura). Jogjakarta was in Mataram, Surakarta in Padjang. If a precedent were to imply reunification,

> tjondra-sangklanipun
> pamudjine ingkang nurat
> pan antuka supangat andika Nabi
> mjang sabate sakawan.

Ff. 398ᵛ and 399ʳ: Lack writing, except for the last line of XCVIII: 46, which runs on to f. 398ᵛ. But they have border decorations identical to those at the beginning and the end of this MS., with the centre sections in which the text was to be written left blank.

F. 399ᵛ: A left-hand page, is blank.

F. 400ʳ: Canto XCVIII, beginning in the middle of stanza 41, exactly as on f. 398ʳ, and ending with stanza 44. Stanzas 45 and 46, with the date of completion, are omitted. Instead the text begins an entirely new Canto XCIX (Durma):

XCVIII: 44. . . .
          ngundurakĕn arahan.
XCIX: 1. kawarnaha Sri Naradipa Ngalaga
          risĕndĕngnja tinangkil
          andĕr kang punggawa
          . . . .

The intention was clearly that ff. 398ʳ to 399ᵛ should have been removed from the final MS., in which case there would have been no indication that an earlier ending had been planned but then abandoned.

[91] See HB I's references to this sixteenth-century precedent cited in Chap. II above, and especially p. 62, n. 63.

only reunification by Mataram would do. But by A.J. 1703 reunification had already become a goal which no one thought capable of achievement. What was needed was not a precedent for temporary division, but one for permanent division. Djajengrat's original conclusion of *Babad Kraton* at a time of division seems intended to demonstrate that two *kratons* existing side-by-side at the start of a new century-cycle was perfectly correct. But the tradition that divisions always ended in reunification seems to have been too strong to be displaced so simply. In any case, it was known what had happened in the previous century. The idea that there should ideally be two *kratons*, rather than that there simply must be two, would not take root. There was no precedent.

A new ending was therefore devised. Djajengrat again took up the narrative and wrote for three more months. Now he ended his text not with the foundation, but with the fall of Kartasura in A.D. 1742.[92] Thus the author of *Babad Kraton*, who clearly knew of the theory of the rise and fall of *kratons* in preceding centuries, now ended his chronicle with the destruction of Kartasura, the last Javanese court to have been founded in accordance with the theory, in A.J. 1603 (A.D. 1680), and the last *kraton* to have fallen. The theory of the rise and fall of courts in time with the changing centuries was restated, but without the implication that at the start of a new century there should be two courts. The implication of this new ending was simply that the last major event before

---

[92] *BK*, ff. 714^v–715^r, Canto CLXIX (Asmaradana), stanzas 16–18. The date given for this event has an inaccurate *sěngkala*: paṇḍita wong rasaning rat, which gives A.J. 1617 rather than the correct A.J. 1667. The writer must have intended to produce a *sěngkala* for A.J. 1667, however, for he says that the year was Alip, which was true of A.J. 1667 but not of A.J. 1617, which was Wawu.

The text was completed on 'Friday-Wage, 25 Rabingulakir, Be, A.J. 1704' but since 25 Rabingulakir was Saturday-Kliwon, either the date was 24 Rabingulakir (22 May A.D. 1778) or the day was Saturday (23 May):

BK, f. 715^v, Canto CLXX (Midjil):

1. Tatkalanira tamat tinulis
   něnggah wajah lahor
   anudju dina Sukra-Wagene
   wuku Sita tanggal Rabijulakir
   gangsal likur singgih
   mongsa kasapuluh

2. taun Ěbe angkane winulis
   sěngkalanira non
   tjatur musna paṇḍita gade [A.J. 1704]
   . . . .

the writing of the *babad* in A.J. 1703, the last event which had concluded an era in Javanese history, was the fall of Kartasura, just as the last major event before A.J. 1703 should theoretically have been the fall in A.J. 1700 of the *kraton* founded in A.J. 1603.

Thus the structure of *Babad Kraton* perhaps suggested to those courtiers who heard it that the old theory was still functioning. Kartasura, the *kraton* founded in A.J. 1603, had fallen. It was known that it had done so over thirty years before the theory prescribed, but nevertheless it had fallen. By ending *Babad Kraton* of A.J. 1703 with that event, the author was perhaps reflecting a *kraton* view which regarded the fall of Kartasura as a sufficient fulfilment of the demands of state theory; it was the end of the previous age. *Babad Kraton's* omission of all events subsequent to Kartasura, such as the foundation of Surakarta, Mangkubumi's rebellion, his accession as ruler, the division of the kingdom, and the foundation of Jogjakarta, implied further that for the purposes of a court chronicle written at an important time in state theory, these events could be left to be described in other books, such as Jogjakarta versions of *Babad Gijanti* and the Crown Prince's *Babad Mangkubumi*. This would seem to carry the implication that, as the new era began in A.J. 1703, Jogjakarta could be seen as a new court, without a past and without a peer, carved from the virgin forest. In other words, Jogjakarta was the rightful and direct successor to the *kraton* of Kartasura, in accordance with the theory which had defined the state significance of the turn of the century for at least three hundred years.

The difference in implication between the old and the new endings of *Babad Kraton* was crucial. The original ending would have implied that there should be two *kratons*. It would have explained in theory what now existed in fact. The new ending, however, implied instead that, as had always been the case, there should be only one court but that Jogjakarta was it. The fact of division was ignored. Jogjakarta was made legitimate, but the simultaneous existence of two courts was not. Thus it seems that the theory of dynastic change, which carried with it the possibility of radical political upheaval at the turn of each century, had been adapted to legitimate the existence of Jogjakarta. By doing so it only indirectly justified the existence of both *kratons*, for no courtier of Surakarta would have accepted that his king and court were any less legitimate thereby. It did not justify the concept of two legitimate *kratons* existing at the same time. The further implications of this will be considered in Chapter XII.

The impact upon eighteenth-century Javanese politics of the cycle of dynastic change at each century is now more clear. The impending crisis of the year A.J. 1700 perhaps explains the sudden concern for stability within the Javanese courts in the years immediately before. Thus were agreed in self-defence the land regulations and law codes which greatly reduced the level of instability in Central Java. Then, in *Sěrat Surja Radja* and *Babad Kraton* the Jogjakarta court left a record of the way in which it met and surmounted the years of crisis, emerging in A.J. 1703 as a legitimate *kraton* for the new century.

There is an obvious and important difference, however, between *Sěrat Surja Radja* and *Babad Kraton*. The former was apparently a bold prophetic document, decreeing a *scenario* of change for the new century to be presided over by the Crown Prince, who would reunify the kingdom and witness the integration of the Dutch. The latter, after an unsuccessful attempt to make division itself seem to be legitimate, became a conventional history which appears to have done no more than take a view of the past making the existence of Jogjakarta seem legitimate, while neither explaining the fact of Surakarta nor requiring that it cease to exist as a *kraton*. *Sěrat Surja Radja* looked forward; *Babad Kraton* looked back. The explanation for this difference may lie in a revision of the Sultan's political intentions between A.J. 1700 and 1703. If, as has been suggested above, the Sultan considered abdication in favour of the Crown Prince sometime in the period A.J. 1700–3 in order not to offend the laws of history, the Crown Prince may have written *Babad Mangkubumi* in A.J. 1699 and *Sěrat Surja Radja* in A.J. 1700 because he anticipated he would soon be Sultan. In particular, he may have written *Sěrat Surja Radja* in the confidence that the new century would see a new ruler, as each new century should. This new monarch would be himself, who, like Pudjakusuma, would lead his followers to victory. Whether or not the Crown Prince genuinely expected these things to move from the realm of prophecy to that of fact is, of course, quite another question. Then perhaps the idea of abdication was abandoned, most likely because the Dutch seemed unwilling to recognize the Crown Prince as his father's successor. The *kraton* perhaps then took the view that Kartasura could be

considered to suffice for the *kraton* which should have fallen in
A.J. 1700, as indeed it should have fallen, being the *kraton* founded
in A.J. 1603. And Jogjakarta could be considered its successor of
A.J. 1703. This view, reflected in the final version of *Babad Kraton*,
could meet the requirements of dynastic theory and at the same
time legitimize Jogjakarta's existence, while involving no perilous
political measures such as abdication.

If this latter suggestion is correct, the documents of A.J. 1700–3
help to clarify one of the most significant developments of Modern
Javanese history. An anomalous political situation, the divided
kingdom, ultimately existed because Dutch military intervention
had prevented the resolution of the underlying cause of the division, the disunity and crisis of leadership among the Javanese
élite. Yet the Dutch Company's financial and consequently military
position in the second half of the eighteenth century was so weak
that a combined Javanese army could almost certainly have expelled the Company from Central Java, if not from the island
entirely. The Javanese could then have fought their way to the
customary conclusion: the elimination of all but a single contender for the support of the Javanese élite. Thus the problem was
potentially soluble. The Javanese princes, however, either had
come to believe that their most vital interests lay with the new
political structure which had evolved since the 1750s, or had sufficiently lost their sense of initiative after a century of crisis, that
the inherent impetus to resolve the anomaly was sublimated. They
turned to traditional ideas to explain and to justify the irregular
situation instead of attempting to correct it. Formalized traditional
perceptions became a refuge from the necessity for action rather
than a guide to understanding problems and a set of models for
resolving them. Rather than dealing finally with the problems
which prevented the expulsion of the Dutch and reunification of
the kingdom, the *kraton* of Jogjakarta, and presumably Surakarta
as well, chose to pretend that the problems did not exist. The
powerful and dynamic Mataram kingdom was already on its way
to becoming two rather passive and introspective principalities.

This process was not, however, without its creative aspects.
The new century after A.J. 1700 seems also to have required a new
corpus of literature. The late eighteenth century is believed to have
witnessed a great burst of literary production which, because it
also involved the re-editing and translating of Old Javanese classics

into Modern Javanese, Dr. Pigeaud has described as a Literary Renaissance. Almost the entire body of Modern Javanese manuscripts dates from the period of this Javanese Literary Renaissance and after. Texts verifiably older than Surakarta-Jogjakarta times are extremely rare. But the implication in several sources that the Literary Renaissance began to flourish when peace returned to Java after the Gijanti treaty (A.D. 1755)[93] does not, in fact, adequately explain the phenomenon. It is notable that the great bulk of dated Javanese manuscripts, and therefore presumably of undated texts as well, began more than twenty years later. In the Javanese calendar, the texts originate not from A.J. 1680 (A.D. 1755), but rather from the period after the end of the century, with the great increase of dated texts coming after A.J. 1703 (A.D. 1777).

This pattern may be seen in an analysis of dated Javanese manuscripts in the older European collections. Among the earliest such collections are those of John Crawfurd (official in Java, 1811–16),[94] Thomas Stamford Raffles (Lieutenant-Governor of Java, 1811–16),[95] J. F. C. Gericke (missionary-scholar in Java, 1827–37),[96] Taco Roorda (Professor of Oriental Languages in Amsterdam, Delft, and Leiden, 1828–74; the founder of Javanese studies in the Netherlands),[97] the collection of the Delft Academy for training East Indies civil servants (1842–64),[98] and that of the Delft Ethnographic Museum.[99] These collections contain over two hundred manuscripts on which the dates are clearly given. Of these, 150 were written before the Java War (A.J. 1753/A.D. 1825). Without attempting to verify absolutely the dates of all these texts or to ascertain which are of *kraton* origin and which from elsewhere, and ignoring such items as letters, the manuscripts

---

[93] e.g. Pigeaud, *Literature*, vol. i, pp. 235–7; Soebardi, 'Jasadipura I', p. 83; Uhlenbeck, *Critical Survey*, p. 137.

[94] Now in the British Museum, London. See Ricklefs, 'Inventory of the Javanese Manuscript Collection in the British Museum'.

[95] Now in the Royal Asiatic Society, London. There is not yet a published inventory of this collection. I have examined the MSS. myself, and have made use of R. O. Winstedt and P. Voorhoeve, 'Royal Asiatic Society. Raffles's Javanese MSS. Hand List 1950' (typescript in RAS).

[96] Collection of the Netherlands Bible Society, now on loan to the Leiden University Library. See Pigeaud, *Literature*, vol. ii, pp. 13, 712–55.

[97] Now in the Leiden University Library, LOr 2097–2188. See ibid., pp. 8, 66–83.

[98] Now in the Leiden University Library, LOr 1786–1882. See ibid., pp. 8, 25–49.

[99] Now on loan to the Leiden University Library. See ibid., pp. 13, 757–61.

may be employed to give a rough picture of the chronological distribution of dated Modern Javanese literature.

Of the texts in these six collections dating from before A.J. 1753 (A.D. 1825), the earliest were written in A.J. 1640 and 1680 (A.D. 1715, 1754), and two copies of another text perhaps dated A.J. 1651 (A.D. 1726) also exist.[100] Only two were dated in the period between A.J. 1681 and 1698 (A.D. 1755–72; i.e. between the treaty of Gijanti and the end of the century), one being a law code.[101] The vast majority of these manuscripts (144; 96 per cent of the total) were dated after A.J. 1699. Five were written between A.J. 1699 and 1703 (A.D. 1773–7), including two copies of the *Anggĕr-Arubiru* law code,[102] *Babad Balambangan*,[103] a *Sewaka* moralistic text,[104] and *Babad Kraton*. Most of the pre-Java War manuscripts in these collections (139; 93 per cent of the total) were written after A.J. 1703 (A.D. 1777). Twelve were written in the decade A.J. 1704–13 (A.D. 1778–86), twenty-three in A.J. 1714–23 (A.D. 1787–96), thirteen in A.J. 1724–33 (A.D. 1797–1806), forty-five in A.J. 1734–43 (A.D. 1807–15), and forty-six in A.J. 1744–53 (A.D. 1816–25). This distribution of manuscripts is altered somewhat if the collection of Colin Mackenzie, who served under Raffles in Java (1811–13), is included. This collection has not yet been completely catalogued but preliminary information suggests that addition of these texts to the sample would lower the percentage of dates after A.J. 1703 from 93 per cent to 89 per cent. But of the total expanded sample of 183 dated manuscripts

---

[100] NBS 95 (see ibid., 738–9); LOr 1828 (7) (see ibid., p. 37). Raffles Java MS. 33 (C) and Royal Asiatic Society Java 45 (A) are two copies of a legal text in which the date is internally inconsistent but seems to be A.J. 1651.

The dates A.H. 955 and 958 (A.D. 1548, 1551) on LOr 1841, LOr 2173, and BM Add. MS. 12290 refer to the date the original Arabic text was supposed to have been written upon, not to the date of the Javanese translations; see ibid., pp. 40, 80; Ricklefs, 'Inventory of the Javanese Manuscript Collection in the British Museum', p. 247; L. de Vries, ' "Kitab Toehpah" en Tuḥfat al Muḥtādj li sjarkh al Minhādj. Resultaten van een voorlopig Onderzoek, met Vertaling van den "Kitab Toehpah" ', *VBG*, vol. 68, pt. 4 (1929), p. 11.

[101] NBS 75 (6), Jogjakarta *Anggĕr-Agĕng*, dated A.J. 1691 (A.D. 1765) (see Pigeaud, *Literature*, vol. ii, p. 728); NBS 152, *Djaka Salewah* from Tĕgal, dated A.H. 1176 (A.J. 1688/A.D. 1762) (see ibid., pp. 746–7).

[102] Dated A.J. 1699. LOr 1843 (5), 2154 (1); see ibid., pp. 40, 76.

[103] LOr 2185, dated A.J. 1699–1700; see ibid., p. 83; Vreede, *Catalogus*, pp. 119–23.

[104] NBS 57, dated A.J. 1702. *Sewaka*, NBS 73 (3), is a much later prose version, although it maintains the older date. See Pigeaud, *Literature*, vol. ii, pp. 723–4, 727.

written before the Java War, 170 (93 per cent) would still be posterior to A.J. 1699 (A.D. 1773).[105] Only about 4 per cent were written between the treaty of Gijanti and A.J. 1699.

It is unlikely that this grouping of manuscripts after the end of the century is entirely due to the accidental ravages of the Javanese climate or to the destruction of warfare. The life expectancy of a book, particularly one written on the heavy European paper in use in the eighteenth century, was considerably longer than the four decades between A.J. 1703 (A.D. 1777) and the arrival of the first British collectors. The *Sěrat Surja Radja* of A.J. 1700 has survived two centuries in Java and seems capable of withstanding several more. Properly preserved, even Javanese paper (*dluwang*) should have lasted several decades. Moreover, although this sample of manuscripts is neither large enough nor susceptible to satisfactory controls on origin and date, it is notable that there is not a regularly increasing number of documents beginning in A.J. 1680 (A.D. 1755), which one would expect had the Literary Renaissance begun after the restoration of peace, with the paucity of manuscripts in early years due entirely to climatic attrition. Instead, there are only a few manuscripts dated before the end of the century. And warfare is not an adequate explanation for the absence of older manuscripts, for peace had been restored two decades before the increase of literary works after the end of the Javanese century. It is also noticeable that the volume of texts does not increase at a regular rate after A.J. 1699: there were considerably more texts dated in the decade A.J. 1714–23 (A.D. 1787–96) than in the following decade.[106]

[105] The Mackenzie MSS. are now housed in the India Office Library, London, but have not yet been completely catalogued. An inventory of a part of the collection has been compiled by Professor D. E. Weatherbee, and a preliminary communication from him supplemented by a personal investigation of the MSS. yields the following result: there seem to be 33 MSS. the dates of which are clear, all written before A.D. 1813. Two are dated before A.J. 1681/A.D. 1755. Five are dated between the treaty of Gijanti and the close of the century (A.J. 1681–98/A.D. 1755–72; 15 per cent of this collection). One was written between A.J. 1699 and A.J. 1703 (A.D. 1773–7; 3 per cent of the collection). Twenty-five (76 per cent) were written after A.J. 1703/A.D. 1777.

[106] This also suggests that the evident pattern of literary production may reflect political events. The productive years A.J. 1714–23 (A.D. 1787–96) were a time of potential and of actual crisis (see Chaps. IX and X below), including the death of PB III and the accession of PB IV (A.D. 1788), and the deaths of HB I (A.D. 1792) and MN I (A.D. 1795). The less productive decade A.J. 1724–33 (A.D. 1797–1806) was rather a lull before the storms which began with Daendels' arrival in A.D. 1808.

Undoubtedly many, if not most, of the books written after A.J. 1699 went back to much older versions, a few of which have found their way into various public collections. But the rapid increase in dated manuscripts which began at the turn of the century suggests that most books were recopied or rewritten after the end of the old century, thereby acquiring dates after A.J. 1699. There is no other reasonable explanation to account for this pattern of dates. The vast majority of Modern Javanese literary works is therefore posterior to the beginning of the new century.

If the dates of the eighteenth-century Javanese manuscripts reflect the importance of the change of the century rather than the return of peaceful conditions after A.D. 1755, there is a further implication that the Javanese Literary Renaissance may not have the significance which it seems to have for Javanese literary history. The Dutch Company had been in contact with the Javanese since the end of the sixteenth century and a few of its officials were knowledgeable in Javanese culture. Two in particular were noted collectors of manuscripts in the seventeenth century, but their collections have since been lost.[107] The oldest collections of Javanese manuscripts to have survived are those which derive from the British occupation of Java in A.D. 1811–16. If the Javanese courts customarily rewrote their books in each new century, it would follow that books collected several years after the turn of a century would also be dated thereafter. Had Raffles, Crawfurd, Mackenzie, and the later Dutch collectors been in Java a century earlier, their collections might give the impression that a great literary flowering had begun in A.J. 1600 (A.D. 1677). Thus the Javanese Literary Renaissance may to some extent be an illusion created by the fact that the pre-nineteenth-century collections of manuscripts did not survive. The impression of a great renaissance after a period of little literary activity may be an inaccurate deduction based upon the historical accident that large-scale collecting of Javanese manuscripts began only in the nineteenth century and

---

[107] The two were Herbert de Jager (1636–94) and Isaac de Saint Martin (d. 1696); Gonda, 'Grepen', pp. 94–5. Gonda was incorrect in his belief that these MSS. were later taken by Raffles, which was based upon the views of Ph. S. van Ronkel, 'Over een oude Lijst van Maleische Handschriften', *TBG*, vol. 42 (1900), pp. 309–22. De Saint Martin's collection is listed in F. de Haan, 'Uit oude Notarispapieren I', *TBG*, vol. 42 (1900), pp. 298–303, but the compilers of this list seem not to have known Javanese and the titles of Javanese books are not given.

that only thereafter were such collections carefully preserved, largely in European libraries, for later scholarly examination.

It must be said here, however, that the idea of a Literary Renaissance is not entirely based upon the chronological distribution of the literary works now known to scholarship, although that distribution has reinforced the concept. It depends also upon Javanese literary tradition as preserved in the *Conversations* of C. F. Winter, Sr., representing information from Surakarta from the first half of the nineteenth century. In one of these conversations,[108] a Surakarta scholar lists thirty great Javanese literati and the works they produced, emphasizing in particular the role of the great Surakarta court poets Jasadipura I and II, the latter being the informant's own *guru* (teacher). He lists also the Surakarta royal authors Pakubuwana III and IV, and several other poets of the Surakarta period, to which thirteen of the writers belonged. These authors are represented by many works still known, some of which are available in published form.[109] It is these works which mark the flowering of the Renaissance. But the *Conversations* also include a number of other authors who pre-date the late eighteenth century. In particular, two poets of the Kartasura period (A.D. 1680–1742), Pangeran Adilangu II and Tjarik Badjra, are emphasized and a large number of works is ascribed to them.[110] The Javanese speaker seems to have ranked these two authors with Jasadipura I, whose works are among the most beautiful and most important in Modern Javanese literature. Yet, so far as is known to the present writer, no manuscripts ascribed to them are now known to exist. This may be most readily accounted for by suggesting that there was an interruption in the preservation of older literary works, resulting in the loss of original

[108] Winter, *Zamenspraken*, vol. i, pp. 352–65.
[109] The reader may refer to Pigeaud, *Literature,* for works by the various authors. Surakarta authors additional to those mentioned in the text are Sastrawidjaja, Judasara, Ronggawarsita, Rongga Amongsastra, Rongga Sutrasna, Adipati Sěmarang, Adipati Pangeran Sěmarang, Paněmbahan Madura, and Kěrtadiwirja.
[110] Tjarik Badjra is said to have written *Babad Kartasura, Damar Wulan, Dasa Nama, Tjaraka Basa, Pandji Murtasmara, Kuda Narawongsa, Sasana Prabu, Judanagara Wulang, Prabangkara,* and *Djaka Krewed.*
Pangeran Adilangu is credited with *Babad Padjadjaran, B. Madjapahit, B. Děmak, B. Padjang, B. Mataram, Radja Kapakapa, Seh Malaja, Djatikusuma,* and *Djajabaja* (from an earlier work by Sunan Giri II).
On these two, see Hoesein Djajadiningrat, *Critische Beschouwing van de Sadjarah Banten: Bijdrage ter Kenschetsing van de Javaansche Geschiedschrijving* (Haarlem, 1913), pp. 221–4.

works by the authors who wrote before Surakarta times and the preservation of their works only in rewritten or recopied form. If dated, these texts would have been in most cases redated; if the author was named, it would usually be the name of the writer who had produced the new version. The Javanese speaker in Winter's *Conversations* says many earlier works were rewritten (*kaanggit malih*) at several stages, including the late eighteenth and early nineteenth centuries. But he does not suggest that there was a 'renaissance' in the latter period. This term implies a rebirth, a revival after an interregnum, but for Winter's informant the Javanese literary tradition was long and continuous. Books were often rewritten and the older copies apparently abandoned. This would readily account for the loss of earlier works.

The important question for a study of eighteenth-century Javanese history is to ascertain when works were rewritten, or whether there was simply an ongoing process of recopying. Here one can only turn to the dated manuscripts as the single source of information which is reasonably specific. And when the dated manuscripts are examined, one is forced to regard the turn of the century as the important watershed, rather than the treaty of Gijanti in A.D. 1755. Had the process of recopying been general and ongoing, one would expect the dated manuscripts to increase in number after A.D. 1755, when the return of peace was favourable to their production and preservation. But this is not the case. The increase in dated manuscripts begins with the turn of the century. And this, in turn, suggests that the writing or rewriting of these works at this time was to some extent a conscious act inspired by the new century.[111]

It may be suggested, then, that there is a case for reconsidering the implications of the term 'renaissance'. The late eighteenth and early nineteenth centuries witnessed the writing of some of the greatest works of Modern Javanese literature now known. But there is reason to suspect that the significance of this period in Javanese literary history may perhaps seem exaggerated because of a conscious rewriting of the literature after the start of the new century (A.J. 1700/A.D. 1774), which has left the literary world

[111] Cf. Berg, 'Māyā's Hemelvaart', p. 332: 'The failure to hand down writings at the crossing of a *bhawacakra*-boundary is not in conflict with the continuity of the *bhujangga*-tradition, for in the one case it is a matter of manuscripts which can be viewed as cult-objects and linked to the lot of the dynasty, in the other case of unalienable, individually-ineradicable knowledge.'

largely ignorant of the earlier writers listed in Winter's *Conversations*. This is a question best left for scholars of Javanese literature. But there is clearly strong evidence to suggest that the turn of the century had an importance for Javanese literature, as it seems also to have had for Javanese politics.

When all of this literary evidence is compared with the political developments in the last decade of the old century (A.J. 1690–1700/A.D. 1764–74), the conclusion seems unavoidable that the changing century meant a very great deal to Jogjakarta, and probably to both Javanese courts. Those years witnessed the regularization and legitimation of the divided kingdom after two decades of doubt about the permanence of the division. Taken together, the weight of evidence indicates that perhaps the most important factor which made such regularization possible was the traditional belief in the importance of each new century. That is not to say that the existence of a tradition of political change at the turn of each century predetermined the legitimization of two contemporaneous courts. It merely predetermined that the Central Javanese élite would regard the turn of the century as a time when major political change was likely; it was not a time when the uncertain conditions of the preceding decades could merely be allowed to go on unaltered. The *kratons* and their supporters expected change, but it was still within their power to affect the nature of these changes. But this new century differed significantly from the preceding ones, according to Javanese tradition. There were two courts, in each of which there lived a legitimate heir to the throne. At the same time, the long-standing if now again peripheral involvement of the Dutch in Central Javanese politics had led the major Javanese princes to conclude that a military resolution of the division was unlikely to succeed. The traditional denouement therefore seemed impossible. No single court would emerge in the new century. But in defence against any possible attempt by another to upset the *status quo*, each court was concerned to achieve stability for itself. At least in Jogjakarta this involved not only concrete political measures such as the land and legal regulations, but a careful observation of tradition as well. The result was the emergence in the new century of two courts, each considering itself and being considered by its supporters to be legitimate in accordance with the old expectations.

Only then was the kingdom truly divided.

VIII

THE PERMANENTLY DIVIDED KINGDOM
1774–1787

As the years of the eighteenth Javanese century passed, the princes who had engineered the division of the kingdom accepted and adjusted to the new circumstances of Javanese politics. The main problem of organizing a divided kingdom, that of relationships between the two main courts, had been largely resolved by the events since A.J. 1694 (A.D. 1768). Only Mangkunĕgara's position in the state system remained somewhat undefined. Now, in the years after A.J. 1700 (A.D. 1774), the primary attention of the Javanese principals was directed towards regulating the internal affairs of their own courts and maintaining a correct and advantageous relationship with the Dutch East India Company. Although old antagonisms lived on, the direct armed confrontations between Surakarta and Jogjakarta which had typified previous decades now ceased. Indeed, having divided the kingdom, both courts preferred to ignore as much as possible the fact of the other's existence. Amidst various intrigues and animosities, it seems that the one fact no one during this period seriously questioned was that Mataram had become two kingdoms.

The generation of Sultan Hamĕngkubuwana I, Susuhunan Pakubuwana III, and Prince Mangkunĕgara was primarily concerned to reap the fruits of a peaceful compromise. But a new generation was emerging in both Surakarta and Jogjakarta, sons and grandsons of the main princes, whose memories of warfare and destruction could not be as vivid as their elders'. As they grew older and more influential, these younger princes posed a potential threat to the stable functioning of the system of division. They could hardly fail to perceive the difference between the system which they observed and the ideal unified state of Sultan Agung which the court *babads* still described. Should one of them attempt to restore that unified state, Java might again be plunged into the anarchy of the 1740s and 1750s. Such a crisis was not likely to emerge until one of these younger princes should succeed to a position of power. For the meantime, their elders lived on. But the potential for disruption grew during the period 1774–87. It will be seen in Chapter IX that when one of the younger generation finally succeeded to the throne of Surakarta, the divided state system was exposed to the first major threat since 1757.

As the 1770s and 1780s passed, one of the highest priorities for the elder generation of Javanese notables was the preparation of the younger for the day when it would wield authority. In the events inspired by the change of the Javanese century, the question of succession had been of great importance to Mangkunĕgara, Pakubuwana III, and Hamĕngkubuwana I. Having survived the potential crisis of A.J. 1700–3, there was no longer the urgency to abdicate or to confirm the right of succession which these three seem to have felt before. Rather, things now took a more natural course, young princes coming to assume greater authority as their fathers or grandfathers grew older. Because this took place within *kraton* walls and was a natural process, it is insufficiently documented by the Dutch and only occasionally commented upon by the Javanese sources. Yet it is clear that this was an ongoing process in these years, if the details remain obscure.

This transition to a new generation thus raised the possibility of eventual discontinuities in political behaviour. As in many other things, so also in this matter Jogjakarta had the advantage in this period. Sultan Mangkubumi exercised greater general authority than did the Susuhunan in Surakarta, and the Crown Prince of Jogjakarta was already an adult and more familiar with the troubled years since 1755 than the Crown Prince of Surakarta, who had been born only in 1768. The former was more likely to understand the reasons for the division of Mataram. The transition to the younger generation was therefore potentially less disruptive in Jogjakarta.

But both the older and the younger generations were heirs to the traditional Javanese ideas of the functioning of the state. Certain themes were therefore to remain long after Mangkubumi and the Susuhunan were laid to rest at Imagiri. Most importantly, the instinctive dislike of the divided kingdom persisted even among many who believed it to be the only solution in the circumstances. Old animosities lived on, particularly between the Sultan and Mangkunĕgara, for these two had greater prestige than the Susuhunan among the political élite and both must have known that should the unification of the state ever again become possible, they would still be the main contenders.

The contest for prestige was an important part of the continuing struggle of each prince to stabilize his domain. Within the Javanese political context, this was one of the few means which a prince or ruler had to increase his authority. The Dutch understood this only imperfectly and consequently interpreted many of the events of these years as merely childish intransigence or wearisome posturing by the Javanese.

In 1773 (A.J. 1699) the Sultan decided to send a mission to the Sultan of Bantĕn. This may or may not have been associated with the preparations for the new Javanese century, but it was almost certainly a part of the general process of demonstrating Mangkubumi's royal standing, in this case by sending a mission to another Indonesian potentate. The Sultan of Bantĕn was without real authority in his own kingdom, which had been under the influence of near-by Batavia since the late seventeenth century and where since the 1750s the Dutch had imposed a peace which, in Dr. de Graaf's opinion, had much in common with the peace of death.[1] But he was nevertheless another Indonesian Sultan and was known moreover to be a pious Muslim.[2] A mission to Bantĕn required Dutch approval, however, for the normal route from Central Java was by sea past Batavia. But the Dutch constantly feared any hint of an Indonesian Muslim alliance against themselves. They therefore attempted to postpone granting Mangkubumi's request for the Company to carry his emissaries to Bantĕn, although they dared not refuse him outright.[3]

Mangkubumi was not so easily put off. In 1777 (A.J. 1703) the Dutch discovered that the *bupati* of Banjumas, belonging to Surakarta, had secretly carried out a mission to Bantĕn by the difficult overland route. The Susuhunan was furious to learn of this, put the *bupati* in confinement, and in 1780 removed him from his position.[4] Although the Company seems never to have

[1] De Graaf, *GI*, p. 271.
[2] J. Reynouts, Tegenwoordigen staat van het Bantamse Rijk, 20 Jan. 1779 in dJ xi, p. 375.
[3] HB I to Sĕmarang, 22 Sept. 1773, in KA 3310 (OB 1775); Sĕmarang to Batavia, 5 June 1774, in KA 3310 (OB 1775); id., 10 March 1779, in KA 3448 (OB 1780).
[4] Sĕmarang to Batavia, 22 Nov. 1777, in KA 3392 (OB 1778); id., 22 Dec. 1777, in KA 3389 (OB 1778); van der Burgh, Memorie, 19 Sept. 1780, in dJ xi, p. 412.

understood the connection, it is clear that this was in fact the Sultan's mission, for the Banjumas *bupati* was the son of Danurĕdja, Mangkubumi's *patih*, who had himself been *bupati* of Banjumas before entering the Sultan's service in 1755.[5] The Susuhunan's firm reaction to the incident suggests that he recognized in such a mission a threat to his own authority, not only because one of his *bupatis* had acted on the Sultan's behalf, but also because the prestige for Jogjakarta of contact with Bantĕn perhaps implicitly threatened the balance of legitimation between Surakarta and Jogjakarta which was the basis of the division.

The most familiar theme of the first years of the new century was the continuing animosity between Mangkubumi and Mangkunĕgara. There were no longer the constant military intrusions into each other's lands. Now the conflicts centred instead about the most vexing problem of a peacefully divided kingdom: subjects who simply chose to desert one court for another. One of the most important expressions of royal authority was the obvious presence of princes, officials, and assorted courtiers who chose to live under the ruler's authority. The desertion of such people from the court had always been a sign of danger. In a divided kingdom the problem was still greater, for there was always another prince willing to receive and to protect such refugees and to extract from them the additional legitimacy which their presence implied. Thus desertion was now both easier for the subjects and less palatable for the monarchs. The problem was not to be entirely solved until the final regulation of the full structure of the divided kingdom in a treaty of 1790, discussed in Chapter X.

In 1776, six or seven of Mangkunĕgara's subjects fled to the Sultan's *kraton* and by mid-1777 the number of these refugees had climbed to twenty-nine, including several court musicians and *ḍalangs*. The latter were particularly important figures in Javanese cultural life. Mangkunĕgara made furious protestations to the Dutch for assistance, but they merely referred him back to the Surakarta *patih* Sasradiningrat. The latter wrote to Danurĕdja demanding the return of the people and the 987 rijksdaalders they had taken with them. But the problem cut both ways, and Danurĕdja replied with a request for the return of four *mantris* (officials)

[5] Van der Burgh, Memorie, 19 Sept. 1780, in dJ xi, p. 412.

PERMANENTLY DIVIDED KINGDOM, 1774-1787   231

of Jogjakarta who had taken refuge with Mangkunĕgara, leaving behind debts of 1,500 rijksdaalders.[6]

The Sultan was unwilling to be co-operative in returning Mangkunĕgara's subjects. His intransigence in this matter was strengthened by a report he was given by Danurĕdja in 1776 after the latter's return from a mission of felicitation to the new Governor-General at Batavia, Jeremias van Riemsdijk (1775-7). Danurĕdja reported that he had told the Governor-General that it was the right of all Javanese to live where they liked so long as they were free men. Van Riemsdijk was said to have replied that this was also the custom in the Netherlands. But he hoped the Sultan would not do anything in such matters which was unfair, which Danurĕdja assured him the Sultan would not do.[7]

In previous years such a conflict would have ended in marching troops and plundered villages, but this was no longer so. Certain appropriate gestures were made, with the public exercising of troops on each side, but no hostilities resulted.[8] In 1777 a village headman under Jogjakarta, who had been demoted by order of the Sultan, undertook a bit of minor plundering and then disappeared. Mangkubumi claimed the man had been put up to this by Mangkunĕgara and uttered various threats about the retaliatory steps he would take. But he took none worthy of note.[9] The stability

[6] HB I to Sĕmarang, 17 Djumadilakir A.J. 1702 (received at Sĕmarang 5 Aug. 1776), in KA 3362 (OB 1777); Sĕmarang to Batavia, 29 Sept. 1776 and 24 Dec. 1776, in KA 3362 (OB 1777); id., 15 April 1777 and 2 June 1777, in KA 3391 (OB 1778); Danurĕdja to Sasradiningrat and Sasradiningrat to Danurĕdja (copies received at Sĕmarang, 22 June 1777), in KA 3391 (OB 1778); van Rhijn to Sĕmarang, 27 June 1777, in KA 3391 (OB 1778); Sĕmarang to Batavia, 5 July 1777 and 31 July 1777, in KA 3391 (OB 1778) (see also dJ xi, p. 308 n. 1).

[7] Danurĕdja, Report to HB I, 2 Dulkangidah A.J. 1702 (copy received at Sĕmarang, 23 Dec. 1776), in KA 3362 (OB 1777). See also van der Burgh, Memorie, 19 Sept. 1780, in dJ xi, p. 404.

[8] Sĕmarang to Batavia, 15 April 1777, 5 July 1777, and 31 July 1777, in KA 3391 (OB 1778); van Straalendorff to Sĕmarang, 27 Aug. 1777, in KA 3391 (OB 1778).

[9] There was never any very clear proof of Mangkunĕgara being connected with the man and he vigorously denied the allegation. The only military action taken was the abduction by Jogjakarta forces of the man's wife from one of the Susuhunan's villages and of his daughter, her husband, and the village headman from a VOC village. See van Rhijn to Sĕmarang, 22 May 1777, in KA 3391 (OB 1778); Sĕmarang to Batavia, 2 June 1777, in KA 3391 (OB 1778); Sĕmarang to van Rhijn, 7 June 1777, in KA 3391 (OB 1778); van Straalendorff to Sĕmarang, 18 June 1777 and 28 July 1777, in KA 3391 (OB 1778); Sĕmarang to Batavia, 22 Dec. 1777, in KA 3389 (OB 1778); id., 23 Dec. 1777, in KA 3392 (OB 1778); Batavia to H.XVII, 31 Dec. 1777, in dJ xi, pp. 307-8; Sĕmarang to Batavia, 12 June 1778, in KA 3420 (OB 1779).

of the division of the kingdom was quite remarkably clear throughout this episode.

In 1777 (A.J. 1703) the Sultan attempted to convince the Company that Mangkunĕgara's customary plotting lay behind the disputes and tried, as he had in 1762, to get the Dutch to exile Mangkunĕgara from Java. The Sĕmarang Governor van der Burgh was, however, of the opinion that Mangkunĕgara was a 'necessary evil' to maintain the balance of forces in Java and that the Sultan only wished him exiled

in order better to carry out his desire for greatness, in order to exert himself over the Susuhunan and in order to arrange everything according to the *adat* (custom) of the previous rulers and to his pleasure, to be able to have a free rein.[10]

This was, of course, an accurate assessment of the Sultan's aims. Mangkubumi wished to be rid of his main competitor. The Company refused to exile Mangkunĕgara, as it had fifteen years before,[11] and the Sultan was forced to accept the decision since he clearly had no intention of taking direct action himself. By the end of 1777 the ominous threats and rumours had ceased.[12] The refugees from each court were not returned by their new protectors, although two had returned to Jogjakarta of their own free will.[13]

The problem of subjects fleeing from one court to another was seen to be essentially insoluble in the absence of a formal agreement between Mangkunĕgara and the Sultan and it continued to plague the divided kingdom until 1790. But it was troublesome only in the case of Jogjakarta subjects who took refuge with Mangkunĕgara or subjects of the latter who fled to the Sultan. Between the Sultan and the Susuhunan there were few such incidents and the records suggest there was no problem in settling them amicably.[14]

[10] Sĕmarang to Batavia, 5 July 1777, in KA 3391 (OB 1778).
[11] Van Rhijn to Sĕmarang, 27 June 1777, in KA 3391 (OB 1778); Sĕmarang to Batavia, 5 July 1777, in KA 3391 (OB 1778); HB I to Sĕmarang, 12 Dulkangidah A.J. 1703 (12 Jan. 1778), in KA 3420 (OB 1779); Sĕmarang to HB I, 19 Jan. 1778, in KA 3420 (OB 1779); HB I to Sĕmarang, 1 Muharram A.J. 1704 (30 Jan. 1778), in KA 3420 (OB 1779).
[12] See Sĕmarang to Batavia, 23 Dec. 1777, in KA 3392 (OB 1778); Batavia to H.XVII, 31 Dec. 1777, in dJ xi, pp. 307–8.
[13] Sĕmarang to Batavia, 31 July 1777, in KA 3391 (OB 1778).
[14] One example was the case of Raden Wirjakusuma, who for unknown reasons fled from Jogjakarta to Surakarta but was returned to the Sultan by the Surakarta *patih*; van Rhijn to Sĕmarang, 19 Dec. 1777, in KA 3420 (OB 1779); Sĕmarang to van Rhijn, 22 Dec. 1777, in KA 3420 (OB 1779).

PERMANENTLY DIVIDED KINGDOM, 1774-1787

There were probably three reasons for this difference in relationships. First, and most importantly, the personal animosity between Mangkunĕgara and Mangkubumi abated not at all with the passage of time. Both were more than pleased to give refuge to the courtiers of the other and probably encouraged such defections whenever possible. Secondly, although the *kratons* of Jogjakarta and Surakarta had arranged a successful administrative system for a divided kingdom in the years before the turn of the century, that system did not expressly recognize Mangkunĕgara's domain as a special or equal principality. Those legal agreements therefore did not reflect Mangkunĕgara's very influential position in Central Javanese politics. Jogjakarta was hardly likely now to recognize Mangkunĕgara as a more-than-usually influential figure by treating protests from him in the same way as complaints from the Surakarta *kraton*. Nor was it in the Susuhunan's interest to allow Mangkunĕgara to behave like a king in such matters and it may be that the Susuhunan's defence of Mangkunĕgara's rights was not as vigorous as the latter would have preferred. Finally, the flow of refugees from Mangkunĕgara to the Sultan seems to have been greater than that in the opposite direction. This tendency was in the Sultan's favour and since he had the superior legal position as a monarch recognized both by the Susuhunan and by the Dutch it was possible for him simply to take no action and to continue to offer refuge to any Mangkunĕgaran courtier who desired it. He could thus continue to strengthen his already advantageous legitimative position *vis-à-vis* Mangkunĕgara who, should hostilities again erupt for any reason, would still be the Sultan's main competitor.

In 1779, more of Mangkunĕgara's subjects joined those already at Jogjakarta. The Sultan refused to return these people, informing Governor van der Burgh that he and the Susuhunan readily returned refugee subjects to each other, but that he could not agree to do this with the subjects of Mangkunĕgara, 'for you as well as the Company know well enough what trouble there is between Mangkunĕgara and me'.[15] Instead he suggested that Mangkunĕgara should visit him in Jogjakarta for one or two nights 'to renew the old friendship'. This proposal both Mangkunĕgara and the Dutch viewed with justified suspicion and it went

[15] HB I to Sĕmarang, 15 Rĕdjĕb A.J. 1705 (29 July 1779), in KA 3448 (OB 1780).

without reply.[16] In 1780, two more court musicians fled the Mangkunĕgaran for Jogjakarta, but this time they were not allowed to stay. They were not, however, turned over directly to the Company or to Mangkunĕgara but were simply put out of the Sultan's *kraton*.[17] The Sultan persistently refused to return the group who had fled to him in 1776–7, however, and although there is little documentation on such matters after 1781 it is clear that this problem continued until it was specifically resolved in 1790. Mangkubumi took the convenient view that any of his subjects who should prefer to live under Mangkunĕgara were by definition 'a pile of vagabonds' and therefore he wished never to see them again.[18]

The fact of refugees flowing from one court to another is of importance not only as evidence of continuing animosity between Mangkunĕgara and the Sultan. It also suggests something of the internal situation within courtly life. Courtiers did not depart one court for another unless they believed their lot would be bettered thereby. Thus the general direction of this refugee traffic should suggest which court had greater appeal to courtiers and which therefore was stronger in terms of legitimation. The most notable element here is the relationship between the Sultan and the Susuhunan, who apparently returned fled subjects to each other without difficulty. This worked so smoothly that there is very little mention in the Dutch Company's archives concerning such incidents, presumably because there was no need for the Dutch to take any interest in a trouble-free arrangement between the Susuhunan and the Sultan. Thus, Hamĕngkubuwana I and Pakubuwana III were in fact treating each other as equals and maintaining the equality and reciprocity which underlay the division of the kingdom since the turn of the Javanese century. Again, there is clear evidence here that the division was now accepted in the two *kratons* and was made to work.

Mangkunĕgara's position was quite different. He was losing courtiers to the Sultan and not regaining them. Although there is

---

[16] HB I to Sĕmarang, 22 Rĕdjĕb A.J. 1705 (5 Aug. 1779), in KA 3448 (OB 1780); Sĕmarang to Batavia, 10 Aug. 1779, in KA 3448 (OB 1780).

[17] Van Rhijn to Sĕmarang, 7 Nov. 1780, in KA 3478 (OB 1781); Sĕmarang to Batavia, 20 Dec. 1780, in KA 3478 (OB 1781); id., 28 April 1781, in KA 3494 (OB 1782).

[18] Sĕmarang to Batavia, 5 Sept. 1781, in dJ xii, pp. 4–5. See also Batavia to H.XVII, 31 Dec. 1779, in dJ xi, pp. 391–2; Siberg, Memorie, 18 Sept. 1787, in dJ xii, p. 87.

ample evidence that Mangkunĕgara was still a very respected and influential person, this slow trickle of court musicians and artisans away from him was symptomatic of his beginning to fall behind in the appeal for an élite consensus. Since the turn of the Javanese century there were clearly seen to be two Javanese kings and the division of the kingdom was clearly going to last for some time. But Mangkunĕgara was not one of those kings and this in itself placed him at an immediate disadvantage. And there was no longer the alternative possibility of proving his leadership in battle. He could only observe the Sultan and the Susuhunan make a greater display, showing more pomp and glory than was possible for him. His attempts to do otherwise had ended with the regulation of the relationship between himself and the Susuhunan in 1772 (A.J. 1698). It would seem that the next 'constitutional' element in the divided kingdom was now beginning to take form: a subsidiary principality at Surakarta, less than a kingdom but more than an ordinary prince's domain. Mangkunĕgara could never again be just another *pangeran*. Yet neither, it seems, was he any longer seriously in the contest to be a king. In 1790, this position would finally receive formal recognition, as will be seen in Chapter X.

Within the *kraton* of Jogjakarta affairs were in general going well. There are some hints, however, of a growing autocracy in the Sultan's government which might potentially threaten the stability of the Sultanate, as it had caused the collapse of Javanese kingdoms before. This is a difficult matter to judge, for the level of autocracy which could threaten a kingdom was a relative matter to some extent dependent upon the mood of princes and courtiers and the extent to which they felt a king's authority to be legitimate, desirable, or necessary. If Mangkubumi was more popular and more respected as a military leader than the Susuhunan, which seems to have been the case, then the degree of autocratic authority which the Sultan could safely employ would have been greater than that which was possible for the Susuhunan. The amount of autocracy which a divided kingdom could tolerate was theoretically less than that which was tolerable in a unified kingdom, for dissident dignitaries could decide to change allegiance to another king without risking their fates in rebellion. Hence the cooperation between the Susuhunan and the Sultan in returning to each other courtiers who had fled their *kratons* was an essential part of maintaining the stability of the kingdom. Nevertheless, the Sultan may have been stretching his authority to levels which were beginning to cause tensions within the Sultanate, a development which had ample precedent in Javanese history and which was very probably connected with the monarch's advancing age and presumably decreasing flexibility. This did not result in any major problems within Jogjakarta during Mangkubumi's reign, but there may have been considerable low-level dissatisfaction upon which there is no specific documentation and which may have provided a background to the turbulent reign of the second Sultan.

The Governor of Sĕmarang J. R. van der Burgh (1771–80) provided a somewhat critical but nevertheless useful description of Hamĕngkubuwana I in 1780:

> The Sultan, ... now nearly 65 years old, has an estimable appearance and royal bearing, and is also an intelligent man, but is at the same time a capricious and irascible person ... for, always mindful of everything which fosters his glory and ambition, he is also always bent on asserting himself over the Susuhunan and winning anything by which in outward appearance his greatness is increased and his dependence [on the Company] decreased, and if one goes against him in this or doesn't give him his way, he easily becomes peevish and then sometimes for many days neither speaks nor allows himself to be seen. ... Nevertheless I have respect for him and ... he has means to inspire everyone and moments in which he can be extremely charming. ... Yet he is assiduous ... to increase his standing and influence and in everything to adopt and to follow the usages of his forefathers, including that of requiring from his subjects as much as they can possibly bear, on the basis of the rule of statecraft among Oriental kings that it is easy to rule a poor people.[19]

Some of van der Burgh's implied criticism of course derived from Mangkubumi's care to keep the Company from exerting any real control over the affairs of the Sultanate, a policy which from the Javanese point of view deserved commendation. But this report does suggest that the Sultan was governing his kingdom

---

[19] Van der Burgh, Memorie, 19 Sept. 1780, in dJ xi, p. 402. See also ibid., pp. 403–4.

On this 'rule of statecraft among Oriental kings that it is easy to rule a poor people', it is interesting to cite HB I's own statement in 1785 that 'the custom of the Javanese is not to oppress his subjects'; HB I to Sĕmarang, 7 Sapar A.J. 1712 (received 13 Dec. 1785), in KA 3630 (OB 1787). The courtly *babads* give ample illustration of the incorrectness of van der Burgh's statement. He who oppressed his subjects was a bad king by Javanese standards. Specifically, *babads* regularly describe the rule of a good king as a period in which, among other things, prices were low and the 'little man' (*wong tjilik*) was happy.

PERMANENTLY DIVIDED KINGDOM, 1774-1787

with firmness, which in excess could be dangerous. Van der Burgh also pointed out that Mangkubumi took a more direct personal concern with the affairs of state than did the Susuhunan, and that lesser Javanese dignitaries at Surakarta displayed greater authority and independence than at Jogjakarta.[20] While from the Dutch viewpoint this state of affairs was complimentary to Jogjakarta, by Javanese standards it could portend possible troubles for the Sultanate in the future.

The Sultan expended much energy and many resources in maintaining his royal glory, the key to his power, an activity in which the Crown Prince now joined him. In addition to the usual tournaments and other public diversions, there was much building at Jogjakarta by both the Sultan and his son and the Dutch provided various paraphernalia, among them trumpets and a boat which *Babad Mangkubumi* says gave the Sultan daily pleasure on the waters of *Taman Sari*.[21]

In the years after the beginning of the new Javanese century, only one important rebel appeared. But this man, one Pangeran Rongga, was of very great importance and the aftermath of his activities was to lead to a serious test of strength between the Sultan and his son the Crown Prince. Both the Dutch and the Javanese took great interest in Pangeran Rongga and his family and there is thus considerable documentation on them. But much of this information is confusing, unreliable, and contradictory. It is clear that the court of Jogjakarta was adept at feeding the Company false and misleading information. This was made easier by the apparent incompetence of the Resident at Jogjakarta, J. M. van Rhijn (1773-86). Because the Jogjakarta Crown Prince later became involved with the daughter of Pangeran Rongga, his *Babad Mangkubumi* is also not above suspicion. It is, however, possible to reconstruct with confidence at least the general outlines of the episode.[22]

[20] Van der Burgh, Memorie, 19 Sept. 1780, in dJ xi, p. 412.

[21] Van Rhijn to Sĕmarang, 22 Aug. 1778, in KA 3420 (OB 1779); Sĕmarang to Batavia, 24 Dec. 1778, in KA 3418 (OB 1779); Sĕmarang to HB I, 21 July 1779, in KA 3448 (OB 1780); Sĕmarang to Batavia, 20 Dec. 1779, in KA 3447 (OB 1780); van der Burgh, Memorie, 19 Sept. 1780, in dJ xi, p. 417; *B. Mang.*, pp. 467-8 (there seems to be an error in the *sĕngkala* here; it should be A.J. 1707/A.D. 1780). See also *Babad Sangkalaning Momana*, p. 272.

[22] The following reconstruction up to the death of Rongga is based upon these sources:

Sĕmarang to van Rhijn, 29 Nov. 1777, in KA 3420 (OB 1779); van Rhijn to

Pangeran Rongga was a descendant of Sunan Kalidjaga, one of the nine *walis* of Javanese Islam. He also apparently possessed important *pusakas*. In 1761 he had caused trouble in the Pati area, under Dutch jurisdiction, but had then retired to a village called 'Djadjar' in the Děmak area.[23] In 1777, the Governor of Sěmarang ordered the arrest of two of Rongga's sons for murder and theft. *Babad Mangkubumi* supports the view that 'Djadjar' had become a refuge for various kinds of criminals. Now the family moved to the Central Javanese kingdoms. The two *bupatis* of Děmak, who were subject to the Company, were fined for allowing them to escape and were later removed from their positions when they again seemed unco-operative in pursuing the Rongga family.

It seems Rongga first took refuge in districts controlled by Pangeran Prabu Amidjaja, the eldest son of Mangkuněgara. The Susuhunan ordered their arrest upon Sěmarang's request and the family then apparently fled to Grobogan, under Jogjakarta. The Dutch informed Mangkubumi of what was believed to be the precise location of the family and the Sultan promised assistance. But thereafter Jogjakarta merely procrastinated, searching for the Pangeran in areas where it seems he was known not to be, all the

---

Sěmarang, 4 Dec. 1777, 19 Dec. 1777, and 5 Jan. 1778, in KA 3420 (OB 1779); Sěmarang to van Rhijn, 9 Jan. 1778, in KA 3420 (OB 1779); van Rhijn to Sěmarang, 12 Jan. 1778, in KA 3420 (OB 1779); Sěmarang to Batavia, 15 Jan. 1778, in KA 3420 (OB 1779); Sěmarang to HB I, 19 Jan. 1778, in KA 3420 (OB 1779); van Rhijn to Sěmarang, 18 Jan. 1778, in KA 3420 (OB 1779); Sěmarang to van Rhijn, 19 Jan. 1778 and 23 Jan. 1778, in KA 3420 (OB 1779); van Rhijn to Sěmarang, 27 Jan. 1778, in KA 3420 (OB 1779); HB I to Sěmarang, 1 Muharram A.J. 1704 (30 Jan. 1778), in KA 3420 (OB 1779); van Rhijn to Sěmarang, 3 Feb. 1778, in KA 3420 (OB 1779); Sěmarang to van Rhijn, 4 Feb. 1778 and 10 Feb. 1778, in KA 3420 (OB 1779); Sěmarang to HB I, 10 Feb. 1778, in KA 3420 (OB 1779); Sěmarang to Batavia, 23 March 1778, in KA 3420 (OB 1779); HB I to Sěmarang, 25 May 1778, in KA 3420 (OB 1779); Sěmarang to HB I, 27 May 1778, in KA 3420 (OB 1779); Sěmarang to Batavia, 12 June 1778, in KA 3420 (OB 1779); HB I to Sěmarang, 22 Djumadilakir A.J. 1704 (17 July 1778), in KA 3420 (OB 1779); Sěmarang to HB I, 19 July 1778, in KA 3420 (OB 1779); Sěmarang to Batavia, 22 July 1778, in KA 3420 (OB 1779); Batavia to H.XVII, 31 Dec. 1778, in dJ xi, p. 349; van Rhijn to Sěmarang, 10 Aug. 1778, in AN Djokjo 34, 'Djokjokarta Brieven naar Samarang, 1770-1780'; Raden Sumajuda, Report, 14 Aug. 1778, in AN Djokjo 34, 'Djokjokarta Brieven naar Samarang, 1770-1780'; HB I to Sěmarang, 11 Dulkangidah A.J. 1704 (1 Dec. 1778), in KA 3421 (OB 1779); Sěmarang to Batavia, 26 Dec. 1778, in KA 3421 (OB 1779); *B. Mang.*, pp. 437-50. See also Poensen, 'Mangkubumi', pp. 300-1, where either Poensen's *babad* or his reading of it is somewhat confused.

[23] On the location of this village, see n. 26 below.

while insisting that any troubles caused by Rongga were entirely due to the machinations of Prabu Amidjaja. The Sultan and his officials were meanwhile providing the Resident van Rhijn with so much false information that Governor van der Burgh completely lost his patience with the gullible Resident.

In June 1778 Mangkubumi took a different position. He told van der Burgh that, because Rongga was a figure of such distinguished lineage, he wished to give him the opportunity to submit and to live in peace at Jogjakarta, to which proposal van der Burgh immediately agreed. The Company in 1778 was in no financial position to undertake expensive military expeditions if cheaper solutions were possible. The Sultan then sent Raden Ronggaprawiradirdja, his main military commander, to Pangeran Rongga with a message the content of which is recorded in *Babad Mangkubumi*. Rongga was told, as other rebels had been told before, that if the rumour were true that he was aspiring to become king, the troops of Jogjakarta would attack him. But if this were not the case, he was invited to submit to the Sultan.[24] Rongga is said to have agreed to submit, but his children were reportedly suspicious of the proposal and convinced him not to do so. Raden Ronggaprawiradirdja then tired of Rongga's procrastination, attacked and defeated him. Three of Rongga's family were killed in the fighting. *Babad Mangkubumi* describes the final capture of Pangeran Rongga himself, who had been wounded. According to the *babad*, Raden Ronggaprawiradirdja and all the commanders of the

---

[24] The message was delivered to Rongga by Raden Tuměnggung Sasraněgara, the *Bupati* of Grobogan, as emissary of Ronggaprawiradirdja. *B. Mang.*, p. 444, Canto LXVII (Ḍanḍanggula):

10. ...
    Pangran amba dinuta
    ing rinta Pukulun
    kangmas Dyan Rongga [prawiradirdja] ing Djipang
    kinen mangjěktosna ing Paduka jukti
    kawarta maděg Radja

11. jen saestu umaděga Adji
    rinta kinen amukula ing prang
    ḍatěng Panduka wijose
    lamun tan maděg Prabu
    pan Paduka dipunaturi
    siweng ḍatěng Ngajogja
    Djěng Sultan Měntarum
    saręnga lawan arinta
    ....

montjanĕgara troops performed the *sĕmbah*, paying obeisance to the spiritual authority of their adversary. Rongga then announced he was about to meet his end, took leave of the dignitaries who sat before him, and died. The body was thereupon cleansed by the *bupatis* of the *montjanĕgara* and laid to rest in 'Djadjar'.[25] In July 1778 the Dutch were informed of the deaths of Rongga and the three family members.[26]

It seems that Mangkubumi had hoped to enlist Pangeran Rongga and the spiritual power he represented in the cause of Jogjakarta's authority. In this he had failed. It is a moot question whether the failure was because Rongga had greater aspirations for himself than being the subject of someone else, or whether it was because he was uncertain whether the Sultan of Jogjakarta was the ruler whose authority he wished to recognize. The Dutch reported that the Sultan's troops made the final assault when they saw Rongga was about to withdraw to the Susuhunan's territory and feared he might fall into the hands of Pakubuwana III.[27] In any case, Rongga was a spiritual force the Sultan had respected and feared. *Babad Mangkubumi* says that when he was informed of Rongga's death,

LXVIII: 25. . . .
>Happy was His Highness
>within his heart,
>exceeding His Highness' delight,
>for this was the descendant of a sage, indeed,
>Pangeran Rongga,
>a descendant of Sunan Kalidjaga.[28]

[25] *B. Mang.*, pp. 448–9. The story that Rongga wished to submit to HB I but was dissuaded by his followers was also repeated in Raden Sumajuda, Report, 14 Aug. 1778, in AN Djokjo 34, 'Djokjokarta Brieven naar Samarang, 1770–1780'. Indeed, Sumajuda's story was very possibly the basis for the narrative in *B. Mang.*

[26] HB I to Sĕmarang, 22 Djumadilakir A.J. 1704 (17 July 1778), in KA 3420 (OB 1779). This letter says the body was buried at Serang. Since *B. Mang.* says the place was 'dusun Djadjar' one at first might suspect the village in question was present-day Kĕdjadjar, in the district Wonosobo, in which the under-district Kĕdjadjar also includes a village called Serang. Yet the fighting took place nowhere near Wonosobo, but rather in Grobogan, and the desa Serangan, under-district Bonang, district Dĕmak, must surely have been the location. Yet if there is a village there called Djadjar, I am unaware of it. There are also rivers named Serang and Djadjar in the Dĕmak region.

[27] Sĕmarang to Batavia, 22 July 1778, in KA 3420 (OB 1779).

[28] *B. Mang.*, p. 450, Canto LXVIII (Durma):
>25. . . .
>suka Sri Narapati
>ing sadjroning drija

PERMANENTLY DIVIDED KINGDOM, 1774-1787

In August 1778 the Sultan's troops captured further members of Rongga's family and took them to Jogjakarta where the Sultan pardoned them. It is notable that these were not in fact subjects of Jogjakarta, since they originated from the Company area of Děmak. But the Sultan took the view that they were his to pardon and the Dutch did not oppose him. Indeed, after Rongga's descendants had sworn their allegiance to Mangkubumi they went to Sěmarang to swear to the Company and were then allowed to return to Jogjakarta. In September, further members of the rebel family, led by Rongga's son Surjakusuma, were defeated by Company dragoons in Děmak and Surjakusuma and several others were killed. Thereafter, no more was heard of the remnants of Rongga's rebellious band, except for the capture of a few of the troublemakers at the end of 1778 and a report nearly a year later that they had caused some trouble again in Děmak.[29]

Now, however, a serious crisis developed within the Jogjakarta *kraton* about the person of Raden Aju Rongga, the daughter of Pangeran Rongga. A major test of strength between the Sultan and the Crown Prince resulted and was to be settled in favour of the younger generation.

The Sultan prepared to take Raden Aju Rongga and the other captured women into his own residence. But the Crown Prince had fallen in love with the girl, according to *Babad Mangkubumi*, and wished to marry her. The *babad* says he feared to ask his

---

langkung ngungun Sang Nata
dening trah ing guru jukti
Pangeran Rongga
turune Sunan Kali.

[29] Van Rhijn to Sěmarang, 10 Aug. 1778, in AN Djokjo 34, 'Djokjokarta Brieven naar Samarang, 1770–1780'; HB I to Sěmarang, 18 Rědjěb A.J. 1704 (12 Aug. 1778) and 20 Rědjěb A.J. 1704 (22 Aug. 1778), in KA 3420 (OB 1779); van Rhijn to Sěmarang, – Aug. 1778, in KA 3420 (OB 1779); Sěmarang to Batavia, 12 Sept. 1778 and 23 Sept. 1778, in KA 3420 (OB 1779); id., 5 Nov. 1778 and 26 Dec. 1778, in KA 3421 (OB 1779); id., 10 March 1779 and 3 Dec. 1779, in KA 3448 (OB 1780); id., 20 Dec. 1780, in KA 3476 (OB 1781); id., 9 Feb. 1782, in KA 3519 (OB 1783).

In 1778, at PB III's request the VOC arrested further members of the family and banished one of them from Java; Sěmarang to Batavia, 29 Aug. 1788, in KA 3708 (OB 1789); Hartsinck to Sěmarang, 1 Sept. 1788, in KA 3708 (OB 1789); Sěmarang to PB III, 4 Sept. 1788, in KA 3708 (OB 1789); Hartsinck to Sěmarang, 5 Sept. 1788, in KA 3708 (OB 1789); Sěmarang to Batavia, 10 Sept. 1788, in KA 3708 (OB 1789).

father for her hand, although Dutch correspondence suggests he did in fact request this of the Sultan. In either case, the Sultan did not apparently favour the marriage. *Babad Mangkubumi* says this was because she was a descendant of Sunan Kalidjaga, and it will be recalled that in 1759 the Sultan himself had been dissuaded from marrying a descendant of Kalidjaga because such a union conflicted with the *adat*. The Dutch also opposed the marriage for fear it would make the Rongga family 'respectable', a concern which illustrates clearly how little the Company understood of the influence such a lineage automatically had in Javanese society.[30]

The Crown Prince now displayed his displeasure by retiring from the court to his pleasure garden (the *Rěksakusuma*) while the Sultan shut himself up at least for much of the time in *Taman Sari* and, fearing his son's intentions, entrusted all the preparation of his food to his eldest daughter Ratu Běndara. The Prince shortly left for the South Coast, the abode of the Goddess of the Southern Ocean, relaxing *en route* with his wives and courtiers.[31] Such behaviour was not the childish posturing the Dutch apparently believed it to be, for both the Sultan and his son were retiring to places of spiritual power to gather their strength and to receive inspiration. Since the woman involved in the conflict was of spiritually powerful lineage, this was more than a conflict of the passions. The Crown Prince was in effect claiming some degree of precedence by demanding such a distinguished woman from his father's own seraglio.

Babad Mangkubumi, which was apparently written by the Crown Prince himself, describes his progress in the direction of the South Coast. Such princely wanderings through Nature were common in Javanese literature. This was basically a spiritual exercise and, according to *Babad Mangkubumi*, the goal of the pilgrimage was 'Sela Gilang'.[32] This is a holy stone near the village of Lipura (to the south of Jogjakarta, in Bantul), upon which

[30] HB I to Sěmarang, 20 Rědjěb A.J. 1704 (22 Aug. 1778), in KA 3420 (OB 1779); van Rhijn to Sěmarang, 22 Aug. 1778, in KA 3420 (OB 1779); HB I to Sěmarang, 13 Saban A.J. 1704 (5 Sept. 1778), in KA 3420 (OB 1779); Sěmarang to Batavia, 12 Sept. 1778, in KA 3420 (OB 1779); van der Burgh, Memorie, 19 Sept. 1780, in dJ xi, pp. 402–3; *B. Mang.*, pp. 451–4.
On the 1759 episode, see p. 103 above.
[31] Van Rhijn to Sěmarang, 22 Aug. 1778, in KA 3420 (OB 1779); Sěmarang to Batavia, 12 Sept. 1778, in KA 3420 (OB 1779); *B. Mang.*, pp. 454–6.
[32] *B. Mang.*, pp. 454–8, 460–1.

PERMANENTLY DIVIDED KINGDOM, 1774–1787

Senapati supposedly lay when the falling star descended and addressed him, prophesying the rise of Mataram.[33]

But before reaching Sela Gilang, the Crown Prince and his party stopped at a Chinese-run toll-port called Trajĕm, near the Praga river in a district belonging to Surakarta. They plundered the site and robbed the goods of the Chinese. *Babad Mangkubumi* not surprisingly describes this as an incident forced upon the Crown Prince by the hostility of the Chinese.[34] It seems more likely that the Prince intended this as a demonstration to all parties, his father, the Susuhunan, and the Dutch, of the power he possessed.

The Dutch Resident attempted to intercede in the dispute by informing the Crown Prince that one of the Ten Commandments exhorted him to honour his father and mother. This had, predictably, no effect. The Crown Prince was dealing in more important matters than those over which the Dutch had any semblance of influence. The Governor of Sĕmarang took the view that if the marriage took place the Company would have no choice but to remain silent.[35]

Finally the Sultan gave in. The Crown Prince returned to Jogjakarta and received Raden Aju Rongga as his wife, although the Sultan did succeed in having the marriage carried out with less than the usual princely ceremony. The Sultan forgave the Crown Prince for the incident at Trajĕm and the stolen goods were returned to the Chinese.[36]

The Crown Prince had succeeded in demonstrating his power within Jogjakarta. The Sultan in succeeding years seems to have deferred more and more to his son, although the documentation of this is not entirely adequate. The Dutch had indirectly suffered a defeat in this quarrel. A major test of power had taken place

[33] See *BTDj*, trans. pp. 78–9, text pp. 75–6. See also p. 13 above and p. 398 below for the Senapati story.

In *BTDj* the stone is called 'sela gĕgilang' and 'sela kumlasa', translated as 'een glanzende steen' and 'een platte steen'. These are accurate translations but it would have been more correct to treat these as synonymous proper names for the site Sela Gilang. Present-day Javanese *literati* still speak of the making of holy *kris*-blades there.

[34] Van Rhijn to Sĕmarang, 5 Sept. 1778, in KA 3420 (OB 1779); Sĕmarang to Batavia, 12 Sept. 1778, in KA 3420 (OB 1779); *B. Mang.*, pp. 458–60.

[35] Van Rhijn to Sĕmarang, – Aug. 1778, in KA 3420 (OB 1779); Sĕmarang to Batavia, 12 Sept. 1778, in KA 3420 (OB 1779).

[36] Van Rhijn to Sĕmarang, 15 Sept. 1778, in KA 3420 (OB 1779); Sĕmarang to Batavia, 23 Sept. 1778, in KA 3420 (OB 1779).

without their understanding even the nature of the conflict. Their intervention had been hesitant, inappropriate, and ineffectual. In the coming years the Dutch were to be taken progressively less seriously in Jogjakarta, probably because of the growing power of the Crown Prince, who never, it seems, viewed the Company as a power to be managed with care. While this was not a dangerous view to take in the late eighteenth century, the Crown Prince would later come to grief when as Sultan Hamĕngkubuwana II he faced early-nineteenth-century European administrations with sufficient power to make their will felt within the *kraton*. The ostensible object of the dispute of 1778, Raden Aju Rongga, was turned out of his residence by the Crown Prince in 1787.[37] Having made his point and, by 1787, having established a firm position within the *kraton*, the Crown Prince apparently lost interest in the woman, who was no longer of value to him.

The Sĕmarang Governor van der Burgh, who had helplessly observed all these manœuvrings, had no reason to regard the Crown Prince with affection. In 1780 he described him as the Sultan's 'favourite son',

now thirty-one years old, who indeed has his intellect and judgement, but who is a proud and conceited Javanese and has yet given little evidence that much good is to be expected of him, but rather that he is pregnant with desires for the crown and cherishes the notion that everything he wishes must be done.[38]

The Dutch, who had been unable to affect the course of the crisis between the Sultan and the Crown Prince, in general were rarely given the opportunity to intervene in Javanese affairs in these years during which the system of division worked successfully for the first time. The Company's progressively more precarious financial circumstances did not encourage the Dutch to over-extend themselves in pursuit of an ideal of 'sovereignty' over Central Java. So long as there was no renewal of warfare and the Company received purchases of crops without excessive delay or difficulty Batavia was not concerned to interfere in the affairs of the Javanese courts. In fact the Company was now taking up a position which was similar in function to that of a Javanese sovereign; Batavia was becoming the remote overlord one of whose

[37] Siberg, Memorie, 18 Sept. 1787, in dJ xii, pp. 86, 91.
[38] Van der Burgh, Memorie, 19 Sept. 1780, in dJ xi, p. 402.

PERMANENTLY DIVIDED KINGDOM, 1774-1787 245

main roles was simply to keep the Javanese courts from attacking one another. The Javanese élite, however, did not see Batavia as an overlord but rather as a senior ally, as will be seen in Chapter XI. So long as the relationship was remote, differing perceptions of it caused no conflict.

Dutch relations with both Jogjakarta and Surakarta were correct, but only Surakarta showed any real willingness to be co-operative. The Sultan took a less cordial view of Dutch interference and was never hesitant to oppose the Company's wishes if they threatened his position or prestige.[39] The Company's worsening financial circumstances favoured the Sultan's independent views, for their army was terribly short of both men and equipment. Van der Burgh in 1780 said that both rulers were aware that if they should go to war against each other the Dutch would hold the balance. If, however, both Javanese monarchs joined together against the Company, they were also aware that the latter would probably go down to defeat. This was particularly true because the Company was so short of manpower just at a time when the increase and prosperity of the Central Javanese population continuously augmented the power of the monarchs.[40] In fact a Surakarta-Jogjakarta alliance against the Company was so unlikely as to be irrelevant. The Javanese never identified the Dutch as their main enemy, partly because by the latter half of the eighteenth century the Company's army seemed so weak that no Javanese prince was apt to regard it as an important military power in Central Java.

But if the Company was no longer so significant as a military force within Central Java, there were still reasons for the Javanese rulers to accept Batavia's friendship. Traditional views of the world encouraged this, as will be seen in Chapter XI. On a more mundane level, one of the most powerful attractions of the Dutch was that they still paid cash for the *pasisir*. Money was important to the rulers, whose truncated domains could never produce the revenues which had previously come from a unified kingdom. The Dutch were also a source of the paraphernalia of royal display: elephants, Persian horses, trumpets, drums, firearms, etc. The funds paid for the *pasisir* were not always adequate, however,

[39] Van der Burgh, Memorie, 19 Sept. 1780, in dJ xi, p. 398; Sĕmarang to Batavia, 20 Dec. 1780, in KA 3478 (OB 1781); Batavia to H.XVII, 29 Dec. 1781, in dJ xii, p. 9.
[40] Van der Burgh, Memorie, 19 Sept. 1780, in dJ xi, p. 398.

and the Sultan at least did not hesitate to demand loans from the Company. In 1777 he received an extra 5,000 reals and by 1781 his debt to Batavia was apparently 10,000 reals. In the latter year this debt was repaid, but already he had been advanced another 10,000 reals. The Governor of Sĕmarang was himself so short of cash at this time that the coins had to be sent from Batavia overland.[41] A full investigation of the economic effect of dividing the kingdom and separating it from the *pasisir* has not yet been done. It already seems clear, however, that the consequently decreased income of each Javanese ruler continued to make the lucrative friendship of the Dutch East India Company all the more essential.

Thus both rulers were willing to accept the friendship of Batavia, but both were alert to any intrusion into their own internal affairs. This was, again, particularly true of Hamĕngkubuwana I. In 1776, for instance, the Dutch unwittingly offended against Javanese *adat* in the realm of princely titles, which both rulers saw as their prerogative alone. On 23 December 1776, the Governer of Sĕmarang notified the *kratons* that, because of their faithfulness to the Company, Pangeran Tjakraningrat of Madura had been given the title *panĕmbahan adipati* and the aged *bupati* of Sĕmarang, Adipati Sura Adimĕnggala, had been titled *pangeran adipati*. The title given to Tjakraningrat was acceptable to the Javanese rulers, for his family was an old and distinguished one. But both expressed displeasure at the title for Sura Adimĕnggala. The Sultan sent a strong letter on the subject to Sĕmarang, saying that the title *pangeran* could be given only to royal children standing in the line of succession to the throne. He would not have objected had the Company given Sura Adimĕnggala larger landholdings as a reward for his faithful service, but he could not accept the giving of the title *pangeran*. This potentially serious problem was soon resolved, for on the third of January 1777 Sura Adimĕnggala suddenly died. He was an aged man and his death may

[41] HB I to Sĕmarang, 20 Sapar A.J. 1703 (20 March 1777), in KA 3391 (OB 1778); Sĕmarang to HB I, 9 April 1777, in KA 3391 (OB 1778); Sĕmarang to Batavia, 31 July 1777, in KA 3391 (OB 1778); Sĕmarang to van Rhijn, 1 Aug. 1777, in KA 3391 (OB 1778); Sĕmarang to Batavia, 20 Dec. 1780, in KA 3478 (OB 1781); id., 15 March 1781, in KA 3492 (OB 1782); Resolutien genoomen in Raade van Politie, Sĕmarang, 20 March 1781, in KA 3492 (OB 1782); Sĕmarang to Batavia, 17 Sept. 1781, in KA 3492 (OB 1782).

There is some confusion in the VOC records over the sum borrowed in 1777, which varies between 5,000 and 10,000 reals.

PERMANENTLY DIVIDED KINGDOM, 1774-1787

have been perfectly natural. But such coincidences in a land where poison was an easy remedy to embarrassing situations were never above suspicion. The Dutch reported that the 'superstitious natives' saw Sura Adiměnggala's death as punishment for his wrongful use of the title *pangeran*. Regardless of the reasons for the death, the problem had been solved, and when the Dutch appointed Sura Adiměnggala's nephew as his successor (with the name Sura Adiměnggala), he was merely given the old title *adipati*.[42]

A more serious conflict arose over the question of the 'homage' the rulers were expected to pay to each new Governor-General of Batavia. When P. A. van der Parra (1761-75) became Governor-General, both rulers sent embassies of felicitation to Batavia in 1762.[43] When J. van Riemsdijk (1775-7) took over that post, embassies came to the Dutch headquarters in 1776. The historian M. L. van Deventer commented particularly upon this latter episode as the clearest demonstration that 'the dominion which the Company exercised over the native rulers and regents was a real one'. On that occasion, the *patihs* and other dignitaries of Surakarta and Jogjakarta came to Batavia, and the *pangeran* of Madura appeared in person, as did Sultan Sěpuh and the son of Sultan Anom of Tjirěbon. The *patih* and dignitaries of Banten and some thirty north-coast Javanese *bupatis* were also present. Around the city camped four thousand armed Javanese troops, three thousand Madurese, and several thousand more from Tjirěbon, Banten, and the Javanese coastal districts. Three hundred ships sat in the harbour. Batavia's twelve thousand inhabitants were meanwhile guarded by a small military force of whom only 187 were European troops, many of whom were ill.[44]

It is something of a misrepresentation to see this as a demonstration of Batavia's 'dominion', as van Deventer has done. Rather, it demonstrates the remarkable military weakness of the Company in its latter decades and the overwhelming military power of the Indonesian princes. At least in the case of the Javanese rulers, embassies were sent to the new Governors-General not because

---

[42] Sěmarang to HB I, 23 Dec. 1776, in KA 3362 (OB 1777); HB I to Sěmarang, 7 Dulkangidah A.J. 1702 (31 Dec. 1776), in KA 3362 (OB 1777); Sěmarang to Batavia, 8 Jan. 1777, in KA 3391 (OB 1778); van der Burgh, Memorie, 19 Sept. 1780, in dJ xi, pp. 427-8. See also n. 108 below.

[43] Sěmarang to Batavia, 30 Oct. 1762, in KA 2957 (OB 1763).

[44] Id. 29 Sept. 1776, in KA 3362 (OB 1777); Batavia to H.XVII, 31 Dec. 1776, in dJ xi, p. 286; dJ xi, pp. lvii-lviii (see also ibid., p. 317).

of Dutch dominion, but because it was part of their royal role to send greetings to their ally, their 'grandfather' as they called him, the Governor-General in Batavia. Pending a more full discussion of this in Chapter XI, here it may simply be pointed out that to the Javanese rulers the Governor-General of Batavia was a respected ally whose friendship they valued. The sending of an embassy to Batavia was for them less an onerous obligation than an opportunity to display their power, glory, and imperial stature. Indeed, it was more onerous for the Company, which had to see to the transportation and maintenance of these enormous missions.

It was important that these embassies were received in Batavia, for that was the Dutch capital in the west of Java, a fitting place to receive royal emissaries. A revealing crisis in this matter developed when the Dutch decided, apparently for financial reasons, that the Javanese rulers' embassies would pay their respects at Sĕmarang instead of Batavia. The limitations of Dutch 'dominion' soon became apparent.

In 1777 Reinier de Klerk became Governor-General (1777–80) and the Company informed the Javanese monarchs that their felicitations would be received at Sĕmarang rather than Batavia. Mangkubumi refused. He would send an embassy only to Batavia. The Governor-General wrote to the Sultan that he wasn't well and could not receive the Sultan's ambassadors, to which Mangkubumi replied that he would await de Klerk's recovery or pay his greetings to the Director-General, the next in rank. But he would send no missions to Sĕmarang. The Company's embarrassment became acute when the Susuhunan proceeded to send his own embassy to Sĕmarang as requested. Mangkubumi persistently refused to give in and the Governor of Sĕmarang was reduced to telling the Sultan that he could not arrange transport for a mission to Batavia. The Dutch finally were forced to drop the issue. The Sultan also stopped requesting that he be allowed to send his embassy to Batavia but would not hear of a mission to Sĕmarang instead. Jogjakarta never sent greetings to Reinier de Klerk.[45]

[45] HB I to Sĕmarang, 22 Rĕdjĕb A.J. 1705 (5 Aug. 1779), in KA 3448 (OB 1780); Sĕmarang to Batavia, 10 Aug. 1779 and 4 Oct. 1779, in KA 3448 (OB 1780); HB I to Sĕmarang, 28 Sawal A.J. 1705 (8 Nov. 1779), in KA 3448 (OB 1780); Sĕmarang to HB I, 19 Nov. 1779, in KA 3448 (OB 1780); Sĕmarang to Batavia, 3 Dec. 1779, in KA 3448 (OB 1780); Batavia to H.XVII, 31 Dec. 1779, in dJ xi, p. 392; Sĕmarang to Batavia, 26 April 1780 and 15 Sept. 1780, in KA 3476 (OB 1781); van der Burgh, Memorie, 19 Sept. 1780, in dJ xi, p. 404.

The Dutch had hardly decided to drop the issue when de Klerk died and was replaced as Governor-General by the former Director-General, Willem Arnold Alting (1780–96). Again Pakubuwana III willingly sent his mission of felicitation, which included the Crown Prince, to Sĕmarang.[46] The new Governor of Sĕmarang, Alting's son-in-law J. Siberg (1780–7), said that a similar mission from the Sultan was 'more to be hoped for than expected'. He resolved to speak personally with Mangkubumi on the subject.[47] But Siberg was one of the most arrogant men to occupy the Sĕmarang governorship and his representations to the Sultan were to come to nothing.

Governor Siberg, to whose installation at Sĕmarang both rulers had sent representatives,[48] made the customary tour of Central Java in July and August 1781. At Jogjakarta he met the Sultan, whom he found to be in 'a very cheerful mood'. It seemed to Siberg an opportune moment to raise the subject of paying homage at Sĕmarang. The Sultan, however, sat quietly for a moment, then answered that this was impossible. The resultant conversations between the Sultan and Siberg[49] provide a revealing illustration both of the inability of the Company to enforce its will in Central Java and of the differing perceptions of the relationship between the Dutch and the *kratons*. Siberg viewed the Sultan as a vassal; the Sultan had no such illusions. Whereas the Dutch thought of *hulde* (homage, tribute), the Javanese apparently thought of felicitations, or even of 'sanctioning the authority of the Governor-General'.[50] The Sultan's conversations with Siberg also reveal Mangkubumi's concern to maintain his prestige in Java, and

[46] Sĕmarang to Batavia, 9 July 1781, in KA 3494 (OB 1782); id., 8 Nov. 1781, in KA 3492 (OB 1782).
[47] Id., 9 July 1781, in KA 3494 (OB 1782).
[48] Id., 15 Sept. 1780, in KA 3476 (OB 1781).
[49] Id., 5 Sept. 1781, in KA 3494 (OB 1782). The edited version of this document in dJ xii, pp. 1–6, omits the descriptions of the conversations summarized here. *B. Mang.*, pp. 466–7, cursorily records Siberg's installation at Sĕmarang and mentions his visit to Jogjakarta, but gives no details.
[50] See BM Add. MS. 12323 (B) (an early-nineteenth-century Surakarta *sĕngkala*-list), f. 44r–v:
Angkatipun dipati Sasradiningrat, tumĕnggung Mangkujuda, tumĕnggung Maospati, tumĕnggung Tjakradipura, mring Bĕtawi ngestreni djĕnĕnging Djendral, Jeremijas pan Rimĕndek [Jeremias van Riemsdijk], . . . [A.J.] 1702 . . .
Dipati Sasradiningrat mring Sĕmawis, matĕdakakĕn kurmat tabe-dalĕm, datĕng Djendral, Renĕr de Kerĕk [Reinier de Klerk], . . . [A.J.] 1705.

suggest the personal difficulties which were possible whenever a Dutch official, particularly one as arrogant as Siberg, attempted to deal with the refined circumlocutions of a Javanese aristocrat who meant 'no' but wished to say it politely.

The Sultan rejected the idea that his embassies should be received anywhere but at Batavia. Siberg replied that there was no suggestion that the reception of the embassies at Sĕmarang should be a permanent arrangement, saying there was nothing in the Contracts to prevent the Sultan and the Dutch from making any new arrangements on such matters that they wished. In any case, the place where the embassies were received had nothing to do with the act of homage itself. Siberg said that the Sultan could hardly care about the location and there must therefore be some other reason for his objection. Furthermore, he recklessly went on, the Sultan's behaviour was not a fitting response to the requests which the Company had often granted him or to the beneficence for which he was indebted to the Company, to whom, next to God, he owed his present status. The Sultan should also consider that not only he during his lifetime, but also his son the Crown Prince after him, would have need of the Company's protection and good will. While saying this, Siberg stood up from his chair, took the Crown Prince's hand and brought him before the Sultan.

An ill-considered reprimand and warning of this nature was bound to infuriate Mangkubumi, who knew that he owed his throne to the consensus of Javanese notables which he had enjoyed long before he had finally forced the Dutch to recognize his position in 1755. The implicit threat to the Crown Prince's succession could only make matters worse. One wonders at the ineptness of Siberg, who probably failed to appreciate how fortunate he was that the Javanese no longer made a regular habit of murdering Dutch officials. This speech is so remarkable that one suspects Siberg very possibly exaggerated it for Batavia's consumption, as he exaggerated other reports. But his further description of Mangkubumi's reaction has the ring of truth.

The Sultan seemed pained by Siberg's statement. He turned to the *bupati* of Sĕmarang, Sura Adimĕnggala, who had accompanied the Governor to the conference at Mangkubumi's request, and told him, 'Your Governor has said to me many things which concern me closely. But I feel an attachment for him which obliges me to listen in silence.' Thereupon the Sultan withdrew into what

Siberg called a 'fit of silence', was observed to subdue his passions, and slowly began to come to himself again. Then he spoke very softly to the Governor, as if he were whispering in his ear. He said he very much wished to please the Governor-General and the Council of the Indies and to comply with Siberg's request. But having previously refused to pay his respects at Sĕmarang he could not now agree to do so without being shamed and being laughed at by his enemies in Surakarta. But, he said, if Siberg could contrive a means whereby he could agree to the request without being shamed, he would gladly do so. Siberg attempted to argue that there would be no reason for the Sultan to feel shame. Indeed, it must be an honour for him to be able to fulfil so easily the request of the Governor-General and the Council of the Indies, who were after all greater than he. The Sultan would not give in and again asked Siberg to devise a means whereby shame could be avoided. Siberg could not, however, think of anything which the Sultan would accept and the Governor therefore asked Mangkubumi to make proposals on the subject himself.

A more perceptive man than Siberg would have realized that there was no possibility of the Sultan agreeing to send his mission to Sĕmarang. He did not wish to do so because such a lesser embassy would be a blow to his prestige. Even if by 1781 he had truly wished to change his mind, which seems unlikely, there was indeed no way to back down without public embarrassment. And in Javanese politics the public embarrassment of the king was more than unpleasant; it threatened the sinews of royal authority. Mangkubumi was refusing the Dutch request, but Siberg was too imperceptive to understand.

Having been asked to make his own proposals, Mangkubumi put forward three suggestions which he surely knew were unacceptable to the Dutch. First, he proposed that while Siberg was at Jogjakarta he should accept Mangkubumi's felicitations there on behalf of the Governor-General. Siberg rejected this, saying it was improper that the Governor-General, whose person he represented, should come to the Sultan to receive homage. Rather the Sultan was obligated to send a mission to the Governor-General. Then Mangkubumi proposed that only a small boat, even with only three or four emissaries, be sent to Batavia. This, too, was rejected as inappropriate and insulting even to the Sultan's own dignity. Finally the Sultan made the absurd proposal that his emissaries should be carried by sea as far as Pĕkalongan, and then brought back to Sĕmarang on the excuse that the ship was leaky and unseaworthy. Felicitations would then be paid at Sĕmarang. This, too, Siberg rejected. In any case, he said, the Company's ships were too much needed to be employed for such unnecessary excursions, since the Dutch were then expecting the British to attack, war with England having broken out in Europe (1780-4).

The Sultan then asked that they discuss the matter no further, so that he could consider it for a few days. Siberg agreed, but again did not recognize this as an opportunity to drop the subject gracefully. The day before his departure from Jogjakarta, Siberg took his leave of the Sultan and again asked him whether he would not now give him the pleasure of agreeing to pay homage at Sĕmarang. Mangkubumi replied that since his proposals were unacceptable and there was no other means to avoid shame, he must persist in refusing to send his embassy anywhere but to Batavia.

Finally Siberg saw that there was no hope. He told the Sultan that his 'inflexible determination' was a source of great sorrow, but the Company would regard the homage which the Sultan offered and to which he was obligated (to which the Sultan replied, 'Yes') on this occasion as if it had actually taken place at Sĕmarang. The Sultan said, 'What is there for me to do? But it is good, let my presentation be regarded as if it had taken place, then I will not need to be shamed before my enemies.'

The matter was at an end. Having lost several opportunities to drop the subject, Siberg had instead forced it to a conclusion which can only be seen as a victory for Mangkubumi. Like Reinier de Klerk, W. A. Alting never received a mission of felicitation from Jogjakarta.

Fortunately, Governor-General Alting outlived the Sultan and the problem of presenting felicitations to a new Governor-General did not recur during the reign of Hamĕngkubuwana I. All levels of the Company administration agreed that if there should be a change of Governor-General they would have no choice but to give in to the Sultan. They would regard the felicitations which he offered to the Governor of Sĕmarang at Jogjakarta as if they had been presented to the Governor on behalf of the Governor-General at Sĕmarang.[51] It was a complex face-saving

[51] Batavia to H.XVII, 29 Dec. 1781, in dJ xii, pp. 9-10; Sĕmarang to Batavia, 20 Dec. 1783, in KA 3543 (OB 1784); H.XVII, Extract Patriaasche Generaale

PERMANENTLY DIVIDED KINGDOM, 1774-1787

formula which hardly masked the fact that the Sultan had had his way.

The Company decided the only solution to this problem was to alter the contracts with the rulers when the opportunity presented itself. Accordingly, when Pakubuwana III died in 1788 his son Pakubuwana IV signed a new contract with the Dutch, Article Twenty-four of which stipulated that the Susuhunan would pay tribute to each new Governor-General at Batavia or, if the Governor-General wished, at Sĕmarang instead.[52] When the Crown Prince of Jogjakarta was asked to sign an identical agreement upon the death of Hamĕngkubuwana I in 1792, he objected. Finally, however, Hamĕngkubuwana II also accepted Article Twenty-four.[53] Yet these agreements hardly ensured Dutch 'dominion'. Both Hamĕngkubuwana II and Pakubuwana IV gave European administrations greater worries than had either of their fathers since 1755. By the time these two young rulers had died, both *kratons* had been besieged by European troops and Sultan Hamĕngkubuwana II had had the unique distinction of being twice deposed and thrice inaugurated. The matter of paying felicitation to the new Governor-General was merely symptomatic of an underlying conflict between the Dutch and Javanese understandings of the relationship between themselves.

So long as the Company did not try actually to enforce some form of a vassal relationship upon Jogjakarta, which in any case they were powerless to do and largely uninterested in attempting, there was no serious conflict. This was to come later, when nineteenth-century European regimes attempted more direct control over Javanese affairs. There is no entirely clear explanation, however, why in the late eighteenth century Surakarta should have been so ready to send missions to Sĕmarang when Jogjakarta considered the proposal so insulting. One reason was probably the different personalities of the Susuhunan and the Sultan. The former was

---

Missive (30 Nov. 1784), 24 Dec. 1785, in KA 3595 (OB 1786); Siberg, Memorie, 18 Sept. 1787, in dJ xii, pp. 86-7; Sĕmarang to Batavia, 9 May 1788, in KA 3708 (OB 1789).

[52] PB IV-VOC Contract, 29 Sept. 1788, in dJ xii, p. 143. The new contracts had been prepared as early as 1783; see van der Burgh, Memorie, 19 Sept. 1780, in dJ xi, pp. 410-11; Sĕmarang to Batavia, 18 Aug. 1783 and 20 Dec. 1783, in KA 3545 (OB 1784); Batavia to H.XVII, 31 Dec. 1783, in dJ xii, p. 44; Siberg, Memorie, 18 Sept. 1787, in dJ xii, pp. 88-9.

[53] Sĕmarang to Batavia, 25 April 1792, in dJ xii, pp. 252-5.

always more amenable to Dutch wishes than the latter, whom the Dutch were now not very affectionately calling 'the old greybeard'.[54] Mangkubumi was inflexible on the question of his prestige, the key to his power within Java, and would never allow the Dutch to threaten it. Perhaps the Susuhunan, who in the years before 1755 had lost the recognition of virtually everyone but the Dutch, not only felt more grateful to the Company than did Mangkubumi, but also had a less firm élite consensus supporting him and could therefore subordinate himself to the Dutch without any appreciable further erosion of his already lukewarm support. Quite apart from personalities, it has been generally true of Javanese history during the two centuries since the founding of Jogjakarta that the latter was consistently more troublesome for the Dutch than was Surakarta.

Crises only occurred if the Dutch happened to overstep the limitations of their position as the Javanese saw it. Otherwise, friendship and co-operation between allies was the rule. For instance, in 1780 Jogjakarta and Sĕmarang quite amicably agreed a set of legal arrangements for dealing with crimes which crossed the boundaries between the Dutch-controlled *pasisir* and Jogjakarta.[55] The Sultan apparently accepted the Dutch presence on the coast and was willing to regularize their position there in law.

The most notable episode involving co-operation between the *kratons* and the Dutch illustrated graphically the weakened military position of the Company in Java and contributed greatly to the growing understanding among Javanese notables of the Company's precarious financial and military condition. On 20 December 1780 England declared war on the Netherlands. The news of the declaration reached Java in June 1781. The Company was seriously worried about an English assault upon their posts in the East Indies, knowing all too well that they had no hope of defending even Batavia. The resounding success of a British Indian force against Manila in 1762 amply justified the Company's

[54] Sĕmarang to Batavia, 20 Dec. 1783, in KA 3543 (OB 1784).
[55] Danurĕdja to Sĕmarang, received 26 Oct. 1780, in KA 3478 (OB 1781); HB I to Sĕmarang, received 15 Nov. 1780, in KA 3478 (OB 1781); Sĕmarang to Batavia, 20 Dec. 1780, in KA 3478 (OB 1781). The Dutch text of the agreement is attached to the Sĕmarang letter of 20 Dec. 1780 in KA 3478 (OB 1781). A Javanese text is to be found in 'Journal', BM Add. MS. 12303, f. 83^{r-v}. The Dutch text is undated, but the Javanese is dated 13 Bĕsar A.J. 1706 and 1 December A.D. 1780. If the Javanese date is correct, however, the Western date should be 10 December A.D. 1780.

PERMANENTLY DIVIDED KINGDOM, 1774-1787   255

apprehension. They therefore decided to ask troops from their Indonesian 'vassals'.[56] The reactions of the Susuhunan and the Sultan to this request were consistent with the different attitudes these two rulers took towards their relationship with Batavia. Dutch records on this matter also suggest the differing conditions within the two courts at this time.

Both the Sultan and the Susuhunan immediately agreed to assist in the defence of Batavia. Each initially offered five thousand troops, although the Dutch only asked and in fact received about one thousand from each.[57] The Susuhunan signed a capitulation (*Capitulatie*) by which his troops were loaned to the service of the Company. His commanders were given Dutch military ranks and the salaries paid to indigenous troops serving in the Company's forces.[58]

The Sultan, while equally willing to come to the defence of the Governor-General, refused absolutely to sign any agreement turning over the formal control of his troops to the Company. Nor would he allow that his troops be assigned European military ranks or receive European salaries. They were to be paid, but only in the form of necessities for the journey. The Dutch did not approve of these irregularities, but the Sultan told them firmly that he would not depart from his *adat* (custom). If it were otherwise, he would gain not honour but shame among his people. He was experienced and old, he said, and knew too well the nature of Javanese soldiery not to understand how they must be handled and how best they could fulfil the Company's purpose. The Dutch gave in.[59]

All of this took place at the same time as Siberg was attempting unsuccessfully to get Mangkubumi to pay homage to the Governor-General in Sĕmarang, and the Sultan's intransigence in both

[56] Sĕmarang to Batavia, 19 May 1781, in KA 3494 (OB 1782); Resolutien genoomen in Raade van Politie, Sĕmarang, 25 June 1781, in KA 3492 (OB 1782).
B. *Mang.*, pp. 468–75, describes the events surrounding the Jogjakarta assistance to Batavia very cursorily, as it does most events after A.J. 1699 (A.D. 1773). See also Poensen, 'Mangkubumi', pp. 305–6.
[57] Sĕmarang to Batavia, 9 July 1781, in KA 3494 (OB 1782); id., 5 Sept. 1781, in dJ xii, pp. 1–4; id., 20 Oct. 1781, in KA 3495 (OB 1782).
[58] PB III, Capitulatie, 19 Oct. 1781, in KA 3495 (OB 1782); Sĕmarang to Batavia, 26 Oct. 1781, in KA 3495 (OB 1782).
[59] HB I to Sĕmarang, 26 Sawal A.J. 1707 (received 17 Oct. 1781), in KA 3495 (OB 1782); Sĕmarang to Batavia, 20 Oct. 1781, in KA 3495 (OB 1782); HB I to Batavia, 11 Dulkangidah A.J. 1707 (received at Sĕmarang, 31 Oct. 1781), in KA 3495 (OB 1782); Sĕmarang to Batavia, 6 Nov. 1781, in KA 3495 (OB 1782).

matters derived from the same considerations. He was willing, even pleased, to be an ally of the Governor-General but he would not be treated as a vassal. The Sultan even proposed that Danurĕdja should accompany his troops to Batavia and there convey his felicitations to the Governor-General. But the Dutch turned this down, saying they considered that matter to be settled.[60] *Babad Mangkubumi* says that the Governor-General 'respectfully requested the assistance of His Highness the Sultan' in providing one thousand mounted troops.[61] This was the Javanese view of the matter; it also depicts more accurately the true nature of the episode than did the Dutch picture of Javanese vassals responding to the command of Batavia.

When the Dutch began to assess the military value of the Javanese troops now at their disposal, they discovered further important differences between the two *kratons*. The Dutch estimate of the troops from Surakarta was very favourable, largely it seems because they were attired in European style. But it was soon learned that the troops from Jogjakarta were better trained, better disciplined, and had better commanders. They were expected to be of greater value than those from Surakarta if an attack should come, because the latter were less accustomed to a firm military discipline.[62] Thus, Jogjakarta was apparently a more martial kingdom. The weapons of neither contingent much impressed the Company, many of the pistols and flintlock rifles being almost unserviceable. But both monarchs asked that their soldiers be allowed to keep their own weapons, partly for fear that they would be worse off if the Dutch insisted on an exchange for other armament, partly because of the almost religious respect with which Javanese regarded their personal weaponry.[63]

At the end of October 1781, the Susuhunan's troops set off for Batavia by the land route along the north coast. There were

[60] Sĕmarang to Batavia, 20 Oct. 1781, in KA 3495 (OB 1782).
[61] B. *Mang.*, p. 469, Canto LXXII (Pangkur):

10. . . .
. . . kang ejang Djendral
ing mangke karsanja ugi

11. nuwun bantu Kangdjĕng Sultan
pratiwa keh sewu tumameng wadjik
. . . .

[62] Sĕmarang to Batavia, 5 Sept. 1781, in dJ xii, pp. 2–4.
[63] Id., 26 Oct. 1781, in KA 3495 (OB 1782).

1,206 troops in all, divided into ten companies, six from the Susuhunan, two from his principal wife, and two from the Crown Prince. Early in November, the Sultan's troops also marched to Batavia, totalling 1,132 men of which 1,000 were common soldiery and the rest officers. A company of 100 men was provided by the Jogjakarta Crown Prince.[64] For the first time in 152 years, Javanese troops were marching to Batavia in expectation of battle. But now it was as the ally, not the enemy, of the Company. But nothing happened. The English did not attack, and the only noteworthy development at Batavia was the necessity to arrest two of Pakubuwana III's commanders for misconduct.[65]

The Dutch dragoons who normally served at the Dutch Residencies in Surakarta and Jogjakarta had accompanied the rulers' troops to Batavia. In their absence, the Susuhunan accepted a life-guard at the *kraton* composed of infantry. The Sultan, however, would not hear of a similar measure at his court. Unlike the Susuhunan, the Sultan did not desire the personal protection of Dutch arms, being interested only in the preservation of his prestige. Dragoons made an impressive display, infantry did not.[66]

By October 1782, Mangkubumi had grown weary of the purposeless absence of his troops at Batavia. He informed the Dutch he wished them returned. Sěmarang and Batavia temporized, knowing there was little point in arguing with the Sultan, whose mind they had never succeeded in changing. They realized they would have to give in if he insisted, but hoped to postpone the matter until the reinforcements they expected from the Netherlands had arrived.[67] The Sultan was concerned less for his own military strength than for the possible effect of a long stay at Batavia upon the minds of his subjects. He told Siberg, 'My brother [Siberg] will be well acquainted with the ways of the

[64] Id., 20 Oct. 1781, 26 Oct. 1781, and 6 Nov. 1781, in KA 3495 (OB 1782). B. *Mang.*, p. 473, gives an incorrect date for the departure of the troops from Jogjakarta, 17 Dulkangidah A.J. 1707 (4 Nov. 1781). The Dutch records say they had already arrived at Sěmarang, a four- or five-day trip, on 2 November.

[65] Sěmarang to Batavia, 26 March 1782, in KA 3519(OB 1783); id., 5 Oct. 1782, in KA 3520 (OB 1783); Batavia to H.XVII, 31 Dec. 1782, in dJ xii, pp. 24–5.

[66] Sěmarang to Batavia, 19 Dec. 1781, in KA 3495 (OB 1782). See p. 156, n. 44 above, on a possible assassination attempt on PB III in 1773. This may have been the reason for PB III's greater desire for VOC troops at his court.

[67] Sěmarang to Batavia, 23 Oct. 1782, in KA 3520 (OB 1783); Sěmarang to HB I, 4 Dec. 1782, in KA 3545 (OB 1784); Sěmarang to Batavia, 23 Dec. 1782, in KA 3545 (OB 1784); Batavia to de Gecommitteerden tot de zaken van den oorlog te Amsterdam, 31 Dec. 1782, in dJ xii, p. 35.

Javanese, that whenever they are long separated from their homes, sometimes some of them develop different inclinations.'[68]

After the customary displays of silent bad humour on the Sultan's part, the Dutch were finally saved embarrassment by news of the armistice in Europe. They had already begun to promise the return of the Sultan's troops and in June 1783 had allowed nearly 300 of them to return to Jogjakarta.[69] In August they informed both rulers that the armistice was signed and their troops would return shortly.[70] In October 1783 the Javanese troops returned home and the Dutch thanked Haměngkubuwana I and Pakubuwana III for their assistance. They were subsequently sent various gifts in gratitude.[71]

Immediately new problems erupted. The Sultan discovered that some of the weapons his troops had taken to Batavia had after all been exchanged for armaments of the Company. On the return of his troops many of the weapons, which he claimed were *pusakas*, had been left behind. It seems most unlikely that there were any royal *pusakas* left behind, and the Sultan was apparently using the excuse of this exchange of weapons to his advantage, as he used every other opportunity. The Company hurriedly apologized for the exchange, which it blamed upon uninformed lower officials. The Sultan demanded that he be repaid with some twenty cannon from the Jogjakarta Residency. The Dutch had planned to exchange their three-pounders for heavier cannon in any case and therefore gave the Sultan a dozen of them. Apparently it was possible to have cannon cast in Java, for the Company feared that if they did not satisfy the Sultan he would order the casting of 'other metal ordnance, possibly of heavier calibre and greater merit than the old three-pounders at Jogjakarta'. The Sultan was satisfied, however, with his twelve three-pounders.[72] The Dutch also com-

[68] HB I to Sěmarang, 10 Sura A.J. 1709 (received 17 Dec. 1782), in KA 3545 (OB 1784).
[69] Sěmarang to Batavia, 23 Dec. 1782 and 20 May 1783, in KA 3545 (OB 1784); id., 30 June 1783, in KA 3543 (OB 1784).
[70] Id., 11 Aug. 1783, in KA 3545 (OB 1784).
[71] Id., 24 Sept. 1783 and 14 Oct. 1783, in KA 3543 (OB 1784); id., 20 Dec. 1783, in KA 3545 (OB 1784); Batavia to H.XVII, 31 Dec. 1783, in dJ xii, p. 44; Sěmarang to Batavia, 27 Jan. 1784, in KA 3630 (OB 1787); id., 4 Sept. 1784, in KA 3568 (OB 1785).
[72] Id., 27 Jan. 1784, in KA 3630 (OB 1787); id., 4 Sept. 1784, in KA 3568 (OB 1785).
On the casting of cannon, see also Raffles (1830), vol. i, p. 330: 'Previous to the reduction of Yúgya-kérta [Jogjakarta], in 1812, by the British forces, the

mented that at this time the number of flintlocks which the Sultan's armoury contained was 'very formidable'.[73]

But if Jogjakarta was showing every sign of increasing power, prosperity, and stability in the new century, Surakarta was not. The problem there was almost surely Pakubuwana III himself. He was a ruler of little administrative authority, but that was usually true of Javanese kings. Much more important was the fact that he still apparently inspired little esteem among the Javanese élite. In this the contrast with the Sultan was clear. The result was a generally less stable and less secure political life in Surakarta. Had both *kratons* not accepted the division of the kingdom after A.J. 1700 (A.D. 1774), one wonders how much longer the Susuhunan could have retained his position. As the years passed, the internal troubles and intrigues which had often surrounded the Surakarta *kraton* continued unabated. And as always, Mangkunĕgara's role in these affairs was often suspect but rarely clear. But now only Mangkunĕgara, his family, and the other dignitaries of Surakarta were directly involved. Jogjakarta stood aloof from the Surakarta troubles. There were no more military intrusions, no more plundered villages. The kingdom had been divided.

In the outlying districts and within the Surakarta *kraton* itself there were signs of trouble. There were cases of thieves, murderers, or vagabonds,[74] who in at least one instance ultimately proved to be in the pay of one of the highest Surakarta court officials. The latter, Raden Tumĕnggung Tjakradipura, had apparently tried to make Jogjakarta seem to be responsible for the troubles but was found out and banished from Surakarta on the Susuhunan's orders.[75]

The most serious defection within *kraton* circles was that of Raden Mas Mangkukusuma, the Susuhunan's nephew. He was the son of Pangeran Purbaja, Pakubuwana's eldest half-brother and a man whose influence in court affairs seems to have been growing in these years. Mangkukusuma's mother was a daughter of

---

Sultan cast brass guns of considerable calibre, and at Grésik [Grĕsik] they are still manufactured for exportation.'

[73] Sĕmarang to Batavia, 27 Jan. 1784, in KA 3630 (OB 1787).

[74] Examples may be found in id., 31 July 1777, in KA 3391 (OB 1778); id., 12 Sept. 1778, in KA 3420 (OB 1779).

[75] Id., 7 April 1779, 13 July 1779, 4 Oct. 1779, and 3 Dec. 1779, in KA 3448 (OB 1780). Tjakradipura had been one of the four leaders of PB III's mission of felicitation to GG van Riemsdijk in 1776; see n. 50 above.

Sunan Kuning, the exiled 'Chinese' Susuhunan of the 1740s, and he was therefore related also to the rebel Raden Mas Guntur of the 1760s. Before his birth, his father had sent his pregnant mother away and the child was subsequently raised by the daughter of Mangkunĕgara who had been married to Raden Mas Guntur before the latter's death in 1762. He was thus by adoption also a grandson of Mangkunĕgara. A more explosive family background could hardly be imagined. Even Mangkunĕgara had reportedly found the youth too troublesome to handle and had abandoned trying to discipline him. Upon Dutch insistence the Susuhunan had taken him into his service in an attempt to lead him to a quieter life. In December 1780 Mangkukusuma left Surakarta and quickly gathered as many as three hundred armed men under him in Sokawati. There is some suggestion that he may have been offered refuge in a village under Pangeran Prabu Amidjaja, Mangkunĕgara's eldest son. But within a few weeks the Susuhunan's and Sultan's troops sought him out and killed him. After Dutch officials at Surakarta had carefully identified the body, it was buried near the old *kraton* of Kartasura where others of Mangkukusuma's relatives were also reportedly buried.[76]

Princely rebellion was always a problem even for the best of kings. More significant was Mangkukusuma's immediate gathering of three hundred followers, which suggests there were still significant numbers of discontented and vagabonds in the countryside who were ready to join a rebel with a powerful ancestry. That someone like Mangkukusuma should leave the Surakarta *kraton* suggests, too, that perhaps all was not well there, although his ancestry and upbringing hardly prepared him for the role of the obedient subject.

Van der Burgh's description of the Susuhunan in 1780 is revealing of the problems which seem now to have been developing in Surakarta. One recalls the *Babad Tanah Djawi*'s criticism of Susuhunan Amangkurat I that 'he often employed violence

---

[76] Van Straalendorff to Sĕmarang, 15 Dec. 1780, in KA 3478 (OB 1781); Sĕmarang to Batavia, 20 Dec. 1780, in KA 3478 (OB 1781); Batavia to H.XVII, 31 Dec. 1780, in dJ xi, p. 492.

See also *B. Mang.*, pp. 464–6, where the story of Mangkukusuma is briefly told, without details. He is said to have been 'possessed' by Dasamuka, the giant king of Ngalĕngka in the *wajang* stories. For an illustration of Dasamuka, see Anderson, *Mythology*, p. 64.

On Raden Mas Guntur, see pp. 123–7 above.

PERMANENTLY DIVIDED KINGDOM, 1774-1787   261

against others and continually held executions in public'.[77] In the seventeenth century that had meant that trouble was approaching. Now, eight years before his death, Pakubuwana III seems also to have begun adopting a more arbitrary and therefore more dangerous form of government. Van der Burgh wrote,

> The Susuhunan or Emperor, now some fifty years old, has always been and always will be a true-hearted friend of the Company, a lover of right and justice, and so strongly satisfied with and attached to the Company that his loyalty and adherence are not to be doubted. But over his subjects he is less mild than in the past, punishing evil without distinction of person, immediately and severely, and he is also less indulgent than formerly in matters in which the Sultan is mixed up and which touch his imperial authority.[78]

A ruler with a strong consensus could afford to be strict. For Pakubuwana III the wisdom of such firmness was less obvious.

The main character in the Surakarta intrigues had long been Mangkunĕgara and now his descendants, too, were becoming important. The main goal of Mangkunĕgara's machinations was somehow to ensure the status and prosperity of these descendants. His son Prabu Amidjaja had by now become something of a trouble maker,[79] and Mangkunĕgara's hopes and affections seem to have passed to his grandson, who was eventually to succeed him as Mangkunĕgara II (1796-1835). The Dutch were, as always, rather unsure what attitude to take towards Mangkunĕgara. Siberg denied that he could possibly be guilty of all the misbehaviour of which the Jogjakarta *kraton* constantly accused him.[80] Yet the Company was not willing that Mangkunĕgara should have too much influence in Surakarta and was still unwilling to give his domain the status of an independent inheritable principality. Mangkunĕgara was not difficult to control indirectly, however, for the Company's great influence over the Susuhunan meant that Dutch advice to the ruler usually procured the desired end and kept Mangkunĕgara from gaining all he wished from Pakubuwana III.

[77] *BTDj*, text p. 154. See p. 19 above.
[78] Van der Burgh, Memorie, 19 Sept. 1780, in dJ xi, pp. 399-400.
[79] Siberg ordered the Surakarta Resident van Straalendorff to keep a close eye on Prabu Amidjaja, whom he called an 'evil subject'; Sĕmarang to Batavia, 9 Feb. 1782, in KA 3519 (OB 1783). Van der Burgh earlier used the same description of Prabu Amidjaja; van der Burgh, Memorie, 19 Sept. 1780, in dJ xi, p. 401.
[80] Van der Burgh, Memorie, 19 Sept. 1780, in dJ xi, p. 406.

In 1780 Mangkunĕgara desired that his grandson be given the name and title Pangeran Surja Mataram ('Sun of Mataram'), a name which had never before been known in Mataram. The Dutch feared it was so grandiloquent that it would arouse suspicions and give offence in Jogjakarta and elsewhere. Mangkunĕgara also wished his grandson's inheritance of his domains to be confirmed. The Susuhunan seemed willing to grant these wishes but the Dutch successfully dissuaded him. Mangkunĕgara was told by the Company that he could dispose of his personal goods as he wished but not of the lands and people which he held as a fief from the Susuhunan and the Company. And his grandson must find another name. All of this Mangkunĕgara accepted.[81]

In the following year, Mangkunĕgara conceived the fantastic proposal that he should wed a princess of Bandjĕrmasin, the widow of the grandfather of the reigning Bandjĕrmasin Sultan. Mangkunĕgara apparently believed her to be wealthy, the truth of which is difficult to ascertain, and hoped by this marriage to compensate for the loss of his wife Ratu Bĕndara, Mangkubumi's daughter. In any case, the Dutch told him the Bandjĕrmasin woman was both old and poor and convinced him to abandon the scheme.[82] As flamboyant in submission as he had formerly been in opposition, Mangkunĕgara was reported by Siberg to have stood

with tears rolling down his cheeks, in the presence of the Susuhunan and the Resident van Straalendorff, falling upon my neck, [he] assured [me] that henceforth he would always submit to the orders and consent of the Company, the Susuhunan, and me, without deviating in any way.[83]

Siberg was so often the source of similar graphic scenes that one sometimes suspects his imagination played a significant role in the reports he sent to Batavia. Yet undoubtedly Mangkunĕgara was by now more submissive to the Company. This was presumably

[81] MN to Sĕmarang, 18 Oct. 1780, in KA 3478 (OB 1781); Sĕmarang to MN, 30 Oct. 1780, in KA 3478 (OB 1781); Sĕmarang to Batavia, 20 Dec. 1780, in KA 3478 (OB 1781).

[82] MN to Sĕmarang, 31 Jan. 1781 and 17 Feb. 1781, in KA 3494 (OB 1782); Sĕmarang to MN, 20 Feb. 1781, in KA 3494 (OB 1782); Sĕmarang to Batavia, 15 March 1781, in KA 3494 (OB 1782); Batavia to H.XVII, 29 Dec. 1781, in dJ xii, p. 10.

In 1782, the VOC also rejected MN's proposal that his son Surjakusuma, the head of Pranaraga, should marry the widow of the Panĕmbahan of Madura; Sĕmarang to Batavia, 22 June 1782, in KA 3519 (OB 1783).

[83] Sĕmarang to Batavia, 5 Sept. 1781, in dJ xii, p. 3.

because he was genuinely worried for his descendants' future and, having firmly renounced warfare, he could only guarantee their prosperity by soliciting the favour of the Susuhunan and the Dutch.

With the Susuhunan Mangkunĕgara now maintained a close relationship which was directed primarily to ensuring the welfare of his family. This relationship was sufficiently good that when the Susuhunan's wife Ratu Kĕntjana, the mother of the Crown Prince, had another child in 1780 the infant was given to Mangkunĕgara to be raised by him.[84] In 1781, the Susuhunan made one of Mangkunĕgara's sons the head of the Crown Prince's subjects (i.e. presumably the *Bupati Kadipaten Anom*),[85] gave positions and incomes to two others of his sons,[86] and gave a recently widowed daughter in marriage to a fourth son of Mangkunĕgara.[87]

But if Mangkunĕgara was no longer such a major, or at least obvious, source of opposition to Pakubuwana III, there were still sufficient signs of instability in Surakarta. In a series of connected incidents between 1781 and 1783 it became clear that several factors were preventing political stability there. One was the Susuhunan's increasing arbitrariness and, perhaps, what may have been an advancing mental infirmity. Another was the general incompetence of the Surakarta administration which was the fault both of Pakubuwana III's inability to select the proper men for important positions and of his incapacity to inspire loyalty. It also

[84] Sĕmarang to Batavia, 26 April 1780, in KA 3476 (OB 1781); van der Burgh, Memorie, 19 Sept. 1780, in dJ xi, pp. 407-8.
Van der Burgh's original report of April says the child was a son but his memorandum of September says it was a daughter.
[85] The Dutch records describe this son, Raden Arja Surjatruna, as 'groot Loera[h] over de onderhoorige van den kroonprins'; PB III to Sĕmarang, 19 Sapar [A.J.] 1707] (Feb. 1781), in KA 3494 (OB 1782); Sĕmarang to Batavia, 15 March 1781, in KA 3494 (OB 1782).
[86] The sons were Raden Mas Surjakusuma and Raden Mas Surjadipura; Sĕmarang to Batavia, 5 Sept. 1781, in KA 3494 (OB 1782). This is edited out of the version of this report in dJ xii, pp. 1-6. But see Batavia to H.XVII, 29 Dec. 1781, in dJ xii, p. 10, where 'Surjakusuma' has been read incorrectly as 'Soeria Reksoemo'.
[87] This son was Raden Mas Slobok; Sĕmarang to Batavia, 5 Sept. 1781, in KA 3494 (OB 1782).
This is edited out of the version of this document in dJ xii, pp. 1-6. The report is summarized in Batavia to H.XVII, 29 Dec. 1781, in dJ xii, p. 10. On the latter page, however, the editors have misread the name 'Slobok' as 'Hobok' and have added a footnote which says, understandably, that 'Deze uitdrukking is voor de beste kenners der Javaansche taal onverstaanbaar'.

seems that Dutch influence over the Susuhunan was expressed in such a way as to lessen the ruler's authority. More than once he was forced to retract orders already made public or to revise intentions which were already known after the Company had convinced him he was behaving unreasonably. And finally, the pressure for good land to use as princely appanages was continuing to grow and contributed to the proliferation of princely intrigues.

In 1781, an Islamic mystical teacher named Hadji Abdul Kamil was turned over to the Dutch by the Susuhunan, who wished him exiled from Java. In 1778, according to his own testimony, Abdul Kamil had returned from the Mecca pilgrimage and had gone to the Susuhunan telling him that he was a 'priest',

and having studied at Mecca thereby not only understood the religion of the Muslims but in particular could bring it about that everyone live forever most enjoyably in peace, freed from fire, disunity, or strife, and all misfortune, in such a manner that none of all these was able to touch the man.[88]

The Susuhunan made him head (*lurah*) of a village near Purwarĕdja, but his magical prowess soon brought him to grief. In 1781, one of the Susuhunan's favourite sons-in-law died and Pakubuwana somehow became convinced that Abdul Kamil and the *patih* Sasradiningrat had killed him by magic. Abdul Kamil admitted he had been in touch with the *patih*, but only in order to instruct him in the mystical sciences and to give him an amulet which would bring him prosperity and spare him misfortune through fire, disunity, or other vicissitudes, as advertised.[89]

The Susuhunan decided Abdul Kamil must die and Sasradiningrat must be removed as *patih*, the latter step requiring Dutch agreement. But the rather more sceptical Company could see no evidence to support the Susuhunan's accusations. They convinced him instead to send Abdul Kamil to Sĕmarang for interrogation and to put up with Sasradiningrat until Siberg could

---

[88] Hadji Abdul Kamil, Relaas, given at Sĕmarang 1 June 1781, in KA 3494 (OB 1782).

[89] Ibid.; Sĕmarang to Batavia, 30 June 1781, in KA 3494 (OB 1782).

Abdul Kamil was made head of 'Jollo Toendo', which was certainly the Djalatuṇḍa in Purwarĕdja district, North Banjumas, and not the famous Old Javanese bathing sanctuary Djalatuṇḍa on Mt. Pĕnanggungan in East Java, which was beyond PB III's authority and would have been too far from Surakarta for Abdul Kamil to have maintained contact with the *patih*.

The deceased son-in-law was Raden Arja Martadipura.

come to Surakarta to discuss the matter personally. Abdul Kamil was soon on his way to Batavia and exile, his guilt or innocence being unproved since they were irrelevant to the necessity of his removal. Siberg suspected all of these rather bizarre ideas might have been put into the Susuhunan's head by some unknown conspirator.[90] If this was true, he might have needed to look no farther than the Susuhunan's elder half-brother Pangeran Purbaja. This is, however, no more than a surmise based on the very few fleeting glimpses of Purbaja in the Dutch records, when he seems always to be whispering in his brother's ear. Another strong candidate for suspicion was, of course, Mangkunĕgara.

Sasradiningrat had been Surakarta *patih* since the removal of the incompetent Mangkupradja in 1770. Like his predecessor he was known to be a true friend of the Company but a man of no great ability. In 1780, van der Burgh described him as

a simple, worthy man, as good and true-hearted towards the Company as his master, but rather too mild, complaisant, and slow for the post that he occupies.[91]

The Susuhunan now wished to rid himself of yet another *patih*. He accused Sasradiningrat of interfering in the carrying-out of royal orders, of being generally too lax, of acting in a conspiratorial fashion which twice gave great offence to Mangkunĕgara, and of having dealt with Abdul Kamil and other magicians in a way which aroused Pakubuwana's suspicion and fear. He was so firm in his intention to remove the man that not even Siberg's personal presence in Surakarta in September 1781 could dissuade him. Sasradiningrat remained for several months in Surakarta but in October 1782 he was sent to live at Batavia, after the Susuhunan had threatened to banish him to an inhospitable area of Banjumas. The Susuhunan provided funds for his maintenance in Batavia until Sasradiningrat's death in 1789. The Company was worried that the removal of Sasradiningrat, like that of Mangkupradja before him, would suggest to the Javanese élite that being a true friend of the Company brought no dividends, since the Company was unable to offer them any real security even in the post of *patih*, which was by treaty a joint appointment of the Dutch and the Susuhunan.

[90] Sĕmarang to Batavia, 30 June 1781, in KA 3494 (OB 1782).
[91] Van der Burgh, Memorie, 19 Sept. 1780, in dJ xi, pp. 411–12.

Sasradiningrat's successor as the fourth *patih* in Pakubuwana III's reign was the head of Kĕḍu, Mangkujuda, who now received the name and title Raden Adipati Sindurĕdja. He was the Susuhunan's personal preference, and, when Pakubuwana told Siberg he left the choice entirely to him, the latter had the wisdom to propose the man. Like his predecessors, he was said to be a friend of the Dutch. Sindurĕdja took over the *patih*'s responsibilities sometime in or before October 1782.[92] He was to last less than two years. In July 1784 he died, apparently of natural causes, without having shown any greater administrative merit than his predecessors. His successor was one of the Susuhunan's sons-in-law, who now became Pakubuwana III's fifth *patih*, Raden Adipati Djajaningrat, who survived in his post until he was removed by Pakubuwana IV in 1796.[93]

The net of the Susuhunan's suspicions was now widely spread. The next to fall into disgrace after Sasradiningrat was Raden Tumĕnggung Arungbinang, the powerful *wĕdana* of Bagĕlen.[94] He was accused of extorting money from his subjects and of being involved with Sasradiningrat in his alleged plots. Mangkunĕgara was also rumoured somehow to have been involved. Sometime in or before October 1782, Pakubuwana banished Arungbinang to live in Kĕḍiri under the supervision of the head of Kĕḍiri who was, strangely enough, a son of Sasradiningrat married to the Susuhunan's second-eldest daughter. The Susuhunan then warned all of his officials that similar conduct by any of them, regardless of person, would be equally strictly punished. The Company was

---

[92] Sĕmarang to Batavia, 30 June 1781 and 5 Sept. 1781, in KA 3494 (OB 1782) (the edited, version of the document of 5 Sept. 1781 in dJ xii, pp. 1-6, omits these sections); id., 20 Oct. 1781, in KA 3495 (OB 1782); PB III to Batavia, received at Sĕmarang 7 Jan. 1782, in KA 3519 (OB 1783); Sĕmarang to Batavia, 14 Jan. 1782 and 26 March 1782, in KA 3519 (OB 1783); id., 5 Oct. 1782, in KA 3520 (OB 1783); Batavia to H.XVII, 31 Dec. 1782, in dJ xii p. 25; Sĕmarang to Batavia, 8 March 1783, in KA 3545 (OB 1784); id., 18 April 1789, in KA 3754 (OB 1790).

[93] Id., 27 July 1784, in KA 3630 (OB 1787); id., 30 Oct. 1784, in KA 3568 (OB 1785); id., 22 July 1796, in dJ xii, p. 412.

[94] In 1774, Bagĕlen was recorded as having a total of 25,713 *tjatjahs*, one of the largest areas; see dJ xi, p. lv. Arungbinang would, of course, have controlled only a part of this area as PB III's official. I do not have figures for the number of *tjatjahs* under his control, but it must have been sizeable, probably in the vicinity of 6,000 *tjatjahs* to judge from Siberg's comment cited below (pp. 267-8) on Arungbinang's successor. On the use of the *tjatjah* figure as an indication of military and therefore of political power, see pp. 422-3 n. 3 below.

told that Mangkunĕgara was much surprised by Pakubuwana's banishment of so powerful a man as Arungbinang, 'assuming that the ruler hadn't enough courage to do so'.[95]

The Dutch were also surprised at the Susuhunan's action and forced him to retract in a fashion which could hardly have enhanced his authority. Having dared to take such a courageous step and having apparently succeeded in it, he must now back down. By early 1783 Siberg had convinced Pakubuwana that the accusations against Arungbinang were not sufficiently proved and the Susuhunan allowed him to return to live in Surakarta in a suitable status. Arungbinang did not long survive. He was an old man and after his return to the court he was observed to weaken continuously. In October 1783 he died. The Dutch were sufficiently suspicious to investigate but were told by Arungbinang's children that their father had died after a rat-bite had become inflamed.[96] Like other timely deaths in Java, this one may not have been entirely above suspicion.

The vacant post in charge of Bagĕlen had gone to a most unusual person, Pangeran Ngabei, one of the Susuhunan's own sons. He was highly thought of by the Dutch for his 'yielding' disposition, but it was unusual for a prince of the royal blood to be given such a powerful position.[97] In a previous age this might have been tantamount to inviting his rebellion. But conditions in Java were now much changed, as Siberg's observations on this appointment correctly reported:

> One has no suspicions about the government and good management there [in Bagĕlen]. Although in the past, before the division of the Java highlands between the rulers took place, it certainly aroused suspicion to place the ruler's blood-relations in such Regencies as Bagĕlen and others, I nevertheless believe that now that the collective lands and Regencies are so very divided between the rulers and both the Susuhunan and the Sultan seldom entrust the full government, much less the incomes, of one of the Regencies to a single individual of their court dignitaries but for a part also favour their court servants or *tumĕnggungdalĕms* therewith in order to have their subsistence therefrom, in the

[95] Van Straalendorff to Sĕmarang, 2 March 1782, in KA 3519 (OB 1783); Sĕmarang to Batavia, 26 March 1782, in KA 3519 (OB 1783); id., 23 Oct. 1782, in KA 3520 (OB 1783).
[96] Id., 22 Feb. 1783, 20 May 1783, and 20 Dec. 1783, in KA 3545 (OB 1784).
[97] Id., 23 Oct. 1782, in KA 3520 (OB 1783); id., 22 Feb. 1783, in KA 3545 (OB 1784).

268 JOGJAKARTA UNDER SULTAN MANGKUBUMI

same way one can reckon that the Surakarta Pangeran Ngabei also has but a quarter of the Bagĕlen district under his control and one need not fear about any following to be made or any detrimental results.[98]

The pressure for good land was growing continuously, so that the already-divided administrative districts must be further divided by each monarch in order to maintain as many dignitaries and royal servants as possible. The amount of land under cultivation was certainly growing as the population rapidly increased, but nevertheless many princes and dignitaries probably wondered how much longer they could maintain themselves and their retinues in a fitting style. The competition among the courtly élite to maintain themselves must have made the Javanese *kratons* more than ever hot-houses of intrigue. Only a ruler who could inspire obedience and keep a steady grip on the state could prevent trouble. Pakubuwana III was never such a ruler. Perhaps his most dangerous characteristic was that he was becoming erratic. In 1782 he had dared to remove Arungbinang from Bagĕlen. In 1784 he dared not execute a village head in Bagĕlen who had committed highway robbery against travelling merchants there because the delinquent was in some way related to Pangeran Ngabei, although apparently not to the Susuhunan, and he feared to give his son offence. Instead the robber was exiled.[99]

The Dutch in Surakarta had great influence but all was not well for them there. In the late 1770s and 1780s the Company was burdened with a series of incompetent and even corrupt Residents at Surakarta. This had several unfortunate results. The Dutch sources of information now began to grow somewhat unreliable, which is as unwelcome to the modern historian as it was to some of the higher Company officials when they discovered the inaccuracy of the reports they received. Secondly, some of the Residents became involved in the complex Surakarta *kraton* intrigues, thus drawing the Company deeper into a world beyond its control. In the following chapter, it will be seen how this led to the suspicious and possibly violent death of one Resident and to serious doubts about where lay the loyalties of another. And finally, corruption and incompetence cost money, of which the Company had little to spare in the 1780s, less than two decades away from its dissolution. In 1783–4, for instance, the financial

[98] Sĕmarang to Batavia, 22 Feb. 1783, in KA 3545 (OB 1784).
[99] Id., 30 Oct. 1784, in KA 3568 (OB 1785).

records for the Dutch posts at the courts revealed a loss of nearly 50,000 guilders in Surakarta and over 35,000 in Jogjakarta.[100]

F. C. van Straalendorff had been Resident at Surakarta since 1767 and had given his superiors great satisfaction.[101] But after his death in 1784 it was reported that the Surakarta fortress, the successful completion of which had been such a pleasant change from the procrastination in Jogjakarta, was not in a satisfactory state. Van Straalendorff was apparently to blame. It was observed that 'just at the same time that the fortress was being built, the late van Straalendorff was possessed of a desire for private carpentry'.[102] The Susuhunan was asked to provide building materials to complete the fortress properly but he refused, saying he had provided van Straalendorff with enough for the task. The Dutch were forced to accept this and decided instead to confiscate the late Resident's estate to pay the costs, along with that of the Engineer who had also died.[103] It is impossible to say whether the accusations against van Straalendorff were correct since they depended largely on the evidence of his successor W. A. Palm, who will be seen in the following chapter to have been a most doubtful source of information.

Mangkunĕgara was, of all the Surakarta dignitaries, most particularly concerned to maintain the Company's favour. He was now in his sixties and in 1786 he was for a time seriously ill.[104] It was imperative that some regulation be made for his descendants beyond the placement of individual sons and daughters in lucrative posts or advantageous marriages. But Mangkunĕgara was caught between an ageing Susuhunan over whom he had great influence but who was becoming unpredictable and the Dutchmen who had never really trusted him and who were now represented by Residents of very doubtful abilities or trustworthiness. It was

[100] Staatreekeningen, 21 Dec. 1784, in KA 3567 (OB 1785).
[101] See Vos, Memorie, 24 July 1771, in dJ xi, p. 170; Siberg, Memorie, 19 Sept. 1780, in dJ xi, p. 413.
[102] Sĕmarang to Batavia, 22 Dec. 1784, in KA 3597 (OB 1786). The precise date of van Straalendorff's death is uncertain.
[103] Sĕmarang to Batavia, 4 Sept. 1784, in KA 3630 (OB 1787) (the same letter is to be found also in KA 3568 [OB 1785]); id., 22 Dec. 1784, in KA 3597 (OB 1786); id., 24 Dec. 1785, in KA 3630 (OB 1787).
[104] On his age, see Poensen, 'Mangkubumi', p. 228. On the illness of 1786, see Sĕmarang to Batavia, 11 July 1786 and 2 August 1786, in KA 3630 (OB 1787); B. Mang., p. 481. The Dutch sources describe his illness as a serious intestinal ailment; B. Mang. describes it as frambesia (katrapan).

becoming more difficult for Mangkunĕgara to control his environment. Moreover, his enemies in Jogjakarta were apparently polishing their technique of feeding false information against him to the Dutch via Jogjakarta's gullible Resident van Rhijn (1773–86). In 1785, for instance, the Sultan accused one of Mangkunĕgara's sons of having led a fatal attack upon some Jogjakarta subjects coming from East Java for *Garĕbĕg Mulud*. Upon investigation the accused proved to be too ill to have done this, and Mangkunĕgara reportedly told the Surakarta Resident that he had had enough of Mangkubumi's machinations. 'Now his main aim is to make me and mine black and hated by the Company', Mangkunĕgara is reported to have said, 'and thus [when I am] detached therefrom and abandoned, if possible to carry out his proud notions of independence and absolute supremacy.'[105]

Mangkunĕgara was able sometimes to win Dutch favour. He was successful in getting the Dutch to return some of the banished princes from the Cape of Good Hope to Java. After initially refusing to support this request, in 1785 the Susuhunan lent his weight to the project and the Company agreed. Among the group was a brother of Mangkunĕgara[106] who, rumour had it, had managed to stow away upon a Dutch ship bound from the Cape for the Netherlands. Upon his arrival there, the story went, he had even been received by the Prince of Orange before the Directors of the East India Company had sent him back to the Cape. The truth of this story was apparently as unknown to Dutch officials in Java at the time as it is to the present writer. Pangeran Danupaja, whom Pakubuwana III had turned over to the Dutch for banishment on the occasion of his accession in 1749, was also returned. The group arrived in Surakarta sometime in early 1787.[107]

But in the familiar conspiratorial field of marriage politics Mangkunĕgara again found himself at odds both with the Dutch and with the Susuhunan, the result being that Mangkunĕgara ended by binding himself ever more closely to the Company

[105] Sĕmarang to Batavia, 1 March 1785, in KA 3597 (OB 1786).
[106] He is called 'Kretta', 'Maas Karetta', or 'Maas Carettie' in the VOC documents. This looks like Javanese *kreta*, but it was more likely 'Mas Krĕta' or 'Mas Krĕti'. He had apparently been born on the Cape to MN's exiled father, who had subsequently died.
[107] Sĕmarang to Batavia, 8 March 1783, in KA 3545 (OB 1784); id., 10 Oct. 1785, in KA 3597 (OB 1786); id., 24 Dec. 1785, in KA 3595 (OB 1786); id., 26 April 1787, in KA 3655 (OB 1788); id., 28 July 1787, in KA 3705 (OB 1789).

PERMANENTLY DIVIDED KINGDOM, 1774-1787   271

and to his sovereign. In 1785-6, Mangkunĕgara failed to get the Susuhunan's youngest and reputedly very beautiful daughter for one of his sons. She was married instead to a son of the Regent of Dĕmak, one of the Company's coastal officials.[108] Mangkunĕgara was most displeased at this turn of events. When in 1787 Pakubuwana III again refused a proposed marriage between one of his daughters and a son of Mangkunĕgara, the latter was furious.[109] The conspiracies within the court were by now so complex that one cannot take the Dutch documents at face value. One may presume that not only Mangkunĕgara, his family, and the Susuhunan were involved, but also the Crown Prince, possibly the Susuhunan's elder brother Pangeran Purbaja, and very likely the Dutch Resident Palm himself, upon whom the Company depended for its information.

The Resident Palm was ordered by Sĕmarang to intervene in the dispute, which had reportedly caused complete estrangement between Mangkunĕgara and Pakubuwana III. The result was not only that the Susuhunan finally approved of the marriage but that Mangkunĕgara also signed a new 'Act of Submission' to the Company and the Susuhunan. It is a comment on the Company's confused bureaucratic machinery that they now, in 1787, believed this to be the first time Mangkunĕgara had ever signed a formal act of submission. No previous act could be found in the Company's archives,[110] although Mangkunĕgara had formally sworn submission upon the *Qur'ān* to the Susuhunan, the Company, and the Sultan in 1757 and had then sent a formal letter of submission to Batavia, and in 1772 had signed a further declaration binding himself to obedience to the Susuhunan and the Company.[111]

---

[108] Id., 30 Nov. 1785, in KA 3597 (OB 1786); id., 6 May 1786, in KA 3630 (OB 1787).

PB III had asked the VOC to raise the groom to *pangeran* but Siberg refused to do so. He almost certainly recalled the trouble over the giving of that title to Sura Adimĕnggala in 1776, discussed earlier in this chapter, and told PB III that he could raise the man to *pangeran* himself but the VOC would not do so for fear of offending HB I, who would see it as VOC intrusion on his prerogatives. PB III subsequently did raise the man, previously called Raden Purbawidjaja, to the name and title Pangeran Rongga.

[109] Sĕmarang to Batavia, 23 March 1787, in KA 3655 (OB 1788).

[110] Ibid.; Siberg, Memorie, 18 Sept. 1787, in dJ xii, pp. 87-8; Batavia to H.XVII, 29 Dec. 1787, in dJ xii, p. 125.

[111] See Batavia to H.XVII, 31 Dec. 1757, in dJ x, p. 316; 'Paccoenagara' [MN] to Batavia, n.d. [March 1757], in KA 2802 (OB 1758); Sĕmarang to Batavia, 28 Aug. 1772, in KA 3256 (OB 1773).

It is a further comment on the Dutch bureaucracy, and specifically upon Governor Siberg, that later in 1787 Siberg's Memorial to his successor at Sĕmarang made this new act of submission appear to have been a result of his own initiative, whereas it was apparently achieved by Palm without a specific directive.[112] Eventually even the Company's Directors in Amsterdam came to regard Siberg as untrustworthy. They vetoed the proposal from Batavia that he succeed his father-in-law W. A. Alting as Governor-General in 1796, although he subsequently gained that position in 1801.[113] A later writer on Dutch administration dismissed Siberg as 'one of the most corrupt members of the old gang' who during his Governor-Generalship (1801–4) was 'content to line his pockets and allow his subordinates to line theirs'.[114] For the historian the general situation of the Dutch Company in its later years poses progressively greater problems in assessing the value of official Dutch reports.

In the late 1780s both Surakarta and the Dutch were thus running downhill. The former in particular was becoming involved in a mesh of intrigue. Before the end of the decade both would become entangled in the last great crisis of the eighteenth century, the subject of the following chapter. But in Jogjakarta the situation was very different indeed. Siberg's valedictory Memorial provides a picture of the difference between the two Javanese courts which is consistent with all other evidence:

> The present *patih* [of Surakarta], installed in 1785 [*sic*, actually 1784] and named Raden Adipati Djajaningrat, is a man of low origin, certainly diligent, but of no great or penetrating intellect. And since the remaining ministers at the Surakarta court are also no statesmen and the Susuhunan concerns himself less with government than does the Sultan, so one finds a considerable difference in the political life of the two courts, which immediately shows itself in Jogjakarta as much in the greater splendour as in the precision with which all matters are handled in that place.[115]

The Sultan of Jogjakarta was, in 1787, already in his seventies.[116]

[112] Siberg, Memorie, 18 Sept. 1787, in dJ xii, p. 88. At the time, Batavia's report to H.XVII made it clear this Act was Palm's accomplishment rather than Siberg's; Batavia to H.XVII, 29 Dec. 1787, in dJ xii, p. 125.

[113] See dJ xii, pp. xlix, liv-lv, lxiii-lxiv.

[114] J. S. Furnivall, *Netherlands India: A Study of Plural Economy* (Cambridge, 1967), p. 64.   [115] Siberg, Memorie, 18 Sept. 1787, in dJ xii, p. 89.

[116] See above, p. 83 n. 39.

PERMANENTLY DIVIDED KINGDOM, 1774-1787

In the previous decade he had been seriously ill on several occasions, most notably in 1777, 1781, 1786, and 1787. Each time he had recovered, rather to the wonderment and greatly to the relief of the Dutch.[117] As the Sultan's age advanced, the Crown Prince, already in his thirties,[118] more and more took a position of power alongside his father. This, too, provides documentary problems. Since the Crown Prince was apparently less willing than his father to deal with the Dutch, as his control over *kraton* affairs increased the amount of information which the Dutch obtained from the court, reliable or otherwise, decreased proportionately.[119] One is forced more frequently to turn to Javanese sources alone. But these consist, first of all, of *Babad Mangkubumi*, which represents the Crown Prince's own views and is hardly disinterested. Moreover, these years are contained in that section of the *babad* apparently added to the original text of 1773 sometime after 1792, and the description is extremely brief.[120] The other main source is the *babad* summarized by Poensen, of Pakualaman origin, reflecting the views of the Crown Prince's brother Pangeran Natakusuma, who came in later years to be much opposed to his brother. Thus, this source, too, is biased,[121] and seems generally less reliable than

[117] Van Rhijn to Sěmarang, 19 Dec. 1777, in KA 3392 (OB 1778); Sěmarang to Batavia, 23 Dec. 1777, in KA 3392 (OB 1778); id., 13 Jan. 1778 and 15 Jan. 1778, in KA 3420 (OB 1779); id., 6 Nov. 1781 and 19 Dec. 1781, in KA 3495 (OB 1782); Batavia to H.XVII, 31 Dec. 1782, in dJ xii, p. 25; Sěmarang to Batavia, 21 Dec. 1786 and 23 March 1787, in KA 3655 (OB 1788); Siberg, Memorie, 18 Sept. 1787, in dJ xii, p. 85; Sěmarang to Batavia, 27 Sept. 1787, in KA 3707 (OB 1789); id., 22 Dec. 1787, in KA 3708 (OB 1789).

HB I's first wife, the Ratu Kěntjana (the mother of Ratu Běndara) died in 1777; the Crown Prince's mother, the Ratu Kadipaten, was still alive in 1787; Sěmarang to Batavia, 8 Dec. 1777, in KA 3392 (OB 1788); Siberg, Memorie, 18 Sept. 1787, in dJ xii, p. 85.

[118] See Poensen, 'Mangkubumi', p. 289.

[119] For instance, in 1786 the seriousness of one of the Sultan's illnesses was apparently intentionally kept from the Dutch Resident; Sěmarang to Batavia, 21 Dec. 1786, in KA 3655 (OB 1788).

The Dutch post at Jogjakarta was also not free of the troubles which plagued the Surakarta detachment, and which make the objectivity of the reports sometimes doubtful. The Jogjakarta Resident van Rhijn (1773-86) was not only somewhat incompetent but also unpopular with his colleagues. Shortly before his retirement as Resident in 1786, he was involved in an incident in which he arrested several of his own dragoons and tried to bribe others, in a case of insubordination. He was not supported by his superiors and shortly left for the Netherlands; Sěmarang to Batavia, 7 June 1786, in KA 3628 (OB 1787); id., 12 June 1786, in KA 3630 (OB 1787).

[120] See Ricklefs, 'Authorship', especially p. 271 n. 7; and pp. 167-9, n. 87 above.   [121] See Ricklefs, 'Authorship', pp. 264-5.

Babad Mangkubumi. Nevertheless, one can gain a fairly clear view of at least the main outlines of Jogjakarta history in the 1780s, although perhaps one may not see all of the picture.

Two incidents, in 1783 and 1785, suggest that the Jogjakarta élite were regarding the Dutch less seriously than before, which was probably a reflection of the Crown Prince's increasing influence. At the celebrations of *Garěběg Mulud* in February 1783 the Captain of the Company's dragoons at Jogjakarta was stabbed in the hip by one of the Sultan's officers. The Sultan investigated the incident and claimed it was an accident. He sent money to pay for medication for the wound but this was returned to him. The Dutch were convinced that the wounding was intentional. There then followed a *kraton* gathering in which the Sultan publicly told the Javanese officer that he had earned the death penalty for wounding the Dutchman. But the Resident van Rhijn then interceded to plead for clemency. The Sultan did not at first answer him but with a gesture made it clear that he wished this proposal repeated via Danurědja. This van Rhijn did. Danurědja, now a very elderly man of about seventy, was so confused by this turn of events that he could repeat the plea for clemency only with the help of Ronggaprawiradirdja. After a lengthy silence the Sultan announced that this time he would show mercy, but never again. The Javanese officer asked and received the forgiveness of the wounded captain and the Sultan pardoned his officer. Thereupon, Mangkubumi firmly admonished the Javanese present not to commit any such excesses upon Europeans. To celebrate the restoration of the friendship, the Sultan then took the Dutch Resident as his guest to a fight between a tiger and a water buffalo, telling the Resident that the accused would have had to perform this work if pardon had not been asked for him.[122]

The Dutch were familiar with the many public diversions of the Javanese élite, from dancing to tournaments, but they never apparently understood that the tiger-and-buffalo fight was a special event. Van Rhijn did not appreciate the significance of the Sultan's statement to him:

'Come along,' continued the Sultan, 'having forgiven and forgotten

---

[122] Van Rhijn to Sěmarang, 20 March 1783, in KA 3545 (OB 1784); Sěmarang to Batavia, 14 April 1783, in KA 3545 (OB 1784).
See also the comments on the aged Danurědja in Siberg, Memorie, 18 Sept. 1787, in dJ xii, p. 89; and Sěmarang to Batavia, 25 April 1792, in dJ xii, p. 265.

PERMANENTLY DIVIDED KINGDOM, 1774-1787

the crime, I shall now put it between the tiger and the buffalo and thereby consider the reconciliation to be settled.'[123]

Just as *Sĕrat Surja Radja* and other works of literature presented the real world in mythologized form, so too the tiger-and-buffalo fights were visual allegory representing the confrontation of Dutch and Javanese power. The Dutch were represented by the tiger: quick, deadly, but without staying power. The buffalo was a living metaphor for the Javanese: powerful but restrained in its movements, and almost always victorious. Raffles was the first to report the symbolic significance of the tiger and the buffalo:

A favourite and national spectacle is the combat between the buffalo and the tiger. . . . It seldom fails that the buffalo is triumphant, and one buffalo has been known to destroy several full grown tigers in succession. . . . In these entertainments the Javans are accustomed to compare the buffalo to the Javan and the tiger to the European, and it may be readily imagined with what eagerness they look to the success of the former. The combat generally lasts from twenty minutes to half an hour, when, if neither of them is destroyed, the animals are changed, and the tiger, if he survives, is removed to be destroyed in the manner called *rampog*, which is as follows . . .

A hollow square of spearmen, four deep, is formed on the *alun-alun*, in the centre of which are placed the tigers in small separate cages . . . Two or three men, accustomed to the practice, at the command of the sovereign, proceed into the centre of the square, . . . and drawing the wooden door up, throwing it to one side, themselves retreat from the spot at a slow pace, to the sound of music. As soon as the tiger . . . [endeavours] to make his way through the spearmen [he] is generally received upon their weapons. . . . The smaller species of tiger is generally selected for this amusement.[124]

---

[123] Van Rhijn to Sĕmarang, 20 March 1783, in KA 3545 (OB 1784).

[124] Raffles (1830), vol. i, pp. 386-8. This symbolism seems to have had wide application. In the *wajang kulit* one of the most important puppets is the *kajon* (*gunungan*), which starts and ends the performances, marks changes of scene, and can represent forests, mountains, a palace, or whatever location is required. Often the complex decoration of the *kajon* includes in the centre a depiction of a buffalo confronting a tiger. For illustrations, see Kats, *Wajang Poerwa*, p. 24; Anderson, *Mythology*, p. 77 (the same *kajon* is depicted in Hardjowirogo, p. 6); Brandon, *Thrones*, p. 83 *et passim*; W. H. Rassers, *Pañji, The Culture Hero. A Structural Study of Religion in Java* (The Hague, 1959), plate I.

The symbolic conflict of tiger and buffalo probably has roots deep in the Javanese past, pre-dating acquaintance with Europeans. Rassers, p. 184, interprets these conflicting figures on the *kajon* as 'the emblems of the two

Thus, in 1783 the Sultan apparently viewed the wounding of the Dutch officer and the subsequent investigation of the incident as a Dutch–Javanese confrontation. He therefore 'put it between the tiger and the buffalo' and considered the matter to be reconciled. It may be that the Crown Prince's rather more belligerent view of the Dutch had forced the Sultan to treat the incident as a confrontation which required such a symbolic resolution, in the same way as the Crown Prince's *Sĕrat Surja Radja* of A.J. 1700 had been dedicated in part to such a symbolic statement.

A similar confrontation occurred again in late 1785, when it appeared that the Dutch Resident had allowed the sale in front of his house of a *baṭik* pattern (*Parang Rusak*) which had just been announced as attire forbidden to all but the Sultan (*awisaning Ratu/larangan-Dalĕm*). The discovery of this by the Sultan's officials led to a clash in which one of Mangkubumi's men and the Resident's coachman were wounded. The Sultan and the Dutch each blamed the other's subjects. But the matter was ultimately dropped.[125]

---

sides of the [primitive sacred men's] house and thus, as it were, the totems of the rival phratries of this community; . . . only thus can the hostile attitude which is characteristic of these animals be understood'. Chap. XI below considers other areas in which traditional ideas which probably pre-dated European contact were adapted by the eighteenth-century courts to explain their relationships with the Dutch.

In the twentieth century the buffalo (*banteng*) came to symbolize Indonesian nationalism and was adopted as the official emblem of the Indonesian Nationalist Party (PNI). Mrs. Claire Holt has also suggested that this symbolism may have had very deep prehistoric roots; see Holt, pp. 22–3. But see also Rinkes, 'Heiligen VI', *TBG*, vol. 55 (1913), p. 3, where the Dutch and not the Javanese are referred to as 'albino buffaloes' (*kĕbo bule*); and the Baron Sakendĕr story summarized in Chap. XI below, where in Canto XI Kasebĕr takes on the form of a white wild buffalo (*kĕbo kamale*) with a human head. See also NBS 87 (IX and XXII) in Pigeaud, *Literature*, vol. ii, p. 735, where the comparison of the Javanese with buffaloes is pejorative.

[125] HB I to Sĕmarang, 7 Sapar A.J. 1712 (received 13 Dec. 1785), in KA 3630 (OB 1787); Sĕmarang to HB I, 17 Dec. 1785, in KA 3630 (OB 1787); van Rhijn to Sĕmarang, 24 Dec. 1785, in KA 3630 (OB 1787); Sĕmarang to Batavia, 3 March 1786, in KA 3630 (OB 1787); Poensen, 'Mangkubumi', pp. 304–5 (where the details of the incident are rather inaccurate).

Later in 1786 another incident occurred which seems, however, to have had no political significance. One of the Sultan's troops went mad, attacked the Dutch dragoons, and single-handedly wounded three of them, one of whom later died. The man was prevented from committing suicide, and the Sultan promised to punish him; Sĕmarang Raade van Politie, Resolutien, 21 Dec. 1786, in KA 3654 (OB 1788). That one Javanese soldier could single-handedly

That such confrontations were more in the spirit of the Crown Prince than in that of the aged Sultan is suggested by the Resident's interview with the Sultan on the matter. Siberg's letter to Mangkubumi, blaming his officials for the incident, was read in the court. The Sultan found it difficult to follow because the reader was stammering over its contents and rain was falling outside. He therefore ordered the reading to be stopped and called the Resident to him. He put his hand on van Rhijn's arm and said he had understood enough, and declared van Rhijn innocent: 'Your coachman and my *mantris* have fought, both have wounds and also guilt. Let us leave it at that and stop all the unpleasantries.' Van Rhijn replied that he had been ordered to discipline his coachman. Mangkubumi said he didn't wish that, but merely that the Resident, the *patih*, and the Sultan's officials should arrange whatever was necessary 'so that I will no more be disturbed'.[126]

In the late 1780s the younger generation was already beginning to dominate Jogjakarta *kraton* affairs. When Siberg described the Crown Prince in 1787, the latter was in his late thirties and had many children and even grandchildren. His eldest son was already some eighteen years old and would later rule as Sultan Hamĕngkubuwana III (1810–11, 1812–14). The latter, too, was already a father, his infant son of some two years of age being the future Pangeran Dipanĕgara, the rebel leader of the Java War (1825–30).[127] Already in Mangkubumi's last years the *dramatis personae* of the turbulent nineteenth-century history of Jogjakarta were entering the stage. And the aged Sultan was, it seems, usually content to take his ease and to enjoy the growing number of his descendants, leaving court affairs to others unless some unusual crisis required his personal intervention.

The Crown Prince was not believed by the Dutch to have his father's intelligence[128] and was already being commented upon for being 'ill-mannered and not very familiar (*gemeensaam*) with

---

account for three dragoons suggests that the VOC troops were not always of the highest professional competence, which is also suggested by other VOC documentation.

[126] Van Rhijn to Sĕmarang, 24 Dec. 1785, in KA 3630 (OB 1787).

[127] Siberg, Memorie, 18 Sept. 1787, in dJ xii, pp. 85–6. The date of Dipanĕgara's birth is not absolutely certain but seems to have been in 1785; see Louw and de Klerck, *Java-Oorlog*, vol. i, p. 89 n. 1.

[128] Siberg, Memorie, 18 Sept. 1787, in dJ xii, p. 86.

the Europeans'.[129] He was clearly a man of strong ideas and to say that he made many enemies before he died in 1828 is a considerable understatement. Yet in these later years of his father's reign he seems to have retained Mangkubumi's confidence. It is true that there is no entirely clear evidence on this point. In the 1780s the Sultan was not in a position to discipline an adult son with his own large family and following even had he wished to do so. He could certainly not attempt to dispose of a Crown Prince by poison, as he had in 1758, without running an unacceptable risk of serious rebellion. Poisoning a prince within his own domain would in any case have been extremely difficult to arrange. Thus it is possible that Mangkubumi did not approve of the Crown Prince but could do nothing about it, which is the view of the nineteenth-century *babad* reflecting the position of the Prince's ambitious brother Natakusuma.[130] But had this been the case, even if the Crown Prince could have managed to keep his father a virtual prisoner within the *kraton* walls, it is unlikely that the Dutch would not at least have heard rumours of the situation and filled volumes of correspondence with speculation. Mangkubumi was not a prisoner of his son and the Dutch records are silent on any estrangement between the two.

In early 1785 the first clear example of the Crown Prince's actual direction of affairs came to light. Suddenly, within less than two weeks, a formidable fortress-wall was flung up around the *kraton*, probably defended by the same cannon the Dutch had given the Sultan upon the return of his troops from Batavia in 1784.[131] *Babad Mangkubumi* was apparently written by the Crown Prince and therefore is not above criticism. But its description of the decision to fortify the *kraton* and of the political outcome of this decision is worth citing. Mangkubumi is said to have convened the court to solicit opinions on a building project. The old man wished to add to his system of pleasure gardens, but the Crown Prince opposed him. It would be better, he said, to put up a fortress. Had his father forgotten the example of Mataram's first ruler, Senapati, who had similarly fortified his city at Kuṭa Gĕḍe? The Sultan said he remembered the story. His eldest son

[129] Kuvel, Report, 28 Oct. 1788, in dJ xii, p. 150.
[130] See Poensen, 'Mangkubumi', especially pp. 306–8 ff. For further consideration of the relations between HB I and his sons, and among the sons themselves, see Chap. X below.
[131] The VOC sources on these fortifications are cited in n. 135 below.

PERMANENTLY DIVIDED KINGDOM, 1774-1787

Pangeran Arja Ngabei and Danurĕdja also agreed with the Crown Prince.[132]

[132] *B. Mang.*, pp. 475-7, Canto LXXIII (Midjil):

30. ...
    Ngandika Sang Prabu

31. Ki Dipati sira sun timbali
    miwah kang ponang wong
    si Ngabei Danurdja maninge
    ija botjah sun bupati
    paḍa ingsun tari
    apa sira rĕmbug

32. ingsun arsa jasa kubon maning
    kidul Gaḍing kono
    satus tjĕngkal iku pasagine
    Kangdjĕng Gusti matur awotsari
    Paduka Ramadji
    karsa ja Sang Prabu

33. langĕn kubon sakidul Gaḍing
    sumongga Sang Katong
    kung prijogi dados langĕn Radjeng
    nanging kula nuwun duka Adji
    punika akĕḍik
    ing pikantukipun

34. dene ingkang pikantuk nglangkungi
    djawi karsa Katong
    luhung inggih ngarsakna Ramadjeng
    amĕnĕdi panggenan nĕgari
    beteng kang prijogi
    ing sakdjagangipun

35. amawija baluwer prijogi
    marijĕm amanggon
    mila ulun matur Djĕng Ramadjeng
    mĕnawi kasupen Djĕng Ramadji
    mirseng amba nguni
    kala ing Mĕntarum

36. ejang Senapati ing Mĕntawis
    akĕkiṭa kadjor [*sic*]
    mapan inggih punika tanḍane
    Sri Narendra angandika aris
    ija ingsun eling
    tjritanejangamu

37. Kuṭa Gĕḍe ejang Senapati
    akĕkuṭa kadjor
    ingsun rĕmbug putrengsun ature
    Danurĕdja apa mrijogeni
    miwah si Ngabei
    apa sira rĕmbug

38. ingature ija ki Dipati
    kabeh rĕmbug kono

Now, says *Babad Mangkubumi*, the Sultan not only agreed to the building of the walls, but formally surrendered authority over the kingdom to the Crown Prince:

LXXIII: 40. . . .
'I surrender everything, all
of the burdens of the kingdom
to the Noble Hero.

41. 'Yes, my son Dipati [the Crown Prince],
this is my wish:
indeed, all of the affairs of the kingdom
I turn over to you,
the burdens of the country,
the whole of them.'

42. The Crown Prince performed the *sĕmbah*,
beseeching the favour
of his Father the King.
His Highness commanded softly,
'Danurĕdja and Pangeran Ngabei,
and the *bupatis*
and *najakas*, all,

43. 'be loyal, all. I command:
the Crown Prince,
because I have already entrusted all,
every burden of the kingdom
and my trust [to him],
for the future I entrust to his care

    Pangran Bei tur sĕmbah nuljage
    kjana patih matur awotsari
    pratiwanung sami
    manĕmbah umatur

39. inggih abdi-dalĕm njuwaweni
inggih Djĕng Sang Katong
aturipun Putra-dalĕm mangke
sabab kula Gusti njuwaweni
kang atur Djĕng Gusti
rumĕksyeng Pradjagung

40. dadi kabeh paḍa mangrĕmbugi
ture putraningong
ki Dipati wus kĕna pikire
sun pasrahi saksaniskaraning
. . . [see n. 133]

44. 'the brothers and sisters of the Crown Prince;
I have entrusted [them].'
Those who were addressed spoke, saying,
'Yea, exceedingly do your servants submit.'
His Highness spoke,
'You! Make known

45. 'to the Resident this my wish.'
He who was ordered performed the *sĕmbah*.
His Highness commanded softly,
'My boy, I entrust [this] to you.
Take charge, then,
of the fortifications and moat.'

46. The Crown Prince made the *sĕmbah*: 'As you wish.'
. . .[133]

[133] *B. Mang.*, p. 477, Canto LXXIII (Midjil):

40. . . . [see n. 132]
sun pasrahi saksaniskaraning
bobot ing pradja di
kang mrih Prawiranung

41. ija kaki putrengsun Dipati
mĕngko karsaningong
ija sakeh obah pradja kije
ingsun pasrah marang sira kaki
bobot ing nĕgari
saniskaranipun

42. Kangdjĕng Gusti manĕmbah nuwun sih
ing Rama Sang Katong
Sri Narendra arum timbalane
Danurĕdja miwah ki Ngabei
miwah prabupati
najaka sadarum

43. mituhuwa kabeh prentah mami
ki Dipati Anom
sabab ingsun wus pitaja kabeh
saniskareng bobot ing pradja di
lan pitaja mami
sun titipi besuk

44. kadang-kadange ki Dipati
wus pitaja ingong
ingkang sinung djarwa samja ture
gih saklangkung patikbra suwawi
ngandika Sang Adji
sira sunga wĕruh

45. mring si Oprup ja karsengsun iki
tur sĕmbah kang kinon

That this story of the Sultan turning over authority to the Crown Prince may not be entirely accurate is suggested by the absence of any corroboration in the Dutch records now extant. Yet it is not impossible that van Rhijn was informed of this, as *Babad Mangkubumi* says, but misunderstood what was happening, just as the Dutch may also have misunderstood Mangkubumi and Mangkunĕgara when in A.J. 1700 they perhaps wished to abdicate in favour of their sons. Or the news may simply have lost its way in the Dutch bureaucracy. Although this seems unlikely, neither van Rhijn nor his superior Siberg were notable for their accurate reporting. Whatever the case, there can be little doubt that the Crown Prince was responsible for the Jogjakarta fortifications, and that his influence within the *kraton* was now very great.

The Dutch records confirm the Crown Prince's role in the construction of the fortifications. The main architect was reportedly Tumĕnggung Wiraguna, the Crown Prince's *patih*. To his residence at Batavia as the commander of the Crown Prince's troops (1781–3)[134] was attributed the fact that these walls so closely resembled the fortifications of the Dutch headquarters. The Dutch initially feared the fortifications were directed against themselves but upon investigation found that the cannon were not in a position to fire on the (still incomplete) Dutch fortress, although their own cannon were equally incapable of breaching the new walls. Siberg sent four students of the Sĕmarang Marine Academy to measure the fortifications. The Sultan not only took no offence at this but even gave orders to facilitate the students in their task, viewing it as a matter of pride that the Company showed such concern. The conclusion of this report was that the walls were too enormous for the Sultan's cannon to defend them,

---

  Sri Narendra arum timbalane
  kulup sira ingsun pitajani
  garapĕn tumuli
  beteng djagangipun
 46. Kangdjĕng Gusti sandika wotsari
  . . . .

 The descriptions of subsequent events in *B. Mang.* clearly picture the Crown Prince as being in control of affairs. Poensen, 'Mangkubumi', p. 354, includes a story of HB I surrendering authority to the Crown Prince, but it is placed chronologically *c.* 1791.

[134] Sĕmarang to Batavia, 20 Oct. 1781, in KA 3495 (OB 1782).

although more expert inspectors in 1791 regarded the fortifications rather more seriously. Mangkubumi himself told the Company that the defences were directed against those who might wish to break the peace, but not against the Dutch.[135] It is almost certainly to be assumed that the Crown Prince and the younger generation of Jogjakarta princes were less worried about the Europeans than about their counterparts in Surakarta. It will be seen in the following chapter that this was a reasonable concern.

In the late 1780s the history of Central Java was coming more and more to be directed by younger men. Those who had stabilized the system of division to their mutual advantage were beginning to lose their grip on state politics. When Pakubuwana III died in 1788, the weakest of the triumvirate of Mangkubumi, Mangkunĕgara, and Pakubuwana III and the first to die, a major crisis threatened the divided state for the first time since the stabilization of the 1770s. And this time it would be a potential military threat for the first time since the end of major rebellion in the 1750s. But the division of the kingdom was by now able to withstand such a challenge. This is the subject of the following chapter.

In the preceding pages of this chapter many subjects familiar to the student of Javanese history have appeared, but there has been one notable omission. The most important subject of preceding chapters has disappeared: the attempt either to reunify Java or to justify its continued division. For the first time, the histories of

[135] Sĕmarang to HB I, – Feb 1785, in KA 3597 (OB 1786); HB I to Sĕmarang, 3 Rabingulakir A.J. 1711 (received 17 Feb. 1785), in KA 3597 (OB 1786); J. P. Pilon (VOC engineer), Jogjakarta, to Sĕmarang, 25 Feb. 1785, in KA 3597 (OB 1786); Sĕmarang to Batavia, 1 March 1785, in KA 3597 (OB 1786); id., 24 Dec. 1785, in KA 3630 (OB 1787).

The inspection by the 1791 Commissioners for Military Affairs is described on pp. 345–6 below; their report is described in Sĕmarang to Batavia, 20 Oct. 1791, in KA 3859 (OB 1793).

See also Poensen, 'Mangkubumi', p. 306, which is as critical of the Crown Prince in the building of the fortifications as in all other matters. Here is found the story that the Jogjakarta *bupatis* were required to pawn their gold and silver *kris*-sheaths to buy construction materials.

B. *Mang.*, p. 478, says HB I gave the Crown Prince 10,000 reals to reward the troops (for their efforts). In Poensen, 'Mangkubumi', p. 311, 'Kjai Wiraguna' is identified as the *patih* of the Crown Prince.

The walls may be found on map III of Louw and de Klerck, *Java-Oorlog*. Some sections of the walls still stand in Jogjakarta and their similarity to the old Batavia fortifications in Djakarta is readily seen.

The VOC fortress in Jogjakarta was still incomplete two years after the *kraton* walls were built; see Siberg, Memorie, 18 Sept. 1787, in dJ xii, p. 91.

JOGJAKARTA UNDER SULTAN MANGKUBUMI

Surakarta and Jogjakarta have been capable of treatment as separate subjects. Only rarely did events cross the boundaries of the kingdoms, as in the case of courtiers who fled from Mangkunĕgara to Jogjakarta or vice versa. The legal agreements of A.J. 1697–9 (A.D. 1771–3) which guaranteed the functioning of the divided kingdom were renewed regularly by the *patihs*.[136] But aside from such matters there seems to have been little or no contact between the two *kratons*.[137]

The elder generation of the Javanese courtly élite had accepted the fact of division. But some of the younger generation had not yet learned the lesson of its necessity. They were soon to do so.

[136] The codes are discussed in Chap. VI above. For references to copies, see p. 163 nn. 69 and 70.

[137] Two Jogjakarta sources describe the sending of a troop of dancers to Surakarta in 1785; *B. Mang.*, pp. 479–81; Poensen, 'Mangkubumi', pp. 330–1. In the latter source, this is said to have been HB I's idea. *B. Mang.* says PB III had requested the dancers.

It was later claimed that PB III had opposed this mission of dancers, but had been forced to accept it by the corrupt Resident Palm; see p. 298 below.

IX

CRISIS IN SURAKARTA AND THE VINDICATION OF THE DIVISION
1787–1790

IN the late 1780s the histories of Surakarta and Jogjakarta again converged in a crisis so complex that the truth of the matter is difficult to establish. The Dutch and the two *kratons* of Central Java both saw this as a major event and the amount of documentation is consequently enormous. But because of the complexity of the crisis and the extent to which various parties were involved in it, a great deal of this information is unreliable. Certain details must therefore remain uncertain, but it is nevertheless clear that this crisis was one of the most important episodes of Javanese history in the late eighteenth century. It was in part the first major test of the permanence of the division and the first major lesson to the younger generation on its necessity. It also reflected the tensions of the last years of Pakubuwana III, when dissatisfaction among high Javanese officials was apparently widespread, largely because of the Susuhunan's increasing loss of control over affairs. A general political disintegration had resulted and it will be seen that Dutch Residents of highly dubious natures took this opportunity to engage in unprecedented extortion and corruption, thus also causing widespread aversion to the Europeans. The Dutch were subsequently manipulated by the Javanese upon whom they depended for information and were led to believe that the Company and its officials were in serious danger unless they took immediate action. Thereby the Dutch were brought to act on behalf of Mangkubumi and Mangkunĕgara to prevent an attempted reunification of Mataram by the new Susuhunan, a design which was viewed with such apprehension that it drove the Sultan and Mangkunĕgara to make common effort for the first time in four decades.

The religious element in all this will be considered in some detail below. It may be suggested in advance that religious ideas certainly played a role in this crisis, but they were traditional Javanese religious concepts and not imported anti-European Wahhābī puritanism, which M. L. van Deventer long ago cautiously suggested as a possible explanation.[1]

This crisis emerged from a background of general and advancing disintegration in Surakarta, described in the preceding chapter. Susuhunan Pakubuwana III was more and more incapable of controlling the affairs of his kingdom. He was sometimes seriously ill[2] and, just as in Jogjakarta, the Crown Prince of Surakarta was taking an increasingly influential part in *kraton* affairs.

But the Crown Prince of Surakarta was rather different from his Jogjakarta counterpart. Most importantly, he was younger. He had been born in 1768 and in 1787 was thus not yet twenty. Moreover, his birth had been one of the developments which had signalled the end of the attempts to reunify the kingdom. Thus, by the time he was old enough to have his own impressions of the world about him, Java was peacefully divided. Unlike his elders, including the Jogjakarta Crown Prince, he could not remember the chaos of warfare, the tensions of an uncertain division, or the experience of seeing Company troops at war. He was thus less likely to appreciate why the permanent division of the kingdom was the solution which had emerged after a century of chaos.

The Crown Prince's behaviour had begun to arouse suspicion as early as 1785, when he was just seventeen. He had then been married for two years to the daughter of Tjakradiningrat, the ruler of Paměkasan (Madura). The girl's mother was a sister to the Paněmbahan of Madura and therefore also a sister to the wife whom Pakubuwana III had divorced in 1762. The Susuhunan and others in the court had been somewhat sceptical of the marriage, saying marriages between the Susuhunan's house and Madura had always brought marital misfortune and strife. But the marriage was carried out and in February 1785 there was born to the Crown Prince a son who lived to rule as Susuhunan Pakubuwana V (1820–3). But the child's mother fell ill during childbirth and died in August 1785.[3] Thereafter the young Crown

---

[1] DJ xii, pp. xix–xxii.
[2] e.g. Sěmarang to Batavia, 1 March 1785, in KA 3597 (OB 1786).
[3] Id., 5 Sept. 1781, in KA 3494 (OB 1782) (This section is omitted from the edited version in dJ xii, pp. 1–6); id., 19 Dec. 1781, in KA 3495 (OB 1782); Batavia to H.XVII, 29 Dec. 1781, in dJ xii, p. 9; Sěmarang to Batavia, 14 Jan. 1782 and 26 March 1782, in KA 3519 (OB 1783); id., 23 Oct. 1782, in KA 3520 (OB 1783); Batavia to H.XVII, 31 Dec. 1782, in dJ xii, p. 24; Sěma-

CRISIS IN SURAKARTA, 1787-1790

Prince reportedly began to lead a dissolute and irregular life, becoming involved with women in a fashion which led the Susuhunan to complain to the Dutch. A second marriage was then arranged in 1786 between the Crown Prince and a daughter of the Susuhunan's brother Pangeran Purbaja.[4] Thereafter, the prince seems to have led a more settled life, but it was observed that he grew more secretive and restrained towards Dutch officials in Surakarta.[5]

It was in 1787 that the Crown Prince for the first time became seriously involved with religious zealots, much to the concern of his father and of the Dutch. The leader of this religious circle was reportedly Wirjakusuma, the son of Raden Mas Krěti. The latter was the brother of Mangkuněgara who had been returned to Java from exile on the Cape of Good Hope in 1787. Wirjakusuma had thus presumably just arrived in Java for the first time in his life.[6] But immediately he became the leader of what seems probably to have been a traditional Javanese religious movement, which counted among its adherents Pangeran Kadjoran, whose predecessor had been instrumental in fomenting the rebellion of Trunadjaja over a century before.[7] That Wirjakusuma became so quickly involved in such a group suggests the extent to which Javanese rebels and religious leaders could maintain their traditions even in exile.

Raden Mas Krěti, who was supposed to have visited the Netherlands as a stowaway during his banishment,[8] reportedly returned to Java in European dress, complete to the wearing of a wig. The Susuhunan allowed him to continue in this attire, but reportedly the Crown Prince forbade it. He ordered Krěti to

---

rang to Batavia, 20 May 1783, in KA 3545 (OB 1784); id., 1 March 1785 and 9 Sept. 1785, in KA 3597 (OB 1786); Siberg, Memorie, 18 Sept. 1787, in dJ xii, p. 84.
On PB III's divorce of his wife in 1762, see pp. 108-9 above.

[4] Sěmarang to Batavia, 30 Nov. 1785, in KA 3597 (OB 1786); id., 3 March 1786, in KA 3630 (OB 1787); Siberg, Memorie, 18 Sept. 1787, in dJ xii, pp. 84-5.
[5] Sěmarang to Batavia, 26 April 1787, in KA 3655 (OB 1788).
[6] For sources on the return of these exiles, see above, p. 270 n. 107.
[7] Pangeran Kadjoran had paid homage to Wirjakusuma by presenting a set of *gamělan*-instruments; Palm to Sěmarang, 2 May 1787, in KA 3655 (OB 1788). See also H. J. de Graaf, 'Het Kadjoran-Vraagstuk', *Djåwå*, vol. 20 (1940), pp. 273-325.
[8] See above, p. 270 nn. 106 and 107, on R. M. Krěti and sources concerning his return from exile.

throw away his wig, to grow his hair, and to take up a religious life, which he apparently did. Then on three occasions Jogjakarta rice-lands were captured by Surakarta subjects. The blame for this was also laid by the Resident Palm at the door of the Surakarta Crown Prince, whom he believed to have ordered this under the influence of Krĕti's son Wirjakusuma. Jogjakarta fortunately left the matter to the Company to settle. Since the highly unreliable Palm was the source of all information on these episodes, the truth of the case is largely impossible to establish. He asked and obtained Sĕmarang's permission to arrest and banish Wirjakusuma and four other subjects of the Crown Prince. The Susuhunan also agreed to this,[9] but subsequent events would show that the Susuhunan's agreement was no guarantee that Palm's version of events was reliable.

The Crown Prince's entourage was by now said to be 'swarming with priests (*paepen*)', and he was reportedly showing ever greater aversion to Europeans and their ways. Wirjakusuma and four followers, one of them a *hadji*, were therefore arrested in April 1787 and sent for banishment to Batavia. With them were captured various *djimats* (amulets), including Wirjakusuma's 'chronicle' ('babbat', i.e. *babad*).[10] The use of amulets suggests that, whatever their intentions or religious leanings, these men were not Wahhābīs. Palm then claimed to have convinced the Crown Prince that Wirjakusuma had been misleading him and even stealing from him. Thereupon, Palm claimed, the Prince thanked him effusively for showing him the error of his ways.[11]

But the troubles in Surakarta had hardly begun. In December 1787 there were discovered in Surakarta two extraordinary letters, posted in public in a court *gamĕlan*-building (*pagongan*). The letters were very long and their contents similar. It will suffice here to present extracts:

> This letter is written by the Susuhunan Ajundjaja Adimurti Senapati Ingalaga, coming from Mecca, who has obtained the blessing of God.

[9] Palm to Sĕmarang, 19 April 1787, in KA 3655 (OB 1788); Sĕmarang to Palm, 21 April 1787, in KA 3655 (OB 1788); PB III to Sĕmarang, 5 Rĕdjĕb A.J. 1713 (received 25 April 1787), in KA 3655 (OB 1788); Sĕmarang to Batavia, 26 April 1787, in KA 3655 (OB 1788).
[10] Palm to Sĕmarang, 24 April 1787, in KA 3655 (OB 1788); Sĕmarang to Batavia, 26 April 1787, in KA 3655 (OB 1788).
[11] Palm to Sĕmarang, 2 May 1787, in KA 3655 (OB 1788); Sĕmarang to Batavia, 15 May 1787, in KA 3655 (OB 1788).

CRISIS IN SURAKARTA, 1787-1790

On Thursday evening, being *pasaran* [day in the five-day week] Lĕgi, this blessing came from Heaven, at a time when all men slept, accompanied by lightning flashes, whereupon on Saturday morning, being *pasaran* Kliwon, a violet rainbow appeared, after which this rainbow was washed by many angels in the Mecca Sea. On Sunday fell also all the stars from the Heavens. And on Thursday evening the rainbow was blessedly altered into a form which thereupon came down, and another rainbow appeared of red and white colours. Wherepon in the night came a Prophet. Wherefore this Friday, the eleventh of the month, the year *wawu*, one must not put out of one's memory. The red and white rainbow reached with its end precisely in the sun. This shall firmly be a sign of a King of Mecca.

This letter is written by the Susuhunan Ajundjaja Adimurti Ingalaga [*sic*], residing in Mecca. First I greet you, King of Sala [Surakarta] most graciously, and I say to you that you are no longer permitted to be a king. You are descended from respectable and priestly rulers, and why do you not do right? Thus are you a king of the Devil. Is that the Will of God? Why know you not the Countenance of God? What sort of king are you? A king of the Europeans, you please God no more; it is finished with you; get out, you apostate from the Faith! You must no longer be in Java. I am nominated [*g'eligeerd*] as King of Java, who maintains the Faith of the Prophet. . . . Moreover, King of Sala, call together my coastal people and say to the Europeans that I will come here when the sun is embellished with a white border and a rainbow, then shall I come from Mecca, sanctioned with the Blessings of Heaven. The twenty-fifth of the coming month Djumadilawal shall I ask of you in the name of God the price[12] of the lands, being a sum of ten times nine hundred thousand, for God has repudiated you and has commanded me that all creditors and debtors need not be grieved, for I am their king. Whoever does not support the king who comes from Mecca shall have neither prosperity nor blessing and shall be declared an enemy of my kingdom . . .

Also, the king coming from Mecca must be proclaimed by the so-called *bĕnde* or gong-alarm; these shall be the ceremonies of the coming king from Mecca, springing from the rainbow of red and white colours. The following persons have been sent for the transmission of this letter: Raden Tedjakusuma, Raden Kuwungkusuma, Raden Megakusuma, Raden Djajakusuma, Raden Malangkusuma, Raden Tandjunganom, Mangmangdana, and Banaspati.[13] These are together royal children, therefore is it seemly that you consider this fully and be not at ease and

---

[12] The other letter (see n. 18 below) refers to the same figure as the 'rents' (*pagt penningen*) of the land.

[13] The other letter (see n. 18 below) lists Tedjakusuma, Kuwungkusuma, Megakusuma, Djajakusuma, and Lintangkusuma.

carefree. Furthermore, you must announce this my letter and collectively consult over it.

I have for a long time, already on the fifteenth of the month Puasa, intended to come here with my retinue, for the King of Sala was then already declared unworthy.... Think you that no one is more powerful than you, King of Sala? Think you that no one pleases God but the King of Sala alone? Shall the Europeans, then, indeed be more powerful than God? Ask your *sĕntanas* or children, or he who still thinks one day to become king, if he dares venture to undertake anything against God. I ask you this, you King of Sala, in the Presence of God. It is finished with your kingdom, you are a king of the Devil . . .

Call together your *sĕntanas* and priests to solve my riddle.[14] I desire this. And if you do this not, then shall the thunder cruelly pursue you and the damned spirits, spectres, devils, stars, sun, moon, and clouds shall all hostilely pursue you. But, King of Sala, know you the *pajung* [parasol] made of the Devil's bread? You do not belong in Heaven if you know it not. You shall be hated of God. And can you, like me, command the clouds, the rainbow, stars, sun, and moon? This power have I received from God when I became king. God gave me the Devil's bread-*pajung* up upon the mountain. The crossed clouds [*dwarse wolken*] and the sun are my signs that I am a King of God . . .

If you know this not, then shall a Prophet come down in the night with lightning flashes. Above all must you not be at ease or carefree, for the rainbow shall be visible in the month Sapar, towards the southwest and directly in the west, then shall the King of Mecca come and the sky shall also be unvarying dark. . . . You, King of Sala, can indeed appoint *tumĕnggungs* and *mantris* everywhere but do you not sense that you are a creature of God? You are finished as king. Therefore is your land in disorder and food and clothing are expensive and it seldom rains, and all is sickness. Where then is the evidence that you are a king of God? You, King of Mataram,[15] can appoint *tumĕnggungs* and *mantris*; why do you not feel the Recompense of God? You are finished with your kingdom, although you are King of Sala, descended from Mataram. But so may it not be, for we are all together creatures of God. Whoever lives and is a king, is king by God thereto appointed. I need not say this to you, for as a king you do know this yourself.[16]

---

[14] The other letter (see n. 18 below) gives the riddle as: 'Can you give orders to the clouds, can you see the stars by day, know you the sun, the moon, the clouds, and the commands of God, know you God's blessing, know you Heaven and Earth?'

[15] See n. 17 below.

[16] Appendix to Sĕmarang to Batavia, 1 Jan. 1788, in KA 3708 (OB 1789) (pp. 60–4).

CRISIS IN SURAKARTA, 1787-1790

The second letter had essentially the same eschatological message. Its contents were rather more confusing, however, and it is slightly unclear to whom it was intended to be addressed. It was primarily directed to Pakubuwana III, but at times it seems also to address the Sultan of Jogjakarta, as the 'King of Mataram'. The latter phrase, however, probably referred to the Susuhunan of Surakarta even though that would have been a less correct usage of 'Mataram'.[17] This letter more clearly criticized the Dutch, as may be seen in the following extract:

I shall also drive from Java the Europeans if they do not behave well. What have the Europeans to do here? Shall they then be more powerful than God? Are the Europeans your God? All right, just stay with your Europeans. You are a Devil's king, for you uphold no justice. Do you think not to die and to be buried in the earth? Do you not sense that you are a creature of God? And you, Adipati [Sura Adiměnggala] of Sěmarang, must command the coastal peoples to come to meet me. You, King of Mataram, do you think to be a wise king? Do you believe that no one is more powerful than the King of Mataram, or do you think that I am afraid of your people? You are no king of God and also are no merciful king. If I were no more powerful king than you, what good would it do me to be a creature of God? Do you then so firmly trust your comrades the Europeans? You are altogether no king ...

Further, King of Mataram, you must say to all the priests that I shall come here, and if you offer resistance you act against the Will of God. And if the Europeans do not wish to acknowledge me or to follow my orders, so say to them that I shall take my coastal people from them. The Europeans are always giving you advice, but if one day they are no longer here you will have to be prudent.[18]

The discovery of these letters understandably excited the Susuhunan greatly. Although one of the two letters was perhaps addressed to the Sultan as well as to Pakubuwana III, copies were found only in Surakarta,[19] unless similar documents were seized

---

[17] 'Mataram' was consistently used in the eighteenth century to refer to Jogjakarta, which was located in Mataram. Surakarta was located in Padjang. Yet in this letter (see n. 18 below) it seems that 'Mataram' was used to refer to Surakarta. In the absence of the original Javanese text, however, it is impossible to judge this matter with complete confidence. In the first letter (extracted above), which is clearly addressed to PB III, there are two references to Mataram, the first of which (not included in the extract here) makes little sense but the second of which (at n. 15) seems to refer to Surakarta.

[18] Appendix to Sěmarang to Batavia, 1 Jan. 1788, in KA 3708 (OB 1789) (pp. 54-9).

[19] Van Ijsseldijk to Palm, 30 Dec. 1787, in KA 3708 (OB 1789).

in Jogjakarta and kept from Dutch knowledge. The letters were of considerable significance.[20] The first comment to be made upon them is that their author was very possibly mad. But the boundary between the insane and the prophetic has often been difficult to draw, and nowhere was it more so than in traditional Java. Mad or not, such documents had the power to spread apprehension widely among the Javanese élite and common-folk, who lived in a world thickly inhabited by spirits and supernatural powers. The letters not only reflected criticisms of the state of Surakarta which were presumably current, but also encouraged further speculation about the possibility of divine intervention to set right the affairs of Java. The expectation of the coming king who would institute a reign of justice (the *Ratu Adil*) had considerable attraction for Javanese living in times of trouble. It was similar to the Islamic idea of a messiah (the *Mahdi*) and Buddhist concepts of the coming Buddha (*Maitreya*) but it was at the same time a thoroughly Javanese idea basic to that culture's perceptions of a troubled time and of the solutions which were to be found.[21] These letters, with their appeal to messianic traditions, must have increased the tensions which, as was seen in the previous chapter, were already serious within the Surakarta court.

Moreover, these criticisms apparently came from within indigenous Javanese circles and were not imported from the international world of orthodox Islam. Were it not for the references to Mecca and to the Prophet, there would indeed be little reason even to call the letters Islamic. The phraseology and images might have come from any Javanese *babad* or mystical text. The general mysticism of the text is consistent with Javanese ideas and is specifically inconsistent with the puritanical thrust of the Wahhābīs.

[20] In analysing such documents, probably written in the rather obscure idiom of Javanese mysticism, one is at the mercy of the VOC translators. I am generally confident of these translations, although errors of detail may exist. Documents in the Algemeen Rijksarchief, the Hague, preserve only the translations, but among the volumes which have found their way to the Djakarta Arsip Nasional are records of the crisis described in this chapter which include both the original Javanese letters and statements and the Dutch translations. Thus it is possible to compare the Javanese and Dutch versions. I have not had the opportunity to undertake a large-scale verification of such translations, but wherever I have compared original texts with translations, the latter have proved to be of sufficient reliability. One should not, however, place too great stress on some detail of expression or upon some particular choice of words in the absence of the Javanese original.

[21] On the *Ratu Adil* tradition, see Drewes, *Drie Javaansche Goeroe's*, pp. 129-93.

The self-asserted title of the author, Susuhunan Ajundjaja Adimurti Senapati Ingalaga, is thoroughly Javanese, with etymological roots in Old Javanese, Sanskrit, and Modern Javanese rather than Arabic words. The symbolism of the red-and-white rainbow will also be familiar to modern Indonesians, whose national flag (*Sang Merah-Putih*) bears those colours.[22] The dates mentioned in the letter are calculated in the Javanese system of five- and seven-day weeks and eight-year (*windu*) cycles, as well as in the Javanese-Islamic lunar months.

The Dutch did not bother to work out the several dates mentioned in the letters but the Javanese would hardly have failed to understand them. The coming of the King of Mecca was at hand. Several of the events mentioned were past when the letters were found.[23] But more was to come. On 'the twenty-fifth of the coming month Djumadilawal' the author would demand 'ten times nine hundred thousand' (reals) from the Susuhunan (25 Djumadilawal A.J. 1714/3 March A.D. 1788). And the King of Mecca would come as the rainbow stood in the darkened sky 'in the month Sapar', which would most likely have been understood as Sapar A.J. 1715 (November A.D. 1788). In less than a year, divine intervention would bring a just ruler to the throne of Surakarta. But by the time November 1788 arrived, Pakubuwana III was to be dead.

The nature of these letters' criticisms is most important. While the writer clearly disliked the Dutch, it will be noted that there

[22] Prof. Muhammad Yamin has attempted to show that this banner has precedents as a national flag deep in the Javanese and Indonesian past. See Muhammad Yamin, *6000 Tahun Sang Mérah-Putih* (Djakarta, 1958).

[23] The second letter (see n. 18 above) has some different dates. The suggestion here is not that the dates referred to any real events, but that in a time of uncertainty they would tend to convince the Javanese reader of the authenticity of the letter and that the events had actually taken place. All the dates would be seen to occupy the months of late 1787 and 1788. The blessing from Heaven was said to have come on 'Thursday-Lĕgi', which would probably have been interpreted as Thursday-Lĕgi, 5 Puasa A.J. 1713 (21 June 1787). There followed on 'Saturday-Kliwon' the washing of the rainbow by the angels (Saturday-Kliwon, 14 Puasa A.J. 1713/30 June 1787). The great day in the letter was apparently Sunday-Lĕgi, 15 Puasa A.J. 1713 (1 July 1787). On that day the stars fell from the Heavens ('on Sunday'), the angels washed the writer in the Mecca Sea ('on Sunday-Lĕgi'), and the writer first intended to come to Java '(on the 15th of the month Puasa')' because PB III had been declared unworthy. 'On Thursday,' 19 Puasa A.J. 1713 (5 July 1787), the red-and-white rainbow appeared. On 'Friday, the eleventh of the month, the year *wawu*' the Prophet came down and the red-and-white rainbow reached to the sun (Friday, 11 Sawal, *wawu* A.J. 1713/27 July 1787).

was no absolute threat to expel them so long as they behaved well and followed orders. It was the Susuhunan rather than the Europeans who bore responsibility for Java's problems. This was consistent with the general inability of the Javanese in the late eighteenth century to see that their circumstances were now affected by factors outside the immediate sphere of Javanese affairs. They believed their problems were basically internal, having to do primarily with relations among themselves. If there was an external problem, it was ultimately the fault of those who were at the centre of the Javanese state. This was a thoroughly traditional view, unaffected by the problem of the Dutch presence. The Susuhunan was denounced for being proud and unrighteous, and it was from this that Mataram's misfortunes were believed to flow. The writer of the letters perhaps did not even appreciate the extent to which the Dutch controlled the *pasisir*: he addressed the Javanese *bupati* of Sĕmarang when he wanted the *pasisir* people summoned, rather than the Dutch Governor of Sĕmarang.

The Dutch Resident and the Susuhunan immediately undertook a search for the writer of the letters. It was a case of the corrupt guiding the infirm. The Dutch Resident Palm found a mystic named Kjai Alim Dĕmak and pronounced him guilty. Siberg had meanwhile been replaced by the more perceptive and reliable, but hardly more virtuous, Jan Greeve as Governor of Sĕmarang (1787–91), and the latter was sceptical of the accusations. Kjai Alim Dĕmak was a man of no particular distinction or influence and since he was illiterate he could hardly have done the actual writing himself. When he was arrested he told an obscure tale about awaiting the Susuhunan's summons, whereupon he would tell the Susuhunan to construct various buildings at prescribed places upon the *alun-alun*. Greeve told Palm to counsel patience upon the Susuhunan until further investigation could reveal the important dignitaries who, Greeve believed, must surely stand behind Kjai Alim Dĕmak, if the latter was involved at all. But royal 'justice' was swift. Kjai Alim Dĕmak was tortured to death. His skin was cut from his body in strips, the letters he was accused of having written being burned under his face.[24]

[24] Palm to Sĕmarang, 31 Dec. 1787, in KA 3708 (OB 1789); Sĕmarang to Palm, 1 Jan. 1788, in KA 3708 (OB 1789); Sĕmarang to Batavia, 12 Jan. 1788, in KA 3708 (OB 1789); Singawidjaja, Declaration, [Jan. 1788], in AN Solo 36, 'Diverze Verklarings'; Sĕmarang to Batavia, 29 Jan. 1788, in KA 3708 (OB 1789).

Also arrested was one Tandjunganom, whose name appeared among those who were ordered to transmit one of the letters. He was said to have been an expert in poisons who was responsible *inter alia* for the death of the wife of one of the Surakarta Crown Prince's officials. He was burned to death.[25] It was shortly discovered that the Susuhunan himself had not been pleased with this treatment of the accused.

Both Greeve at Sĕmarang and his superiors in Batavia were dissatisfied with the evidence adduced against Kjai Alim Dĕmak and Tandjunganom. They were displeased with the precipitate executions, believing quite reasonably that there was more behind these letters than the amateur machinations of an illiterate mystic and a poisoner.[26] Their suspicions of their Resident, Palm, were already beginning, and did nothing to allay the Company's general sense of unease at the discovery of such letters.

The Dutch were becoming concerned at this time over what appeared to be growing anti-European sentiments throughout Java and Madura. From Bantĕn, Tjirĕbon, and Madura came reports of Islamic agitators preaching against the foreign infidels.[27] Much more research would be necessary to clarify the origins, intentions, and influence of these various individuals. It is not unreasonable to suppose in the meantime that more and more Indonesians were coming to believe that the Company was not as strong as it had been in earlier years and were thus less afraid to speak against the Dutch. The Dutch commented that some of these 'priests' were 'foreigners', which raises the further possibility of non-Indonesian Muslims now beginning to stir up latent indigenous animosity towards the Company. The Company feared that the letters discovered in Surakarta were part of the same pattern. They therefore encouraged Pakubuwana III to forbid the continued residence of 'foreign priests' in Surakarta, which he pretended to do. But six months later Greeve reported this command had had no effect,[28] and it was shortly learned that the

---

[25] Sĕmarang to Batavia, 29 Jan. 1788, in KA 3708 (OB 1789).
[26] Id., 5 July 1788, in KA 3708 (OB 1789); Batavia to H. XVII, 30 Dec. 1788, in dJ xii, p. 161.
[27] See dJ xii, pp. xix–xxi. One of these agitators is described as an Arab.
[28] Sĕmarang to Batavia, 29 Jan. 1788 and 5 July 1788, in KA 3708 (OB 1789).
Batavia to H.XVII, 30 Dec. 1788, in dJ xii, p. 161, reported PB III's decree but omitted to inform the Company's Directors that it had had no effect.

Susuhunan had in fact suspended his own order. In any case, the true root of these letters was primarily to be sought within Surakarta circles and not among outside religious zealots, whatever the situation elsewhere in Indonesia.

At the same time as these letters were discovered, in December 1787, Palm also reported another intrigue of a more familiar nature. Mangkunĕgara had been divorced from the Sultan's eldest daughter Ratu Bĕndara in 1763 and two years later she had remarried Pangeran Dipanĕgara of Jogjakarta.[29] Mangkunĕgara had never ceased to complain at what he believed to have been the injustice of the entire affair. In July 1787 Pangeran Dipanĕgara died. Then in December Palm reported the discovery of a secret correspondence between Mangkunĕgara, now about sixty-three years old, and the widowed Ratu Bĕndara, who was now about fifty. There was supposedly a plan for Ratu Bĕndara to flee Jogjakarta to live again with Mangkunĕgara.

Images of renewed hostility between the Sultan and Mangkunĕgara sprang into Dutch minds. They immediately and extensively investigated the matter in both Surakarta and Jogjakarta, taking great pains to keep the allegations from the old Sultan for fear of arousing his rage. It was, of course, extremely unlikely that the Sultan, or at least the Crown Prince, could have been unaware of the entire investigation. Van Ijsseldijk, the Resident in Jogjakarta, soon began to doubt Palm's report, as did Greeve in Sĕmarang. By January 1788, Greeve had begun to doubt Palm's general reliability and by July he would come to believe that the entire correspondence was a complete fabrication. Palm claimed Mangkunĕgara had admitted to the correspondence, but later Mangkunĕgara furiously denied the allegations when he met Greeve personally in August 1788. Danurĕdja gave his assurance that it was impossible for Ratu Bĕndara to be involved in such a correspondence, since she was constantly attended by other members of the Sultan's family. In any case, there was no discernible reason why she should wish to abandon her privileged position in Jogjakarta. Van Ijsseldijk suggested that the rumour may have been fabricated by Mangkunĕgara in hopes of insulting the Sultan. Alternatively, he thought it possible but not very likely that the Jogjakarta Crown Prince had been responsible, hoping to bring his father to take military action against Mang-

[29] See pp. 110–15, 117–18 above on these matters.

CRISIS IN SURAKARTA, 1787-1790

kunĕgara. But Greeve was by now convinced that Palm was responsible for the rumours himself.[30]

Palm's abilities to deceive his superiors and to use his position in Surakarta to his own advantage and profit were now suddenly disclosed and even more suddenly brought to a halt. On 11 May 1788 Palm died. The Dutch reported he died of illness[31] but a later Jogjakarta source raises the possibility that he was poisoned. It says he died by drinking spirits (*er kras*) 'and immediately thereupon expired'.[32] It is possible to reconcile these sources by suggesting that he died of alcoholism, which Professor Boxer believes was probably the largest single cause of mortality among Europeans in the tropics.[33] Yet it will be seen below that Palm was not the only one to die suddenly amidst accusations of gross misconduct from the Surakarta *kraton*, and poisoning should not be ruled out as a possible or even probable cause of death.

After Palm's death the channels of communication between the Surakarta *kraton* and the Dutch hierarchy were suddenly thrown open as they had not been for several years. It became clear that normal communications had been blocked more and more in the years of Palm's Residency since 1784. Communications were also facilitated by the fact that Jan Greeve was a more perceptive Governor of Sĕmarang than his predecessor Siberg (1780-7), who had confidently informed Batavia in 1787 that Palm had the gift to make himself beloved by the Javanese.[34] With the floodgates thus reopened, a torrent of accusations against Palm poured forth from the *kraton*. He was accused of serious extortion. He had forced the docile old Susuhunan to appoint one of Palm's favourites as scribe to the *patih* in place of one of the Susuhunan's own

[30] Siberg, Memorie, 18 Sept. 1787, in dJ xii, p. 86; van Ijsseldijk to Palm, 30 Dec. 1787, in KA 3708 (OB 1789); Palm to van Ijsseldijk, 31 Dec. 1787, in KA 3708 (OB 1789); Palm to Sĕmarang, 31 Dec. 1787, in KA 3708 (OB 1789); Sĕmarang to Batavia, 1 Jan. 1788, in KA 3708 (OB 1789); van Ijsseldijk to Sĕmarang, 4 Jan. 1788, in KA 3708 (OB 1789); Palm to Sĕmarang, 6 Jan. 1788, in KA 3708 (OB 1789); Sĕmarang to Palm, 8 Jan. 1788, in KA 3708 (OB 1789); van Ijsseldijk to Sĕmarang, 9 Jan. 1788, in KA 3708 (OB 1789); Sĕmarang to van Ijsseldijk, 12 Jan. 1788, in KA 3708 (OB 1789); Sĕmarang to Batavia, 12 Jan. 1788, 29 Jan. 1788, 5 July 1788, and 29 Aug. 1788, in KA 3708 (OB 1789).
[31] Sĕmarang to Batavia, 12 June 1788 and 5 July 1788, in KA 3708 (OB 1789).
[32] Poensen, 'Mangkubumi', p. 317 n. 2: sanalika ladjeng pĕdjah.
[33] Boxer, *Dutch Seaborne Empire*, p. 209: 'I think it no exaggeration to say that most of the Dutch and English males who died in the tropics died of drink, even making due allowance for the heavy toll taken by malaria and dysentery.'
[34] Siberg, Memorie, 18 Sept. 1787, in dJ xii, p. 90.

sons-in-law. This man had then diverted *kraton* funds from their rightful recipients. After Palm's death he was banished to the wilderness. Palm had also wrongly appropriated Javanese labourers to work without pay upon the Dutch fortress and upon his own residence and garden to such an extent that he was said to be the ruin of the land, the people, and the officials. The Susuhunan complained of Palm's manner of speaking to him, and said the Resident had frequently insulted Mangkunĕgara and the Crown Prince, the latter for instance by sending one bottle of spoiled wine as a gift on the occasion of a marriage in the royal house. He had forced the Susuhunan to receive a corps of Jogjakarta *kraton* dancers in 1785, although Pakubuwana III said he had wanted nothing to do with the other *kraton* of the divided kingdom. Palm was said to have personally carried out the hasty investigation of the letters discovered in 1787, over Pakubuwana III's objections, and had then introduced the barbaric punishment of burning Tandjunganom, a form of execution said to be unknown to the Javanese, who preferred banishment, dismemberment, or battle with tigers. It was also Palm who had told the Susuhunan to forbid all 'foreign priests' to live in Surakarta, but Pakubuwana III had realized this could lead to trouble and had himself stopped the carrying-out of his own command.[35]

All of this had been possible only because Pakubuwana III had by now almost completely lost control over his own court and kingdom. Lesser Javanese officials had so feared Palm's influence over the Susuhunan that much of the extortion and oppression did not even reach the Susuhunan's ears until after Palm's death. The effect of the whole affair was thus increased dislike among the élite both for the Susuhunan and for the Dutch. When Greeve visited Central Java in August 1788, he encountered widespread hatred of Palm's memory and he feared it would be difficult to restore the Dutch position in Surakarta. Palm's behaviour was also believed, probably rightly, to be the principal cause of the Crown

---

[35] E. A. de Wilde and J. A. Faupelle (Acting Surakarta Residents) to Sĕmarang, 2 June 1788, 3 June 1788, and 12 June 1788, in KA 3708 (OB 1789); Sĕmarang to Batavia, 5 July 1788, in KA 3708 (OB 1789); PB III to Sĕmarang, [June–July 1788], in KA 3708 (OB 1789); Sĕmarang to Batavia, 29 Aug. 1788, in KA 3708 (OB 1789).

On Javanese sources for the dance mission of 1785, see above, p. 284 n. 137. It is unclear why Palm should have desired such a mission.

See also Batavia to H.XVII, 30 Dec. 1788, in dJ xii, pp. 161–2.

Prince's aversion to Europeans. The young heir had reportedly complained to his father about Palm but the Susuhunan regretfully said he had turned a deaf ear.³⁶

The old Susuhunan now also complained to Greeve about the behaviour of the Second Resident, E. A. de Wilde, who was said to be encouraging the younger princes to take to drink and enticing them to 'bad places' by night. But before Greeve could take steps to remove de Wilde, he, too, suddenly died on 23 August 1788, after a sickness of short duration.³⁷ The sudden death of de Wilde shortly after that of Palm greatly increases the possibility that both had been poisoned, probably by their Javanese servants upon the orders of some Surakarta dignitary.

An explosive situation was building in 1788 in Surakarta, with hatred of the Dutch now added to a general political disintegration and to the growing influence of a Crown Prince who favoured mystics and disliked Europeans. Moreover, the life of Pakubuwana III was now drawing to a close and the usual tensions which surrounded times of succession were added to the ferment. Nor was the Dutch position improved in any way by the deaths of Palm and de Wilde. The new Resident at Surakarta was Andries Hartsinck (1788–90),³⁸ whose career there was to be even more nefarious than Palm's.

By the time Greeve made the customary new Governor's tour of the Central Javanese courts (19 July–20 August 1788) the tensions in Surakarta were beginning also to produce significant conflict between Surakarta and Jogjakarta, for the first time since the permanent division of the kingdom in A.J. 1700–3 (A.D. 1774–7). The first major cause of renewed animosity was in the old mould of the Mangkubumi-Mangkunĕgara hatred, but to judge from later events it is probable that the Surakarta Crown Prince was the true instigator.

In June 1788 a grandson of Mangkunĕgara, the later Mangkunĕgara II (1796–1835), was raised to the rank of *pangeran* and was given a new name as was customary. But this was no ordinary name: he was called Surja Mangkubumi. The use of 'Mangkubumi' infuriated the Sultan, whose own name it was, and he

---

³⁶ Sĕmarang to Batavia, 5 July 1788 and 29 Aug. 1788, in KA 3708 (OB 1789).
³⁷ Id., 29 Aug. 1788, in KA 3708 (OB 1789).
³⁸ Hartsinck's appointment is reported in id. 12 June 1788, in KA 3708 (OB 1789).

took this as an affront to his dignity. But he left the matter to the Dutch to adjudicate, merely threatening to stop all official correspondence with Surakarta if the name was not changed. The Dutch were reluctant to interfere in this sensitive area of royal names and titles, but nevertheless they urged Pakubuwana III to withdraw the name. The latter saw this as an intrusion into his own prerogatives and Mangkunĕgara took it as an insult to himself. But the Company's influence over the old Susuhunan had usually been sufficient to achieve the desired end and in September 1788 the name was withdrawn. Mangkunĕgara's grandson was now renamed Surja Prangwadana.[39] For the second time the Dutch had forced this grandson to be renamed, having prevented the use of the name Surja Mataram in 1780.[40]

When Greeve was in Surakarta in late July 1788, he spoke with Mangkunĕgara about the various complaints concerning his behaviour. He was said to be unduly quick to take offence and was accused of not behaving in general as a loyal subject of the Susuhunan. For instance, a few days previously one of Mangkunĕgara's subjects had been arrested for horse-stealing and Mangkunĕgara had sent an armed party to take back the culprit from Pakubuwana III's officials. Greeve spoke, too, of Palm's reports about the supposed secret correspondence with Ratu Bĕndara, which Mangkunĕgara entirely denied. He seemed indeed to be unaware that he had even been so accused, which seems somewhat unlikely although not impossible. In any case, Greeve believed him completely. Mangkunĕgara said he would henceforth regard Ratu Bĕndara as if she were dead and would never again ask for her as his wife, a promise which he did not fulfil,

[39] Sĕmarang to Batavia, 12 June 1788, 27 Aug. 1788, and 29 Aug. 1788, in KA 3708 (OB 1789); Hartsinck to Sĕmarang, 26 Aug. 1788, in KA 3708 (OB 1789); Sĕmarang to HB I, 29 Aug. 1788, in KA 3708 (OB 1789); HB I to Sĕmarang, 1 Bĕsar A.J. 1714 (received 4 Sept. 1788), in KA 3708 (OB 1789); Hartsinck to Sĕmarang, 5 Sept. 1788, in KA 3708 (OB 1789); Sĕmarang to Batavia, 10 Sept. 1788, in KA 3708 (OB 1789); Poensen, 'Mangkubumi', p. 313.

The official correspondence which HB I threatened to stop was that concerning the enforcement of legal agreements between the courts, notifications of marriages, deaths, etc.

The name Prangwadana came to be used in the nineteenth century as a title for the princes Mangkunĕgara until about their fortieth year, when they took the full title of Pangeran Adipati Arja Mangkunĕgara; see Rouffaer, 'Vorstenlanden', pp. 266-8.

[40] On the 1780 episode, see above, p. 262.

CRISIS IN SURAKARTA, 1787-1790

as will be seen below. Mangkunĕgara also made clear to Greeve that he, too, had reason for complaint. He specifically listed the insults done to him by the divorce of Ratu Bĕndara and her subsequent remarriage, by the failure to return to him subjects who fled to Jogjakarta, and by the necessity twice to retract names given to his grandson. But Greeve's personal conversation with Mangkunĕgara seems to have calmed the old prince, who was apparently reassured that the Company would not abandon him from its continued protection.[41]

Greeve then proceeded to visit Jogjakarta, where his reception was hardly of the kind which was to be expected during a visit by the Sĕmarang Governor to a Javanese court. The visit was so full of danger and animosity that Greeve began seriously to fear that trouble was to come from Jogjakarta rather than from Mangkunĕgara or the Surakarta Crown Prince. The Jogjakarta Crown Prince was now the dominant influence in the *kraton*, although the old Sultan was presumably still capable of exerting a moderating influence. Mangkubumi had never feared the Dutch, but he knew it was more profitable to manipulate than to offend them, a lesson which his son, to judge from his later career as Sultan, never learned until it was too late. Apparently because of the Crown Prince's influence, Greeve had to undergo a series of comedy-of-errors events at the Jogjakarta *kraton* which seriously threatened the well-being and even the lives of himself and his companions.

The first notable event of Greeve's visit was pleasant enough: a tour of the ninth-century ruins of Tjaṇḍi Prambanan and Tjaṇḍi Sewu. There he and his party saw

> many remains of heathen temples, some of which were already entirely dilapidated, but others still displayed themselves very well, and wherein various images of idols were placed which were maintained to have originated from the Brahmins, whereas the temples as well as the images have very much in common with those which up to the present are still found on the Coromandel Coast and Malabar . . .
>
> According to the evidence of the Javanese, the entire area . . . is strewn with thousands of such remains.

But Greeve's formal reception in Jogjakarta on 5 August 1788 was very much less entertaining. Accompanied in his coach by

---

[41] Sĕmarang to Batavia, 29 Aug. 1788, in KA 3708 (OB 1789); MN, Memorie, under date 10 Sept. 1788, in KA 3708 (OB 1789).

the new Surakarta Resident Hartsinck, Greeve passed between two rows of armed Jogjakarta soldiers who proceeded to fire a welcoming salute. Their weapons, however, were pointed not into the air but directly at the coach carrying the Dutchmen. The troops must have had no shot in their guns, for the Governor could hardly have escaped assassination if that had been intended. His horses panicked but were eventually brought under control. The Susuhunan's son Pangeran Ngabei, who had accompanied the Governor from Surakarta, flung himself from the second coach in the procession and climbed into the door of Greeve and Hartsinck's coach, ready to defend them. But the salute had only, it seems, been intended as a gesture. Greeve had been welcomed to the Jogjakarta of the Crown Prince.

When the Governor was formally received by the court, Mangkubumi excused himself from drinking wine, thereby escaping the usual series of formal toasts, in which the Sultan did not even pretend to join by raising an empty glass. And the Crown Prince failed to accompany the Governor back to his coach, as the Surakarta Crown Prince had done during Greeve's visit there. The Jogjakarta Resident subsequently told the Sultan and the Crown Prince that the Governor was displeased with these changes in protocol and they agreed to conform with the usual procedures thereafter. But again, a gesture had been made.

The following day Mangkubumi proposed that on 8 August they should have a fireworks display in front of the still incomplete Dutch fortress. In Surakarta Greeve had observed a similar exhibition which had ended by setting alight and destroying a large collection of building materials intended for the construction of a new mosque. He now feared that a similar fate awaited the Jogjakarta fortress and told Mangkubumi that he would allow a fireworks display if it took place in front of the *kraton*, but not before the fortress. The Sultan said there had been no fires started on previous occasions, but the rather nervous Greeve again refused. Mangkubumi insisted. If anything were damaged, he would pay for its rebuilding. Greeve refused, and Mangkubumi now dropped the subject. But the Governor's misadventures had only begun.

On Wednesday 6 August, Greeve was treated to a tour of the new *kraton* fortifications which had so alarmed the Dutch in 1785. He was accompanied by the Crown Prince himself and a troop of armed men, as well as by the Susuhunan's son and the Dutch Resident van Ijsseldijk. They went to the walls on horseback but rather than stopping at the foot of the fortifications the horses were ridden up to the top of the wall itself. There the Governor surveyed his precarious position and deemed it prudent to dismount and to continue the tour on foot, no doubt to the delight of the Crown Prince. Again the Governor had been forced to show fear.

On Thursday a tiger-and-buffalo fight was staged. Greeve was, of course, unaware of the symbolic significance of these contests for the Javanese, in which the tiger represented the Dutch and the buffalo the Javanese. The tiger engaged the buffalo but as usual soon lost its taste for battle and retired to a corner. The Governor was apparently bored with the progress of the contest and proposed to the Sultan that a second tiger also be introduced to see if it would join forces with the first against the buffalo. The Governor 'opined that the fight would not only be rather more amusing, but also it would be all the buffalo could do to defend himself'. The Sultan approved of this innovation and was 'exceedingly curious' to see the outcome. The new tiger was introduced and it attacked the buffalo furiously but without encouraging the first tiger to take any part. The new tiger soon retreated to a resting place where it was joined by the first tiger. As was the usual practice, the tigers were now prodded with burning brands to get them to return to battle. But this only infuriated them and they ferociously fought each other rather than the buffalo.

Shortly both tigers expired, battered as much by one another as by the buffalo. Greeve's diary reports:

All of this not a little amused the Sultan as well as the Governor and the remaining party, and gave rise to various allusive conversations about previous events . . .
After this fight was thus ended, the Sultan affirmed once again his pleasure at the Governor's innovation, saying that in the future he would do this more often, . . . which compliment was replied to by the Governor in a friendly fashion.

One can only regret that Greeve did not record the nature of these 'allusive conversations'. But it seems reasonably certain that once again a tiger–buffalo contest had been a symbolic resolution of a Dutch–Javanese confrontation. And as usual the 'Javanese' buffalo had won. In this case, the 'Dutch' tiger had even had reinforcements but this had only resulted in the two tigers assisting the buffalo in killing each other. It is hardly surprising that Mangkubumi said he intended to do this again.

On Friday Greeve took gifts to the Sultan and his women, including two silver spittoons for the Sultan, rather improbably adorned with silver filigree tulips. Mangkubumi then took Greeve to see the pride of his old age, the pleasure-garden complex of *Taman Sari*. But not even there could Greeve take his ease. The Governor and the Sultan rode in a gilded boat to one of the buildings which rose out of the water. The Sultan displayed a remarkable vitality for his age by climbing the steps from the water and hiding himself in one of the rooms, forcing his companions to play hide-and-seek. In another building the old Sultan began to dance and animated the entire company to join him. Finally they returned to the *kraton* and observed that evening a fireworks display, well away from the walls of the Company's fortress.

Greeve must have been by now rather exhausted and perhaps more than a little intimidated. Fortunately the weekend was a quiet one, but on Monday 11 August the formal festivities resumed their careening course. A hunt of stags (*hartebeesten*) took place, in which the animals were driven past the huntsmen. The Dutch troops from Sĕmarang were invited by Mangkubumi to try capturing some of the animals alive, but Greeve had to order a halt to the exercise when one of the Sĕmarang dragoons was trampled underfoot and slightly wounded. The following Wednesday, Greeve visited one of the Crown Prince's retreats (the *Radjawinangun*). A salute was fired by the Prince's troops, whereupon one of the Javanese guns exploded and wounded a nearby European artilleryman. Greeve must have been relieved when he was finally able to leave Jogjakarta on Friday 15 August, having extended his stay by several days to please the Sultan.[42]

[42] The description of the visit to Jogjakarta is taken from Greeve, Dagregister, 20 Aug. 1788, in KA 3708 (OB 1789). Selections from Greeve's Dagregister are to be found in the notes to Frederik Jacob Rothenbühler, 'Dagregister of dagelijksche Aanteekeningen van het Voorgevallene ter Geleegentheid van de Verwisseling van de . . . vacant geraakte Troon van het Djocjocartasche Rijk, en de daartoe gedane Reis door den Wel. Ed. Gestr. Heer Mr. Pieter Gerardus van Overstraten . . .', *TBG*, vol. 27 (1882), pp. 353–9.

During his visit to the *Radjawinangun*, Greeve also saw for the first time the Crown Prince's corps of mounted female troops, for which the Prince later gained some notoriety during his reign as HB II.

The visit to Jogjakarta was not entirely dedicated to the intimidation of the Governor, although that seems to have been one of its most important aspects for the Jogjakarta court. The Sultan and the Crown Prince were also concerned to arrange several matters of importance as they wished them, in an atmosphere conducive to the Governor's agreement. Danurědja was by now old, and sometimes ill, and the Governor suggested a successor should be named. Mangkubumi agreed, but appointed as the *patih's* assistant and successor in case of death his own choice, Raden Tuměnggung Natajuda, who was Mangkubumi's son-in-law and who had formerly been married to a daughter of Danurědja who had died. The Sultan rejected Greeve's candidate, who was Danurědja's son Arja Mandura. Greeve told Batavia it was best to leave the choice to Mangkubumi, even though the *patih* was the single appointment over which the Dutch shared control by treaty.[43]

Mangkubumi was also concerned about the succession of his son as the next Sultan. The old Sultan was periodically unwell now, although Greeve nevertheless had good cause to comment on the Sultan's vitality. Mangkubumi was also developing the useful elderly attribute of selective attention:

For hours he can sit and day-dream and immediately forget that which occurred a moment before, while again concerning matters relating to ceremony and splendour he shows surprising evidence of memory.[44]

The question of the succession was one of the subjects which earned the Sultan's full attention. The Dutch were still unwilling to bind themselves absolutely to recognize the succession of the Crown Prince, whose general conduct had not given them much cause for satisfaction. Nevertheless, they had long since learned there was little point in disagreeing with the Sultan. He pressed Greeve for Dutch confirmation of the succession, and finally, at the end of October 1788, the Company relented and gave the Sultan what he desired, a written act guaranteeing the succession of the Crown Prince, providing of course his conduct remained proper.[45]

[43] Sěmarang to Batavia, 9 May 1788 and 29 Aug. 1788, in KA 3708 (OB 1789).
[44] Id., 29 Aug. 1788, in KA 3708 (OB 1789). HB I's illnesses are mentioned in van Ijsseldijk to Sěmarang, 6 Sept. 1788 and 6 Nov. 1788, in KA 3708 (OB 1789); Sěmarang to Batavia, 10 Nov. 1788, in KA 3708 (OB 1789).
[45] Id., 29 Aug. 1788 and 20 Sept. 1788, in KA 3708 (OB 1789); HB I to Sěmarang, 7 Muharram A.J. 1715 (received 11 Oct. 1788), in KA 3708 (OB 1789); van Ijsseldijk to Sěmarang, 6 Nov. 1788, in KA 3708 (OB 1789);

The Sultan also objected again to the revised ceremonial whereby felicitations were to be paid to each new Governor-General at Sĕmarang rather than Batavia, to which Mangkubumi had never agreed. Greeve said the Company's position on this had not changed since 1781, when Siberg had unsuccessfully attempted to convince Mangkubumi to send his emissaries to Sĕmarang.[46] Mangkubumi still wished to send Danurĕdja to greet Governor-General Alting (1780–96), but the Company was now in the curious position of actually refusing one of its 'vassals' a mission to Batavia to pay 'homage', as it would have been seen by the Company. That the Sultan's concern was for his own position as seen by his subjects rather than for any obligations of vassalage is suggested by Greeve's report. He said Mangkubumi wanted to send a mission 'in order that it should again appear to his subjects that he still lived, even as before, in close friendship with his grandfather the Governor-General and the Council of the Indies'. The traditional ideas which lay behind this view of the relationship with Batavia are discussed in Chapter XI. But in 1788 the Dutch would not arrange for a mission to Batavia. Mangkubumi therefore took the view that the Company now considered the situation to be the same as if his *patih* had been to Batavia, although of course he had gone nowhere at all. The Dutch simply dropped the subject.[47]

The result of this most unpleasant trip to Jogjakarta was a fear on the part of the Dutch that the Sultan was preparing to make trouble when Pakubuwana III died in Surakarta. Greeve told Batavia:

> This conduct of the Sultan seems to me so strange and improper that I can ascribe it to nothing other than to his old age and the obstinate, trifling fickleness which accompanies his advanced years, and of which I encountered so many tokens during my presence in Jogjakarta that it should be regarded as a desirable matter for the Company's interest

---

Sĕmarang to Batavia, 10 Nov. 1788, in KA 3708 (OB 1789) (the 'Acte', dated 31 Oct. 1788, is an appendix to this letter); id., 24 Dec. 1788, in KA 3754 (OB 1790).

[46] Discussed above, pp. 249–53.
[47] Sĕmarang to Batavia, 29 Aug. 1788, in KA 3708 (OB 1789); HB I to Sĕmarang, 1 Bĕsar A.J. 1714 (received 4 Sept. 1788), in KA 3708 (OB 1789).

if the Sultan's death should anticipate that of the Susuhunan, since it would not surprise me if, because of his growing peevishness, one from time to time became embroiled by this aged ruler in cases which could be most pernicious for the peace of Java.[48]

Greeve had made two mistakes. The first was to believe Mangkubumi was primarily responsible for the unpleasantries in Jogjakarta, whereas they were almost surely a result of the Crown Prince's initiative. His second and more dangerous error was to identify Jogjakarta as the most probable source of crisis in Central Java. An explosion was by now building in Surakarta but the Dutch were looking in the wrong direction.

Despite the Surakarta Crown Prince's previous suspicious conduct and his well-known dislike of Europeans, the Company took a cautiously favourable view of him. His reception of Greeve at Surakarta had been outwardly friendly[49] and by September 1788 Greeve had begun to propose to Batavia that it would be best if the Susuhunan, who was by then very ill, should abdicate in favour of his son.[50] While in Surakarta, Greeve had heard various dignitaries express the opinion that the Sultanate of Jogjakarta would revert to Surakarta control upon Mangkubumi's death,[51] but he does not seem to have recognized this as a forewarning that trouble was to come from the direction of Surakarta.

At the beginning of September 1788, the Jogjakarta Crown Prince undertook a pleasure-trip which seemed to confirm the Company's view that Jogjakarta was to be the source of conflict. Accompanied by some of his brothers and sons and a small retinue which included his women, the Crown Prince rode to Dĕlanggu, well within the boundaries of Surakarta. The following day he returned peaceably to Jogjakarta. But the Surakarta Resident, Mangkunĕgara, and the Susuhunan's court reacted strongly, perhaps seeing this as the first step of an invasion designed to reunify Java. They sent out troops to guard the old Kartasura *kraton*, which seems to have been considered the site where such a reunification would begin. The Sultan and the Jogjakarta Resident denied that the Crown Prince had any such intent and the

[48] Sĕmarang to Batavia, 29 Aug. 1788, in KA 3708 (OB 1789).
[49] Ibid.; see also Siberg, Memorie, 18 Sept. 1787, in dJ xii, p. 84.
[50] Sĕmarang to Batavia, 20 Sept. 1788, in KA 3708 (OB 1789).
[51] Id., 29 Aug. 1788, in KA 3708 (OB 1789).

Company did not pursue the matter.[52] If the Prince had had any warlike intentions, he would surely have gone with a larger force and without female companions. That is not to say this excursion was without significance as a gesture of independence and authority by the Crown Prince. But the most important effects of this incident were again to focus Dutch apprehensions upon Jogjakarta and to raise the general level of tension across the boundaries of the two Javanese kingdoms.

By now Susuhunan Pakubuwana III was fast approaching the end of his reign. He had been in poor health for much of his life. In 1787 and 1788 he had often been very ill, and was now also growing blind. In 1787, with Batavia's approval, the Crown Prince had begun to represent his father on public occasions.[53] On 21 September 1788, Pakubuwana III asked Greeve to hasten to Surakarta, for his end was near. The Governor arrived on 25 September and the following morning the Susuhunan died. Greeve immediately secured the *kraton* with the 181 troops he had brought from Sĕmarang and called all of the Surakarta dignitaries to the court to hold them under observation, excepting Mangkunĕgara. He had been discovered making preparations to go to the *kraton* with a large armed party, and the Crown Prince claimed he had also attempted to get possession of the Susuhunan's *pusaka kris*. Mangkunĕgara was therefore ordered to stay in his *dalĕm*, which he did.[54]

On 29 September the Crown Prince became Susuhunan Pakubuwana IV (1788–1820). He signed and swore to the Contracts

[52] Hartsinck to Sĕmarang, 2 Sept. 1788, in KA 3708 (OB 1789); Sĕmarang to Batavia, 3 Sept. 1788, in KA 3708 (OB 1789); Sĕmarang to Hartsinck, 3 Sept. 1788, in KA 3708 (OB 1789); Hartsinck to Sĕmarang, 3 Sept. 1788, in KA 3708 (OB 1789); van Ijsseldijk to Sĕmarang, 6 Sept. 1788, in KA 3708 (OB 1789); van Ijsseldijk to HB I, 6 Sept. 1788, in KA 3708 (OB 1789); HB I to van Ijsseldijk, 6 Sept. 1788, in KA 3708 (OB 1789); Sĕmarang to Batavia, 10 Sept. 1788, in KA 3708 (OB 1789); Batavia to H.XVII, 14 Nov. 1788, in dJ xii, pp. 151–6. See also Poensen, 'Mangkubumi', pp. 326–7.
[53] Sĕmarang to Batavia, 27 Sept. 1787, in KA 3707 (OB 1789); Palm to Sĕmarang, 27 Nov. 1787, in KA 3707 (OB 1789); Sĕmarang to Batavia, 30 Nov. 1787, in KA 3707 (OB 1789); id., 22 Dec. 1787, in KA 3708 (OB 1789); Palm to Sĕmarang, 23 Dec. 1787, in KA 3708 (OB 1789); Sĕmarang to Batavia, 29 Jan. 1788, 12 June 1788, 5 July 1788, 29 Aug. 1788, and 10 Sept. 1788, in KA 3708 (OB 1789).
[54] PB III to Sĕmarang, 19 Bĕsar A.J. 1714 (21 Sept. 1788), in KA 3708 (OB 1789); Sĕmarang to Batavia, 21 Sept. 1788, in KA 3708 (OB 1789); Greeve, Surakarta, to Batavia, 26 Sept. 1788, in KA 3708 (OB 1789); Batavia to H.XVII, 14 Nov. 1788, in dJ xii, pp. 156–8.

CRISIS IN SURAKARTA, 1787-1790

with the Company and Greeve proclaimed his accession. Mangkunĕgara was brought by Greeve to the *kraton* and there paid homage to his new king. But in his manner he made clear his reluctance to recognize the succession and Greeve was forced to threaten him with the Company's displeasure. To ensure their good conduct, Mangkunĕgara and the new Susuhunan's brothers, his father-in-law Pangeran Purbaja, and other princes were required to add their signatures to the Contract.[55] Greeve did not leave Surakarta until 7 October, by which time he felt that the tensions of succession had been successfully surmounted. The rice which Javanese farmers had begun to hide away shortly before the old Susuhunan's death, in anticipation of the disorder which was expected to attend that event, had again begun to appear on the markets.[56] Before departing, Greeve took the opportunity to instruct the new Susuhunan how his kingdom should be governed.[57]

The Company was relieved that there had been none of the expected trouble from Mangkunĕgara or the Sultan. The Company's military forces in Java in 1788 were limited and in a major war could hardly have achieved even the stalemate which had produced the treaties of Gijanti and Salatiga over three decades before. The Company had, however, recently received reinforcements in the form of Netherlands government naval forces, the squadrons of van Braam and Staringh.[58] In September 1788 the Dutch frigates *Scipio* and *de Valk* were sent to Governor Greeve at Sĕmarang. Greeve decided to send the Captains of these frigates, Abraham Kuvel and Engelbertus Lucas, on a visit to the Javanese courts to impress upon the rulers, in particular upon the Sultan, that no matter how weak the Company appeared there were Netherlands government forces ready to defend the Dutch

---

[55] PB IV–VOC, Acte van Verband, 29 Sept. 1788, in KA 3708 (OB 1789); PB IV–VOC, Contract van Vriend- en Bondgenootschap, 29 Sept. 1788, in dJ xii, pp. 133–45; VOC Proclamatie, 29 Sept. 1788, in KA 3708 (OB 1789); Greeve, Surakarta, to Batavia, 1 Oct. 1788, in KA 3708 (OB 1789); A. Kuvel, Report, 28 Oct. 1788, in dJ xii, p. 148; Batavia to H.XVII, 14 Nov. 1788, in dJ xii, pp. 157–9.

The death of PB III and the succession of PB IV are described in *B. Mang.*, pp. 482–5, including a death-bed speech in which PB III admonishes his son not to break with the VOC or HB I. See also Poensen, 'Mangkubumi', pp. 331–2.

[56] Sĕmarang to Batavia, 15 Oct. 1788, in KA 3708 (OB 1789).
[57] Batavia to H.XVII, 14 Nov. 1788, in dJ xii, p. 159.
[58] See dJ xii, pp. ix–x.

position. The two Captains thus prepared to depart with a large retinue 'in order to impress [the rulers] as much as possible'.[59]

These Captains accompanied Greeve to Surakarta when Pakubuwana III died and his son succeeded. When Greeve returned to Sěmarang, the two naval officers proceeded to visit Jogjakarta. The Sultan's reception suggested that this display of Dutch power was rather ineffective. He at first refused to receive them with any special honours such as they had enjoyed at Surakarta, but then changed his mind. Their talk with the Sultan, however, consisted largely of listening to a denunciation of Mangkunĕgara.[60] The Sultan seems not to have been much intimidated by his visitors. The Pakualaman *babad*, although not always a reliable source, adds a detail which is illuminating if it is true. After the two Captains had departed, the Sultan reportedly called his sons to him and spoke to them of the visitors. Then he read from a *babad* the story of the *tĕnung Wĕlanda* (Dutch magician) from the time of Pakubuwana I (1703–19).[61] This story, to be found in the various versions of the *Babad Tanah Djawi*,[62] describes an encounter between Pangeran Pugĕr (Pakubuwana I) and the *tĕnung Wĕlanda*, who was sent out by Batavia to defeat the Javanese king in supernatural powers (*kasĕkten*) and then to kill him. By mistaken identity the *tĕnung* believed Pugĕr rather than Amangkurat III (1703–8) to be the king. But Pugĕr's *kasĕkten* was greater than that of the *tĕnung Wĕlanda* and the latter was reduced to the size of a child. Pugĕr than ordered him to return whence he came, to *sabrang* (overseas). If it is true that Mangkubumi read the *tĕnung* story to his children, he must have intended it as a lesson that, no matter how powerful the naval captains seemed to be, the might of a true Javanese ruler was sufficient to overpower them. The Jogjakarta notables seem by now to have become convinced that the Company was no longer a serious military threat to them. The officials of the Company were not likely to have disagreed.

[59] Sěmarang to van Ijsseldijk and Hartsinck, 19 Sept. 1788, in KA 3708 (OB 1789); Sěmarang to Batavia, 20 Sept. 1788, in KA 3708 (OB 1789); A. Kuvel, Report, 28 Oct. 1788, in dJ xii, pp. 145–6. Quotation from Kuvel's Report.
[60] A. Kuvel, Report, 28 Oct. 1788, in dJ xii, pp. 147–50.
[61] Poensen, 'Mangkubumi', pp. 329–30.
[62] *BK*, ff. 513^v–515^r; *BTDj(BP)*, vol. xvi, pp. 52–5; *BTDj*, text pp. 264–5, trans. pp. 272–4.

The details of these various versions differ slightly. The *BK* text is perhaps the very book from which HB I read this story.

The military ascendancy of Jogjakarta in Central Java was now at a peak. During his forty years of rule the old Sultan had built up a powerful and unified kingdom which contrasted sharply with the general decline and dissolution experienced both by Surakarta and by the Company. The succession of the younger generation with its rivalries and intrigues would greatly weaken Jogjakarta. But in the late 1780s, in the Indian summer of his reign, Mangkubumi ruled what was probably the most powerful Javanese state since the time of Sultan Agung. In October 1788, Greeve described the general Javanese political situation in this way:

Mangkunĕgara, and after him his children, will always remain the boundary-wall between the two rulers and a convenient means for the Company to make use of, as matters require, against the ascendancy of the Jogjakarta kingdom, which within a quarter-century stands to become rather considerable if that kingdom increases as greatly under the second and third rulers as it has under the present founder. At the least, if the present Susuhunan [Pakubuwana IV] does not take great pains as rapidly as possible to restore all that which has fallen into a pitiable decay because of the prolonged sickness of his father and other collateral reasons, then for certain will the kingdom of Surakarta always remain considerably inferior in power to that of Jogjakarta.[63]

Greeve also observed, as had earlier Dutch reporters, that the officials and dignitaries of Jogjakarta 'take the greatness of the kingdom to heart, just so much as those of Surakarta are to the greatest degree ignorant and indifferent'.[64]

For the first several months of his reign, the new Susuhunan undertook nothing to redress this imbalance between Surakarta and Jogjakarta. His youth, his personal mildness, and his physical weakness[65] did not suggest much was to be expected from him. The only noteworthy event of this period was the compilation upon his order of a new recension of the *Babad Tanah Djawi*. This was begun on 14 December 1788.[66] Dutch officials were uninformed

[63] Greeve, Surakarta, to Batavia, 1 Oct. 1788, in KA 3708 (OB 1789).
[64] Sĕmarang to Batavia, 15 Oct. 1788, in KA 3708 (OB 1789).
[65] Greeve, Surakarta, to Batavia, 1 Oct. 1788, in KA 3708 (OB 1789); Sĕmarang to Batavia, 11 June 1790, in KA 3802 (OB 1791).
[66] NBS 224, *Babad Tanah Djawi*, dated Ahad-Pon, 15 Rabingulawal, Alip, margeng nata kaswareng dasih [A.J. 1715]; see Djajadiningrat, *Sadjarah Bantĕn*, p. 229; Pigeaud, *Literature*, vol. ii, p. 751 (Dr. Pigeaud has confirmed that the reading of the date as A.J. 1755/A.D. 1827 is a mistake).

PB IV has a considerable reputation as a Javanese littérateur and several

of and uninterested in such courtly matters and did not consider that, in a culture in which the historical tradition is cyclical, to learn of the past is to some extent to foresee the future. The Susuhunan's new chronicle extended from early mythological history to the building of a wall around the *kraton* by Senapati, the same event which the Jogjakarta Crown Prince used as a precedent for the fortification of the Jogjakarta *kraton* in 1785. Perhaps Pakubuwana IV was particularly interested in the story of Senapati's forging of the united Mataram hegemony, the culmination of an era of partition in Javanese history. The younger generation had still to learn that, in spite of Senapati's example, the division of Mataram was a necessary solution to the long-standing problems of Javanese political life. Now one of the younger generation was actually in control of a *kraton* and he would soon reveal how unpalatable he found the partition. But the Dutch, unaware of all this, continued to focus their attention upon Jogjakarta.

Events in Jogjakarta continued to suggest to the Company that the Sultanate was the primary source of instability in Java. There were, indeed, tensions there. In particular, Mangkubumi's advancing age was apparently making him less subtle in his political affairs. He and the Crown Prince sent emissaries to the new Susuhunan to urge him to take some sort of action against Mangkunĕgara. This was a misjudgement of the new ruler, who was not amenable to pressure from his great-uncle the Sultan. He informed the Dutch of these overtures and, with Dutch encouragement, then refused to receive a formal mission of felicitation from Jogjakarta.[67] Mangkubumi also tried to convince the Company that Mangkunĕgara was their main enemy, comparing him with Surapati. He said Hartingh had assured him at Gijanti that the Company would be the enemy of Mangkunĕgara's family to the seventh

---

texts are ascribed to his authorship. See Poerbatjaraka, *Pandji-Verhalen onderling Vergeleken* (Bandung, 1940), p. 361 n. 3; and Pigeaud, *Literature*, at the pages cited under PB IV's name in vol. iii, Index. These should, however, be compared with J. W. Winter's highly critical description of PB IV in 'Beknopte Beschrijving', pp. 38, 41.

[67] Van Ijsseldijk to Greeve, Surakarta, 2 Oct 1788, in KA 3708 (OB 1789); Greeve, Surakarta, to van Ijsseldijk, 3 Oct. 1788, in KA 3708 (OB 1789); PB IV to HB I, 3 Oct. 1788, in KA 3708 (OB 1789); van Ijsseldijk to Greeve, Surakarta, 5 Oct. 1788, in KA 3708 (OB 1789); Sĕmarang to Batavia, 15 Oct. 1788, in KA 3708 (OB 1789); HB I to Sĕmarang, under date 15 Oct. 1788, in KA 3708 (OB 1789).

generation. But the Dutch were now firmly committed to maintaining Mangkunĕgara as the makeweight of the Javanese balance-of-power, which they knew was the only guarantee of their continued presence in Java.[68] They had again demonstrated that their three decades of alliance with Mangkubumi meant nothing when it came to the main point of the alliance, the destruction of Mangkunĕgara. It is a comment upon the Sultan's intransigence that he could still not accept this fact.

Two developments late in 1788 and early in 1789 also suggested that the aged Sultan felt he was perhaps losing some of his authority within Jogjakarta, which he now wished to regain. There can be little doubt that the Crown Prince was by now virtually in control of court affairs, whether or not he had formally been given such control by his father in 1785 as was claimed in *Babad Mangkubumi*.[69] Rumours from Surakarta may already have begun to suggest that there were doubts about the legitimacy of the Sultanate, which perhaps led Mangkubumi to feel that he must now retake personal control of the affairs of state and re-enhance his authority. In December 1788 Mangkubumi, who had used the Islamic titles *Sultan* and *Kalipatulah* (God's caliph) for over thirty-three years, suddenly asked the Dutch to provide transport for a mission to Mecca. He desired to solicit there 'priestly investiture' (*priesterlijke waardigheid*) and to repair a 'consecrated house' which his ancestors had constructed. The Dutch agreed, and by February 1790 a mission of five was on its way by a Dutch ship to Ceylon, whence they would make their own way to Mecca.[70] It seems unlikely that these emissaries could have returned to Jogjakarta before the Sultan's death in 1792. Such a mission may have reflected a heightened religious awareness in the aged Sultan, but it is equally likely that it reflected a sense of insecurity about the élite recognition of his titles and, therefore, of his position as ruler.

In January 1789, Mangkubumi reacted more directly against his son's authority in Jogjakarta. It is to be presumed that the

---

[68] Greeve, Surakarta, to Batavia, 1 Oct. 1788, in KA 3708 (OB 1789); HB I, Geschrift, under date 1 Oct. 1788, in KA 3708 (OB 1789); van Ijsseldijk to Greeve, Surakarta, 7 Oct. 1788, in KA 3708 (OB 1789).

[69] See above, pp. 280-2.

[70] Sĕmarang to Batavia, 24 Dec. 1788, in KA 3754 (OB 1790); id., 14 March 1789, in KA 3753 (OB 1790); id., 27 Feb. 1790, in KA 3800 (OB 1791).

Sultan Agung (1613-45), the only previous Mataram ruler to use the title Sultan, had solicited it from Mecca; see de Graaf, 'Sultan Agung', pp. 264-8.

intrigues among the Sultan's sons which typified the reign of Hamĕngkubuwana II were already well under way. The old Sultan was possibly incapable of controlling the machinations of several adult sons, and reacted by trying to take back all authority to himself. He may also have been encouraged to do this by early reports of the impending threat from Surakarta. Mangkubumi accused the aged Danurĕdja and the *kraton* functionaries of showing too much deference to the Crown Prince. He took from them all their *upatjara* (*cieraaden*, regalia of authority) and made them sit in the open on the *alun-alun* for more than two days in the midst of monsoon downpours before forgiving them. He sent the dignitaries home without receiving them in person, commanding them never to obey orders from the Crown Prince until they had fulfilled any orders given them by himself.[71] This incident suggested that Mangkubumi had not lost the fire of his youth, but it is unlikely that the Crown Prince's influence would have been greatly or for long diminished. The Prince must have handled his father with greater care thereafter and tolerated more overt direction of affairs by the Sultan. But the old Sultan was now well over seventy and had in fact only three more years to live. The courtly élite would have been inclined to attach themselves to rising, not setting, stars.

The Dutch were meanwhile finding the Sultan to be difficult in all manner of minor questions. He was, for example, constantly urging them to provide more pistols and carbines for himself and the Crown Prince. His health was doubtful, and Greeve expected he would very soon have to proceed to Jogjakarta to regulate the succession of the Crown Prince.[72]

With Dutch apprehensions fixed firmly on Jogjakarta, the crisis in Surakarta began almost unnoticed in the first months of 1789. From early 1789 until late 1790 Java approached the brink of renewed civil war. The new Susuhunan was not the inconsequential youth so many had believed him to be and he now took steps which posed the first great threat to the divided kingdom and to the position of the East India Company on the coasts. A detailed treatment of this crisis will require a separate monograph. It

[71] Sĕmarang to Batavia, 2 Feb. 1789, in KA 3754 (OB 1790). In 1792 Danurĕdja was said to be 79 years old; id., 25 April 1792, in dJ xii, p. 265.

[72] Id., 14 March 1789 and 18 April 1789, in KA 3754 (OB 1790); id., 30 Dec. 1789, in KA 3802 (OB 1791).

CRISIS IN SURAKARTA, 1787-1790

cannot be done justice as a subsidiary part of a study of the reign of Mangkubumi. But since such a monograph does not yet exist, the main developments of the crisis will be described here with emphasis on the role of Jogjakarta.[73]

In early 1789 Pakubuwana IV began to show an unusual inclination for public demonstrations of religious conviction, and was reported to have taken on a 'gloominess of spirit'. The Company suspected this had to do with the recent death of his wife, the daughter of Pangeran Purbaja.[74] But high Surakarta officials said it was a result of the oath which rulers took to observe religious affairs, which was carried out with greater exactitude by some than by others. At first the Dutch regarded this as a matter of no great importance, but in March 1789 the Susuhunan suddenly began to remove high officials from office and to replace them with members of a new group of religious advisers in the *kraton*, whom the Dutch as usual called 'priests' (*paepen*). By September 1789, reports had begun to connect some of these new advisers with Wirjakusuma, whom the Dutch had banished in April 1787 for turning the then-Crown Prince against themselves. The Susuhunan was now said to be surrounded by *santris* (religious) and was diligent in his attendance at the mosque on Fridays. Religious influence was also seen in his forbidding his officials to use opium, a step which the Dutch disliked for mercantile reasons since opium was controlled by them. The Susuhunan was also reported to be making secret nocturnal visits to the residence of his new chief adviser, Arja Manduraredja, or to the mosque, for unknown but apparently suspicious purposes. The Dutch Resident Hartsinck reported late in April 1789 that these visits had stopped but the Company was soon to learn that once again it had a Resident in Surakarta upon whom it could not rely. Late in 1789, Pakubuwana

[73] The documentation on this crisis is enormous and it would be impossible to cite here each individual item of correspondence. In the following pages, individual items will be cited where they are of particular importance. Otherwise, the general narrative depends upon the correspondence and reports contained in the following volumes: KA 3754 (OB 1790); KA 3802 (OB 1791); KA 3833 (OB 1792); AN Solo 5, 'Soerakarta Afgaande Brieven, 1773-93'; AN Solo 36, 'Diverze Verklarings'; AN Java's Noord-Oost Kust 162, 'Bijlagen 1790'. See also dJ xii, pp. 165 ff.; Poensen, 'Mangkubumi', pp. 331 ff.; *B. Mang.*, pp. 485 ff.; *Babad Pakĕpung* (Sana Budaja MS. 123).

[74] According to a Surakarta *sĕngkala*-list written later in the reign of PB IV, she died on 21 January A.D. 1789; BM Add. MS. 12323 (B), f. 46^v: seda Kangdjĕng Ratu Purbajan, Rĕbo, ping 23 Rabingulakir, Alip, marga tunggal wiku ning rat 1715.

IV began to construct a new mosque, which was to be a replica of the famous mosque at Děmak.

The Company received a severe shock in July 1789. Their commandant at Salatiga was told by two of his Javanese soldiers with relatives in the Surakarta *kraton* that the Susuhunan and his religious advisors were plotting to slaughter all Europeans in Java. No matter how improbable the plot at first seemed, the Dutch officials began slowly to believe in it. Resident Hartsinck denied there was any substance to the rumour, but opposition to the Susuhunan and his advisers was beginning to grow within Surakarta *kraton* circles and the Dutch began to suspect that this meant very serious schemes were indeed being discussed.

In July, Mangkunĕgara expressed his firm attachment to the Company in such extensive terms that the Dutch now thought something very pernicious indeed must be brewing in the *kraton*. He proposed at the same time that trouble could be avoided by killing the Susuhunan's new advisers, but to their regret the Dutch could conceive no practical means to achieve this. The 'second *pěngulu*' of Surakarta meanwhile reported that he had admonished the Susuhunan that these advisers taught a false doctrine and as a ruler and a Muslim he should not listen to them, but Pakubuwana IV ignored this advice. It was said that the entire court were disciples of the new teachers, excepting Mangkunĕgara, the Susuhunan's uncle Pangeran Purbaja, and Pangerans Mangkudiningrat and Rongga.

The Governor of Sĕmarang, Greeve, wrote to the Susuhunan in August 1789, warning him that the new advisers, particularly two named Mandurarĕdja and Wiradigda, were dangerous to himself and to the Company. The Susuhunan replied that his courtiers assured him there was nothing to fear from these two, and thanked the Governor for his advice. Greeve wrote again, saying he was glad the Susuhunan had accepted his advice, but he had expected him to act upon it. He said the Company was unconcerned if these new advisers merely directed the Susuhunan's religious life. But their growing influence over the administration of the kingdom was a matter for Dutch concern. But the advisers' influence over the young ruler grew steadily. There was nothing the Dutch could do in the situation. Although large numbers of officials had been replaced, the Susuhunan had not yet replaced the *patih*, in whose appointment alone the Company had a voice.

The second great shock to the Dutch came in September 1789. Greeve had begun to suspect the reliability of the Surakarta Resident, Hartsinck, because the latter's reports of calm and normal conditions in the *kraton* conflicted so greatly with the rumours from all other sources. On 5 September 1789, the Second Resident at Surakarta reported that Hartsinck had been observed in the company of several of the Susuhunan's new advisers, clad in Javanese dress, going by night to a secret conference in the *kraton*. Hartsinck's explanation that he was merely assisting in the composition of letters to the Governor was not believed and in November 1789 the Company discharged him. But, incredibly, he was allowed to remain in his post for nine more months in Surakarta to finish personal affairs. Hartsinck's role in the nebulous *kraton* plotting was never made entirely clear. At the time, it was of most importance that the web of intrigue was now believed to reach even to within the Company's garrison at Surakarta. Whatever the truth of the matter, this occasioned understandable apprehension in Dutch circles. Greeve was now prepared to believe anything.[75]

By late 1789 rumours were spreading in Central Java that the Susuhunan had been endowed with supernatural powers by his new teachers. He was said to have been invisibly present in the Jogjakarta mosque. At the same time, minor rebels were beginning to appear throughout the area, responding to and further contributing to the sense of crisis. All manner of suspicious stories came to the Dutch from various quarters. It was said in Tĕgal that the religious advisers had been bribed by some high personage, whom the sources would not name but who was by implication Mangkunĕgara, to assassinate the Susuhunan. But the Susuhunan rejected this report when the Dutch used it in an attempt to persuade him to banish his advisers. Other sources said the Crown Prince of Jogjakarta had been invited to join in a plot against the Europeans, but that he had refused to do so. At the same time, both the Susuhunan and Mangkunĕgara were reported to be forming new companies of troops.

[75] Greeve was not the only victim of disloyalty to be in Java in September 1789. On the 13th of that month there arrived at Surabaja a two-master under the command of the Englishman Lt. William Bligh, the former commander of H.M.S. *Bounty*. He had made his way there after the mutiny aboard his ship in the South Pacific, and now requested passage to Batavia and on to Europe; Sĕmarang to Batavia, 25 Sept. 1789, in KA 3754 (OB 1790).

318 JOGJAKARTA UNDER SULTAN MANGKUBUMI

By now the Dutch position was extremely difficult. There was no way for them to contact the Susuhunan in order to discern the truth of the various rumours. They could not write him letters for these would be read in open court gatherings in the presence of the *santris*. A contingency plan to meet the Susuhunan secretly at Salatiga or some similar location could not be used, because the rumours had said that Pakubuwana IV's departure from the *kraton* would be the signal for the slaughter of Europeans to begin. They could not demand the surrender of the *santris* for this would merely embitter further the Susuhunan, who was prepared to defend them. They could not arrange any means of murdering the *santri* advisers without the Susuhunan learning who was responsible. They could not even be sure of the security or reliability of their own garrison in Surakarta. And the Company simply did not have the military power to march to Surakarta and capture the *kraton*, the Susuhunan, and all of the dignitaries and officials of the court.

The Jogjakarta court was meanwhile observing carefully these developments in Surakarta. *Babad Mangkubumi* describes the Jogjakarta understanding of these events:

> LXXV: 1. After two years, it is said,
> of the reign of the Susuhunan in Surakarta,
> there was a devil's plague,
> the teachings of evil men.
> Pangeran Mangkunĕgara conspired
> with his Highness the Susuhunan
> because of the teachings of
> Wiradigda and Panĕngah,
> Amad Saleh, Bahman, and Kanḍuruwan, and
> the one named Sudjanapura,
>
> 2. with Martadjaja by name:
> They advised the conquest of the kingdom of
> Jogjakarta.[76]
> . . .

---

[76] *B. Mang.*, p. 485, Canto LXXV (Ḍanḍanggula):

   1. sampun angsal kalih warsa nguni
   djumĕnĕnge Sunan Surakarta
   jwantĕn pangriḍu bĕlise
   tur ing wong tjorah wau
   Pangran Mangkunĕgara kait
   kalijan Kangdjĕng Sunan

A later comment adds further details:

LXXVII: 53. ...
   (They) undertook to annihilate the Dutch
   and to demand back the lands
  54. of the *pasisir* and Jogjakarta.[77]
   ...

Poensen's later Pakualaman *babad* confirms the view that Jogjakarta understood this to be a plot designed to reunify Central Java,[78] a direct threat to the Sultanate. This was both correct and incorrect. As will be seen below, the plot definitely involved the relegation of Jogjakarta to a secondary position junior to that of Surakarta. But it seems unlikely that the Susuhunan envisaged actual conquest of Jogjakarta or the physical annihilation of the Dutchmen. He disliked the division of the kingdom but he lacked the determination or, perhaps, the imagination to attempt a military reunification. Nevertheless, the Sultan and the Crown Prince were correct in seeing the plot as a threat to their position and they began to take steps to counter it. One of the most essential measures to be taken was to convince the Dutch after over thirty years of fruitless alliance finally to act in the interest of Jogjakarta. But this was made more difficult by the fact that the Company, although it was greatly worried about the Susuhunan's activities, had become accustomed to assume that trouble in Central Java usually originated with the Sultan.

The Dutch Resident in Jogjakarta, W. H. van Ijsseldijk (1786–99), a rather more capable man than his gullible predecessor, now

   sangking aturipun
   Wiradigda lan Paněngah
   Amad Saleh Bahman Kanḍuruwan maning
   aran Sudjanapura
  2. lan Martadjaja iku araning
   rěmbug ngrajud nagri Ngajogja
   ....

[77] Ibid., p. 510, Canto LXXVII (Pangkur):

 53. ...
   saguh njirnakěn Wělonda
   andjaběla kang něgari
  54. pasisir miwah Ngajogja
   ....

[78] Poensen, 'Mangkubumi', pp. 333, 340.

became the channel for various rumours about the plans of the *santris*. He was told that the Crown Prince of Jogjakarta had learned the *santris* were promising to drive the Europeans from Java. The Crown Prince was supposed to have declared his opposition to such an idea, saying he would always be true to the Company. He supposedly prophesied this would lead to the Susuhunan's downfall. Van Ijsseldijk doubted the entire story, saying: 'I daily experience more and more how learned are the Javanese in dissembling.' But he began to suspect there was some truth in it after all when one of the Crown Prince's brothers repeated it to him, while Danurĕdja and the Sultan took the trouble to deny it.[79] It is probable that Jogjakarta was now employing its skill in manipulating the information which the Dutch were allowed to receive. The effect was to heighten Dutch fears of the Susuhunan's plans.

In September Greeve 'secretly' solicited the Sultan's opinion of events in Surakarta. Mangkubumi encouraged his suspicions while at the same time flattering him. Greeve reported that Mangkubumi,

> this discerning ruler, by no means approves the Susuhunan's devotion to the 'priests' and indeed expressed his opinions thereupon in a manner which is not at all flattering for the Susuhunan, although at the same time he declared that he also regards my concessionary procedure towards the Susuhunan as corresponding to the conduct of a father towards his son and that the Susuhunan should be in every way grateful therefore, by making use of my advice.[80]

The Sultan was carefully manœuvring the Dutch into firmer opposition to the Susuhunan, while placing himself in position as their adviser, the elder statesman of Javanese politics.

In the first months of 1790 the Susuhunan moved towards direct confrontation with Jogjakarta. In late April or early May he gave his brother, Pangeran Arja Mataram, a new name: Pangeran Mangkubumi. The Sultan was furious, as he had been in 1788 when Mangkunĕgara's grandson had been given that name. He declared that no one but himself might use it until after he was dead. He further proposed as a general principle that the dignitaries of Jogjakarta and Surakarta should not have identical

---

[79] Van Ijsseldijk to Hartsinck, 28 July 1789, in KA 3754 (OB 1790); Sĕmarang to Batavia, 30 Sept. 1789, in KA 3754 (OB 1790); van Ijsseldijk to Sĕmarang, 4 Aug. 1789, in KA 3754 (OB 1790).

[80] Sĕmarang to Batavia, 30 Sept. 1789, in KA 3754 (OB 1790).

names. The Dutch tried to convince Pakubuwana IV to retract the name, but to no avail. It was the Company's view that this incident was Pakubuwana IV's revenge for the Sultan's success in getting the name retracted shortly before Pakubuwana III's death. They believed, quite correctly, that the matter of princely titles was entirely within the Susuhunan's prerogatives. Although they would have preferred to have the name withdrawn in order to avoid conflict, the Dutch were inclined to take the Susuhunan's side. The name was not retracted and the matter was only settled in October when the Sultan named one of his own grandsons, the son of the Crown Prince, Mangkubumi.[81] But the Sultan was correct in seeing this incident as an indication of growing belligerence in Surakarta.

More important and bellicose developments were now occurring. The right of succession of the Crown Prince of Jogjakarta was openly denied in Surakarta. The Surakarta *kraton* was said to believe that the existence of Jogjakarta was only temporary and that it would be re-absorbed under Surakarta upon Mangkubumi's death. In May 1790 Mangkunĕgara wrote to the Company claiming that he had been promised by the Dutch Resident in A.J. 1700 and again in A.J. 1710 (A.D. 1774 and 1783) that upon Mangkubumi's death he, Mangkunĕgara, would succeed to the throne of Jogjakarta. Rumours spread that the Susuhunan and Mangkunĕgara planned to block the roads to prevent the Sĕmarang Governor from reaching Jogjakarta to oversee the succession if the Sultan should die, as he was expected at any time to do. They would then take control of Jogjakarta themselves. Greeve doubted these rumours, but reported that the western route to Jogjakarta via Sĕtjang (Magĕlang) was indeed occupied by large numbers of armed forces. If this were blocked, he would be obliged to take the eastern route passing near Surakarta.

The Company quickly surveyed the military situation and found to their dismay that Mangkunĕgara had nearly 1,400 men under arms, and could summon another 4,000 immediately and more than 10,000 in two to three days. The total force available to Sĕmarang to attempt to break through to Jogjakarta was 243

[81] Van Ijsseldijk to Sĕmarang, 29 April 1790, in KA 3802 (OB 1791): Sĕmarang to Batavia, 19 May 1790, in KA 3802 (OB 1791); van Ijsseldijk to Sĕmarang, 20 May 1790, in KA 3802 (OB 1791); Sĕmarang to Batavia, 27 May 1790, 11 June 1790, 24 June 1790, 26 June 1790, and 29 July 1790, in KA 3802 (OB 1791); Greeve, Diarium, 1 Dec. 1790, in KA 3833 (OB 1792).

officers and men.⁸² Greeve told Batavia that he dared not deny Mangkunĕgara's claims outright, for he feared this would set the clock back to 1757, with the land ruined and the country flowing with blood. The Company would once again be unable to defeat Mangkunĕgara. Unlike some later historians, Greeve was fully aware that the treaties of the 1750s had not been the result of victories by Company arms. Not until September 1790 did the Company dare to deny directly Mangkunĕgara's claims.

The relationship between Mangkunĕgara's pretensions and the rumours emanating from the Susuhunan's court was not clarified at this time. It later emerged that Mangkunĕgara had been encouraged, perhaps even forced, to make these claims by the Susuhunan's *santri* advisors. But in May 1790 it was only clear that a serious threat to Jogjakarta existed.

The Sultan reacted quickly. In June he called all the princes and dignitaries to *Taman Sari*. He told them that the Dutch had assured him they regarded the Jogjakarta *kraton* as permanent, as indeed they had. He denied the Surakarta view that Jogjakarta was a temporary fief and rejected Mangkunĕgara's pretensions to his throne. The Dutch had proposed that all threats could be removed if he were to abdicate now in favour of the Crown Prince, but this Mangkubumi refused to do. He declared that if the Dutch should ever have need of his assistance he would then show them how capable he was still of demonstrating his attachment to the Company. He asked the Crown Prince whether he wished to succeed while his father lived and the Prince replied under oath that he did not. Mangkubumi told the Prince that he was a son of the Company, who had made his father Sultan, and he did not doubt that after his own death the Company would have equal regard for his son. 'If the Company is your support, who shall dare resist you?' he said. Mangkubumi gave the Crown Prince a copy of the Gijanti Contract of 1755 and told him to see whether anything in it suggested that Jogjakarta was a temporary fief. Then he required all of the officials to swear a new oath of faithfulness to himself, the Crown Prince, and the Company. The princes, sons of the Sultan, were required to go after the *Taman Sari* meeting to the Crown Prince's residence where they swore to be faithful to him, their brother. And at *Taman Sari*

---

⁸² Sĕmarang to Batavia, 19 May 1790, in KA 3802 (OB 1791); list of MN 'gewapend volk', 21 May 1790, in AN Solo 36, 'Diverze Verklarings'.

CRISIS IN SURAKARTA, 1787–1790 323

they were required to swear eternal loyalty to the Company, promising to follow all its good advice. The Sultan proceeded to denounce the use of the name Mangkubumi in Surakarta, calling it an insult to himself, the oldest living member of the entire Mataram line in Java. The dignitaries then departed.

This meeting may have been stage-managed primarily for Dutch consumption. A report of the meeting was immediately dictated by two *bupatis* to the Dutch translator. The Resident then repeated it word-for-word to Danurědja and his assistants, who attested the contents of the statement.[83] The Sultan wished to be sure there were no mistakes. That is not to suggest that no such meeting was held, for it is also mentioned in the Pakualaman *babad* although not in *Babad Mangkubumi*. But the descriptions of the meeting in the *babad* and in the report given to the Dutch Resident are rather different. Both versions were presumably designed to support particular points of view.[84] In 1790, the purpose of the report was to encourage the Dutch to see the Sultan as the offended party and to accept his view of the situation.

The Sultan was worried for very good reasons. Although Jogjakarta was more powerful than Surakarta, an attack from the latter would cause widespread destruction even if Jogjakarta troops ultimately won the day. And there were still fears that Mangkunĕgara could claim the allegiance of many Jogjakarta notables 'among whom', Greeve said, 'not a few malcontents are to be found, as much on account of the harsh administration of the Sultan as because of the stern character of the Crown Prince'.[85] Mangkunĕgara claimed that he had set up three companies of troops composed entirely of refugees from Jogjakarta.[86]

In these uncertain circumstances, the only guarantee that Java would not again be laid waste by civil war and that the Sultan might not have to test the strength of his support against Mangkunĕgara was the maintenance of the system of division. With the Susuhunan and Mangkunĕgara apparently unwilling to maintain it, the Sultan's only recourse was to win the support of the body which had made the division a necessary compromise and

[83] Relaas van het heeden morgen in de Taman voorgevallene, 20 June 1790, in KA 3802 (OB 1791).
[84] In Poensen, 'Mangkubumi', pp. 335–6, the Crown Prince is unfavourably depicted, as he is throughout this text.
[85] Sěmarang to Batavia, 19 May 1790, in KA 3802 (OB 1791).
[86] MN to Sěmarang, 11 Sawal A.J. 1716 (25 June 1790), in KA 3802 (OB 1791).

was still its ultimate arbiter, the Dutch East India Company. In the 1740s and 1750s, Mangkubumi opposed the Dutch because they prevented the ultimate victory which was nearly within his grasp. Now, several decades later, he turned to them to convince his enemies that they, too, could expect no ultimate victory. He told the Resident,

if the Susuhunan thinks to have given this my kingdom of Jogjakarta in temporary fief only to me, [then] I have also only given the kingdom of Surakarta to him in temporary fief. And if he should request of the Company that he might have back this kingdom, then shall I also ask of the Company that I might have back the kingdom of Surakarta and that Java come back under me alone.

He added that if Mangkunĕgara wished to destroy Jogjakarta then he would destroy Mangkunĕgara.[87] In other words, the system of division depended upon its continued acceptance by the Javanese élite. The role of the Dutch when members of that élite questioned the system was to deny their pretensions. If they would not do so, then Mangkubumi had as much right to expect Dutch support as had anyone else.

The Sultan's manœuvring of the Dutch had so far been relatively successful. They were growing increasingly sympathetic towards his views. But now his impatience got the better of his diplomacy; he could wait no longer for the Company to act. In June and July 1790 the troops of the Sultanate were being publicly exercised, 4,000 being reviewed on one occasion by the Crown Prince. The tensions in Central Java noticeably increased.[88] The Dutch now grew rather confused about the source of the troubles, being inclined to shift the blame alternately from Mangkunĕgara to the Sultan. In July they strengthened their garrisons at both courts, each of which included something under 200 officials of all types, but then discovered that both the Susuhunan and the Sultan refused to supply the expanded garrisons with their necessary provisions. Mangkubumi finally gave in and provided the required rice in September, but when the Dutch asked him how many men he had under arms in case it should be necessary to move against Mangkunĕgara, he refused to tell them.[89]

[87] HB I to van Ijsseldijk, 7 Sawal A.J. 1716 (21 June 1790), in KA 3802 (OB 1791).
[88] Sĕmarang to Batavia, 24 June 1790, 3 July 1790, and 29 July 1790, in KA 3802 (OB 1791).
[89] Id., 29 July 1790, in KA 3802 (OB 1791); van Ijsseldijk to Sĕmarang, 3 Sept. 1790, in KA 3833 (OB 1792).

CRISIS IN SURAKARTA, 1787-1790

On 22 July 1790, the Sultan ordered all correspondence with Surakarta to be stopped,[90] thus bringing to a halt the administration of the system of division. In June the old pattern of rebels with princely patronage had already reappeared when several brigands were apparently offered the protection and support of Mangkunĕgara's grandson Prangwadana. And by August small-scale clashes of arms were beginning to be reported.

Early in September, Jogjakarta forces attacked several Surakarta villages, which provoked reprisals from the Surakarta side. Danurĕdja confirmed to the Dutch Resident that the Sultan and the Crown Prince had ordered the conquest of all of Mangkunĕgara's lands, and the Crown Prince was said to be leading some of the troops. The Dutch, who found it difficult to know which side to take, ordered their Residents to observe an absolute neutrality but to be prepared to defend themselves. Both sides told the Company that they would withdraw if their demands were met. The Sultan demanded an oath from Mangkunĕgara and his descendants never to undertake anything against Jogjakarta. He demanded also the retraction of the name Mangkubumi for the Susuhunan's brother. Mangkunĕgara said he was ready for a reconciliation with the Sultan, but if the Company could not arrange a real and lasting *rapprochement*, which he professed to prefer, then he wished leave to take his own revenge for a lifetime of wrongs done him by the Sultan. The two senior figures were still seeking final solutions. The Susuhunan merely said his troops would withdraw if the Sultan's did.[91]

The Dutch confusion at this point about their own proper role was attributable to a basic misconception. The Company, like any bureaucracy, was unable to consider the possibility that it was

[90] Id., 27 July 1790, in KA 3802 (OB 1791).
[91] Van Reede to Sĕmarang, 2 Sept. 1790 (2 letters), in KA 3833 (OB 1792); van Ijsseldijk to Sĕmarang, 3 Sept. 1790 (2 letters), in KA 3833 (OB 1792); Danurĕdja to van Ijsseldijk, 22 Bĕsar A.J. 1716 (3 Sept. 1790), in KA 3833 (OB 1792); Sĕmarang to Batavia, 4 Sept. 1790, in dJ xii, pp. 191-4; van Reede to Sĕmarang, 6 Sept. 1790, in KA 3833 (OB 1792); Sĕmarang to Batavia, 7 Sept. 1790, in KA 3833 (OB 1792); van Ijsseldijk to Sĕmarang, 7 Sept. 1790, in KA 3833 (OB 1792); Sĕmarang to Batavia, 9 Sept. 1790, in KA 3833 (OB 1792); van Ijsseldijk to Sĕmarang, 9 Sept. 1790, in KA 3833 (OB 1792); van Ijsseldijk to van Reede, 9 Sept. 1790, in KA 3833 (OB 1792); Sĕmarang to van Ijsseldijk, 10 Sept. 1790, in KA 3833 (OB 1792); HB I to van Ijsseldijk, 9 Sura A.J. 1717 (19 Sept. 1790), in AN Java's Noord-Oost Kust 162, 'Bijlagen 1790'; various reports on hostilities, dated Bĕsar A.J. 1716 (10 Aug.-10 Sept. 1790), in AN Solo 36, 'Diverze Verklarings'.

fundamentally unreliable. The Dutch considered that the Sultan had no justification for reacting militarily against Surakarta, since they had made clear to him that they intended to ensure the regular succession of the Crown Prince of Jogjakarta. Although Surakarta was the origin of provocative claims and rumours, Jogjakarta appeared to them to be the aggressor. They could not appreciate that their years of alliance with the Sultan had convinced him that the Company could not be relied upon. The Sultan, therefore, was hardly likely to be satisfied with assurances of good faith which were not backed up by marching armies. But events were now moving very quickly indeed, and the Dutch were soon to accept completely the idea that the Susuhunan, not the Sultan or Mangkunĕgara, was the cause of all the trouble.

Early in September the Susuhunan again took a threatening step. He wrote to Greeve that he was worried about the succession in Jogjakarta, where all of Mangkubumi's sons were after their father's throne. He proposed that Jogjakarta should therefore be subdivided among those of the Sultan's sons who were of good nature. Greeve recognized that such a fragmentation was an exceedingly dangerous proposal. Not only would Jogjakarta thereby be easily dominated by Surakarta, but the principle of equal division, 'the corner-stone of the Company's dominion', would be destroyed.[92]

Greeve decided he must go personally to Central Java to settle the disputes before full-scale war began. He undertook this step with great hesitation. The Company was so weak militarily that he feared it would simply be sucked into a conflict which it had no hope of controlling. Of the small Sĕmarang garrison, 100 men were in hospital, as were many of the Surakarta and Jogjakarta garrisons. When Greeve took the able-bodied troops to Central Java, he would have to leave the defence of Sĕmarang itself largely to 'the burghers and Moors'.[93] To make his situation still more difficult, Greeve was by now acting entirely on his own, since Batavia no longer had either the time or the information to give orders to cover the situation as it changed from day to day.

[92] PB IV to Sĕmarang, 27 Bĕsar A.J. 1716 (received 9 Sept. 1790), in KA 3833 (OB 1792); Sĕmarang to Batavia, 9 Sept. 1790, in KA 3833 (OB 1792).

[93] Id., 11 Sept. 1790, in KA 3833 (OB 1792). The Diarium of Greeve, 15 Sept.– 1 Dec. 1790, is in KA 3833 (OB 1792). Selections from this diary for the dates 21 Oct.–1 Dec. are to be found in dJ xii, pp. 209–28. Unless otherwise indicated, the following description of events up to the encirclement of Surakarta and the surrender of the *santris* is based upon Greeve's diary.

CRISIS IN SURAKARTA, 1787-1790

From 16 September until 6 October 1790, Greeve was at Surakarta. He was told every sort of tale about the conflicts, which assigned the blame variously to the Sultan, the Susuhunan, Mangkunĕgara, their offspring, the *santri* advisers, and the Dutch Resident Hartsinck. And more and more Greeve's imagination was dominated above all by the growing fear that his own life was in danger. On the 26th of September the Surakarta *patih* Djajaningrat came to Greeve and asked with tears in his eyes to be relieved of his duties. With him came Pangeran Ngabei, who had thrown himself into the door of Greeve's coach in 1788 when the troops of Jogjakarta seemed about to assassinate him, whose countenance told Greeve that the *kraton* discussions must be taking a highly suspicious turn.

On the 29th the Susuhunan's uncle Pangeran Purbaja called upon Greeve and warned him of matters which Greeve felt were so serious that he feared to write them in his diary, which was being sent in instalments to Batavia. Purbaja was now becoming the leader of the *kraton* group opposed to the *santri* advisers and the main Dutch ally within Surakarta circles. Mangkunĕgara was also approaching Greeve, particularly via one Corporal Pieter Bloemhart who served as his attendant (*oppasser*), to suggest that his recent belligerent stance concerning the Jogjakarta throne had been forced upon him by the Susuhunan's advisers. He had had no choice but to go along out of fear for his and his descendants' future. He reiterated the hoary demand that Ratu Bĕndara be returned to him. Failing this, he said, he should be given 4,000 *tjatjahs* of Jogjakarta land. He would then be independent of the Susuhunan and immune to *kraton* pressure. Greeve tried to get him to accept instead 4,000 reals annually from the Company, without success. But it was clear to Greeve that Pangeran Purbaja and Mangkunĕgara, as well as other important parties within Surakarta, could be detached from the Susuhunan's party, which he was coming more and more to suspect.

On 6 October Greeve went to Jogjakarta. The Sultan and the Crown Prince met him and immediately inquired about 100 carbines which had long ago been promised by the Company. Greeve, who no doubt remembered his last eventful visit to Jogjakarta two years before, realized he could no longer postpone the matter and promised he would send the carbines upon his return to Sĕmarang.

On 7 October Greeve attempted to bluff the Sultan into cooperation, hoping he might agree to give Mangkunĕgara 4,000 *tjatjahs*. He said if Mangkubumi and the Crown Prince were unwilling to discuss Mangkunĕgara's claims, which they had rejected out of hand, then there was no point in his continued presence in Jogjakarta. He would leave the next day and the Company would take no responsibility for the consequences. This seemed at first to surprise the Sultan, but then Mangkubumi said it was good for the Governor to go and he ordered Danurĕdja to make the necessary preparations. Danurĕdja had begun to play the role of mediator between the Sultan and the Company, and it was he who had earlier advised Greeve that such a bluff might succeed. It is not clear whether or not he had done so at the orders of the Sultan, with the intention of placing the Governor in an embarrassing position to remind him who had the upper hand. In any case, Danurĕdja now protested that he had no time to prepare for a suitable departure the following day. Greeve then spoke up and said, in that case, he would wait until the day after.

Greeve, proceeding from surprise to surprise, now learned that he was about to be bribed. According to the Dutch translator, the Sultan was going to give 2,000 reals to Greeve, 1,000 to the Resident van Ijsseldijk, and a sum[94] to the translator. Greeve let it be known he could not accept this, and was told the next day (8 October) that Mangkubumi was satisfied. He had only intended the money as a sign of friendship and a contribution to Greeve's expenses. The Sultan was clearly trying anything which came to mind to get the Company finally to act.

On 10 October Greeve was back in Surakarta. On his departure from Jogjakarta he had learned that Mangkubumi was ill and he feared an imminent succession crisis. He therefore told the Jogjakarta Resident to see that three to four thousand troops of the Sultanate were sent out to occupy the Jogjakarta–Surakarta road if the Sultan should die, so that he could get back to Jogjakarta.

On 11 October the Susuhunan received Greeve, 'with so many signs of friendliness and apparent sincerity that I found myself in extreme irresoluteness and inner conflict what I should believe'. But the same day a report came through the Jogjakarta Resident that the Surakarta *kraton* had again attempted to get Jogjakarta

---

[94] Greeve's diary, 1 Dec. 1790, in KA 3833 (OB 1792), is badly soiled and the figure for the sum to be given to the translator is illegible.

CRISIS IN SURAKARTA, 1787–1790

to join in 'dangerous projects' against the Company. Mangkunĕgara was meanwhile telling Greeve that he depended on the Company to give him satisfaction against the Sultan, and full-scale war seemed about to break out at any moment. Limited hostilities were meanwhile continuing, especially in Gunung Kidul.

The Susuhunan subsequently announced he had planned a reception for Greeve on the evening of 13 October. Greeve's suspicions were aroused and the Resident told the Susuhunan that midday would be preferable 'for the darkness of the evening would detract greatly from the amusement'. The Susuhunan was then informed that Greeve intended to leave on the thirteenth, but he insisted nevertheless that the reception be held. The much-confused and much-intimidated Governor agreed.

On the evening of 12 October further ominous reports came via the Jogjakarta Resident. Greeve was now led to believe that he would be murdered on the occasion of the Susuhunan's reception. He decided to feign indisposition to avoid the affair. He told Batavia it would be necessary to join with the Sultan for an assault on the Susuhunan if the latter would not give up his *santri* advisers. He would also try at all costs to win the support of Mangkunĕgara, if necessary by promising him the Susuhunan's throne. There was no time, he said, to await the orders of Batavia.[95]

Greeve had decided the Susuhunan was the cause of the disturbances in Central Java and that extreme action was required against him. He had done so on the basis of a mass of rumour fed him by Surakarta officials who had lost their jobs to the *santris* or who feared they would lose them, by dissatisfied *pangerans*, by Mangkunĕgara, and by the Jogjakarta *kraton*. There had been not a single shred of reliable evidence to support these rumours.

On 12 October Greeve was greatly pleased to find he was suffering from haemorrhoids and, by the following morning, a fever. The Surakarta *Babad Pakĕpung* says, perhaps more truthfully, that he 'acted as if he suffered from haemorrhoids'.[96] On

---

[95] Greeve, Surakarta, to Batavia, 12 Oct. 1790, in KA 3833 (OB 1792).
[96] B. *Pakĕpung*, p. 7, Canto II (Asmaradana):
    27. Idlir neng Sala tri latri
        prapta Kad-rĕbo pamitnja
        api-api sakit dobol
    . . . .

Ibid., p. 8, Canto II (Asmaradana), quotes Greeve saying to Djajaningrat, 'I'm not really sick': 32. ingsun jĕktine tan sakit / . . .

the thirteenth he excused himself from the Susuhunan's reception and immediately departed, which would hardly have been the usual response to his ailments. He hastened back to Sĕmarang, taking leave of Pakubuwana IV by letter. The *patih* Djajaningrat accompanied Greeve out of the city, speaking darkly of his fears for the future and of his intention to resign if these fears proved justified. He complained bitterly of the influence of the *santris*, who excluded him almost entirely from the inner councils of state. On 14 October Greeve arrived back in Sĕmarang, 'with no great reason to rejoice at the result of my continuous endeavours'. Both Mangkubumi and Mangkunĕgara had greater reason to be pleased, for they had finally begun to manœuvre him in the desired directions.

Rumours continued to spread. By the end of October, Greeve was even prepared to believe that Pakubuwana IV contemplated an assault on Batavia.[97] Trapped in his increasingly irrational panic, Greeve had never asked himself whence it was that all these rumours came. Nor had he tried to ascertain exactly what plans were being formed in the Susuhunan's court. The latter is all the more remarkable because Greeve had been told what Pakubuwana IV and his advisers desired. But his apprehensions were too great for him to consider these desires dispassionately, and his knowledge of Javanese politics too limited for him to understand them.

On 11 October, before leaving Surakarta, Greeve had heard unofficially of the Susuhunan's demands. On 25 October he received a document setting them out more exactly. The Susuhunan wanted above all that Batavia should confirm in writing that Surakarta was the senior *kraton* of Java (i.e. *ingkang sĕpuh*). Communications between Batavia and Jogjakarta should be transmitted via Surakarta and the money for the *pasisir* should be paid entirely to Surakarta. The *pĕngulus* of Sĕmarang and Jogjakarta should acknowledge the seniority of the *pĕngulu* of Surakarta.[98] Javanese sources, from both Jogjakarta and Surakarta, confirm in varying detail that the primary aim was to establish Surakarta as the main court.[99] This was a most explosive plan,

[97] Greeve, Diarium, 1 Dec. 1790, in dJ xii, p. 213.
[98] See ibid., pp. 210–11, giving the contents of the communication received on 25 October. Further information is to be found in the Diarium in KA 3833 (OB 1792), under the dates 11 and 12 Oct.; and in Sĕmarang to Batavia, 8 Nov. 1790, in KA 3833 (OB 1792).
[99] See *B. Mang.*, cited in nn. 76 and 77 above; *B. Pakĕpung*, pp. 2–4; Poensen, 'Mangkubumi', pp. 332–3, 339–41.

for it would have destroyed the balance which underlay the division of Java. Jogjakarta would go to war to prevent this. The proposals from time to time were even more extreme, particularly when the Susuhunan proposed that Jogjakarta be subdivided upon Mangkubumi's death. But there was no evidence that the Susuhunan ever contemplated a slaughter of Europeans, much less an assault on Batavia. Indeed, he wished Batavia's confirmation of his status, not its destruction.

Students of Javanese history will recognize in this a conception similar to the traditional view of the Dutch–Javanese relationship as it was described in the *Sĕrat Baron Sakenḍer*: a bipartite division of the island between the Dutch in the west of the island (Batavia) and the Javanese king in the Javanese-speaking areas of Central and East Java (in this case, Surakarta). Similar conceptions underlay the *Sĕrat Surja Radja*. This ideal system will be discussed in Chapter XI below. It was this which Pakubuwana IV apparently wished to restore. To achieve it, both Jogjakarta and Sĕmarang must be relegated to secondary positions. There was no absolute necessity to conquer or to destroy them, for the Javanese state had never been a monolithic structure intolerant of countervailing powers. Power was always dispersed, but it had always been assumed that one single power must be greater than the others. In other words, Pakubuwana IV was attempting in the first two years of his reign what his elders had attempted in the first two decades of the division: to restore a single state to supremacy in Central Java. But the vested interest in the division was by now too great for it to be set aside. If the Susuhunan persisted, he would plunge Java into total civil war. Pakubuwana IV, the first second-generation ruler of the permanently divided kingdom, was about to be taught the lesson his elders had learned, that division was the only answer.

There remains the question of religion. On the basis of partial documentation, M. L. van Deventer very cautiously suggested in 1884 that these *santris* might be connected in some way with the puritanical Wahhābī movement.[100] But there is no evidence to support this. Van Deventer referred to the statement of the 'second *pĕngulu*' of Surakarta, that the *santris* taught a 'false teaching' to which Pakubuwana IV, as a ruler and a Muslim, should not

[100] dJ xii, pp. xix–xxii. For a brief statement on the Wahhābīs in the Near East, see Hitti, *History of the Arabs*, pp. 740–1.

listen.¹⁰¹ Rather than inverting this to mean that the *santris* were more fundamentalist Muslims than the *pěngulu*, who was a *hadji*,¹⁰² van Deventer might have done better to take the statement at face value. In the opinion of a *hadji* who was a high religious official, their teachings were unworthy to be heard by a Muslim king. Javanese and Dutch sources alike describe these *santris* as men who used magical formulae, who claimed supernatural powers, and who visited holy grave-sites.¹⁰³ None of this would have been acceptable to a Wahhābī.

But if it is probable that they were not Wahhābīs, it is more difficult to say what they were, what the nature of their 'false teaching' may have been in religious terms. This question may be unanswerable, for so far as is known to the present writer all available documentation, both in Dutch and in Javanese, derives from their enemies. Furthermore, the Javanese courtly élite did not customarily draw fine theological boundaries around various schools of thought. Definition thus becomes difficult. The Javanese sources usually denounce these men only in general terms, as 'devils' and 'evil men'. There is, however, reason to suspect that the second *pěngulu* may have meant by 'false teaching' that the *santris* were literally not Muslims, or at least were less orthodox than himself. The term *santri* indicated their status as students of religion but it did not necessarily reflect upon the question of orthodoxy. The courtiers' criticisms of the *santris* certainly suggest that they did not share the Islamic-Javanese traditions of Central Javanese court life. And since none of these men were described as *hadjis* their doctrines were unlikely to have been of Arabic origin. There remains the possibility of pre-Islamic Javanese traditions or of less sophisticated non-*kraton* traditions. *Babad Mangkubumi* quotes the Susuhunan's uncle Pangeran Purbaja, perhaps apocryphally, calling their doctrines 'sorcery which is far from the Law of the Prophet'.¹⁰⁴ In August 1789, when the

¹⁰¹ Hartsinck to Sěmarang, 26 July 1789, in KA 3754 (OB 1790). This statement is repeated in Batavia to H. XVII, 15 Oct. 1789, in dJ xii, pp. 166–7.

¹⁰² His name is given as 'Hadjie Moesa' in Hartsinck to Sěmarang, 9 Aug. 1789, in KA 3754 (OB 1790).

¹⁰³ e.g. *B. Pakěpung*, pp. 37–8; *B. Mang.*, p. 523 (see n. 104 below); Poensen, 'Mangkubumi', pp. 332–3, 340–1.

¹⁰⁴ *B. Mang.*, p. 523, Canto LXXIX (Měgatruh):

    58. kados sikir kang těbih Sarengat Rasul
        batal karam den rampědi
        . . . .

Dutch Resident spoke with the Susuhunan about the *santris*, Pakubuwana IV replied that it was untrue that their teachings were evil. 'I adhere absolutely to the Islamic *Qur'ān*,' he said,[105] thereby apparently denying a specific charge that they were not Muslims. Furthermore, Pakubuwana IV was the same ruler who two decades later joined Raffles's Hindu sepoys in what Raffles believed to be a conspiracy to restore Hindu rule.[106]

This question is perhaps best left for a full study of the entire crisis. For the present, it seems wisest to conclude that these men were very unlikely to have been Wahhābīs. And there is some evidence to suggest that, whatever these teachers regarded their own doctrinal allegiance to be, they were regarded by those whom they displaced in court affairs as non-Muslims. On the other hand, the Susuhunan's attendance at the mosque on Fridays, the prohibition of opium, and the construction of a replica of the Děmak mosque all suggest at least nominal commitment to Islam. This problem was not, however, at the centre of the crisis. Whatever the nature of their religious teachings, the main opposition to the *santris* was on political rather than theological grounds. They had displaced many important Surakarta dignitaries and now they were planning to restore the Surakarta *kraton* to a central position, which would plunge Java into civil war.

The Dutch had by now been manœuvred into a position in which they believed that the Susuhunan's main aim was to attack themselves. The decision had therefore been taken to stop, and if necessary to attack, the Susuhunan. The Company's army was in poor condition, with new forces arriving only to go directly into hospitals, while many senior officers were, in Greeve's opinion, too old to perform field duties. By November, Greeve had been told that Batavia could provide no more European troops and he had decided to hire troops from Madura, in as small numbers as possible to reduce costs.

In late October and early November 1790, the Dutch assured

[105] Hartsinck to Sěmarang, 9 Aug. 1789, in KA 3754 (OB 1790).

[106] Raffles (1830), vol. ii, p. 5. See also Raffles to Gov.-Gen. of British India, 8 Dec. 1815 and 8 Feb. 1816, in M. L. van Deventer, *Het Nederlandsch Gezag over Java en Onderhoorigheden sedert 1811*, vol. i: *1811–1820* ('s-Gravenhage, 1891), pp. 58–63. In the letter of 8 Dec. 1815, Raffles made the perceptive comment that 'the Susuhunan himself is of too cautious a character, to commit himself so openly'.

See also H. D. Levyssohn Norman, *De Britsche Heerschappij over Java en Onderhoorigheden (1811–1816)* ('s-Gravenhage, 1857), pp. 78–9.

themselves of Mangkunĕgara's support. He failed to get the 4,000 *tjatjahs* he wanted from the Sultan, but the Company promised him and he now accepted an annual payment of 4,000 reals, thereby greatly increasing his independence of the Susuhunan. He then swore an oath of reconciliation with the Sultan and the Crown Prince of Jogjakarta on the sixth of November, to which the Crown Prince swore the following day in Jogjakarta.[107]

On 28 October the Sultan told the Dutch Resident that he agreed with the Company that the surrender of the *santris* must be demanded. Since he was partly responsible for the idea, his agreement was hardly surprising. The Dutch had told him they were worried that monsoon rains would hamper military operations, but the Sultan said, 'If my subjects and those of the Company get rain, then the enemy will get it, too, and therefore if the Company has plans it is best that they be carried out directly.'[108] He also joined in the *rapprochement* with Mangkunĕgara and was pleased when Mangkunĕgara had sworn the act of reconciliation. He specifically withdrew his curse upon Mangkunĕgara and his descendants.[109] It is a comment upon the seriousness with which the Susuhunan's plans were regarded that it could drive even

[107] MN, Geschrift, [*c.* 20 Sura A.J. 1717/30 Sept. 1790], in AN Java's Noord-Oost Kust 162, 'Bijlagen 1790'; van Reede to MN, 31 Oct. 1790, in AN Java's Noord-Oost Kust 162, 'Bijlagen 1790'; Sĕmarang to Batavia, 1 Nov. 1790, in KA 3833 (OB 1792); van Ijsseldijk to Sĕmarang, 7 Nov. 1790, in AN Java's Noord-Oost Kust 162, 'Bijlagen 1790'; Sĕmarang to Batavia, 8 Nov. 1790, in KA 3833 (OB 1792); Greeve, Diarium, 1 Dec. 1790, in dJ xii, pp. 213–14, 218–19. The VOC-PB IV–MN–HB I settlement of 1790 is discussed in Chap. X.

[108] HB I to van Ijsseldijk, 18 Sapar A.J. 1717 (28 Oct. 1790), in AN Java's Noord-Oost Kust 162, 'Bijlagen 1790'; Sĕmarang to Batavia, 1 Nov. 1790, in KA 3833 (OB 1792); Greeve, Diarium, 1 Dec. 1790, in dJ xii, p. 213.

[109] HB I to MN, 14 Sura A.J. 1717 (24 Sept. 1790), in AN Java's Noord-Oost Kust 162, 'Bijlagen 1790'; Greeve, Diarium, 1 Dec. 1790, in dJ xii, pp. 215–16, 219, 221.

The letter of HB I to MN, 14 Sura A.J. 1717 (24 Sept. 1790), seems to be dated rather too early for the withdrawal of the curse. It is preserved in the AN only in Dutch translation and the date may be wrong. A more likely date would be 24 Sapar A.J. 1717 (3 Nov. 1790). See Greeve, Diarium, 1 Dec. 1790, in dJ xii, p. 215, announcing the arrival of a document from HB I of 2 Nov., indicating HB I's willingness for reconciliation with MN. But the date might also be 14 Sapar A.J. 1717 (24 Oct. 1790). See Greeve, Diarium, in dJ xii, p. 210, reporting a letter of 24 Oct. which said that MN–HB I hostilities in Gunung Kidul had already ceased.

Copies of various acts of friendship (not originals) between HB I, the Jogjakarta Crown Prince, and MN are to be found in AN Java's Noord-Oost Kust 162, 'Bijlagen 1790'.

CRISIS IN SURAKARTA, 1787-1790   335

Mangkubumi and Mangkunĕgara to co-operate for the first time in forty years. The warfare between the two had ceased before the end of October.[110] *Babad Mangkubumi* even says that for a time Mangkunĕgara wished to shift his allegiance to Jogjakarta,[111] which seems a somewhat exaggerated picture of the reconciliation.

By early November the Company's last hope of a peaceful settlement was removed, again by information provided through the Resident at Jogjakarta. It was said that the Susuhunan's advisers held the opinion that an oath given to a Christian was not binding on a Muslim. The Company could not therefore be satisfied with an 'act of recantation' (*acte van retractie*).[112] The die was cast. The Sultan meanwhile urged the Dutch to move quickly, before the celebrations of *Garĕbĕg Mulud* could begin (12 Mulud A.J. 1717/20 November A.D. 1790), when the Susuhunan's *bupatis* with their retinues and troops would gather in Surakarta. By mid-October the troops of Banjumas had already arrived. The Company now began to fear that *Garĕbĕg Mulud* would be the occasion for an assault on their Surakarta garrison.[113]

The Dutch initially set 19 November as the day on which action would be taken. Troops of the Sultanate and of the Sultan's *montjanĕgara*, over 4,500-strong (including nearly 3,500 cavalry), began to move into position around Surakarta. From Madura came 500 troops in the service of the Company, but their late arrival meant that the 19 November date had to be extended. Of the European troops sent from Batavia, which included 30 artillery, many were ill on their arrival in Sĕmarang. Greeve took men from his own garrison to supplement them and sent them on to Surakarta. He was extremely fortunate to be offered in addition the assistance of Dutch Government forces aboard Staringh's squadron, who marched to Surakarta on 4 November.[114]

[110] Greeve, Diarium, 1 Dec. 1790, in dJ xii, p. 210.
[111] B. *Mang.*, p. 507, Canto LXXVII (Pangkur) (MN addressing van Reede):
34. ...
    ngandika malih mring Uprup
    aku datan gĕlĕma
    angawula ija marang anak-Prabu [PB IV]
    sun balik marang Mĕntarum
    ingkang santosa ing budi.
[112] Greeve, Diarium, 1 Dec. 1790, in dJ xii, p. 216.
[113] Ibid., in KA 3833 (OB 1792) (see also dJ xii, pp. 215, 221, 222).
[114] Sĕmarang to Batavia, 29 July 1790, in KA 3802 (OB 1791); id., 16 Oct. 1790, in KA 3833 (OB 1792); Danurĕdja to van Ijsseldijk, 18 Sapar A.J. 1717

The encirclement of Surakarta was beginning. Greeve was so anxious about this, the first significant military effort by the Company in Central Java for over thirty years, that his records began to grow disorganized. It is difficult to know how many troops were in position around the city, and how many Indonesian and European troops were in the Company's fortress, facing the *kraton* across the *alun-alun*. But the Surakarta *kraton* could have no doubt that it was about to be besieged by several thousand troops of the Sultanate supported by several thousand more from Mangkunĕgara. These were clearly allied with several hundred Indonesian and European troops of the Company within the city itself. And once hostilities had begun, there could be no way of knowing how much the attacking armies might swell as they took in disaffected elements from within Surakarta.

The pressure on the Susuhunan was great and he tried to seek an exit. Various proposals were put by him and by the Dutch Resident to each other: that the *santris* be surrendered or sent on pilgrimage to Mecca, which Pakubuwana IV refused; that none be surrendered, that only some of them be surrendered, or that some be murdered, which the Dutch refused, although they began to think that the execution of the leaders might be a satisfactory compromise. The Dutch meanwhile postponed the giving of a final ultimatum because they felt militarily unprepared.[115]

(28 Oct. 1790), in AN Java's Noord-Oost Kust 162, 'Bijlagen 1790'; Sĕmarang to Batavia, 8 Nov. 1790, in KA 3833 (OB 1792); Greeve, Diarium, 1 Dec. 1790, in dJ xii, pp. 209, 215, 222, 224.

The new troops arriving in Java were now largely non-Dutch mercenaries hired from the lowest levels of European society. They were a motley band, and sickness was common among them. In his letter of 29 July 1790, Greeve said that he had been excited to hear of the impending arrival of the Württemberg troops, consisting of German mercenaries. He expected at least 300, but found he received slightly over one-third of that figure, some having died on the trip and many others being ill, with sickness daily increasing. He was able to carry out the strengthening of the Surakarta and Jogjakarta garrisons by 100 men each, but only by keeping at Sĕmarang troops who were supposed to be sent to Malacca. On the army of the VOC at this time, see de Graaf, *GI*, p. 169; see also Clive Day, *The Policy and Administration of the Dutch in Java* (Kuala Lumpur, 1966), pp. 107-8.

[115] Van Ijsseldijk to Sĕmarang, 10 Oct. 1790, in AN Java's Noord-Oost Kust 162, 'Bijlagen 1790'; Sĕmarang to Batavia, 14 Nov. 1790, 20 Nov. 1790 and 25 Nov. 1790, in KA 3833 (OB 1792); Greeve, Diarium, 1 Dec. 1790, in dJ xii, pp. 218, 220-1, 223, 225-6, and ibid., in KA 3833 (OB 1792) (several important passages are omitted from the text in dJ xii).

It is impossible to know precisely what consultations now took place within the *kraton*, but the general direction of events is clear. As the besieging forces gathered, the Susuhunan's uncle Pangeran Purbaja and the ruler's brothers Buminata and Mangkubumi, with others, began to urge the Susuhunan to give in to the demands and to surrender his advisers.

With the Dutch now firmly on the side of Jogjakarta, the Sultan and the Crown Prince began to exert pressure as well. The Dutch were asked how they would react if, in the eventuality the Susuhunan were deposed, the Crown Prince of Jogjakarta were put forward as a candidate for the throne of Surakarta. Upon Mangkubumi's death, Mataram could then be reunited. This they refused to consider. The Dutch had already decided secretly to make Mangkunĕgara the new Susuhunan if it came to a deposition, and in no circumstance were they willing to contemplate a reunification of Mataram. They were fully aware that this would be the end of the Company's position in Java.[116] The Sultan could hardly take any steps towards reunification without Dutch support. If he attempted to do so, his new reconciliation with Mangkunĕgara would immediately turn into a general blood-bath, with no guarantee that he would in the end be victorious over Mangkunĕgara and the Dutch.

The growing pressure upon the Susuhunan finally succeeded without the necessity of a military assault on the *kraton*. Pangerans Purbaja, Mangkubumi, Buminata, and Ngabei, along with the *patih* Djajaningrat and others, convinced the young Susuhunan to surrender the leading *santris*: Wiradigda, Panĕngah, Kanḍuruwan, Ahmad (or Nur) Saleh, and Bahman. On 26 November they were turned over to Purbaja, who immediately took them under arrest to the Dutch fortress. On the twenty-seventh they were sent to Sĕmarang and on the twenty-eighth the Company began to withdraw its forces and paid off its Buginese and Malay troops. The Susuhunan begged Batavia's forgiveness and the Company, relieved to be spared the expenses of war, speedily granted it to him on 29 November.[117] A Surakarta *sĕngkala*-list written later in the reign

[116] Van Ijsseldijk to Sĕmarang, 19 Oct. 1790, in AN Java's Noord-Oost Kust 162, 'Bijlagen 1790'; Greeve, Diarium, 1 Dec. 1790, in dJ xii, pp. 218–19 n. 1, 222, 224.
[117] Sĕmarang to Batavia, 25 Nov. 1790, in KA 3833 (OB 1792); H. Hartman and van Reede to Sĕmarang, 26 Nov. 1790 and 27 Nov. 1790, in AN Java's Noord-Oost Kust 162, 'Bijlagen 1790'; Sĕmarang to Batavia, 29 Nov. 1790,

of Pakubuwana IV gives the chronogram for these events: 'The teachers of the King (spread) terror in the world.'[118] But they would spread no more. As far as Surakarta was concerned, things had been put aright. Pangeran Purbaja and the older Surakarta dignitaries were again in control of *kraton* affairs, the kingdom was still safely divided, and there had been no major war.

Jogjakarta had again been trapped by the turn of events. On the verge of a full-scale assault on Surakarta, the Dutch allies had again been easily satisfied and had immediately withdrawn, without taking significant action. From their own point of view, the Dutch had been wise to avoid steps which might have made war unavoidable. The Sultan could only make two more small requests of his dubious allies. Still apparently fearing a last-minute reunification attempt, he said he would not withdraw his troops until the *santris*, under Dutch escort, had passed the site of the old Kartasura *kraton* on their way to Sěmarang. The Dutch had no objection. His second proposal was rejected absolutely. He said, since the Susuhunan had behaved so badly, the Dutch should consider Jogjakarta as 'the oldest, and therefore also as the first in rank' (i.e. *ingkang sěpuh*). The Resident told him there was no hope of a favourable response to this and the Sultan did not even bother to take the proposal to higher levels of the Dutch bureaucracy.[119]

Mangkuněgara also had not done as well as he might have hoped. He had missed being made Susuhunan by the last-minute surrender of the *santris*. But he had won firm assurances of Dutch

---

in KA 3833 (OB 1792); Greeve, Diarium, 1 Dec. 1790, in dJ xii, pp. 224–5, 227.

See also Poensen, 'Mangkubumi', pp. 347–50; *B. Mang.*, pp. 516–35; *B. Pakěpung*, pp. 39–50. No other source, Dutch or Javanese, supports the story told in *B. Pakěpung* that Jasadipura I was an important figure in the anti-*santri* group.

[118] BM Add. MS. 12323 (B), f. 47ᵛ: Djumungah, ping 18, Mulud Djimawal, Tuměnggung Wiradigda, Tuměnggung Kanḍuruwan, lan Pangran Paněngah, Bagus Bahman, Nur Saleh, sami katjěpěng ladjěng kaselong, panḍita radja gora ning rat, 1717. The date given here is that on which the *santris* were turned over to Purbaja and taken to the VOC fortress: Friday, 18 Mulud A.J. 1717/26 Nov. A.D. 1790.

[119] Van Ijsseldijk to Sěmarang, 28 Nov. 1790, in AN Java's Noord-Oost Kust 162, 'Bijlagen 1790'; van Ijsseldijk to HB I, 28 Nov. 1790, in AN Java's Noord-Oost Kust 162, 'Bijlagen 1790'; van Ijsseldijk to Sěmarang, 29 Nov. 1790, in AN Java's Noord-Oost Kust 162, 'Bijlagen 1790'; Greeve, Diarium, 1 Dec. 1790, in dJ xii, p. 228.

support, a reconciliation with the Sultan, and an independent source of income from the Company.[120]

The Dutch had not quite heard the last of the *santris*. On 29 November the Dutch government brig *de Zwaluw* left Sĕmarang with the five deportees aboard. On 10 December it returned to Sĕmarang, having failed to make the passage to Batavia. Greeve found these men back on his hands, much to his regret. He feared the impact which news of the failed voyage might have upon the Javanese and particularly upon the Susuhunan, who had been fed for two years with tales of the *santris'* supernatural powers. It would be five months before a second attempt could be made, presumably because of weather conditions. Greeve therefore immediately put the *santris* under escort and sent them by the land route along the north coast to Batavia.[121] The following September, 1791, Greeve retired. His four years as Governor of the Northeast Coast (1787–91) had been more harrowing than the administration of any Governor since von Hohendorff (1748–54) and Hartingh (1754–61). But they had not been without compensation, for Greeve had unofficially amassed a personal fortune said to exceed a million guilders.[122]

The effect of the years of crisis between 1787 and 1790 was to vindicate the system of division. The courts of Jogjakarta and Surakarta, and the lesser principality of Mangkunĕgara, were all sustained by firm bodies of supporters, by committed lines of allegiance and patronage. The balance of power in Central Java was real and the vested interests in each of the constituent elements was too great for the system to be overturned. Anyone who attempted to do so would automatically face the opposition of the

---

[120] The inheritance of MN's grandson was not yet definitely determined, although Greeve advised Batavia on 10 Nov. 1788 that it would probably be in the interest of the VOC to confirm it so that the Mangkunĕgaran would become a permanent principality dependent directly upon the VOC and immune to pressure from the Susuhunan. In 1792, the inheritance of the 4,000 *tjatjahs* in MN's house was finally fixed. See Sĕmarang to Batavia, 10 Nov. 1788, in KA 3708 (OB 1789); id., 25 April 1792, in dJ xii, pp. 271–4; id., 3 Nov. 1792, in dJ xii, pp. 286–90; id., 22 July 1796, in dJ xii, pp. 413–14; Rouffaer, 'Vorstenlanden', p. 271.

[121] Sĕmarang to Batavia, 11 Dec. 1790, in KA 3833 (OB 1792). On the violent weather conditions along the coast of Java from late November until April, as described by a Dutch Admiral, see John Splinter Stavorinus, *Voyages to the East-Indies* (trans. Samuel Hull Wilcocke; 3 vols.; London, 1798), vol. i, pp. 224–6.

[122] dJ xii, p. xlvi.

other two principal Javanese figures and almost surely of the Company as well. The chances of success against such opposition were so small as to render an attempted reunification unlikely. When someone contemplated such an attempt, as had the Susuhunan, even his own closest family members would oppose him and, under pressure, would act to stop him. Although the divided state offered courtiers and princes limited opportunities for incomes and influence, they preferred to maintain the stability they enjoyed than to risk losing all in a new conflagration. Pakubuwana IV had been taught a lesson already learned by his elders. That he did not learn easily is suggested by the fact that he apparently considered a second reunification attempt during the British administration (1811–16).[123] But the persistence of an instinctive dislike of the division of Mataram could not change the fact that it had become the only way in which Central Java had proved governable by the Javanese élite. Not even a Susuhunan could change the past.

The Dutch now realized more clearly than ever that the division of Mataram was the only guarantee of their continued presence in Java. But they never appreciated, or at least admitted, the extent to which they had been the pawns in a game of Javanese power politics. When Greeve wrote his final report on the episode, he was forced to observe that the events at Surakarta had not been sufficiently clear to arrive at 'complete conviction' about the Susuhunan's intentions. But there had been, he said, more than a 'moral certainty' and it had had to be acted upon.[124] One wonders if he ever looked back upon his own reports and realized how completely he had allowed himself to rely upon the advice and information of the court of Jogjakarta and of disaffected members of the Surakarta élite.

The last great crisis of Mangkubumi's life was now surmounted, if not entirely successfully, at least satisfactorily. The permanence of the division, and therefore of Jogjakarta, had been reconfirmed. There remained only for the old Sultan to die.

[123] See the sources cited in n. 106 above.
[124] Sěmarang to Batavia, 1 Dec. 1790, in KA 3833 (OB 1792).

X

THE SUCCESSION OF THE YOUNGER GENERATION
1791–1792

THE aftermath of the crisis of 1787–1790 was readily cleared up. The two *kratons* of Java began again to ignore each other except in those administrative matters which were required by the fact of division. Normal administrative correspondence between the two *patihs*, as established by the law codes of A.J. 1697–9 (A.D. 1771–3), was presumably restored immediately. The lands which had been occupied by Jogjakarta forces during the early hostilities and as they prepared to besiege the *kraton* were returned to Surakarta control beginning in December 1790. Before the end of February 1791, all such lands had been handed over.[1] In May 1791, the Dutch helped to negotiate a final settlement of the various claims for damages. Surakarta had laid claims against Jogjakarta for 16,000 reals and Mangkubumi had demanded up to 11,000 reals in compensation. In the final settlement, the Sultan agreed to pay 4,000 reals to Pakubuwana IV.[2] It must be a comment upon Mangkubumi's advanced age and his desire simply to wash his hands of the entire Surakarta affair that he should have allowed the payment of any damages at all.

One of the results of the conflict had been a new contract agreed to by the Susuhunan, the Sultan, Mangkunĕgara, and the Company. It was a major landmark in the history of the permanent division of Java, and seems to have originated in Dutch initiatives to maintain the peace in the crisis of 1790. During Greeve's trip to Surakarta in September 1790, he had with some difficulty convinced the Susuhunan to agree to the contract. Danurĕdja had then come to Surakarta as the Sultan's representative and the contract had been signed and sworn there on 28 September.

[1] Sĕmarang to Batavia, 29 Nov. 1790, 13 Dec. 1790, and 28 Feb. 1791, in KA 3833 (OB 1792); *B. Mang.*, pp. 535–8.
[2] Sĕmarang to Batavia, 10 May 1791, in KA 3833 (OB 1792).

Danurědja insisted and it was agreed that, to avoid giving the impression that the Sultan had come to the Susuhunan, the Surakarta *patih* should pay a reciprocal visit to the Sultan as soon as possible. On 6 November, Mangkunĕgara signed the contract as well. He saw this as part of his alliance with the Sultan and insisted that no witnesses from the Susuhunan's *kraton* be present at the signing. Needless to say, the new contract was a dead letter in so far as it affected relations between the Surakarta and Jogjakarta *kratons* until after the *santris* had been surrendered to the Dutch. It was apparently not finally ratified by the Susuhunan and the Sultan until early December 1790. The Company ratified it shortly thereafter.[3]

The new contract was not a departure in principle from past agreements, for it reconfirmed and recommitted the signatories to the general structure of the divided kingdom. But the details of that system now reached a new level of formal definition. The preamble of the treaty named Governor Jan Greeve, Pakubuwana IV, Hamĕngkubuwana I, and Mangkunĕgara as the parties to the agreement, arrived at through the intercession of the Company. Articles One and Two ended the hostilities between the Susuhunan and the Sultan and declared all disputes to be forgotten and forgiven. In Article Three the Sultan accepted the continued use of the name Mangkubumi in Surakarta and said he would regard it as if it had been granted by the Company. The Susuhunan recognized the right of succession of the Jogjakarta Crown Prince

[3] Sĕmarang to Batavia, 8 Nov. 1790, in KA 3833 (OB 1792); Greeve, Diarium, 1 Dec. 1790 (under dates 22–4 Sept., 27–8 Sept.), in KA 3833 (OB 1792) (see also dJ xii, p. 226); Sĕmarang to Batavia, 13 Dec. 1790 and 28 Feb. 1791, in KA 3833 (OB 1792); Batavia to H.XVII, 31 Dec. 1791, in dJ xii, p. 234.
The Jogjakarta copy of the text, which is the basis of the summary given here of the treaty, is in 'Journal', BM Add. MS. 12303, ff. 93^r–97^v.
The contract is also discussed in *B. Pakĕpung*, p. 2. The trip of Danurĕdja to Surakarta is mentioned in *B. Mang.*, p. 498.
PB IV later showed some reluctance to send his *patih* on a reciprocal visit to HB I. He argued that Danurĕdja had not been in Surakarta to pay him compliments, but had been summoned there by the Company to sign the contract. The Dutch insisted, however, and PB IV finally agreed to send his *patih* to Jogjakarta in July 1791. But HB I was by that time very ill. By February 1792, one month before HB I's death, the visit had still not taken place. It is nearly certain that there was no such visit until after the accession of HB II. *B. Mang.* says that after the surrender of the *santris*, PB IV asked the Dutch to convey his greetings to HB I and to his 'uncle' the Crown Prince. See Sĕmarang to Batavia, 28 Feb. 1791, in KA 3833 (OB 1792); id., 20 July 1791 and 28 Oct. 1791, in KA 3857 (OB 1793); id., 17 Feb. 1792, in KA 3859 (OB 1793); *B. Mang.*, p. 536.

in Article Four, and in Article Five the Sultan affirmed his support of a regular succession in Surakarta if that throne should fall vacant. In Article Six the Susuhunan and the Sultan agreed that if their mutual peace and prosperity should be disturbed in the future they and their *patihs* would settle the matter with justice; but if either should not accept the settlement, rather than seeking revenge himself he would submit the dispute to the judgement of the Company. In Article Seven the two rulers bound themselves to punish those who had recently engaged in highway robbery. In Article Eight they affirmed that in the future they would live in 'truth, good friendship, and good order as before'.[4]

The reconciliation between the Sultan and Mangkunĕgara commenced in Article Nine. There it was stated that original responsibility for the hostilities could not be established; all damages had therefore been cancelled, all conquered lands restored, and all incidents forgotten. In Article Ten the Sultan and Mangkunĕgara both reconfirmed their commands to end all hostilities, upon the advice and at the desire of the Company, and agreed to live in amity for the future. In Article Eleven the Sultan discarded all complaints against Mangkunĕgara and all harmful intentions towards him. Mangkunĕgara renounced any harmful intent against the Sultan in Article Twelve. Article Thirteen confirmed Mangkunĕgara's agreement to the succession of the Crown Prince of Jogjakarta and bound him, his children, and his grandchildren not to cause the slightest displeasure to the future Sultan. In Article Fourteen, one of the key passages of the agreement, the Sultan and Mangkunĕgara agreed not to accept or to conceal refugees from each other's courts, but to return them whence they came. In Articles Fifteen and Sixteen was established the procedure for settling disputes between the Sultan and Mangkunĕgara. The Sultan would communicate complaints against Mangkunĕgara via his *patih* to the Susuhunan's *patih*, who would investigate the matter. Mangkunĕgara would communicate his protests against the Sultan to the Susuhunan's *patih*, who would transmit this to the Sultan's *patih*. But if either Mangkunĕgara

---

[4] 'Journal', BM Add. MS. 12303, f. 95ʳ: Mila para Ratu Kangdjĕng Susuhunan, kalih Kangdjĕng Sultan, inggih sami angangkĕni, jen tuhu tĕmĕn ing bendjingipun, agĕsang kalajan tuhunipun, pawong-sanak, sarta apĕpĕnĕdan kadi rumijin.

or the Sultan did not accept the settlement, he would not seek justice through violence, but would submit the dispute to the decision of the Company.

In Article Seventeen the Susuhunan and the Sultan agreed that their *patihs* should swear to the new agreement as their representatives, in the presence of the Governor of Sĕmarang. Mangkunĕgara agreed to swear to those parts of the agreement which affected him, binding also all his descendants. Danurĕdja was also to offer an oath on the Sultan's behalf to the reconciliation with Mangkunĕgara. The text was dated 28 September 1790 for the agreement between Pakubuwana IV and Hamĕngkubuwana I, and 6 November 1790 for that between Mangkunĕgara and Hamĕngkubuwana I.

The system described in the new contract was still one in which the Sultan and the Susuhunan ignored each other as much as possible. The division required considerable administration, for questions often crossed the boundaries of the states, but this was left to the *patihs*. If they failed to achieve a settlement, the conflicts would have to be submitted to the Company, as had always been the case if hostilities were not to result. But whereas this appeal to Dutch arbitration had previously been rather unofficial, it was now made formal and permanent by its detailed exposition in the text of the new contract. The Company was now formally recognized as the last court of appeal for problems which crossed the boundaries between the Javanese rulers.

There was another very important new departure. Now Mangkunĕgara was admitted as a signatory along with the Susuhunan, the Sultan, and the Company. And it was specifically agreed between the Sultan and Mangkunĕgara that subjects who fled from one to the other would be returned to their places of origin rather than given refuge. Thus, Mangkunĕgara's position in Javanese affairs had now been officially recognized.

The contract of 1790 was thus an explicit recognition of all the constituent elements of the divided kingdom, including Mangkunĕgara, and of the procedures by which that kingdom was governed, including most importantly final appeal to the Company as arbiter. The system which it described was not new, but its formalized structure had now evolved beyond the agreements of A.J. 1697–9 (A.D. 1771–3) by including Mangkunĕgara and the Dutch. This was a further step in the process of regulating formally a system which still conflicted with the essential dynamics of Javanese politics. The latter had always required the unrivalled legitimative glory of a single monarch in order to bind together a consensus of Javanese notables in allegiance to the central state. But this ideal system had been abandoned by the older generation in favour of the more practicable and peaceful alternative of accepting the fact of division on a permanent basis. When the Dutch proposed the contract of 1790, the Javanese presumably agreed to it not because they were compelled to do so, such compulsion being beyond the capacity of the Company, but rather because the contract's provisions made sense in terms of the issues which they saw as important. They required a more formal definition of the divided state system which they were then seeking to preserve. It may therefore be suggested that the new contract is further documentation of the Javanese élite's increasing dependence on rigid and formalized structures as a means of bolstering the stability of the partitioned kingdom and as a refuge from the uncomfortable irregularity of it all. It was the Dutch presence which had made the partition necessary by preventing the emergence of a single central *kraton*. The new contract formally recognized not that the Dutch had made the partition necessary but that their presence was required to make the partition viable.

The Sultan's personal contacts with Dutch officials were few in these last months of his life. By mid-1791 he had, it seems, already left the *kraton* for the more secluded comforts of Krapjak, to the south of Jogjakarta, which was presumably the site of a resting-place.[5] Only once in the months of 1791 and 1792 did Mangkubumi receive formal emissaries from the East India Company, they being the Commissioners for Military Affairs sent out from Europe by the Netherlands Government to inspect the precarious state of the Company's military forces. The Sultan met them at the end of September 1791. He received them personally but, because of his general weakness, only briefly. He gave them permission to inspect the *Taman Sari* complex and before their departure they were treated to a tiger–buffalo fight, which by now had become a regular feature of Europeans' visits to

[5] See Sĕmarang to Batavia, 20 July 1791, in KA 3857 (OB 1793), speaking of HB I's 'seclusion, being engaged in partaking of the sun'. *B. Mang.*, p. 539, says HB I's terminal illness began in Krapjak, whence he was brought back on a palanquin to the *kraton* to die. Poensen, 'Mangkubumi', pp. 358–60, also says HB I had gone to Krapjak, where his terminal illness began.

Jogjakarta. They were then sent on their way with *krises* as gifts.⁶

The Pakualaman *babad* gives a graphic description of the tiger–buffalo contest which, it will be remembered, was apparently regarded by the Javanese as a symbolic confrontation between themselves (the buffalo) and the Europeans (the tiger). The commissioners supposedly presented to Mangkubumi a white, particularly strong and ferocious tiger as a gift. The animal was then put to battle with a buffalo, which of course defeated even this powerful adversary, much to the Sultan's pleasure. The Dutch Resident then asked and received the body of the dead tiger as a gift.⁷ Contemporary Dutch records confirm that a tiger–buffalo fight was held, but the details of the story in the *babad* may be apocryphal. The story does, however, seem to represent clearly the views of the younger generation of Jogjakarta dignitaries, who were now almost completely in charge of the kingdom: the white tiger was a powerful beast but the buffalo was always the stronger.

The Dutch Commissioners were impressed by the military strength of the Jogjakarta *kraton*. They

> expressed their surprise at the *kraton* of the Sultan, for having found it very well fortified, indeed such that in case of hostilities not much could be done against it with any effect from the [Company's] fort.⁸

Their general impression of the Company's military position throughout the Indonesian archipelago was highly pessimistic and their hopes of amelioration under the Company's bankrupt, inefficient, and corrupt bureaucracy were small.⁹ They thus regarded with considerable wonderment the contrast between the Company's defences and the impressive fortifications at Jogjakarta, the broad and perfectly levelled *alun-alun* in front of the *kraton* which could be flooded with water to keep down the dust for tournament days, and the 'particularly beautiful water-works and conduits' of the Sultan's pleasure-gardens.¹⁰

---

⁶ HB I to Sĕmarang, 8 Sapar A.J. 1718 (received 9 Oct. 1791), in KA 3859 (OB 1793).
See dJ xii, p. 297 n. 1, on the background of this Commission.
⁷ Poensen, 'Mangkubumi', pp. 357–8.
⁸ Sĕmarang to Batavia, 20 Oct. 1791, in KA 3859 (OB 1793).
⁹ See Militaire Commissie to Batavia, 8 Jan. 1793, in dJ xii, pp. 297–303.
¹⁰ Report of C. F. Reimer, in Bosboom, 'Waterkasteel', pp. 520–5.

But all of this had little to do with Mangkubumi. His remaining days were few and his illnesses became progressively more regular and more serious. Indeed, this present chapter is less an integral part of Mangkubumi's history than it is an appendix to that history and a prologue to the troubled reign of his son, Hamĕngkubuwana II. The old Sultan was dying and the younger generation were moving into position for the conflicts which would come when the last restraints of their father's influence were gone.

The intrigues among the younger generation of Jogjakarta dignitaries were already very extensive and of long standing. Various interested parties passed their views of the situation to the Dutch, who were apparently insufficiently perceptive to discern what intrigues lay behind various biased reports. It is thus difficult to discern the truth of the situation. It should be pointed out, too, that these were not the amateur intrigues of adolescents or young men. The Crown Prince was already in his forties,[11] his brother Pangeran Ngabei was still older, and several other princes were not far behind them.

By 1790 the Dutch were receiving very critical comments on the Crown Prince, who was said to be 'despotic' and much disliked by his brothers and the dignitaries of the Sultanate. They began to worry about the possibility of conflict upon the death of Mangkubumi and therefore urged him to abdicate in favour of his son while he still lived, to ensure a peaceful succession. The Company did not reveal any suspicion at the fact that some of the strongest denunciations of the Prince came from Danurĕdja's son Arja Mandura. It was this man whom Greeve had proposed as Danurĕdja's assistant and eventual successor in 1788, but whom Mangkubumi had turned down for that post. He preferred instead his own son-in-law Raden Tumĕnggung Natajuda. Danurĕdja himself had approved this choice, saying his own son was insufficiently 'tough' (*zwaar*) for the position. Arja Mandura thus had cause for grievance and reason for hoping the Dutch might prefer someone else as the second Sultan who would give him his father's position as *patih*. He artfully told Greeve in 1790, when he accompanied his father to Surakarta to sign the new contract, that Danurĕdja had not found the opportunity to speak with Greeve about the Crown Prince. But, he said, his father had

[11] HB II was born about 1749; see Poensen, 'Mangkubumi', p. 289; and p. 101 n. 14 above.

ordered him to enlighten the Governor on the subject in strictest secrecy, to which Greeve bound himself. The Governor recorded his gratitude to this 'honest' (*eerlijke*) informant.[12]

Mangkubumi consistently rejected the Dutch suggestion that he should abdicate in the interests of a peaceful succession. There are some hints that he refused to do so precisely because he feared this would provoke premature conflicts among his sons, and perhaps because he was himself not entirely pleased with the conduct of the Crown Prince. It was said that he had often told Danurĕdja he did not find in the Crown Prince the necessary qualities for the welfare of his kingdom and his subjects, and that he had even at times considered naming another of his sons Crown Prince. But since this report came through Danurĕdja's son its veracity is impossible to judge.[13]

In June 1790, as the crisis with Surakarta was entering its final stages, the Company had asked Mangkubumi whether he felt he could rely upon his subjects to support the succession of the Crown Prince. He replied,

I trust in them. But because mortals are inconstant and therefore perhaps they would not conform to their statements to me, they have sworn their loyalty to my son the Crown Prince after my death.

And when, in the course of time, by God's Will I have come to my end, I trust in full upon the Company regarding the confirmation of my kingdom upon my son the Crown Prince and further posterity.[14]

If the Sultan had any doubts about the Crown Prince's ability or rightness to rule after him, he never communicated them directly to the Dutch. He continued until his death to maintain his choice of a successor. But he was clearly worried about the machinations within his kingdom and depended upon the Dutch, his unreliable allies, at least to do him the service of assisting in the Crown Prince's succession. It was to be one of the few obligations of their alliance with Mangkubumi which they fulfilled.

The Dutch were even convinced, by what parties is not clear, that the Crown Prince himself did not believe that he was the

---

[12] Sĕmarang to Batavia, 11 June 1790, in KA 3802 (OB 1791); Greeve, Diarium, 1 Dec. 1790 (under date 23 Sept.), in KA 3833 (OB 1792).

The appointment of Natajuda over Arja Mandura is discussed on p. 305 above.

[13] Sĕmarang to Batavia, 11 June 1790, in KA 3802 (OB 1791).

[14] HB I to van Ijsseldijk, 14 Sawal A.J. 1716 (29 June 1790), in KA 3802 (OB 1791).

SUCCESSION, 1791-1792

lawful successor 'by right of birth'. This tale was so inconceivable that one wonders that the Jogjakarta Resident bothered to report it in all seriousness to his superiors. Greeve even went so far as to tell Batavia that this report 'may be held for a certainty and . . . is beyond all doubt'.[15] The Crown Prince had been chosen by his father over other sons, had a mother as distinguished as any of the wives of Mangkubumi, had been maintained by his father even when there had been differences of opinion, and had been allowed extensive control over the affairs of state. Even had Mangkubumi grown displeased with his son in his later years, of which there is no reliable evidence, it is inconceivable that the Crown Prince would be the one to question his own fitness to succeed. He was undoubtedly fully aware that there were others among his own brothers who were intriguing against him and he could not have been unconcerned about the possibility of opposition. Nevertheless, his behaviour in this period leading up to his own succession suggests he was confident of his rights and of his ability to control his Javanese opponents. If he was uncertain of his dominance over anyone, it was the Company. But about the Dutch he need not have worried, for after 115 years of intervention their only policy for ensuring stability in Java was to support the succession of the designated Crown Prince.[16]

The rumour that the Crown Prince doubted the legality of his own succession 'by right of birth' pointed to his elder brother Pangeran Ngabei as a possible source. It was only he who would have been likely to base a claim to the succession on priority of birth-rights. Ngabei's age is not certain, but if van der Burgh was

[15] Van Ijsseldijk to Sĕmarang, 4 Sept. 1790, in KA 3833 (OB 1792); Sĕmarang to Batavia, 7 Sept. 1790, in KA 3833 (OB 1792).

[16] One of the more euphoric conclusions which Greeve drew from the success of the efforts against the Surakarta *santris* in 1790 was: 'That, if there are thus princes at the Jogjakarta court who have ambitious designs to the detriment of the arranged succession, which one certainly cannot doubt, these will be readily subdued with an adequate force (which the Company should always keep here)'; Sĕmarang to Batavia, 29 Nov. 1790, in KA 3833 (OB 1792).

The only times the Company did not support the incumbent ruler or the designated Crown Prince were when they took the side of Pakubuwana I (1703-19) against Amangkurat III (1703-8) and when they were forced to compromise with Mangkubumi and Mangkunĕgara in 1755 and 1757. In 1719 they supported Amangkurat IV (1719-27), who had been designated Crown Prince some time before the death of Pakubuwana I, against Pangeran Blitar, whom the Susuhunan had been persuaded to name as his successor a few days before his death. On these matters, see de Graaf, *GI*.

correctly informed in 1780,[17] he was in his mid-fifties by the period 1791–2. In 1758 he had been passed over for the Crown Prince's position when the first holder of that title had died. Ngabei was then said variously to be too unintelligent to be chosen as Mangkubumi's successor, to have been involved in some scandal, or to be ineligible because his mother's status was considered to be too low.[18] In later years he was said to be out of his father's favour.[19] Yet in *Babad Mangkubumi*, representing the Crown Prince's views, Ngabei appears regularly and his opinions are often consulted.[20] From the time the Dutch began to worry about the Jogjakarta succession as early as the 1770s until the Sultan's death, they consistently identified Pangeran Ngabei as one of the most likely sources of trouble.[21]

After Pangeran Ngabei and the Crown Prince, the next most important son of Mangkubumi was Pangeran Natakusuma. He was Mangkubumi's child by Raden Aju Srĕnggara, who was also the mother of the wife of Natajuda, the assistant to the *patih*. Another of Natakusuma's full sisters was married into the family of Ronggaprawiradirdja, *bupati-wĕdana* of the *montjanĕgara*.[22] Natakusuma was thus in a position to exert a considerable influence throughout the kingdom via his family. It is not clear when Natakusuma was born, but he must have been at least thirty by the end of Mangkubumi's life. At the end of 1780 he had been raised to the status of a *pangeran* and had been given an appanage of 1,000 *tjatjahs*.[23]

[17] Van der Burgh, Memorie, 19 Sept. 1780, in dJ xi, p. 403, giving Ngabei's age at that time as 43.

[18] On these matters see Chap. IV above and the sources cited in p. 101 n. 13.

[19] See Ossenberch, Memorie, 13 May 1765, in dJ xi, p. 36; van der Burgh, Memorie, 19 Sept. 1780, in dJ xi, p. 403; Siberg, Memorie, 18 Sept. 1787, in dJ xii, p. 86.

[20] e.g. *B. Mang.*, pp. 336, 364–5, 394, 396, 450, 468, 475–6, 508, 509, 511, 536, 540, 544–5.

[21] See Sĕmarang to Batavia, 23 Dec. 1777, in KA 3392 (OB 1778); id., 25 April 1792, in dJ xii, pp. 244–6, 248–9.

[22] See Dwidjosoegondo, *Serat Dharah*, pp. 97–8; *Putra-dalĕm Sinuwun Sapisan* (Jogja kraton MS. A.24).

[23] Sĕmarang to Batavia, 20 Dec. 1780, in KA 3478 (OB 1781); *B. Mang.*, p. 474.

Rouffaer, 'Vorstenlanden', p. 268, believes Natakusuma to have been born *c.* 1760, which is a reasonable assumption. He would thus have been about twenty when he was raised to the rank of Pangeran. Before receiving the name Natakusuma he had been known as Raden Mas Adi.

It is impossible to judge the role which Natakusuma played during his father's lifetime, except to conclude that he was certainly involved in the intrigues of the later years. He has won an exceptionally 'good press', largely because C. Poensen chose to use a *babad* reflecting Natakusuma's point of view as the basis for his articles on the reigns of Haměngkubuwana I and II.[24] From these articles one learns of the boundless perfidy of the Crown Prince (Haměngkubuwana II) and of the virtue of Natakusuma, who supposedly stood highest of all the sons in his father's favour. But it is impossible to judge with confidence the truth of this. The Dutch occasionally received rumours which would support this view[25] but they were no more reliable than other rumours heard by the Company, and they cannot be verified. Near the end of the Sultan's life Natakusuma, along with Pangerans Ngabei and Děmang, was seen as one of the main opponents of the Crown Prince.[26] But it seems that Natakusuma only emerged as a main element in the *kraton* intrigues shortly before his father's death. Whereas *Babad Mangkubumi* often mentions Pangeran Ngabei, Pangeran Natakusuma does not figure largely.[27] His greatest success was to come in 1813, when the British administration of Java raised him to become Pangeran Pakualam I (1813–29), with an independent income from the European government and 4,000 *tjatjahs* as appanage from the Sultan. Thus, for his 'fidelity, attachment, and public services' to the English,[28] this prince and his descendants became the Jogjakarta mirror-image of the princes Mangkuněgara in Surakarta, thereby completing the

[24] Poensen, 'Mangkubumi' and 'Amăngku Buwånå II'. Poensen's source material is also discussed in Ricklefs, 'Authorship', pp. 264–5.

[25] Sěmarang to Batavia, 2 Feb. 1789, in KA 3754 (OB 1790): 'It is said that the Sultan's second [sic] son Natakusuma, who now in particular is regarded and beloved by his father far above the Crown Prince, constantly tries to dispose the old ruler against his brother . . .'

Greeve, Diarium, 1 Dec. 1790, in KA 3833 (OB 1792), under the date 28 Oct. (not excerpted in dJ xii), is badly soiled but seems to suggest that van Ijsseldijk had reported 'the probability that upon his death the Sultan gladly [? would see that his] son next in age after the Crown Prince, Natakusuma [sic], was chosen by the Company thereto [presumably, as the next Sultan]'.

[26] Sěmarang to Batavia, 24 July 1789, in KA 3754 (OB 1790); id., 25 April 1792, in dJ xii, pp. 244–6.

[27] He appears relatively infrequently, and mostly in the later part of the *babad*, after c. 1790; see *B. Mang.*, pp. 474, 509, 536, 540, 546.

[28] Copies of the contract of 17 March 1813 are to be found in van Deventer (ed.), *Java en Onderhoorigheden sedert 1811*, p. 333–5; and in Soekanto, *Sekitar Jogjakarta*, pp. 201–2.

quadripartite partition of Mataram. Natakusuma (Pakualam I) is remembered as a Javanese littérateur of some distinction,[29] but a full and reliable assessment of his life and character must await further research into the reign of Hamĕngkubuwana II.

The only remaining son to figure largely in these early intrigues was Pangeran Dĕmang. By 1791 he was apparently about thirty-five years old and was married to a daughter of Danurĕdja. Perhaps, therefore, it was Dĕmang who was most closely associated with the rumours spread by Danurĕdja's son Arja Mandura. Although the Dutch feared Dĕmang's machinations at the end of Mangkubumi's life, their reports consistently said he was held in low regard by *kraton* circles.[30] Of the other surviving sons of Mangkubumi, of whom there were at least fifteen in all,[31] most were just reaching an age to indulge successfully in *kraton* intrigues when their father died. Two years before his death, Mangkubumi raised four more to the rank of *pangeran*.[32]

While Mangkubumi lived, the intrigues among his sons led to no serious conflicts. But he had not long to live. For several years the Dutch had been expecting the death of the Sultan, who in 1791 was in his seventies or early eighties.[33] In 1788 Greeve had somewhat cold-bloodedly spoken to him of his 'probably far away, but with just as much reason probably near by, end'.[34]

[29] See Ki Hadjar Dewantara, *Beoefening van Letteren en Kunst in het Pakoe-Alamsche Geslacht* (Djokja, 1931), pp. 11–14.

[30] Van der Burgh, Memorie, 19 Sept. 1780, in dJ xi, p. 403; Siberg, Memorie, 18 Sept. 1787, in dJ xii, p. 86; Sĕmarang to Batavia, 9 May 1788, in KA 3708 (OB 1789); id., 25 April 1792, in dJ xii, pp. 245–6.
See also Poensen, 'Mangkubumi', p. 296.

[31] See Louw and de Klerck, *Java-Oorlog*, vol. vi, pp. 458, 465, listing:

1. The first Crown Prince, who died in 1758,
2. Ngabei,
3. HB II,
4. Dĕmang,
5. Dipasonta,
6. Natakusuma/Pakualam I,
7. Kusumajuda,
8. Muhamad Abubakar,
9. Panular,
10. Mangkukusuma,
11. Adikusuma,
12. Dipasana,
13. Danupaja,
14. Blitar,
15. Santakusuma,
16. Dipawidjaja.

[32] Van Ijsseldijk to Sĕmarang, 29 April 1790, in KA 3802 (OB 1791). The Sultan listed the names Silarong (whose name does not appear in the list in n. 31 above, but who may have been the same as no. 8, Muhamad Abubakar), Panular (no. 9 in n. 31 above), Mangkukusuma (no. 10 in n. 31 above), and Adikusuma (no. 11 in n. 31 above).

[33] On the birth of HB I, see p. 83 n. 39 above.

[34] Sĕmarang to Batavia, 29 Aug. 1788, in KA 3708 (OB 1789).

SUCCESSION, 1791-1792

The Company was primarily concerned that ample notice should be given if the Sultan was about to die, so that the Governor of Sĕmarang could hasten to Jogjakarta before the Sultan's death. The Company believed that the presence of the Governor at the deaths of Pakubuwana II in 1749 and Pakubuwana III in 1788 had been the only guarantee of a peaceful succession. Mangkubumi assured the Company that he would give the Governor ample notice.[35] But perhaps he never regarded this as a serious or important assurance. In any case, it was impractical. If he was ill, the Sultan usually secluded himself with only a favourite *sĕlir* (concubine),[36] and there was little likelihood in the event of a terminal illness that he would be able to send notice to the Dutch. Furthermore, whenever Mangkubumi was ill the Crown Prince was in control of the *kraton* and he was not a man who regarded the Dutch with affection. Very likely he would prefer to arrange his own succession than to chance that the Europeans might have been won over to the cause of one of his brothers. When Mangkubumi finally died, the Governor remained uninformed in Sĕmarang while the Resident of Jogjakarta sat uninformed in the fortress.

In 1790 Greeve had prepared to go to Jogjakarta when the Sultan was reported to be seriously ill with a fever. But Mangkubumi recovered and the trip was cancelled.[37] By January 1792, however, the Sultan's final illness had begun. He was clearly aware of this. He distributed among his sons various *krises*, rings, and other possessions, and commanded them to be loyal to the Crown Prince. But he refused to discuss with the Dutch the likelihood of his death and refused to allow the new Governor of Sĕmarang, P. G. van Overstraten (1791–6), to come to Jogjakarta because, he said, the trip might be in vain. Van Overstraten felt it inadvisable to go before he was summoned. He feared that to do so would give offence to the Sultan and would lead him to suspect that the Crown Prince hoped to mount the throne while his father still lived. Mangkubumi reassured van Overstraten that if his end were near, he would give notice.[38] The Dutch insistence

[35] Ibid.; HB I to Sĕmarang, 7 Muharram A.J. 1715 (received 11 Oct. 1788), in KA 3708 (OB 1789); A. Kuvel, Report, 28 Oct. 1788, in dJ xii, p. 150.

[36] Sĕmarang to Batavia, 24 Dec. 1788, in KA 3754 (OB 1790).

[37] Id., 19 May 1790 and 11 June 1790, in KA 3802 (OB 1791).

[38] Id., 5 Jan. 1792, in KA 3859 (OB 1793). See also *B. Mang.*, pp. 540–1; Poensen, 'Mangkubumi', p. 355.

that the Sultan notify them of his own impending death, before which notification the Governor could not travel to Jogjakarta without arousing suspicions, had now made it possible for the Sultan and the Crown Prince to ensure that the Governor would not be present when the event came. They need simply omit to give notice. By mid-February, the Sultan had recovered slightly but he remained very weak, with continued swelling of his hands and feet.[39]

It was probably during this illness that the Sultan was brought back on a palanquin from Krapjak to the *kraton*. He could no longer ride.[40] *Babad Mangkubumi*, giving the Crown Prince's version of these events, describes what the Sultan is supposed to have said when he called together his children:

LXXXII: 13. . . .
>   His Highness said,
>   'Ngabei, Natakusuma, and
>   indeed all my children,
>
> 14. 'after I have come to the promised end,
>   yes, all of you watch over
>   the Crown Prince
>   in his ascending the throne,
>   succeeding to my *kraton*.
>   Do no wrong
>   to the Crown Prince hereafter.
>   If there be those who cause disturbance
>   to the rule of the Crown Prince
>   may they meet no good fortune.'
>
> 15. Those who were commanded spoke,
>   the children saying, 'As you wish,'
>   with tears in their eyes, all.
>   His Highness spoke sweetly
>   to his son the Crown Prince,
>   'My last instruction to you:
>   absolutely, my son, must you
>   watch over your family,
>   go not so far as to cause difficulties in
>   their hearts,
>   provide equally for their good fortune.

---

[39] Sĕmarang to Batavia, 17 Feb. 1792, in KA 3859 (OB 1793).
[40] *B. Mang.*, pp. 539–40; Poensen, 'Mangkubumi', pp. 355, 359–60.

16. 'And furthermore, I entrust you
    to Sindurĕdja [the *patih djĕro*]. Please his
      heart,
    an aged person, how many are his years.
    Moreover, my final instruction:
    Become not estranged, my son,
    from the armies of the Dutch,
    go along with them truly.
    The legacy of grandfather's
    grandfather, Sultan Agung of Mataram,
    must you support.'

17. The Crown Prince made the *sĕmbah*, saying,
    'Indeed, your servant will do as you wish,
      all you command.'[41]
    ...

---

[41] *B. Mang.*, pp. 540–1, Canto LXXXII (Ḍanḍanggula):

13. ...
    Sri Narendra angandika
    ki Ngabei Natakusuma pa dening
    ja kabeh putraningwang

14. sapungkur ngong jen tĕka ing djandji
    ija sira kabeh dirumĕksa
    marang ki Dipati Anom
    gonira madĕg Ratu
    anggĕnteni kĕraton mami
    adjana gawe ala
    mring ki putra besuk
    jen ana gawe rubeda
    ija marang djĕnĕnge Kijadipati
    adja nĕmu rahardja

15. ingkang samja kĕḍawuhan angling
    para putra aturnja sandika
    prasamja rawat luh kabeh
    Sang Nata ngandika rum
    mring kang putra Pangran Dipati
    wĕkas ingwang marang sira
    pema sira kulup
    dirumĕksa sanakira
    adja nganti susah ing atine sami
    paḍa prihĕn rahardja

16. lawan maning kaki ingsun titip
    mring Sindurdja enakna atinja
    wong tuwa pira ngumure
    lan maning wĕkas ingsun
    adja sira apisah kaki
    marang bola Wĕlonda

The 'legacy of Sultan Agung' presumably referred to Agung's statement to Pangeran Purbaja concerning the siege of Batavia (1628–9). According to the eighteenth-century Jogjakarta *Babad Kraton*, Agung said that it was his will that the Company should become the ally of his descendants. It was the Dutch who would install kings, and in the future the Javanese would not dare to oppose them. Agung then withdrew his troops from Batavia, for which the grateful Dutchmen paid tribute to Mataram.[42]

> kanṭinĕn satuhu
> wasijate ejangira
> ejang Sultan Ngalaga Karta Mĕntawis
> pema sira tuokna
>
> 17. Kangdjĕng Gusti umatur wotsari
> gih sandika saḍawuh patikbra
> . . . .

Cf. Poensen, 'Mangkubumi', pp. 355–6.

[42] *BK*, ff. 271ᵛ–272ᵛ, Canto LIX (Durma):

> 6. . . .
> Sri Naranata
> nulja ngandika aris
>
> 7. lah ta uwa Purubaja karsaningwang
> sun kon mundur kang djurit
> lah ta wong Mataram
> ing bendjang wruhanira
> ing sapungkur-pungkur mami
> nak-putuningwang
> lunga tĕkeng Mĕtawis
>
> 8. ija iku kang atulung tĕḍak ingwang
> besuk sapungkur mami
> ija si Wĕlonda
> ingkang akarja Nata
> ngulihakĕn mring Matawis
> wong Djawa bendjang
> tan wani mring Kumpĕni
> . . .
>
> 13. sampun bubar wadya pasisir sadaja
> Wĕlonda aningali
> langkung sukanira
> sampun angrasa gĕsang
> wus angrasa wong Kumpĕni
> jen Kangdjĕng Sultan
> ingkang asru ngalimi
>
> 14. pira-pira sukanira wong Wĕlonda
> wus olih rĕmbug bĕtjik
> tan njana jen gĕsang

SUCCESSION, 1791–1792

Mangkubumi had thus enunciated to his son the principles upon which he advised him to base his government: to maintain unity among his brothers and not to antagonize the Company. Mangkubumi's view of the Dutch relationship was primarily that of an alliance rather than of vassalage, as will be seen more clearly in Chapter XI. According to *Babad Mangkubumi*, after instructing his sons, the Sultan spoke to the *patih* Danurědja and his assistants, entrusting to them the responsibility to ensure the succession of the Crown Prince.[43]

At midday of 14 March 1792 the Sultan collapsed while being carried about in his palanquin in the rice fields. He never recovered. He was taken to the *kraton* where he survived the night and, much to everyone's wonderment, the following ten days. He lay peacefully, his breathing steadily diminishing. The Company prepared for van Overstraten's trip to the *kraton* by sending twenty-five additional infantrymen and twenty-eight dragoons from Surakarta to Jogjakarta. Further reinforcements were sent to Salatiga and Bajalali, on the road between Sěmarang and Central Java. The north and south watches at the outer entrances to the *kraton* were occupied by Dutch troops and the other *kraton* entrances were

> dandanan sampun tělas
> marmane sira nusuli
> maring Mataram
> ngaturi bulu-pěkti.

The edited version of this story in *BTDj*, text pp. 138–9, trans. p. 143, is somewhat changed from the original, substituting 'Allah's will' (*karsa Allah*) for 'my will' (*karsaningwang*), etc. The text in *BTDj(BP)*, vol. x, pp. 15–16, is nearly identical to the *BK* text, except that *BK*'s stanza 8 is omitted.

[43] B. Mang., p. 541, Canto LXXXII (Ḍanḍanggula):

> 18. . . .
> Danurdja sun titěp [*sic*] bae
> marang sira wong tělu
> sapungkur ngong těka ing djandji
> mulih mring Rahmatolah
> wus pitaja ingsun
> Danurdja marang ing sira
> Ki Dipati manděge Nata nak-mami
> mongsa boḍowa sira
>
> 19. karo sira Mangundipura ning
> Natajuda sun titip ing sira
> putrengong maděga Radjeng
> . . . .

Cf. Poensen, 'Mangkubumi', pp. 355–6.

closed. All the princes and high officials of the court were billeted in separate temporary residences (*pondok*) on the *alun-alun*. But the Crown Prince told van Overstraten not to come to Jogjakarta until he had been informed of the Sultan's death. Van Overstraten decided to wait.[44]

At eleven p.m. on 24 March 1792 Mangkubumi died.[45] *Babad Mangkubumi* describes, perhaps with poetic licence, the Sultan's death in the presence only of his son:

LXXXII: 22. . . .
      His Highness then said,

23. 'My son, I give one last instruction:
may you be able to care well for the kingdom;
discharge this alone, my child.
It is finished. Remain behind, my son,
I take my leave of you.
I have reached my promised end;
I return, my child,
to the Mercy of God.'
The Crown Prince's words were mixed with
    weeping;
he wiped away a deluge of tears.

24. Then His Highness passed away.
The Crown Prince bowed deeply before his father.[46]
. . .

---

[44] Sěmarang to Batavia, 21 March 1792, in KA 3859 (OB 1793); id., 25 April 1792, in dJ xii, pp. 242–3; Rothenbühler, 'Dagregister', pp. 295–302. See also Poensen, 'Mangkubumi', pp. 359–60.

[45] Sěmarang to Batavia, 25 March 1792, in KA 3859 (OB 1793); id., 25 April 1792, in dJ xii, p. 246; Rothenbühler, 'Dagregister', p. 302 (where '21 Maart' is a misprint for '25 Maart'); *B. Mang.*, pp. 543–4; Poensen, 'Mangkubumi', p. 360; *Sěrat Djuměněngan S.D.I.S. Kg. Sultan Haměngkubuwana I* (Jogja kraton MS. A.22), pp. 4–5; *Babad Sangkalaning Momana*, p. 272.

The Javanese date was Sunday-Kliwon, 1 Ruwah, Dje, A.J. 1718. Because the death occurred after sunset, it was regarded by the Javanese as falling upon Sunday-Kliwon, although by Western reckoning 11 p.m., 24 March, was still Saturday (-Wage).

[46] *B. Mang.*, p. 542, Canto LXXXII (Ḍanḍanggula):

22. . . .
    malih Nata ngandika

23. Ki Dipati ingsun měkas malih
ja dibisa angěmong ing pradja
mung iku estokna angger
uwis karija kulup

Mangkubumi's body was bathed and prayed for by the religious leaders and the following day was laid to rest at the royal grave-site of Imagiri.[47]

Thus ended the reign of one of the greatest rulers of the House of Mataram. Mangkubumi had become king in 1749, had forced the Dutch to recognize him six years later, had overseen the foundation and legitimization of a great and powerful kingdom where his descendants still rule, and had passed on to his son the reins of authority. When he died in 1792, he was in the vicinity of eighty years of age. His reign since 1749 had been the longest in the history of Mataram, perhaps in all of Javanese history. Not until the twentieth century would Javanese kings reign longer.[48] Rarely had they ruled more successfully.

The old Sultan was dead and a new age now began. The reign of Haměngkubuwana II was to be one of the most turbulent in the history of Java, as conflicts among the sons of Mangkubumi as well as between the *kraton* and the Europeans grew in intensity. The Crown Prince of Jogjakarta, soon to become the new Sultan,

       ingsun pamit mring sira kaki
       wus těka djandjeningwang
       sun mulih putrengsun
       ija marang Rahmatolah
       Narpa Putra aturnja awor lan tangis
       waspa drěs ingusapan
24. sampun surud Sang Sri Narapati
       gja nungkěmi Djěng Gusti mring Rama
    ....

[47] *B. Mang.*, p. 543; Poensen, 'Mangkubumi', pp. 360–1; van Overstraten, Jogjakarta, to Sěmarang, 29 March 1792, in KA 3859 (OB 1793).

[48] HB I's reign (1749–92) was 43 years. PB III (1749–88) had reigned for 39. Both Sultan Agung (1613–45) and Amangkurat I (1645–77) had ruled for 32 years. Javanese history before the seventeenth century is exceedingly obscure and always open to revision. Dates for such earlier Javanese kings are therefore uncertain in the extreme. But it is not impossible that HB I's reign had been the longest in Javanese history. Krom, *HJG*, pp. 470–2, indicates no reigns longer than that of Wikramawardhana, to which he assigns the years 1389–1429 (40 years).

In the twentieth century, Haměngkubuwana VII (1877–1921) reigned for 44 years and Pakubuwana X (1893–1939) for 46.

De Graaf, *GI*, p. 482, lists kings in Bantěn and Tjirěbon in the sixteenth and seventeenth centuries with longer reigns than any of the Javanese kings: Abdul Kadir, 1596–1651 (55 years) and Paněmbahan Ratu, 1570–c. 1650 (80 years).

On the date of HB I's birth, see above, p. 83 n. 39.

was a different man than his father had been and he was to face different problems.

The Dutch soon learned that the Jogjakarta *kraton* was in the hands of a different and less cordial ruler. Van Overstraten was informed of the Sultan's death the following evening, 25 March, by which time the Sultan had already been buried. He set off the next morning and arrived in Jogjakarta on 29 March, his trip having been slowed somewhat by unusually hot weather.[49] In the meantime, according to *Babad Mangkubumi*, the Crown Prince called a conference with Danurĕdja, the *najakas* (highest court advisers), and his brothers. He asked whether it was necessary to await the arrival of van Overstraten or whether he should simply ascend the throne himself. Danurĕdja reminded him of his father's instruction not to estrange himself from the Company. In order to avoid such estrangement, he insisted that the Company must be allowed to declare the Crown Prince to be Sultan. The Crown Prince then asked the *najakas* Natajuda, Mangundipura, Danukusuma, and Dipakusuma for their advice, whereupon they agreed with Danurĕdja. Pangerans Ngabei and Natakusuma also said that the Governor's arrival must be awaited. The Crown Prince then accepted their advice and ordered the preparation of a letter to summon van Overstraten from Sĕmarang. *Babad Mangkubumi* ends as the Javanese awaited the arrival of the Governor.[50]

It is unclear whether the Crown Prince actually considered installing himself as Sultan before the Governor could arrive in Jogjakarta. But it may be significant that the Dutch Resident went to a *kraton* gathering at which were present the Crown Prince, Danurĕdja, the Crown Prince's son Mangkubumi (later Sultan Hamĕngkubuwana III), and the *najakas* Natajuda, Mangundipura, Danukusuma, and Dipakusuma. At this gathering van Ijsseldijk informed the Crown Prince that it was Batavia's intention to declare him Sultan Hamĕngkubuwana II, but that the installation could not take place until the Governor had arrived from Sĕmarang and all the contracts and acts of alliance had been renewed. The Crown Prince declared his pleasure at this and said he would await the Governor's arrival.[51] If the Prince had

---

[49] Sĕmarang to Batavia, 25 March 1792, in KA 3859 (OB 1793); id., 25 April 1792, in dJ xii, p. 247; Rothenbühler, 'Dagregister', pp. 302–14.
[50] *B. Mang.*, pp. 544–9.
[51] Sĕmarang to Batavia, 25 April 1792, in dJ xii, pp. 246–7.

considered a precipitous declaration of his succession, its necessity was presumably removed by this assurance of Company support.

Van Overstraten arrived in Jogjakarta on 29 March with more than 600 European troops. On 2 April 1792, he formally declared Mangkubumi's son to be Sultan Haměngkubuwana II. But the troubles between the Europeans and the *kraton* had already begun. Before his accession, the new Sultan had objected to various details of the ceremonial and of the contracts he was expected to sign. He had forced van Overstraten to recognize that there were discrepancies between the Dutch and Javanese texts of the agreements, which the Governor agreed to rectify.[52]

The various disagreements were sufficiently settled for the installation of the Sultan to take place. But the first steps had been taken on a bitter road which in the coming decades would lead to intrigues, murders, rebellions, depositions, and, finally, to the Java War (1825–30). These matters must await further investigation into the thousands of pages of European and Javanese records before they will be understood even partially. But some of the roots of these conflicts may be found in the tradition of greatness which Mangkubumi bequeathed to his heirs, and which the younger generation found it ever more difficult to emulate.

[52] Van Overstraten, Jogjakarta, to Sěmarang, 29 March 1792 and 2 April 1792, in KA 3859 (OB 1793); Sěmarang to Batavia, 25 April 1792, in dJ xii, pp. 242–76; Rothenbühler, 'Dagregister', pp. 314 ff.

XI

JOGJAKARTA AND THE DUTCH

Preceding chapters have been primarily a study of internal Central Javanese history. The late-eighteenth-century *kratons* were most concerned with relations among themselves, as they struggled to resolve the problem of seemingly permanent disunity among the élite. The outcome of this was the permanent division of Java into two *kratons* and one subsidiary princedom, which system had come by 1813 to include a second subsidiary princedom. It was suggested in Chapter I that the persistent inability of the Javanese to unite behind a single ruler and thereby to restore stability was partly a result of the Dutch intervention. By supporting rulers whom the Company regarded as legitimate because of their heredity but who had lost legitimacy in Javanese eyes, which could only be gained by forging a consensus of élite support, the Dutch disrupted the martial process by which new Javanese monarchs had traditionally emerged in times of crisis. But the Javanese did not apparently analyse their dilemma sufficiently to recognize the role played by the Company. Indeed, the Dutch did not perceive their own role in this way. They simply felt frustration when actions intended to restore stability produced the opposite effect.

Thus the important issues of the latter half of the eighteenth century seemed to the Javanese to involve primarily themselves. The Dutch were regarded as important but peripheral to the great issues of Javanese politics. Although policy towards the explosive situation in Central Java had become one of the main preoccupations of the Company, that priority was not reciprocated in Javanese eyes.

The Javanese were nevertheless concerned that their relationship with the Europeans should be properly regulated. Since 1619 Company officials had been permanently established at Batavia and since 1680 there had been Dutchmen present at the *kratons*, except for short periods. The relationship with these individuals could not go unregulated. The purpose of the present chapter is to consider the form into which this relationship had evolved. It is, like previous chapters, concerned primarily with Jogjakarta, although reference will be made also to Surakarta. It should be remembered, however, that despite the customary European conviction that Westerners were the most important element in the calculations of others, as they were in their own, this relationship was for the Javanese secondary in importance to the issues which have been discussed in previous pages.

It is necessary to begin by removing a historical red herring. The treaty of 1749, discussed in Chapter II, formally surrendered sovereignty over Mataram to the Company. There is considerable uncertainty about Pakubuwana II's intentions in this matter and reason to doubt that he, or any other Javanese, would have accorded that treaty the significance which it has been given by Westerners accustomed to European ideas of sovereignty over non-Western peoples. Whatever the case, the treaty had no significant impact upon the Dutch–Javanese relationship until the early nineteenth century, when administrators like Daendels and Raffles decided to impose a genuine exercise of Western sovereignty upon the Javanese courts. Until that time, the treaty was of far less significance than, for instance, the original decision of Amangkurat I in 1677 to solicit Dutch military support or the surrender of the *pasisir* in 1746. It should already be apparent from preceding chapters that the Company had neither the power nor, except in unusual circumstances, the inclination to attempt any genuine control over Central Javanese affairs. The Dutch presence was a more important political factor than the Javanese realized, but there can be no question of regarding the latter half of the eighteenth century as part of Dutch colonial history. Colonialism in Central Java is a matter for nineteenth-century historians.

Two further preliminary caveats are necessary. As is clear from preceding chapters, Jogjakarta and Surakarta were very different courts and their differences increased as the years passed. It was in the relationship with the Company that one of these many differences could be seen. Despite the problems with Pakubuwana IV discussed in Chapter IX, Surakarta was usually much more friendly towards the Dutch and very much more co-operative in all matters than Jogjakarta. The reader should take care not to assume that what is said here about Jogjakarta may be applied without further consideration to Surakarta. And the reader must also not assume that what is said about the late eighteenth century applies to any other period. The assumption that Javanese society was static over centuries[1] is based upon a paucity of specific historical studies and cannot be accepted *a priori*. The relationship described here may have applied in other periods, but it cannot be assumed to have done so until further research has been completed. Like the rest of this volume, the present chapter is based upon materials which are contemporaneous to the period discussed, in so far as possible. Thus this discussion relates only to a specific period in time and its generality or otherwise should be investigated rather than assumed.

The preceding chapters have described the way in which the court of Jogjakarta, and to a lesser extent that of Surakarta, dealt with specific issues concerning the Dutch. It is clear that Mangkubumi wished the relationship with the Company to be amicable, but that he never placed that goal above the more pressing concerns of Jogjakarta politics. The general understanding which underlay his view of that relationship will now be considered. In Chapter I the general Javanese perception of Westerners was discussed. It was suggested that the Europeans were perceived in a manner similar to that in which the Javanese saw the *panakawan*, the 'clown'-retainers of the *wajang*. Thus, individual Dutchmen might be both humorous and worthy of respect. But this was primarily a matter of individual relationships, while the present chapter is intended to consider more formal institutionalized relations between the *kraton* and the three main levels of the Dutch Company: the Residencies at the courts, the Government of Java's Northeast Coast at Sĕmarang, and the Company's headquarters in Batavia.

The Company's establishments at the *kratons* varied somewhat, but were usually in the vicinity of 150 to something over 200 men, as far as can be established without a detailed examination of the Dutch personnel records. An attempt was made to keep

[1] e.g. Schrieke, *Sociological Studies*, vol. ii, p. 4: 'The assumption which is basic to these studies . . . is that the structure of the Java of around 1700 was not appreciably different from that of the Java of around 700 . . .'
Moertono, *State and Statecraft*, p. 6: 'During these four hundred years [the late sixteenth century to the present] no basic changes seem to have taken place in the structural organization of the Mataram state, nor in the ideological bases of state-life.'

both Residencies at about the same strength as part of the Company's policy to maintain a balance between Jogjakarta and Surakarta. It was recognized that the Residencies served less to influence affairs at the courts than simply to display a Dutch presence, which was also made available to the rulers for largely ceremonial purposes. Thus, in 1773 a Second Resident was insisted upon by the Sultan for purely ceremonial reasons. A Second Resident had been appointed at Surakarta who accompanied Mangkunĕgara on formal occasions, but there was no one to perform an equivalent function for the Crown Prince of Jogjakarta. The Dutch Governor, van der Burgh, supported the Sultan's case.[2] And in 1781, the Jogjakarta garrison was increased by 57 men to bring it up to the same strength as that in Surakarta, not for military reasons but because 'the equality between the Susuhunan and the Sultan was judged necessary in all things'.[3]

The personnel at the Residencies included First and Second Residents, clerical and medical staff, students of Javanese, carpenters and locksmiths, as well as coachmen and trumpeters who were officially placed in the service of the Javanese monarchs. Roughly ninety per cent of the garrisons consisted of military personnel of various kinds. But these troops were of little military value and the Dutch recognized that their role was, like that of the Residency in general, largely ceremonial.[4] Whenever the Residencies were expected to have a genuine military role to play, the first priority was a large increase in the numbers of troops. But even then they were of dubious independent value, isolated in the midst of vast Javanese armies. The sad tale of the repeatedly

[2] Sĕmarang to Batavia, 5 April 1773, in KA 3281 (OB 1774). Cf. Norodom of Cambodia's complaint to Aymonier in 1879 that the Siamese king had 'a court of consuls; here there is only one representative'; cited in Milton E. Osborne, *The French Presence in Cochinchina and Cambodia: Rule and Response (1859–1905)* (Ithaca, 1969), p. 177.

[3] Van der Burgh, Memorie, 19 Sept. 1780, in dJ xi, pp. 414–16; Resolutien genoomen in Raade van Politie, Sĕmarang, 14 June 1781, in KA 3492 (OB 1782).

[4] See van der Burgh, Memorie, 19 Sept. 1780, in dJ xi, pp. 414–15; Siberg, Memorie, 18 Sept. 1787, in dJ xii, pp. 90–1.

See also Hartingh, Memorie, 26 Oct. 1761, in dJ x, pp. 368–9: 'The dragoons serve as the [Susuhunan's] life-guards, of whom a detachment always escort him whenever he goes out and is accompanied by the Resident. . . . The Sultan also has a company of dragoons as life-guards'; van der Burgh, Memorie, 19 Sept. 1780, in dJ xi, p. 415: 'The . . . servants are more than necessary, the dragoons as pomp and as guards for the rulers, the infantry and artillery to occupy the fortress, and the rest for other services.'

postponed construction of the Jogjakarta fortress, discussed in Chapter V, will be recalled. The position of that fortress was considered particularly exposed in case of hostilities,[5] and Dutch records document amply the weakened state of the Company's defences in general in the latter half of the eighteenth century. This should also be clear from preceding chapters.

Life at the *kraton* Residencies must have been a strange affair for the small European communities in the centre of the exotic *kraton* towns. In particular the Residents, who often served for many years at the *kratons*, must occasionally have come to lose something of their sense of identity. The cases of Palm and Hartsinck in Surakarta will be recalled.[6] Of the latter the Company was even prepared to believe that he was conspiring with the Susuhunan to slaughter all Europeans. The Jogjakarta Resident J. M. van Rhijn, who had been Second Resident at Surakarta for four years before being made First Resident at Jogjakarta, retired after thirteen years at the Sultan's court in 1786. By that time Europe was apparently more foreign to him than Java. He asked to be repatriated to the Netherlands with his Dutch wife, but wished to be allowed to return to Java if either of them should prove unable to adapt to a European climate.[7] His replacement as First Resident was the former Second Resident W. H. van Ijsseldijk, who served for a further thirteen years (1786–99). The Surakarta Resident van Straalendorff (1767–84) took an Indonesian mistress, by whom he had eight children. He applied to Batavia to have these children declared legitimate, which was granted.[8]

These men lived a life curiously suspended between two greatly dissimilar cultures. The Residents were often men of low origins, as were many of the Company's servants. To them, extended tours in strange Javanese cities often meant primarily a chance to increase their own power and wealth. The Resident who was not corrupt, incompetent, or debauched was perhaps more the exception than the rule. One should not place them in the postures

[5] Sĕmarang to Batavia, 1 March 1785, in KA 2597 (OB 1786).
[6] Palm and Hartsinck are discussed in Chap. IX above.
[7] Batavia to H.XVII, 31 Dec. 1769, in dJ xi, p. 104; Resolutien genoomen in Raade van Politie, Sĕmarang, 14 June 1773, in KA 3280 (OB 1774); Sĕmarang to Batavia, 12 June 1786, in KA 3630 (OB 1787).
[8] Id., 4 Nov. 1779, in KA 3447 (OB 1780); Resolutien genoomen in Raade van Politie, Sĕmarang, 18 Jan. 1780, in KA 3476 (OB 1781).
The woman is simply referred to as an 'indigenous woman', and she may not necessarily have been Javanese.

of the dedicated colonial civil servant who came to be the ideal of much later periods. The Company's Residents had such opportunities to supplement their salaries unofficially that they were said sometimes to enjoy incomes greater than the Governor of Sĕmarang,[9] who stood considerably higher than they in the scale of official salaries and who was not without his own means to supplement his income. Salaries were not particularly good and 'corruption' was an established element in Company life from the top of its bureaucracy to the bottom. A Resident, who usually had the rank of *opperkoopman* (senior merchant), received from about 80 to 100 guilders per month in salary, which was what an *opperkoopman* had received a century before.[10] And even that salary could suddenly be reduced. F. C. van Straalendorff had been in the service of the Company for thirty-one years in 1781, for the last fourteen of which he had been First Resident at Surakarta and for the last six of which he had received 100 guilders per month. Suddenly his salary was reduced to 80 guilders per month, prompting the Governor of Sĕmarang to take his case to the Governor-General.[11]

The somewhat equivocal position of the Residents was reflected in the nature of their official post, which was rather similar to that of an ambassador. The Resident was a servant of the Company, which paid his salary and offered him opportunities to supplement it. His primary responsibility was to provide information to his superiors concerning affairs in Central Java[12] and to act as a channel of communication in both directions between the Company and the rulers. He had commercial duties to fulfil as well, and was responsible for administering the affairs of the Europeans under him. But although he was a servant of the Company, the Resident was at the same time recognized to be a servant

[9] See Hartingh, Memorie, 26 Oct. 1761, in dJ x, p. 358; Vos, Memorie, 24 July 1771, in dJ xi, p. 171. See also Day, *Dutch in Java*, pp. 113–15.

[10] The general salary structure in the latter half of the eighteenth century may be found in Mossel, Reglement op het benoemen en ontslaan van Compagnie's dienaren, 31 July–6 Aug. 1753, in J. A. van der Chijs (ed.), *Nederlandsch-Indisch Plakaatboek, 1602–1811* (17 vols.; 's Hage, 1885–1900), vol. vi, pp. 456–93. Salary scales for the latter half of the seventeenth century may be found in Boxer, *Dutch Seaborne Empire*, pp. 300–2.

[11] Sĕmarang to Batavia, 19 Dec. 1781, in KA 3492 (OB 1782).

[12] See van Ossenberch's comment that the Residents' 'principal duty, after all, is to investigate and examine secretly the rulers' designs'; Sĕmarang to Batavia, 19 Sept. 1762, in KA 2957 (OB 1763).

of the Javanese ruler, not only by the Javanese but also by the Dutch. One of the most important commendations that his superiors could give to a Resident was that he possessed the gift to make himself 'beloved by the Javanese'. It seems that the Residents actually took an oath of faithfulness to the ruler to whose court they were assigned as well as to the Company.[13]

The Javanese rulers treated the Residents as their servants, and the conversations recorded in the court *babads* between Javanese rulers and the Residents reflect this attitude. The Javanese monarch would address his Resident in *ngoko* ('low Javanese', used for addressing inferiors) while the latter would reply in *krama* ('high Javanese', used to address superiors).[14] There is no reason to think that this procedure was not actually followed. There was not yet any question of the Resident at the court representing the person of the Governor-General, and therefore requiring the protocol observed with regard to the latter. The Residents are also described in the court *babads* as acting as the Javanese ruler's emissaries.[15]

That the Company accepted, or at least tolerated, this view of the Resident as a joint servant of the Javanese ruler and the Com-

---

[13] A letter from Siberg to HB I of 1785 refers to the Resident's oath of faithfulness to HB I and the VOC; Sĕmarang to HB I, 17 Dec. 1785, in KA 3630 (OB 1787).

[14] e.g. *B. Mang.*, pp. 21, 52, 486. The *babads* are written in verse and the distinction between *ngoko* and *krama* is sometimes ignored for metrical reasons. In some cases, however, the authors took the trouble to make clear the difference in the level of spoken Javanese. For example:
B. Mang., p. 53, Canto X (Asmaradana) (HB I and VOC Resident Donkel speaking, Donkel speaks first):

8. ...
inggih kĕlangkung prajoga
punapa sakarsendra
Kumpni tumut sĕdarum
[HB I answers:] ora Dongkĕl karsaningwang

9. sira lan kang djaga mami
kabeh Kumpni karija
adjagaha barisane
apan ingsun ora lawas
....

[15] e.g. *B. Mang.*, p. 26. See also *B. Mang.*, p. 437, cited above, p. 174 n. 102, in which one of the elements of Jogjakarta's prosperity was that 'Resident van Rhijn was ever more proficient in serving every wish of His Highness'; and the role of von Hohendorff in the *Babad Gijanti* story of the founding of Surakarta, translated in Soepomo and Ricklefs, 'Establishment of Surakarta'.

pany is reflected in Dutch promotion procedures. Company officials were, of course, promoted by the Company for Company reasons. But an additional procedure was observed in the case of servants at the *kraton* garrisons. The Susuhunan or the Sultan often informed the Dutch that various individuals, including lower officials and soldiers as well as the Residents, were deserving of promotion to a higher rank in the Dutch bureaucracy (e.g. to *sergeant* or *opperkoopman*). This was either because that individual was said to have served the ruler well or because it had been discovered that the man who performed an equivalent role in the other *kraton* had the higher rank. The Company would agree to the promotion and raise the individual's rank upon the Susuhunan's or the Sultan's nomination. This apparently came to be accepted as a standard procedure for the *kraton* garrisons, even in the case of nominations for the position of the Resident itself.[16]

The Resident's position as the joint servant of the Javanese and the Company was a Dutch mirror-image of that of the Javanese *patih*. By the treaties of 1743 and 1755, the *patih* owed joint loyalty to the Company and to his ruler.[17] Like the Resident, of course, the *patih* also had many responsibilities not connected with *kraton*–Company relations. And preceding chapters have shown that when new *patihs* were nominated the actual procedure was for the Company merely to approve the Sultan's or the Susuhunan's appointment even when that appointment was not the Company's own first choice. Nevertheless, the *patih* was seen to fit, with the Resident, into a dual position consisting of two men, one from each side, each owing loyalty to both sides. A twentieth-century genealogy of the Sultan's *patih* Danurĕdja suggests that the duality of this position may have had a genealogical expression. It will be seen below that the Dutch were considered to be the

---

[16] e.g. Hartingh, Memorie, 26 Oct. 1761, in dJ x, p. 369; HB I to Batavia, 15 Dulkangidah A.J. 1687 (8 June 1762), in KA 2956 (OB 1763); id., 3 May 1765, in KA 3048 (OB 1766); Sĕmarang to Batavia, 1 June 1779 and 10 Aug. 1779, in KA 3448 (OB 1780); id., 8 Nov. 1781, in KA 3492 (OB 1782).

The Sĕmarang letter of 1 June 1779 says that van der Burgh had attempted to end this procedure but both PB III and HB I continued to make such nominations and van der Burgh finally submitted them with his approval to Batavia. The Sĕmarang letter of 8 Nov. 1781 refers to PB III's request for the promotion of three low-level military officers as being submitted 'according to custom' (*na het gebruijk*).

[17] See PB II–VOC Treaty, 11 Nov. 1743, in dJ ix, p. 436; HB I–VOC Treaty, 13 Feb. 1755, in dJ x, p. 300.

legitimate successors of the ancient kingdom of Padjadjaran, which had ruled the area including Batavia. Padjadjaran was seen as the equivalent in the West of Java, ruling a non-Javanese (Sundanese) population, to the great kingdom of Madjapahit in the East of Java, ruling the ethnic Javanese. Thus it is not surprising to find that Danurĕdja traced his ancestry to a union between a daughter of the last king of Padjadjaran and a son of the last king of Madjapahit.[18] Whether the genealogy was correct and Danurĕdja was therefore the most appropriate man for the *patih*'s position or whether, as is considerably more likely, the genealogy evolved afterwards as an expression of the *patih*'s dual position, cannot be asserted with complete confidence.

Thus, the immediate channel of communication at *kraton* level between the Sultan or the Susuhunan and the next level of the Dutch bureaucracy went through both the *patih* and the Resident. Along this channel flowed gifts, letters, reports, and intelligence in both directions. The *patih* and the Resident carried primary responsibility to both sides for keeping open these lines of communication.

The next important level in the Dutch hierarchy was Sĕmarang. From 1748 to 1808, the Dutch maintained a 'Government of Java's Northeast Coast' at Sĕmarang, headed by a 'Governor and Director of Java's Northeast Coast', whose position was intermediate between Batavia and the Dutch posts on Java east of Tjirĕbon, including the *kraton* Residencies. Communications between the courts and Batavia passed through Sĕmarang. In addition, new Governors customarily made a tour to the Central Javanese courts as soon as possible after their installations and also travelled there whenever unusual circumstances seemed to demand their presence. Thus there was often direct personal communication between the Javanese rulers and the Governor. Many such meetings have been described in preceding chapters, and it

---

[18] Th. Pigeaud, 'Kangdjeng Pangeran Arja Adipati Danoeredja VII, Papatih Dalem ing Karaton Ngajogjakarta, Toemboek 1798/1869–1862/1931', *Djåwå*, vol. 11 (1931), nos. 5–6, p. 35.

The princess was Rĕtna Pamĕkas, daughter of Prabu Siliwangi of Padjadjaran; the prince was Raden Saputra Arja Baribin alias Paṇḍita Putra Pangeran Ngabei, son of Prabu Brawidjaja (IV) of Madjapahit.

In other Javanese sources, 'Arja Baribin' is the name of the Muslim Bupati of Madura who was among the enemies of the last king of Madjapahit; see *BTDj(BP)*, vol. iii, p. 11, cited and translated in Ricklefs, 'Consideration', pp. 308–9; see also Djajadiningrat, *Sadjarah Bantĕn*, p. 23.

will be clear that the nature of this relationship varied greatly according to the nature of the individuals who held the Governorship. Within internal Javanese politics the Governor of Sĕmarang on several occasions served an important function as the outsider who arbitrated disputes between the two *kratons*.

The Javanese courtly view of the position of Sĕmarang does not seem as clear as that of the Residencies and of Batavia. This may be because of the short duration of the Government of the Northeast Coast. The institution lasted for only sixty years and only ten men held the Governor's post, of whom eight were involved in the period described in the present study.[19] Perhaps this was not long enough for the *kratons* to evolve an official view of the relationship. Moreover, Sĕmarang was something of an anomaly in Javanese eyes. As will be seen below, the Javanese accepted a bipartite division of the island between Batavia and Central Java, which corresponded historically to the division between Padjadjaran and Madjapahit and ethnically to the distinction between the Sundanese and the Javanese. The *patihs* and the Residents at the *kratons* were the local expression of this duality. The *pasisir*, however, was Javanese ethnically and historically but was governed by the Dutch after 1746. Perhaps, then, there was some difficulty in placing the Sĕmarang Government into a consistent view of the over-all Dutch–Javanese relationship. It will be recalled that the designs of Pakubuwana IV, discussed in Chapter IX, seem to have been opposed as much to Sĕmarang as to Jogjakarta, but not to Batavia.

In their relations with the Governor, the Javanese rulers addressed him as *saudara*, which appears in Dutch translations of official Javanese letters as 'brother'. In *Babad Mangkubumi*, the form of address is often *saudara*,[20] but it is also sometimes *bapak dĕler*,[21] meaning literally 'father *edele Heer*', the latter being the Dutch form of address for the Governor and other 'gentlemanly' officials. Neither of these forms is very helpful in understanding the Javanese view of the Governor. *Saudara* did mean literally 'brother', being derived from the Malay, but in Javanese it came to be used as a form of address only for non-Javanese, in which

[19] See Appendix I.
[20] e.g. *B. Mang.*, pp. 14, 28, 337, 344, 537.
[21] e.g. ibid., pp. 335, 344 (on the latter page, HB I refers to 'saudara mami bapak dĕler').

circumstance it was more equivalent to English 'Mister' or 'you'. It is a problem for historical semantics whether in the eighteenth century the rulers really meant to call the Governor their 'brother' (hence, their equal in protocol) or merely 'Mister (non-Javanese)'. The problem is further complicated by the fact that personal oral communication would in most cases have taken place in Malay while written correspondence was in Javanese. The term *bapak dĕler* does not necessarily suggest that the Javanese ruler was addressing the Governor as a superior ('father'); indeed *Babad Mangkubumi* includes speeches in which the Sultan apparently addresses the Governor in *ngoko*, used only for close equals or inferiors.[22] Thus the relationship is unclear. But it is significant that *Babad Mangkubumi* describes van Ossenberch's trip to Jogjakarta in 1763 as a visit to 'pay homage' to the Sultan.[23] And in 1788, when Mangkubumi wrote to Governor Jan Greeve concerning an assurance of the succession of the Jogjakarta Crown Prince, he called the Prince 'my brother's [Greeve's] son'.[24] Since he was Mangkubumi's son, this suggests that the Sultan was placing the Governor on the same protocol level as himself. On the whole, then, it seems that the Governor's position was somewhat irregular, but that it was not generally seen as being superior to that of the Sultan.

The most important person in the Javanese view of the relationship with the Company was the far-away Governor-General in

---

[22] e.g. *B. Mang.*, p. 14, Canto II (Pangkur) (HB I addresses Hartingh):

10. . . .
    Djĕng Sultan angandika
    saudara ingsun iku ora wĕruh
    angluwih ingsun pitaja
    karone iku pe mami

11. ingsun bangĕt apitaja
    marang iku Tumĕnggung Judanĕgari
    . . . .

See n. 14 above on the general problem of *ngoko* and *krama* in Javanese verse.

[23] Ibid., p. 328, Canto L (Sinom):

49. pĕsṭi aku nuli prapta
    aseba Kangdjĕng Sang Adji
    . . . .

[24] HB I to Sĕmarang, 7 Muharram A.J. 1715 (received 11 Oct. 1788), in KA 3708 (OB 1789). The letter is preserved only in Dutch translation. The Javanese phrase was presumably *putra* or *anak saudara*.

Batavia, whom they addressed as their 'grandfather' (*ejang*).²⁵ This was not, however, a close personal relationship. After the trip of Governor-General van Imhoff to Surakarta in 1746, which was the occasion of Mangkubumi's rebellion, there had been no personal meetings between the Javanese rulers and any Governor-General in the period of this study. It had been the practice to send missions of felicitation to each new Governor-General in Batavia, but when the Dutch decided in 1777 that such missions would thereafter be received at Sĕmarang instead, Mangkubumi even stopped sending embassies although Pakubuwana III complied with the new ceremonial.²⁶ The Governor-General was clearly perceived as a senior figure ('grandfather'). But it was important that he should reside in Batavia, and at least Jogjakarta felt it was inappropriate that greetings be sent to him in Sĕmarang instead. These missions of felicitation were not seen by Mangkubumi as a colonial obligation but as a right of alliance. As late as 1788 he complained that the revised ceremonial made it impossible for him to send an embassy to Batavia so that his subjects could see 'that he still lived, even as before, in close friendship with his grandfather the Governor-General and the Council of the Indies'.²⁷ The embassies to Batavia had been part of the Sultan's royal role as a king in the Indonesian world of which the Governor-General was an important part.

An important key to understanding the Governor-General's position as it was seen by Jogjakarta lies in the location of Batavia, as is suggested by the Sultan's reluctance to send greetings to him at any other city. According to traditional Javanese views of history, there had long been a kingdom in West Java called Padjadjaran, roughly contemporaneous with Madjapahit. The actual history of Padjadjaran is exceedingly obscure. Krom placed its foundation in the early fourteenth century and the remnants of the kingdom were known to the Portuguese early in the sixteenth

---

²⁵ e.g. PB III to Batavia, 30 Mulud A.J. 1688 (19 Oct. 1762), in KA 2956 (OB 1763); Sĕmarang to Batavia, 29 Aug. 1788, in KA 3708 (OB 1789); *B. Mang.*, pp. 363, 469.

See also *B. Mang.*, p. 340, where HB I and PB III are called 'children' of the VOC, and MN is called the 'grandchild' of the VOC.

²⁶ This matter is discussed in detail, pp. 247–54 above.

²⁷ Sĕmarang to Batavia, 29 Aug. 1788, in KA 3708 (OB 1789). See also p. 249 n. 50, citing Javanese sources which depict these embassies in terms of 'sending royal felicitations to' or 'sanctioning the authority of' the GG.

century before it was displaced by Islamic states.[28] Whatever the actual history of Padjadjaran, it is preserved in a highly mythical fashion in the Modern Javanese *babads* as the kingdom of the Sundanese, as distinct from the Javanese kingdoms farther to the east on the island. It occupied the highlands above present-day Djakarta, and its port was Sunda Kalapa, renamed Djajakarta (Djakarta) by the successor Islamic rulers. There in 1619 the Dutch established their headquarters, renaming it Batavia.[29]

By taking over control of Batavia and, eventually, of the adjacent regions, the Dutch became in fact the successors to Padjadjaran, and the Javanese apparently saw the Company's position in precisely that way. This was made clear in one of the treaties of 1677, by which Amangkurat II confirmed Dutch support against Trunadjaja's rebellion. The Susuhunan formally ceded to the Company 'the ancient Djakartan, now Batavian, jurisdiction and limits, from the river Krawang eastwards to the river Pamanukan and then directly overland reaching to the Southern Ocean'.[30] The Dutch had been ceded the Sunda-lands, the ancient kingdom of Padjadjaran.

Several writers have described and commented upon Javanese texts which actually attribute Padjadjaran ancestry to the Dutch, via a Padjadjaran princess.[31] Here, in the interest of historical precision, the discussion will centre upon a major text which was almost certainly written shortly after the period studied here and is very probably of Jogjakarta *kraton* origin, the *Sĕrat Sakoṇḍar*. Here is found a version of the mythical 'Baron Sakender' story. The Jogjakarta courtly texts *Sĕrat Surja Radja* and *Babad Kraton* will also be employed. The reader should be warned in advance of the exceeding complexity of this matter. It was not simply a case of fabricating a false genealogy for the Dutch East India Company.

Padjadjaran was the 'other kingdom' on Java and, because it was Sundanese and not Javanese, it had always been a foreign kingdom.

[28] Krom, *HJG*, pp. 405–6, 458.
[29] On these matters, see de Graaf, *GI*, pp. 93, 149–51.
[30] Amangkurat II–VOC Treaty, 19–20 Oct. 1677, in dJ vii, pp. 166–7. See also *BTDj*, text p. 208, trans. p. 214.
[31] See Cohen Stuart, *Baron Sakéndhèr*, pp. 160–2, and the literature cited there; Djajadiningrat, *Sadjarah Bantěn*, pp. 285–8; Schrieke, *Sociological Studies*, vol. ii, p. 12; Brandes, 'Pararaton', pp. 66–7; Raffles (1830), vol. ii, p. 104; Pigeaud, *Literature*, vol. ii, p. 249.
See also the slightly different statements of such myths in W. H. Rassers, *De Pandji-Roman* (Antwerpen, 1922), pp. 335–7.

JOGJAKARTA AND THE DUTCH

Now new foreigners were there. But the position of Padjadjaran was more than that of a political counterbalance to the Javanese kingdoms. Apparently it was also, in Javanese eyes, a place of particular spiritual significance. Much more research is required before this aspect will be clear, but the broad outlines may be suggested. Padjadjaran/Batavia ruled the high mountains of West Java, the 'Priangan' as it is known today. This toponym seems to be derived from *parahjangan* or *prajangan*, meaning apparently 'the (abode of the) spirits'.[32] Thus, it was apparently a place associated with the spirit world of Java. That spirit world was dominated by the authority of the Goddess of the Southern Ocean. The important connection here is that the Padjadjaran princess who was the ancestor of the Dutch was apparently, according to Javanese tradition, of the same royal line of descent as the Goddess herself.[33] Both were descended from the royal house of Padjadjaran.

Thus the Dutch ruled a place of spiritual significance and were related to the Goddess of the Southern Ocean, who played an important role in Mataram *kraton* mythology. She was the wife of

[32] *Parahjangan* or *prajangan* is apparently derived from *hjang* (god, spirit) and hence means 'the (abode of the) spirits'. See Berg, 'Māyā's Hemelvaart', p. 377. Gericke-Roorda (1901), vol. i, p. 158, gives: '*Prajangan*, a spirit of the female sex, also name of the Preanger-Regencies'. But van Hien, *Javaansche Geestenwereld*, vol. i, p. 253, says the *prajangan* or *prijangan* may be of either sex.

It has been suggested to me that *parahjangan* might also be derived from the Old Javanese *rahyang* ('holy man'). *Pa-rahyang-an* could then mean 'hermitage(s)'. This might then be a synonym for 'Padjadjaran', since the latter toponym could originally have evolved from *adjar* ('holy man') via *pangadjaran* ('hermitage(s)'), to *Padjadjaran*. Nevertheless, the use of the word *parajangan* in Modern Javanese texts clearly shows that the Javanese authors understood it as 'the spirits' or 'abode of the spirits', not 'hermitage'.

[33] In the *Babad Tanah Djawi* stories Raden Susuruh, the future founder of Madjapahit, encounters the hermit Tjĕmara Tunggal, who reveals herself to him as a princess of Padjadjaran who has left her father's court because she refused to marry. She has magical powers, and can be male or female, young or old. She announces she will become queen of all the spirits (*prajangan lan ĕdjin*) and will serve Raden Susuruh and his descendants, who will reign to the south of Mt. Mĕrapi and to the north of Mantjingan (i.e. in Mataram). She is, thus, the Goddess of the Southern Ocean. In *BTDj* and *BTDj(BP)* she also promises to marry all those who become ruler of all Java, but this is not the case in the Jogjakarta *BK*. See *BK*, ff. 45^v–48^r; *BTDj(BP)*, vol. i, pp. 58–66; *BTDj*, text pp. 16–17, trans. pp. 16–17; van Iperen, 'Sadjara Radja Djawa', *TBG*, vol. 3 (1781), pp. 125–30.

See also Cohen Stuart, *Baron Sakéndhèr*, pp. 162–3; Raffles (1830), vol. ii, p. 104; Pigeaud, *Literature*, vol. ii, p. 249.

Official Jogjakarta *kraton* mythology still has it that the Goddess is a Padjadjaran princess.

Senapati and Sultan Agung, and the evidence of *Taman Sari* very strongly suggests that Mangkubumi was her mystical spouse as well.[34] Thus, in theory, the Sultan of Jogjakarta was related by marriage also to the Dutch 'kings' of the spiritually significant lands of West Java. The Dutch position in West Java was thus part of a complex mythological system which assured the Sultan of Jogjakarta that the spirit forces of Java would not turn against him. By assuring other Javanese of this as well, it contributed to the legitimation of royal authority. And just as the Goddess had promised her aid to the House of Mataram, so it was appropriate that the Dutch, her relatives, should also be the allies of the Javanese kings.

Babad Kraton contains an early story of the foundation of Batavia which takes place in the Southern Ocean. It seems primarily intended to explain the name 'Batavia' and provides the transition by which, in other texts, the *babad* story moves from early Javanese mythical history into the Baron Sakender stories. The story is found in the early mythological sections of the book, where the Javanese king (of the kingdom of Galuh) has gone to war and has been defeated by his younger brother, the king of the Sundanese in Padjadjaran. He sets off to the south-east, coming to the coast of the Southern Ocean. Having walked across the sea to the island Nusa Tumbini, he encounters a personage who is black, with large red eyes, clad only in a loin-cloth. After a conversation concerning the baking of bricks, the king of Galuh decides to settle on Nusa Tumbini. He changes the name to 'Batawijah', meaning in Javanese 'common bricks' (*bata wijah*).[35] Since it is in the Southern Ocean, Nusa Tumbini (which is not identifiable as an actual location) is obviously on the wrong side of the island for the location of Batavia. But the location makes sense in terms of the connection between the Goddess of the Southern Ocean and the Dutch position which was set out above.

In a Jogjakarta *Babad Tanah Djawi* written in 1821, the text proceeds from the story about the founding of 'Batawijah', which is identical with the *Babad Kraton* text, directly to the story of Baron Sakender.[36] The latter story is not included in

[34] *Taman Sari* is discussed in Chap. III. See especially p. 85.
[35] *BK*, ff. 33^r–34^r.
[36] NBS 158 includes a text identical (with small variations) to the *BK* text cited in n. 35 above. In both cases, the story is in Canto V of the text. A second copy of NBS 158 (LOr 6483, dated 1851) also has this story. Both

JOGJAKARTA AND THE DUTCH

Babad Kraton, but another text is available which will be described here. The *Sĕrat Sakondar* (BM Add. MS. 12289) describes the story of Raden Baron Kasender, as he is called in this text. The paper on which it is written, the handwriting, the use of special characters found in other Jogjakarta *kraton* texts, and the large amount of the text which is similar to later Jogjakarta versions all suggest it is a Jogjakarta *kraton* manuscript.[37] It is undated, but since it was part of John Crawfurd's collection it can have been written no later than Crawfurd's departure from Java in 1816. It was probably written before 1812, when the English captured the *kraton* while deposing Sultan Hamĕngkubuwana II, and since it mentions both French and English troops it was perhaps composed after the arrival of Daendels in 1808. It is thus, most probably, a text from the court of Sultan Hamĕngkubuwana II, who was Crown Prince during the period described in the preceding chapters, and it was perhaps composed between 1808 and 1812. It is the oldest manuscript of the story known to the present writer.[38]

---

texts proceed in Canto VI (NBS 158, vol. i, p. 58; LOr 6483, p. 55) to the Baron Sakender story which occupies both texts to Canto XXXV. *BK*, Canto VI, begins the story of Mundingsari of Padjadjaran.

[37] The MS. is on Javanese paper (*dluwang*). Since those texts in the BM which Crawfurd had copied for himself are on English paper, this MS. may have been taken in the capture of the Jogjakarta *kraton* in 1812. It is possible, of course, that the MS. may have been presented to Crawfurd as a gift by someone, but this is unlikely since it is not a refined work of art. It is very sloppily written, and the scribe switched back and forth between different styles of handwriting, which would not have been done in a presentation copy. The hand is similar to that in 'Journal', BM Add. MS. 12303, which was certainly taken from the *kraton*. The MS. also employs special characters for *nga* and *e*, not found in other MSS., but similar in construction to the special characters for *a* and *i* used in the various MSS. of *Sĕrat Surja Radja*. Dr. Pigeaud has confirmed my impression that the use of such characters is peculiar to Jogjakarta *kraton* MSS. (letter of 5 Aug. 1971). Several cantos in the BM *Sĕrat Sakondar* MS. seem to be identical with those in the Jogjakarta MSS. NBS 158 and LOr 6185, although a complete comparison of the texts has not been possible.

[38] The other MSS. used for comparison here are the following:

NBS 158 and LOr 6483, dated respectively 1821 and 1851. Both Jogjakarta *Babad Tanah Djawi* texts, including the Baron Sakender stories (see n. 36 above).

LOr 1800, *Baron Sakender*, Cohen Stuart's published text, dated 1845. Much of the text, especially in the middle portions, is nearly identical with BM Add. MS. 12289. See n. 54 below.

LOr 6185, *Baron Sakender*, dated 1936. At least Cantos VIII–X seem, on

JOGJAKARTA UNDER SULTAN MANGKUBUMI

It cannot be known with certainty how old the first versions of the Baron Sakenḍer story may have been. Because of the complete absence of manuscripts older than the eighteenth century, it is impossible to answer the question which was raised somewhat more successfully in Chapter VII: did myth explain events after they had occurred, or did myth pre-date events and thereby dispose the Javanese to accept them? Although there are hints of some antiquity in the Baron Sakenḍer stories, it seems unlikely that the stories in the forms now known could have been written before the mid-eighteenth century. An earlier origin is seemingly implied by the prominence in the stories of the 'Spanish' (*wong Spanjol*), which led the editor of the only published text and translation of this work, A. B. Cohen Stuart, to suggest an early-seventeenth-century origin, although the manuscript he used was dated 1845.[39] If it derived from some hypothetical seventeenth-century work, however, one would have expected to find not the Spanish but the Portuguese, who were much more important in Javanese history. Although some elements may have been taken from an older text about foreign nations, it is more probable that the Spanish were included because the Javanese had heard from Dutchmen the role which Spain had played in the

---

quick comparison, to be nearly identical with the same cantos in BM Add. MS. 12289.

Several other MSS. include the story or versions of it, but none seems to be older than BM Add. MS. 12289. See the MSS. listed in the index in Pigeaud, *Literature*, vol. iii, under 'Sakèṇḍèr' and Kasèṇḍèr'.

Most of the MSS. containing the story seem to be of Jogjakarta origin and none is verifiably from Surakarta. This leads one to suspect that the story may be a creation of the Jogjakarta literati. This has further implications for the question of the antiquity of the stories. If the tale was older than the division of the kingdom in the eighteenth century it would have been part of the common literary heritage of both Surakarta and Jogjakarta. In that case, it would seem strange that there do not seem to be any MSS. verifiably from Surakarta. This suggests that the tale is instead an eighteenth- or early-nineteenth-century Jogjakarta text in its original form. It is possible, therefore, that BM Add. MS. 12289, besides being the most appropriate text for the present study, may also be the most original version of the text now available.

Winter, *Zamenspraken*, vol. i, pp. 353, 364, ascribes the story to one Ngabei Judasara, a Surakarta poet. This, too, confirms that the text was written after the mid-eighteenth century, but it is curious that Judasara is mentioned in no MS. known to me, and that none is verifiably from Surakarta. Yet it is certain that the text was known to the great Surakarta court poet Jasadipura I, for there is a clear reference to the story in *BG*, vol. viii, p. 57 (see n. 46 below). On the antiquity of the story, see also nn. 44 and 45 below.

[39] Cohen Stuart, *Baron Sakéndhèr*, p. ix.

history of the Netherlands. Aside from the problem of the Spanish, Baron Sakenḍer stories could hardly have been known until after the failed Mataram sieges of Batavia in 1628 and 1629, before which a formal view of the Dutch–Javanese relationship would have been unlikely to have evolved. And the relationship as it is pictured in this story seems to include the idea of a Dutch Resident at the *kraton*; it must therefore be posterior to 1680.

Whenever the first versions may have been composed, the title 'Baron' clearly indicates that the Baron Sakenḍer story in its present form is unlikely to be older than the middle of the eighteenth century. The title could hardly have been known to the Javanese until the arrival of the first Barons to serve in Java, the Governor-General G. W. Baron van Imhoff (1743–50) and J. A. Baron von Hohendorff, commandant at Kartasura and Surakarta (1741–8) and first Governor at Sĕmarang (1748–54).[40] Furthermore, the names of Dutchmen which appear in the story include several from the middle years of the eighteenth century, and again point to that period as a possible time when the story took on something like its shape in the *Sĕrat Sakonḍar* text. But this is all speculation. Although it is not without philological interest, in the absence of documentation it is of small historical value.[41] Here will be described the story as it was known in the early years of the nineteenth century. The text is the closest version available to the *kraton* myth of the reign of Mangkubumi. It has much in common with Cohen Stuart's text, but there are important differences as well, particularly at the beginning and the end. The following summary, therefore, follows the *Sĕrat Sakonḍar* manuscript rather than Cohen Stuart's later version.

The *Sakonḍar* story is long and exceedingly involved. As in the *Sĕrat Surja Radja*, much of it is an extensive description of adventures, magical events, and battles. The Baron Sakenḍer texts may be profitably compared with other works of Javanese literature,[42] but the intention here is merely to summarize those

[40] This has already been pointed out by Dr. de Graaf in 'Sultan Agung', p. 157.

[41] Further technical matters relating to the antiquity of the story, all of which suggest that in its present form it can be no older than the mid-eighteenth century, are discussed in nn. 38, 44, and 45.

[42] See Th. Pigeaud, 'Alexander, Sakèndèr en Sénapati', *Djåwå*, vol. 7 (1927), pp. 321–61; Berg, 'Māyā's Hemelvaart', pp. 26, 224, 269, 331, 340.

Prof. Berg has commented on the Baron Sakenḍer tales in several of his earlier publications. See especially his article 'De Zin der tweede Babad-Tanah-Jawi', *Indonesië*, vol. 8 (1955), pp. 361–400. See also n. 55 below.

elements of the book which help to clarify Jogjakarta's understanding of the more mythical aspects of the relationship with the Company.

The text begins as follows:

I: 1. Be it forgiven by those who will,
for of the characters many are alike,
spidery, ugly in manner,
indeed [the work of] a student,
daring to thwart (the rules of) poetry.
It is a story from overseas
which begins the tale.
At the beginning there emerged from a cave,
like ants, one after the other without interruption,
the first Dutchmen.

2. Exceedingly many, counting thousands, tens and
    hundreds of thousands,
for long they increased continuously,
overflowing the great kingdom,
all becoming kings,
each sufficient in power.
Commerce was their work,
equal their wealth.
One there was who became King,
a Dutchman exceedingly wise,
Sungadjrit his name.

3. Exceedingly heroic in battle,
his wives, indeed, a thousand princesses,
together war-booty, all;
but he had yet no children.
All the lands were his property,
because of the exceeding greed
of the King of the great land.
Spain was his kingdom.
All submitted, the kings of other lands,
all were ruled.

4. Many were the subject lands of His Highness,
England and France, Malawa [?] and the
    Netherlands [?],
many are not told of. Governed were
the lands of the coasts, mountains,
and the interior, all paid court,

offering tribute
in jewels, great horses,
and raiment.
Ever more was submitted to the King of Spain.
Now, great was his might,

5. with supernatural powers, overbearing, proud,
following the religion of the Prophet Moses;
in Spain, the King.[43]
...

[43] *Sĕrat Sakonḍar*, BM Add. MS. 12289, ff. 2ᵛ–3ᵛ, Canto I (Ḍanḍanggula):

1. apuranĕn dera kang sudyapti
   dene sastranja kaṭah mĕmaḍa
   angongga awon tanduke
   tantu wong sisinau
   tjumĕṭaka amunggĕl kawi
   tjarita saking sabrang
   kang pinurweng tutur
   purwanja midjil sing guwa
   kadya sĕmut adulur tansah anggili
   Wĕlandi ingkang purwa

2. langkung kaṭah ewon lĕksan kĕṭi
   mangke lami sing saja atangkar
   angradon nĕgari gḍe
   prasamja madĕg ratu
   sowang-sowang ingkang kawawi
   karjanja mradagangan
   sami sugihipun
   wontĕn kang djumnĕng Nata
   wong Wĕlando pabjanta witjĕksoneki
   Sungadjrit ingkang nama

3. sakĕlangkung prawira ing djurit
   garwanira nĕnggih putri sasra
   samja tĕtawanan kabeh
   nanging dereng susunu
   sakjeh nagri samja kamelik
   kĕlangkung dening murka
   Nata nagri agung
   Sĕpanjol ingkang nĕgara
   samja sujud para nata nagri lain
   sadaja kawisesa

4. kaṭah bawahipun Sri Bupati
   Nganggris Prasman ngaMalawa Nelan [? ngamal lawan Nelan]
   kaṭah tan winarna winreh
   nagri pasisir gunung
   ing tĕngahan sami anangkil
   atur bulupĕktinja
   rĕtna turangga gung
   miwah kang busana wastra

382 JOGJAKARTA UNDER SULTAN MANGKUBUMI

Now is told of the land of the Dutch, of the first Tuwan Governor of Holland, the land of the mountains. He was an orphan, cut from the womb before birth. He became famous in battle and rich as a merchant, and all of the kings became deeply indebted to him. He took as wives twelve daughters of the kings, of great beauty. One of these wives exceeded the others in beauty, the princess from the land Ngabĕsah (*putri saking nĕgari Ngabĕsah*), but she was sent to live apart in the cooking-place (*pawon*). There she forewent food and sleep, continuously practicing asceticism, deeply upset by her fate. (Canto I: 7–10)

This Nakoda (ship captain), named 'bas pan Rudyah Kawit', ruled the kingdom of Mabukit Ambin.[44] But he was unhappy because his wives had borne him no children. No one could seem to help him. Then a voice came to the Nakoda in his sleep, saying if he wished children he should go to the mountains and ask the hermit (*bĕgawan*) Mintuna. Certainly his wives would then give birth to sons. Upon waking, the Nakoda called together his wives, but the wife who was sent to live

---

      langkung kaṭah katur Spanjol Sang Adji
      nahan gĕng prakosanja
5. sakti guna udjubrija kibir
      anut agamanja Nabi Mungsa
      Sĕpanjol ika Sang Radjeng
      . . . .

The kingdom Malawa mentioned in stanza 4, if that is the correct reading, is a mythical land taken from the *Bratajuda* stories, an ally of the Kurawa.

It is interesting that the text notes the different religion of the foreigners, but calls it the religion of the Prophet Moses (Nabi Mungsa) rather than that of the Prophet Jesus (Nabi Ngisa). Presumably the Javanese understanding of Christianity was as unsophisticated as the Dutch understanding of Islam. See also n. 65 below.

[44] *Sĕrat Sakonḍar*, f. 4ᵛ, Canto I (Ḍanḍanggula):

    11. ki nakoda bas pan Rudyah Kawit
        reh Mabukit Ambin nagrinira
        . . . .

This is clearly a Dutch name. *Bas* is the Dutch *baas* ('boss, master') and *pan* is the Dutch *van*. But the name is difficult to identify among the Europeans who were known to the Javanese. It may have derived from J. Fr. Baron *van Reede tot* de Parkeler, who was Resident at Surakarta from 1790 to 1796 and Governor at Sĕmarang from 1796 to 1801. This would suggest a late-eighteenth-century origin for this version. But the identification is an extremely dubious one.

Later in *Sĕrat Sakonḍar* (f. 109ʳ; see n. 62 below), Kasenḍer says his father's name was 'Baron Kawit Prispruranjah' and his kingdom 'Bukit Tarbi'. In Cohen Stuart's text, stanza 2, the Nakoda is called Baron Kawit Paru and his kingdom Bukit Tarbi.

JOGJAKARTA AND THE DUTCH

apart (the princess of Ngabĕsah) was not summoned. He took leave of his wives and went to Mintuna. Through Mintuna's magical means, eleven of his wives subsequently became pregnant and when their time was due they gave birth to eleven sons. Great was the joy of the Nakoda. (Canto I: 11–61)

The Nakoda gave (Dutch) names to his sons: Baron Patrasmin, Raden Baron Sapilman, Baron Isrek, Raden Baron Emup, Baron Irdijan, Baron Malĕk, Baron Tasminten, Baron Djangkung, Baron Simunan, Baron Intedeng, and Baron Mabĕlum.[45] He was exceedingly

[45] These are all Dutch names, but it has been impossible to identify all of them. Those which are reasonably clear are the following:

Patrasmin: Abraham Patras, GG 1735–7.

Sapilman: Admiral Cornelis Speelman, leader of the VOC expedition against Trunadjaja, GG 1681–4.

Isrek: Perhaps W. H. van Ijsseldijk, Jogjakarta Resident 1786–99. In *B. Mang.*, p. 479, however, van Ijsseldijk is called 'Salĕdik'. It might also be Isaac de Saint-Martin (d. 1696), captain in Speelman's expedition against Trunadjaja, later a member of the Council of the Indies and a noted collecter of Indonesian-language MSS.

Emup: G. W. Baron van Imhoff, GG 1743–50. In *BG*, vol. iii, p. 32, he is called 'Baron pan Emut'.

Irdijan: Perhaps Adriaan Valckenier, GG 1737–41, or Adriaen Antheunisz., who was wounded in the second siege of Batavia, 1629. The latter was suggested by F. de Haan, 'Uit Oud-Batavia: Kota Tahi', *TBG*, vol. 42 (1900), p. 576. 'Irdijan' also appears as one of the Dutch 'Admirals' during the attack on Djakarta in *Sĕrat Sakondar*, f. 141ᵛ, which is an argument in favour of identifying this with Adriaen Antheunisz.

Tasminten: Perhaps Pieter Gerard van Overstraten, Governor of Sĕmarang 1791–6. See 'Journal', BM Add. MS. 12303, f. 164ʳ, where he is called 'Tuwan Idler Mester Piter Gĕrardus pa [*sic*] Opĕrsĕtrantĕn', and *B. Mang.*, p. 548, where he is called 'Tuwan Girardus Sĕtratĕn'. The change from (Opĕr) Sĕtrantĕn or Sĕtratĕn to Tasminten is not an obvious one, but it is perhaps possible. This text transposes Sakender to Kasender (or other texts do the reverse). If Sĕtrantĕn is changed to Tĕsrantĕn, or something similar, the possibility of further change to Tasminten can be seen. But this identification remains extremely uncertain. The name of Abel Jansz. Tasman, explorer of Australia, Tasmania, and New Zealand in the 1640s, suggests itself, but it seems impossible for the Javanese to have known his name.

Djangkung: Jan Pietersz. Coen, founder of Batavia and GG 1619–23, 1627–9. See *BK*, f. 267ʳ, where he is called 'Kapitan Djangkung'. The *Sĕrat Sakondar* MS. is not concerned about the introduction of Coen a second time at the end of the story. See n. 78 below.

Simunan: Johannes Simong, VOC merchant and translator in the 1740s. See *Sĕrat Babad Pakunĕgaran*, f. 101ʳ, where he is called 'Simun' (djuru basa wastanipun Simun kapitan Wĕlandi).

Of these, Sapilman, Emup, Djangkung, and Simunan may be regarded as firm identifications. It will be noted that Emup (van Imhoff) and Simunan (Simong) were both involved in the Third Javanese War of Succession of the

pleased with his offspring. But Sang Rĕtna (the princess of Ngabĕsah) had borne no child. After fourteen years, she produced not a child but a sea-shell (*kuwuk samodra*). Her attendant, who was also pregnant, produced a mango-pit (*pĕlok*). Eventually there

---

1740s, and the list of names cannot therefore be older than that period. If the very much more uncertain suggestions regarding pan Rudyah Kawit (as van Reede tot de Parkeler; see n. 44 above), Isrek (as van Ijsseldijk rather than de Saint-Martin), and Tasminten (as van Overstraten) are correct, the list took its present form in the 1790s. See also n. 38 above.

None of the sons are named in Cohen Stuart's text, although in stanza 693 four 'Admirals' are named: Tomas, Ilman, Ardijan, and Falĕk. On these, see de Haan, 'Kota Tahi', p. 576. The Admirals are also in *Sĕrat Sakondar*, f. 141^r, where they are named Tomas, Mabĕlum, Ilman, Palĕk, and Irdijan.

Related lists of names for the 11 sons are given in the Jogjakarta *Babad Tanah Djawi* MSS. NBS 158 and LOr 6483, dated respectively 1821 and 1851. But here twelve names are given for the eleven. The second text is an almost exact copy of the first and the names are given together below, followed by suggested identifications. The first of the two names in each case is from NBS 158, vol. i, p. 62, the second from LOr 6483, p. 60 (in both cases, Canto VII: 23–4). Where the texts are identical, the name is given only once:

Apiman/Alpiman: Speelman? Cf. 'Sapilman' above.

Kastedeng: presumably *Sĕrat Sakondar's* 'Intedeng', unidentified.

Ardiman/Ardijan: Adriaan Valckenier or Adriaen Antheunisz. Cf. 'Irdijan' above.

Pitanja: Unidentified. Perhaps from '(Ka)pitan'.

Tanemut: Van Imhoff. Cf. 'Emup' above. 'Tanemut' means roughly 'forget-(ful).'

Driansah: Jan Albertsz. Sloot, captain under Speelman against Trunadjaja. Despite the apparent improbability of this identification it is in fact beyond doubt. See *BK*, f. 513^v, where he is called 'Sĕlut Hendrik Ansah'; *BTDj* (*BP*), vol. xvi, p. 52, where he is called 'Sĕlut Hendrik Jansah'; and *BTDj*, text p. 227, trans. p. 223, where he is called 'Sĕlup Driansah'. I am grateful to Dr. H. J. de Graaf for bringing this curious identification to my attention. The derivation of this name for Sloot is unknown. The Javanese seem to have given him the spurious Christian names 'Hendrik Janszoon'.

Makrĕsmin: Unknown.

Surang/Sura: Unknown.

Arte: Nicolaas Hartingh, Sĕmarang Governor 1754–61.

Kaseman: Unknown.

Kasberah: Probably W. H. van Ossenberch, Sĕmarang Governor 1761–5. See *B. Mang.*, p. 362, where he is called 'Saberah'.

Sĕmit: Might be anyone named Smit, or perhaps David Joan Smith, a member of the Council of the Indies in the 1780s.

The selection of names for these lists probably reflects those individuals whose activities most struck the Javanese. But it presumably also reflects which names happened to have the most interesting sound, regardless of the importance

appeared two sets of twins from the sea-shell and the mango-pit. From the princess's shell came Raden Baron Sukmul, the elder [sic] of the twins, and Raden Baron Kasenḍer, the younger. In beauty they exceeded their eleven brothers. From the mango-pit came twins named Suhulman and Kasebĕr,[46] who became the retainers (*ponakawan*) of

---

of the individual. Biographical information on these individuals may be found in dJ by use of the index volume.

Given the fact that these are clearly Dutch personal names, there seems no reason not to accept also that 'Baron' is the European title of nobility (see Pigeaud, *Literature*, vol. i, p. 162). If one accepts that the versions of the Baron Sakenḍer story now known are all later than the mid-eighteenth century, the use of the title presents no puzzles.

[46] In Cohen Stuart's text Kasebĕr is called 'Sakebĕr', which Dr. Pigeaud ('Alexander', p. 323 n. 3) suggested was derived from the Dutch *gezaghebber* (person in authority), a rank for VOC officials below those of Governor, Director, Commander, or *opperhoofd* (chief). For such ranks, see Mossel, Reglement, 31 July–6 Aug. 1753, in van der Chijs (ed.), *Plakaatboek*, vol. vi, pp. 456–93.

Kasenḍer (Sakenḍer) is usually presumed to have derived from 'Iskandar', the Malay and Javanese form for Alexander (the Great) (Iskandar dhu-al-Qarnayn of the *Qur'ān*). But there seems little reason to associate the Sakenḍer story with the Malay and Javanese stories about Iskandar, which are quite different in content. See the summary of a Javanese *Sĕrat Iskandar* (LOr 1805) from Surakarta, dated A.J. 1717/A.D. 1790, in Vreede, *Catalogus*, pp. 32–6.

It was seen above (nn. 44 and 45) that other names given to Dutchmen in this MS. seem to be derived from those of individuals with whom the Javanese were acquainted. In the absence of such identifiable names before the final portions of the published Cohen Stuart text (see n. 45, citing Cohen Stuart's stanza 693), it has never been asked whether Sakenḍer, Sakebĕr, Sukmul, and Suhulman might not also be Javanese versions of actual Dutch names. Suhulman might easily be, for instance, Schulman or Schuurman, but I am unaware of anyone of those names whom the Javanese are likely to have known. Problems of identification notwithstanding, it is noteworthy that Sakebĕr appears in *Babad Gijanti* as a Dutch Major in the war against Mangkubumi; *BG*, vol. iii, pp. 68–9: Sakebĕr, Kebĕr; ibid., vol. x, p. 42: Major Sakebĕr.

Baron Sakenḍer's name also appears in *BG*, but only as a reference to the Baron Sakenḍer stories. The Surakarta commandant Toutlemonde is said to have marched to battle against Mangkubumi like Baron Sakenḍer in the Spanish wars; *BG*, vol. viii, p. 57: Totlomondo pan unḍagi . . . / gĕlar Baron Sakenḍer ingkang kinarja / duk prang Sĕpanjol nguni / mungsuh satus radja.

As befits their status as foreigners (non-Javanese), Sukmul, Kasenḍer, Suhulman, and Kasebĕr commonly speak Malay among themselves throughout this text. For example, *Sĕrat Sakonḍar*, f. 16ʳ, Canto II (Asmaradana) (Kasenḍer speaking to Sukmul) (cf. Cohen Stuart's stanza 37):

23. mari kakak luwar manḍi
ini tĕrlalu apanas
suḍah manḍi makan kuwih
ĕmakku suḍah tiḍur inak
ingkang raka [Sukmul] angutjap
baik aḍek saja turut
wong sĕkawan sampun mĕdal.

the first two. But the Nakoda knew nothing of these twins, born in the cooking-place. After fourteen years, the sage-king (*radja paṇḍita*) Mintuna came to the Nakoda. He demanded the fulfilment of the promise that he might choose to have one of the Nakoda's children, born because of his (Mintuna's) magic. Accusing the Nakoda of bad faith for not having sent immediate notice of the birth of the sons, Mintuna demanded that they be called before him for his selection. The eleven sons were assembled, and the Nakoda said, 'These are my sons'. But Mintuna flew into a rage: 'You said you had twelve wives; here are only eleven (sons)!'[47] Mintuna then informed the Nakoda that his twelfth wife, who had been sent to live apart and had then been completely forgotten, had given birth to twins. There were also two retainers. Now the Nakoda recalled the princess and summoned her. She broke into tears when she was called, knowing from a dream that it would be her beloved Kasenḍer whom Mintuna would choose. Kasenḍer took leave of his bereaved mother, placing her in Sukmul's care. The latter he ordered to join the eleven other brothers. When they entered the presence of the Nakoda and Mintuna, the latter was overjoyed and selected Kasenḍer for himself. (Canto II: 1–72)

Mintuna set off with his 'grandson' Kasenḍer, accompanied by his retainer Kasebĕr. After Kasenḍer had defeated four demons who tried to block their passage, they arrived at the mountain hermitage. During a temporary absence of Mintuna from the hermitage, Kasenḍer investigated a forbidden building and discovered there much to his dismay, amid a heap of human bones, the imprisoned demon king (*radja kala*) Singgunkara, formerly ruler of the land Guwa Sonjagiri.[48] Singgunkara

---

[47] The conversation takes place in Malay. E.g. *Sĕrat Sakoṇḍar*, f. 20ʳ, Canto II (Asmaradana):
    56. anulja Sang Wiku adji
        aningali mring darmadja
        winitjal kirang tjatjahe
        Sang Maha Jĕkti ngandika
        Nakoda sira dora
        ini katinggalan satu
        lu bilang bini ḍuwablas

    57. ini sablas lu sĕmbuni
        ĕlu tiḍak kabĕtulan
        nakoda djrih lingira lon
        ija bĕtul tuwan kata
        sĕmbuni saja tiḍak
        traḍa anak lahin itu
        . . . .

[48] In Cohen Stuart's text he is called the former ruler of Nusa Tĕmbini (see stanza 87). He is thus associated with the later figure of Sajĕmpraba, ruler of Nusa Tĕmbini (see n. 55 below), who as Mintuna's daughter had presumably replaced Singgunkara there when he was taken captive by her father. *Sĕrat*

told Kasenḍer that the bones were those of princes like Kasenḍer himself whom Mintuna had brought to his hermitage and then eaten. He sprinkled magical water upon the skull of the Prince of Cambodia (*Putra Kĕmbodja*) which then came to life and confirmed its identity, convincing the sceptical Kasenḍer of the truth of Singgunkara's story. When Mintuna returned to the hermitage, Kasenḍer, now aware of his impending fate, managed to kill him. All the devoured princes were then brought back to life and were sent back to their own kingdoms. To Singgunkara Kasenḍer turned over control of the hermitage. (Canto III: 1–60)

Singgunkara's gratitude to Kasenḍer was great and he swore eternal obeisance to his saviour. He advised Kasenḍer to set out from the hermitage and to go to Spain where he would one day become a great warrior, the commander-in-chief (*senapati*) of the armies, and the son-in-law of the Spanish king. But he must beware, for many were his enemies. His dead 'grandfather' (Mintuna) had four daughters, each a sovereign, and he must take care. Kasenḍer took this advice and with Kasebĕr he set off for Spain. Eventually they arrived there. (Canto III: 61–74, Canto IV: 1–17)

When they had nearly reached the Spanish capital city (*kiṭa*), a horse appeared and spoke to them. Baron Kasenḍer asked what manner of horse was this that could speak like a man. The horse replied that he was Kuda Sĕmbrani. 'I was told by my parents that I have a human brother named Raden Baron Kasenḍer,' said Sĕmbrani. 'Can it be you?' Kasenḍer replied that he had no equine brother. Sĕmbrani replied softly that this was true. Yet his parents had said they were brothers at birth and he had been sent to serve Kasenḍer.[49] Thus

---

Sakonḍar does not make clear this association, but in both texts Singgunkara becomes Kasenḍer's ally against Mintuna and his family, who are their shared enemies.

[49] *Sĕrat Sakonḍar*, f. 33ʳ, Canto IV (Sinom):

19. Baron Kasenḍer ngandika
    djaran apa sira dening
    njĕluk bisa tata djalma
    apa arsa amet kardi
    angling Kuda Sĕmbrani
    ing mangke kawula matur
    wartine jajah rena
    ulun darbe kadang djalmi
    inggih Raden Baron Kasenḍer kang nama

20. punapa inggih panduka
    Raden Kasenḍer nahuri
    sun tan darbe kadang djaran
    Sĕmbrani umatur aris

Sĕmbrani entered the service of Kasenḍer, who sprinkled him with magical water given him by Singgunkara, wherepon Sĕmbrani turned to gold. Then appeared a great bird named Garuḍa. He, too, announced he was a brother to Kasenḍer, sent to serve him. Garuḍa was sprinkled with the magical water, was turned to gold, and entered Kasenḍer's service. Kasenḍer ordered Garuḍa and Sĕmbrani, both of whom could fly, to watch over him from on high. He and Kasebĕr then continued their adventures. But suddenly there appeared from the earth a serpent, who announced he was Kasenḍer's brother. He was turned to gold with the magical water, and was told to await the summons of Kasenḍer. Kasenḍer and Kasebĕr again set off, for Kasenḍer wished to see the Diamond City (*kiṭa intĕn*). (Canto IV: 17–33)

In Spain the king was great and all monarchs offered him tribute. But he was deeply disturbed because enemies were gathering. The king of Sasranĕgara (the thousand lands), named Prabu Ngabĕsah,[50] wished to marry the king's only child, a daughter of surpassing beauty. But she refused to marry him, having learned in a dream of Baron Kasenḍer, a warrior of supernatural powers who would cause the kingdom to prosper. Her father was furious and sent her away from the court amidst great sobbing on the part of his wives, who were greatly distressed. The princess set off, her tears showering down. (Canto V: 1–29)

The King of Sasranĕgara, Prabu Ngabĕsah, summoned his subject kings and told them of these events. He ordered that Spain be attacked and his five hundred kings set off to war. The troops of Spain fell back before the enemy, taking refuge in the city. Informed by his *patih* that the city was surrounded, the Spanish king ordered the manning of the city walls, the setting up of the cannon large and small, of the grenades and bombs. Battle commenced. (Canto V: 30–50)

Meanwhile, the Spanish princess continued on her sorrowful way, thinking day and night of the hero of her dreams, Baron Kasenḍer. Suddenly she encountered Kasenḍer and Kasebĕr. After hearing of her expulsion from the court by her father and of her dream of himself,

---

inggih lĕrĕs ta nanging
wĕlingipun bapa babu
kadang sarĕng lahirnja
mila ulun kinen ngabdi
jen sĕmbada kawula angestupada.

Cf. Cohen Stuart, *Baron Sakéndhèr*, stanzas 134–6.

[50] Thus, he is Kasenḍer's and Sukmul's grandfather, since their mother was the Putri Ngabĕsah. It will be seen below that this Ngabĕsah lineage is important in the genealogy of these myths.

Dr. Pigeaud has pointed out to me that the toponym Ngabĕsah (Abĕsah) apparently derives from the Arabic *al-ḥabasha* (Abyssinia, Ethiopia).

Kasender made his identity known to her.[51] Amid a deluge of tears she told Kasender that she wished to return to her father, whose city was besieged. If he received no help the kingdom would fall. The princess, Kasender, and Kasebĕr then set off for the city, accompanied by Sĕmbrani and Garuḍa. (Canto V: 50–86)

On their way to the city the party was set upon by enemy troops. But Kasender, Kasebĕr, Sĕmbrani, and Garuḍa won the day. Prabu Ngabĕsah was amazed to hear of this defeat and ordered to war his troops (*kumpĕni*) without number. Kasender and his party had meanwhile arrived at the court, where the princess was received by her father. She introduced Kasender and told of his heroism on the way to the court. Kasender promised the king to defeat his enemies. The Spanish king declared Kasender to be commander-in-chief (*senapati*) and gave him the name Prabu Anom (the Young King). To the sound of a thirteen-gun salute, the troops set forth. The enemy king Ngabĕsah also collected his forces, which included among others the peoples of Persia, of the East (of Arabia), of the West (North Africa), the Chinese, the Turks, and the Quraysh (the tribe inhabiting Mecca and the family of the Prophet Muḥammad).[52] (Canto VI: 1–67)

[51] Kasebĕr plays a role here very much like the *wajang panakawan*'s. He speaks loudly and coarsely, in Malay, calling the princess insolent ('putri kurang adjar') and telling Kasender not to excuse her ('djangan kasih ampun tuan'). Both Kasebĕr and Suhulman behave in this fashion throughout both *Sĕrat Sakondar* and Cohen Stuart's text. It was pointed out in Chap. I above that the Javanese seem to have perceived the behaviour of individual Europeans in much the same terms as those in which they saw the conduct of the *panakawan*.

[52] *Sĕrat Sakondar*, f. 54ᵛ, Canto VI (Durma):
    67. bala Ngidjam wong Parasi Masrik lawan
        wong Dustam sampun prapti
        wong Turki Kuresan
        wong Tjina lan wong Bulgan
        wong Mahrib sadaja prapti
    . . . .

Thus, the battles in which Baron Kasender is about to take part amount to a confrontation between largely Islamic peoples (including the family of the Prophet Muḥammad) and the Christian (or, as this text has it, the Mosaic—see n. 43 above) state of Spain. This view of events would not have been inconsistent with a general knowledge of the centuries-long confrontation between the Muslims and the Iberian Christian states. Now Kasender is about to do battle on behalf of Spain against these Islamic peoples. The situation is made more complex by the fact that the leader of Kasender's enemies is Prabu Ngabĕsah, who is apparently the grandfather of Kasender, the son (via the sea-shell) of the princess of Ngabĕsah. It should be remembered that the Javanese view of such great wars, as is also to be seen in the *Bratajuda* stories, does not allow of a simple Western-style division into the forces of evil *vs.* the forces of virtue. Although one side may be generally more heroic, virtue is not a monopoly of either side and neither can exist without the other.

The important point here is that *Sĕrat Sakondar* has divided the foreign,

The great battle was soon engaged, with Kasenḍer, Kaseběr, Sěmbrani, and Garuḍa fighting the enemy kings, who included the kings of England, France, and China. The enemy fell before them. Eventually Prabu Ngaběsah, astride a great elephant, locked himself in personal combat with Kasenḍer, who rode the golden Sěmbrani. Sěmbrani and the elephant grappled furiously while in the midst of the battlefield Prabu Anom (Kasenḍer) and Prabu Ngaběsah contended in mystical powers (*kasěkten, wignja*). Kasenḍer bested his opponent and from on high Sěmbrani fell upon Prabu Ngaběsah. His head was severed from his body, he fell dead, and his army disappeared. The conquered armies all submitted to Kasenḍer. (Canto VI: 68–167)

The victorious Prabu Anom (Kasenḍer) then returned to the city, where he was welcomed by a fifteen-gun salute. He was received with joy by the king of Spain and by his daughter, who was Kasenḍer's wife. She had feared for her husband's life and now fell overjoyed at his feet. Prabu Anom (Kasenḍer) was taken into the palace where he offered the king the spoils of war. The king then proposed that Prabu Anom should take the throne while he retired to a hermitage. But Prabu Anom politely declined. He was pleased, he said, to be a warrior and to serve the king, but he had never dreamt that he would become king himself. The ruler finally gave in. After a time, Prabu Anom grew distressed because he had heard of the land of Java, a fruitful land where food and clothing were cheap and commerce excellent. For this alone did he yearn.[53] (Canto VI: 168–79)

---

non-Indonesian, world into two great alliances partly distinguished by religion: Ngaběsah and the Spanish-Dutch side. And Kasenḍer, the hero, carries the blood of both sides. It will be suggested below that this is genealogically symmetrical to the division of the Indonesian world into two great kingdoms: Padjadjaran and Madjapahit. See also n. 60 below.

[53] *Sěrat Sakonḍar*, f. 67ᵛ, Canto VI (Durma):

176. Angandika Sang Nata wis djumněnga
    Prabu Sapanjol nagri
    běgawan manira
    Prabu Anom aturnja
    nuhun lěnggona wak-mami
    datan supna
    jen nědya adadya Dji

177. lěga ulun jen mradjurit anjatrija
    ataḍah karsa Adji
    Sang Nata ngandika
    angur dadija Nata
    Prabu Anom anuhun sih
    angling Sang Nata
    ija kaki sun iring

178. tuluseňa kaki Prabu mukti sjara
    Prabu Anom wotsari

Meanwhile,[54] the four daughters of the king of Lĕbur Gongsa, the dead Mintuna, had learned of their father's death at Kasenḍer's hands. Their uncle was summoned and one of the sisters, Rĕtna Sajĕmpraba, queen of Nusa Tambini,[55] consulted with him. It was decided that the murder of their father must be avenged although Kasenḍer's supernatural powers, his victory over Prabu Ngabĕsah, and the existence of his powerful brothers Sĕmbrani and Garuḍa were known and aroused

> anuhun aturnja
> wus lami kang winarna
> Prabu Anom gĕng prihatin
> dening miarsa
> wartine Tanah Djawi
>
> 179. loh-djinawi mirah sanḍing lawan boga
> dagangan kjeh nglangkungi
> ku kang dadi brongta
> ....

[54] From this point (Canto VII) the Cohen Stuart text (stanza 191, also Canto VII) follows the *Sĕrat Sakonḍar* text very closely, with many identical or nearly identical stanzas. It continues to do so until the end of Cohen Stuart's text (stanza 723), which corresponds with *Sĕrat Sakonḍar*, Canto XIV: 10 (f. 145ᵛ). The *Sĕrat Sakonḍar* text, however, has two additional stanzas to that canto and a further Canto XV of 19 stanzas. These will be discussed below (see nn. 86, 89, and 90). Since the *Sĕrat Sakonḍar* Cantos VII–XIV are so close to the published text, the description here will be rather more brief. But there are also differences and the summary here still follows the *Sĕrat Sakonḍar* version.

[55] *Sĕrat Sakonḍar*, f. 68ʳ⁻ᵛ, Canto VII (Midjil):

> 5. ingkang paman denaturi prapti
> gupita Sang Sinom
> Nusa Tambini Sang Dyah nagrine
> Rĕtna Sajĕmpraba kang wĕwangi
> ....

Cf. Cohen Stuart's text, stanza 195. There it is the uncle whose kingdom is spoken of, and it is called Guwa Badjra. *Sĕrat Sakonḍar* later speaks of this as well (see the summary of Canto VIII). Not until later in Cohen Stuart's text (stanza 245) is Sajĕmpraba's kingdom identified as Nusa Tambini.

The reader is referred to the story from *Babad Kraton* cited above (n. 35) where Nusa Tumbini is the island which is renamed 'Batawijah'. It is located, according to *BK*, in the Southern Ocean. The implications of this connection are not immediately clear, but it is obvious at least that Nusa Tambini/Tumbini is an important location in the Javanese spirit-world, the domination of which is a part of the spiritual authority of Sajĕmpraba and of the Dutchmen who ruled 'Batawijah'.

Prof. Zoetmulder has pointed out to me that Sajĕmpraba is probably derived from the demonic Swayĕmprabā of the *Rāmāyaṇa* (Sarga 7). There would seem to be good reason to pursue further Prof. Berg's argument that *Rāmāyaṇa* motifs are to be discerned in Baron Sakenḍer texts; see Berg, 'Māyā's Hemelvaart', p. 26. See also H. N. van der Tuuk, *Kawi-Balineesch-Nederlandsch Woordenboek* (4 vols.; Batavia, 1897–1912), vol. iii, p. 225.

the fears of Mintuna's children. Sajĕmpraba departed in the guise of a maiden of surpassing beauty to wreak vengeance upon Kasenḍer. She arrived in Spain, where she claimed to be from Europe (*Prĕnggi*), a daughter of the king who had been driven from the palace. She claimed she had dreamt of the king of Spain and had thereafter refused to marry another. The Spanish king then took her as wife and spent his days and nights in bliss, forgetting his other wives, whom Sajĕmpraba nightly devoured one by one. Sajĕmpraba eventually devised a means to get Kasenḍer into the hands of her sisters by causing the king to send him in quest of a golden banana for herself. Kasenḍer took Kasebĕr, whom he now renamed the Factor Tumĕnggung Rĕksanĕgara, and upon the back of the golden Sĕmbrani they departed from Spain. Soon they arrived at the hermitage where they met Kasenḍer's 'grandfather' Singgunkara. (Canto VII: 1–45)[56]

Through his supernatural powers Singgunkara was already aware of the goal of Kasenḍer's quest. He further informed Kasenḍer that the golden banana in fact existed but that it was the property of Kasenḍer's 'mother' (the queen of Spain), whose true identity Kasenḍer knew not. She was a demon, Singgunkara explained, the daughter of Mintuna whom Kasenḍer had killed, and her kingdom was Nusa Tambini. She had disguised herself as a princess in order to convince the king of Spain to send Kasenḍer on this quest so that revenge could be taken upon him for the killing of her father. Singgunkara instructed Kasenḍer in the magical powers he would need to overcome this danger and to succeed in his quest, whereupon Kasenḍer set off for Nusa Tambini. After a series of supernatural adventures, he ultimately succeeded in launching an assault on the uncle of Mintuna's daughters, the ruler of the demons on the island Guwa Badjra, lying to the south. Kasenḍer, Garuḍa, and Sĕmbrani, reinforced by the princes whom Mintuna had devoured and whom Kasenḍer had brought back to life, fell upon the demon armies. The fallen enemy covered the ground, their bodies severed in battle. Finally fell the king of the demons himself, cut in two by Kasenḍer. The surviving demons fled. When Kasenḍer returned to Spain with this news, Sajĕmpraba fell to grieving for she knew that nothing now could save her. (Canto VIII: 1–76)[57]

Sajĕmpraba nearly convinced the king of Spain to take her part against Kasenḍer but in the end he was informed of her true identity. Sajĕmpraba then took again the form of a demon and announced herself as the queen of Nusa Tambini. She challenged the king and Prabu

[56] Cf. Cohen Stuart, *Baron Sakéndhèr*, stanzas 191–235.
[57] Cf. ibid., stanzas 236–304. The story of the *gĕlaṭik mas*, the golden rice bird (*Tringgila oryzivora Horsf.*) upon which the life of Sajĕmpraba depended, is found in both *Sĕrat Sakonḍar* and Cohen Stuart. It is omitted in the summary here since it is readily accessible in Cohen Stuart's translation and text.

Anom (Kasenḍer) to battle upon the *alun-alun* before the palace. Meanwhile, the Spanish troops (*kumpni Sapanjol*) battled to no avail against her, their muskets with golden bullets having no effect. Then Kasenḍer, who had been sent away from the city, returned and came down astride the golden Sĕmbrani. After nearly losing the contest, Sĕmbrani and Kasenḍer succeeded in murdering the demon queen Sajĕmpraba. Her body was kicked into the sea. Prabu Anom (Kasenḍer) took off into the air, intending to finish the matter. (Canto IX: 1–51)[58]

Sajĕmpraba's three sisters, Ṭaṭaini, Kaladjahar, and Ṭaṭakuṭana, had learned of her death. Suddenly, like a bolt of lightning, Kasenḍer came down before them and announced his identity. They submitted to him, but enticed him then into a game of chess (*prang tjatur*) in which Kasenḍer lost all: his kingdom, his treasures, Garuḍa and Sĕmbrani, his wife the Spanish princess, and, finally, his own life. Thereupon Kaladjahar devoured Kasenḍer and the princess, Garuḍa was devoured by Ṭaṭaini, Kasebĕr and Sĕmbrani by Ṭaṭakuṭana. (Canto IX: 52–4, Canto X: 1–46)[59]

The (Dutch) Nakoda of the mountainous land Bukit Tarbi (i.e. Mabukit Ambin), who began this tale, meanwhile enjoyed ever greater luxury. Ever greater were his riches and all the trade of the world, except for the lands of *Rum* (Turkey), Mecca, and Medina, was in his hands.[60] But his son Baron Sukmul, the son of the princess of Ngabĕsah and Kasenḍer's elder twin, had neither eaten nor slept for seven days. He was considering the words of Kasenḍer who upon his departure had left behind a ring. If the stone should disappear, he had said, it would be a sign of his own death. The stone had now disappeared. Sukmul took leave of his mother and set off, accompanied by his retainer Suhulman, for the hermitage where Kasenḍer had been taken by Mintuna. There he met Singgunkara who told him of his brother's many adventures and of his end at the hands of Mintuna's three surviving daughters.

[58] Cf. Cohen Stuart, *Baron Sakéndhèr*, stanzas 305–50. *Sĕrat Sakonḍar* has some stanzas not found in the Cohen Stuart text.

[59] Cf. Cohen Stuart, *Baron Sakéndhèr*, stanzas 351–90.

[60] *Sĕrat Sakonḍar*, ff. 96ᵛ–7ʳ, Canto X (Mas Kumambang):

> 51. . . .
>   sadagangan donja
>   kadjawi ing Rum nagari
>   lan nagri Mkah Madinah
>
> 52. ingkang lija nagri alit dentĕbasi
>   kinarja ponḍokan
>   padjagad gḍong kinardi
>   nagri alit pan ĕrata.

The text still maintains a clear distinction, commented upon in n. 52 above, between the Spanish-Dutch family on the one hand and the Islamic lands on the other.

Singgunkara told Sukmul how, by defeating Kaladjahar at dice, he could save Kaseṇḍer, the princess, *et al.* Sukmul then went to the home of the demon daughters and defeated Kaladjahar at her game. When she refused to pay, Sukmul drew his sword and slew Kaladjahar, Ṭaṭaini, and Ṭaṭakuṭana. He slashed open their bodies and discovered his devoured twin and companions, as if asleep. Upon their bodies he sprinkled magical water given him by Singgunkara and therepon Kaseṇḍer, the princess, Kasebĕr, Garuḍa, and Sĕmbrani were all restored to life. The party, including Sukmul and Suhulman, then returned to Spain where they were received with joy by the anxious king. (Canto X: 47–59, Canto XI: 1–54)[61]

The king again proposed that Kaseṇḍer should take the throne while he retired in his old age to a hermitage, but again Kaseṇḍer declined: if he took the throne, it would be said that the Spanish king had been conquered by a foreign land. But the king insisted and Kaseṇḍer then agreed, asking only that this should also be approved by his father, who still lived. The king knew nothing of his son-in-law's origins and asked who was his father. He was, said Kaseṇḍer, a Nakoda named 'Baron Kawit Prispruranjah' and his kingdom was 'Bukit Tarbi' (i.e. 'bas pan Rudyah Kawit' of the land 'Mabukit Ambin'). Suddenly the king realized that this was his own elder brother.[62] He summoned Sukmul

---

[61] Cf. Cohen Stuart, *Baron Sakéndhèr*, stanzas 391–459. At stanza 434, Cohen Stuart's text begins a new canto (XII) but the *Sĕrat Sakoṇḍar* Canto XI (171 stanzas) continues to a point equivalent to stanza 623 of Cohen Stuart's text. The *Sĕrat Sakoṇḍar* Canto XII (60 stanzas) extends to Cohen Stuart's stanza 680. Canto XIII of *Sĕrat Sakoṇḍar* is then equivalent to Cohen Stuart's Canto XVI.

[62] *Sĕrat Sakoṇḍar*, ff. 108ᵛ–9ʳ, Canto XI (Ḍanḍanggula):

56. Baron Kaseṇḍer matur wotsari
    kula dewa ndji uhun lĕnggona
    lamun ingadĕgna Radjeng
    mendah potjapanipun
    nĕgari ljan katingal ngĕnḍih
    ḍatĕng Sri Naranata
    ngandika Sang Prabu
    ingsun kaki uwis lila
    lahir-batin sun tan darbe putra malih
    lanang lijane sira

57. Baron Kaseṇḍer nuhun turnja ris
    nanging kaidena sakalijan
    pun bapa maksih jusjane
    Prabu Sapanjol muwus
    sapa rane wong tuwaneki
    Baron Kaseṇḍer turnja
    Nakoda ranipun
    Baron Kawit Prispruranjah

JOGJAKARTA AND THE DUTCH

and sent him to fetch his and Kaseṇḍer's father,[63] his own brother. Sukmul then set off, designated the Admiral[64] and accompanied by the great army (*kumpni agung*). Upon his arrival in Bukit Tarbi he gave the happy news to his father. They returned together to Spain and entered the city by the main gate (*pintu bĕsar*). Seated side by side with his long-lost brother, the Nakoda wished upon the king the blessings of the Prophet Moses.[65] Then the Spanish king surrendered the throne to Kaseṇḍer and retired to a hermitage. (Canto XI: 54–96)[66]

Spain prospered under the rule of Kaseṇḍer, but after a time he grew dissatisfied and gave himself over to spiritual exercises. He wished to travel to another land where commerce was excellent. He therefore surrendered the throne to his elder twin Sukmul. Astride Sĕmbrani and overshadowed by Garuḍa, Kaseṇḍer took leave of Spain. But the eleven other sons of the Nakoda grew jealous of Sukmul and conspired

---

Bukit Tarbi Sang Nata engĕt ing galih
jen putrane kang raka

Cf. Cohen Stuart, *Baron Sakéndhèr*, stanzas 461–3. For the version of the Nakoda's name given earlier, see n. 44 above.

It now appears that Kaseṇḍer is the nephew of the Spanish king as well as his son-in-law. The genealogy of the text now stands as follows:

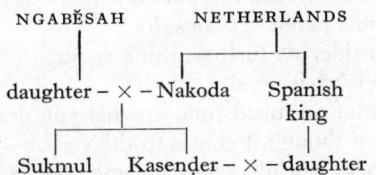

(Unbroken lines indicate direct descent. ' – × – ' indicates marriage.)

[63] The king speaks Malay. *Sĕrat Sakoṇḍar*, f. 110ᵛ, Canto XI (Ḍanḍanggula):

64. ...
ngandika malih Sang Nata
mari anak punja bapak lĕkas panggil
....

[64] Ibid., f. 111ʳ, Canto XI (Ḍanḍanggula) (Kaseṇḍer speaking Malay):

68. djaga urdi baik tu njang pĕgi
ḍari bukit djalan sama kakak
djaḍi Amral sang urdine
....

Urdi is the Dutch 'order.'

[65] Ibid., f. 116ᵛ, Canto XI (Ḍanḍanggula):

94. sewu djumurung manira jaji
mugangsala barkah Nabi Mungsa
....

(See also n. 43 above.)

[66] Cf. Cohen Stuart, *Baron Sakéndhèr*, stanzas 459–505.

together to attack him. Kasender saw this from on high and flew down to Spain, bringing the war to a halt as he came down in the midst of the battlefield. Now Kasender turned the throne over to his father, the Nakoda. (Canto XI: 97–133)[67]

The Nakoda ordered his sons not to become again disunited. He required all of them to swear an oath, which they did. The *plakaats* (edicts), orders, and agreements were completed. Then spoke the Nakoda:

> 135. . . .
> 'Now it is my command:
> all worldly goods, I command,
> these I make to be king,
> adorning the *kraton*;
> my twelve sons, watch over them.
> Be not in discord, let your salaries be the same,
> take the salaries from profits.
>
> 136. 'These worldly goods be regarded as king.
> Be set on your way (you) twelve.
> But be agreed in your consultations;
> if one is not yet consulted
> consider no further, think again,
> do what is good.
> Suffer no misfortune in what you desire,
> even though it comes to thievery.
> These worldly goods I name "The Company."
> But to be consulted over by (you) twelve are
>
> 137. 'all of its affairs:
> commerce, war, the destroying of cities.
> These worldly goods be salaries then,
> but omit not to calculate,
> write up precisely
> the profits and the losses,
> remember these calculations.'
> This was the beginning of the existence
> of the twelve *edele heeren* [Members of the
>   Council of the Indies]; honoured even now is
> this ancient order.[68]

[67] Cf. Cohen Stuart, *Baron Sakéndhèr*, stanzas 505–42.
[68] *Sěrat Sakondar*, ff. 124ᵛ–5ʳ, Canto XI (Dandanggula):

> 135. sampun sinung kang palěkat urdi
> pradjangdjejan ingkang katah-katah

JOGJAKARTA AND THE DUTCH

With the establishment of the Company (i.e. the Dutch East India Company) completed, Baron Kasender again departed from Spain. He left now for the rich and prosperous land of Java. (Canto XI: 133–9)[69]

Kasender, Kaseber, Garuda, and Sembrani soon arrived over Java, which was governed by the kingdom of Mataram. But suddenly they fell to the ground, robbed of their powers to fly. Seven times they tried to fly and seven times failed. Unsure what to do in the face of this threat, Kasender *et al.* decided to disguise themselves by their supernatural powers and to enter the service of the Mataram king and his officials.

     Sri Nakoda andikane
     wis ta parentah ingsun
     donja kabeh parentah mami
     iki sun djundjung nata
     ngrenggani kadatun
     putrengsun rolas tungguwa
     dja salaja lenggaho gadjije sami
     gadjih amet batinja

136. dunja iku kang minongka adji
     teka nglungakena ja wong rolas
     nging ta dengujuba rembuge
     jen sidji durung rembug
     enengena pikiren maning
     kang btjik lakonana
     adja sjaleng kajun
     nadyan silih anjolonga
     dunja iku ingsun arani Kumpni
     nging dirembug wong rolas

137. samubarang pakarjanereki
     adagang aprang abedah kita
     dunjaku gadjihna mangke
     nanging dja sepi petung
     tulisona dipun atiti
     batine lawjan tuna
     petunge diemut
     iku kawitane ana
     deler rolas denwewuri dalah mangkin
     urdine ingkang kina

Cf. Cohen Stuart, *Baron Sakéndhèr*, stanzas 546–51, and p. 143 n. 80.

The Council of the Indies (*Raad van Indië*) was an institution which very much struck the Javanese, perhaps because they perceived in it the familiar pattern of consultation and consensus so essential to their own political life (see Chap. I above). In Javanese texts the Council was called *Rat pen Indija*, or something similar, and from that derived the shorter form *Ratpeni* which was used as a synonym for *Kumpeni* (Company). The number of councillors was not fixed at twelve, but the figure was usually about that number when the various Extraordinary Councillors were included.

[69] Cf. Cohen Stuart, *Baron Sakéndhèr*, stanzas 542–57.

Kasender took the guise of a white *lawejan* (a legendary beast), Garuda became a golden serpent, Sěmbrani the cow Andini with body of gold, and Kasebĕr a white wild buffalo (*kĕbo kamale*) with a human head. They arrived at Mataram and there encountered the ruler Senapati, a king of supernatural powers. Unseen by Senapati, Kasender and the serpent (Garuda) accompanied him to Lipura where he went to pray. He suddenly saw them and, after discussion, accepted their offer to serve him. Senapati then slept upon the stone at Lipura.[70] Meanwhile Senapati's servants Djuru Martani and Ki Nitik Wongsadipradja had encountered Andini (Sěmbrani) and the white buffalo with the human head (Kasebĕr), and had accepted them into their service. The latter party went then to Lipura and there found Senapati asleep. But above his head there suddenly descended a falling star. Djuru (Martani) awakened Senapati, whereupon the star began to speak: 'I give you to know that blessed is our union; it has been determined by God that you be king, governing the land of Java. But when it comes to your great-grandchild the kingdom will fall, conquered by your own people; the final age unrest. But still your descendants shall be (kings). Now, farewell!' And then the star rose into the air; great was the pleasure of Senapati at its words.[71] But Djuru (Martani) advised his master not to end his meditative exercises but to continue them in the sea, while he himself would go to the mountains. They set off. But first the white

---

[70] Lipura is the site of the holy stone Sela Gilang, the goal of the Jogjakarta Crown Prince's pilgrimage in 1778, discussed in Chap. VIII. See p. 243 n. 33.

[71] *Sěrat Sakondar*, f. 131^r, Canto XI (Dandanggula):

    165. . . .
        sumaur lintang manira
        asung djarwa njamadi wor kita mami
        wus pinasṭi Jwang Sukma

    166. sira Nata mĕngku ing rat Djawi
        prapteng bujut rusak nagrinira
        rinĕbat pada bangsane
        djaman ahir dauru
        maksih turunira kang dadi
        wis ta sira karija
        punang lintang mumbul
        Senapati langkung ṭusṭa
        amiarsi pituture lintang nguni
    . . . .

Cf. Cohen Stuart, *Baron Sakéndhér*, stanzas 612–14. For other versions of this prophecy, see also *BTDj(BP)*, vol. v, pp. 20–1; *BTDj*, text pp. 75–6, trans. pp. 78–9.

The greatgrandson (*bujut*) referred to is Amangkurat I, whose *kraton* fell to Trunadjaja in A.J. 1600/A.D. 1677.

JOGJAKARTA AND THE DUTCH

lawejan (Kasender) was placed in a garden and given the name Ki Djuru Taman (the 'garden keeper').[72] (Canto XI: 140–68)[73]

Baron Sukmul (still in Spain) had decided to go to Java to trade. Ten ships were prepared, laden with goods, and then set off on the three-months' journey to Java. The Dutchmen[74] landed at Djakarta, to the wonderment of the inhabitants and to the pleasure of the Pangeran of Djakarta. The Dutch established themselves on the island *Undrus* ('Onrust', the Dutch name for an island in the bay of Batavia). (Canto XI: 168–71, Canto XII: 1–6)[75]

When Padjadjaran had been conquered (by the successor Islamic states of West Java, i.e. by the Pangeran of Djakarta in this text), one of the princesses had fled to the mountains, where she became pregnant by the *adjar* (holy man) Sukarsi. When her time was due, she gave birth to a daughter of surpassing beauty. This daughter was taken by the Pangeran of Djakarta, but when he tried to sleep with her flames came out of her genitals.[76] She was therefore banished to an island. In turn

---

[72] *Sĕrat Sakondar*, f. 131ᵛ, Canto XI (Dandanggula):

168. wus mĕsat rĕbat paraneki
samja ngiring mĕngamĕnganira
lawejan seta purwane
pinĕrnahkĕn genipun
neng udyana sinung kĕkasih
wasta Ki Djuru Taman
gĕnti kang winuwus
. . . .

Cf. Cohen Stuart, *Baron Sakéndhèr*, stanza 617, where the change of name to Djuru Taman is omitted.

Djuru Taman also appears in the *babad* stories concerning the reigns of Senapati and Sultan Agung. Dr. de Graaf ('Sénapati', p. 88) has suggested that the mythical figure of Djuru Taman is perhaps to be associated with an Italian who was in the service of Sultan Agung's father Krapjak, according to Agung's statement to Dr. de Haan in 1622. Whether or not Kasender in his new identity as Djuru Taman is to be associated with a European adventurer in the service of the early kings of Mataram (a role which is consistent with Kasender's role in *Sĕrat Sakondar*), it is clear that at least in this text he is not to be associated with the distinct character Djuru Martani, as was suggested by Dr. Pigeaud in 'Alexander', p. 360.   [73] Cf. Cohen Stuart, *Baron Sakéndhèr*, stanzas 557–617.

[74] Again the family are clearly Dutch (*Wĕlandi*), not Spanish. But this distinction is not important within the context of *Sĕrat Sakondar*, which sees Spain and the Netherlands as being essentially identical. See the genealogy in n. 62 above, and the beginning of the text (Canto I: 1–3), cited in n. 43 above.

[75] Cf. Cohen Stuart, *Baron Sakéndhèr*, stanzas 618–29.

[76] The princess with flaming genitals is a theme elsewhere in Javanese literature (Ken Dĕdĕs in the *Pararaton*) and it is accepted that she represents the powers of sovereignty. Only the rightful successor to sovereignty (Ken Angrok, Sukmul) is able to sleep with her. See Brandes, 'Pararaton', pp. 13–14, 57–8, 66; Berg, 'Vijfvoudige Buddha', pp. 142–3, 273; Schrieke, *Sociological Studies*, vol. ii, pp. 12, 70–4.

both the Sultan of Tjirĕbon and the Sultan [sic] of Mataram[77] took the girl but could not sleep with her because of the flames. The Sultan of Mataram again sent her back to the island, where she lived in sorrowful isolation for three years. Then she was sold by the Pangeran of Djakarta to the Dutch. It was Sukmul who bought her, for the price of three cannon. These three became regalia (*wasijat*, literally 'heirlooms'), Guntur Gĕni going to the *kraton* of Mataram, Ki Pamuk to Bantĕn, and Njai Sĕtomi to Tjirĕbon. Sukmul took his new wife home (to Spain) where she became pregnant and in time bore Sukmul a son, named Mur Djangkung (i.e. Jan Pietersz. Coen, 1587–1629; the founder of Batavia, 1619).[78] When Mur Djangkung had grown to become a famous warrior, he asked his mother about his origins. She told him[79] that she was not of that land (Spain), but a princess of Padjadjaran, which had been destroyed by the Muslims. Having heard the whole of her tale, Mur Djangkung announced he would go to take revenge upon the Pangeran of Djakarta. He fitted out fifteen ships, loaded with beer, wine, bread, and strong drink of all sorts, as well as war materials, and set sail for Java. Soon he arrived there. (Canto XII: 6–31)[80]

[77] The use of the title Sultan (see also Cohen Stuart's stanza 720) indicates that the author no longer has in mind Senapati, but rather Sultan Agung (1613–45). This is confirmed later in *Sĕrat Sakondar*, f. 145^v (Canto XIV: 11, cited in n. 86 below), where the ruler of Mataram is called 'Sultan Karta', i.e. Sultan Agung.

[78] The genealogy derived by putting together this text and the information about the Padjadjaran family (see nn. 33 and 62 above) now stands as follows:

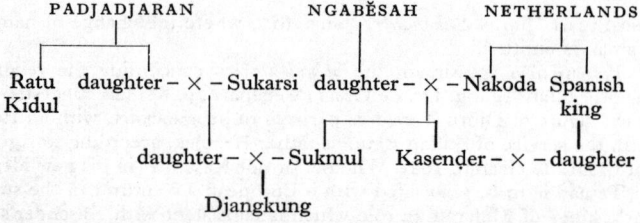

(Unbroken lines indicate direct descent. '–×–' indicates marriage.)

That the author meant Djangkung as the Javanized version of Jan Coen (see Pigeaud, 'Alexander', p. 325 n. 5) can be seen in the use of 'Djangkung' for Jan Coen in the *Babad Kraton* story about the Dutch in Batavia (f. 267^r: Kapitan Djangkung). In the same story in *BTDj(BP)*, vol. x, p. 7, is mentioned 'Kapitan Djakwes'. This apparently refers to the VOC commander Jacques Lefebvre; see J. Brandes, 'Djakuwès in de Babad, tijdens de Belegering van Batavia = Jacques Lefebvre', *TBG*, vol. 44 (1901), pp. 286–8. (Cf. 'Djakuwes' in *BTDj*, text p. 136, trans. p. 141.)

The word *djangkung* has several meanings in Javanese, but in these literary texts it is most often used as 'to watch over from on high'. In *Sĕrat Sakondar*, Sĕmbrani and Garuda *djangkung* over Kasender.

[79] Both Djangkung and his mother speak Malay, since both are non-Javanese.

[80] Cf. Cohen Stuart, *Baron Sakéndhèr*, stanzas 629–51.

Mur Djangkung was well received by the Pangeran, and the Dutch settled in Djakarta. They mixed with the local people, who liked their language and were all able to speak Malay.[81] But Mur Djangkung was all the while making military preparations for his revenge. His practising with cannon ultimately aroused the Pangeran's anger when cannon-balls fell within the *kraton* grounds. He was told to leave Djakarta, but Mur Djangkung protested that he would suffer great commercial loss and did not wish to leave. Instead he begged forgiveness, which was granted.[82] To get away from the Dutch and their cannon, the Pangeran then moved from Djakarta to Gunung Sari (within the boundaries of modern Djakarta), which was in accord with the Will of God. Mur Djangkung was greatly pleased at this and proceeded to build a castle called *Kuṭa Tai*.[83] He prepared for his revenge. (Canto XII: 31–60)[84]

The Dutch now attacked the Pangeran of Djakarta and great losses were suffered on both sides. The Pangeran's younger brother Pangeran Purbaja, a warrior of supernatural powers, led the people of Djakarta. The tide of battle flowed back and forth and proceeded for several days, the air filled with missiles. Mur Djangkung could not gain the victory. In Spain, Baron Sukmul (Djangkung's father) learned of his son's difficulties. He set off for Java and soon arrived at Batavia (*Bĕtawi*). There he advised his son to use guile to win the day: instead of shot, the cannon were to be loaded with coins (*rejal kĕton lan Anggris talen rupijah*). Djangkung gave the order and for several days money rained down on the people of Djakarta. They ran out from Gunung Sari to collect this money but then the cannon were suddenly loaded again with cannon-balls. The people of Djakarta fell in great numbers and in Gunung Sari the defenceless Pangeran Djakarta was filled with anxiety. (Canto XIII: 1–36)[85]

Now, it was the Will of God that the Pangeran of Djakarta should

---

[81] *Sĕrat Sakondar*, f. 136ᵛ, Canto XII (Asmaradana):

   38. Wĕlandi awor wong bumi
   samja rĕmĕn basanira
   wong Djakarta bisa kabeh
   tjara Lumaju basanja
   . . . .

Cf. Cohen Stuart, *Baron Sakéndhèr*, stanza 658.

[82] Again he speaks Malay: 'djadi rugi bĕtul-bĕtul . . . saja mentak ampun banjak', etc.

[83] This may be translated as 'Fort Faeces'. It was a pejorative indigenous nickname for the Maeghdelins Reduijt, also called Hollandia, a small fortress in the south of seventeenth-century Batavia; see de Haan, 'Kota Tahi', on the origin of this picturesque name. The story is also mentioned in Raffles (1830), vol. ii, p. 168.

[84] Cf. Cohen Stuart, *Baron Sakéndhèr*, stanzas 651–80.

[85] Cf. ibid., stanzas 681–713.

depart with all his troops and relatives. He settled in the mountains south of Djakarta and Gunung Sari was taken by the Dutch. But the latter remained on guard against Pangeran Purbaja, shooting even the clouds for fear they should be he. Ever greater was the sorrow of Pangeran Bĕtawi (*sic*; i.e. Djakarta) and of his troops and relatives. He thought to himself that he had never suspected things would go so far with the Dutch. Now he had given his place to the foreigners (*wong Sabrang*) and lived in the mountains. What would happen to him, he thought, when this came to the Sultan of Mataram? Surely he would be killed. He had been long in the mountains when his troops departed, leaving him with only his relatives. He became a mere rebel with the *wong parajangan* ('the people of Priangan', or 'the spirits') as his companions, all practising asceticism, with supernatural powers were all their descendants. But they were unable to conquer any lands. The Pangeran thought then of his errors, in ever greater sorrow. He recalled the princess, the daughter of *adjar* Sukarsi (by the princess of Padjadjaran), whom he had sold to the Dutch. Great was his sorrow; he neither slept nor ate. Within his heart he asked, 'What is the Will of God for my course of life? Here am I found without honour; what am I to do? Certainly I will suffer misfortune from Sultan Agung; certainly I will die; many are my sins. The Dutchmen in Batavia grow ever worse, setting forth their designs, creating a city surrounded by water. Indeed the river Tjiliwung has been enclosed within the city.' (Canto XIV: 1–12)[86]

[86] The last several stanzas differ from Cohen Stuart's text, stanzas 714–23. They are therefore given here: *Sĕrat Sakondar*, ff. 145r–6r, Canto XIV (Asmaradana):

    8. wadya alit sami mulih
       kantun sĕntana kewala
       dadya angaraman bae
       wong parajangan kanṭinja
       pan sami apratapa
       asĕkti saturunipun
       tan bisa ngrĕbat nĕgara

    9. Pangran kang katjipteng galih
       lĕpatipun kang sarira
       karantan-rantan nalane
       ketang Sang Putri ing kina
       anake djar Sukarsa
       duk winade Sang Dyah Aju
       tinumbas datĕng Wĕlonda

   10. angraos pikir kasilib
       mila Pangeran Djakarta
       asangĕt ing pangungune
       tan arsa ḍahar lan nendra
       ngandika ing djro nala

JOGJAKARTA AND THE DUTCH

1. 'I, a young man,[87] will list
   the spirits of the island Java

       baja karsane Jwang Agung
         lĕlakone wak-manira

11. ing mĕngko iki pinanggih
    sarira tanpa adjija
    koja paran polah ingong
    ora wande oleh ala
    mring Kangdjĕng Sultan Karta
    pasṭi ingsun tĕkeng lampus
    akaṭah dosa manira

12. Wĕlandi kang neng Bĕtawi
    ing mangke sangsaja dadra
    anutugakĕn karĕpe
    apan sami karja kiṭa
    kinubĕngan ing toja
    anĕnggih Lepen Tjaliwung
    ingubĕngakĕn djro kiṭa

    Cohen Stuart's translation of his stanza 721 renders the phrase *ngrĕbat kaḍatun* as 'de herovering van den rijkszetel', by which he means 'the reconquest of Batavia'. In stanza 8 above, I understand *ngrĕbat nĕgara* as 'to conquer (any) lands', i.e. in a general rather than a singular and specific sense. This, then, makes more clear the rather sudden transition to Canto XV (see n. 87) which concerns those spirits who *angrĕksa nĕgara* ('watch over the lands'). The *nĕgara* of stanza 8 might be Batavia, but since Canto XV lists the spirits of many *nĕgara*, I prefer to understand both the *nĕgara* of Canto XIV: 8 and those of Canto XV in a plural and general sense.

[87] The transition from Canto XIV to Canto XV (text in n. 89 below) is explicable only if (*a*) the Pangeran of Djakarta is continuing to soliloquize in the midst of his sorrow, or (*b*) the author of the *Sĕrat Sakonḍar* MS. added the list of spirits as a kind of addendum, referring to himself as a 'young man' (*wong anom*). In the latter case, the identity of the 'young man' is unknown. The author nowhere refers to himself by name. On f. 3^v (Canto I: 6), he calls himself the 'Honourable Poet' (*Sang Kawi*).

    The transition to the last canto in any case is not clear. Up to the end of Canto XIV the text is a pseudo-historical narrative. In Canto XV it suddenly becomes a sort of spiritual geography of Java. Canto XV can be considered separately from the preceding cantos as another version of the *Kidung Lalĕmbut*, of which several texts exist (see n. 89 below and Pigeaud, *Literature*, vol. i, pp. 92–3). But it is desirable here to attempt to understand why the author of *Sĕrat Sakonḍar* felt this to be a fitting text with which to finish his book.

    The logical relevance of this final canto to the foregoing text is perhaps apparent if one recalls that one is here dealing with a story full of supernatural events and wondrous characters which describes the Dutch position in West Java in terms of the descent from the Padjadjaran Princess, who is connected genealogically with the Goddess of the Southern Ocean (see nn. 33 and 78 above). The spiritual forces of Java are essential to explain the significance of the tale as a whole and it is not therefore illogical that the author of *Sĕrat Sakonḍar* should complete his story by setting out the whole spiritual geography of the island. Nevertheless, a sense of discontinuity remains.

who watch over the lands,
the kings of the spirits,
and great is their beneficent power.
If they are all memorized
they will become a defence,
will be made watchmen over the ill;
inauspicious grounds and strange trees shall
   become harmless.'

(There follows a list of 142 spirits and the places they watched over. It begins with 'Durga, who bewitched Madjapahit', and Radja Baurĕksa, the king [and queen?] of the spirits. The list includes Djuru Taman [who according to this text is Baron Kasendĕr],[88] *adjar* Sukarsi, and the family of the Goddess of the Southern Ocean. It ends with Ki Burĕng and Ni Burĕng 'who suckled all the devils.')[89]

[88] See n. 72 above. Djuru Taman's place may be on the northern *pasisir*. Does *Sĕrat Sakondar* therefore see the Dutch rulers of the north coast at Sĕmarang as being under the protection of Baron Kasendĕr? This has obvious attractions but I prefer not to argue such an interpretation. In the first place, the text has *Tundjung Bang*, which is unknown to me. It would seem to be either Tratebang (*trate* and *tundjung* are synonyms), a north coast village near Pĕkalongan, or Tandjung Bang, a cape on the north coast. The latter is found in *Lijst van de voornaamste Aardrijkskundige Namen in den Nederlandsch-Indischen Archipel* (Weltevreden, 1923), p. 309, where it is said to be in the Bandjaran district of the Djĕpara division. But the location of Tundjung Bang in the list (see no. 22 in the list in n. 89 below) suggests that it should be in the Jogjakarta area, as are the toponyms which surround it. A location near Jogjakarta would also be consistent with the text of the story, since Senapati would have been near Lipura when he renamed Kasendĕr 'Djuru Taman'. And it will be suggested below that Kasendĕr seems to occupy not the position of the Governor at Sĕmarang, but that of the Resident at the *kraton*, which would also seem to call for a place near Jogjakarta rather than one on the north coast. Furthermore, the Dutch coastal headquarters at Sĕmarang has quite a different spirit of its own named Kĕlasong (see no. 78 in the list in n. 89). This sounds rather like a Dutch name (Claeszoon?), as do several others in the list (e.g. nos. 21, 54, 79, 102, 127), and perhaps Sĕmarang does have the protection of a Dutch spirit even if it is not Kasendĕr's.

[89] *Sĕrat Sakondar*, f. 146ʳ, Canto XV (Sinom):

1. wong anom ingsun angetang
   lĕlĕmbut ing nungsa Djawi
   ingkang angrĕksa nĕgara
   para ratu ning dĕdĕmit
   agung sawabe ugi
   jen apal sadajanipun
   apan dadi tĕtulak
   kinarja tunggu wong sakit
   lemah sangar kaju aeng dadi tawa

2. ingkang rumijin bang wetan
   Durga nĕluh Maospait

19. 'Honour, all (of you), the history of the spirits,

lawan Radja Baurĕksa
iku ratu ning ḍĕḍĕmit
. . . .

Rather than giving the text, the list of places and their spirits will be summarized here in the order in which they appear. The first in each case is the toponym, usually a village but often a larger district, a cave, a mountain, etc. The reader can find these locations in Schoel, *Alphabetisch Register*, or in *Lijst van de voornaamste Namen*. Some of the spirits are known in other sources, many are not. For information on Javanese spirits, see van Hien, *Javaansche Geestenwereld*. The list as a whole can be compared with a closely related text, the *Kidung Lalĕmbut*, LOr 4000 (2), which is published in full in J. Brandes, *Beschrijving der Javaansche, Balineesche en Sasaksche Handschriften aangetroffen in de Nalatenschap van Dr. H. N. van der Tuuk* (4 vols.; Batavia, 1901–26), vol. ii, pp. 56–8. This text has been consulted here to clarify some uncertain readings.

1. Madjapahit: Durga; Baurĕksa (ratu ḍĕḍĕmit).
2. Balĕmbangan: Sang Balabatu.
3. Kĕḍiri: Pun Sĕntjaja.
4. Pranaraga: Si Koreg.
5. Patjitan: Sidakari.
6. Kaduwang: Kalĕnting.
7. Magĕtan ('Kĕmagĕtang'): Endrajĕksa.
8. Djĕnggala: Si Tundjungpuri.
9. Surabaja: Prangmuka.
10. Pĕnanggungan: Aburabur.
11. Djipang: Sapudjagat.
12. Madiun: Kalasĕkti.
13. Pasuruan: Prabujĕksa.
14. Gĕgĕlang: Ngamaita.
15. Gĕgĕsang: Si Ḍaḍungawik.
16. Padjang: Buta Sulewah.
17. Mataram: Mondarmandir.
18. Plered: Radjĕgnĕsi.
19. Kuṭa Gĕḍe: Njai Panggung.
20. Karta: Pulunggana.
21. Djombor: Si Kabĕr (cf. no. 79 below).
22. 'Tundjung Bang' (see n. 88 above): Djuru Taman.
23. Kreteg: Si Sĕndal.
24. Bleberan: Sapu Angin.
25. 'Brangkudan' [?]: Sinatpada.
26. Sari: Si Nandansari.
27. Wonopĕti: Malangkarsa.
28. Sawangan: Si Sanḍung.
29. 'Pamasuhan' [?]: Dudukwarih.
30. Tĕgalajang: Buta Tukang.
31. Kajulanḍejan [text has 'Taju . . .']: Ki Daruna; Ni Daruni.
32. Roban: Baguskarang.
33. Dĕlĕpe: Widanongga.
34. Pandjalin: Ḍĕnḍĕngrawa.
35. Kuwu: Kĕnḍunggurunggung.
36. Loḍaja: Arja Tiran.
37. 'Kalu Djaja Widana Prih' [?].
38. Pĕnaruban ('Panaroban'): Sontapura.
39. Brian ('Barejan'): Tjitranajaka.
40. Rawabĕning ('Pning'): Sarpabongsa.
41. Kĕsongo: Si Pĕrang Tandang.
42. 'Galĕbug' [?]: Si Ondarandir.
43. Talaga Pasir: Pun Djalilu.
44. Tuntang: Kalangadang.
45. Gunung Prau ('Ardi Baita'): Bantjuri Kalabantjuri.
46. Djĕnar: Nini Galuh.
47. Bandjarsari: Wĕwasi.
48. Watukuro: Si Lĕngkung.
49. 'Rukĕs' [?]: Si Oragarig.
50. Loano: Ni Djĕnggi; Ki Pun Djĕnggi.
51. Patalan: Si Gĕndrug.
52. Rĕngas: Buta Kumbari.
53. Banjumas: Kalanaḍah.
54. (Pa)mantjingan: Si Dulĕk.
55. Guwa Langse: Raden Putri.
56. Parangwedang: Raden Arja Djajengwesṭi.
57. All along the south coast are the family of the Goddess of the

at night be it remembered;
it will become a defence for the ill.

Southern Ocean ('sakjeh urut pasisir / kulawarga Ratu Kidul').
58. Surakarta ('Sala'): Djim Sětja.
59. Děmak: Djim Santri.
60. Jogjakarta ('Jugdja'): Ratu Aju Dyarawati.
61. Kaliurang: Si Lombo.
62. Lěmah Ḍuwur: Bagus Djěḍig.
63. Galuh: Rara Panḍita.
64. 'Pagasděndji' [?]: Si Ḍuwung.
65. Kawu: Buh Rěnggin; Ki Děmalung.
66. Patje: Bagus Ambar.
67. Warung: Kjai Basuki.
68. Grobogan: Ki Sěburung.
69. Pěkalongan: Njai Marbot.
70. Wiradesa: Bagus Kutjir.
71. Těgal: Si Gigil.
72. Karangasěm: Pun Tjaluri.
73. Kalangbret: Si Umik.
74. Gunung Lawu: Tunggul Wulung.
75. Pěmalang: Pun Gutuk Api.
76. Girilaja: Raden Giwang.
77. Batang: Si Lumrah.
78. Sěmarang: Kělasong (see n. 88 above).
79. Kenḍal: Setan Kaběr (cf. no. 21 above).
80. Batavia: Si Arimili.
81. Kaliwungu: Djim Kurwit.
82. Kudus: Ki Bělarong.
83. Djuwana: Raden Bantrik.
84. Wringinputih: Ni Kěmanḍang Ragawati.
85. Siluman: Gěnawati.
86. Tjěngkalsewu: Kalasrěnggi.
87. Lasěm: Setan Karungbang.
88. Paṭi: Djuwalpajal.
89. Brěběs: Badjobali.
90. Tjirěbon: Batutjatur.
91. Sunda-lands ('Pasunḍan'): Raden Oglang.
92. Gěbang: Buta Kikili.
93. Děrmaju: Buta Arikumba.
94. 'Kaběḍulan' [?]: Buta Kakab.
95. 'Demrě Radja Bolang Bali' [?].
96. Kali Djaga: Raden Ina.
97. Krawang: Sang Radja Srěnggi.
98. Suměḍang: Raden Tělik.
99. Tjiandjur: Buta Sinawur.
100. Bajabang: Kurung.
101. Bantěn: Sang Tungguldjati.
102. Bagor: Buta Peběr ('Buta Peběr kang ruměksa Bagor djadjar').
103. Gunung Prawata: Lambahur.
104. Gunung Sumbing: Megatara.
105. Ajah: Kusumangumbara.
106. Sundara: Rangsangpati.
107. Sela: Djatisari.
108. Tuban: Si Nalasaut.
109. Bonang: Arja Srěnggara.
110. Ngampel: Sambělsungil.
111. Sidaju: Raden Běṭak.
112. Lumadjang: Umbulselang.
113. Rawi: Raden Lěngkur.
114. [Pa]měkasan: Kěntjanawungu.
115. Madura: Raden Sěngkali.
116. Pandjěr: Ni Muhili.
117. Prabalingga: Agulagul.
118. Pědjarakan: Raden ('dyan') Sarat.
119. Kartasura: Ki Abru.
120. Padjadjaran: Saraděnta.
121. Gunung Karatjak: Si Patjět.
122. Tjarěme: Adjar Sukarsi.
123. Kanḍangwěsi: Raden Djaka.
124. Galunggung: Rara Api.
125. Gunung Djati: Dasjara.
126. Kanḍanghaur: Djaka Karjor.
127. Krangkeng: Djakawisa.
128. Gunung Gěḍe: Radja Bukit.
129. 'Nungsa Běrambang' [?]: Ratu Kěnja.
130. Karangbalong: Djaka Kalang.
131. 'Larbok' [?]: Djaka Mukilking.
132. Gunungputri: Djim Salewah.
133. Bulupitu: Raden Pěri.
134. Waturupit: Pun Tjěngklung.
135. Sidopěkso: Guntur Suwuk.
136. Djrebeng ('Djěrebe'): Wewepěṭak.
137. Ki Burěng and Ni Burěng, who suckled all the devils ('Ki Burěng Ni Burěng něnggih / pan punika kang nusoni setan kabeh').

Be feared the spirits,
all, none dare oppose.
And when travelling,
the spirits and devils, none shall dare to oppose:
in the forests savage beasts do run.'[90]
  (Canto XV: 1-19. End of *Sĕrat Sakonḍar*)

Thus, somewhat enigmatically and chillingly, *Sĕrat Sakonḍar* comes to an end. As is the case with *Sĕrat Surja Radja*, there is a great deal in this text of interest to scholars of Javanese myth and literature which cannot be discussed fully here. For the purposes of the present study, the main interest is in the Javanese view of the Dutch East India Company. It should be pointed out that although this text sometimes reveals some understanding of European history, in such matters as the general nature of the Crusades and the origins of the Company in the necessity to end competition among Dutch shippers, it is above all a mythical tale. It should be compared not with actual history but with other mythical statements concerning the Dutch. In particular, the story should be compared with the latter parts of the *Sĕrat Surja Radja*, summarized in Chapter VII above. Indeed, it might be argued that in some ways the story of *Surja Radja* follows upon that of *Sĕrat Sakonḍar* in a mythical chronological order. *Sĕrat Sakonḍar* tells of the foreigners up to their first adventures in Java; *Surja Radja* describes mythical events thereafter. But clearly the stories do not actually follow one another except in a general way, in that the characters and details are quite different.

The heroes of *Sĕrat Surja Radja* and *Sĕrat Sakonḍar*, Pudjakusuma and Kasenḍer respectively, share some adventures. In particular, both are killed and later returned to life. But the differences between the two are more important. Pudjakusuma is a Javanese prince. Indeed, he is identified with the text's author,

---

[90] *Sĕrat Sakonḍar*, f. 149ᵛ, Canto XV (Sinom):

19. den samja angestokĕna
sĕdjarahe kang ḍĕḍĕmit
jen dalu den apalĕna
dadi tĕtulak wong sakit
kinadjriha ḍĕḍĕmit
sadaja tan ana purun
miwah jen kekesahan
djim setan tan ana wani
aneng wona sato galak pan lumadjar.

the Crown Prince of Jogjakarta.[91] Kasender, on the other hand, is a foreigner descended from both the foreign lands of Ngabĕsah (apparently Islamic) and of the Netherlands and Spain (Mosaic, i.e. Christian).[92] In the end he is not a king but rather a servant of the Javanese king. Indeed, it is curious that Kasender suddenly disappears from the story after he enters the service of Senapati. Thereafter the interest is focused upon Sukmul and the activities of the Dutch in West Java. A suggestion regarding the significance of Kasender in the formal Javanese–Dutch relationship will be made below.

Both *Sĕrat Surja Radja* and *Sĕrat Sakondar* end with statements of Javanese–Dutch relations. But the point of view is different. *Sĕrat Surja Radja* describes the relationship between the Javanese king and the king of Tanah Sabrang at the end of the wars. They are friends and, indeed, their relationship is that of elder brother (Tanah Sabrang) and younger brother (Javanese king). *Sĕrat Sakondar* ends with the conflict between the Dutch and the Pangeran of Djakarta, who is displaced by them. But implicit in the latter is also a depiction of the Mataram–Dutch relationship. By marrying the princess with the flaming genitals Sukmul demonstrated that the Dutch were the legitimate successors of Padjadjaran, whose sovereignty was represented by the princess's supernatural characteristic.[93] Thus they were the successors to the position of Padjadjaran in Javanese eyes. They therefore became the rightful rulers of the West of Java, of the Sundanese, and of the *parahjangan*. They represented the legitimate line of West Java, as opposed to the illegitimate line of the Pangeran of Djakarta. As will be seen below, this relationship, too, could be depicted in family terms in which the Dutch were the senior members. It is thus consistent with the final Dutch–Javanese relationship depicted at the end of the *Sĕrat Surja Radja*.

Both the *Surja Radja* and *Sakondar* stories depict the difference in the religion of the foreigners. In the former, a story predominantly about Java, the Javanese are Muslims and the people of Sabrang something else which is not precisely defined. In the end, the main element in the reconciliation of Sabrang and Java is the conversion of the foreigners to Islam. In *Sĕrat Sakondar*

[91] See Chap. VII above, especially p. 210.
[92] See above, nn. 43, 50, 52, 60, 62, 65.   [93] See above, n. 76.

JOGJAKARTA AND THE DUTCH

the text concerns primarily the history of the foreign lands and therefore the Indonesians and their religion are not emphasized. The Dutch and Spanish religion is said to be that of the Prophet Moses. But it will be noted that Kasenḍer and Sukmul, by virtue of their descent from the princess of Ngabĕsah, seem also to carry the blood of Islamic lands in their veins.[94] They are thus descended from foreigners on both their parents' sides, but in the one case the line is Mosaic (Christian) and in the other apparently Islamic.

It is always dangerous to assume that several Javanese sources together represent a consistent body of myth. There is a considerable danger of discovering parallels and forcing comparisons which do not exist, or of ignoring contradictions which may be significant. Nevertheless, it would seem appropriate here to attempt to draw together the various aspects of Jogjakarta *kraton* myth regarding the Dutch and to associate this with the more mundane documentation employed at the beginning of this chapter.

There are four interrelated subjects involved in these myths. They are the foreigners, the Sundanese, the Javanese, and the spirits. Several Jogjakarta *kraton* sources deal with these topics. *Sĕrat Sakonḍar* concerns itself primarily with the foreigners, the Sundanese, and the spirits. *Sĕrat Surja Radja* is primarily interested in the foreigners (after they have come to Java), the Javanese, and the spirits. *Babad Kraton* shares a *kraton* origin with these two manuscripts. In its earlier portions it is concerned with the Sundanese, the Javanese, and the spirits. In the course of this chapter, relevant passages of these three texts have been described and discussed. Now they will also be associated with the various Dutch and Javanese documents from the eighteenth century which clarify how Dutch–Jogjakarta relations actually functioned.

There are several ways of considering these matters, but here genealogy seems the most appropriate, since the Javanese usually expressed the relationship with the Dutch in family terms. Here will be put together the main portions of the genealogies of Sukmul, Kasenḍer, and Djangkung, of the Sultans of Jogjakarta, of their *patihs* Danurĕdja, and of the Goddess of the Southern Ocean.[95]

[94] See above, nn. 43, 50, 52, 60, 62, 65.
[95] The genealogy of the Mataram rulers is to be found in any *babad* text and in several standard published sources; e.g. see de Graaf, 'Sénapati', p. 5. For sources on the other genealogies, see above, nn. 18, 33, 78.
In the following genealogical table, unbroken lines indicate direct descent,

410 JOGJAKARTA UNDER SULTAN MANGKUBUMI

The genealogy which results is divided into two segments, Indonesian and foreign (Sabrang). It will be seen that these two halves come together only in the person of Djangkung and hence, presumably, in the position of the Governors-General of Batavia:

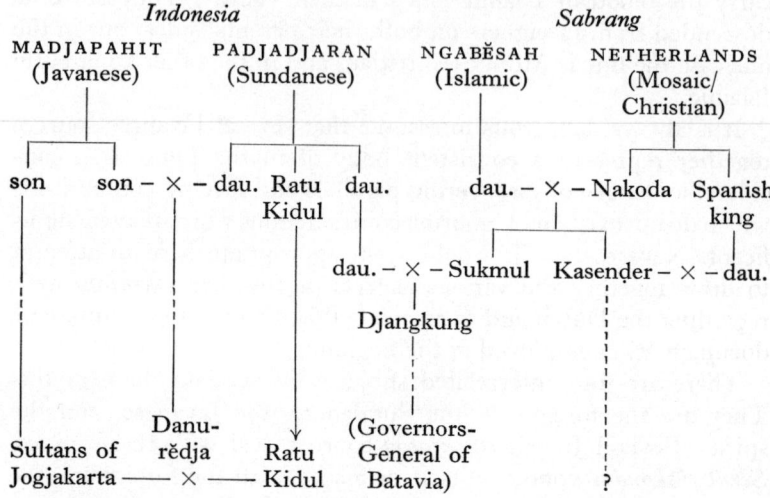

Thus the position of the Governors-General in Batavia, as it was explained by Jogjakarta courtly myth, becomes more clear. Djangkung and his successors carried the blood of both the foreign royal houses and also inherited the legitimate sovereign rights of Padjadjaran in West Java. In this treble royal ancestry they had no equal. By their descent from Padjadjaran they were also related to the Goddess of the Southern Ocean and hence indirectly (by the Goddess' marriage to the Javanese kings) to the rulers of Mataram. They were therefore foreigners of the most honourable origins, legitimate successors to Padjadjaran, rightful occupants of Batavia, natural allies of the Javanese kings, and very senior figures in *kraton* mythology. But they carried no rights of sovereignty over Mataram.

---

broken lines direct descent over several unenumerated generations. ' – × – ' indicates marriage. Ratu Kidul (the Goddess of the Southern Ocean) is an eternal figure who will live until the Judgement Day, and this is indicated by an arrow connecting the two points at which she appears in this genealogy. 'Daughter' is abbreviated 'dau'.

A question mark has been placed where descendants of Kasenḍer ought to be. No text presently known ascribes descendants to him, although that is not to say that such a text may not have existed. But descendants are not required to see the position which Kasenḍer fills in this mythological scheme. It is important to remember that at the end of the *Sĕrat Sakonḍar* tales about him, Kasenḍer entered the service of the Javanese king. He was also a descendant of both the Ngabĕsah and Netherlands lines. He was related by the marriage of his twin to the Padjadjaran line but had no blood relationship with the Indonesian families. His position has important parallels with that of Danurĕdja. Danurĕdja was related to the foreign families by marriage in a collateral line, and both to the Padjadjaran line and to the Madjapahit line by direct descent. He had no blood relationship with the Dutch but as *patih* he served both the Sultan and the Company. Thus, Danurĕdja and Kasenḍer occupy analogous positions. Each is the descendant of both major family lines on his side of the genealogy and each serves the ruler of the other side of the genealogy. The suggestion then follows that Kasenḍer represents the position of the Dutch Resident at the court, as it was set out earlier in this chapter. He was the Dutchman who served the Sultan as well as the Company (to whom he was related), just as the *patih* served the Company as well as the Sultan (to whom he was related).[96]

Thus the complex mythological framework of the Jogjakarta *kraton* texts helped to explain and to justify the relationship, as the Sultans saw it, with the Dutch East India Company. The *patih* and the Resident occupied the dual positions, one from each side of the relationship, each owing loyalty to both sides. And the central position of the entire framework was occupied by the Governor-General, who alone bridged the genealogical gap

[96] Danurĕdja was also connected to the line of HB I by marriage (HB I and Danurĕdja were brothers-in-law), just as Kasenḍer was additionally connected to the Spanish line by marriage.

There is, however, a certain lack of symmetry here. Danurĕdja and the foreign rulers whom he serves have in common direct descent from Padjadjaran. But Kasenḍer shares no direct descent with the Mataram (Jogjakarta) line which he serves. But this merely reflects the general asymmetry of the whole genealogy. The structure has an 'Indonesia-centric' bias; its point is to explain and to justify a foreign presence in West Java, not a Javanese presence abroad. Hence the foreigners have Sundanese blood, but there is no need for the Javanese kings to have Sundanese or foreign blood, the Javanese position in Mataram being a simple matter of direct descent. Thus Kasenḍer, a foreigner, shares no direct ancestry with the Javanese.

between the indigenous and the foreign royal families. It was this very senior figure whom the Javanese rulers addressed as their 'grandfather'.

This mythological system is significant not only to understand the general relationship between the *kratons* and the Company. It also assists in understanding the crisis at the beginning of Pakubuwana IV's reign, which was the subject of Chapter IX. Pakubuwana IV's intention seems to have been a restoration of a bipartite division of Java between Batavia and Surakarta. In other words, this would have been a restoration of the structure of the Baron Kasenḍer story without the additional complications of the Dutch Government at Sěmarang and a second Javanese court at Jogjakarta. Poensen's Pakualaman *babad* contains several possible and one fairly clear literary reference to the Kasenḍer myth in its description of that crisis. The author says that one of the Susuhunan's *santris* claimed various magical abilities. Among them, he possessed the flying horse Sěmbrani upon which he flew every night over the Dutch fortress. Sěmbrani was, of course, Baron Kasenḍer's golden mount. Kasenḍer's supernatural powers were expressed in his possession of Sěmbrani and his decision to enter the service of Senapati came after Sěmbrani was unable to fly over Mataram, thereby demonstrating Senapati's superior powers. The *santri* who said in 1790 that he flew on Sěmbrani over the fortress was claiming superior supernatural powers over the Dutch. The Pakualaman *babad* rejects this claim as nonsense, saying the horse was in fact made of leather to deceive the gullible.[97] And there is no evidence from the Surakarta side which confirms that the *santris* actually laid claim to Sěmbrani. But the *babad* reference does suggest either that the *santris*' teachings were based upon Baron Kasenḍer myths or, more likely, that their teachings were sufficiently similar to Jogjakarta Baron Kasenḍer stories that the *babad* author fell into terminology from the latter to describe the plots.[98]

The present chapter does not, of course, exhaust the subject of Dutch–Javanese relations in the latter part of the eighteenth century. Javanese myth is so complex and extensive that one can

[97] Poensen, 'Mangkubumi', p. 341. Poensen should have treated 'kapal Sěmbarani' as a proper name rather than translating it as 'een gevleugeld paard'.

[98] Sěmbrani is not exclusive to the Baron Sakenḍer stories. See Poerbatjaraka, *Agastya in den Archipel* (Leiden, 1926), p. 30.

only begin by studying particular texts and specific aspects. But the over-all Jogjakarta *kraton* view of the matter should now be more clear. The structure described in this chapter should be of assistance in understanding why, although the Company enjoyed considerable respect and authority in Java, Sultan Mangkubumi never regarded himself as being in a colonial situation. This was not a question of the Jogjakarta court failing to comprehend its position as a 'colonial' dependency. In the later eighteenth century, in usual practice not even the Dutch treated their relationship with the Jogjakarta court as colonial, nor was it so in any sense in which a colonial relationship would have been understood in the nineteenth and twentieth centuries. The relationship was complicated but clear: it took the form of alliance rather than dependency, and this was depicted in *Sĕrat Sakonḍar* in a fashion appropriate to the power relationships of the later eighteenth century. The substantive history of the period 1749–92, described in preceding chapters, should be useful in explaining why this view was particularly suitable in a period when the Dutch Company declined more and more while the Jogjakarta *kraton* grew ever more powerful. The Governor-General in Batavia was a most senior and respected ally, with an important position in *kraton* mythology, but he had no rights of sovereignty in Mataram.

XII

THE CONSEQUENCES OF THE PERMANENT DIVISION OF JAVA

THE permanent division of Java was a process, not an event. Temporary divisions had been a common circumstance over centuries of Javanese history (Chapter I) and when Mangkubumi was declared Susuhunan in 1749, thereby introducing a renewed division, there was nothing to suggest a new departure had been taken (Chapter II). But events took a somewhat unusual turn between 1755 and 1757 when the warfare between Mangkubumi and Pakubuwana III and between both of them and Mangkunĕgara came to an end in formal agreements of partition (Chapter III). Thereafter these Javanese principals attempted without success to reunify the kingdom by marriage diplomacy. The failure of these attempts reduced the likelihood that any arrangement other than a continuation of the division of the kingdom would evolve as the long-range framework of Javanese political life (Chapter IV). As the years passed, other potential reunifiers from the ranks of rebellion were meanwhile eliminated and the birth of the future Pakubuwana IV ensured that there would be regular successions in both *kratons* (Chapter V). The divided state had thus taken on considerable inertia, and in the period 1768 to 1775 the Javanese notables, encouraged by traditional ideas concerning the patterns of history, began to take administrative steps which made possible the continuation of the division on a permanent basis (Chapter VI). The new court of Jogjakarta, and perhaps Surakarta as well, evolved an official courtly view of history which made the existence of the two *kratons* seem not to be in conflict with the traditions of the past (Chapter VII).

Thereafter the permanent division of Central Java was accepted as the appropriate means to govern the island. Although problems persisted, they were not allowed to overturn the system of division itself (Chapter VIII). Only when one of the next generation succeeded to the throne of Surakarta in 1788 was the system

CONSEQUENCES OF PERMANENT DIVISION

threatened, but it was by then sufficiently stable that not even the new Susuhunan could win enough support to overthrow it (Chapter IX). This threat having been resolved, the Javanese in 1790 completed the formal regulation of the permanent division by explicitly admitting Mangkunĕgara to its structure and by accepting that the Dutch must be final arbiters to problems which could otherwise be solved only by warfare. Two years later, Sultan Mangkubumi, the main cause of the division and one of its primary architects, passed on the *kraton* of Jogjakarta to a younger generation with different concerns and other problems (Chapter X).

The significance of this process must be seen in a broad perspective dominated by the underlying factor which had so greatly influenced the shape of Javanese history for centuries: the inability of the Javanese élite to unite behind a single monarch or, once united, long to remain so. The immediate crisis from which the division evolved began with the rebellion of 1675, over the questions of how and by whom the kingdom was to be ruled. It followed upon Sultan Agung's relatively recent and fragile reunification of Java after more than a century of disunity and warfare, and was precipitated by Amangkurat I's more recent misuse of his authority. The Dutch intervention, which began in 1677 at the invitation of the beleaguered Mataram kings, had the effect of preventing the traditional denouement of such a crisis. Neither Trunadjaja nor any of his successor rebels could carry their followers swiftly to the conquest of the kingdom. For eighty years the crisis persisted, nearly exhausting both the Dutch and the Javanese. In the 1750s both finally abandoned warfare and turned to diplomacy. For the Dutch the treaties of 1755 and 1757 were initially a means to extricate themselves from a crisis which had proved beyond their control. Only afterwards did they discover that these treaties also made easier their continued presence in Java, for the partition of the kingdom rendered unlikely a uniting of Javanese armies against themselves. For the Javanese, the problem remained what it had been for decades: how to reunify the kingdom. But the abandonment of warfare for formal diplomacy as a means to resolve this problem was an unprecedented step for them.

It was ironic that the Javanese should have decided warfare could not resolve their central problem just at that point in history when it might have done so. In the latter half of the eighteenth century, prolonged and major warfare might very possibly have disposed the declining Dutch Company to withdraw to distant Batavia, leaving the Javanese free of the effects of its intervention. The result of such a move would probably have been to carry Mangkubumi to sole possession of the Susuhunan's throne. Whether he would not in turn have been toppled by a rebellion led by Mangkunĕgara is a question which leads one too far into the realm of speculation. The Javanese princes and their followers were, however, exhausted by the decades of civil war and they accepted the division of the kingdom as a *modus vivendi*. As further decades passed, it became clear that Java was never likely to be reunited. Other means to achieve this proved abortive and no one dared re-initiate another full-scale war.

Through an adaptation of traditional concepts the Javanese court élite were finally able to accept and to legitimize the permanent division of Central Java. This new system was a successful means of dealing with the centrifugal realities of Javanese politics. If Java continuously collapsed into its component political units, there was nothing inappropriate in a state system which allowed a greater formal expression of the dispersal of power and of the fragmentation of loyalty. But the Javanese were tied by the limitations of tradition, which was predicated upon the assumption that there could be only a single sovereign in Java, whose unrivalled legitimative glory was essential to hold the kingdom together. These traditional views were never changed. No new theory of history or of kingship evolved which said that there should ideally be two equal Javanese *kratons*. Rather, each of the two *kratons* seems to have continued to believe that there should be a single superior court, but each believed itself to be it. In matters of courtly life, each ruler ignored the other as much as possible. A complex legal system administered by the *patihs* was constructed to deal with the necessity of considerable co-operation between the *kratons* if the system were to function. But each ruler could only behave like a traditional monarch so long as he affected not to notice the existence of his equal in protocol in another court. Each monarch might refer to the other ruler and give commands which affected his subjects' relationship with him, but neither would go beyond the barest minimum of direct communication with the embarrassingly equal king of the other *kraton*. The situation was not unlike that of modern divided nations in which two governments are aware of each other's existence and must deal with that fact, but cannot allow themselves to accord each other an equality in law.

This implied a disparity between the administrative fact of an accepted and regulated bipartition of the kingdom and the legitimative theory of a single monarch. The theory never evolved into political concepts capable of explaining the new political circumstance, into a system in which two equal sovereigns could accept each other's equality in matters of courtly protocol and regal glory. Co-operation at the highest levels became exceedingly difficult in this situation. It will be recalled that in the period of this study no Javanese monarch met his royal counterpart in person after the acutely embarrassing encounter at Djatisari in 1755. This difficulty virtually excluded the possibility that the Sultan and the Susuhunan could ever, for instance, stand together as joint commanders against a common foe. They were more likely always to regard each other as the major enemy and to ally themselves with any outsiders against each other.

It may be that this inconsistency between administrative fact and legitimative theory resulted in an administrative system which required ever more precise and extensive formal regulation, since it lacked a theoretical life of its own. Javanese administration had probably functioned in previous centuries without requiring voluminous treaties and legal texts regulating the *minutiae* of jurisdictional relationships among Javanese rulers and local notables. The principles of jurisprudence were always studied and there is a considerable corpus of juridical literature in Old and Modern Javanese. But the matter of jurisdiction had probably never required such careful definition. Where the political divisions of the island reflected the real power on the ground of various notables and where state theory recognized the legitimative centrality but administrative dispersal of authority, the jurisdiction of various powers was probably instinctively understood. When disagreements arose, they were more likely to have been resolved by resorting to arms or the threat of arms than by referring to treaties. But with Central Java permanently and peacefully divided between two *kratons*, each of which preferred to regard itself as the senior court but neither of which wished to risk everything in a new war to defend its prestige, the question of jurisdiction became very difficult. What was to be done with a thief captured in Jogjakarta who was a subject of Surakarta; or who must decide matters of family rights where each of a married couple came from opposite parts of the kingdom? Still more difficult, what was the procedure to be followed if Mangkunĕgara had a complaint against the Sultan or his officials? And what should he do when the agreed procedure produced no satisfaction but resource to arms was excluded?[1] Each case, and each step in its settlement, must be defined and agreed, for no logic flowing from an over-all view of the nature of the state made it possible to deduce the manner for settling such cases as they arose. In land as in law, no logical conclusions from theory could define the complex cadastral structure of the kingdom, which must therefore be agreed by administrative act. Thus arose the complicated and much-argued land settlements of the Book of Klĕpu (*Sĕrat Buk Kalĕpu*) and the New Book (*Sĕrat Ĕbuk Anjar*). One of the most important elements in maintaining the permanent division of Java was the determination by both sides that these land and legal settlements must function successfully. If they did not do so, each minor incident might become a test of royal prestige, which in Javanese politics meant a test of royal authority.

This discrepancy between legitimative theory and administrative reality perhaps meant, therefore, a growing formalism in Javanese state life. This argument is to a large extent subjective, for the almost complete lack of Modern Javanese sources before the latter half of the eighteenth century makes it impossible to reconstruct confidently the nature of earlier political life in Modern Java. But it seems likely that the turbulent rough-and-ready warrior kings of Dĕmak, Padjang, and early Mataram probably rose and fell in accord with natural laws of Javanese politics. If they made themselves sufficiently attractive to enough of the élite and managed to destroy those who opposed them, they became kings. If they offended too many or were outdone by others, they ceased to be so. Within this system one could be either a strong or a weak king, but the system itself defined the role of kingship with sufficient clarity and consistency so that Java-

---

[1] These are not hypothetical problems. Each is among the subjects arranged in the eighteenth-century law codes. See Soeripto, *Vorstenlandsche Wetboeken*, pp. 86, 98, 99; and the summary of Articles Fifteen and Sixteen of the 1790 treaty on pp. 343–4 above.

nese kingdoms had probably continued to function in roughly the same way for centuries. This system was outlined in Chapter I. In the late eighteenth century, however, the theory which defined the ideal king was inadequate to explain why there were now two kingdoms and two kings, with an almost independent subsidiary princedom.

Walls which stand on their own need no exterior buttresses. But now the structure of Javanese political thinking must be shored-up with complex supporting agreements which masked the changing role of kingship itself. In Javanese thinking there could not be two 'shadows of God upon the earth' in Java; there could not be two competing claimants who were both protégés of the Goddess of the Southern Ocean. Yet there were. The consequence of this was, it seems, a necessary dependence upon rigid administrative agreements which camouflaged the underlying inappropriateness of the unchanged but no longer adequate perception of the nature and scope of royal authority. This meant that the vitality of Javanese politics came to be enclosed in a rigid framework which made the divided kingdom function but could not explain in theoretical terms why it did so. And perhaps now the Javanese courts also placed even greater emphasis than before upon the external forms of royal glory in defensive reaction to the erosion of the cult of glory as the central functioning prop of royal legitimation. When content begins to lose relevance, form is sometimes emphasized in defence.

Thus, it may be in the permanent division of the kingdom that the roots of the over-elaboration of courtly protocol, the 'Byzantine' artificiality of élite life which so many have observed, are to be sought. It was not, then, the result of 'nearly sixteen centuries of urban living', as was suggested by one observer.² It resulted,

² Geertz, *Religion of Java*, p. 231. There is no explanation given, and none suggests itself, for the conclusion that Javanese urban life is a phenomenon of sixteen centuries' duration.

The idea of Javanese culture as 'Byzantine' in its courtly artificiality is found in several sources. Its clearest exposition in English is in D. H. Burger, *Structural Changes in Javanese Society: the Supra-Village Sphere* (trans. Leslie H. Palmier; Ithaca, 1956), pp. 11 ff. Burger's views were based to a large extent upon those of Rouffaer. It seems to me, however, that there is a tendency to project backwards into the Kartasura period (1680–1742) and even before a characteristic which was observable in the nineteenth and twentieth centuries but which was perhaps of more recent origin (as a 'hypertrophic development', in Burger's terms) than Kartasura. This cannot, however, be settled until some historical investigation of the Kartasura period has taken place.

rather, from the fact that the traditional court élite decided after a century of crisis that for the first time in Javanese history their central problem, their own disunity, simply could not be resolved, no matter how temporarily. They derived new administrative structures to deal with this crisis, but failed to achieve new legitimative and theoretical formulae which were relevant to it. It was perhaps then that Javanese courts began to become what many nineteenth- and twentieth-century observers have incorrectly assumed they had always been: rather quaint, somewhat desiccated museum pieces. But while *kraton* life grew more artificial it preserved its glory. Indeed, this glory was probably enhanced by the encouragement later Dutch colonial regimes gave to these apparently harmless ritual establishments. When in 1945 Indonesian life was thrown into the maelstrom of revolution, it was discovered that Mangkubumi's line could still turn the traditional power of the royal cult of glory to the resolution of political issues.

The permanent division of Central Java resulted from the primary crisis of élite disunity. But it was necessitated also by the secondary factor of the Dutch presence which made disunity permanent. This neither the Javanese nor the Dutch appreciated at the time, although by the end of the eighteenth century the Company believed that its position in Java depended upon the élite's continued disunity. The Javanese continued to concentrate on the primary problem, and evolved the permanent division as the only means of dealing with it. But in doing so they ensured that the secondary problem could never be resolved, for the complicated administrative structure had one absolutely essential need which only the Dutch could satisfy. There must be an outside authority to arbitrate those clashes of royal prestige which from time to time must occur. Royal politics was prestige politics and if a crisis of royal prestige developed, warfare or the threat of war were the traditional system's only means of resolution. But now the élite were determined that there must be no more of the inconclusive fratricide they had endured for decades. Hence the Dutch must be available to act as an outside power whose authority to arbitrate could be accepted by all. The Javanese rulers' 'grandfather' at Batavia and his officials thus not only caused the permanent division to be evolved, but were invoked by the Javanese to guarantee its continued functioning. In the treaty of 1790 this mediatory role was expressly defined. This was not because the

Dutch possessed sufficient military power to dominate the Javanese princes, who could muster armies of tens of thousands and who had fought the Dutch to a stalemate in the 1750s. Indeed, Central Javanese history in the eighteenth century is a comment upon how little military or economic 'power' is required for an external factor thoroughly to disrupt the functioning of an indigenous political system. The increasing dependence upon rigid formalized administrative agreements was no doubt further encouraged by this fact that the ultimate arbiters of insoluble disputes were the Dutch, a nation who themselves emphasized formal legalistic thinking and who insisted that their relations with the Javanese must be clearly formulated in precise agreements.

By instituting the permanent division of Central Java, the élite could divert their own attention from the underlying political crisis. The problem of disunity seemed now to have gone away, but it was never resolved. Other goals than unity were given a higher priority, of which the highest was given to the preservation of peace. Probably for the first time since the fall of Madjapahit, perhaps for the first time in Javanese history, Central Java saw no major warfare for nearly seventy years (1757–1825). The fruits of peace could be seen by all, and the determination that the peace must not be broken seems to have been shared by the vast majority of the élite.

The permanent division, coupled with the determination that Java must remain at peace, had, it seems, at least one major consequence for the deterioration of the traditional role of royal authority. Rebellion had always been the ultimate sanction against royal despotism and it had been resorted to with devasting regularity. But this sanction was now virtually removed. The aspirant rebel now had to consider an entirely new set of circumstances. In previous ages, he had pitted himself against the central monarch and replaced him if he won, or fled to the hills if he lost and was lucky enough not to lose his head. Now he might throw one of the halves of Central Java into chaos, but the consequence might very possibly be that the other court would be unable to resist the temptation to attack a rival in trouble. The results were unforseeable, but one outcome might be the conquest by the other monarch of the king against whom the rebel had launched his own attack. The rebel who assaulted the Sultan might assume that the most likely victor would be the Susuhunan. And the Company would presumably be drawn in as well, with the only predictable result being renewed devastation. If the co-operation between the two *kratons* was such as to make them allies against a particular rebel, he had little chance of conquering both *kratons* and the Dutch. There were still rebels, but in these circumstances it was exceedingly difficult to convince others to follow them. The difficulty of the rebel's role was increased by the dominant opinion that peace must be maintained at all costs. Not until Dipanĕgara led the Java War (1825–30) was a major rebel with a large following to appear in Java, and he was to be the last.

Thus the acceptance of a permanent peaceful division of Mataram had the effect of raising considerably the threshold of rebellion. This also raised the degree of royal absolutism which the élite would tolerate. The administrative agreements made certain that a courtier could not even shift his allegiance to another ruler, for the three principals accepted that it was in their mutual interest for all such refugees to be returned to their court of origin. The dissatisfied member of the élite could neither seek another protector nor, with any expectation of success, could he rebel. This must have made possible much greater royal absolutism, for some of the principal sanctions against it were now removed. Despots there had often been, of whom the best-known is probably Amangkurat I (1646–77). But it should be remembered that Amangkurat I lost his *kraton* to an indigenous rebellion. No Javanese ruler after 1749 ever suffered a similar fate.

The end of rebellion and the desire and necessity to maintain the peace meant that the military role of the Javanese state grew less important. In the nineteenth century it was to lose this military role almost entirely. This was a change of the most fundamental proportions for, in this writer's opinion, the Javanese kingdoms had in past centuries been predominantly military organizations. For many state institutions war had been the *raison d'être*.[3] The *kratons* had important ceremonial roles and

[3] This may perhaps be seen in the use of the ubiquitous term *tjatjah*. In this study it has been translated as 'household'. It has several extended meanings, depending upon context, and in its origins means a counting unit (see Rouffaer, 'Vorstenlanden', pp. 303–4). In Javanese administration it meant a household, or the amount of land necessary to support a household. But I suspect that one of its primary functions as an administrative unit was military: from each household was levied in the first instance one armed man. The number of *tjatjahs* controlled by a king, prince, or local notable was therefore a statement of the size of his immediately available army. Thus a ruler who had

CONSEQUENCES OF PERMANENT DIVISION

were presumably important economic foci as well, although the latter subject is much in need of detailed research. But the ceremonial and legitimative functions were primarily intended to attract the loyalty of powerful men who had settled populations under their direct control. They were designed to ensure that legitimation flowed down a long chain of authority so that armies would flow back in the opposite direction when needed. War and the threat of war were the normal fare of Javanese politics; political power was military power. With the removal of the military function, the substance of state life began to wither and the Javanese were more and more left with a vestigial form.

Thus the latter half of the eighteenth century was a time when Javanese leadership was adjusting to changing circumstances. This adaptation was only partial and clearly very serious problems remained unresolved. But political systems and cultures do not change overnight. Given more men of the leadership qualities of Mangkubumi and Mangkunĕgara, and more time, a changed political system with a new view of the nature of authority might have developed which would have given the Javanese a successful structure for the future. But the Javanese had few men of great leadership qualities. Indeed, the end of rebellion substantially eliminated any means for such men to reach the top of Javanese

---

just under 100,000 *tjatjahs*, as HB I had in 1774 (see dJ xi, p. lvi n.), could levy an initial armed force of nearly 100,000 armed men (assuming, of course, that those under him with immediate control over these *tjatjahs* supported him). The number of *tjatjahs* therefore expressed with some precision the military and hence political power of a given dignitary.

One piece of evidence to support this view is found in the VOC archives. The Dutch sometimes listed the number of troops under arms in various *kraton* companies, but only once to my knowledge did they ascertain and report a specific figure for the potential levy available to a prince. That was in May 1790, when they assessed MN's military strength. He had at that time 1,380 men actually under arms, but it was reported that he could assemble a force of 4,000 men within a short time and given two to three days could call up more than 10,000. The important figure here is the initial levy of 4,000, for it will be remembered that MN's appanage was 4,000 *tjatjahs*. This suggests that the figure of *tjatjahs* in someone's appanage gives the figure for the immediately available force of armed men, assuming that the appanage-holder could depend upon the loyalty of his subordinates. The lists of MN's troops are in Sĕmarang to Batavia, 19 May 1790, in KA 3802 (OB 1791); and List of MN 'Gewapend volk', 21 May 1790, in AN Solo 36, 'Diverze verklarings'.

Moertono, *State and Statecraft*, pp. 137–41, prefers to emphasize *tjatjah* as a unit of taxation, which is not inconsistent with its simultaneous use as a calculation of military strength. See also Widjojo Nitisastro, *Population Trends in Indonesia* (Ithaca, 1970), pp. 12–13.

political life except by genetic good fortune. And of time there was little. While the Javanese and the Dutch Company manœuvred to defend the division against the threats of Pakubuwana IV in 1789, half a world away the Bastille fell. If there is tragedy in the history of Java in modern times it is to be sought in this unfortunate coincidence. No Javanese ruler, no matter how wise, could have foreseen the consequences for Java of the French Revolution. Sixteen years after Mangkubumi died, the Napoleonic Governor-General H. W. Daendels arrived in Java and a new chapter in the history of Javanese relations with the West began. Just when Javanese society was in a time of uncertain transition it was exposed to the threat of a virulent and dangerously expanding Europe, with which it was not then prepared to cope.

Javanese history in the later eighteenth century is not a story of decline; it is merely a story of change. Of benefits there were several, of which the greatest was peace. The cultivators tilled their crops and the harvests came in season after season. The main element in the traditional Javanese picture of a prosperous time was preserved: the 'little man' (*wong tjilik*) was at peace, his lands untouched by marching armies, his sons at home to till the fields. Yet, in a time of fundamental changes, not even peace was without disadvantage. More and more members of the élite needed supporting, appanages were divided into ever smaller parcels to maintain them, and as their economic opportunities became more restricted their demands upon the cultivators under them probably grew.

This time of political change was also an age of cultural initiative. Again, this is difficult to document because of the absence of Javanese records from before the latter half of the century. Whatever traditions were inherited by the *kratons*, and they were certainly rich, the Javanese went on in the late eighteenth century to produce the greatest works of Modern Javanese literature now known. Several of them have been used in this study and many more mentioned in passing. The chronicles *Babad Mangkubumi*, *Babad Kraton*, and the exceptionally beautiful *Babad Gijanti* were composed in this time, as was also the extraordinary *Sĕrat Surja Radja*. Historians may, indeed, ask themselves whether there is not some peculiarity about times of political change and uncertainty which makes them congenial to cultural progress.

CONSEQUENCES OF PERMANENT DIVISION

The Central Javanese were about to face a new age, with the problems of the past age not yet laid entirely to rest. In the nineteenth century they would be subjected to the full force of European colonialism, from which they would not free themselves until the new city of Jogjakarta was nearly two centuries old. The history of Jogjakarta over those two centuries was dominated by several themes, not a few of which were the legacy of its founder. Jogjakarta was always the city less willing than Surakarta to tolerate European domination and more ready to adapt to the opportunities of changing times. Yet in its cultural life it consciously conserved traditional forms, considering its arts more 'authentic' than those of Surakarta, while the latter regarded them as more 'antiquated'. In 1945, Jogjakarta would declare for the Indonesian Revolution and become the capital of the revolutionary state. On 27 December 1949—two hundred years and fifteen days after Mangkubumi declared himself ruler of Mataram—the Dutch would formally acknowledge Indonesian independence and Jogjakarta would be recognized as an important part of an independent Indonesian state. Thus would begin a new chapter in the history of Mangkubumi's kingdom.

APPENDIX I

MAJOR OFFICIALS OF THE DUTCH EAST INDIA COMPANY IN THE LATER EIGHTEENTH CENTURY[1]

Governors-General
1743–1796

Gustaaf Willem Baron van Imhoff	1743–1750
Jacob Mossel	1750–1761
Petrus Albertus van der Parra	1761–1775
Jeremias van Riemsdijk	1775–1777
Reinier de Klerk	1777–1780
Willem Arnold Alting	1780–1796

Governors of Java's Northeast Coast, Sĕmarang
1748–1796

Johan Andries Baron von Hohendorff	Feb. 1748–April 1754
Nicolaas Hartingh	April 1754–Oct. 1761
Willem Hendrik van Ossenberch	Oct. 1761–May 1765
Johannes Vos	May 1765–July 1771
Johannes Robbert van der Burgh	July 1771–Sept. 1780
Johannes Siberg	Sept. 1780–Sept. 1787
Jan Greeve	Sept. 1787–Sept. 1791
Pieter Gerard van Overstraten	Sept. 1791–Oct. 1796

First Residents at Surakarta
1741–1796

Johan Andries Baron von Hohendorff	1741–Feb. 1748
Balthasar Toutlemonde	Feb. 1748–1752

[1] There are some uncertain or incomplete dates and names in these lists which it has not been possible to remove entirely. The lists, unless otherwise indicated, are based upon the volumes in the Algemeen Rijksarchief; the printed documents in dJ; Louw, *Successie-Oorlog*; and Rouffaer, 'Vorstenlanden', pp. 264–5 (which is not completely accurate).

MAJOR OFFICIALS

J. H. Abrahams	1752–Oct. 1757[2]
Duurveldt	? Oct. 1757–1761
Jan Christoffel Beuman	1761–Sept. 1767
Frederik Christoffel van Straalendorff	Sept. 1767–1784
Willem Adriaan Palm	1784–11 May 1788
Andries Hartsinck	June 1788–31 Aug. 1790 (relieved of many of his responsibilities after Nov. 1789)
J. Fr. Baron van Reede tot de Parkeler	Sept. 1790–Sept. 1796

First Residents at Jogjakarta
1754–1799

C. Donkel	Sept. 1754 (at Pědagangan)–early 1761
Jacob Cornelis van der Sluijs	Early 1761 (May or before)–1764 (after March)
Jan Lapro	1764–Oct. 1773[3]
Jan Mathijs van Rhijn	Oct. 1773[4]–Sept. 1786[5]
Wouter Hendrik van Ijsseldijk	Sept. 1786[6]–early 1799

[2] According to BM Add. MS. 12323 (B), f. 41ʳ.
[3] According to Rouffaer, 'Vorstenlanden', p. 264. I have been unable to verify this, but I have no reason to doubt its accuracy.
[4] See n. 3.
[5] According to Rouffaer, 'Vorstenlanden', p. 264. I can only verify that van Rhijn requested retirement and repatriation in June 1786, and that van Ijsseldijk's surety bond of 2,000 rijksdaalders as First Resident was paid in November 1786.
[6] See n. 5.

APPENDIX II

PATIHS OF SURAKARTA AND JOGJAKARTA IN THE EIGHTEENTH CENTURY

Surakarta, 1742–1796

Pringgalaja	21 Dec. 1742[1]–early Oct. 1755
Mangkupradja	Early Oct. 1755–April 1770 (in disfavour after late 1769)
Sasradiningrat	April 1770–in or before Oct. 1782 (in disfavour after mid-1781)
Sindurĕdja	In or before Oct. 1782–July 1784
Djajaningrat	July 1784–1796

Jogjakarta, 1746–1799

Mas Said (Mangkunĕgara I)	1746–1752[2]
Natakusuma	1752[3]–13 Feb. 1755
Danurĕdja (I)	13 Feb. 1755–19 Aug. 1799

[1] According to Rouffaer, 'Vorstenlanden', p. 277.
[2] The dates for Mas Said and Natakusuma, the two wartime *patihs*, are not entirely certain. Neither of them actually served in the city of Jogjakarta, which had not yet been founded.
[3] See n. 2.

APPENDIX III

PRINCIPAL MEMBERS OF THE HOUSE OF MATARAM IN THE LATER EIGHTEENTH CENTURY[1]

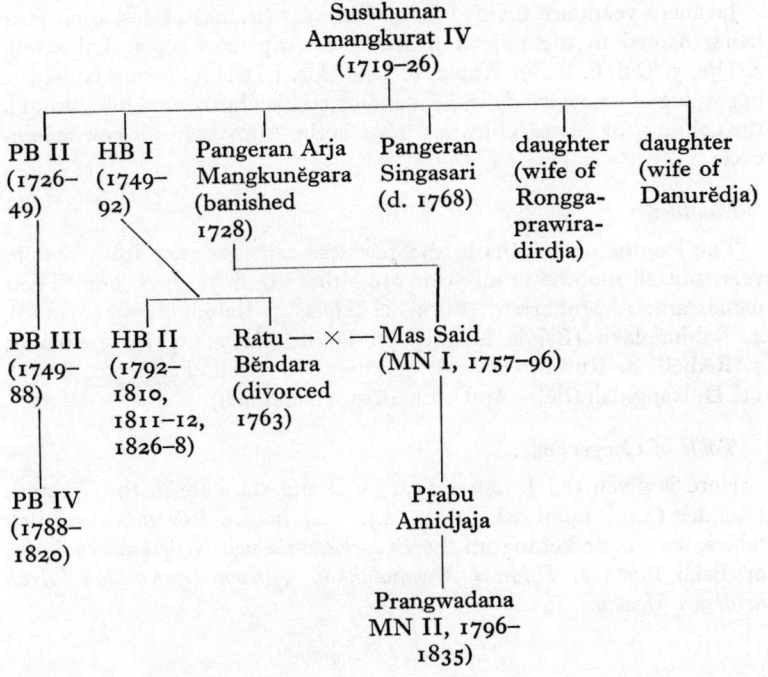

[1] See abbreviations listed on pp. xiii–xiv. Unbroken lines indicate direct descent. '– × –' indicates marriage.
The children of Amangkurat IV listed here were not from the same mother.

APPENDIX IV

JAVANESE AND WESTERN CHRONOLOGY
A.D. 1749–1792

Windu-cycles:

Javanese years are divided into eight-year (*windu*) cycles, each year being named in the following order: 1. Alip, 2. Ehe, 3. Djimawal, 4. Dje, 5. Dal, 6. Be, 7. Wawu, 8. Djimakir. In the following table, the beginning of a new *windu*-cycle is indicated by a horizontal line through the columns of years. Thus, A.J. 1691 is the Alip-year of a new *windu*-cycle.

Months:

The lengths of months in the Javanese calendar vary from year to year, but all months in all years are either 29 or 30 days long. Their names are: 1. Muharram (Sura), 2. Sapar, 3. Rabingulawal (Mulud), 4. Rabingulakir (Bakda Mulud), 5. Djumadilawal, 6. Djumadilakir, 7. Rědjěb, 8. Ruwah (Saban), 9. Puasa (Ramělan, Pasa), 10. Sawal, 11. Dulkangidah (Sěla, Apit), 12. Běsar (Dulkidjah).

Table of Conversions:

Here is given the Javanese year (A.J.) and the date in the Western calendar (A.D.) upon which the A.J. year began. For more detailed tables, see 'Tijdrekening' in the *Encyclopaedia van Nederlandsch Indië*, or Balai Pustaka, *Djidwal Memindahkan Tahoen Djawa dan 'Arab ketahoen Maséhi*.

'Thursday Calendar'[1]

A.J.	A.D.
1675	11 Dec. 1749
1676	30 Nov. 1750
1677	20 Nov. 1751
1678	8 Nov. 1752
1679	28 Oct. 1753

[1] The 'Thursday Calendar' was used in Surakarta from 11 Dec. 1749. Dates in Jogjakarta were one day behind until the calendar was adjusted there sometime between December 1749 and November 1755. See pp. 54–5 n. 42, and p. 80 n. 31.

CHRONOLOGY, A.D. 1749-1792

A.J.	A.D.
1680	18 Oct. 1754
1681	7 Oct. 1755
1682	25 Sept. 1756
1683	15 Sept. 1757
1684	4 Sept. 1758
1685	25 Aug. 1759
1686	13 Aug. 1760
1687	2 Aug. 1761
1688	23 July 1762
1689	12 July 1763
1690	30 June 1764
1691	20 June 1765
1692	9 June 1766
1693	30 May 1767
1694	18 May 1768
1695	7 May 1769
1696	27 April 1770
1697	16 April 1771
1698	4 April 1772
1699	25 March 1773
1700	14 March 1774
1701	4 March 1775
1702	21 Feb. 1776
1703	9 Feb. 1777
1704	30 Jan. 1778
1705	19 Jan. 1779
1706	8 Jan. 1780
1707	28 Dec. 1780
1708	17 Dec. 1781
1709	7 Dec. 1782
1710	26 Nov. 1783
1711	14 Nov. 1784
1712	4 Nov. 1785
1713	24 Oct. 1786
1714	13 Oct. 1787
1715	2 Oct. 1788
1716	21 Sept. 1789
1717	11 Sept. 1790
1718	31 Aug. 1791

GLOSSARY OF JAVANESE WORDS

Note: These definitions give only those senses in which the words have been used in the present study.

adat	custom
alun-alun	great square before the *kraton*
awisaning Ratu	attire forbidden to all but the king, also known as *larangan-Dalĕm*
babad	Javanese text written in chronicle form; as a verb, 'to clear' (the forest)
baṭik	intricately-designed dyed fabric
bupati	high administrative official; the title was used both for officials within the *kraton* and for officials in the countryside
ḍalang	puppeteer in the *wajang* theatre
dalĕm	princely residence
desa	village
djimat	amulet
gamĕlan	Javanese orchestra, consisting almost entirely of percussion instruments
garĕbĕg	thrice-annual Islamic festivals, consisting of *Garĕbĕg Mulud* in celebration of the birth of the Prophet Muḥammad, *Garĕbĕg Puasa* to celebrate the end of the fasting-month, and *Garĕbĕg Bĕsar* in commemoration of Abraham's willingness to sacrifice his son and of the pilgrimage to Mecca
hadji	pilgrim who has been to Mecca
kafir	infidel, non-Muslim
krama	'High Javanese', one of the two basic forms of Modern Javanese (see *ngoko*); used to address superiors
kraman	rebel
kraton	court, residence of a ruler
kris	Javanese dagger, often considered to possess supernatural powers
larangan-Dalĕm	see *awisaning Ratu*
mantri	official of lower rank
mas	title of nobility
montjanĕgara	outer regions of the kingdom
najaka	adviser to the king

GLOSSARY

nĕgara agung	core regions of the kingdom, surrounding the court
ngelmu gaib	secret mystical truth
ngoko	'Low Javanese', one of the two basic forms of Modern Javanese (see *krama*); used to address close equals or inferiors
panakawan	literally 'retainer'; the clown-servant-adviser attached to a *wajang* character
paṇḍita	wise man, teacher
panĕmbahan	high princely title
pangeran	prince
pasisir	coast, in particular the north coast of Java
patih	chief administrator of the Javanese kingdom; his full title was *patih djaba*, to distinguish him from the *patih djĕro* who had primary administrative responsibility over affairs within the *kraton*
pĕngulu	chief religious functionary
pusaka	holy regalia, heirloom
raden	title of middle-rank nobility
raden mas	title of higher nobility
Ratu Kidul	Goddess of the Southern Ocean, also referred to as 'Njai Rara Kidul'
santri	student of religion, follower of a religious way of life
sĕmbah	gesture of respect performed by placing the palms of the hands together before the nose
senapati	commander-in-chief
sĕngkala	chronogram
sĕntana	member of a ruler's family of lesser rank
tapa	to engage in asceticism; an ascetic, mystic, man of religion
tjatjah	household
tumĕnggung	high administrative rank
wajang	Javanese puppet theatre, of several types. Those mentioned in this study are: *wajang-kulit*, shadow theatre with flat leather puppets; *wajang-pantjasila*, an adaptation of the former used for nationalist purposes during the Indonesian Revolution; and *wajang-topeng*, a masked dance
wali	early apostle or saint of Islam in Java; the *walis* are usually said to have been nine in number
wĕdana	high administrative official; the title, like *bupati*, was used both for officials within the *kraton* and for officials in the countryside

BIBLIOGRAPHY

I. PRIMARY SOURCES

A. MANUSCRIPTS

1. *Javanese*

[*Babad Kraton.*] BM Add. MS. 12320. Dated A.J. 1703 (A.D. 1777). 717 ff. 170 cantos. Written in Jogjakarta.

Babad Mangkubumi. LOr 2191. Dated A.H. 1187 (A.D. 1773). 549 pp. 84 cantos. Written in Jogjakarta.

Babad Pakĕpung. Sana Budaja Museum (Jogjakarta) MS. 123. Undated. 61 pp. 10 cantos.

Babad Sangkalaning Momana. A copy of a MS. in Museum Pusat, Djakarta, provided by Dr. H. J. de Graaf. Completed in A.D. 1912. 70 pp. (pp. 208–78). Written in Jogjakarta.

Babad Tanah Djawi. LOr 1786. Dated A.J. 1764 (A.D. 1836). 18 volumes. Written in Surakarta.

Babad Tanah Djawi. LOr 6483. Dated A.J. 1780 (A.D. 1851). 627 pp. 154 cantos. Written in Jogjakarta.

Babad Tanah Djawi. NBS 158. Dated A.J. 1749 (A.D. 1821). 2 volumes. 176 cantos. Written in Jogjakarta. Parallel text to LOr 6483.

Baron Sakenḍer. LOr 6185. Dated A.J. 1867 (A.D. 1936). 64 ff. 15 cantos.

'A Journal kept by the late Sultan of Java [Hamĕngkubuwana II].' BM Add. MS. 12303. 180 ff. Written in Jogjakarta.

Putra-dalĕm Sinuwun Sapisan. Jogjakarta *kraton* MS. A.24. Undated.

[*Sĕngkala* list.] BM Add. MS. 12323 (B), ff. 31^v–59^v. Last date A.J. 1743 (A.D. 1815). From Surakarta.

[*Sĕngkala* list.] BM Add. MS. 12325 (C), ff. 44^v–9^v. Last date A.J. 1741 (A.D. 1813). From Jogjakarta.

Sĕrat Babad Pakunĕgaran. BM Add. MS. 12283. Original dated A.J. 1705 (A.D. 1779); this copy dated A.J. 1740 (A.D. 1813). 365 ff. 90 cantos. Written in Surakarta.

Sĕrat Djumĕnĕngan Sampejan-Dalĕm Ingkang Sinuhun Kangdjĕng Sultan Hamĕngkubuwana I. Jogjakarta *kraton* MS. A.22. Last date A.J. 1840 (A.D. 1910).

Sĕrat Konḍa, also called *Sĕrat Gĕnḍing Bĕksan,* consisting of selections from *Sĕrat Surja Radja.* Undated. BM Add. MS. 12325 (B), ff. 10^r–43^r. Written in Jogjakarta.

Sĕrat Sakonḍar. BM Add. MS. 12289. Undated. 149 ff. 15 cantos.

Sĕrat Suluk Surja Djaja Amisesa. Jogjakarta *kraton* MS. F.1. Undated. Pages unnumbered (approx. 800–1000).

Sĕrat Surja Radja. Jogjakarta *kraton* MS. F.7. Dated A.J. 1841 (A.D. 1911). 1,029 pp. 124 cantos. A copy of this MS. made in 1969 is in the library of the School of Oriental and African Studies, London.

Surja Radja, Kangdjĕng Kjai. MS. preserved in *Prabajĕksa, kraton* Jogjakarta. Dated A.J. 1700 (A.D. 1774). 2 volumes.

2. *Dutch*

Volumes in the Algemeen Rijksarchief, The Hague:

Gemeen & Secret Afgaand Briefboek van Batavia: KA 912 (1755); KA 913 (1756); KA 914 (1757); KA 915 (1758).

Overgekomen Brieven en Papieren (Batavias Inkomend Briefboek). Relevant volumes from KA 2735 to KA 3859 (1755 to 1793).

Volumes in the Arsip Nasional Republik Indonesia, Djakarta:

Java's Noord-Oost Kust:

161, 'Dagregister 1791.'
162, 'Bijlagen 1790.'

Solo:

5, 'Soerakarta Afgaande Brieven, 1773-93.'
26, 'Soerakarta Brieven, 1754-91.'
36, 'Diverze Verklarings.'
38, 'Diverze Verklarings.'
43, 'Register der landen van den Soesoehoenang (met het tractaat van 2 November 1773).'
52.
53.

Djokjo:

32, 'Djokjokarta Brieven naar Samarang, 1756-61.'
33, 'Djokjokarta Brieven naar Samarang, 1761-64.'
34, 'Djokjokarta Brieven naar Samarang, 1770-1780.'
35, 'Djokjokarta Brieven naar Samarang, 1785-1799.'
42, 'Register der landen van den Sultan (met het tractaat van 2 November 1773).'
86, 'Aankomende Brieven, 1786-89.'
Unnumbered volume containing Jogjakarta contracts.

Documents from the Arsip Nasional Republik Indonesia used in the form of typed copies provided to the author by Dr. H. J. de Graaf:

I. van Suchtelen, Lijst der thans in wezen zijnde kinderen, broeders, en susters, mitsgaders de afkomst van den Soesoehoenang Pakoeboewana, de Hooftregenten en mindere bedienden, die zig aan 't Hoff zoo aan de stranden als binnen en bovenlanden bevinden; Kartasura, November 1743; in Solo 42.

Hugo Verijssel, Eerbiedig kort bericht in forma van rapport, opgedragen aan ... G. W. van Imhoff; Samarang, 14 December 1743; in Solo 42.

J. A. Baron von Hohendorff, Dagregister . . . gehouden op desselfs Rheijse na het Soeracartasche Hoff; Samarang, 31 December 1749 [volume number unknown].

B. PUBLISHED SOURCES

Balai Pustaka. *Babad Tanah Djawi*. 31 vols. Batavia, 1939–41.

Bataviaasch Genootschap van Kunsten en Wetenschappen. *Dagh-Register, Gehouden int Casteel Batavia vant Passerende daer ter Plaetse als over geheel Nederlandts India*. 31 vols. 's-Hage, 1887–1931.

Brandes, J. L. A. (ed.). 'Pararaton (Ken Arok) of het Boek der Koningen van Tumapĕl en van Majapahit', 2nd ed., ed. N. J. Krom, *VBG*, vol. 62 (1920).

Chijs, J. A. van der (ed.). *Nederlandsch–Indisch Plakaatboek, 1602–1811*. 17 vols. 's-Hage, 1885–1900.

Cohen Stuart, A. B. (ed. and trans.). *Geschiedenis van Baron Sakéndhèr, een Javaansch Verhaal*. Batavia, 1850.

Deventer, M. L. van (ed.). *Het Nederlandsch Gezag over Java en Onderhoorigheden sedert 1811*. Vol. i: *1811–1820*. 's-Gravenhage, 1891.

[Imhoff, G. W. van.] 'Reis van den Gouverneur-Generaal van Imhoff, over Java, in het Jaar 1746', *BKI*, vol. 1 (1853), pp. 291–440.

Iperen, Josua van. 'Begin van eene Javaansche Historie, genaamd, Sadjara Radja Djawa', *VBG*, vol. 1 (1779), pp. 134–72; vol. 2 (1780), pp. 262–88; vol. 3 (1781), pp. 117–33.

Jasadipura. *Babad Gijanti*. 21 vols. Batavia, 1937–9.

—— *Serat Rama*. Ed. J. Kats. 3 vols. Weltevreden, 1925.

Jonge, J. K. J. de and M. L. van Deventer (eds.). *De Opkomst van het Nederlandsch Gezag in Oost-Indië: Verzameling van onuitgegeven Stukken uit het Oud-koloniaal Archief*. 16 vols. 's-Gravenhage, 1862–1909.

[Munnik, H. de.] 'Kort Verhaal van de Javasche Oorlogen, welke met onderscheidene Prinsen gevoerd zijn, sedert den Jare 1741, tot den algemeenen Vrede, gesloten in den Jare 1757', *VBG*, vol. 12 (1830), pp. 75–254.

Olthof, W. L. (ed. and trans.). *Babad Tanah Djawi. In Proza. Javaansche Geschiedenis*. 2 vols. 's-Gravenhage, 1941.

Ossenberch, W. H. van. 'Memorie opgestelt door den Raad Extraordinair van Nederlands India en afgaande Gouverneur en Directeur van Java's Noord Oostcust Willem Hendrik van Ossenberch, om te strekken tot Narigt van zijnen Successeur, den Heer Johannes Vos, aankoomende Gouverneur en Directeur van Java's Noord Oostcust', ed. R. W. Tadama, *Berigten van het Historisch Genootschap te Utrecht*, vol. 5, pt. 2 (1857), pp. 178–203.

Poensen, C. 'Amăngku Buwånå II (Sĕpuh). Ngajogyåkartå's tweede Sultan. (Naar Aanleiding van een Javaansch Handschrift)', *BKI*, vol. 58 (1905), pp. 73–346.

―― 'Mangkubumi. Ngajogyakarta's eerste Sultan. (Naar Aanleiding van een Javaansch Handschrift)', *BKI*, vol. 52 (1901), pp. 223-361.

Roorda, T. (ed.). *Javaansche Wetten, namelijk de Nawålå-Pradåtå, de Anggĕr-Sadåså, de Anggĕr-Agĕng, de Anggĕr-Goenoeng en de Anggĕr-Aroebiroe.* Amsterdam, 1844.

Rothenbühler, Frederik Jacob. 'Dagregister of dagelijksche Aanteekeningen van het Voorgevallene ter Geleegentheid van de Verwisseling van de, door het Overlijden van den Sulthan Hamangkoe Boeana Seno Pattij Ingalaga Abdul Rachman Sahidin Panatto Gama Califatollah, vacant geraakte Troon van het Djocjocartasche Rijk, en de daartoe gedane Reis door den WelEd. Gestr. Heer Mr. Pieter Gerardus van Overstraten, Raad Extra-Ordinair van Nederlandsch Indië, mitsgaders Gouverneur en Directeur op en langs Java's Noord-oostkust, gehouden door den Onderkoopman en Secretaris van Politie te Semarang Frederik Jacob Rothenbühler, 20 Maart-13 April 1792', *TBG*, vol. 27 (1882), pp. 295-362.

Soeripto. *Ontwikkelingsgang der Vorstenlandsche Wetboeken.* Leiden, 1929.

C. JAVANESE MANUSCRIPTS MENTIONED ONLY BRIEFLY

Asṭa Brata. NBS 87-XXIV.

Babad Balambangan. LOr 2185.

Babad Dipanagaran Surja Ngalam. LOr 6488.

Babad Pakunĕgara. Raffles Jav. MS. 16, Royal Asiatic Society, London.

Babad Prajud. LOr 6755.

Babad Tanah Djawi. NBS 224.

Baron Sakenḍer. LOr 1800.

Buku Kĕḍung Kĕbo. Athenaeum Library, Deventer, DvT V 1.

Djaka Salewah. NBS 152.

Kidung Lalĕmbut. LOr 4000 (2).

Pralambange Tanah Djawa. LOr 6536.

Rama Badra Djawi. LOr 2105.

Sĕrat Iskandar. LOr 1805.

Sĕrat Kanḍaning Ringgit Purwa. LOr 6379.

Sĕrat Rama. NBS 4.

Sĕrat Rama. NBS 149.

Sĕrat Surja Radja. BG 164, Museum Pusat, Djakarta.

Sĕrat Surja Radja. LOr 8604.

Sewaka. NBS 57.

Sewaka. NBS 73 (III).

Unḍang-unḍang. NBS 75 (6).

BM Add. MS. 12341. Letters, land lists, etc.

BM Add. MS. 12342. Letters, land lists, etc.

BM Add. MS. 14397. Letters, land lists, etc.
LOr 2052. Bantĕn Sultanate census materials.
LOr 2055. Bantĕn Sultanate census materials.
LOr 7709. Bantĕn Sultanate census materials.
CB 146 (5–8) (Berg collection, Leiden University library). Palembang census materials.
LOr 7489. Notes on mysticism.
NBS 77. Life of Abdul Kadir Djaelani.
Raffles Jav. MS. 33 (C). Royal Asiatic Society. Legal text.
Royal Asiatic Society Java 45 (A). Legal text.

II. SECONDARY SOURCES

Ahmat, Sharom. 'The Political Structure of the State of Kedah 1879–1905', *JSEAS*, vol. 1, no. 2 (Sept. 1970), pp. 115–28.

d'Almeida, William Barrington. *Life in Java: With Sketches of the Javanese*. 2 vols. London, 1864.

Anderson, Benedict R. O'G. *Mythology and the Tolerance of the Javanese*. Ithaca, 1965.

Arberry, Arthur J. *The Koran Interpreted*. 2 vols. New York, 1955.

Balai Poestaka. *Djidwal memindahkan tahoen Djawa dan 'Arab ketahoen Maséhi*. Batavia, 1932.

Balé Poestaka. *Babad Gijanti. Pratélan Namaning Tijang lan Panggénan*. Batavia, 1939.

Basham, A. L. *The Wonder that was India: A Survey of the Culture of the Indian Sub-Continent before the Coming of the Muslims*. New York, 1959.

Bataviaasch Genootschap van Kunsten en Wetenschappen. *Rapporten van de Commissie in Nederlandsch-Indië voor Oudheidkundig Onderzoek op Java en Madoera, 1907*. 's-Gravenhage, 1909.

Berg, C. C. 'De Arjunawiwāha, Er-langga's Levensloop en Bruiloftslied?', *BKI*, vol. 97, no. 1 (1941), pp. 19–94.

—— 'Javaansche Geschiedschrijving', vol. ii, pp. 5–148 in *Geschiedenis van Nederlandsch Indië*, ed. F. W. Stapel. 5 vols. Amsterdam, 1938–40.

—— 'The Javanese Picture of the Past', pp. 87–117 in *An Introduction to Indonesian Historiography*, ed. Soedjatmoko *et al*. Ithaca, 1965.

—— 'Kraton-Bouw in de Wildernis', *Indonesië*, vol. 10, no. 6 (1957), pp. 506–32.

—— 'Māyā's Hemelvaart in het Javaanse Buddhisme', *Verhandelingen der Koninklijke Nederlandse Akademie van Wetenschappen, Afd. Letterkunde*, vol. 74, nos. 1 and 2 (1969).

—— 'Het Rijk van de Vijfvoudige Buddha', *Verhandelingen der Koninklijke Nederlandse Akademie van Wetenschappen, Afd. Letterkunde*, vol. 69, no. 1 (1962).

—— 'Twee nieuwe Publicaties betreffende de Geschiedenis en de Geschiedschrijving van Mataram', *Indonesië*, vol. 8 (1955), pp. 97–128.

—— 'De Weg van Oud- naar Nieuw-Mataram', *Indonesië*, vol. 10, no. 5 (1957), pp. 405–32.

—— 'De Zin der tweede Babad-Tanah-Jawi', *Indonesië*, vol. 8 (1955), pp. 361–400.

Berg, L. W. C. van den. *De Inlandsche Rangen en Titels op Java en Madoera*. 's-Gravenhage, 1902.

Bezemer, T. J. (ed.). *Beknopte Encyclopaedie van Nederlandsch-Indië, naar den tweeden Druk der Encyclopaedie van Nederlandsch-Indië*. 's-Gravenhage, 1921.

Boedihardjo. 'Grepen uit de Wajang', *Djåwå*, vol. 2 (1923), pp. 22–8.

Bosboom, H. D. H. 'Het verdwenen Waterkasteel te Djokdjokarta (uit oude Papieren)', *TBG*, vol. 45 (1902), pp. 518–29.

Boxer, C. R. *The Dutch Seaborne Empire, 1600–1800*. London, 1965.

Brandes, J. *Beschrijving der Javaansche, Balineesche en Sasaksche Handschriften aangetroffen in de Nalatenschap van Dr. H. N. van der Tuuk*. 4 vols. Batavia, 1901–26.

—— 'Bladvulling: Eenige foutieve Eigennamen in de door Meinsma uitgegeven Prozabewerking van den Babad Tanah Djawi', *TBG*, vol. 35 (1893), pp. 127–8.

—— 'Djakuwès in de Babad, tijdens de Belegering van Batavia = Jacques Lefebvre', *TBG*, vol. 44 (1901), pp. 286–8.

—— 'Iets over een ouderen Dipanegara in Verband met een Prototype van de Voorspellingen van Jayabaya', *TBG*, vol. 32 (1889), pp. 368–430.

Brandon, James R. (ed.). *On Thrones of Gold: Three Javanese Shadow Plays*. Cambridge, Mass., 1970.

Bratakèsawa. *Katrangan Tjandrasangkala*. Djakarta, 1952.

Burger, D. H. *Structural Changes in Javanese Society: the Supra-Village Sphere*. Trans. Leslie H. Palmier. Ithaca, 1956.

Chijs, J. A. van der. *Inventaris van 's Lands Archief te Batavia (1602–1816)*. Batavia, 1882.

Coedès, G. *The Indianized States of Southeast Asia*. Trans. Susan Brown Cowing. Ed. Walter F. Vella. Honolulu, 1968.

Coolhaas, W. Ph. *A Critical Survey of Studies on Dutch Colonial History*. 's-Gravenhage, 1960.

Cortesão, Armando (ed. and trans.). *The Suma Oriental of Tomé Pires and the Book of Francisco Rodrigues*. 2 vols. London, 1944.

Covarrubias, Miguel. *Island of Bali*. London, 1937.

Damais, Louis-Charles. 'L'Épigraphie musulmane dans le Sud-Est Asiatique', *BEFEO*, vol. 54 (1968), pp. 567–604.

—— 'Études javanaises: I, Les Tombes musulmanes datées de Trålåjå', *BEFEO*, vol. 48 (1957), pp. 353–415.

Day, Clive. *The Policy and Administration of the Dutch in Java*. Kuala Lumpur, 1966.
Dewantara, Ki Adjar. *Beoefening van Letteren en Kunst in het Pakoe-Alamsche Geslacht*. Djokja, 1931.
Djajadiningrat, Hoesein. *Critische Beschouwing van de Sadjarah Bantĕn: Bijdrage ter Kenschetsing van de Javaansche Geschiedschrijving*. Haarlem, 1913.
Drewes, G. W. J. (ed. and trans.). *The Admonitions of Seh Bari*. The Hague, 1969.
—— *Drie Javaansche Goeroe's: Hun Leven, Onderricht en Messiaspredi-king*. Leiden, 1925.
—— (ed. and trans.). *Een Javaanse Primbon uit de Zestiende Eeuw*. Leiden, 1954.
—— 'Javanese Poems dealing with or attributed to the Saint of Bonaṅ', *BKI*, vol. 124, no. 2 (1968), pp. 209–40.
—— and Poerbatjaraka. *De Mirakelen van Abdoelkadir Djaelani*. Bandoeng, 1938.
—— 'New Light on the Coming of Islam to Indonesia?', *BKI*, vol. 124, no. 4 (1968), pp. 433–59.
—— 'Over werkelijke en vermeende Geschiedschrijving in de Nieuw-javaansche Litteratuur', *Djåwå*, vol. 19 (1939), pp. 244–57.
—— 'The Struggle between Javanism and Islam as Illustrated by the Sĕrat Dĕrmagaṇḍul', *BKI*, vol. 122, no. 3 (1966), pp. 309–65.
Dwidjosoegondo. *Serat Dharah inggih 'Seseboetan Radèn'*. Malang, 1941.
Encyclopaedia van Nederlandsch-Indië. 9 vols. 's-Gravenhage, 1917–40.
Furnivall, J. S. *Netherlands India: A Study of Plural Economy*. Cambridge, 1967.
Geertz, Clifford. *The Religion of Java*. Glencoe, Ill., 1964.
Gericke, J. F. C., and T. Roorda. *Javaansch–Nederduitsch Woordenboek*. Amsterdam, 1847.
—— —— *Javaansch–Nederlandsch Handwoordenboek*. Ed. A. C. Vreede and J. G. H. Gunning. 2 vols. Leiden, 1901.
Goeje, M. J. de. 'Aanwinsten der Verzameling van Oostersche Handschriften te Leiden', *De Nederlandsche Spectator*, 21 November 1874, pp. 379–80.
Gonda, J. *Ancient Indian Kingship from the Religious Point of View*. Leiden, 1966.
—— 'Eenige Grepen uit de Geschiedenis der Beoefening van de Maleische Taal- en Letterkunde', *Verslag Provinciaal Utrechtsch Genootschap van Kunsten en Wetenschappen* (1935), pp. 93–113.
Graaf, H. J. de. 'Beknopte Overzicht der Geschiedenis van het Sultanaat Jogjakarta', *Historia*, vol. 12, no. 12 (December 1947), pp. 275–85.
—— 'De eerste Moslimse Vorstendommen op Java: Studiën over de Staatkundige Geschiedenis van de 15de en 16de Eeuw.' Forthcoming publication.

—— *Geschiedenis van Indonesië.* 's Gravenhage, 1949.
—— 'Gevangenneming en Dood van Raden Truna-Djaja, 26 Dec. 1679–2 Jan. 1680', *TBG*, vol. 85 (1952), pp. 273–309.
—— 'De Historische Betrouwbaarheid der Javaanse Overlevering', *BKI*, vol. 112 (1956), pp. 55–73.
—— 'Het Kadjoran-Vraagstuk', *Djåwå*, vol. 20 (1940), pp. 273–325.
—— *De Moord op Kapitein François Tack, 8 Febr. 1686.* Amsterdam, 1935.
—— 'De Opkomst van Raden Troenadjaja', *Djåwå*, vol. 20 (1940), pp. 56–86.
—— 'De Regering van Panembahan Sénapati Ingalaga', *VKI*, vol. 13 (1954).
—— 'De Regering van Sultan Agung, Vorst van Mataram, 1613–1645, en die van zijn Voorganger Panembahan Séda-ing-Krapjak, 1601–1613', *VKI*, vol. 23 (1958).
—— 'De Regering van Sunan Mangku-Rat I Tegal-Wangi, Vorst van Mataram, 1646–1677', *VKI*, vols. 33, 39 (1961, 1962).
—— 'Titels en Namen van Javaanse Vorsten en Groten uit de 16e en 17e Eeuw', *BKI*, vol. 109 (1953), pp. 62–82.
—— 'De verdwenen Tjandi te Salatiga', *BKI*, vol. 114 (1958), pp. 117–20.
—— (ed.). *De Vijf Gezantschapsreizen van Rijklof van Goens, naar het Hof van Mataram, 1648–1654.* 's-Gravenhage, 1956.
Groeneveldt, W. P. 'Notes on the Malay Archipelago and Malacca, Compiled from Chinese Sources', *VBG*, vol. 39, pt. 1 (1877).
Groneman, J. *De Garĕbĕg's te Ngajogyåkartå.* 's-Gravenhage, 1895.
—— 'Het Waterkasteel te Jogjåkartå', *TBG*, vol. 30 (1885), pp. 412–34.
Gullick, J. M. *Indigenous Political Systems of Western Malaya.* London, 1965.
Gunning, J. G. H. (ed.). *Een Javaansche Geschrift uit de 16de Eeuw handelende over den Mohammedaansche Godsdienst, naar een Leidsch Handschrift uitgegeven en met Aanteekeningen voorzien.* Leiden, 1881.
Haan, F. de. 'Uit Oud-Batavia: Kota Tahi', *TBG*, vol. 42 (1900), pp. 567–83.
—— 'Uit oude Notarispapieren I', *TBG*, vol. 42 (1900), pp. 297–308.
Hageman, J. 'Geschied- en Aardrijkskundig Overzigt van Java, op het Einde der Achttiende Eeuw', *TBG*, vol. 9 (1860), pp. 261–419.
Hall, D. G. E. (ed.). *Historians of South East Asia.* London, 1961.
—— *A History of South-East Asia.* 3rd ed. New York, 1968.
Hardjowirogo. *Sedjarah Wajang Purwa.* Djakarta, 1952.
Hien, H. A. van. *De Javaansche Geestenwereld.* 3 vols. Batavia, [1933–5].
Hitti, Philip K. *History of the Arabs, from the Earliest Times to the Present.* London, 1968.

Holt, Claire. *Art in Indonesia: Continuities and Change.* Ithaca, 1967.
Irwin, Graham. 'Dutch Historical Sources', pp. 234–51 in *An Introduction to Indonesian Historiography*, ed. Soedjatmoko et al. Ithaca, 1965.
Jansonius, H. *Groot Nederlands–Engels Woordenboek.* 2 vols. Leiden, 1950.
Johns, A. H. 'Muslim Mystics and Historical Writing', pp. 37–49 in *Historians of South East Asia*, ed. D. G. E. Hall. London, 1961.
—— 'Sufism as a Category in Indonesian Literature and History', *JSEAH*, vol. 2, no. 2 (July 1961), pp. 10–23.
Juynboll, H. H. *Supplement op den Catalogus van de Javaansche en Madoereesche Handschriften der Leidsche Universiteits-Bibliotheek.* 2 vols. Leiden, 1907–11.
Kartodirdjo, Sartono. 'The Peasants' Revolt of Banten in 1888, its Conditions, Course and Sequel, A Case Study of Social Movements in Indonesia', *VKI*, vol. 50 (1966).
—— *Tjatatan tentang Segi-segi Messianistis dalam Sedjarah Indonesia.* Jogjakarta, 1959.
Kats, J. *Het Javaansche Tooneel.* Vol. i: *Wajang Poerwa.* Weltevreden, 1923.
Kern, H. (ed.). *Rāmāyaṇa, Oudjavaansch Heldendicht.* 's-Gravenhage, 1900.
Keyzer, S. 'De Javaansche Handschriften te Londen', *BKI*, vol. 2 (1854), pp. 330–44.
Klinkert, H. C. *Nieuw Maleisch–Nederlandsch Woordenboek, met Arabisch Karakter.* [Leiden, 1893.]
Kraemer, H. *Een Javaansche Primbon uit de Zestiende Eeuw. Inleiding, Vertaling en Aanteekeningen.* Leiden, 1921.
Krom, N. J. *Hindoe-Javaansche Geschiedenis.* 's-Gravenhage, 1931.
—— (ed.). 'Oud Javaansche Oorkonden. Nagelaten Transscripties door wijlen Dr. J. L. A. Brandes', *VBG*, vol. 60 (1913).
Leur, J. C. van. 'Eenige Aanteekeningen betreffende de Mogelijkheid der 18e Eeuw als Categorie in de Indische Geschiedschrijving', *TBG*, vol. 80 (1940), pp. 544–67.
Levyssohn Norman, H. D. *De Britsche Heerschappij over Java en Onderhoorigheden (1811–1816).* 's-Gravenhage, 1857.
Lijst van de voornaamste Aardrijkskundige Namen in den Nederlandsch-Indischen Archipel. Weltevreden, 1923.
Linden, A. L. V. L. van der. *De Europeaan in de Maleische Literatuur.* Meppel, 1937.
Lohuizen-de Leeuw, J. E. van. 'The Beginnings of Old-Javanese Historical Literature', *BKI*, vol. 112 (1956), pp. 383–94.
Lombard, Denys. 'Jardins à Java', *Arts Asiatiques*, vol. 20 (1969), pp. 135–83.

Louw, P. J. F. *De derde Javaansche Successie-Oorlog(1746–1755)*. 's Hage, 1889.

—— and E. S. de Klerck. *De Java-Oorlog, 1825–30*. 6 vols. 's Hage, 1894–1909.

Moertono, Soemarsaid. *State and Statecraft in Old Java: A Study of the Later Mataram Period, 16th to 19th Century*. Ithaca, 1968.

Mollema, J. C. *De eerste Schipvaart der Hollanders naar Oost-Indië, 1595–1597*. 's-Gravenhage, 1935.

Moquette, J. P. 'De Datum op den Grafsteen van Malik Ibrāhīm te Grissee', *TBG*, vol. 54 (1912), pp. 208–14.

—— 'De oudste Mohammedaansche Inscriptie op Java, n.m. de Grafsteen te Leran', pp. 391–9 in *Handelingen van het eerste Congres voor de Taal-, Land- en Volkenkunde van Java*. Weltevreden, 1921.

Noto Soeroto. 'Beknopt Geschiedkundig Overzicht van het Sultanaat Jogjokarto', *Nederlandsch Indië Oud en Nieuw*, vol. 5 (1920–1), pp. 197–207, 241–56, 335–52.

Osborne, Milton E. *The French Presence in Cochinchina and Cambodia: Rule and Response (1859–1905)*. Ithaca, 1969.

Pigeaud, Th. G. Th. 'Alexander, Sakèndèr en Sénapati', *Djåwå*, vol. 7 (1927), pp. 321–61.

—— *Javaans-Nederlands Handwoordenboek*. Groningen, [1938].

—— *Java in the 14th Century: A Study in Cultural History*. 5 vols. The Hague, 1960–3.

—— 'Kangdjeng Pangeran Arja Adipati Danoeredja VII, Papatih Dalem ing Karaton Ngajogjakarta, Toemboek 1798/1869–1862/1931', *Djåwå*, vol. 11 (1931), no. 4, pp. 127–32; nos. 5–6, pp. 34–40.

—— *Literature of Java*. 3 vols. The Hague and Leiden, 1967–70.

Poerbatjaraka. *Agastya in den Archipel*. Leiden, 1926.

—— 'Lijst der Javaansche Handschriften in de Boekerij van het Kon. Bat. Genootschap', *Jaarboek, Koninklijk Bataviaasch Genootschap van Kunsten en Wetenschappen* (1933), pp. 269–376.

—— *Pandji-Verhalen onderling Vergeleken*. Bandoeng, 1940.

Poerwadarminta, W. J. S. *Baoesastra Djawa*. Groningen, 1939.

Praag, S. van. *Onrust op Java. De Jeugd van Dipanĕgara. Een Historisch-Literaire Studie*. Amsterdam, 1947.

Prabhavananda, Swami, and Frederick Manchester (ed. and trans.). *The Upanishads, Breath of the Eternal*. New York, 1963.

Pringgadigda, A. K. *Dhoemadhos saha Ngrembakanipoen Pradja Mangkoenagaran*. Surakarta, 1939.

[——] Pringgodigdo, A. K. *Geschiedenis der Ondernemingen van het Mangkoenagorosche Rijk*. 's-Gravenhage, 1950.

Raffles, Thomas Stamford. *The History of Java*. 2 vols. London, 1830.

Rassers, W. H. *De Pandji-Roman*. Antwerpen, 1922.

Rassers, W. H. *Pañji, the Culture Hero. A Structural Study of Religion in Java*. The Hague, 1959.

Ravaisse, Paul. 'L'Inscription coufique de Léran à Java', *TBG*, vol. 65 (1925), pp. 668–703.

Reid, Anthony. 'Nineteenth Century Pan-Islam in Indonesia and Malaysia', *Journal of Asian Studies*, vol. 26, no. 2 (Feb. 1967), pp. 267–83.

Ricklefs, M. C. 'A Consideration of Three Versions of the *Babad Tanah Djawi*, with Excerpts on the Fall of Madjapahit', *Bulletin of the School of Oriental and African Studies*, vol. 35, pt. 2 (1972), pp. 285–315.

—— 'An Inventory of the Javanese Manuscript Collection in the British Museum', *BKI*, vol. 125, no. 2 (1969), pp. 241–62.

—— 'On the Authorship of Leiden Cod. Or. 2191, Babad Mangkubumi', *BKI*, vol. 127, no. 2 (1971), pp. 264–73.

—— Review of *State and Statecraft in Old Java*, by Soemarsaid Moertono, *JSEAS*, vol. 1, no. 1 (March 1970), pp. 116–17.

Rijckevorsel, E. van. *Brieven uit Insulinde*. 's-Gravenhage, 1878.

Rinkes, D. A. 'De Heiligen van Java', *TBG*, vol. 52 (1910), pp. 556–89; vol. 53 (1911), pp. 17–56, 269–300, 435–581; vol. 54 (1912), pp. 135–207; vol. 55 (1913), pp. 1–201.

Rockhill, W. W. 'Notes on the Relations and Trade of China with the Eastern Archipelago and the Coast of the Indian Ocean during the Fourteenth Century', *T'oung Pao*, vol. 14 (1913), pp. 473–6; vol. 15 (1914), pp. 419–47; vol. 16 (1915), pp. 61–159, 236–71, 374–92, 435–67, 604–26.

Ronkel, Ph. S. van. 'Over een oude Lijst van Maleische Handschriften', *TBG*, vol. 42 (1900), pp. 309–22.

Rouffaer, G. P., and W. C. Muller. *Catalogus der Koloniale Bibliotheek van het Kon. Instituut voor de Taal-, Land- en Volkenkunde van Ned. Indië en het Indisch Genootschap*. 's-Gravenhage, 1908. Supplements *1–4*, 's-Gravenhage, 1915, 1927, 1937, 1966.

—— and J. W. Ijzerman (eds.). *De eerste Schipvaart der Nederlanders naar Oost-Indië onder Cornelis de Houtman, 1595–1597*. 3 vols. 's-Gravenhage, 1915, 1925, 1929.

—— 'Het Tijdperk van Godsdienstovergang (1400–1600) in den Maleischen Archipel: Wanneer is Madjapahit gevallen?', *BKI*, vol. 50 (1899), pp. 111–99.

—— 'Vorstenlanden', *Adatrechtbundels*, vol. 34, pp. 233–378.

Schoel, W. F. (ed.). *Alphabetisch Register van de Administratieve- (Bestuurs-) en Adatrechtelijke Indeeling van Nederlandsch-Indie*. Vol. i: *Java en Madoera*. Batavia, 1931.

Schrieke, B. J. O. *Het Boek van Bonang*. Utrecht, 1916.

—— *Indonesian Sociological Studies, Selected Writings of B. Schrieke*. 2 vols. The Hague, 1955–7.

Selosoemardjan. *Social Changes in Jogjakarta.* Ithaca, 1962.

Seno Sastroamidjojo. *Renungan tentang Pertundjukan Wajang Kulit.* Djakarta, [1964].

Skinner, C. (ed. and trans.). 'Sja'ir Perang Mengkasar (The Rhymed Chronicle of the Macassar War) by Entji' Amin', *VKI*, vol. 40 (1963).

Soebardi. 'Raden Ngabehi Jasadipura I, Court Poet of Surakarta: His Life and Works', *Indonesia*, no. 8 (Oct. 1969), pp. 81–102.

Soedjatmoko et al. (eds.). *An Introduction to Indonesian Historiography.* Ithaca, 1965.

Soedjono Tirtokoesoemo. *De Garebegs in het Sultanaat Jogjakarta.* Jogjakarta, 1931.

Soekanto. *Hubungan Diponegoro-Sentot.* Djakarta, [1959].

—— *Sekitar Jogjakarta, 1755–1825 (Perdjandjian Gianti-Perang Dipanagara).* Djakarta, [1952].

Soepomo Poedjosoedarmo and M. C. Ricklefs. 'The Establishment of Surakarta, a Translation from the *Babad Gianti*', *Indonesia*, no. 4 (Oct. 1967), pp. 88–108.

Stavorinus, John Splinter. *Voyages to the East-Indies.* Trans. Samuel Hull Wilcocke. 3 vols. London, 1798.

Teeuw, A. *Register op de Tekst en Vertaling van de Babad Tanah Djawi (Uitgave 1941).* ['s-Gravenhage, 1946.]

Tjabang Bagian Bahasa, Djawatan Kebudajaan pada Kementerian P. P. & K., Jogjakarta. *Riwajat Kjahi Jasadipura I: Pudjangga Djawa di Surakarta.* [Jogjakarta, 1952.]

Het Triwindoe-Gedenkboek Mangkoe Nagoro VII. 2 vols. Soerakarta, 1939–40.

Tuuk, H. N. van der. *Kawi–Balineesch–Nederlandsch Woordenboek.* 4 vols. Batavia, 1897–1912.

Uhlenbeck, E. M. *A Critical Survey of Studies on the Languages of Java and Madura.* 's-Gravenhage, 1964.

Verdam, J. *Middelnederlandsch Handwoordenboek.* 's-Gravenhage, 1964.

'Vertaling van een Javaansch Handschrift, behelzende eene Geschiedkundige Schets der Splitsing van het Rijk van Soerakarta en der Stichting van het Rijk van Djockjokarta', *Tijdschrift voor Neêrland's Indie,* vol. 12, pt. 2 (1839), pp. 204–11.

Veth, P. J. *Java, Geographisch, Ethnologisch, Historisch.* 3 vols. Haarlem, 1875–82.

Vreede, A. C. *Catalogus van de Javaansche en Madoereesche Handschriften der Leidsche Universiteits-Bibliotheek.* Leiden, 1892.

Vries, L. de. '"Kitab Toehpah" en Tuḥfat al Muḥtādj li sjarkh al Minhādj. Resultaten van een voorloopig Onderzoek, met Vertaling van den "Kitab Toehpah"', *VBG*, vol. 68, pt. 4 (1929).

Widjojo Nitisastro. *Population Trends in Indonesia.* Ithaca, 1970.

Winstedt, R. O., and P. Voorhoeve. 'Royal Asiatic Society. Raffles's Javanese MSS. Hand List 1950.' Typescript in Royal Asiatic Society, London.

Winter, C. F., Sr. *Javaansche Zamenspraken*. Vol. i. Ed. T. Roorda. 5th ed. Leiden, 1911.

—— *Javaansche Zamenspraken*. Vol. ii. Ed. S. Keyzer. Amsterdam, 1858.

Winter, J. W. 'Beknopte Beschrijving van het Hof Soerakarta in 1824', *BKI*, vol. 54 (1902), pp. 15-172.

Wiselius, J. A. B. 'Djåjå Båjå, zijn Leven en Profetieën', *BKI*, 3rd series, vol. 7 (1872), pp. 172-217.

Worsley, Peter John. *Babad Buleleng: A Balinese Dynastic Genealogy*. 's-Gravenhage, 1972.

Yamin, Muhammad. *6000 Tahun Sang Mérah-Putih*. Djakarta, 1958

Zoetmulder, P. J. 'Kalangwan: A Survey of Old Javanese Literature.' Forthcoming publication.

—— *Pantheisme en Monisme in de Javaansche Soeloek-Litteratuur*. Nijmegen, 1935.

—— and Waldemar Stöhr. *Die Religionen Indonesiens*. Stuttgart, 1965.

INDEX

Where an item appears in both the text and the notes of a page, no separate reference is made to the notes.

abdication: perhaps contemplated by Mangkubumi, 139, 167–70, 174–5, 187, 210, 218, 282; rejected by Mangkubumi, 322, 347–8; perhaps contemplated by Mangkunĕgara, 171–3, 174–5, 210, 282
Abdul Kadir (rebel), 127–9, 134
Abdul Kadir (Sultan of Bantĕn), 359 n.
Abdul Kadir Djaelani, 127 n.
Abdul Kamil, Hadji, 264–5
Abdullah, 152
Abrahams, J. H., 71, 427
Abū Bakr, 152
Abyssinia, 388 n.
Adam, 138, 212, 214
adat, 19, 42, 45, 50–2 n., 77, 103, 149, 232, 242, 246, 255
Adi, Raden Mas (Natakusuma/Pakualam I), 350 n.
Adikusuma, Pangeran, 352 nn.
Adilangu, *see* Kadilangu
Adilangu II, Pangeran, 224
Adinĕgara, Pangeran, 43 n., 102, 149 n.
Adiprakosa, Susuhunan, *see* Mangkunĕgara I
Adiwidjaja, Pangeran, 43 n.
agricultural deliveries, 73
Agung, Sultan, 12, 13, 15–16, 17, 21, 22, 61, 76 n., 83, 85, 126 n., 129, 158, 180 n., 184, 213, 227, 355–6, 359 n., 376, 399 n., 400 n., 402, 415
Ajogja, 81 n.
Ajundjaja Adimurti Senapati Ingalaga, Susuhunan, 288–9, 293
Alexander the Great, 385 n.
Algemeen Rijksarchief, xvii
'Alī, 152
Alit, Pangeran, 18
Alpiman/Apiman, 384 n.
Alting, W. A., 249, 252, 272, 306, 426
alun-alun, 124, 166, 201, 294, 314, 336, 346, 358, 393

Amad (Nur) Saleh, 318, 337, 338 n.
Amangkurat I, Susuhunan, 18–20, 25, 26, 45, 69 n., 70, 180–1, 186 n., 260–1, 359 n., 363, 398 n., 415, 422
Amangkurat II, Susuhunan, 20, 123, 125, 127, 214–15, 374
Amangkurat III, Susuhunan, 26, 38, 123, 136, 310, 349 n.
Amangkurat IV, Susuhunan, 83, 130, 349 n., 429
Ampel, *see* Ngampel
Andajaningrat, Adipati, *see* Djaka Tingkir
Andini, 398
anem, 77–8
Anggĕr-Agĕng, 162–3, 221 n.
Anggĕr-Arubiru, 163–5, 221
Angrok, Ken, 399 n.
Anom, Sultan, of Tjirĕbon, 247
Antheunisz., A., 383–4 n.
anti-Europeanism, 154–5, 295–6
Arabia, Arabs, 59, 199, 295 n., 332
Arabic language, 134, 150–1, 153, 155, 293, 388 n.
Ardijan, 384 n.
Ardiman, 384 n.
Arjunawiwāha, 189
Arsip Nasional Republik Indonesia, xviii
Arte, 384 n.
Arungbinang, Raden Tumĕnggung, 266–7
Asmara, Sang, 200
Asṭa Brata, 81 n.
Atjeh, 127 n.
Australia, 383 n.
autonomy, local, 23 ff.
awisaning Ratu/larangan-Dalĕm, 163–5, 276
Aymonier, E., 365 n.
Ayodhyā, 80

INDEX

baas, 382 n.
Babad Balambangan, 221
Babad Děmak, 224 n.
Babad Dipanagaran Surja Ngalam, 189
Babad Dipaněgara, 87
Babad Gijanti, xix-xx, 41-6, 50, 51 n., 53, 55, 88, 103-4, 217, 378 n., 385 n., 424
Babad Kartasura, 224 n.
Babad Kraton, xxiii, 5-6, 9-10, 11, 29-30, 85, 185, 212-19, 221, 356, 376-7, 409, 424
Babad Madjapahit, 224 n.
Babad Mangkubumi, xx, *et passim*; written by Crown Prince of Jogjakarta, xx, 167-8, 187, 218; apparently written in two sections, xx, 168-9 n., 273
Babad Mataram, 224 n.
Babad Nitik, 17 n.
Babad Padjadjaran, 224 n.
Babad Padjang, 224 n.
Babad Pakěpung, xxi-xxii, 329, 338 n.
Babad Pakuněgara, 93 n.
Babad Prajud, 138
Babad Sangkalaning Momana, xxii, 188, *et passim*
Babad Tanah Djawi: versions, xxiii; Meinsma version, xxiii, 5, 18, 19, 20, 260-1; NBS 158 and LOr 6483, 376, 377 n., 384 n.; NBS 224, 311-12; Surakarta version, xxiii, 5, 132 n., 138, 214. See also *Babad Kraton*
Badjra, Tjarik, 224
Bagělen, 43, 71, 157, 159, 266-8
Bagong, 28
Bagus Kuda, 128-9, 135-6
Bahman (Bagus Bahman), 318, 337, 338 n.
Bajalali, 357
Bajat, Sunan, 4 n., 16, 17
Balěmbangan, 39, 130, 135, 137, 146, 405 n.
Bali, Balinese, 1, 23 n., 27, 29 n., 48, 130, 135, 179, 182, 193 n.
Banaspati, 289
Banda, 90 n., 102 n.
Bandjar Binangun, 209 n.
Bandjar Rukma, 209 n.
Bandjěrmasin, princess of, 262
Bangsal Manis, 194 n.
Banjumas, xx, 69-70, 71, 146, 159, 229-30, 265, 335, 405 n.

Banjumas, *bupati* of, *see* Judaněgara (son of Danurědja I)
Bantěn, 13, 57, 127 n., 158, 247, 295, 359 n., 400, 406 n.
Bantěn, Sultan of, 105, 229-30
banteng, 276 n.
Bantul, 242
bapak děler, 371-2
Baraburdur, 1, 100, 177
Bari, Seh, Admonitions of, 6-7
Baribin, Arja, 370 n.
Baribin, Raden Saputra Arja, 370 n.
Baron (title), 379, 385 n.
Baron Sakenḍer: LOr 1800, 377 n.; LOr 6185, 377-8 n.
Baron Sakenḍer stories, xxiv, 27, 276 n., 331, 374-413; age, 378-9, 385 n.; alluded to in *Babad Gijanti*, 378 n., 385 n.
Baṭara Guru, 29
Batavia, 15, 18, 35, 38, 76 n., 149, 247, 248, 356, 373-5, 379, 410, *et passim*; name, 376; spirit of, 406 n.
'Batawijah' (Batavia), 376, 391 n.
baṭik, 60, 276
Bauręksa, Radja, 404, 405 n.
beer, *see* Dutch, drink and drinking
Beganonda, 202
Bei, *see* Ngabei
běksa djěběng, 192
běksa djěmparing, 192
běnde, 289
Bengal, 103, 193 n.
Berg, C. C., 12, 81-2, 177, 178, 181 n., 182 n., 189; quoted, 225 n.
Běsar, Tuwan Sajid *or* Sarip, *see* Ibrahim, Seh
Běsari, Hadji, 154
Běstam, Ki, *see* Kartabasa (Ki Běstam)
Bětawi (Batavia), 401-2
Bětok, Kjai, 76 n.
Beuman, J. C., 427
bhawacakra, 225 n.
bhujangga, 225 n.
Bima, princess of, 104
Bintara (Děmak), 5
Bintara, Pangeran (rebel), *see* Buminata
Bintara, Sultan/Adipati, *see* Patah, Raden, *and* Trěnggana, Sultan
birds' nests, 97
Bligh, W., 317 n.

INDEX

Blitar, 132
Blitar, Pangeran (son of Mangkubumi), 352 n.
Blitar, Pangeran (son of Pakubuwana I), 349 n.
Bloemhart, P., 327
Blora, 124
Boltze, C. P., 153 n.
Bonang, 126, 240 n., 406 n.
Bonang, Sunan, 4 n., 6
Bontit, Kjai, 125 n.
Book of Klĕpu (*Sĕrat Buk Kalĕpu*), 89, 143, 144, 157, 158, 418
Borneo, 14
Bounty, H.M.S., 317 n.
Boxer, C. H., 297; quoted, 29 n., 87 n.
Braam, J. A. van, 309
Brandes, J. L. A., 177
Bratajuda, 382 n., 389 n.
Brawidjaja, Prabu, 3, 370 n.
Brian, 405 n.
Bringan, 80 n.
Buddhism, 4, 82, 100, 292
Buginese, 193, 337
Bukit Tarbi, 382 n., 393, 394-5
Buku Kĕḍung Kĕbo, 190 n.
Buminata, Pangeran (brother of Pakubuwana IV), 337
Buminata, Pangeran (rebel), 43 n., 90
bupati, passim
Bupati Kadipaten Anom, 263
Burĕng, Ki and Ni, 404, 406 n.
Burgh, J. R. van der, 120, 121, 140, 146-50, 156, 157, 161, 165, 166, 170, 171, 175, 232, 233, 236-7, 239, 244, 245, 260-1, 265, 349, 365, 369, 426

calendar, Islamic, xxv
calendar, Islamic Javanese, xxv, 17, 126 n., 138, 142, 155, 165, 174, 184, 213 n., 293, 430-1. *See also* 'Thursday Calendar', 'Friday Calendar', *and* century-cycles
calendar, solar, xxv, 17, 184
Cambodia, 365 n., 387
cannon, given to Mangkubumi, 258, 278
Cape of Good Hope, 102 n., 109, 270, 287
census-taking, 158
century-cycles, 75, 138, 142-3, 155, 175, 176 ff.

Ceylon, 38, 75, 90, 102, 103, 109, 124, 149, 313
Champa, 3
Chandogya-Upanishad, 7
Cheng Ho, 2
chess, 393
China, Chinese, 1, 2, 38, 100, 102, 243, 389-90
Chinese massacre, 38
Chinese War, 21, 33, 38-9, 41, 49, 58, 102, 123-4
Christianity, Christians, 127, 335, 382 n., 389 n., 408-9, 410. See also *kafir*
chronogram lists, xxii
Claeszoon, 404 n.
Clausewitz, K. von, 94
Coen, J. P., 29 n., 383 n., 400
Cohen Stuart, A. B., 378, 379
Coleridge, S. T., 84
Commissioners for Military Affairs (1791), 283, 345-6
consensus, 19, 22 ff., 55, 83, 250, 362, 397 n., *et passim*
construction-projects at the turn of the century, 165-6, 170, 175
Coromandel, 301
corruption of Dutch Residents, 268-9, 285, 297-9, 366-7
Council of the Indies, 396, 397 n.
Couper, J., 182 n.
Crawfurd, J., MSS. collection of, xxii, xxiv, 220, 223, 377
Crown Prince of Jogjakarta, first, *see* Ĕnṭo, Raden Mas
Crown Prince of Jogjakarta (Hamĕngkubuwana II), *passim*; compared to Joseph, 82, 190; accession as Crown Prince, 101; titles, 101, 202 n.; birth, 101 n.; described in 1765, 102; circumcision, 102; proposal to marry Surakarta princess, 102, 104, 111, 115-17; visit to Surakarta in 1763, 111; visit to Surakarta in 1765, 116-17; marriage to daughter of Pangeran Pakuningrat in 1765, 117-18; proposal to marry girl from *pasisir*, 139-40; identified with Pudjakusuma, 210, 407-8; described in 1780, 244; attitude towards Dutch, 244, 273-4, 277-8, 301, 353, 360-1; Mangkubumi's attitude towards, 278, 313-14, 348-9; and

Crown Prince of Jogjakarta (*cont.*):
fortifications of 1785, 278–83; perhaps assumes authority in 1785, 280–2, 313; influence in Jogjakarta, 273–4, 301, 313–14; reconciliation with Mangkunĕgara I in 1790, 334–5; criticisms of, 347–9, 351; accession as Sultan in 1792, 253, 360–1; later deposed by English, 213, 377. See also *Babad Mangkubumi* and *Sĕrat Surja Radja*
Crown Prince of Surakarta, joins rebels in 1753, 58
Crown Prince of Surakarta, see Pakubuwana IV

Daendels, H. W., 192, 222 n., 363, 377, 424
ḍalang, 28, 67–8, 105, 150, 190, 192, 230
Damar Wulan, 224 n.
Danaradja, 198
Danasukma, 198–9
dancers, Jogjakarta, sent to Surakarta, 284 n., 298
Danukusuma, 360
Danuningrat, 164 n.
Danupaja, Pangeran (brother of Mangkubumi), 43 n., 102, 270
Danupaja, Pangeran (brother of Pakubuwana III), 149
Danupaja, Pangeran (son of Mangkubumi), 352 n.
Danurĕdja (*patih* of Kartasura), 38
Danurĕdja I, Raden Adipati (*patih* of Jogjakarta), *passim*; appointment, 69–70, 74; genealogy, 369–70, 409–10
Darawati/Dyariwati, 3 n. See also Dyarawati, Ratu Aju
Dasakusuma, 198 ff.
Dasamuka, 260 n.
Dasa Nama, 224 n.
dating, xxv, 430–1. See also calendar, Islamic Javanese; calendar, solar; 'Thursday Calendar'; 'Friday Calendar'
Ḍĕḍĕs, Ken, 399 n.
Dĕlanggu, 89 n., 307
Delft Academy, MSS. collection of, 220
Delft Ethnographic Museum, MSS. collection of, 220

Dĕmak, 1, 8–10, 11, 14, 61, 75, 125, 126, 179, 211, 213, 238, 240 n., 271, 316, 333, 406 n., 418
Dĕmak, Kjai Alim, 294–5
Dĕmak, Sultan of, see Patah, Raden *and* Trĕnggana, Sultan
Dĕmang, Pangeran, 351, 352
deva, 16 n.
Deventer, M. L. van, 247, 286, 331–2
Dewa, 204, 206
Dewi Sinta, 30
dice, 394
Dipakusuma, 360
Dipanĕgara, Pangeran (husband of Ratu Bĕndara), 117–18, 296
Dipanĕgara, Pangeran Arja (rebel), 60, 87, 136, 189–90, 277, 422
Dipasana, Pangeran, 352 n.
Dipasanta, Pangeran (brother of Pakubuwana II), 43 n.
Dipasonta, Pangeran (son of Mangkubumi), 352 n.
Dipawidjaja, 352 n.
division of Java, *passim*; precedents for, 33–5, 61, 62, 66, 75, 78, 214–18, 312; of 1749, 56, 65; of 1755, 64–6, 67 ff.; lack of precedents for permanent, 35, 142–3, 214–18, 416–20
'Djadjar', 238, 240
Djajabaja prophecies, 81 n., 183–4 n., 186 n., 210 n., 224 n.
Djajakarta, 374
Djajakusuma (in *Sĕrat Surja Radja*), 198
Djajakusuma, Raden (in letters of 1787), 289
Djajalĕlana, Ngabei, 129 n.
Djaja Midjaja, 210 n.
Djajaningrat, Raden Adipati, 164 n., 266, 327, 330, 337, 428; described in 1787, 272
Djajasumadi, 201
Djajawinata, 79
Djajengrat, Raden Tumĕnggung, xxiii, 212, 214–16
Djaka Krewed, 224 n.
Djakarta, 399 ff.
Djakarta, Pangeran of, 399 ff., 408
Djaka Salewah, 221 n.
Djaka Tingkir, 11, 75, 179, 187
Djakwes, Kapitan, 400 n.
Djalatuṇḍa, 264 n.

INDEX

djam-djam water, 154
djangkung, meaning of, 400 n.
Djangkung, Mur/Baron, 383, 400 ff., 409–10
Djatikusuma, 224 n.
Djatisari (place), meeting of 1755 at, 74–7, 103, 417
Djatisari (spirit), 406 n.
Djatiwisesa, 199
Djĕnar, 405 n.
Djĕnggala, 405 n.
Djĕpara, 14, 39
djimat, 152, 153, 202, 288
Djipang, 124, 405 n.
Djuru, Pangeran, see Natakusuma (patih of Kartasura)
Djuru, Raden Aju, 102, 104
Djuru Martani, 398, 399 n.
Djuru Taman, Ki (Kasenḍer), 399, 404, 405 n.
Djuwana, 46, 406 n.
Donkel, C., 63, 71, 92, 100, 368 n., 427
Dradjat, Sunan, 4 n.
Drewes, G. W. J., 6, 184 n.
Driansah, 384 n.
ḍukun, 150 n.
Durga, Baṭari, 190, 404, 405 n.
Dutch, passim; drink and drinking, 29, 74, 77, 112, 135, 297, 298, 299, 302, 400; first expedition, 13; intervention of, 20, 21, 26 ff., 37, 39, 219, 362, 415, 420–1; Javanese views of, 26–30, 293–4, 362 ff., see also Tanah Sabrang; Balinese depictions of, 29 n.; Malay view of, 29 n.; manipulated by Javanese, 237, 239, 270, 285, 320, 324, 329, 333, 340
Dutch East India Company, 15, et passim; sources, xvi-xviii; decline, 30, 37, 54, 99, 219, 244–5, 254, 272, 333, 346, 366, 416, 421, et passim; establishment according to Sĕrat Sakonḍar, 396–7; fortress at Jogjakarta, 120–2, 133, 302, 304, 366; fortress at Surakarta, 120–1, 166, 269, 298; fortresses on road to Jogjakarta, 122; Jogjakarta garrison, 120–2, 257, 273 n., 276–7 n., 324, 326, 336 n., 357, 364–9; Kartasura garrison, 38, 48; loans to Mangkubumi, 121, 246; Sĕmarang garrison, 148, 321–2, 326, 335; Surakarta garrison, 48, 257, 268–9, 324, 326, 335, 336 n., 364–9; promotion procedures, 369
Dutch government armed forces, 309, 335
Duurveldt, 427
Dyarawati, Ratu Aju, 406 n.

economics, xvi, 73, 108, 246, 421, 423
Edam island, 149
ejang, 373
elephants, 58, 87, 88, 245
élite, 22, et passim
embassies, Javanese to Governor-General, 99, 231, 247–54, 255–6, 306, 373
Emup, Raden Baron, 383
Enḍangrĕtnasasi, 201
England, English, 121, 192–3, 252, 254–8, 317 n., 340, 351, 377, 380, 390
Ênṭo, Raden Mas, 72 n., 100, 128, 352 n.
Erlangga, 189
Erutjakra, Panĕmbahan, 132 n.
Ethiopia, 388 n.
Europe (Prĕnggi), 392

Falĕk, 384 n.
falling star and Senapati, 13, 242–3, 398
financial problems, 68, 97–8, 245–6. See also economics
formalism, 418–21
fortifications of Jogjakarta (1785), 122, 278–83, 302–3, 312, 346
fragmentation of Java, 10–11, 19. See also division of Java, precedents for
frambesia, 269 n.
France, French, 192–3, 377, 380, 390
French Revolution, 424
'Friday Calendar', 53 n., 54–5 n., 80 n., 213 n.
Furnivall, J. S., quoted, 272

Gadjah Mada, 182 n.
Gadjah Oja, 201
Galuh, 376, 406 n.
Galuh, Nini, 405 n.
gamĕlan, 74, 103 n., 203, 287, 288
Gamping, 79–80
Garĕbĕg Bĕsar, 146–7, 157
Garĕbĕg Mulud, 133, 270, 274, 335

Garĕndi, Raden Mas (Sunan Kuning), 38, 123–4, 126, 260
Gareng, 28
Garuḍa, 388 ff.
Gĕḍong Pulo Arga, 166
Geertz, C., quoted, 419
Gĕgĕsang, 126, 405 n.
gĕlaṭik mas, 392 n.
Gĕnawati, 406 n.
gĕntos taun, 181 n.
Gericke, J.F.C., MSS. collection of, 220
Germans, 336 n.
Gĕsĕng, Sunan, 4 n.
gezaghebber, 385 n.
Gijanti, 68, 74, 77, 79, 80, 86, 91, 150, 312. *See also* treaties
Giri, 126, 202
Giri, *paṇḍita* of, 199, 201
Giri, Sunan, 4 n., 7, 17–18, 179 nn., 224 n.; *kris* of, 5 n.
Goddess of the Southern Ocean, 13, 15, 23, 25, 34, 200, 203, 242, 375–6, 400 n., 403 n., 404, 405–6 n., 409–10, 419; and *Taman Sari*, 85, 376; names of, 200 n., 203 n.
Goens, R. van, 18–19
Gonda, J., 223 n.
Gonda Pura, 200
Gonda Sukma Misesa, 191
Gordijn, J., 212
Governor-General, Javanese view of, 247–8, 306, 372–3, 410, 411–12, 413
Graaf, H. J. de, xxii, 10, 11, 12, 17, 176–7, 179, 181, 229, 399 n.; quoted, 15, 38
Greeve, J., 121–2, 294–300, 307–11, 314, 316–17, 320, 322, 323, 326, 330, 333, 335–6, 339–40, 342, 347–8, 349, 352, 353, 372, 426; visit to Jogjakarta in 1788, 301–7; visit to Central Java in 1790, 326–30, 341; wealth, 339
Grĕsik, 14, 259 n.
Grobogan, 46, 60, 126, 238, 239 n., 240 n., 406 n.
Gunawan, 126
Gunter, Raden Mas, 123–7, 129, 134, 145 n., 260
Guntur Gĕni, 400
guntur pawatugunung, 178
Gunungdjati, Sunan, 4 n.
Gunung Kidul, 159, 329
Gunung Sari, 401–2

Guwa Badjra, 391 n., 392
Guwa Langse, 405 n.
Guwa Sonjagiri, 386

Haan, H. de, 399 n.
ḥabasha, al-, 388 n.
hadji, 150, 154, 155, 288, 332
haemorrhoids, 329
Hageman, J., 71–2
Hajam Wuruk, 3, 178 n.
Ḥallāj, al-, 8
Hamĕngkubuwana I, Sultan, *see* Mangkubumi, Sultan/Pangeran Arja
Hamĕngkubuwana II, Sultan, *see* Crown Prince of Jogjakarta
Hamĕngkubuwana III, Sultan, *see* Mangkubumi, Pangeran
Hamĕngkubuwana V, Sultan, 191–2
Hamĕngkubuwana VII, Sultan, 359 n.
Hamĕngkubuwana VIII, Sultan, 178–9 n.
Hamĕngkubuwana IX, Sultan, 178–9 n., 200 n.
Hamĕngkunĕgara, Pangeran Adipati, *see* Mangkunĕgara I
Hamĕngkunĕgara, Pangeran Adipati Anom, *see* Crown Prince
Ḥanafī, 152
Ḥanbalī, 152, 153
Hartingh, N., 39, 58, 65, 84, 90, 91, 92, 99, 100, 107, 312, 339, 384 n., 426; negotiations with Mangkubumi in 1754, 59–63; at Gijanti in 1755, 66, 67–74, 150; at Djatisari in 1755, 74–5, 77; at Salatiga in 1757, 92
Hartsinck, A., 299, 302, 315–17, 327, 366, 427
Hinduism, 4, 16, 130, 333
'Hobok', 263 n.
Hohendorff, J. A. Baron von, 43, 47, 48–54, 58, 339, 368 n., 379, 426
Hollandia, 401 n.
Holy War, 134, 151–4
hulde, 249

Ibrahim, 152
Ibrahim, Seh, 59
Ibrahim Asmara, 103
Ijsseldijk, W. H. van, 296, 303, 319–20, 328, 360, 366, 383 n., 427
Ilman, 384 n.
Imagiri, 1, 100, 228, 359
Imhoff, G. W. Baron van, 40–3, 45, 47, 373, 379, 383–4 n., 426

INDEX

Ina, Raden, 406 n.
Indian Ocean (Southern Ocean), 374, 376, 391 n. *See also* Goddess of the Southern Ocean
Indonesian Revolution, 190, 420, 425
infidel, see *kafir*
Intedeng, Baron, 383, 384 n.
Irdijan, Baron, 383, 384 n.
Iskandar (dhu-al-Qarnayn), 385 n.
Islam, *passim*; heresy in, 7–8, 200; Hindu-Javanese concepts in, 6, 7–8; and Hinduism, 82
Ismaja, Sang Hjang, 28
Isrek, Raden Baron, 383
Italian, 399 n.

Jager, H. de, 223 n.
Janssens, J. W., 192
Jasadipura I, Raden Ngabei, xix-xx, 45, 80–1 n., 224, 338 n., 378 n.
Jasadipura II, Raden Ngabei, xxi, 81 n., 224
Java Institute, xxiii
Javanese language: Dutch knowledge of, xvi, 58, 74, 107, 292 n.; levels, 368, 372
Javanese sources, xviii-xxiv
Java War, 100, 189–90, 220–2, 277, 361, 422
Jenever, 29 n.
Jesus, Prophet (Nabi Ngisa), 382 n.
Jīlānī, 'Abd-al-Qādir al-, 127 n.
Jogja, 47, 54, 79, 84
Jogjakarta, *passim*; establishment of court, 80; name of city, 80; spirit of, 406 n.
Jong, W. H. de, xx
Joseph, 82, 190, 198, 201
'Journal kept by the late Sultan of Java, A', xxii-xxiii
Judanagara Wulang, 224 n.
Judanĕgara (son of Danurĕdja I), 70, 146, 229–30
Judanĕgara, Raden Tumĕnggung, see Danurĕdja I, Raden Adipati
Judasara, Ngabei, 224 n., 378 n.
Judgement Day, 410 n.

Kabanaran, Sunan, 55 n.
Kadilangu (Adilangu), 75, 103 n., 126
Kadisono, 144 n.
Kadjoran, Pangeran, 287
Kaduwang, 159–60, 405 n.

kafir, 8, 27, 127, 151, 192, 193, 200, 209–11, 295
kajon (gunungan), 275 n.
Kajulandejan, 405 n.
Kaladjahar, 393–4
kala sakti, 81 n., 405 n.
Kalidjaga, 126, 406 n.
Kalidjaga, Sunan, 4 n., 103, 238, 240, 242; *kris* of, 74–6, 103
Kalinjamat, 126
Kalipatulah (title), 78, 313
Kaliwungu, 127, 406 n.
Kanduruwan, Tumĕnggung, 318, 337, 338 n.
Kanwa, Mpu, 189
Karta/Kĕrta, 12, 400 n., 403 n., 405 n.
Kartabasa, 153 n.
Kartabasa (Ki Bĕstam), 68, 153 n.
Kartasura, 12, 20–1, 33, 37–8, 123, 125, 126, 130, 182, 184, 211, 214–15, 216–17, 218–19, 224, 260, 379, 419 n.; as symbol of united kingdom, 126–7, 307, 338; spirit of, 406 n.
Kartodirdjo, Sartono, 184 n.
Kasberah, 384 n.
Kasebĕr, 276 n., 385 ff.
kasĕkten, sĕkti, 203, 310, 390
Kaseman, 384 n.
Kasender (Sakender), Raden Baron, 377, 385 ff., 407–10, 412; as Dutch Resident, 404 n., 411
Kastedeng, 384 n.
Kawit Paru, Baron, 382 n.
Kawit Prispruranjah, Baron, 382 n., 394
kawula-gusti, 200
Kĕdah, 23 n.
Kĕdiri, 14, 20, 90, 132, 133 n., 266, 405 n.
Kĕdjadjar, 240 n.
Kĕdu, 43, 71, 88, 100, 127, 157, 159, 266
Kĕlasong, 404 n., 406 n.
Kĕlut, Mount, 138
Kĕmbodja, Putra, 387
Kĕndal, 127, 406 n.
Kĕrtadiwirja, 224 n.
Keyzer, S., 165 n.
Kidung Lalĕmbut, 403 n.; LOr 4000 (2), 405 n.
Kilen, Raden Aju (of Surakarta), 140 n.
kitab, 206

Kitab Tupah, 221 n.
kiṭa intĕn, 388
Klaten, 89 n.
Klĕpu, 89 n. See also Book of Klĕpu
Klerk, R. de, 248–9, 252, 426
Kopek, Kjai, 74–6
Kraemer, H., 6
krama, 368, 372 n.
kraman, 123, 156 n.
Krapjak, 345, 354. See also Seda ing Krapjak, Panĕmbahan
Krawang, 406 n.
Krawang river, 374
Krĕsna, 81
Krĕti, Raden Mas, 270, 287–8
Krom, N. J., 373
Kuda Narawongsa, 224 n.
Kudus, 1, 109 n., 126, 406 n.
Kudus, Sunan, 4 n.
Kumalawati, 198
Kumbakarna, 132
Kuning, Sunan, see Garĕndi, Raden Mas
Kurawa, 382 n.
Kusumajuda, Pangeran (son of Mangkubumi), 352 n.
Kusumajuda, Pangeran Arja (nephew of Mangkubumi), 148
Kuṭa Gĕḍe, 12, 14, 47, 278, 405 n.
Kuṭa Tai, 401
Kuvel, Abraham, 309–10
Kuwu, 405 n.
Kuwungkusuma, Raden, 289

land, shortage of, 105, 108, 160, 264, 267–8
land lists, Javanese, 158 n.
land-settlements: of 1755, 71, 143; of 1756 (Klĕpu), 89, 143, 157, 418; of 1768, 144–5, 218; of 1770, 145, 218; of 1773–4, 157–61, 163, 218, 418
Lapro, J., 427
larangan-Dalĕm, see *awisaning Ratu*
Laroh, 159
lawejan, 398–9
laws, legal codes, xxii–xxiii, 161–5, 218, 284, 341, 417–18; Dutch-Jogjakarta of 1780, 254
Lawu, Mount, 68, 124, 406 n.
Lĕbur Gongsa, 391
Lefebvre, J., 400 n.
legitimacy, 23 ff., *et passim*
Lembu Amidjaja, 210 n.

Lĕngkara, Mount, 191
Leran gravestone, 3 n.
letters: Arabic of 1772, 150–4; found in Surakarta in 1787, 288–96, 298
Lintangkusuma, 289 n.
Lipura, 242, 398, 404 n.
Loḍaja, 405 n.
Lodewijks, W., 12 n.
Louw, P. J. F., 47, 65
Lucas, E., 309–10
Luzac, P., 119 n.

Mabĕlum, Baron, 383, 384 n.
Mabukit Ambin, 382, 393, 394
Mackenzie, C., MSS. collection of, 221, 223
Madiun, 60, 124, 405 n.
Madjapahit, 1–6, 8, 9, 126, 127, 132 n., 175, 177–8, 184, 185, 191, 212, 370, 371, 373, 375 n., 390 n., 404, 405 n., 410–11, 421
Madura, Madurese, 20, 39, 57, 90, 286, 295, 333, 335, 370 n., 406 n.
Madura, Panĕmbahan/Pangeran of, 88, 104, 108, 246–7, 262 n., 286; as author, 224 n.
Maeghdelins Reduijt, 401 n.
Magĕlang, 321
Mahdi, 292
Ma Huan, 2
Maitreya, 292
Makasar, 193
Makrĕsmin, 384 n.
Malabar, 301
Malacca, 14, 336 n.
Malang, 106–7, 123, 124, 129–38, 145 n.
Malangkusuma, Raden, 289
Malawa, 380, 382 n.
Malaya, Malays, 23 n., 134, 152, 337
Malay language, 371; spoken by Dutch, 28–30, 193, 372; in *Sĕrat Sakonḍar*, 385 n., 386 n., 389 n., 395 nn., 400 n., 401
Malĕk, Baron, 383
Malikī, 152
Malik Ibrahim, 4 n.; gravestone of, 2–3
Mandura, Arja, 305, 347–8, 352
Mandurarĕdja, Arja, 315, 316
Mangkubumi (name): given to Prangwadana, 299–300; given to Pangeran Arja Mataram (brother of

INDEX

Pakubuwana IV), 320–1, 323, 325, 342
Mangkubumi, Pangeran (Haměngkubuwana III), 189, 277, 321, 360
Mangkubumi, Pangeran Arja (brother of Pakubuwana IV), 320–1, 323, 325, 337
Mangkubumi, Sultan/Pangeran Arja (Haměngkubuwana I), *passim*; defeats Mangkuněgara I in 1746, 40; rebels in 1746, 40–6 ff.; alliance with Mangkuněgara I in 1746, 46; accession as Susuhunan in 1749, 54–6; titles in 1749, 55–6; hatred of von Hohendorff, 58; split with Mangkuněgara I c. 1752, 58, 63; negotiations with Dutch in 1754, 59–64; titles as Sultan, 64, 78–9; selection of court-site, 79; establishment of Jogjakarta court, 80; greatness of, 83, 359; birth, 83 n.; attitude towards submission of Mangkuněgara I, 92–4; relations with Dutch, 98–9, 119–20, 155–6, 253–4, 355–7, 362 ff., *et passim*; children, 99–100, 280–1, 322–3, 347–52, 353; administrative reorganization, 104–5; animosity towards Mangkuněgara I, *passim*; described in 1780, 236; illnesses, 273, 305, 328; perhaps surrenders authority to Crown Prince in 1785, 280–2, 313; reconciliation with Mangkuněgara I in 1790, 334–5, 338–9, 342, 343–4; illness and death in 1792, 347, 353–9. *See also* abdication
Mangkudiningrat, Pangeran, 316
Mangkujuda, Tuměnggung, 249 n. *See also* Sindurědja, Raden Adipati (*patih* of Surakarta)
Mangkukusuma, Pangeran (son of Mangkubumi), 352 nn.
Mangkukusuma, Raden Mas (of Surakarta), 259–60
Mangkuněgara I, Pangeran Adipati (Mas Said), *passim*; rebellion, 39; defeated by Mangkubumi in 1746, 40; alliance with Mangkubumi in 1746, 46 ff.; chief general and *patih* of Mangkubumi in 1750, 57, 428; abortive negotiations with von Hohendorff in 1752, 58; split with Mangkubumi in 1752, 58, 63;

names, 90; dislike of Dutch, 90; appearance, 90–1; negotiations in 1756–7, 91–2; submission in 1757, 92–4, 148, 271; at Salatiga in 1757, 92; titles, 92, 173; status, 93, 150, 233–5, 261–2, 344; relations with Dutch, 99, *et passim*; animosity towards Mangkubumi, *passim*; sons married to daughters of Pakubuwana III, 110, 263, 271; agreement of 1772, 150, 271; illness, 172 n., 269; agreement of 1787, 271; alleged correspondence with Ratu Běndara in 1787, 296, 300; Dutch decision to offer Surakarta throne to, 329, 337, 338; given independent income by Dutch in 1790, 334–5, 338–9; reconciliation with Mangkubumi in 1790, 334–5, 338–9, 342, 343–4. *See also* abdication
Mangkuněgara II, Pangeran Adipati Arja, *see* Prangwadana, Pangeran
Mangkuněgara, Pangeran Arja (father of Mangkuněgara I), 38, 39, 109, 270 n., 429
Mangkupradja, Raden Adipati, 108, 144 n., 146, 428; appointment as *patih*, 88; dismissal, 145; exile and death, 149
Mangmangdana, 289
mangsa, 213 n.
Mangundipura, 360
Manila, 254
Mantjingan (Pamantjingan), 375 n., 405 n.
mantri, 19, 230, 277, 290
manuscripts, dated Javanese, 220–5
Maospati, Tuměnggung, 249 n.
Marine Academy, Sěmarang, 282
marriage politics, 24–5, 96–7, 270–1. *See also* Ratu Běndara
Martadipura, Raden Arja, 264 n.
Martadjaja, 318
Martasana, 149
Mas, Sunan, *see* Amangkurat III
Mataram, 11 ff., 43, 47, 71, 159, 214–16, 291, 397–8, 400, 402, 405 n., 412, 418, *et passim*
Mataram, Pangeran (brother of Pakubuwana II), 43 n.
Mataram, Pangeran Arja (brother of Pakubuwana IV), 320. *See also* Mangkubumi, Pangeran Arja

INDEX

Matěsih, 159
Mecca, 17, 103, 134, 150, 152, 153, 154, 264, 288–90, 292, 293, 313, 336, 389, 393
Medina, 152, 154, 393
Mědjagung, Sunan, 4 n.
Megakusuma, Raden, 289
Měgatsari, Raden Arja, 140 n.
Meijer, J. C., 135
Merah-Putih, Sang, 293
Měrapi, Mount, 15, 18, 186, 375 n.
Mintuna, 382 ff.
Moertono, Soemarsaid, 23; quoted, 364 n.
Moluccas, 14, 18
montjaněgara, 43, 71, 86–7, 122, 133, 159–60, 198, 202, 240, 335, 350
Moses, Prophet (Nabi Mungsa), 381, 382 n., 389 n., 395, 408–9, 410
mosque (*Masdjid Agěng*), 166, 317
Mossel, J., 119 n., 426
Muhamad Abubakar, Pangeran, 352 nn.
Muhamad Djenal Ngasik Ngarifin (title), 202
Muhamad Djuwana, 54 n.
Muḥammad, the Prophet, 72, 151–2, 196, 205, 389
Muḥammad, Seh, 152
Muḥammad Idris, 154
Munḍingsari, 377 n.
Mungsa, Nabi, see Moses
Munnik, H. de, 46 n., 111
mupakat, see consensus
Murja, Mount, 126
Murja, Sunan, 4 n.
Murti, Sang, 81 n.
Musa, Hadji ('hadjie Moesa'), 332 n.
Musa Ngidrus, Sajid, 103

Nāgarakěrtāgama, 178, 211 n.
najaka, 41, 69 n., 280, 360
Nakoda, see Rudyah Kawit
names, Dutch, in Baron Sakenḍer stories, 383, 383–4 n., 385 n.
Naqshbandī order, 154
Narada, 29–30
Natajuda, Raden Tuměnggung, 305, 347, 350, 360
Natakusuma (*patih* of Kartasura): banishment, 38, 69 n., 102; return to Java, 75, 102–4; renamed Pangeran Djuru, 103; adventures in Ceylon, 103; daughter married to Pakubuwana III, 110
Natakusuma, Pangeran (*patih* of Mangkubumi), 68, 69, 72 n., 428
Natakusuma, Pangeran (Pakualam I), xxi, 67, 100, 190, 273, 278, 350–2, 354, 360
Nataněgara, Pangeran, 129 n.
Nationalist Party, Indonesian, 276 n.
Nawala-Pradata, 165 n.
něgara agung, 159–60
Netherlands, 36, 231, 254, 257, 270, 287, 345, 366, 380, 382, 408, 410–11
Netherlands Bible Society, MSS. collection of, 220 n.
New Book (*Sěrat Ebuk Anjar*), 158–9, 418
New Zealand, 383 n.
Ngabei, Panḍita Putra Pangeran (son of Brawidjaja), 370 n.
Ngabei, Pangeran (brother of Mangkubumi), 43 n., 102
Ngabei, Pangeran (son of Pakubuwana III), 267–8, 302, 303, 327, 337
Ngabei, Pangeran Arja (son of Mangkubumi), 101, 279, 280, 347, 349–50, 351, 352 n., 354, 360
Ngabei (Sa)loringpasar, Pangeran (at least two individuals), 43 n., 72 n., 117 n.
Ngaběsah, 382 ff., 408–9, 410–11
Ngaběsah, Prabu, 388 ff.
Ngaběsah, princess of, 382 ff.
Ngajodya, 80
Ngajogjakarta Adiningrat, xxiv, 80. See also Jogjakarta
Ngalaga, Susuhunan, see Pakubuwana I
Ngalěngka, 260 n.
Ngambar Sari, 207
Ngampel (Ampel), 126, 406 n.
Ngampel-Děnta (Ampel-Děnta), Sunan, 4 n., 17
ngelmu (*gaib*), 7, 17, 196, 207
Ngendra-Buwana, 191
Ngisa, Nabi, see Jesus
ngoko, 368, 372
Njai Rara Kidul, see Goddess of the Southern Ocean
Norodom, King, 365 n.
Nur Saleh, see Amad (Nur) Saleh
Nur Wahid, 196
Nusa Tambini/Těmbini/Tumbini, 376, 386 n., 391, 392

INDEX

Old Javanese, 1, 80 n., 178, 189, 219, 293, 417
Olthof, W. L., xxiii
Onrust, 399
opium, 108, 315, 333
opperhoofd, 385 n.
opperkoopman, 367, 369
Orange, Prince, of, 270
orthography, xxiv
Ossenberch, W. H. van, 106, 107, 113–14, 116, 117, 119 n., 120, 129, 132–3, 155, 372, 384 n., 426
Overstraten, P. G. van, 139 n., 353, 357–8, 360–1, 383 n., 426

Padjadjaran, 177, 370, 371, 373–6, 390 n., 399 ff., 406 n., 408, 410–11
Padjadjaran, princess of, 399 ff., 408
Padjang, 11, 13, 14, 43, 47 n., 61, 62, 66, 71, 75, 78, 159, 179, 211, 213, 214–15, 291 n., 405 n., 418
Padjang, Sultan of, see *Djaka Tingkir*
Padjangwasista, Raden, xxi
Padris, 153 n.
pagongan, 288
pajung, 290
Pakualam I, Pangeran, see Natakusuma, Pangeran
Pakualaman *babad*, see Poensen's *babad*
Pakubuwana I, Susuhunan, 26, 38 n., 78, 123, 214–15, 310, 349 n.
Pakubuwana II, Susuhunan, 23, 37–53, 54, 65, 67, 69 n., 74, 75, 83, 123, 130, 363; illness and death, 47–53, 353
Pakubuwana III, Susuhunan, *passim*; accession, 52–3; titles, 78–9; revival of court, 87–8; daughters, 97 ff.; relations with Dutch, 99, 253–4, *et passim*; and Madurese wife, 88, 108–9; intemperance, 108; incompetence of *patihs*, 108–9, 263–4, 266; described in 1780, 260–1; illnesses, 286, 308; death in 1788, 308, 310, 353; as author, 224
Pakubuwana IV, Susuhunan, *passim*; birth in 1768, 140–1, 142; installation as Crown Prince in 1775, 170–1; visits Sĕmarang in 1781, 249; growing influence, 286; troubled youth, 286–7; involved with religious zealots, 287–8, 299; dislike of Europeans, 298–9, 307; accession in 1788, 253, 308–9, 310; crisis of 1789–90, 314–40, 412; as author, 224, 311–12 n.
Pakubuwana V, Susuhunan, birth, 286
Pakubuwana VII, Susuhunan, 138 n.
Pakubuwana X, Susuhunan, 359 n.
Pakuningrat, Pangeran, 72 n., 117
Palĕk, 384 n.
Palembang, 134, 150, 158
Palm, W. A., 269, 271–2, 284, 288, 294–9, 366, 427; death in 1788, 297
Pamanahan, Ki, 75, 78
Pamanukan river, 374
Pamĕkasan, 286, 406 n.
Pamĕrden, 159
Pamuk, Ki, 400
panakawan, 28–9, 364, 385, 389 n.
Panangsang, Arja, 75–6 n.
Pandan Arang, Ki, see Bajat, Sunan
Pandawa, 28
paṇḍita, 198–9, 386
Pandjawi, Ki, 75–6 n., 78
Pandji, 116
Pandji Murtasmara, 224 n.
Panĕmbahan (rebel), 129 n.
panĕmbahan adipati (title), 246
Panĕngah, Pangeran, 318, 337, 338 n.
pangeran (title), 246–7, 271 n.
pangeran adipati (title), 126, 173, 246–7
Panggung, Njai, 405 n.
Panggung, Pangeran, 4 n.
Panular, Pangeran (brother of Pakubuwana II), 43 n.
Panular, Pangeran (son of Mangkubumi), 352 nn.
paper, European, xx, 195 n., 222, 377 n.
paper, Javanese, 222, 377 n.
parahjangan, 375, 408
Parang Rusak, 276
Parangwedang, 405 n.
Pararaton, 1, 178–9, 182, 399 n.
Parra, P. A. van der, 119 n., 247, 426
pasisir, 5, 11, 13–14, 18, 19, 20, 27, 57, 61, 62, 75, 139–40, 160, 172, 198, 201, 202, 254, 404 n.; Dutch lease of, 37, 38–9, 40–4, 59, 62, 68, 106–8, 294, 319, 363, 371; Dutch payments for, 43, 62, 63, 68, 70, 73, 79, 98, 245–6, 330

Pasuruan, 106, 136, 405 n.
Patah, Raden, 5, 9–10, 179, 187
Paṭi, 76 n., 140 n., 238, 406 n.
patih, passim; Dutch role in appointing, 38, 69, 70–1, 73, 145, 264–6, 305, 316, 369; position in Dutch–Javanese relations, 369–70, 411
patih djĕro, 86, 355
Patjitan, 156 n., 159, 405 n.
Patras, A., 383 n.
Patrasmin, Baron, 383
Pĕdagangan, negotiations at in 1754, 60–3, 91, 102 n.
Pĕkalongan, 106–7, 252, 404 n., 406 n.
Pĕkih Ibrahim, 87
Pĕmalang, 106, 132, 406 n.
Pĕnanggungan, 264 n., 405 n.
pĕnḍapa, 166
Pĕngging, 10
pĕngulu: of Jogjakarta, 87, 111, 330; of Semarang, 330; second, of Surakarta, 316, 331–2
pepe, 60–1 n.
Persia, 3, 8, 127 n., 200, 389
Petruk, 28
Pigeaud, Th. G. Th., xxv, 190, 220, 377 n., 399 n.
Pitanja, 384 n.
Plered, 12, 47, 180–1, 185, 405 n.
Plered, Kjai, 76 n.
Poensen, C., xv, 45 n., 91 n., 96, 351
Poensen's *babad*, xxi, *et passim*
Poeroebojo, B. P. H., 188 n.
poison, 88, 100, 247, 278, 295, 297, 299
Polanhardjo, 89 n.
Poll, van de, 91
ponḍok, 358
Pontjarĕsmi, 203 ff.
Pontjasona, 202 ff.
population: in 1755, 71–2; in 1773–4, 159; growth of, 108, 157, 159–60, 245
ports, Javanese, 18, 20, 39. See also *pasisir*
Portuguese, 2, 373, 378
Prabajĕksa, 166, 188, 194 n.
Prabalingga, 184 n., 406 n.
Prabangkara, 224 n.
Prabu Amidjaja, Pangeran Arja, 172, 210, 238–9, 260, 261, 429
Prabudjaja, Pangeran Arja, *see* Singasari, Pangeran

Prabudjaka, Pangeran Arja, *see* Singasari, Pangeran
'Prabu Indrapuri', 189
pradjuritan, 61 n.
Praga river, 243
prajangan, 375, 402
Pralambang Djajabaja, *see* Djajabaja prophecies
Pralambange Tanah Djawa, 183 n.
Prambanan, Tjanḍi, 13, 301
Pranaraga (Ponorogo), 60, 262 n., 405 n.
Prangmadana, Pangeran, 43 n.
prang sabil, *see* Holy War
Prangwadana (name), 300 n.
Prangwadana, Pangeran, *see* Mangkunĕgara I
Prangwadana, Pangeran (Mangkunĕgara II), 261–2, 325, 429; named Surja Mangkubumi, 299–300; named Surja Prangwadana, 300
Prau, Mount, 186, 405 n.
Prawata, Mount, 406 n.
Prawata, Sultan/Sunan, 11, 76 n.
Priangan, 375, 402
primbon, sixteenth-century, 6
princes: in 1746, 43 n.; banishment in 1749 and later return to Java, 56, 102, 270, 149 n.
Pringgalaja, Raden Adipati, 40–4, 46, 71, 76 n., 145, 428; death, 88
Pudjakusuma, 198 ff., 210, 218, 407–8
Pudjarĕsmi, 198
Pudjasmara, 198
Pugĕr, Pangeran, *see* Pakubuwana I
Pulo Gĕḍong, 84
Purbaja, Pangeran (brother of Pakubuwana III), 149, 259–60, 265, 271, 287, 309, 315, 316, 327, 332, 337–8
Purbaja, Pangeran (of Djakarta), 401–2
Purbaja, Pangeran (uncle of Sultan Agung), 356
Purbawidjaja, Raden, 271 n.
Purwa Gupita, 197 ff.
Purwa Kanḍa, 198 ff.
Purwa Radja, 200 ff.
Purwarĕdja, 264
Purwa Rukma, 203 ff.
Purwa Tjipta, 197 ff.
pusaka, 23, 34, 74, 87, 90, 103, 123, 125, 175, 188, 194 n., 211, 238, 258, 308; divided at Djatisari in 1755, 76

INDEX

pusaka agĕng of Jogjakarta, 74–5, 76 n.
Putri Tjĕmpa, 3

Qādirite order, 127
Qur'ān, 72, 82, 103, 151–2, 203, 206, 271, 333, 385 n.
Quraysh, 389

Radja Kapakapa, 224 n.
Radjawinangun, 304
Raffles, T. S., 221, 333, 363; quoted, 57 n., 64, 258–9 n., 275; MSS. collection of, 220, 223
Raffles Jav. MS. 33 (C), 221 n.
Rama Badra Djawi, 81 n.
Rāmāyaṇa, 80–1, 391 n.
rampog, 275
Ranamĕnggala, 106–8
Rasamulja, Mount, 198–9, 202
Rassers, W. H., quoted, 275–6 n.
Ratpĕni, 397 n.
Ratu, Panĕmbahan (king of Tjirĕbon), 359 n.
Ratu Adil, 132 n., 183, 292
Ratu Bĕndara, 117, 146, 149–50, 242, 262, 273 n., 300–1, 327, 429; marriage to Mangkunĕgara I, 46, 97; crisis of 1763, 110–15, 119, 123, 138, 143; marriage to Pangeran Dipanĕgara in 1765, 117–18, 155; alleged correspondence with Mangkunĕgara I in 1787, 296, 300
Ratu Kadipaten (of Jogjakarta), 273 n.
Ratu Kĕntjana (of Jogjakarta), 273 n.
Ratu Kĕntjana (of Surakarta), 140 n., 263
Ratu Kidul, *see* Goddess of the Southern Ocean
Reede tot de Parkeler, J. Fr. Baron van, 382 n., 384 n., 427
refugees, 230–5, 301, 323, 343, 422
Rĕksakusuma, 242
Rĕksanĕgara, Faktor Tumĕnggung (Kasebĕr), 392
Rĕmbang, 39
renaissance, literary, 219–26
Residents, Dutch, *passim*; status reduced at Surakarta, 57; positions at court, 366–70, 411. *See also* corruption *and* Dutch East India Company
Rĕtna Dewati, *see* Goddess of the Southern Ocean

Rĕtna Manik Rasa, 191
Rĕtna Pamĕkas, 370 n.
Rhijn, J. M. van, 174, 237, 239, 270, 273 n., 274, 277, 282, 366, 368 n., 427
Riemsdijk, J. van, 231, 247, 249 n., 259 n., 426
Rijckevorsel, E. van, quoted, 183
Roban, 405 n.
Rongga, Pangeran (brother of Mangkubumi), 43 n.
Rongga, Pangeran (of Dĕmak), 271 n.
Rongga, Pangeran (of Surakarta), 316
Rongga, Pangeran (rebel), 237–41
Rongga, Raden Aju, 241–4
Rongga Amongsastra, 224 n.
Ronggaprawiradirdja, Raden Tumĕnggung, 72 n., 86–7, 92, 132–3, 137, 150, 239, 274, 350, 429
Rongga Sutrasna, 224 n.
Ronggawarsita I, Raden, xxi, 224 n.
Roorda, T., MSS. collection of, 220
Rouffaer, G. P., 161, 163 n., 165 n.
Royal Asiatic Society Java 45 (A), 221 n.
Rudyah Kawit, Nakoda bas pan, 382 ff.
Rum, 59, 393. *See also* Turkey

sadjen, 194 n.
Said, Mas, *see* Mangkunĕgara I
Saint Martin, I. de, 223 n., 383 n.
Sajĕmpraba, 386 n., 391 ff.
Śāka era, xxv
Sakebĕr, 385 n. *See also* Kasebĕr
Sakebĕr, Major, 385 n.
Sakenḍer, Baron, *see* Kasenḍer, Raden Baron, *and* Baron Sakenḍer stories
Salatiga, 316, 318, 357; conference at in 1757, 92, 96, 110, 187, 322, 415; stone mosque at, 177
Sanskrit, 1, 80, 293
Santakusuma, Pangeran, 352 n.
santri, 315, 318, 320, 327, 329, 330, 331–3, 334, 336, 337, 338–9, 342, 349 n., 412
Sapilman, Raden Baron, 383
Saraita, 28
Sasana Prabu, 224 n.
Sasradiningrat, Raden Adipati, 163, 164 n., 230, 249 n., 264–6, 428; appointment as *patih*, 145; described in 1780, 265
Sasranĕgara (toponym), 388

Sasranĕgara, Raden Tumĕnggung, 239 n.
Sastranĕgara, Raden Tumĕnggung, xxi
Sastrawidjaja, 224 n.
satrija, 100
saudara, 371–2
Sawangan, 405 n.
Schrieke, B. J. O., quoted, 364 n.
Scipio, 309
Seda ing Krapjak, Panĕmbahan, 14–15, 80 n., 399 n.
Seh Malaja, 224 n.
Sela, 406 n.
Sela Gilang, 242–3, 398
Sĕlangor, 103
Sĕlarong, Pangeran, 43 n.
sĕlir, 353
Sĕmangun, 128–9, 135–6
Sĕmar, 28, 29
Sĕmarang, *passim*; spirit of, 406 n.; Government of Java's Northeast Coast at, 370–2, 426, *et passim*
Sĕmarang, Adipati (author), 224 n.
Sĕmarang, Adipati Pangeran (author), 224 n.
Sĕmbrani, Kuda, 387 ff., 412
Sĕmit, 384 n.
Senapati Ingalaga, Panĕmbahan, 12–14, 23, 85, 243, 278, 312, 376, 398, 399 n., 408, 412
sĕngkala lists, *see* chronogram lists
sĕntana, 19, 41, 290
Sĕntot, 87
sepoys, 333
sĕpuh, 77–8, 330, 338
Sĕpuh, Sultan (of Jogjakarta), *see* Crown Prince of Jogjakarta (Hamĕngkubuwana II)
Sĕpuh, Sultan (of Tjirĕbon), 247
Sĕrambi, 166, 168 n.
Serang, 240 n.
Serangĕn, 126, 240 n.
Sĕrat Achir ing Djaman, 193 n.
Sĕrat Babad Pakunĕgaran, 42 n., 46 n., 90 n., 93 n.
Sĕrat Bonang, 6
Sĕrat Buk Kalĕpu, *see* Book of Klĕpu
Sĕrat Dĕrmagaṇḍul, 183–4
Sĕrat Djajabaja, 81 n.
Sĕrat Djumĕnĕngan Sampejan-Dalĕm Ingkang Sinuhun Kangdjĕng Sultan Hamĕngkubuwana I, xxii

Sĕrat Ĕbuk Anjar, *see* New Book
Sĕrat Iskandar, 385 n.
Sĕrat Jusup, 82
Sĕrat Kaṇḍa, 4 n.
Sĕrat Kaṇḍaning Ringgit Purwa, 4 n.
Sĕrat Koṇḍa (*Sĕrat Gĕṇḍing Bĕksan*), 192–3
Sĕrat Rama, 80–1 n.
Sĕrat Sakoṇḍar, xxiv, 374–413; origin, 377; age, 377–9, 383–4 n.; summary of text, 380–407
Sĕrat Suluk Surja Djaja Amisesa, 190–2
Sĕrat Surja Radja, xxiv, 27, 85, 188–211, 218, 222, 275, 276, 331, 377 n., 379, 407–9, 424; written by Crown Prince of Jogjakarta, xxiv, 169, 188, 196; research conditions, 194–5 n.; summary of text, 195–207; as prophecy, 209–11
Sĕrat Surja Radja (BG 164), 195 n., 211 n.
Sĕrat Surja Radja (LOr 8604), 195 n.
Sĕsela, 126
Sĕsela, Kjai Gĕḍe, 212
Sĕstraprawira, 196
Sĕtjajuda, 128
Sĕtjang, 321
Sĕtjawalantĕn, 128
Sĕtomi, Njai, 400
Sewaka, 221
Sewu, Tjaṇḍi, 301
Shāfi'ī, 152
Siberg, J., 121, 249–52, 255, 261, 262, 264–7, 271 n., 272, 277, 282, 294, 297, 306, 426
Sidiwĕtjana, 201
Silarong, Pangeran, 352 n.
Siliwangi, Prabu, 370 n.
Siluman, 406 n.
Simong, J., 383 n.
Simunan, Baron, 383
Sindurĕdja, Adipati (*patih djĕro* of Pakubuwana II), 41, 43
Sindurĕdja, Raden Adipati (*patih* of Surakarta), 164 n., 266, 428
Sindurĕdja, Raden Rija (*patih djĕro* of Jogjakarta), 86, 355
Sindurĕdja, Tumĕnggung (*patih djĕro* of Jogjakarta), 86
Singasari, Pangeran, 39, 43 n., 57, 90, 107, 123, 130–8, 142, 151 n., 187, 214, 429; death, 135

INDEX

Singgunkara, 386 ff.
Siti Djĕnar, Seh, 4 n., 7–8, 10
Siti Fatimah, 152
Siti Inggil, 166
Siwa, 29
Sleman, 144 n.
Slobok, Raden Mas, 263 n.
Sloot, J. A., 384 n.
Sluijs, J. C. van der, 112, 427
Smith, D. J., 384 n.
Soegiarto, J., 138 n.
Soekanto, 50–2 n.
Soeripto, 161–2
Sokawati, 40, 43–4, 46, 71, 75 n., 159, 260
Solomon, 201
sovereignty of Dutch over Mataram, 37, 49–52, 53, 64, 98, 247, 249, 253–4, 256, 363, 410, 413; treaty texts, 50–1 n.
Spain, Spanish, 378–9, 380–1, 385 n., 387 ff., 408, 410–11
Speelman, C., 20, 383–4 n.
spirits of Java, 402, 403–7, 409; listed, 405–6 n.
Sragen, 40 n.
Srĕnggara, Raden Aju, 350
Sri Mĕnganti, 166 n.
Staringh, 309, 335
Straalendorff, F. C. van, 146–7, 262, 269, 367, 427
succession: Dutch policy towards, 47, 60, 63, 65, 69, 101 n., 139, 167, 170–3, 262, 305, 339 n., 349, 360; in Jogjakarta, 73, 139, 305, 326; in Jogjakarta questioned by Surakarta, 321, 326; in Jogjakarta accepted by Surakarta, 342–3; concern for at turn of the century, 166–73. *See also* abdication
Sudjanapura, 318
Sufis, 4, 127 n.
Suhulman, 385 ff.
Sukarsi, *adjar*, 399, 400 n., 402, 404
Sukmul, Raden Baron, 385 ff., 408–10
Sultan (title), 10 n., 15 n., 17, 59, 61–2, 313
Sumadiwirja, 106–8
Sumatra, 153 n.
Sumbing, Mount, 406 n.
Sumur Gumuling, 85
Sunda, Sundanese, 127 n., 370, 371, 374, 376, 406 n., 408–9, 410–11

Sunda Kalapa, 374
Sundara, Raden Mas, *see* Crown Prince of Jogjakarta (Hamĕngkubuwana II)
Sungadjrit, 380
Supala *and* Supali, 198
Sura, Surang (name), 384 n.
Sura Adimĕnggala, Adipati (a), 143, 144, 271 n.; death, 246–7
Sura Adimĕnggala, Adipati (b), 247, 250, 291
Surabaja, 13–14, 15, 17, 39, 61, 135, 405 n.
Surakarta, *passim*; foundation, 39; spirit of, 406 n.
Suramulja, Raden Mas, *see* Prabu Amidjaja, Pangeran Arja
Surapati, 21, 132, 312; descendants of, 107, 123, 130, 131, 132, 137, 146
Surat, 103
Surja Amidjaja, 198
Surjadipura, Raden Mas, 263 n.
Surja Djaja Amisesa, 190 ff.
Surjakusuma (son of Pangeran Rongga, rebel), 241
Surjakusuma, Raden Mas (son of Mangkunĕgara I), 262 n., 263 n.
Surjakusuma, Raden Mas Arja, *see* Mangkunĕgara I
Surja Mataram, Pangeran, name proposed for Prangwadana (Mangkunĕgara II), 262, 300
Surjanagara, Pangeran Arja, xxii
Surja Prangwadana, name given to Prangwadana (Mangkunĕgara II), 300
Surja Radja, Kangdjĕng Kjai, see *Sĕrat Surja Radja*
Surjatruna, Raden Arja, 263 n.
Surja Wisesa, 198
Susuhunan (title), 17
Susuruh, Raden, 375 n.
Svetaketu, 7
Swajĕmprabā, 391 n.

Tack, F., 132
Taman Asri, 85 n.
Taman Sari, 1, 84–6, 111, 122, 139, 166, 237, 242, 304, 322–3, 345, 376
Tanah Abang, 38
Tanah Sabrang, 192 ff., 408–10
Tandjunganom, Raden, 289, 295, 298
Tandjung Bang, 404 n.

Tandjung Putih, Si, 187 n.
Tanemut, 384 n.
tapa, 90, 123
ṭarīqah, 4, 127 n.
Tasman, A. J., 383 n.
Tasmania, 383 n.
Tasminten, Baron, 383
Ṭaṭaini, 393–4
Ṭaṭakuṭana, 393–4
Tedjakusuma, Raden, 289
Tĕgal, 221 n., 317, 406 n.
Tĕmbajat, 16, 17
Ten Commandments, 243
Tĕngger, 27
tĕnung Wĕlanda, 310
Tĕpasana, Pangeran, 123, 126–7
Tĕrnate, 193
'Thursday Calendar', 53 n., 54–5 n., 80 n., 213 n., 430–1
tiger–buffalo fights, 274–5, 303–4, 345–6
Timur, Raden Mas, *see* Crown Prince of Jogjakarta (Hamĕngkubuwana II)
Tinab, Kjai Agĕng, 128 n.
Tirtanĕgara, Ngabei, 71
tjahja, 199
Tjakradiningrat, 286
Tjakradipura, Raden Tumĕnggung, 249 n., 259
Tjakraningrat, Pangeran / Panĕmbahan, 246–7. *See also* Madura, Panĕmbahan/Pangeran of
Tjaraka Basa, 224 n.
tjatjah, 422–3 n., *et passim*
Tjĕmara Tunggal, 375 n.
Tjĕmpa, 3, 126
Tjĕngkalsewu, 124, 406 n.
Tjiliwung river, 402
Tjirĕbon, 61, 247, 295, 359 n., 370, 400, 406 n.
tobacco, 97
Togog, 28
Tomas, 384 n.
Toutlemonde, B., 53, 385 n., 426
Trajĕm, 243
Tralaja gravestones, 3
transliteration, xxv
Tratebang, 404 n.
Trawulan gravestone, 3
treaties, xxii–xxiii; of 1677, 20, 363, 374; of Kartasura period, 21; of 1743, 39, 40, 49, 51 n., 53, 69, 106, 136, 369; of 1746, 40, 49, 51 n., 53, 363, 371; of 1749, 49–53, 98, 363; of 1755 (Gijanti), 68–73, 91, 94, 98, 99, 118, 120, 130, 143, 158, 162, 164, 187, 220–2, 225, 309, 322, 369, 415; of 1757, *see* Salatiga, conference at in 1757; of 1780, 254; of 1788, 253, 308–9; of 1790, 230, 235, 341–5, 420; of 1792, 253, 360–1
Trĕnggana, Sultan, 10, 11 n., 179
troops loaned by Javanese to defend Batavia, 255–8, 282
Trunadjaja, Raden, 17, 20, 21, 33, 127, 180, 187, 287, 374, 383–4 n., 398 n., 415
Tuban, 126, 406 n.
tumĕnggung, 41, 267, 290
Tundjung Bang, 404 n., 405 n.
Tunggul Wulung, 406 n.
Turkey, Turks, 59, 389, 393

Udajana, 198
Ukiran Tunggak-Sĕmi, 164 n.
'Umar, 152
Unḍang-unḍang, 162 n.
'Unḍang-unḍang Mataram', 161 n.
Ungaran, Mount, 127
upatjara, 314
Urawan, Kjai, *see* Sindurĕdja, Tumĕnggung (*patih djĕro* of Jogjakarta)
'Uthmān, 152

Valckenier, A., 383–4 n.
Valk, de, 309
Veth, P. J., 177, 183 n.
Vos, J., 117, 119 n., 120, 123, 133, 136, 139, 144–5, 155, 426

Wahhāb, Muḥammad ibn-'Abd-al-, 153
Wahhābīs, 153–4, 286, 288, 292, 331–3
wajang, 28–30, 67, 81, 132 n., 188, 190, 203, 260 n., 364, 389 n.
wajang-kulit, 190, 275 n.
wajang-pantjasila, 190
wajang-topeng, 116
wali, 4–6, 7, 9–10, 16, 17, 74, 238; names of, 4–5 n.
Walilanang, Sunan, 4 n.
Wanakĕrta (Kartasura), 182 n.
Wars of Succession, Javanese, 21, 33, 44 ff., 123, 383–4 n.

(Wasi) Djajamurtjita, 201 ff.
Watu-Gunung, 29
Weatherbee, D. E., 222 n.
wĕdana, 68, 86, 88, 124, 266
Widjil, Pangeran, 103 n.
Wikramawardhana, 359 n.
Wilaja, Mount, 201
Wilde, E. A. de, 299
Wilhelmina, Queen, 190
windu-cycles, 167, 213 n., 430–1
Winter, C. F., Sr., *Conversations* of, 224–6
Wiradigda, Tumĕnggung, 316, 318, 337, 338 n.
Wiradirĕdja, 129 n.
Wiraguna, Tumĕnggung, 282
Wiramĕnggala, Pangeran, 123
Wiranĕgara, 131, 132 n., 133 n.

Wiratmĕdja, Raden, *see* Guntur, Raden Mas
Wiratmĕdja, Raden Mas, 124
Wirjakusuma (of Surakarta), 287–8, 315
Wirjakusuma, Raden (of Jogjakarta), 232 n.
Wirjawidjaja, 196
Wisnu, 73, 81–2
Wongsadipradja, Ki Nitik, 398
wong tjilik, 236 n., 424
Wonosobo, 240 n.
Wringinputih, 406 n.
wuku-cycles, 213 n.
Württemberg troops, 336 n.

Zoetmulder, P. J., 8; quoted, 189
Zwaluw, de, 339

MAPS

CENTRAL AND

EAST JAVA

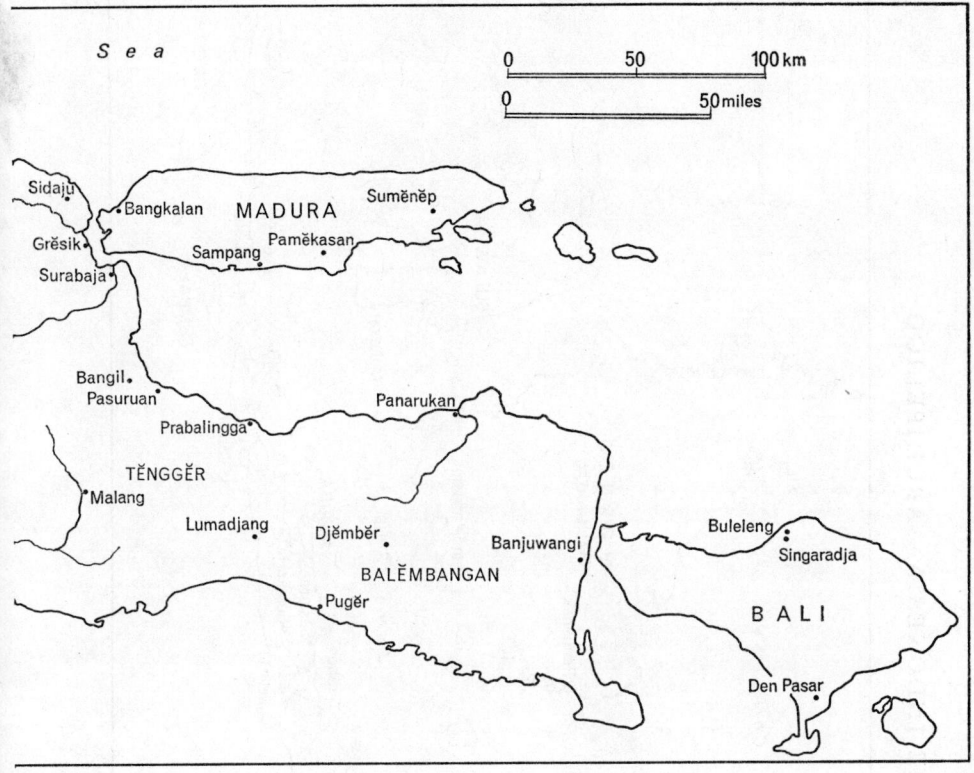

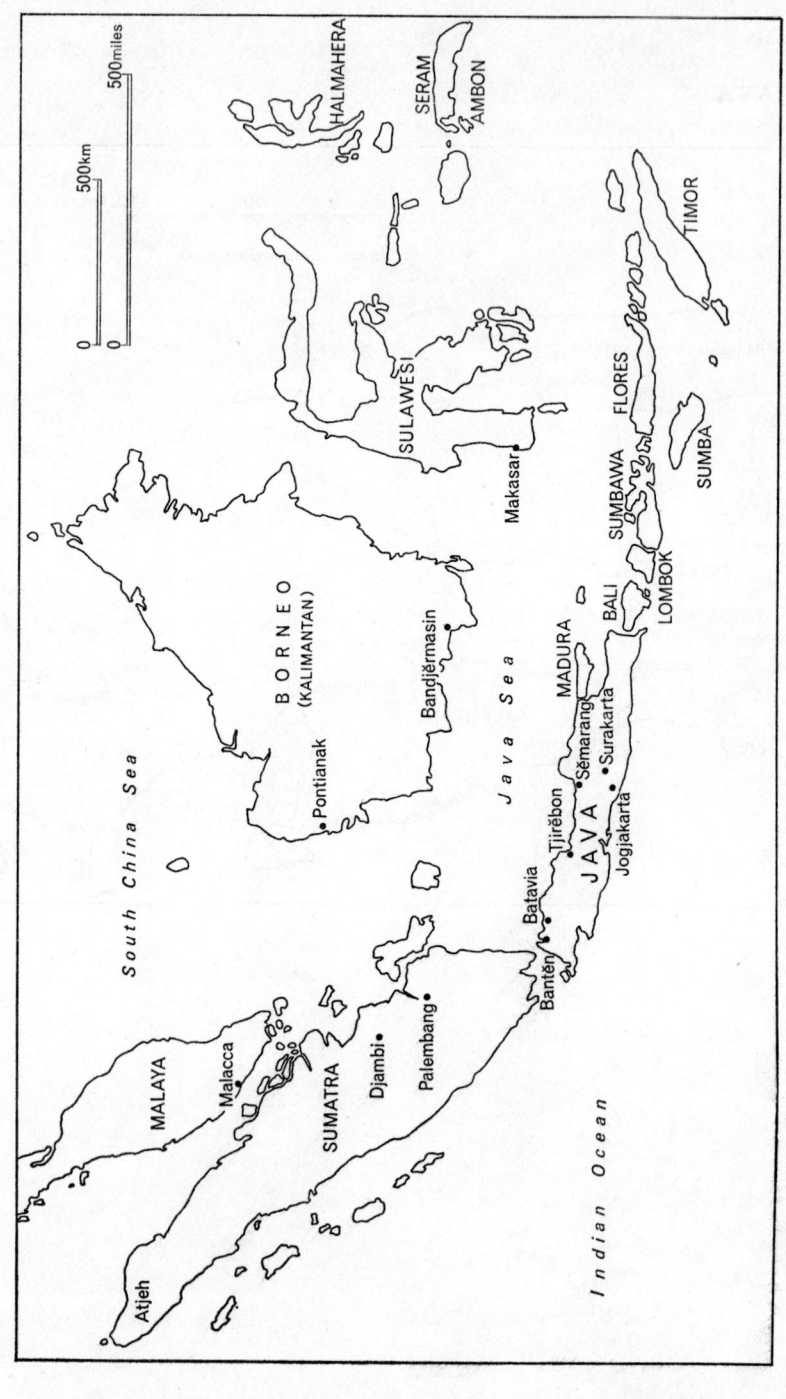